17th Edition

AF685122

Deskbook Encyclopedia of Employment Law

Center for Education & Employment Law

Center for Education & Employment Law
P.O. Box 3008
Malvern, Pennsylvania 19355

Copyright © 2009 by Center for Education & Employment Law
All rights reserved. No part of this publication may be reproduced by any means, electronic or mechanical, including photocopying, without prior written permission from the publisher.
First edition 1993
Seventeenth edition 2009
Printed in the United States of America

"This publication is designed to provide accurate and authoritative information in regard to the subject matter covered. It is sold with the understanding that the publisher is not engaged in rendering legal, accounting or other professional service. If legal advice or other expert assistance is required, the service of a competent professional person should be sought."—*from a Declaration of Principles jointly adopted by a Committee of the American Bar Association and a Committee of Publishers and associations.*

The Library of Congress has catalogued this book as follows:

Employment - 17th ed.
p. cm.
Includes bibliographical references and index.
ISBN 978-1-933043-36-4
1. Labor laws and legislation--United States--Digests.
I. Center for Education & Employment Law
KF3314.D47 2005
344.73'01—dc20
[347.3041] 94-441
CIP

Library of Congress Catalog Card Number: 94-441
ISBN 978-1-933043-36-4

Cover Design by Patricia Jacoby

Other Titles Published by Center for Education & Employment Law:

Deskbook Encyclopedia of American School Law
Deskbook Encyclopedia of Public Employment Law
Federal Laws Prohibiting Employment Discrimination
Higher Education Law in America
Keeping Your School Safe & Secure: A Practical Guide
Private School Law in America
Statutes, Regulations and Case Law Protecting Individuals with Disabilities
Students with Disabilities and Special Education
U.S. Supreme Court Education Cases
U.S. Supreme Court Employment Cases

CHAPTER ONE
Discrimination

CHAPTER TWO
Employer Liability

TABLE OF CONTENTS

CHAPTER THREE
Discipline, Suspension and Termination

CHAPTER FOUR
Employee Benefits

CHAPTER FIVE
Labor Relations

CHAPTER SIX
Employment Practices

CHAPTER SEVEN
Workers' Compensation

CHAPTER EIGHT
Unemployment Compensation

TABLE OF CONTENTS

CHAPTER NINE
Employer Insurance Coverage

INTRODUCTION

The ***Deskbook Encyclopedia of Employment Law*** provides a comprehensive selection of state and federal court decisions that impact employment. It covers a wide range of important topics including discrimination, employer liability, discipline and termination, employee benefits, and labor relations. Our editorial staff reviews court decisions from the past year for inclusion in the deskbook and arranges them topically so you can locate them easily. Within each chapter, the subsections contain explanatory passages to help you develop an overall understanding of the legal issues in that particular area. More importantly, each case summary has been written in everyday language with important facts, issues, and holdings highlighted in boldface type.

For your convenience, we have also included relevant provisions of the U.S. Constitution and compiled a topical list of U.S. Supreme Court decisions, separated into specific topics to allow you to gather more information on areas of particular interest to you.

We have designed the ***Deskbook Encyclopedia of Employment Law*** to provide professionals involved in all areas of employment law with access to important cases in the field. Our aim has been to make the law accessible to you regardless of your level of understanding of the legal system.

Steve McEllistrem, Esq.
Senior Legal Editor
Center for Education & Employment Law

ABOUT THE EDITORS

Steve McEllistrem is the senior legal editor at the Center for Education & Employment Law. He is a co-author of *Students with Disabilities and Special Education Law* and *Higher Education Law in America*, and is the former managing editor of the monthly newsletter *Special Education Law Update*. He graduated cum laude from William Mitchell College of Law and received his undergraduate degree from the University of Minnesota. Mr. McEllistrem is admitted to the Minnesota Bar.

Thomas D'Agostino is a managing editor at the Center for Education & Employment Law and is the editor of *Higher Education Legal Alert* and *School Safety & Security Alert*. He graduated from the Duquesne University School of Law and received his undergraduate degree from Ramapo College of New Jersey. He is a past member of the American Bar Association's Section of Individual Rights and Responsibilities as well as the Pennsylvania Bar Association's Legal Services to Persons with Disabilities Committee. Mr. D'Agostino is admitted to the Pennsylvania bar.

Laurel Kalser is the editor of the monthly newsletters *Employment Law Report* and *Public Employment Law Report*. Ms. Kalser graduated *cum laude* from the University of Pennsylvania, and received her law degree from the University of Miami in Coral Gables, Florida, where she was a member of the Moot Court Board for outstanding appellate advocacy. Ms. Kalser is admitted to the Florida Bar.

Curt J. Brown is the Group Publisher of the Center for Education & Employment Law. Prior to assuming his present position, he gained extensive experience in business-to-business publishing, including management of well-known publications such as *What's Working in Human Resources*, *What's New in Benefits & Compensation*, *Keep Up to Date with Payroll*, *Supervisors Legal Update*, and *Facility Manager's Alert*. Mr. Brown graduated from Villanova University School of Law and graduated *magna cum laude* from Bloomsburg University with a B.S. in Business Administration. He is admitted to the Pennsylvania bar.

HOW TO USE YOUR DESKBOOK

We have designed your ***Deskbook Encyclopedia of Employment Law*** in an accessible format for both attorneys and non-attorneys to use as a research and reference tool toward prevention of legal problems.

Using Your Deskbook to Conduct Research

As a research tool, our deskbook allows you to conduct your research on two different levels by topics or by cases.

➢ *Researching a Topic*

If you have a general interest in a particular **topic** area, our **table of contents** provides descriptive section headings with detailed subheadings for each chapter.

✓ For your convenience, we also include the chapter table of contents at the beginning of each chapter.

Example:

For information on notice under the FMLA, the table of contents indicates that a discussion of that subject takes place in Chapter Six under the section heading, The Family and Medical Leave Act, and begins on page 406.

V. THE FAMILY AND MEDICAL LEAVE ACT 402
- A. "Serious Health Condition" 403
- ➔ B. Notice 406
- C. Employer Paid Leaves and State Statutes 409
- D. Certification 411
- E. Post-Leave Issues 413
- F. Other FMLA Issues 415

If you have a specific interest in a particular **issue**, our comprehensive **index** collects all of the relevant page references to particular issues.

> **Example:**
> For cases involving breach of contract, the index refers you to the page numbers where that issue is discussed.
>
> ➔ Breach of contract, 161-170
> Oral contracts, 165-170
> Oral representations, 166-168
> Written contracts, 161-165

➢ *Researching a Case*

If you know the **name** of a particular case, our **table of cases** will allow you to quickly reference the location of the case.

> **Example:**
> If you wanted to look up the case *Hoffman Plastic Compounds, Inc. v. NLRB*, you would look in the table of cases, which has been arranged alphabetically, under H.
>
> **H**
>
> Hockett v. Sun Co., Inc., 218
> Hodgkins v. New England Telephone Co., 402
> ➔ Hoffman Plastic Compounds, Inc. v. NLRB, 289
> Hoffman v. Professional Med Team, 412
> Hogan v. Allstate Insurance Co., 278
> Hoge v. Honda of America Manufacturing, 415
> Hogue v. Blue Bell Creameries, L.P., 486
> Holbrook v. Harman Automotive, Inc., 120

✓ Each of the cases summarized in the deskbook also contains the case citation that will allow you to access the full text of the case from a law library. *See How to Read a Case Citation, p. 585.*

If your interest lies in cases from a **particular state**, our **table of cases by state** will identify the cases from your state and direct you to the page numbers where they are located.

> **Example:**
> If cases from Texas are of interest, the table of cases by state, arranged alphabetically, lists all of the cases from Texas that have been summarized in the book.
>
> **TEXAS**
>
> Adams v. Travelers Indemnity Co. of Connecticut, 543
> Administaff Companies, Inc. v. New York Joint Board, 355
> Aetna Health Care v. Davila, 229
> Air Line Pilots Ass'n Int'l v. O'Neill, 333
> Alex Sheshunoff Management Services, L.P. v. Johnson, 381
> Altivia Corp. v. Greenwich Insurance Co., 547
> Asarco, Inc. v. NLRB, 202

✓ Remember, the judicial system has two court systems – state and federal – which generally function independently of each other. *See The Judicial System, p. 581.* We have included the federal court cases in the table of cases by state according to the state in which the court resides. However, federal court decisions often impact other federal courts within that particular circuit. Therefore, it may be helpful to review cases from all of the states contained in a particular circuit.

Reference Tool

As a reference tool, the deskbook includes information of a general nature that can be helpful in determining legal rights and responsibilities. For example:

Appendix A contains provisions of the **U.S. Constitution** that are relevant to employment law. The Commerce Clause, for instance, located on page 565, grants Congress the right to regulate commerce and is the source of power for most of the laws enacted by the legislature.

Appendix B contains a list of recent and important **U.S. Supreme Court employment cases**. The cases are arranged by subject matter and have been placed in reverse chronological order (from newest to oldest).

We hope you benefit from the use of your *Deskbook Encyclopedia of Employment Law*. If you have any questions about how to use the book, please contact Steve McEllistrem at smcellistrem@pbp.com.

TABLE OF ABBREVIATIONS

The following abbreviations are used in your *Deskbook Encyclopedia of Employment Law*.

ADA – Americans with Disabilities Act

ADEA – Age Discrimination in Employment Act

ALJ – administrative law judge

CBA – collective bargaining agreement

CEO – chief executive officer

CFO – chief financial officer

CGL – comprehensive general liability

COBRA – Consolidated Omnibus Budget Reconciliation Act of 1985

DOT – Department of Transportation

EEO – equal employment opportunity

EEOC – Equal Employment Opportunity Commission

ERISA – Employee Retirement Income Security Act

FCA – False Claims Act

EPPA – Employee Polygraph Protection Act

FELA – Federal Employers' Liability Act

FLSA – Fair Labor Standards Act

FMLA – Family and Medical Leave Act

FRA – Federal Railroad Administration

HR – human resources

HMO – health maintenance organization

HSA – Hours of Service Act

TABLE OF ABBREVIATIONS

INS – Immigration and Naturalization Service

IRCA – Immigration Reform and Control Act

IRS – Internal Revenue Service

LHWCA – Longshore and Harbor Workers' Compensation Act

LMRA – Labor Management Relations Act

LMRDA – Labor Management Reporting and Disclosure Act

MPPPA – Multi-employer Pension Plan Amendments Act of 1980

NLRA – National Labor Relations Act

NLRB – National Labor Relations Board

OSHA – Occupational Safety and Health Administration

OSH Act – Occupational Safety and Health Act

OWBPA – Older Workers Benefit Protection Act

RIF – reduction in force

RLA – Railway Labor Act

STAA – Surface Transportation Assistance Act

Title VII – Title VII of the Civil Rights Act of 1964

USERRA – Uniformed Services Employment and Reemployment Rights Act

WARN Act – Worker Adjustment and Retraining Notification Act

TABLE OF CASES

A

B

TABLE OF CASES

TABLE OF CASES

C

D

TABLE OF CASES

E

F

G

H

I

J

K

TABLE OF CASES

N

O

P

TABLE OF CASES

Q

R

S

T

U

V

W

Y

Z

TABLE OF CASES BY STATE

TABLE OF CASES BY STATE

COLORADO

CONNECTICUT

DELAWARE

DISTRICT OF COLUMBIA

FLORIDA

GEORGIA

HAWAII

TABLE OF CASES BY STATE

IDAHO

ILLINOIS

INDIANA

IOWA

KANSAS

TABLE OF CASES BY STATE

KENTUCKY

LOUISIANA

MAINE

MARYLAND

MASSACHUSETTS

MICHIGAN

MINNESOTA

MISSISSIPPI

MISSOURI

TABLE OF CASES BY STATE

MONTANA

NEBRASKA

NEVADA

NEW HAMPSHIRE

NEW JERSEY

NEW MEXICO

NEW YORK

NORTH CAROLINA

NORTH DAKOTA

OHIO

OKLAHOMA

OREGON

PENNSYLVANIA

PUERTO RICO

RHODE ISLAND

SOUTH CAROLINA

SOUTH DAKOTA

TENNESSEE

TEXAS

UTAH

VERMONT

VIRGINIA

VIRGIN ISLANDS

WASHINGTON

WEST VIRGINIA

WISCONSIN

WYOMING

CHAPTER ONE

Discrimination

Page

I. RACE AND NATIONAL ORIGIN DISCRIMINATION

Title VII of the Civil Rights Act of 1964 and 42 U.S.C. § 1981 protect against employment discrimination on the basis of race, and Title VII (but not Section 1981) protects against national origin discrimination. State laws also protect workers from race and national origin discrimination.

Under both state and federal law, employers cannot discriminate on the basis of race or national origin in hiring, promotions, benefits, firing, discipline, transfers, etc. In other words: **Never** take race into account when making any employment decision.

You may take national origin into account where you can show that having an employee of a particular national origin is a bona fide occupational qualification for a specific position. However, such situations will be extremely rare.

Even if you don't take race or national origin into account in your employment decision-making, you still could become liable if you make decisions that are designed to be neutral but have a negative impact on persons of certain races or ethnic backgrounds. This is known as disparate impact discrimination.

A. Federal Statutes and Supreme Court Interpretations

Title VII applies to any entity engaged in an industry affecting commerce that has 15 or more employees. Its coverage is limited to employment discrimination based upon race, color, sex, religion or national origin.

The U.S. Equal Employment Opportunity Commission (EEOC) is empowered to enforce Title VII through investigation and administrative complaint procedures or federal court lawsuits. Indeed, a private individual alleging discrimination must pursue administrative remedies within the EEOC before the individual will be allowed to sue an employer under Title VII.

Plaintiffs who prevail in an employment discrimination lawsuit will be entitled, where appropriate, to back pay, front pay, accumulated seniority and other benefits, and attorneys' fees. Further, Title VII allows the recovery of monetary damages for intentional discrimination except for cases of race discrimination where monetary damages are already available under 42 U.S.C. § 1981. Title VII is found at 42 U.S.C. § 2000e *et seq.*

§ 2000e-2. Unlawful employment practices

(a) Employer practices

It shall be an unlawful employment practice for an employer –

(1) to fail or refuse to hire or to discharge any individual, or otherwise to discriminate against any individual with respect to his compensation, terms, conditions, or privileges of employment, because of such individual's race, color, religion, sex, or national origin; or

(2) to limit, segregate, or classify his employees or applicants for employment in any way which would deprive or tend to deprive any individual of employment opportunities or otherwise adversely affect his status as an employee, because of such individual's race, color, religion, sex, or national origin.

* * *

42 U.S.C. § 1981
Equal rights under the law

(a) All persons within the jurisdiction of the United States shall have the same right in every State and Territory to make and enforce contracts, to sue, be parties, give evidence, and to the full and equal benefit of all laws and proceedings for the security of persons and property as is enjoyed by white citizens, and shall be subject to like punishment, pains, penalties, taxes, licenses, and exactions of every kind, and to no other.

(b) For purposes of this section, the term 'make and enforce contracts' includes the making, performance, modification, and termination of contracts, and the enjoyment of all benefits, privileges, terms, and conditions of the contractual relationship.

(c) The rights protected by this section are protected against impairment by nongovernmental discrimination and impairment under color of State law.

* * *

◆ One of the most important Supreme Court cases in the area of civil rights is *Griggs v. Duke Power Co.*, where the Court held that **Title VII forbids not only practices adopted with a discriminatory motive, but also those that have a discriminatory effect**. In *Griggs,* a group of black employees at a North Carolina power plant sued under Title VII, challenging their employer's requirement that employees possess a high school diploma or pass an intelligence test as a condition of employment. Section 703 of the act authorized the use of an ability test, so long as it was not intended or used to discriminate. The district court held that the employer's prior policy of racial discrimination had ended, and the Court of Appeals upheld that determination. The employees appealed to the U.S. Supreme Court, which held that if a practice excludes minorities and that practice cannot be shown to be related to job performance, it is prohibited, even if the employer lacked discriminatory intent. Title VII does not preclude the use of testing or measuring procedures, so long as they are demonstrably a reasonable measure of job performance. In this case, the procedures were not related to job performance. Therefore, they violated Title VII. *Griggs v. Duke Power Co.,* 401 U.S. 424, 91 S.Ct. 849, 28 L.Ed.2d 158 (1971).

◆ The Supreme Court created a shifting burden of proof standard for Title VII discrimination lawsuits in a case where a black civil rights activist engaged in disruptive and illegal activity against his former employer, asserting that his discharge and the employer's general hiring practices were racially motivated. Soon after, the employer advertised for qualified personnel but rejected the activist's reemployment application on the grounds of his illegal conduct. The activist filed a complaint with the EEOC and claimed a Title VII violation. The EEOC found that there was reasonable cause to believe that the decision violated Title VII, which forbids discrimination against applicants or employees for protesting discriminatory employment conditions. The activist then filed suit against the employer, and a Missouri federal district court ruled that the activist's illegal activity was not protected.

The case reached the U.S. Supreme Court, which held that in a private, non-class-action complaint under Title VII, the complaining party has the burden of establishing a ***prima facie* case** of employment discrimination. Therefore, the activist had to show that:

1) he belonged to a racial minority
2) he applied and was qualified for a job the employer was trying to fill
3) he was rejected, and
4) the employer continued to seek applicants with his qualifications.

Even though the activist had done this, the employer had responded to the activist's *prima facie* case by showing that it had a reason for rejecting him. The Court remanded the case with instructions to provide the activist an opportunity to establish his ultimate burden to show that the employer's reason for refusal was simply a pretext for a racially discriminatory decision. *McDonnell Douglas Corp. v. Green*, 411 U.S. 792, 93 S.Ct. 1817, 36 L.Ed.2d 668 (1973).

◆ Two African-American employees in Alabama sued under Title VII when they were passed over for promotions in favor of two white employees. The plant manager called them "boy" when talking to them. A jury ruled in their favor, but the Eleventh Circuit held that the use of the word "boy" by itself was not evidence of discrimination. The U.S. Supreme Court held that **the use of the word "boy" by itself could evidence racial animus**, given the context of the remark, inflection or tone of voice, local custom and historical usage. Also, the employees did not have to prove that their qualifications were so superior to the white employees' that the difference virtually jumped off the page and slapped the court in the face. A better test was needed for determining pretext in the qualifications context – e.g., were the plaintiff's qualifications "clearly superior"? Or could no reasonable person have chosen the selected candidate over the plaintiff? The Court remanded the case. *Ash v. Tyson Foods, Inc.*, 546 U.S. 454, 126 S.Ct. 1195, 163 L.Ed.2d 1053 (2006).

◆ A Missouri halfway house demoted and ultimately discharged an African-American correctional officer, who sued for race discrimination under Title VII. A federal court found that the employer's stated reasons for its actions were pretextual. However, the court held that the officer had failed to carry his ultimate burden of proving that the adverse actions were racially motivated. The case reached the U.S. Supreme Court, which agreed that **even if an employer's asserted reasons for its actions are pretextual, a plaintiff is not necessarily entitled to judgment as a matter of law**. Once the officer established a *prima facie* case of discrimination, a presumption arose that the employer unlawfully discriminated against him. This presumption placed upon the employer the burden of proving that the adverse actions were taken for legitimate, nondiscriminatory reasons. However, the ultimate burden of persuasion remained at all times with the employee. The case was remanded to determine whether the employer intentionally discriminated against the officer. *St. Mary's Honor Center v. Hicks*, 509 U.S. 502, 113 S.Ct. 2742, 125 L.Ed.2d 407 (1993).

◆ A federal court ordered a union to end its discriminatory practices, establishing a 29% nonwhite membership goal (based on the percentage of nonwhites in the relevant labor pool in New York City). After the union failed to comply, the court imposed a fine to be placed in a special fund so as to increase nonwhite membership in the union. The U.S. Supreme Court noted that **Title VII allowed the kind of affirmative, race-conscious relief the district court had ordered**. A court need not order relief only for actual victims of past discrimination, but can also order relief of a broader scope to satisfy the purposes of Title VII. *Local 28 of Sheet Metal Workers v. EEOC,* 478 U.S. 421, 106 S.Ct. 3019, 92 L.Ed.2d 344 (1986).

◆ A union and a Louisiana company entered into a collective bargaining agreement. The agreement included an affirmative action plan designed to raise the percentage of black craftworkers in the company's plants to the percentage of blacks in the local labor force. After some junior black employees were selected for in-plant craft training programs over some senior white employees, a lawsuit was brought, alleging that the affirmative action program violated Title VII. The U.S. Supreme Court stated that **Title VII's prohibition against racial discrimination did not condemn all private, voluntary, race-conscious affirmative action plans**. To do so would defeat the very purpose of Title VII. The affirmative action plan here was permissible. It opened employment opportunities for blacks in areas that were traditionally closed to them, it did not unnecessarily trammel the interests of white employees, and it did not create an absolute bar. Finally, the plan was a temporary measure, designed only to eliminate a manifest racial imbalance. *United Steelworkers v. Weber*, 443 U.S. 193, 99 S.Ct. 2721, 61 L.Ed.2d 480 (1979).

◆ Two white employees of a transportation company were discharged for misappropriating cargo from one of the company's shipments. However, a black employee, charged with the same offense, was not fired. When they sued under Title VII, the U.S. Supreme Court held that **Title VII and Section 1981 apply to whites as much as to nonwhites in the private employment context**. A discipline policy that is applied more harshly to whites than nonwhites violates Title VII. *McDonald v. Santa Fe Trail Transportation Co.,* 427 U.S. 273, 96 S.Ct. 2574, 49 L.Ed.2d 493 (1976).

- A 53-year-old employee of Hungarian descent was fired after he refused to resign. He sued the company under Title VII and the Age Discrimination in Employment Act, asserting that the real reason for the termination was discrimination on the basis of national origin and age. A New York federal court dismissed the complaint because he had not adequately alleged circumstances that supported an inference of discrimination. The Second Circuit affirmed, explaining that the employee failed to set forth a *prima facie* case of discrimination under *McDonnell Douglas*. On further appeal, the U.S. Supreme Court held that in employment discrimination cases, **the pleadings do not need to contain specific facts** detailing the alleged bias in order to avoid dismissal. They need only contain "a short and plain statement" of the case. The Court reversed and remanded the case. *Swierkiewicz v. Sorema N.A.*, 534 U.S. 506, 122 S.Ct. 992, 152 L.Ed.2d 1 (2002).

- A black assistant manager at an Illinois restaurant claimed he was fired because he complained that a white colleague fired a black subordinate for race-based reasons. He sued the restaurant for retaliation under 42 U.S.C. § 1981, which prohibits race discrimination in the making and enforcement of contracts. The case reached the U.S. Supreme Court, which held that **Section 1981 also prohibits employers from retaliating against employees who complain of race discrimination**. The right to "make and enforce contracts" also includes the right to complain of race discrimination without being retaliated against for doing so. *CBOCS West, Inc. v. Humphries*, 128 S.Ct. 1951 (U.S. 2008).

B. Race Discrimination

Most cases of race discrimination get filed under Title VII (intentional and unintentional discrimination) or 42 U.S.C. § 1981 (intentional discrimination only). Under Title VII, employees must first avail themselves of administrative remedies before suing, whereas under Section 1981, employees can proceed to court directly.

Since most employers ensure that intentional race discrimination does not occur, the greater danger often lies in unintentional discrimination – for example, where an employer requires a college degree for a job that does not necessitate such an education. Even though this policy is neutral on its face, it could be construed as discriminatory where more whites than minorities graduate from college.

Affirmative Action: While affirmative action may be permissible in very limited circumstances – for example, where there has been historic discrimination or where a current imbalance is due to past discriminatory practices – you should not assume that an affirmative action policy will comply with Title VII.

- A Massachusetts production supervisor from Jamaica decided to have urgent dental work done in Jamaica. He got another supervisor to cover for him and sent his boss an e-mail confirming the time he'd be off. However, he did not submit a written request for the time off as required by company policy. Once in Jamaica, he realized he needed another week off and left a voice mail message with his boss, but again failed to fill out a computer spreadsheet, as required by company policy. His manager, who had told him he hated Jamaicans and Jamaican music a year earlier, notified HR of his failure to follow company procedures. When the supervisor returned to work, he met with managers to explain his absence. A separate review committee fired him, and he sued under Title VII. A federal court and the First Circuit ruled against him, noting that there was **no evidence of race discrimination in the termination process**. His boss had minimal input into the termination decision. *Thompson v. The Coca-Cola Co.*, 522 F.3d 168 (1st Cir. 2008).

- A black manager at a UPS facility in Indiana dated and then married a white employee who worked in another department. This was in violation of the company's anti-fraternization policy. After UPS fired the manager, he sued under Title VII, **claiming that he was fired because the company didn't want him associating with a white woman**. A federal court granted pretrial judgment for UPS, and the Seventh Circuit affirmed. Here, the manager was warned to "rectify" the situation and failed to do so. Also, he failed to show that similarly situated white couples were treated differently. Another white manager who refused to end a relationship with an employee was fired too. *Ellis v. United Parcel Service*, 523 F.3d 823 (7th Cir. 2008).

- A white assistant coach for a New York university married a black woman and was fired four years later, when the team's performance slipped. The university also fired a black assistant coach, but retained the most junior assistant coach, who was white. When the coach sued under Title VII, **claiming he had been discriminated against because of his association with a black woman**, the Second Circuit held that there were fact issues for a jury as to whether the reason offered by the university was a pretext for discrimination. The coach offered evidence that a vice president was biased against blacks and that there was pressure to fire him to appeal to the university's mostly white alumni. *Holcomb v. Iona College*, 521 F.3d 130 (2d Cir. 2008).

- A security company employed a white female and an Asian male as security officers for a Philadelphia client. Although the two employees met the company's security requirements, they did not meet the client's standards. The African-American company president then decided to meet with all Philadelphia employees to discuss the client's requirements. He made the meeting mandatory and told three African-American employees about it. However, the other two employees were never told about it and failed to show up. After they were fired, they sued for race discrimination. The company sought pretrial judgment, but the court found issues of fact that required a trial. *Adams v. B&B Security Consultants, Inc.*, 2008 WL 375099 (E.D. Pa. 2/12/08).

- A black assistant store manager at a Walgreen store in Illinois was twice offered the manager position at a predominantly black, low-income store. He turned down both offers. **When a manager position opened up in a predominantly white, affluent neighborhood, he sought that promotion.** His supervisor told him that the store "was possibly not ready to have a black manager." A white candidate was selected, and the assistant manager was given differing reasons for why he didn't get the job. He sued. After a federal court granted pretrial judgment to the company, the Seventh Circuit reversed, finding that a jury could conclude that the real reason for the non-promotion was racial bias. *Simple v. Walgreen Co.*, 511 F.3d 668 (7th Cir. 2007).

- A black employee of a rapidly growing company was promoted from sales clerk to assistant manager, but then had an argument with her manager. Although the manager was fired, the assistant manager was passed up for several promotions in favor of less-qualified white candidates. She sued for discrimination and an Arkansas federal court ruled in her favor, awarding her damages of $16,000. The Eighth Circuit largely affirmed, noting that **the company did not have written criteria for the manager position so as to justify its refusal to consider the black assistant manager**. Further, the argument with the manager could not be used as a reason for the non-promotion because a white employee who argued with her manager received a promotion. *Allen v. Tobacco Superstore, Inc.*, 475 F.3d 931 (8th Cir. 2007).

- The African-American corporate purchasing manager for Dr Pepper was passed over for promotion to vice president of purchasing in favor of a white candidate from Coca-Cola who had been a logistics manager. After a rocky relationship with the new vice president, the manager was fired. He then sued for discrimination in the non-promotion as well as the firing. A Texas federal court granted pretrial judgment to Dr Pepper, but the Fifth Circuit reversed in part. Although the deteriorating relationship led to poor performance that justified the termination, the promotion decision may have been discriminatory. **Dr Pepper offered inconsistent explanations for its decision** to hire the white candidate, making a jury trial necessary. *Burrell v. Dr Pepper/Seven Up Bottling Group*, 482 F.3d 408 (5th Cir. 2007).

- An African-American security employee with a Colorado company was fired after a video camera showed him leaving two hours early, and after there was a discrepancy in his weekly log. Not until after he sued for discrimination under Title VII did he offer an explanation for why he had walked out of the store early (to check gas tanks behind the building). A federal court and the Tenth Circuit ruled against him. Here, **the company conducted a reasonable investigation and honestly believed he engaged in misconduct**. His explanation casting doubt on the decision came too late. *Young v. Dillon Companies*, 468 F.3d 1243 (10th Cir. 2006).

- An African-American team leader at a Tennessee plant was fired after cursing at subordinates. He also allegedly falsified time cards and intimidated his subordinates to the point that they sought transfers. A white team leader who also cursed at subordinates wasn't fired, and a Title VII lawsuit erupted. The case reached the Sixth Circuit, which ruled for the company. Here, the two employees' misconduct was not substantially identical. **The white employee only cursed, while the African-American employee allegedly committed other misconduct as well.** And the investigation, while not optimal, led the company to believe the employee had committed the misconduct alleged. *Haughton v. Orchid Automation*, 206 Fed.Appx. 524 (6th Cir. 2006).

- A black woman from Zimbabwe who had permanent resident status worked for a Colorado company. She complained of race discrimination after a comment by her supervisor. Three months later, her supervisor gave her a positive annual review. Five months after that, the employee went to Zimbabwe for a vacation and had a problem with her immigration papers that delayed her return. She reached the company by phone to explain the problem but failed to call in for the next several days, apparently because of problems with international telephone lines. The company considered her to have abandoned her job and discharged her. She sued for race and national origin discrimination, and retaliation under Title VII. A federal court and the Tenth Circuit ruled against her. **The company followed its employee handbook on job abandonment**, and the discharge was not causally connected to the earlier complaint. It came nine months later and after a positive review from her supervisor. *Antonio v. The Sygma Network*, 458 F.3d 1177 (10th Cir. 2006).

- An African-American poker dealer applied for a job at a casino in Mississippi. Even though he was certified and his skills were considered above average, he was not hired. He sued under Title VII for race discrimination. Another dealer at the casino testified that one of her supervisors commented that he didn't like to hire black dealers because the customers wouldn't like it. A federal judge found her testimony not credible and refused to let a jury have the case. The Fifth Circuit reversed, noting that the credibility of the witness was for a jury to determine. The lawsuit was allowed to proceed. **The comment was direct evidence of discrimination** even though the employee could not remember which manager made the statement. *Jones v. Robinson Property Group, d/b/a/ Horseshoe Casino & Hotel*, 427 F.3d 987 (5th Cir. 2005).

- The new CEO of a credit union in Oregon decided to reorganize operations and eliminated the position of an African-American vice president who was responsible for managing bank branches, cash operations and lending. The vice president became the director of lending. The CEO also created a new position (president of sales and branch operations) and planned to promote a lower-level white employee into the position. The former vice president sued for race discrimination under Title VII. A federal court dismissed the case, but the Ninth Circuit reversed in part, finding issues of fact over whether the demotion occurred because of race. Here, **the African-American vice president was the only senior executive to be demoted**. *Cornwell v. Electra Cent. Credit Union*, 439 F.3d 1018 (9th Cir. 2006).

◆ An African-American employee of a company in New Mexico was fired after an HR supervisor examined his personnel file and determined that his refusal to work a Sunday shift warranted discharge. To make the decision, the HR manager relied entirely on the recommendation of the employee's superior, who was allegedly biased. When the EEOC sued for race discrimination, the Tenth Circuit reversed the grant of pretrial judgment for the company, finding issues of fact as to whether the real reason for the firing was discrimination. **Even though the HR supervisor believed the employee had been insubordinate, she relied exclusively on information provided by the biased superior.** *EEOC v. BCI Coca-Cola Bottling Co. of Los Angeles*, 450 F.3d 476 (10th Cir. 2006).

◆ Over two weekends in July 2001, bomb threats were made against a telemarketing center in Missouri. When a sales manager played a tape of one of the phone calls to his team leaders, nine of them identified the voice as belonging to an African-American employee. The company fired the employee and he then sued under Title VII, alleging race discrimination. A federal court and the Eighth Circuit ruled against him. The company may have mistakenly believed he made the calls, but **it had legitimate reasons to believe he had made the threats**, including the voice recognition and the fact that the calls were made to a number that only employees were likely to know. *Johnson v. AT&T Corp.*, 422 F.3d 756 (8th Cir. 2005).

◆ An African-American engineer at a company in Indiana was fired after receiving three disciplinary notices in one year. He claimed he was treated less favorably than a white engineer and sued for race discrimination under Title VII. A federal district court and the Seventh Circuit Court of Appeals ruled against him. Here, the employee had been with the company for four years whereas the white engineer had started only eight months previously and was still learning the job. **The substantial gap in experience meant that the two employees were not similarly situated.** Further, even though the white engineer's supervisor received complaints about his performance for several months before issuing him a disciplinary notice, the black employee's supervisors had received complaints about his performance for several years before giving him his first disciplinary notice. *Bio v. Federal Express Corp.*, 424 F.3d 593 (7th Cir. 2005).

◆ A black female employed by a company in South Carolina applied for a managerial position, which was eventually given to a white woman. The black woman sued for race discrimination, claiming that she was more qualified because she had prior management experience and a master's degree in public administration. The selected candidate did not have a college degree and had been with the company for less than 18 months. The case reached the Fourth Circuit, which ruled in favor of the company. Here, although **the selection process was subjective**, it relied on nine factors for evaluating candidates, and the white employee scored higher in every category. *Diamond v. Colonial Life & Accident Insurance Co.*, 416 F.3d 310 (4th Cir. 2005).

◆ An African-American FedEx driver in Tennessee began a pallet-recycling program to earn money for company parties and other events. He also collected pallets while off duty and sold them to earn spare cash. When the driver later complained about how African-American employees were being treated, he was accused of stealing money from the company. He admitted during a lengthy interrogation that he may have made a few small mistakes in calculating the number of pallets sold. His supervisors then reported that he had confessed to the theft, and the regional manager fired him without verifying the truth of the information she received. When he sued for race discrimination and retaliation under Title VII, a jury awarded him $15,000 in back pay and $100,000 in punitive damages. The Sixth Circuit upheld the award, noting that **the company managers failed to act in good faith**. *Tisdale v. Federal Express Corp.*, 415 F.3d 516 (6th Cir. 2005).

◆ An African-American independent insurance agent sued American Family Insurance Group for race discrimination under 42 U.S.C. § 1981 in an Iowa federal court. The question arose as to whether she could even bring the lawsuit because of her status as an independent contractor, and the court held that she could. **The contractual relationship protected by Section 1981 is not limited to employees.** However, she lost her case because she failed to produce evidence of race discrimination. She only produced an unauthenticated list of transferred accounts that did not identify the race of the transferors or transferees. *Wortham v. American Family Insurance Group*, 385 F.3d 1139 (8th Cir. 2004).

◆ A telephone marketing and calling company in Alabama hired a black employee to work on a gubernatorial campaign to "get out the vote." At the request of the candidates, the company engaged in "race-matched calling," which meant that black callers called only black voters and white callers called only white voters in order to lure the voter groups to the polls on election day. During the race-matched calling, callers were segregated by whom they called. They were also physically separated by race in separate rooms. After the election, the employee was laid off, and she sued the company under 42 U.S.C. § 1981. The court found that the race-matched calling and segregation of the work force violated Section 1981. **Employers are forbidden by Section 1981 from assigning work based on stereotyped assumptions.** On appeal, the Eleventh Circuit held that even though the company had no malicious intent in separating its workers, its actions amounted to intentional segregation of black and white workers. However, punitive damages were not justified. *Ferrill v. Parker Group, Inc.*, 168 F.3d 468 (11th Cir. 1999).

C. Racial Harassment

Like sexual harassment, racial harassment is prohibited by Title VII and state law. Every employer should have a policy banning all harassment. The policy should include a means for employees to report the harassment without fear of retaliation.

◆ A driver for a trucking company in Iowa was married to a black woman. He was subjected to a number of pranks by a co-worker, who also made a number of racially derogatory comments. However, all but one of the comments were made outside his hearing. He only learned of them later from co-workers. When he complained to his supervisor, the supervisor said that if he didn't like the way things were run, he could leave his keys on the supervisor's desk. He quit and sued under Title VII. A federal court and the Eighth Circuit ruled against him. **The comments he did not hear did not rise to the level of a hostile work environment**, and the pranks pulled on him were also pulled on other drivers, even if not to the same extent. *Carpenter v. Con-Way Cent. Express, Inc.*, 481 F.3d 611 (8th Cir. 2007).

◆ An African-American Boeing employee in Maryland was told by his team leader to refer to him as "Massah Dave." He reported the comment to a supervisor and the human resources (HR) department, and requested a written apology. The team leader signed a written apology drafted by HR, and the employee signed a statement indicating that he accepted the apology. No further incidents arose. The employee nevertheless sued Boeing under Title VII. A federal court and the Fourth Circuit ruled against him. **The single comment was not severe or pervasive enough to create Title VII liability.** And the employee had accepted the apology as being a sufficient response. *Lamb v. The Boeing Co.*, 213 Fed.Appx. 175 (4th Cir. 2007).

◆ An advertising manager for a Philadelphia radio station became concerned about a female account executive's unprofessional attire and handed out "Dress for Success" books to all the account executives. He did not read the book himself. The station's only black account executive was offended by some of the statements in the book (telling blacks to "dress very white") and he complained. The station's HR director then collected the books, but the black employee filed a race discrimination complaint. After he won a $610,000 damage award, the Commonwealth Court vacated the award. **The single incident of distributing the book was not severe or pervasive enough to amount to racial harassment**, and the HR manager acted promptly in collecting the books. *Infinity Broadcasting Corp. v. Pennsylvania Human Relations Comm'n*, 893 A.2d 151 (Pa. Commw. Ct. 2006).

◆ A co-worker of a black bank teller in Minnesota called her a monkey and a chimpanzee and other racially derogatory terms eight times in three months. She complained to her supervisor but did not file a formal complaint. Nothing was done until she filed a formal complaint, at which time the co-worker was warned, then fired. When she sued for racial harassment, a federal court and the Eighth Circuit Court of Appeals ruled against her. **Even though the comments were severe enough to constitute racial harassment under Title VII, the bank fired the co-worker within a month after the vice president learned of the comments.** The bank's response, though not ideal, was sufficient to avoid liability. *Green v. Franklin National Bank of Minneapolis*, 459 F.3d 903 (8th Cir. 2006).

◆ The CEO of a company in Oregon **repeatedly called an Arab-American employee "Manny"** even though the employee objected on several occasions. The CEO believed that calling the employee by a "Western" name would increase his chances for success and be more acceptable to the company's clients. The employee sued under 42 U.S.C. § 1981, and a jury awarded him $15,000 in compensatory damages and $15,000 in punitive damages for a hostile work environment. The Ninth Circuit upheld the award. Even though the nickname was not egregiously racial, it was used so frequently and consistently that it created a hostile work environment. *El-Hakem v. BJY*, 415 F.3d 1068 (9th Cir. 2005).

◆ A Hispanic employee at an Indiana plant experienced racially derogatory graffiti as well as name-calling by his mostly white co-workers. He reported the graffiti twice before it was removed and also told his supervisor that he believed he was being harassed because of his race. However, he did not follow the company's formal procedure for reporting harassment. Still, his supervisor told the plant's general manager about the problem. No investigation was conducted until after the employee had filed charges with the EEOC. At that time, the company concluded that the employee was not subjected to harassment. In the lawsuit that followed, a federal court granted pretrial judgment to the company, but the Seventh Circuit reversed. **Even though the employee did not follow the proper complaint procedure, the company knew about the complaint.** A new trial would determine whether the company had acted reasonably to prevent harassment after becoming aware of the problem. *Cerros v. Steel Technologies, Inc.*, 398 F.3d 944 (7th Cir. 2005).

◆ A company in Illinois brought in a new vice president of human resources (HR), who was asked to focus on client dissatisfaction with the unit. She was also informed of concerns that her predecessor and the director of HR had with an African-American employee. She immediately began to document the employee's performance problems, noting that the employee was inaccessible during work hours, missed deadlines, related inaccurate information and failed to keep her credit card account up to date. She put the employee on a performance improvement plan and ultimately fired her. The employee sued for racial harassment under Title VII. A federal court and the Seventh Circuit ruled against her. The vice president carefully documented the employee's poor performance, and **a single comment she made about changing the complexion of the unit was not enough to show harassment**. *Luckie v. Ameritech Corp.*, 389 F.3d 708 (7th Cir. 2004).

◆ Two African-American lead repairmen for an Illinois power company worked independently on one-man trucks responding to customer calls. After a new plant manager took over, a white employee began harassing the two repairmen. The plant manager refused to do anything about the harassment, and one of the repairmen contacted the company's HR department. The plant manager then transferred the two repairmen to construction laborer positions that required them to dig ditches in the snow. They sued the company under Title VII and Section 1981 for race discrimination, and a jury ruled in their favor. The Seventh Circuit agreed, finding that **the reassignment was a "stripping of duties" that amounted to adverse action**. *Tart v. Illinois Power Co.*, 366 F.3d 461 (7th Cir. 2004).

D. National Origin Discrimination

Title VII prohibits discrimination on the basis of national origin by employers, but discrimination against noncitizens on the basis of alienage has been upheld by the U.S. Supreme Court. National origin discrimination claims are very similar to race discrimination claims but are a bit broader in scope and don't offer all the protections of race discrimination claims.

For example, although race can never be a bona fide occupational qualification for a job, national origin can, in very limited circumstances. Still, as a general rule, **never** make employment-related decisions on the basis of national origin.

- A Muslim car salesman in Texas endured a number of harassing comments from his supervisor and co-workers. **His supervisor called him Taliban and Arab even though he was from India**, and also mocked his religious dietary restrictions and his need to pray during the workday. After September 11, his co-workers suggested that he was involved in the terrorist attacks, and one told him he should go back to where he came from because of his beliefs. The supervisor also issued him a written warning for acting like a "Muslim extremist," and banged on his office partition to startle the salesman every time he walked by. When the salesman complained, he was fired. He filed a complaint with the EEOC, which sued for national origin discrimination on his behalf. A federal court granted pretrial judgment to the dealership, but the Fifth Circuit reversed, noting that all these incidents, when added together, could amount to a hostile work environment under Title VII. A trial was required. *EEOC v. WC & M Enterprises*, 496 F.3d 393 (5th Cir. 2007).

- An accountant from Peru who spoke rudimentary English emigrated to America and got a job as a credit union clerk after interviewing for the job in Spanish. Many of the credit union's customers spoke Spanish. Less than a year later, a new CEO took over and the clerk was fired because the CEO couldn't understand the clerk's limited English. The clerk sued for national origin discrimination and the credit union sought pretrial judgment. The District of Columbia Court of Appeals refused to award pretrial judgment to the credit union, finding issues of fact that required a trial. Here, there was evidence that **the CEO may have selectively enforced the credit union's bilingual language requirement against the clerk**, and that the requirement may have been added after the clerk was hired. *Estenos v. PAHO/WHO Federal Credit Union*, 952 A.2d 878 (D.C. Ct. App. 2008).

- An Iraqi supervisor at an Ohio manufacturing plant was fired because of numerous complaints about the demeaning way he communicated with his subordinates and because his superiors saw him ignore potential safety problems. He sued under Title VII, asserting that the real reason was national origin discrimination. He pointed out that employees discussed the Iraq war over lunch, and that, at his termination meeting, the operations manager said, "Maybe it's the people of Northwest Ohio who have a problem with you." A federal court and the Sixth Circuit held that the company provided ample evidence to support its decision to fire the supervisor. **The single comment, in the context of a discussion about his personality and management conflicts, could be construed as a statement about Midwestern congeniality.** The termination was upheld. *Abdulnour v. Campbell Soup Supply Co., LLC*, 502 F.3d 496 (6th Cir. 2007).

- A Hispanic FedEx driver enrolled in the company's Leadership Apprentice Course and twice interviewed for a supervisory position. When he was denied the promotion, he sued for national origin discrimination under Title VII, claiming the customer service manager had told him he would have been promoted except for the human resources (HR) manager's concerns about his accent. A Michigan federal court granted pretrial judgment to FedEx, but the Sixth Circuit Court of Appeals reversed. Here, **the customer service manager's statement about the HR manager's bias was admissible evidence of discrimination** that demanded a trial. It would have to be balanced against FedEx's assertion that he wasn't promoted because he never finished the leadership course and never formally applied for the position. *In re Rodriguez*, 487 F.3d 1001 (6th Cir. 2007).

- An Egyptian-born Muslim worked as a manager trainee at a Minnesota convenience store. After the busy holiday season, he was demoted to assistant trainee based on reports of insubordination. His hours were also cut back. He walked off the job after being accused of harassment, then sued under Title VII, claiming discrimination on the basis of his Arabic race. A federal court and the Eighth Circuit ruled against him. The company had **a legitimate reason for demoting him** and for cutting back his hours. Also, derogatory comments by an assistant manager could not be attributed to the company because the assistant manager was not involved in the decision to demote him. *Elnashar v. Speedway SuperAmerica, LLC*, 484 F.3d 1046 (8th Cir. 2007).

- A Kansas company learned that the Immigration and Naturalization Service was going to inspect its facility and became concerned because it had hired 300 people in a short time and knew it might not have completed I-9 forms for them. A Hispanic employee who had been hired under a more careful screening process was **suspended until he provided documentation of his eligibility to work**. After providing the documentation, he demanded a written apology and a complete explanation of why he had been suspended. The HR manager believed the demand amounted to a voluntary resignation and told the employee to leave the office. The employee, believing he had been fired, sued under Title VII. The case reached the Tenth Circuit Court of Appeals, which ruled in favor of the company. Here, the suspension was legitimate. Further, the HR manager's belief that the employee would not return to work without a written apology justified the termination decision. And the employee failed to show that this reason was actually a pretext for national origin discrimination. *Zamora v. Elite Logistics*, 478 F.3d 1160 (10th Cir. 2007).

◆ After a company in Illinois acquired a major new client, an India-born employee got a new supervisor. Shortly thereafter, amid complaints from the new client and her new supervisor, the company eliminated her position and fired her. When she sued for national origin and race bias under Title VII, the Seventh Circuit ruled against her. **The discretionary bonus she received at the time of her discharge was more like severance pay than an acknowledgement that she was meeting the company's expectations.** Also, her duties and supervision had changed since her last, generally positive performance review, thus giving that review less impact. *Johal v. Little Lady Foods*, 434 F.3d 943 (7th Cir. 2006).

◆ An international manufacturer hired an employee to work at its Brazilian facility, later transferring him to its Indiana facility. He worked as a buyer and eventually learned that he was making less than two senior buyers who had just been hired. His supervisor told him that he might be getting a lower salary because he was Brazilian. He sued for national origin discrimination, claiming that the supervisor's comment proved bias by the company. A federal court and the Seventh Circuit ruled against him. The company proffered a legitimate reason for the difference in pay – the greater education and experience of the senior buyers. **The supervisor's statement was not direct evidence of discrimination because he did not determine the employee's salary.** *Cardoso v. Robert Bosch Corp.*, 427 F.3d 429 (7th Cir. 2005).

◆ An employee of a security company in Pennsylvania was fired when he refused to remove or cover Confederate flag stickers on his lunch box and pickup truck. He sued the company under Title VII, asserting discrimination on the basis of religion and national origin, based on his claim as a "Confederate Southern-American." A federal court dismissed his case and the Third Circuit affirmed. Although national origin usually refers to a country of origin, it could be expanded to include a region. However, **even if "Confederate Southern-American" was a valid national origin, the employee's claim still failed**. The Confederate flag sends out a message that stigmatizes African-Americans by representing the belief that white men have the right to own black slaves. And the employee was not fired because of his status or beliefs, but because he refused to remove or cover the stickers. *Storey v. Burns Int'l Security Services*, 390 F.3d 760 (3d Cir. 2004).

◆ A Hispanic parts salesman for a truck dealership was subjected to numerous derogatory nicknames. When the president of the company heard about the situation, he ordered a review of the dealership's anti-discrimination policies. Subsequently, all but one of the salesman's co-workers stopped using the ethnic slurs. After the salesman was fired, he sued the company under Title VII, alleging national origin discrimination in the form of a hostile work environment. A jury awarded him $25,000 in compensatory damages and $50,000 in punitive damages. The Eleventh Circuit affirmed in part but vacated the award of punitive damages. Here, there was sufficient evidence that **the harassment occurred multiple times each day, thus altering the conditions of employment**. Also, the manager had constructive notice of the harassment because he was present on some of the occasions. Finally, the manager was high enough up the corporate ladder to justify imposing liability on the company. However, there was insufficient evidence of malice or reckless indifference on the company's part, so the punitive damages award could not stand. *Miller v. Kenworth of Dothan, Inc.*, 277 F.3d 1269 (11th Cir. 2002).

◆ A Hispanic employee responsible for inspecting and weeding out damaged or unfit products at a company's Omaha plant learned of two promotions and sought to be advanced into those positions. However, he did not bid for the positions according to the promotion procedure available. Nor was he recommended by the company's human resources (HR) manager as a potential candidate for promotion because: 1) none of his supervisors recommended him for the list; 2) he was not a member of the Hispanic Association of Employees, which recommended Hispanic employee members for certain promotions; and 3) he had not worked with the HR manager so as to become known as a potential candidate. When he failed to get the promotions, he sued the company under Title VII for national origin discrimination and obtained an award of $300,000. The Eighth Circuit Court of Appeals reversed the award, noting that the employee had not proven national origin discrimination because **he failed to abide by the company's procedures for promotion**. Since the procedures were not discriminatory, his Title VII claim failed. *Cardenas v. AT&T Corp., Lucent Technologies*, 245 F.3d 994 (8th Cir. 2001).

◆ A citizen of Mexico, who resided lawfully in the United States, sought employment as a seamstress with a manufacturing company. Her application was rejected due to a longstanding policy against the employment of aliens. After exhausting her administrative remedies with the EEOC, the applicant sued the company in a Texas federal court, asserting that the company had discriminated against her on the basis of national origin in violation of Title VII. The court granted pretrial judgment to the applicant, but the U.S. Court of Appeals, Fifth Circuit, reversed. It determined that the phrase "national origin" did not include citizenship.

The case then came before the U.S. Supreme Court. The Supreme Court held that the company's refusal to hire the woman because of her citizenship was not national origin discrimination in violation of Title VII. Even though it protects aliens against discrimination because of race, color, religion, sex, or national origin, **Title VII does not prohibit discrimination against aliens on the basis of alienage**. Here, the company had not refused to hire the applicant because of her Mexican ancestry, but because she was not a United States citizen. This was not forbidden by Title VII. The Court affirmed the court of appeals' decision against the applicant. *Espinoza v. Farah Manufacturing Co.*, 414 U.S. 86, 94 S.Ct. 334, 38 L.Ed.2d 287 (1973).

II. GENDER DISCRIMINATION

Gender discrimination, like race discrimination, violates Title VII of the Civil Rights Act of 1964. Where an employee proves under Title VII that his or her employer has engaged in unlawful intentional discrimination on the basis of sex, the employee will be entitled to recover money damages in addition to equitable relief.

Where the discrimination is unintentional, money damages are not available (except for equitable relief like back pay).

Where an employer shows that sex is a bona fide occupational qualification for a position, it will be able to legally discriminate against members of one sex. However, such instances will be rare. As a general rule, **never** take gender into account in hiring and promotion decisions.

A. Title VII

◆ One of the few female area managers for an Alabama plant worked for the company from 1979 until 1998. For most of that time, she and all other salaried employees received or were denied raises based on their supervisors' evaluations of their job performance. Initially, her salary was in line with the salaries of male area managers, but over time her pay slipped in comparison. She alleged that the pay disparity began in the 1980s as retaliation because she rejected a supervisor's sexual advances. She also claimed that another supervisor gave her a poor evaluation because of her gender. However, she didn't complain to the EEOC until March 1998. When she finally sued under Title VII, the case reached the U.S. Supreme Court. Over a vigorous dissent, the Court held that she waited too long to sue. **She could not prove that the most current raises she received were the result of any discriminatory intent.** She should have filed an EEOC charge within 180 days after each of the earlier poor evaluations. *Ledbetter v. Goodyear Tire & Rubber Co., Inc.*, 550 U.S. 618, 127 S.Ct. 2162, 167 L.Ed.2d 982 (2007).

◆ A Caesars Palace (Las Vegas) employee claimed she was disciplined and finally fired because of her gender. She was the only woman who worked in the hotel and casino's warehouse. Although her work was regarded as "excellent," she had a number of problems with her co-workers and supervisors. When she complained about being singled out because she was a woman, the human resources (HR) department refused to intervene. At trial, she recounted several incidents of discrimination where she was formally reprimanded for rules infractions while similarly situated male employees were not. Caesars maintained that she was fired because of the disciplinary problems. She countered that, although she was not a perfect employee, her gender was the "real" reason or motivating factor for her discharge. The jury awarded $264,000 to the employee. The Ninth Circuit and the Supreme Court affirmed. **A plaintiff in a discrimination case need not have direct proof of bias to qualify for a "mixed motive" jury instruction.** Title VII provides that "a plaintiff need only 'demonstrate' that an employer used a forbidden consideration with respect to 'any employment practice.'" *Desert Palace Inc. d/b/a Caesars Palace Hotel & Casino v. Costa*, 539 U.S. 90, 123 S.Ct. 2148, 156 L.Ed.2d 84 (2003).

- A female lower-level director of the American Dental Association sought a promotion to the position of legislative director. She competed for the position with a male lower-level director; both had received "distinguished" performance ratings. After she was rejected, she sued in a federal court for gender discrimination, claiming that the male candidate had been pre-selected. A jury found discrimination and awarded her $52,718 in back pay. However, the district court judge refused to allow the jury to consider punitive damages. The case reached the U.S. Supreme Court, which clarified when employers may be liable for punitive damages under Title VII. A plaintiff need not prove that the employer engaged in some extraordinarily egregious behavior independent of the employer's state of mind. Instead, the employer must act with **malice or reckless indifference** to the plaintiff's federally protected rights. In other words, the terms "malice" and "reckless indifference" pertain to "the employer's knowledge that it may be acting in violation of federal law." **Punitive damages** are not warranted where the employer is unaware of the relevant federal prohibition, or where the employer discriminates with the distinct belief the discrimination is lawful, such as where it reasonably believes a bona fide occupational qualification is satisfied. *Kolstad v. American Dental Ass'n*, 527 U.S. 526, 119 S.Ct. 2118, 144 L.Ed.2d 494 (1999).

- An employee of an Illinois educational materials company filed a sex discrimination complaint against her employer with the Equal Employment Opportunity Commission (EEOC) asserting that she should have received a promotion. The employer then fired her. The EEOC sued the employer on her behalf for retaliation under Title VII. The employer moved to dismiss the case, stating that it did not have 15 employees during 20 weeks in the past two years and therefore did not come within the coverage of the act. Before the U.S. Supreme Court, the EEOC argued that the appropriate test is whether the parties have an employment relationship on the day in question. This test was already used by the EEOC in age discrimination regulations and the U.S. Department of Labor in Family and Medical Leave Act regulations. The Court agreed with the EEOC that **an employer has an employee if an employment relationship exists between the parties**. Since the employer had employment relationships with 15 or more employees for 38 weeks of the calendar year in question, it was an "employer" under Title VII. *Walters v. Metropolitan Educ. Enterprises, Inc.*, 519 U.S. 202, 117 S.Ct. 660, 136 L.Ed.2d 644 (1997).

- A senior manager at a nationwide professional accounting firm was refused admission as a partner. She sued the firm under Title VII, charging that it had discriminated against her on the basis of sex in its partnership decisions. The district court found that the firm had discriminated against the manager, but held that it could avoid equitable relief if it could prove by clear and convincing evidence that it would have made the same decision absent a discriminatory motive. The U.S. Court of Appeals, D.C. Circuit, affirmed. The U.S. Supreme

Court held that under Title VII, the employer could avoid liability if it showed by a mere preponderance of the evidence that it would have made the same decision even if it had not taken the manager's gender into account. This preserved the employer's right to freedom of choice. The court then reversed and remanded the case for a determination of whether the same decision would have been made absent the discrimination. *Price Waterhouse v. Hopkins*, 490 U.S. 228, 109 S.Ct. 1775, 104 L.Ed.2d 268 (1989).

Under the Civil Rights Act of 1991, if it is shown that **discrimination is a contributing factor in the employment decision**, then (assuming that the employer can show that it would have made the same decision absent the discrimination) courts will be prohibited from ordering certain injunctive relief – like reinstatement. However, money damages may still be available.

◆ A female employee in Maine had six-year-old triplets and an 11-year-old. She sought a promotion, but the job was given to a female employee with a 10-year-old and a 14-year-old. To soften the blow, a female superior told her she didn't get the job because she had a lot on her plate. She sued for sex discrimination under Title VII, **asserting that she was denied the job because of her status as a female caregiver for her children**. A federal court granted pretrial judgment to the company, finding no way for her to prevail at trial. *Chadwick v. Wellpoint, Inc.*, 550 F.Supp.2d 140 (D. Me. 2008).

◆ A female project engineer in Puerto Rico received poor performance evaluations from two different superiors and failed to sufficiently improve her performance after she was put on a performance improvement plan. She was fired, and sued under Title VII for sex discrimination. A federal court and the First Circuit ruled against her, noting that **the company had documented the performance problems as well as her positive attributes**, and that it had even extended her performance improvement plan by a month. *Garcia v. Bristol-Myers Squibb Co.*, 535 F.3d 23 (1st Cir. 2008).

◆ A female office manager and a male sales manager for an Illinois home furnishings store began having an affair. The office manager's husband found out about the affair and threatened the sales manager, who reported the threats to upper management. The store fired the office manager because of the threats. She then sued for discrimination under Title VII and lost. Despite a jury verdict in her favor, the Seventh Circuit held that she could not prove sex discrimination. She was not fired because of the affair. Rather, **she was fired because of her husband's threats**. Also, the company could choose to retain the male sales manager, whom it believed was more valuable to the corporation. Neither he nor his wife made any threats against the store. *Hossack v. Floor Covering Associates of Joliet, Inc.*, 492 F.3d 853 (7th Cir. 2007).

◆ A New Mexico car dealership disciplined a female manager for unsatisfactory performance because she was chronically late for work, made personal phone calls and frequently wasn't in the office such that the dealership had to assign someone else as her backup. However, the dealership didn't discipline a male manager who was also often tardy. When the EEOC sued on her behalf, the Tenth Circuit ruled in favor of the dealership. Here, the two employees were not similarly situated because **the female's problems affected productivity while the male's did not**. No one had to do extra work for him. Thus, the dealership did not violate Title VII. *EEOC v. PVNF, LLC*, 487 F.3d 790 (10th Cir. 2007).

◆ A funeral director for a Missouri company had seven complaints lodged against her in three years, more than any male employee. The company investigated, then suspended her for five days, warning her that future rudeness and unprofessionalism would result in her termination. Subsequently, the company eliminated five director positions (three males, two females). She was chosen for layoff based on her personnel record and high salary. When she sued for sex discrimination, a federal court and the Eighth Circuit ruled against her. She failed to prove that gender played a role in her termination. Also, she was **not similarly situated to male employees who had complaints filed against them**, but who had not been laid off, because she had more complaints filed against her. *Wells v. SCI Management*, 469 F.3d 697 (8th Cir. 2006).

◆ A department director had to decide which of two managers to keep in a reduction in force. He interviewed the managers for about an hour each, then spoke to their subordinates and supervisors. Afterwards, he chose to retain the male, and the female sued for sex discrimination under Title VII. A Maryland federal court ruled for the company, and the Fourth Circuit upheld that decision. **Even though the selection process was informal, the company had established criteria for the decision** and the male candidate had seemed to be more committed to the position. By contrast, the female stated that she did not see herself with the company in five years. *Luh v. J.M. Huber Corp.*, 211 Fed.Appx. 143 (4th Cir. 2006).

◆ A company told a South Dakota employee it was eliminating her position around the same time she informed it she was pregnant. The company then moved up her evaluation and told her she would have to relocate or leave the company. Two weeks later she had a miscarriage. When she refused the transfer, she was fired. She sued for sex discrimination under Title VII and lost because **the transfer offer was not an adverse action**. Further, the Eighth Circuit held that the company had no liability for causing her miscarriage through the stress of the relocation situation. *Reynolds v. Ethicon Endo-Surgery, Inc.*, 454 F.3d 868 (8th Cir. 2006).

◆ The CEO of the Wisconsin Health Fund became romantically interested in a dentist who worked for the fund and decided to promote her to the position of director of the dental clinic. To do so, he had to fire the current director of the clinic – a male with an MBA as well as a dental degree. After being fired, the male clinic director sued the health fund for sex discrimination under Title VII. A federal district court and the Seventh Circuit Court of Appeals ruled against him. **Favoring a woman because of romantic interest is not sex discrimination** even when the male is more qualified for the job. Here, the decision to fire the male and hire the female was purely personal and not based on a belief that women were superior workers. *Preston v. Wisconsin Health Fund*, 397 F.3d 539 (7th Cir. 2005).

◆ An HR manager for a company in Rhode Island counseled a district manager about his treatment of women after **an investigation revealed that he treated women worse than he treated men**. About a year later, the company hired a woman to manage one of its stores. She worked there for less than a year, then quit and sued the company for sex discrimination. A trial court dismissed the lawsuit, but the Supreme Court of Rhode Island reinstated it. Even though the district manager never referred to her gender when he yelled at her, the company could still be liable for sex discrimination where the HR manager's notes revealed the company's awareness of a potential problem. *DeCamp v. Dollar Tree Stores, Inc.*, 875 A.2d 13 (R.I. 2005).

◆ A Nevada casino instituted a "Personal Best" program under which female bartenders and beverage servers had to wear makeup and nail polish, while male bartenders and beverage servers had to keep their hair short and have clean, trimmed fingernails. A female bartender with excellent performance reviews refused to comply with the makeup policy and never applied for a position that did not require makeup. She was fired, and then sued the casino under Title VII, alleging sex discrimination. A federal court and the Ninth Circuit ruled against her. The policy did not burden female servers more than males. **Different grooming standards are discriminatory only when they impose a greater burden on one sex than the other.** Accordingly, the casino could legally enforce its personal appearance policy. *Jespersen v. Harrah's Operating Co.*, 392 F.3d 1076 (9th Cir. 2004).

◆ A Colorado employee worked as a meat wrapper for a company's retail stores. Subsequently, she was given the opportunity to work as a temporary project employee. The assignment was not considered a promotion, and she was not given higher pay or better benefits. She stayed in temporary assignments for nearly two years. Her supervisor then told her he did not need her anymore, and she was returned to her meat-wrapping position, again with no change in salary or benefits. She sued for sex discrimination under Title VII, alleging that two male employees with less experience were kept in the temporary assignment to complete the work she had been told was done. A federal court dismissed her lawsuit on the grounds that the company had not taken "adverse action" against her, but the Tenth Circuit reversed. **The reassignment could be an adverse action because it resulted in a reduction in responsibility.** A trial was required. *Stinnett v. Safeway, Inc.*, 337 F.3d 1213 (10th Cir. 2003).

◆ In a lawsuit brought by the EEOC against a restaurant for gender discrimination, a Florida federal court found that the restaurant intentionally discriminated against four women even though they did not apply for jobs during the period covered by the lawsuit. The restaurant appealed to the Eleventh Circuit, which affirmed in part. The Eleventh Circuit held when **a plaintiff has not actually applied and been rejected for a job**, a case of discrimination can be established by showing 1) a real and present interest in the job, and 2) that she was effectively deterred from applying by the employer's discriminatory practices. Here, two of the women were unable to show that they had a real and present interest in applying for the jobs during the applicable time period. The other two women showed that they had a real and present interest that was effectively deterred by the restaurant's male-servers-only policy. Those two plaintiffs were entitled to back pay and prejudgment interest. *EEOC v. Joe's Stone Crabs, Inc.*, 296 F.3d 1265 (11th Cir. 2002).

◆ A Washington federal court held that a company could not offer a health plan with a comprehensive prescription medicine benefits package that excluded prescription contraceptives. The court stated that **employers cannot exclude benefits that are available only to women**. Denying prescription contraceptives here was tantamount to denying employee benefits on the basis of sex, in violation of Title VII. *Erickson v. Bartell Drug Co.*, 141 F.Supp.2d 1266 (W.D. Wash. 2001).

◆ An airline instituted a policy that limited male flight attendants to maximum weights that corresponded to large body frames. However, its policy for female flight attendants limited them to maximum weights that corresponded to medium body frames. A number of female flight attendants were unable to keep within the airline's guidelines and were fired or otherwise disciplined. They sued the airline under Title VII for sex discrimination. A California federal court certified the lawsuit as a class action, and the airline then eliminated the policy. The airline also offered to reinstate many of the flight attendants who had been terminated under the policy. After the court ruled in favor of the airline, the Ninth Circuit reversed. The airline had treated females less favorably than males because of their protected status and had **provided no evidence that the weight standard was a bona fide occupational qualification**. *Frank v. United Airlines*, 216 F.3d 845 (9th Cir. 2000).

◆ A New Jersey employer revised its appearance and grooming policy, requiring male employees to maintain traditional hair styles, with hair no longer than mid-collar in the back. Two employees, who both wore ponytails, were fired following warnings and progressive discipline after they refused to cut their hair. They sued the employer for sex discrimination. The Superior Court of New Jersey, Appellate Division, found that the sex discrimination claims failed because **hair length policies do not constitute sex discrimination** under Title VII. The employees could not claim any constitutional protection in their appearance, since the Constitution does not protect individuals from the actions of a private employer. *Rivera v. Trump Plaza Hotel & Casino*, 305 N.J.Super. 596, 702 A.2d 1359 (N.J. Super. Ct. App. Div. 1997).

B. The Equal Pay Act

Enacted by Congress in 1963, the Equal Pay Act requires that employers pay males and females the same wages for the same work. As such, the act applies only to sex discrimination in pay. Race-based equal pay claims must be litigated under the more general provisions of Title VII.

Because the Equal Pay Act is part of the Fair Labor Standards Act, employees are protected by the act as long as the employer is engaged in an industry affecting interstate commerce (in contrast to Title VII's 15-employee minimum for triggering coverage). In other words, most employers are covered.

The employee's burden of proof under the act has been interpreted to require only that the jobs under comparison be substantially equal. Strict equality of the jobs under comparison is not required. Thus, if two jobs are basically the same, male and female workers generally must be paid the same.

The Equal Pay Act, 29 U.S.C. § 206(d), provides in relevant part as follows:

(d) Prohibition of sex discrimination

(1) No employer having employees subject to any provisions of this section shall discriminate, within any establishment in which such employees are employed, between employees on the basis of sex by paying wages to employees in such establishment at a rate less than the rate at which he pays wages to employees of the opposite sex in such establishment for equal work on jobs the performance of which requires equal skill, effort, and responsibility, and which are performed under similar working conditions, except where such payment is made pursuant to (i) a seniority system; (ii) a merit system; (iii) a system which measures earnings by quantity or quality of production; or (iv) a differential based on any other factor other than sex: *Provided,* That an employer who is paying a wage rate differential in violation of this subsection shall not, in order to comply with the provisions of this subsection, reduce the wage rate of any employee.

* * *

- An employee of General Electric (GE) worked in the collections department and received high evaluations. Although she had been with the company for 25 years, she earned less than some male collectors who had been transferred in or been demoted from other positions. At age 60, she was discharged as part of a reduction in force. She sued GE under the Equal Pay Act and the Age Discrimination in Employment Act (ADEA). A Georgia federal court ruled against her, and the Eleventh Circuit Court of Appeals affirmed. Here, **she could not show an Equal Pay Act violation because the company had a salary retention policy** (under which demoted employees earned the same salaries) that had been uniformly applied to both men and women for decades. This policy bolstered employee morale and saved GE the cost of training new employees. Also, she failed to prove an ADEA violation because GE showed that it would have made the same decision absent any discrimination. She was laid off on the basis of a "comparison matrix" score that was not related to her age. *Steger v. General Electric Co.*, 318 F.3d 1066 (11th Cir. 2003).

- A saleswoman for a transportation company was appointed to the position of trade show specialist. She was paid her same wage of $756 a week and had to relinquish her company car, but she was allowed to reduce some of her outside accounts. After she resigned, the company appointed a man to the position, paying him $900 a week and allowing him to use a company car. Four months into the job, he was also given an assistant. The saleswoman sued the company for violating the Equal Pay Act (EPA) and state law. A jury found the company violated the EPA, and a federal court awarded her nearly $10,000 in lost wages, the same amount in liquidated damages, emotional distress damages of $30,000 and punitive damages of $200,000. The Eighth Circuit upheld all but the punitive damages award. The job responsibilities for both employees were substantially similar, and **the evidence supported the jury's finding that gender was the reason she had been paid less**. Even though the man had 100 accounts to the woman's 85, he also had an assistant to help him. *Lawrence v. CNF Transportation, Inc.*, 340 F.3d 486 (8th Cir. 2003).

◆ A female employee failed to prove an Equal Pay Act violation where the court determined that the males who were paid more than her had greater experience, education, or were predicted/planned for advancement. These were **legitimate non-gender-based reasons for the differential in pay**, and the employee did not dispute the veracity of the company's assertions. She merely maintained that she should be paid the same amount based on her skills and knowledge. *Hammock v. Nexcel Synthetics, Inc.*, 201 F.Supp.2d 1180 (N.D. Ala. 2002).

◆ A female human resources coordinator at an Indiana manufacturer's plant was responsible for handling matters for the plant's 50 salaried research and development employees. She was paid less than the human resources (HR) managers at two larger plants (127 and 268 workers, some who were salaried and some who were hourly). One of the larger plants was also unionized. When the manufacturer eventually closed the plant, the HR coordinator sued under the Equal Pay Act, asserting that she had been improperly paid less than the male HR managers at the other two plants. A federal court ruled for the manufacturer, and the Seventh Circuit affirmed. Here, **the female HR coordinator did not perform responsibilities that required the same skill and effort as the male HR managers** in the larger plants. They had more employees to train, union grievances to resolve, hourly wages to track, and a greater number of personnel records to monitor and maintain. As a result, the manufacturer did not violate the Equal Pay Act by paying her less than its male HR managers. *Howard v. Lear Corp. EEDS & Interiors*, 234 F.3d 1002 (7th Cir. 2000).

◆ The University of Southern California (USC) paid its women's basketball coach less than the head coach of the men's team, and refused to agree to pay her the same salary in contract negotiations. After the contract expired, the women's coach sued under the Equal Pay Act, and a federal district court granted pretrial judgment for USC. The Ninth Circuit affirmed because of **the substantially different levels of experience between the two coaches**. The men's head coach had 31 years' experience to the women's coach's 17 years. The men's coach had also coached the Olympic basketball team, had nine years' marketing and promotional experience and had written several books on basketball. Accordingly, this was a legitimate reason "other than sex" for the pay differential, and no Equal Pay Act violation occurred. *Stanley v. Univ. of Southern California*, 178 F.3d 1069 (9th Cir. 1999).

◆ Three female Ohio automobile insurance underwriters, laid off as part of a reduction in force, sued under the Equal Pay Act. The court observed that in order to show a violation of the Equal Pay Act, an employee must demonstrate that compensation rates are unequal by sex in positions requiring equal skill, effort and responsibility and similar working conditions. Although the employees identified **one male underwriter who was paid $10,000 more than the average female** underwriter, this was insufficient to demonstrate a violation of the act. The complaining party must demonstrate that the positions are equal in all material respects and do not simply bear the same job title. *Creech v. Ohio Casualty Insurance Co.*, 944 F.Supp. 1347 (S.D. Ohio 1996).

◆ A computer company hired a Florida woman to work as a technical writer. She learned that she and a female co-worker were earning less than the male technical writers at the facility and complained to her supervisor. She was subsequently placed on probation because of declining work performance and absenteeism. She filed a complaint with the EEOC and was later given an unsatisfactory rating. Eventually she resigned, claiming her supervisors had engaged in a pattern of harassment that constituted constructive discharge in retaliation. She sued the employer under the Equal Pay Act and Title VII, and won. The Eleventh Circuit affirmed the holding under the Equal Pay Act but reversed on the Title VII discrimination claim. Under the Equal Pay Act, once the pay disparity between substantially similar jobs is demonstrated, the burden shifts to the employer to prove that **a factor other than sex is responsible** for the differential. However, under Title VII, the employee must prove that the employer had a discriminatory intent. Here, the lower court had never made a finding of intentional discrimination. However, the employee's claims of constructive discharge and retaliation were supported by the evidence. *Meeks v. Computer Associates Int'l*, 15 F.3d 1013 (11th Cir. 1994).

C. Pregnancy Discrimination

The Pregnancy Discrimination Act (42 U.S.C. § 2000e(k)) amended Title VII of the Civil Rights Act in 1978 to include pregnancy in its general prohibition of discrimination on the basis of sex.

The act prohibits less favorable treatment of pregnancy-related conditions than that afforded to other medical conditions and disabilities. In other words, if you provide paid leave for other kinds of medical conditions, you cannot refuse to provide paid leave for a pregnancy-related condition.

Employers need not provide greater benefits for pregnant employees than they provide for other employees who have non-work-related disabilities. So if you don't provide paid leave for employees who suffer illness or injury outside the workplace, you don't have to provide paid leave for pregnant employees.

◆ A company manufactured batteries made primarily from lead. In 1982, the company began a policy of excluding pregnant women and women capable of bearing children from jobs involving lead exposure. In 1984, a group of affected employees initiated a class action suit against the company, challenging its fetal protection policy as sex discrimination that violated Title VII. A Wisconsin federal court granted pretrial judgment to the company, finding that it had established a business necessity defense. The U.S. Court of Appeals, Seventh Circuit, affirmed, and the case reached the U.S. Supreme Court.

The Court noted that **there was a clear bias in the company's policy allowing fertile men but not women the choice of risking their reproductive health**. Thus, there was clear sex discrimination involved. Even though there was no malevolent motive involved, the policy could not be termed "neutral." Accordingly, the only way for the company to justify the discrimination was by establishing that gender was a bona fide occupational qualification, which it could not do. Decisions about the welfare of future children must be left to parents rather than employers. Since the company complied with the lead standard developed by the Occupational Safety and Health Administration and issued warnings to its female employees about the dangers of lead exposure, it was not negligent, and a future court would have difficulty finding it liable. The Court reversed the lower court decisions and struck down the company's fetal protection policy. *Int'l Union, UAW v. Johnson Controls, Inc.*, 499 U.S. 187, 111 S.Ct. 1196, 113 L.Ed.2d 158 (1991).

◆ A pregnant insurance company employee in Pennsylvania asked about time off for doctor's appointments and was told by a vice president (and part owner) that they would "play it by ear." The company required her to call in every day she was going to be absent. She later learned that her baby had deformities and decided to terminate the pregnancy. Her husband called the vice president and allegedly was told that she could take time off for the abortion and the funeral. However, when she called in after the funeral, she was told she was fired. She sued under the Pregnancy Discrimination Act. A federal court granted pretrial judgment to the company, but the Third Circuit reversed. It held that **the PDA protects a woman who decides to terminate a pregnancy**, and that there was evidence the employee was treated more harshly than male employees who needed time off for medical reasons. *Doe v. C.A.R.S. Protection Plus, Inc.*, 527 F.3d 358 (3d Cir. 2008).

◆ A Michigan fire safety officer claimed that she was promised the supervisor position at Chrysler's Auburn Hills facility. However, when she filled out forms explaining that she was pregnant and needed a new uniform that would fit, she was offered a promotion that was significantly inferior to the one at Auburn Hills. She began a three-month maternity leave several weeks later and did not return to work. Instead, she sued for sex discrimination under state law. A jury found that she was discriminated against because she was pregnant, but it rejected her claim of constructive discharge. The Sixth Circuit affirmed the ruling in her favor, but modified the award, noting that **she was only entitled to pay for the time between when she was offered the inferior position and when she quit**. *Lulaj v. The Wackenhut Corp.*, 512 F.3d 760 (6th Cir. 2008).

◆ A company in Washington advertised for a clerk/order checker, and a woman applied for the job. Although the job had no documented description of its requirements, the applicant was told it had a 25-pound lifting requirement. She was offered the job contingent on passing a preemployment physical. At the exam, she informed the company doctor that she was pregnant, and was told to get a release from her doctor. After she obtained the release allowing her to lift between 20 and 30 pounds, she was told that the lifting requirement was 40 pounds. When she got her doctor to raise her lifting restriction to 40 pounds, an internal expert at the company determined that the lifting requirement was actually 60 pounds. The company then refused to hire the applicant, and she sued for pregnancy discrimination. The Washington Supreme Court ruled in her favor, finding that the company violated state law. **It failed to show that the lifting requirement was a business necessity.** *Hegwine v. Longview Fibre Co.*, 172 P.3d 688 (Wash. 2007).

◆ A railroad offered a health care plan that excluded coverage for all male and female contraceptive methods, both prescription and non-prescription, when those methods were used solely for contraception. The plan allowed coverage for contraception when it was medically necessary for a non-contraceptive purpose. A number of female employees sued for sex discrimination under the Pregnancy Discrimination Act, and a Nebraska federal court ruled in their favor. The Eighth Circuit reversed. Here, **the plan was gender-neutral, excluding all contraception methods**. Further, since contraception prevents pregnancy, it is not "related to pregnancy" as meant by the act. *In re Union Pacific Railroad Co.*, 479 F.3d 936 (8th Cir. 2007).

◆ When a Puerto Rico ex-employee sued for pregnancy discrimination, her former employer alleged it didn't have 15 employees so as to be liable under Title VII. It didn't count the president or vice president, claiming they were directors and shareholders. The case reached the First Circuit, which noted **the six factors set forth by the Supreme Court in the *Clackamas* case for testing employment status**: 1) can the company fire the employee or set rules for work; 2) to what extent can the company supervise the individual's work; 3) does the individual report to someone higher up; 4) to what extent is the individual able to influence the company; 5) did the parties intend the individual to be an employee; and 6) does the individual share in the company's profits, losses and liabilities. The company would have to submit evidence pertaining to these six factors to be entitled to a dismissal. *DeJesus v. LTT Card Services, Inc.*, 474 F.3d 16 (1st Cir. 2007).

◆ A New York employee sued her employer seeking benefits for her infertility treatments. She alleged violations of Title VII, the Pregnancy Discrimination Act and state law based on the employer's refusal to cover certain infertility procedures under its health benefits plan. Although the plan covered some treatments, it expressly excluded surgical impregnation procedures. A federal court ruled in favor of the employer, and the Second Circuit affirmed. Here, **the employer limited coverage equally between men and women**, so there was no violation of Title VII or the Pregnancy Discrimination Act. Despite the fact that surgical implantation procedures would be performed only on women, both male and female employees were denied coverage for such a procedure. *Saks v. Franklin Covey Co.*, 316 F.3d 337 (2d Cir. 2003).

◆ A loan collector with generally outstanding performance goals was forced to miss work due to pregnancy-related problems. As a result, she fell short of her performance goals and was placed on a 90-day probation. Although she was able to improve the status of her accounts, she failed to meet specific performance goals and was fired. She sued the company under Title VII for pregnancy discrimination, and a jury awarded her $1,500 in compensatory damages, $30,000 in back pay and $230,000 in punitive damages. The Fourth Circuit Court of Appeals upheld the award against the company. There was evidence that **the employee was treated differently than non-pregnant employees** with respect to performance goals following a medical leave, and she was fired before the expiration of her 90-day probationary period. Even though the company had an EEO policy, there was evidence that the company was not committed to enforcing it. *Golson v. Green Tree Financial Servicing Corp.*, 26 Fed.Appx. 209 (4th Cir. 2002).

◆ An Arizona employee, who had a difficult relationship with her supervisor, became pregnant and informed her supervisor. She was fired a month before the baby was due. After the child's birth, she unsuccessfully sought substitute employment for several months before deciding to stay home with the baby. When she sued the company for pregnancy discrimination under Title VII and state law, a jury ruled in her favor. The court awarded her $15,000 in back pay and $50,000 in punitive damages. In the appeal that followed, the Ninth Circuit held that **the award of back pay had been properly limited** to the time between her firing and when she decided to stay home with the baby. Also, she was not entitled to more than $50,000 under Title VII because of the cap in 42 U.S.C. § 1981a applicable to employers with fewer than 101 employees. *Caudle v. Bristow Optical Co.*, 224 F.3d 1014 (9th Cir. 2000).

◆ A pregnant entry-level clerk began a probationary period for a Florida company. Partly because of her pregnancy, she missed at least six days of work in her first three months. She also left work early or arrived late on nine other occasions. The company fired her for violating its attendance policy during her probationary period, and she sued under the Pregnancy Discrimination Act. A federal court ruled for the company, and the Eleventh Circuit affirmed. It noted that **the act did not require the company to treat her more favorably than it would treat non-pregnant employees** who missed work. It did not matter that the absences were in part the result of the pregnancy. *Armindo v. Padlocker, Inc.*, 209 F.3d 1319 (11th Cir. 2000).

◆ An employer did not discriminate against an employee under the Pregnancy Discrimination Act or the Family and Medical Leave Act by **firing her two months after she informed her supervisors that she was pregnant** and wanted to continue working part time. The employer needed its employees to work full time because of a new initiative that required it to hire additional staff and increase the work hours of its existing employees. This was not a pretext for discrimination. *Gleklen v. Democratic Congressional Campaign Committee*, 199 F.3d 1365 (D.C. Cir. 2000).

◆ A New Hampshire business was sold and subsequently restructured by its new owner. A production manager, who was retained after the takeover, assumed the duties of two other management employees. The manager later became pregnant and requested maternity leave. Although her supervisor advised her that her position was secure, the company determined during her leave that her job duties could be performed by other employees. Before her six weeks of leave was over, the company advised the manager that her position would be eliminated. The employee sued, and the U.S. Court of Appeals, First Circuit, held that the decision to eliminate the manager's position had been based on business judgment and did not reflect a discriminatory motive. **The Pregnancy Discrimination Act did not prohibit the employer from firing her while she was on maternity leave.** A pregnant employee can be fired for legitimate reasons unrelated to pregnancy. The firing was not discriminatory. *Smith v. F.W. Morse & Co., Inc.*, 76 F.3d 413 (1st Cir. 1996).

D. Sexual Harassment

Three U.S. Supreme Court cases establish important rules relating to sexual harassment. The first, *Oncale*, states that employers can be held liable for same-sex harassment against employees. This means, for example, that if male employees harass another male employee, the employer can be held liable.

The other two cases, *Ellerth* and *Faragher*, state that where no adverse action is taken against an employee, an employer can defend itself by asserting:

> that it exercised reasonable care to prevent and promptly correct any sexual harassment and that the employee unreasonably failed to use the employer's remedies or otherwise avoid harm.

This defense does not work, however, if the employee is fired, demoted, forced to resign or subjected to a hostile work environment.

Note that harassment because of race, national origin, religion, age or disability will be examined the same way as sexual harassment. The same analysis is used to determine whether a hostile work environment exists and to determine whether the employer has made a good-faith effort to prevent the harassment.

1. Supreme Court Cases

◆ An employee at a Louisiana café quit after 10 months, claiming she had been sexually harassed and forced to quit because of that. She sued under Title VII, and a jury awarded her $40,000. Two weeks later, the café sought to have the action dismissed because it did not have 15 employees. It claimed the federal court thus had no jurisdiction to hear the case. A federal court and the

Fifth Circuit agreed, but the U.S. Supreme Court reversed. It ruled that **the 15-employee requirement was not jurisdictional**. In other words, the café had a duty to raise that defense at or before trial. Having failed to do so, it could not later try to assert the defense. *Arbaugh v. Y&H Corp.*, 546 U.S. 500, 126 S.Ct. 1235, 163 L.Ed.2d 1097 (2006).

- When a Tennessee worker sued her employer under Title VII for subjecting her to a hostile work environment, a federal court found that her co-workers' conduct amounted to sexual harassment, that her supervisors were aware of the harassment, that she was forced to take a medical leave of absence, and that she was fired for refusing to return to the hostile work environment. It awarded her over $107,000 in back pay and benefits as well as $300,000 in compensatory damages – the maximum permitted by 42 U.S.C. § 1981a(b)(3). The court determined that the award was insufficient to compensate the employee, but that it was bound by a previous case, which held that front pay was subject to the statutory cap. The Sixth Circuit affirmed. However, the U.S. Supreme Court reversed, holding that **front pay was not an element of compensatory damages** within the meaning of the Civil Rights Act of 1991. As a result, the worker could be awarded $300,000 in compensatory damages as well as an additional amount in front pay (money awarded for lost pay between the time of the judgment and when the employee is reinstated, or as here, money awarded in lieu of reinstatement). *Pollard v. E.I. du Pont de Nemours & Co.*, 532 U.S. 843, 121 S.Ct. 1946, 150 L.Ed.2d 62 (2001).

- An Illinois employee alleged that she was subjected to constant *quid pro quo* sexual harassment from one of her supervisors, a mid-level manager who had the authority to hire and promote, subject to higher approval, but who was not considered a policymaker. The employee refused all of the supervisor's advances, but she suffered no tangible retaliation and was even promoted once. Despite her knowledge of the employer's sexual harassment policy, she never complained to upper-level management about the supervisor's behavior. Instead, she resigned and sued the employer for sexual harassment and constructive discharge in violation of Title VII.

  The U.S. Supreme Court held that Title VII imposes vicarious liability on an employer for actionable discrimination caused by a supervisor with authority over an employee. When a supervisor discriminates in the terms and conditions of a subordinate's employment, his actions draw upon his superior position over the subordinate. However, **where no tangible employment action is taken against the employee, the employer may assert a two-pronged affirmative defense**. First, the employer must prove that it exercised reasonable care to prevent and promptly correct any sexual harassment. Second, it must prove that the employee unreasonably failed to avail herself of any employer remedies or failed to avoid harm otherwise. However, the affirmative defense is not available when the supervisor's harassment culminates in a tangible employment act such as discharge or demotion. The Court remanded the case for trial. *Burlington Industries, Inc. v. Ellerth*, 524 U.S. 742, 118 S.Ct. 2257, 141 L.Ed.2d 633 (1998).

◆ A Louisiana offshore service employed a roustabout to work on oil platforms in the Gulf of Mexico. He claimed that he was forcibly subjected to sex-related humiliating actions, assault and threats of rape by co-workers, including two employees with supervisory authority. When he complained to the employer's safety compliance clerk, the clerk did nothing and stated that he had also been subjected to abuse by the co-workers. Eventually, the roustabout quit and sued the employer for sex discrimination under Title VII. The case reached the U.S. Supreme Court, which stated that sex discrimination in the form of **same-sex harassment that is so objectively offensive that it alters the conditions of employment** is actionable under Title VII. The Court found no language in Title VII that bars a sex discrimination claim when the complaining party and alleged perpetrators are of the same sex, and it rejected the employer's assertion that allowing the claim would transform Title VII into a general code of workplace civility. The Court noted that not all verbal or physical harassment in the workplace is prohibited by Title VII, since it does not cover conduct that is not severe or pervasive enough to create an objectively hostile or abusive work environment. *Oncale v. Sundowner Offshore Services, Inc.*, 523 U.S. 75, 118 S.Ct. 998, 140 L.Ed.2d 201 (1998).

◆ A woman worked for a District of Columbia bank in various capacities over a four-year period. Her supervisor allegedly harassed her during this period, demanding sexual favors, and she accused him of forcibly raping her on several occasions. When the employee took an indefinite sick leave, the bank discharged her. She then sued the bank, claiming that she had been subjected to sexual harassment in violation of Title VII. A federal court ruled for the bank, finding that it did not have notice of any harassment, and that its policies forbade such behavior. The U.S. Court of Appeals reversed. The U.S. Supreme Court stated that **sexual harassment is clearly a form of sex discrimination prohibited by Title VII**. While absence of notice of harassment will not necessarily shield an employer from liability, employers are not always automatically liable for sexual harassment by their supervisory employees. Congress intended agency principles to apply to some extent. The Court affirmed the court of appeals' holding and remanded the case. *Meritor Savings Bank, FSB v. Vinson*, 477 U.S. 57, 106 S.Ct. 2399, 91 L.Ed.2d 49 (1986).

◆ A Tennessee woman worked as a manager of a rental equipment company. The company president often insulted her because of her gender and frequently made her the target of unwanted sexual innuendoes. The employee quit and sued, claiming the president's conduct created an abusive work environment because of gender. A federal court found that the president's conduct did not violate Title VII because it was not so severe as to seriously affect the manager's psychological well-being. The Sixth Circuit affirmed. The U.S. Supreme Court reiterated the standard set forth in *Meritor Savings Bank v. Vinson, FSB*, above. "Title VII is violated when the workplace is permeated with discriminatory behavior that is **sufficiently severe or pervasive to create a hostile environment**." This standard required showing only an objectively hostile environment – one that a reasonable person would find hostile – as well as the victim's subjective perception that the environment was abusive. The Court reversed and remanded the case with instructions for the trial court to consider the psychological harm to the victim as just one factor to be considered. *Harris v. Forklift Systems, Inc.*, 510 U.S. 17, 114 S.Ct. 367, 126 L.Ed.2d 295 (1993).

2. The Affirmative Defense

Having and distributing to every employee a sexual harassment policy is only the first step in avoiding liability. Employers must also ensure that the policy can be implemented effectively. For example, a policy that requires employees to report harassment to their supervisors will not be effective if the supervisors are doing the harassing.

Note also that the affirmative defense does not work if an adverse action has been taken against the employee. Adverse action includes more than termination, demotion or suspension. It can also be found in any action that alters the conditions of employment.

- An entry-level supervisor for a Maine company resigned, then sued for sexual harassment, claiming that her superior harassed her and that she had told a fellow entry-level supervisor about the harassment. However, she never used the company's confidential tip line even though she knew about it. She asserted that her fellow entry-level supervisor's knowledge could be imputed to the company. A federal court and the First Circuit disagreed. Here, **the supervisor unreasonably failed to report the harassment** under *Ellerth/Faragher*, and her co-worker didn't think the superior's comments rose to the level of actionable harassment under Title VII. *Chaloult v. Interstate Brands Corp.*, 540 F.3d 64 (1st Cir. 2008).

- A Missouri employee called the company's hotline to complain that her supervisor had been sexually harassing her for over two years. The company fired the supervisor two days later. The employee nevertheless sued the company under Title VII, claiming that the company's anti-harassment policy wasn't reasonable because it required a corroborating witness to the alleged harassment before the company would take action against the harasser. The case reached the Eighth Circuit, which noted that the company did not actually require a corroborating witness. Instead, it required some evidence to confirm the harassment, or at least an accumulation of uncorroborated allegations. **The employee waited too long to report the harassment.** *Adams v. O'Reilly Automotive, Inc.*, 538 F.3d 926 (8th Cir. 2008).

- A saleswoman at a Minnesota furniture store conflicted with a salesman over customers and, after a run-in with him, made a number of allegations against him, including that he told her she had a "large butt," and that she and another female employee were involved in a lesbian relationship. The store reprimanded the salesman, then met with the saleswoman to discuss the reprimand. A few days later, a store meeting was held to discuss how to assign salespeople to customers. After the meeting, the saleswoman gave two weeks' notice. The store manager asked her not to quit and stated that the salesman wouldn't be working at the store much longer. She nevertheless quit, then sued for sexual harassment, alleging other misconduct by the salesman. A federal court and the Eighth Circuit ruled against her. **She could not include the misconduct she never complained of, and she quit before the company could resolve her internal complaint.** *Anda v. Wickes Furniture Co.*, 517 F.3d 526 (8th Cir. 2008).

◆ A bartender at a Chili's Restaurant in Maine dated a co-worker employed as a cook for a couple of years. When the relationship soured, the cook began harassing the bartender, calling her names. She complained to management but asked that he not be fired because she still cared about him. The restaurant issued him an oral warning, then a written warning two weeks later, and finally fired him a few weeks after that when he refused to stop harassing the bartender. She later resigned, then sued the restaurant for creating a hostile work environment under Title VII. A federal court and the First Circuit ruled against her, finding that **the restaurant acted promptly and appropriately to her complaints**. *Forrest v. Brinker Int'l Payroll Co.*, 511 F.3d 225 (1st Cir. 2007).

◆ An assistant manager at an Iowa restaurant was subjected to sexual advances by her manager. She complained to the company hotline after a company official gave her the number in lieu of taking any action himself. She also talked to a co-manager, who called HR. Ten minutes later, HR called her to get a description of the incidents. The next time the manager was scheduled to work, the HR representative came to the restaurant to talk to him. Later that day, the HR rep told the employee she wanted to resolve the situation and offered to meet with the employee to work out a new schedule or a move to another restaurant nearby. The employee instead quit and sued, refusing further offers to return to work. A federal court ruled for the restaurant, noting that **the employee quit before HR could work out a final solution**. *Brenneman v. Famous Dave's of America, Inc.*, 507 F.3d 1139 (8th Cir. 2007).

◆ An Alabama insurance company employee allegedly endured harassment (including being propositioned) at her manager's hands for a year before reporting it. The company detected the hostility in the relationship, but couldn't verify that there had been harassment. The manager agreed to counseling but the employee refused. She also refused a transfer offer, insisting that her manager be fired. When the company fired her, she sued for harassment under Title VII. The Eleventh Circuit ruled for the company. Here, it acted promptly after learning of the alleged harassment and **offered two reasonable options** to remedy it. Further, the employee waited a year before reporting the harassment, and more than a year after she was propositioned. *Baldwin v. Blue Cross/Blue Shield of Alabama*, 480 F.3d 1287 (11th Cir. 2007).

◆ After enduring three years of harassment at the hands of her supervisor, a New York employee finally complained to the head of human resources (HR). The company then investigated and determined that the supervisor's conduct violated its anti-harassment policy. It issued him a formal reprimand and transferred the complaining employee to another department with the same compensation and benefits. She quit and sued under Title VII. A federal court and the Second Circuit ruled against her because **she unreasonably waited to report the harassment**, and the company acted promptly to end it. *Finnerty v. Sadlier, Inc.*, 176 Fed.Appx. 158 (2d Cir. 2006).

◆ A female employee of a Massachusetts contractor complained that unidentified employees of a subcontractor locked her in a portable toilet while she was using it and peeped at her through a hole. The contractor sought to identify the subcontractor's employees involved in the incident, but the subcontractor and its employees' union refused to cooperate. Vulgar graffiti appeared around the work site. For a while, she used a bathroom facility farther away from the job site, then she accepted a transfer to another work site. She quit and sued the contractor for sexual harassment, but lost when the Massachusetts Supreme Court ruled that the contractor had done enough to avoid liability. **Even though its actions were not entirely successful, it took prompt action** reasonably calculated to end the harassment. *Modern Continental/Obayashi v. Massachusetts Comm'n Against Discrimination*, 833 N.E..2d 1130 (Mass. 2005).

3. Individual Supervisor Liability

As a general rule, supervisors will not be held individually liable for sexual harassment under Title VII. However, they might incur liability under state civil rights laws or under other tort laws (torts are civil wrongs other than breach of contract).

Because employers can be held liable for their supervisors' harassing conduct, employers need to make sure that their supervisors are aware that harassment of any sort will not be tolerated.

◆ After being told that she was fired, a Georgia employee claimed that she had been sexually harassed by the owner of the company. She sued him and the company under Title VII, asserting that he should be held individually liable because even though the company was her official employer, it was in reality the alter ego of the owner. A federal court ruled for the owner, and the Eleventh Circuit affirmed. Here, it would not matter if the company was the owner's alter ego because **Title VII did not allow for individual liability**. Further, there was no allegation that the company was insolvent. In addition, the company was not liable because the employee never availed herself of the *Faragher/Ellerth* defense. Even though the company had a harassment policy in place, she never claimed harassment until she was fired. *Dearth v. Collins*, 441 F.3d 931 (11th Cir. 2006).

◆ An employee sued her employer, a manufacturer with facilities in Rhode Island, for sexual harassment and retaliation in violation of Title VII and state law. She named her immediate supervisor and his supervisor as individual defendants because of their alleged participation in the harassment and their failure to investigate other incidents reported to them. A Rhode Island federal court denied the supervisors' motion to be dismissed from the case. It followed its earlier holding that **supervisors could be personally liable for violations of Title VII** and state law. Because Title VII defines "employer" as a person with 15 or more employees or "any agent of such a person," under traditional agency principles, the employer and the employer's agent could be held jointly and severally liable under Title VII, the court reasoned. The majority of federal appeals courts have ruled that supervisors cannot be personally liable for violations of Title VII, but the First Circuit has not yet ruled on the issue. *Wyss v. General Dynamics Corp.*, 24 F.Supp.2d 202 (D.R.I. 1998).

◆ A Florida employee alleged that the president of the company for which she worked repeatedly made sexual comments and told explicit jokes in her presence. On two occasions, he touched her in an offensive manner. She was allegedly fired for confronting him about his behavior. She sued him and the company, claiming violations of Title VII and the Florida Civil Rights Act. The court dismissed the Title VII and state civil rights act complaints against the president in his individual capacity. **Neither act provided for individual liability.** However, the employee presented evidence that the president had been acting in his capacity as a supervisor when the alleged incidents occurred. If this was proven, the company might be held liable for his conduct. The court denied the company's dismissal motion. *Blount v. Sterling Healthcare Group, Inc.*, 934 F.Supp. 1365 (S.D. Fla. 1996).

◆ A Kentucky federal court held that a supervisor could not be held liable for damages in a Title VII action filed by a restaurant employee who alleged repeated sexual harassment by the supervisor. After a period during which she frequently called in sick to avoid contact with the supervisor, the employee filed an Equal Employment Opportunity Commission complaint against the employer and a federal district court lawsuit against the supervisor. The court observed that while the Sixth Circuit had not expressly ruled on a supervisor's potential liability under Title VII, **Congress' failure to explicitly provide for supervisor liability** indicated that it did not intend such liability. *Winston v. Hardee's Food Systems, Inc.*, 903 F.Supp. 1151 (W.D. Ky. 1995).

◆ A California research specialist claimed that her supervisor sexually harassed and assaulted her on the job. She also stated that her repeated complaints to the company's president and chief executive officer were ignored and that the company fired her in retaliation for taking a one-month leave of absence to avoid further harassment. She filed a lawsuit against the company and the supervisor in a California trial court under the state Fair Employment and Housing Act (FEHA). The trial court held that the supervisor could not be held personally liable for sexual harassment, but the California Court of Appeal held that the FEHA prohibited sexual harassment by an employer, labor organization, employment agency, training program, or any other person. This broad language indicated **legislative intent to bring supervisors within FEHA coverage**. The court rejected the supervisor's arguments that the act did not apply to individuals. *Page v. Superior Court*, 37 Cal.Rptr.2d 529 (Cal. Ct. App. 1995).

4. Low-Level Employees and Third Parties

Although employers generally can escape liability for the harassing acts of low-level employees or third parties where the employers do not know of the harassment, they can be held liable where they have allowed a culture of harassment to exist. For this reason, it is important to make clear to all employees that harassing behavior will not be tolerated under any circumstances.

- A Wisconsin employee complained to a more senior co-worker about harassment by several male employees. The co-worker allegedly informed the plant manager, who told her to notify the company's vice president. Nothing was done. A year later the employee complained to the HR department, which investigated and fired two male employees. The employee believed that she was being ostracized for reporting the harassment and quit. When she sued under Title VII, a federal court granted pretrial judgment to the company. The Seventh Circuit reversed, finding issues of fact that required a trial. Here, **if the plant manager was informed of the harassment, he was negligent in not following up on the complaint**. *Bombaci v. Journal Community Publishing Group, Inc.*, 482 F.3d 979 (7th Cir. 2007).

- A restaurant company owned by two Alabama men obtained a franchise to operate a Western Sizzlin restaurant. After one of the men allegedly harassed female employees, charges were filed with the EEOC. Lawsuits were filed against Western Sizzlin, the restaurant company, and the harassing owner. A state court granted pretrial judgment to Western Sizzlin, and the plaintiffs appealed. They asserted that Western Sizzlin was vicariously liable for the harassing acts of the owner. The Alabama Supreme Court disagreed, noting that **Western Sizzlin was not vicariously liable for the harassment** because the control it retained over the restaurant's operations was limited to ensuring that the restaurant company was complying with the franchise agreement. However, the court reversed the dismissal of the direct negligence claims against Western Sizzlin, finding that issues of fact existed as to whether it had breached a duty to the employees. *Kennedy v. Western Sizzlin Corp.*, 857 So.2d 71 (Ala. 2003).

- A sales associate for a camera company in Georgia alleged sexual harassment and presented a laundry list of all the negative and "hostile" comments and actions taken against her by her co-workers. However, no one with supervisory power abused or even touched her in any way. A federal judge granted pretrial judgment to the employer, stating that while the employee might have found the work environment hostile, a reasonable person in her position would not have agreed with her assessment of the situation. The judge posited that the level of vulgarity in modern society (and particularly in the contemporary workplace) has made it more difficult for plaintiffs to show that inappropriate comments and sexually oriented behavior were severe enough to create a hostile work environment under Title VII. As a result, the **ogling, catcalling and other activity by co-workers was not sufficiently severe** as to amount to actionable harassment. *Breda v. Wolf Camera, Inc.*, 148 F.Supp.2d 1371 (S.D. Ga. 2001).

◆ An Illinois bank employee experienced a series of unsolicited incidents instigated by a co-worker over two-and-a-half years. Finally, the employee complained to bank managers. The bank investigated, but the co-worker denied the allegations and the bank could not corroborate her story. Nevertheless, the bank took steps to address her concerns. However, in the meantime, her work deteriorated. The bank fired her almost a year-and-a-half after the harassment complaints were brought to its attention. The U.S. Court of Appeals, Seventh Circuit, held that the bank had taken appropriate remedial measures. As soon as it became aware of the employee's complaint, **the bank acted promptly and took appropriate steps** to end the harassment. Nor was the bank's action in firing the employee retaliatory. First, the lapse of 15 months between her complaint and her discharge was simply too long to raise an inference of retaliation. In addition, the record contained ample evidence of the employee's substandard performance during those 15 months, including that she was unable to follow instructions and that other employees had to redo her work. *Caudillo v. Continental Bank/Bank of America*, 191 F.3d 455 (7th Cir. 1999).

◆ A Louisiana store security employee suspected some employees of stealing merchandise by concealing it in their clothing. He concealed a television camera in a unisex employee restroom to obtain proof. An employee saw the camera on the first day it was installed, and the employer fired the security employee for violating a company policy. Some employees rejected the employer's explanation that it had no knowledge of the observation plan, and they sued. A jury awarded one employee $10,000 and another $1,000, while 43 others received nothing. The employees appealed to the Court of Appeal of Louisiana, which affirmed. The court found **no evidence that the employer had created a hostile environment for female employees**, as the restroom was a unisex facility. There was also no evidence that the employer or any supervisor had knowledge of the camera but failed to take action. The trial court had committed no error in awarding only limited damages to the two employees who attended psychological counseling. The other employees failed to show that they had ever sought medical or psychological care. *Meche v. Wal-Mart Stores,* 692 So.2d 544 (La. Ct. App. 1997).

5. Damage Awards

Where employers are found liable for harassment under Title VII, money damages can be awarded under 42 U.S.C. § 1981a – an amendment to Title VII. Section 1981a sets damages caps that vary depending on the size of the employer.

◆ An employee at an Arkansas manufacturing facility complained to the plant manager that his female supervisor had made sexual advances toward him, including at a bar after work. The company began a thorough investigation but was unable to verify his most serious assertions. However, it determined that the supervisor acted inappropriately by socializing with employees in bars after work. When she returned from leave, the employee claimed that she retaliated against him by criticizing him in public and giving him too much work. Again the company could not substantiate his claims. He resigned, then sued under

Title VII and state law. A jury awarded him compensatory and punitive damages, but the Eighth Circuit **vacated the punitive damages award because the company did not act with reckless indifference** to the law when it refused to fire the supervisor or transfer the employee. *Dominic v. DeVilbiss Air Power Co.*, 493 F.3d 968 (8th Cir. 2007).

◆ A female Chicago bank manager sued the bank, two shareholders and the bank president for sex discrimination and harassment under Title VII, alleging a steady stream of inappropriate behavior from the three men. She also sued the individual defendants for assault and battery, and intentional infliction of emotional distress. A jury awarded her $200,000 against the bank, which the court **reduced to $50,000 under 42 U.S.C. § 1981a**. The jury also awarded her $200,000 for the assault and battery and $100,000 in punitive damages. The Seventh Circuit upheld the awards, finding that they were not excessive, and that the jury properly considered testimony by a lay-witness friend about her emotional state. *Farfaras v. Citizens Bank and Trust of Chicago*, 433 F.3d 558 (7th Cir. 2006).

◆ An Arizona employee sued under Title VII, alleging that she was subjected to a sexually hostile work environment. The jury agreed and awarded her $100,000 in damages for pain and suffering, mental anguish, shock and discomfort, and $1 million in punitive damages. The court applied **the statutory cap of 42 U.S.C. § 1981a** and reduced the damages award to $200,000. The employee appealed, asserting that the cap on damages violated the Fourteenth Amendment's Equal Protection Clause. The Ninth Circuit upheld the cap as constitutional. Congress legitimately restricted the amount of damages available for public policy reasons. *Lansdale v. Hi-Health Supermart Corp.*, 314 F.3d 355 (9th Cir. 2002).

◆ An employee of a debt collection company in Kansas was subjected to continuing harassment by a number of co-workers and supervisors. She reported the incidents to the office general manager, who had the power to discipline employees and who was responsible for implementing human resource policies, including an anti-harassment policy. He brushed her complaints aside, telling her that the men were revenue producers while she was not and that **she would just have to tolerate their behavior**. When she sued for sexual harassment, a jury awarded her $5,000 in compensatory damages and $1 million in punitive damages. The court reduced the punitive damages award to $295,000 under 42 U.S.C. § 1981a(b)(3), and the company appealed. The Tenth Circuit affirmed, noting that under *Kolstad v. American Dental Ass'n*, 527 U.S. 526 (1999), the standard for punitive damages was not how egregious the employer's conduct was, but rather the employer's knowledge that it might be acting in violation of federal law. Here, the general manager's actions were not merely inadequate; they were reckless and malicious. *Deters v. Equifax Credit Information Services, Inc.*, 202 F.3d 1262 (10th Cir. 2000).

◆ A New York employee claimed that she was subjected to repeated, unwelcome sexual advances and comments from her supervisor and that the company took no action despite her complaints. When she sued the company under Title VII, a jury awarded her $100,000 in punitive damages, but no compensatory (actual) damages. The company appealed to the Second Circuit, asserting that since no compensatory damages were awarded, no punitive damages should have been awarded. The court of appeals joined the Seventh Circuit in holding that **punitive damages could be awarded in a Title VII case even where there is no award of actual or compensatory damages.** The statutory caps imposed by the Civil Rights Act of 1991 eliminated the need for actual damages as a precondition for punitive damages under Title VII. *Cush-Crawford v. Adchem Corp.*, 271 F.3d 352 (2d Cir. 2001).

◆ A checker for a family-owned grocery store in Missouri complained several times about a co-worker's harassment, but the co-worker maintained that the allegations were racially motivated. Faced with this dilemma, the store director transferred the co-worker to the night shift. The checker was fired four months later for failing to pay for food she ate on the job. She sued, claiming that she had been retaliated against for complaining about the co-worker's sexual harassment. A federal court judge dismissed her claims for punitive damages and retaliation, and the jury awarded her $1 in compensatory damages on her hostile work environment claim. The Eighth Circuit affirmed. Here, **there was no evidence that the store managers acted with evil intent** so as to support an award of punitive damages. There was also insufficient evidence that the firing was retaliatory because it happened four months after the complaints and for a valid reason. *Dhyne v. Meiners Thriftway, Inc.*, 184 F.3d 983 (8th Cir. 1999).

◆ A Delaware employee was repeatedly sexually harassed by co-workers, and her supervisors failed to remedy the situation. She chose to be laid off after the harassment continued and filed a lawsuit against the employer for sexual harassment and discrimination in violation of Title VII, and for personal injury under Delaware law. A federal court dismissed the state law claims, ruling that they were barred by the Delaware Workers' Compensation Act. The Supreme Court of Delaware then stated that no exclusion existed under state law for injuries caused by sexual harassment or assault and that mental injury may be compensable under the state workers' compensation act. The conduct alleged in this case arose out of and in the course of employment and was potentially within the scope of the workers' compensation act. Because sexual harassment was not specifically excluded, **the personal injury suit based on sexual harassment was barred by the workers' compensation act**. *Konstantopoulos v. Westvaco Corp.*, 690 A.2d 936 (Del. 1996).

6. Same-Sex Harassment Cases

In the *Oncale* case, (this chapter), the Supreme Court held that same-sex harassment can be actionable under Title VII.

◆ An Illinois nurse was subjected to sexual comments and offensive touching by the facility's executive director. She complained to three different supervisors, per company policy, but the company did not take any action. Despite her complaints, the nurse was on relatively friendly terms with the director, allowing the director's lesbian lover to baby-sit her daughter and providing medical assistance to the director's mother. She was later fired for unrelated reasons, then sued for sexual harassment. The company sought pretrial judgment, which the Seventh Circuit denied. Here, there were questions of fact as to whether the company exercised reasonable care to prevent and correct the director's behavior. *Kampmier v. Emeritus Corp.*, 472 F.3d 930 (7th Cir. 2006).

- A female team leader at a manufacturing plant in Missouri repeatedly blew kisses at another female team leader, attempted to kiss her on the mouth and made suggestive comments to her like "I want you, honey." The second team leader resigned, then sued for same-sex harassment under Title VII. A federal court and the Eighth Circuit ruled against her. This was not sexual harassment because the aggressor was just a sarcastic person who was not motivated by sexual desire or hostility to women. **While her behavior was boorish and vulgar, it was not harassment "because of sex."** *Pedroza v. Cintas Corp.*, 397 F.3d 1063 (8th Cir. 2005).

- A female sales rep for a company in Puerto Rico got a new supervisor – an inexperienced female who had trouble distinguishing personal from professional relationships. The supervisor accused the sales rep of getting her prestigious sales territory because of her good looks, and made other comments about the sales rep's appearance. The sales rep complained and asked to be allowed to work for a different supervisor. The company agreed to the arrangement, which meant that the sales rep had to take a less prestigious territory. She took a six-week leave of absence due to depression and did not return to work. Instead, she sued under Title VII for same-sex harassment. A federal court ruled against her, and the First Circuit affirmed. Here, **the supervisor's actions were neither severe nor physically threatening**, and they were not an impediment to the sales rep's work performance. Thus, they could not be deemed sexual harassment under Title VII. *Lee-Crespo v. Schering-Plough Del Caribe Inc.*, 354 F.3d 34 (1st Cir. 2003).

- A Louisiana technician's supervisor touched the technician's anus while the technician was bending over and told the technician he was jealous that the technician had a girlfriend. When the technician filed an Equal Employment Opportunity Commission complaint, the company's investigation found that two other employees had had similar experiences with the supervisor. The technician resigned and sued the company under Title VII. A Louisiana federal court granted pretrial judgment to the company. The Fifth Circuit reversed in part, noting that Title VII protects against same-sex harassment. Where the victim proves: 1) that the harasser intended to have some sexual contact with him, and 2) that the harasser made sexual overtones to other employees, that constitutes especially credible proof that the **harasser is homosexual** such that the Title VII action can succeed. The court remanded the case for trial. *La Day v. Catalyst Technology, Inc.*, 302 F.3d 474 (5th Cir. 2002).

◆ A male security guard, while acting as a supervisor, disciplined two other male guards, who reacted by launching a campaign of retaliation against him. They slashed his tires, taunted him after he was demoted to a non-supervisory position, and made lewd gestures and obscene remarks. The guard complained, and an investigation revealed that there was no corroborating evidence. Nevertheless, the guard and one of the "harassers" were reassigned. The other "harasser" was fired for unrelated reasons. When the guard sued under Title VII, a federal court ruled for the company. The U.S. Court of Appeals, D.C. Circuit, affirmed. Here, **the guard failed to show that the harassers acted the way they did because of his gender**. They did not treat him differently than women; they treated him differently than all other company employees. This was nothing more than a workplace grudge that could not be classified as same-sex sexual harassment. *Davis v. Coastal Int'l Security, Inc.*, 275 F.3d 1119 (D.C. Cir. 2002).

◆ A waiter at a Washington restaurant was subjected to name-calling and relentless insults because of his effeminate behavior. He reported the harassment to his manager and the company's human resources (HR) director, who conducted several spot checks over the next two weeks and told the waiter to report any further harassment. Shortly thereafter, the waiter got into a heated argument with an assistant manager and walked off the job. He was fired for leaving in the middle of a shift. He sued the restaurant and its parent company under Title VII, and a federal court ruled in favor of the restaurant. The Ninth Circuit Court of Appeals reversed, holding that the waiter had proven that he was harassed in violation of Title VII. No restaurant employee contradicted his testimony that the harassment had occurred, and the restaurant failed to take appropriate remedial action upon his reports of the harassment. Relentless abuse because an employee **fails to conform to gender-based stereotypes** of how a person should act amounts to sex discrimination under federal law. *Nichols v. Azteca Restaurant Enterprises, Inc.*, 256 F.3d 864 (9th Cir. 2001).

7. Other Sexual Harassment Cases

Sexual harassment is the single largest problem area for most employers. As the following cases show, liability for sexual harassment can arise in a wide variety of situations. The lesson to take away is this:

—have and distribute a sexual harassment policy
—make your intolerance of harassing behavior known
—provide a good avenue for employees to report inappropriate behavior
—investigate any claims of harassment promptly and thoroughly, and
—take decisive and meaningful action to eliminate future harassment without punishing the person who reports the harassment.

◆ A secretary at a New York university claimed hostile work environment and retaliation under Title VII, alleging that her boss spent one to two hours every day viewing hardcore pornography. He also used her computer on the weekend to view porn Web sites, and had videotapes containing masochism and sadism shipped to the office, where she had to open them and deliver them to his mailbox. When she reported this activity to the university's EEO director, her boss allegedly retaliated against her by removing virtually all her secretarial functions. A federal court dismissed the case, but the Second Circuit reversed, allowing her claims to proceed. *Patane v. Clark*, 508 F.3d 106 (2d Cir. 2007).

- An Alabama sales rep was the only female in her office. She claimed she was subjected to sexually offensive language on a daily basis, and that the male sales reps kept the radio tuned to a station that aired pornographic talk and advertisements. When she complained, little was done. Every time she changed the channel, the male sales reps would change it back. And the manager used the word "bitch" to refer to other women, including female customers. She finally quit and sued under Title VII. A federal court granted pretrial judgment to the company because the sexually offensive language wasn't directed at her. The Eleventh Circuit reversed, noting that **the conduct was pervasive enough to be deemed illegal harassment even though it wasn't targeted at her**. *Reeves v. C.H. Robinson Worldwide, Inc.*, 525 F.3d 1139 (11th Cir. 2008).

- A female employee got a new male supervisor who insulted her on the basis of her gender at least 18 times over a 10-month period. Most of his comments reflected his views of a woman's place, though he also made a few sexual comments. She complained to the HR director, who promised to take care of the problem. However, her supervisor then cut her hours and gave her the worst review of her career, preventing her from receiving a raise. She resigned and sued under Title VII. An Illinois federal court granted pretrial judgment to the company, but the Seventh Circuit reversed. Here, **the sexist quips could have created a hostile work environment even though they were generally not based on sexual desire**, and the low performance review could be considered an adverse action because it prevented her from getting a raise. *Boumehdi v. Plastag Holdings, LLC*, 489 F.3d 781 (7th Cir. 2007).

- A female youthcare worker at a nonprofit residential care facility for male youths convicted of violent crimes (including rape and murder) claimed that she was sexually harassed by the youths as well as by male co-workers. She asserted that she was retaliated against when she complained, and was thus forced to resign. When she sued under Title VII, alleging constructive discharge, a Minnesota federal court and the Eighth Circuit ruled against her. First, the offensive conduct by her co-workers stopped before she resigned. Second, the restriction imposed on her ability to sanction youths did not amount to retaliation because it was not enforced. Accordingly, **the working conditions were not so intolerable that a reasonable person would have felt compelled to resign**. *Vajdl v. Mesabi Academy of Kidspeace, Inc.*, 484 F.3d 546 (8th Cir. 2007).

- A probationary employee claimed that his female supervisor told him he looked good in his jeans, grabbed his buttocks and asked him out on dates. When he complained, the company removed him from his supervisor's chain of command, but ultimately determined that the complaint was unfounded. He filed an EEOC complaint and two days later, his probationary period was extended. He resigned, then sued for harassment and retaliation under Title VII. A Pennsylvania federal court ruled against him. Here, the allegations, if true, did not rise to the level of severity required by Title VII, and **the extension of the probationary period was not an adverse employment action**. *Swanson v. Northwestern Human Services*, 2006 WL 3354145 (E.D. Pa. 11/2/06).

◆ A Kentucky restaurant manager rejected sexual advances from his two supervisors. Shortly thereafter, he was fired without warning on the grounds that he was not "supporting" his general manager. He called his former district manager, and was told that he could maintain his position if he agreed to transfer to another location 120 miles away. After a month of commuting, he quit to take another job, then sued for sexual harassment. The company claimed that no adverse action was taken against him, but a jury disagreed. The Sixth Circuit upheld the jury's award, noting that although a lateral transfer is not normally an adverse action, the jury permissibly found that **the 120-mile transfer made the action adverse**. *Keeton v. Flying J, Inc.*, 429 F.3d 259 (6th Cir. 2005).

◆ After a part-time waitress sued a restaurant for sexual harassment, an Illinois federal court dismissed the case on the grounds that the restaurant did not have 15 employees for at least 20 weeks a year. The Seventh Circuit reversed, noting that **even though the owner's husband and mother essentially ran the place, making hiring and firing decisions, they still counted as employees** of the restaurant because they received weekly paychecks, and the owner could choose to take over the running of the restaurant at any time. Thus, the restaurant met the 15-employee requirement. *Smith v. Castaways Family Diner*, 453 F.3d 971 (7th Cir. 2006).

◆ Following a year of reprimands about his declining performance, a Kansas insurance agent complained to company officials that his supervisor was sexually harassing him. He cited an occasion where she told him he had nice legs. Three weeks later, he was late for work again and refused to obey his supervisor's order to call old customer leads – the same performance problems about which he had been earlier warned. He was fired the next day. When he sued for discrimination, a federal court and the Tenth Circuit ruled against him. **He was fired for engaging in exactly the behavior he had been warned against**, and the complained-of harassment was extremely mild. *Argo v. Blue Cross and Blue Shield of Kansas*, 452 F.3d 1193 (10th Cir. 2006).

◆ A newspaper employee in Texas complained to her supervisor that a printing press operator was sexually harassing her. Her supervisor spoke with a number of former and current employees to see what they knew, but could not substantiate the employee's allegations. The employee then contacted an attorney, who notified the human resources (HR) director of her intent to file an EEOC complaint. About a week later, the HR director ordered the printing press operator to do his work in a different area and warned him to stay away from the employee. She also investigated the complaint, but could not verify the accusations. When the employee sued for sexual harassment, the Fifth Circuit ruled against her. **The HR director's prompt response in separating the alleged harasser relieved the company of liability.** *Harvill v. Westward Communications, LLC*, 433 F.3d 428 (5th Cir. 2005).

◆ A supervisor for a Missouri company cut a peephole in the women's bathroom wall so he could spy on a female employee. Eventually he was caught when another female employee notified management that something was amiss. Management enlisted the spied-upon female to trap the supervisor. She then sued the company for sexual harassment under Title VII. A federal court and the Eighth Circuit ruled against her because she was not aware of the peeping at the time it was going on. **Title VII requires sexual harassment to be both subjectively and objectively offensive**, which it could not be if the harassed party did not know she was being harassed. *Cottrill v. MFA, Inc.*, 443 F.3d 629 (8th Cir. 2006).

◆ An employee of an Indiana vehicle manufacturer claimed that her manager touched her on several occasions, including **once sliding his hand up her shorts along her thigh and touching her underwear**. When she went to a security checkpoint and called the plant manager for help, he failed to show up. Her manager ordered her to return to work. Instead, she quit and sued for sexual harassment and constructive discharge under Title VII. A federal court ruled that the manager's alleged misconduct could not amount to sexual harassment, but the Seventh Circuit reversed, holding that a reasonable jury could agree that the work environment was sexually hostile and that a reasonable person would quit rather than continue to be subjected to such treatment. A trial was required. *Patton v. Keystone RV Co.*, 455 F.3d 812 (7th Cir. 2006).

◆ On a layover after a flight from New York to Rome, all 17 crew members were driven to a hotel and assigned to a block of rooms rented by the airline. A male flight attendant put a drug in a female flight attendant's drink and raped her. She worked the return flight without telling anyone about the incident. She later told several airline officials about the rape without identifying the assailant. The officials narrowed down the list of suspects and suspended the male flight attendant after another female flight attendant recounted a similar experience. Apparently, there were two other reports filed by flight attendants involving the assailant, but the airline did not take any action until the suspension. When the female flight attendant sued under Title VII, a federal court granted pretrial judgment to the airline on the ground that the hotel room did not constitute a "workplace" under the law. The Second Circuit reversed in part, holding that **the hotel room could be considered a work environment** and that the airline could be held liable for failing to warn. *Ferris v. Delta Air Lines, Inc.*, 277 F.3d 128 (2d Cir. 2001).

E. Sexual Orientation and Identity Issues

Title VII does not protect against sexual orientation discrimination, nor does it protect against gender identity discrimination. However, many state laws provide protections in these areas. There may also be protection for gender identity disorders under disability discrimination laws.

◆ A salon in New York **fired an openly gay assistant stylist** because she got an "extremely unprofessional-looking haircut at a barbershop," which amounted to insubordination. She claimed that she was really fired because she did not conform to gender stereotypes of how a woman should look. When she sued the salon under Title VII, she lost. A federal court and the Second Circuit held that the salon did not violate Title VII. The salon could require her to have her hair cut by its stylists as a means of advertising its techniques. Title VII does not protect against sexual orientation discrimination and this was not gender stereotyping. *Dawson v. Bumble & Bumble*, 398 F.3d 211 (2d Cir. 2005).

◆ A deliveryman for a supermarket chain was also a cross-dresser, though he never assumed his female persona at work. After revealing his disorder to his supervisor, he was fired. He sued the company for violating Title VII, asserting that it engaged in forbidden sexual stereotyping by firing him. He also asserted that no similarly situated females were **discharged for cross-dressing**. A Louisiana federal court ruled in favor of the company. First, although the discharge may have been morally wrong, it was not because of sexual stereotyping. Neither Title VII nor the Supreme Court's decision in *Price Waterhouse v. Hopkins*, 490 U.S. 228 (1989), prohibits discrimination on the basis of sexual identity or gender identity disorders. Also, the deliveryman failed to show that there were any female cross-dressers working for the company, so his disparate impact claim could not succeed either. *Oiler v. Winn-Dixie Louisiana, Inc.*, 2002 WL 31098541 (E.D. La. 2002).

◆ A New York-based telecommunications company instituted a new employee benefits plan, listing as an "eligible dependent" any employee's "same-sex domestic partner." A male employee requested that the company add his girlfriend's name to his benefits plan under the new policy. The request was denied, and he sued, claiming that he had been denied benefits on the basis of his sexual orientation and marital status. In dismissing his claim, a federal court explained that the policy did not discriminate between similarly situated men and women by **distinguishing between same-sex couples and opposite-sex couples** because of the difference in the couples' ability to marry. The policy did not violate Title VII because the male employee could not show that he was treated differently from "similarly situated" persons of the opposite sex. A female employee with a female domestic partner would be differently situated from him because under current law, she would be unable to marry her partner. The male employee was therefore not treated differently "on the basis of sex." *Foray v. Bell Atlantic*, 56 F.Supp.2d 327 (S.D.N.Y. 1999).

F. State Law

State laws generally track the language of Title VII and the Equal Pay Act, and the analyses used to determine whether discrimination has occurred are generally the same as in cases involving the federal statutes.

Sometimes there is more protection under state law – for example, a number of states bar discrimination on the basis of sexual orientation and marital status. Since there is no protection under federal law for these kinds of discrimination, employees in states that protect against this type of discrimination will sue under state law. There also may be individual supervisor liability under state law.

◆ An Ohio employee sued her employer for sexual harassment and lost. The employer then sued her for malicious prosecution and abuse of process. He also sought to recover his attorneys' fees and costs in defending the prior lawsuit. The employee sought to have the case dismissed as illegal retaliation under Ohio law. The case reached the Supreme Court of Ohio, which held that **the mere filing of the lawsuit did not amount to retaliation**. As long as the second lawsuit raised genuine issues of material fact over the employee's motives in filing the first lawsuit, it was not retaliation. The court remanded the case for further proceedings. *Greer-Burger v. Temesi*, 879 N.E.2d 174 (Ohio 2007).

◆ A male employee at a Wal-Mart store in West Virginia brought a sexual harassment complaint against an assistant store manager who was **equally obnoxious to both men and women**. A jury awarded him $80,000, but the Fourth Circuit Court of Appeals reversed the award. Here, even though the manager had clearly harassed the employee, he had not done so on the basis of the employee's gender. As a result, there was no violation of West Virginia's Human Rights Act. *Lack v. Wal-Mart Stores*, 240 F.3d 255 (4th Cir. 2001).

◆ An employee's supervisor coerced the employee into having sex with him by reminding her that he had substantial control over her job. When she sought to end the relationship and threatened to quit, he promoted her and continued to ask for sex, telling her that she "owed" him for promoting her. The employee did not tell company officials about the harassment, but she did tell two co-workers. Her work began to suffer, and she was eventually fired. She sued under state law, and a trial court found the company vicariously liable. It awarded the employee over $400,000 in damages. The Washington Court of Appeals affirmed, noting that it made no difference whether the supervisor was a "manager" or a "supervisor" under the law because **he exercised his authority as an agent of the company when he engaged in the harassment**. *Henningsen v. WorldCom, Inc.*, 9 P.3d 948 (Wash. Ct. App. 2000).

◆ The Texas Supreme Court held that **companies could be liable for employment discrimination under the state's human rights act, even though the aggrieved individual was employed by someone else**. In the case, a hospital contracted with a laboratory to have the lab run its pathology department. When the lab dismissed a female pathologist, she filed a charge with the EEOC and sued the hospital, alleging that it directly controlled how the lab staffed and operated the department and interfered with the lab's decision to keep her employed. The Texas Supreme Court explained that the hospital dictated how the pathology department was to be set up, had the final say over who was named department director, and determined how many pathologists the director could keep on staff. Further, the hospital's CEO, who knew of the sex discrimination charge, allegedly coerced the lab into firing the employee. *NME Hospitals, Inc. v. Rennels*, 994 S.W.2d 142 (Tex. 1999).

◆ A Virginia employee went into premature labor and was ordered to stop working by her doctor. When she was later released for work, her employer stated that she had been fired because she was no longer dependable and that her place was at home with her child. She filed a lawsuit against the employer in a Virginia trial court for wrongful discharge. The court held for the employer, and the employee appealed to the Supreme Court of Virginia. The court held that although Virginia law encompasses the common law rule of at-will employment, the strong public policy against race and gender discrimination reflected in the human rights act constitutes **an exception to the presumption of at-will employment**. Because the employee's allegations reasonably supported an inference of gender discrimination, the trial court had improperly granted judgment to the employer. The case was reversed and remanded. *Bailey v. Scott-Gallaher Inc.*, 480 S.E.2d 502 (Va. 1997).

◆ A New Jersey cable company closed its door-to-door sales department and released all employees of that department after settling a federal court discrimination complaint by one of the department's employees. The employee's mother, sister, and two close friends also had been employed in the department. Eighteen months later, the company resumed door-to-door sales but refused to rehire three of the former department employees. The former employees sued the company for violating the state law against discrimination. The court dismissed the complaint, but an appellate division court reversed and remanded. The employer appealed to the Supreme Court of New Jersey, which found that the state law against discrimination **protected friends and family members of complaining parties** against retaliatory discharge. Here, the door-to-door sales department was small and cohesive, and the complaining parties constituted almost the entire department. Some of the employees had participated in the earlier discrimination claim by giving testimony adverse to the employer, and the law was intended to protect such individuals from reprisal. The court affirmed the decision for the former employees. *Craig v. Suburban Cablevision, Inc.*, 140 N.J. 623, 660 A.2d 505 (N.J. 1995).

III. AGE DISCRIMINATION

The Age Discrimination in Employment Act forbids discrimination against individuals <u>at least 40 years old</u>. This includes not only hiring and firing decisions, but also the provision of benefits. For example, health care benefits for older employees are generally more expensive than the same level of benefits for younger employees.

Thus, employers can provide less benefits to older employees than to younger workers as long as the amount of payment made or cost incurred on behalf of the older employees is equal to or greater than the amount paid or cost incurred on behalf of the younger workers.

Where age is a bona fide occupational qualification, it may be used as a factor in employment decisions. However, for most jobs, age will not be a valid consideration. As a general rule, **never** take age into account in employment decisions.

Age Discrimination in Employment Act

Like the Equal Pay Act, the Age Discrimination in Employment Act of 1967 (ADEA) (29 U.S.C. § 621 *et seq.*) is part of the Fair Labor Standards Act. It applies to institutions that have 20 or more employees and that affect interstate commerce. The ADEA extends its protections to any individual 40 years old or older.

Relevant provisions of the ADEA are as follows:

§ 623. Prohibition of age discrimination

(a) Employer practices

It shall be unlawful for an employer –

(1) to fail or refuse to hire or to discharge any individual or otherwise discriminate against any individual with respect to his compensation, terms, conditions, or privileges of employment, because of such individual's age;

(2) to limit, segregate, or classify his employees in any way which would deprive or tend to deprive any individual of employment opportunities or otherwise adversely affect his status as an employee, because of such individual's age; or

(3) to reduce the wage rate of any employee in order to comply with this chapter.

* * *

(f) Lawful practices; age an occupational qualification; other reasonable factors; laws of foreign workplace; seniority system; employee benefit plans; discharge or discipline for good cause.

It shall not be unlawful for an employer, employment agency, or labor organization –

(1) to take any action otherwise prohibited under subsections (a), (b), (c), or (e) of this section where age is a bona fide occupational qualification reasonably necessary to the normal operation of the particular business, or where the differentiation is based on reasonable factors other than age, or where such practices involve an employee in a workplace in a foreign country, and compliance with such subsections would cause such employer, or a corporation controlled by such employer, to violate the laws of the country in which such workplace is located;

(2) to take any action otherwise prohibited under subsection (a), (b), (c), or (e) of this section –

(A) to observe the terms of a bona fide seniority system that is not intended to evade the purposes of this chapter, except that no such seniority system shall require or permit the involuntary retirement of any individual specified by section 631(a) of this title because of the age of such individual; or

(B) to observe the terms of a bona fide employee benefit plan –

(i) where, for each benefit or benefit package, the actual amount of payment made or cost incurred on behalf of an older worker is no less than that made or incurred on behalf of a younger worker, as permissible under section 1625.10, title 29, Code of Federal Regulations (as in effect on June 22, 1989); or

(ii) that is a voluntary early retirement incentive plan consistent with the relevant purpose or purposes of this chapter.

Notwithstanding clause (i) or (ii) of subparagraph (B), no such employee benefit plan or voluntary early retirement incentive plan shall excuse the failure to hire any individual, and no such employee benefit plan shall require or permit the involuntary retirement of any individual specified by section 631(a) of this title, because of the age of such individual. An employer, employment agency, or labor organization acting under subparagraph (A), or under clause (i) or (ii) of subparagraph (B), shall have the burden of proving that such actions are lawful in any civil enforcement proceeding brought under this chapter; or

(3) to discharge or otherwise discipline an individual for good cause.

* * *

A. Supreme Court Cases

The Supreme Court has decided a number of cases involving age discrimination in the past few years. One of its most important decisions came in the *O'Connor* case, (this chapter), where it held that employees can sue under the Age Discrimination in Employment Act (ADEA) even when they are not replaced by persons outside the protected class.

As long as the reason for an adverse decision is age-based, the decision will subject the employer to potential liability.

The Supreme Court also held, in the *Oubre* case, that waivers and releases must comply with the Older Workers Benefit Protection Act (OWBPA) (an amendment to the ADEA) in order to be valid. Thus, if you offer an employee a severance package in exchange for a promise not to sue, it must comply with the OWBPA.

- An atomic power laboratory in New York was ordered to reduce its workforce and had to cut 31 jobs. It did so in part by ranking employees on job performance, flexibility and criticality. The flexibility factor assessed whether the employees' skills were transferable to other assignments. The criticality factor assessed the importance of the employees' skills to the lab. When 30 of the 31 people laid off were age 40 or older, an ADEA lawsuit ensued. A jury ruled that the layoff process had a disparate impact on older employees, but the Second Circuit reversed, finding the employees should have been required to prove that the selection process was unreasonable. The Supreme Court vacated and remanded the case. Here, **the burden should have been on the employer to prove that its layoff process used reasonable factors other than age**. *Meacham v. Knolls Atomic Power Laboratory*, 128 S.Ct. 2395, 171 L.Ed.2d 283 (U.S. 2008).

- After an older employee in Kansas was fired as part of a reduction in force, she sued for age discrimination. When she sought to introduce testimony from five other employees who claimed that their supervisors discriminated against them because of age, the court refused to allow the "me too" testimony. The Tenth Circuit reversed, but the Supreme Court reversed the court of appeals. It held that such **"me too" testimony can be admitted if it is relevant and not unduly prejudicial**. This is a fact-based inquiry that is best left to the trial court to ascertain. *Sprint/United Management Co. v. Mendelsohn*, 128 S.Ct. 1140 (U.S. 2008).

- A group of senior, longtime police officers with a Mississippi city challenged the city's revised pay policy because it gave proportionately higher raises to officers with less than 5 years' tenure. They claimed that the revised policy had a disparate impact on them. In other words, a facially neutral policy had an adverse effect on them. The case reached the U.S. Supreme Court, which held that **the officers could sue for disparate impact discrimination under the ADEA**. To win, the officers would have to identify a "specific test, requirement, or practice with the pay plan that ha[d] an adverse impact on older workers." The city claimed that the differential was justified by the need to make junior officers' salaries competitive with comparable positions in the market. Here, the Court determined that the policy was based on reasonable factors other than age and therefore did not violate the ADEA. *Smith v. City of Jackson*, 544 U.S. 228, 125 S.Ct. 1536, 161 L.Ed.2d 410 (2005).

- A company and a union entered into a collective bargaining agreement, which eliminated the company's obligation to provide health benefits to subsequently retired employees, except as to then-current workers at least 50 years old. Employees between the ages of 40 and 49 filed charges with the Equal Employment Opportunity Commission (EEOC), claiming that the bargaining agreement violated the ADEA. When the company and union refused to settle, the employees sued in an Ohio federal court, which dismissed the action on the grounds that the ADEA did not cover "reverse age discrimination." The Sixth Circuit reversed, finding that the ADEA did not specifically limit its coverage to older workers. The U.S. Supreme Court then held that the ADEA was never intended to prevent an employer from favoring an older worker over a younger one. Rather, Congress was concerned with discrimination that was directed at older workers. The Court overruled the EEOC's interpretive guidance, which told employers that they could not favor an older worker over a younger one. **Reverse age discrimination is not barred by the ADEA.** *General Dynamics Land Systems, Inc. v. Cline*, 540 U.S. 581, 124 S.Ct. 1236, 157 L.Ed.2d 1094 (2004).

◆ The Supreme Court held that in a lawsuit brought under the ADEA, once the employee presented a *prima facie* case of discrimination and showed that the employer's asserted nondiscriminatory reason for its adverse action was false, **intentional discrimination could be inferred** without further evidence of discrimination. This reaffirmed the holding of *St. Mary's Honor Center v. Hicks*, 509 U.S. 502 (1993), a Title VII case that set forth the same standard. The case involved a supervisor in the "hinge room" of a manufacturer of toilet seats and covers. After he was fired for failing to keep accurate records, he sued under the ADEA and presented evidence that his record keeping had been proper. The district court had properly let the case go to the jury without further evidence of discrimination, and the jury's award of $98,000 should not have been overturned by the court of appeals. *Reeves v. Sanderson Plumbing Products*, 530 U.S. 133, 120 S.Ct. 2097, 147 L.Ed.2d 105 (2000).

◆ The OWBPA imposes specific requirements on employers who discharge employees and seek **a waiver or release of potential claims** against them under the ADEA. The requirements apply where an employee is offered a severance package. A valid OWBPA waiver must provide at least 20 days' notice to the employee to consider the waiver, written advice to consult an attorney prior to executing the waiver, a seven-day period after signing the waiver to revoke consent, and specifically refer to rights or claims arising under the ADEA. A Louisiana employer presented an employee with a severance agreement and waiver after she received a poor performance rating. The employer gave her only 14 days to consider the waiver, failed to allow seven days after signing the release during which to change her mind, and made no reference to ADEA claims. The employee signed the release, waiving all claims against the employer in return for $6,258. She then sued the employer for constructive discharge in violation of the ADEA. The court granted the employer pretrial judgment, ruling that she had ratified the defective release by retaining the severance pay.

The Fifth Circuit affirmed the district court judgment, but the U.S. Supreme Court found that the employee's **retention of the severance pay did not effectively waive the ADEA claim**. The OWBPA amended the ADEA with specific statutory commands forbidding the waiver of an ADEA claim unless the statutory requirements are met. The Court reversed and remanded the case, since the release did not comply with OWBPA standards and was unenforceable. The failure to tender back the severance pay award did not excuse the employer's failure to comply with the OWBPA. *Oubre v. Entergy Operations, Inc.*, 522 U.S. 422, 118 S.Ct. 838, 139 L.Ed.2d 849 (1998).

◆ A 56-year-old North Carolina employee was fired by his employer after 12 years of work and replaced by a 40-year-old man. The discharged employee sued under the ADEA. The U.S. Supreme Court agreed to review the question of whether the employee was barred from proving age discrimination under the ADEA solely because he had been replaced by a worker who was 40 years old and also within the class of persons protected by the ADEA. It stated that, in age discrimination cases, it was **not necessary that the employee be replaced by someone outside the protected class**. Under that logic, a 40-year-old worker replaced by a 39-year-old worker would be entitled to ADEA protection while the 56-year-old employee in this case would gain no relief despite being replaced by an individual who was 16 years younger. Because the ADEA prohibits discrimination on the basis of age, the replacement of an employee by a substantially younger employee was a far more reliable indicator of age discrimination. *O'Connor v. Consolidated Coin Caterers Corp.*, 517 U.S. 308, 116 S.Ct. 1307, 134 L.Ed.2d 433 (1996).

◆ A 62-year-old secretary at a Tennessee publishing company had access to company financial records and made copies of documents when she became concerned that the company would fire her because of her age. The company dismissed the secretary under a workforce reduction plan. She sued under the ADEA, seeking back pay and other relief. When the company learned that she had copied financial documents, it filed a motion for pretrial judgment, which the court granted on the basis of the secretary's misconduct. The Sixth Circuit affirmed, but the U.S. Supreme Court reversed. It rejected the reasoning of the lower courts that the secretary's misconduct constituted proper grounds for termination based on the **after-acquired evidence**. Employee wrongdoing remained relevant and would preclude reinstatement or front pay as an appropriate remedy in this case. However, the district court could not impose an absolute rule barring the secretary's recovery of back pay. The remedy should calculate back pay from the date of the unlawful discharge to the date the company discovered the wrongdoing. *McKennon v. Nashville Banner Publishing Co.*, 513 U.S. 352, 115 S.Ct. 879, 130 L.Ed.2d 852 (1995).

◆ A Massachusetts manufacturing employee was fired at age 62, a few weeks before his pension benefits were due to vest. He sued under the ADEA and the Employee Retirement Income Security Act. The case reached the U.S. Supreme Court, which noted that when **an employer's decision is wholly motivated by factors other than age**, no ADEA violation occurs. This was true even when the motivating factor was correlated with age (such as pension status). Because age and years of service may be analytically distinct, an employer could take account of one while ignoring the other. The Court remanded the case to the court of appeals to determine if the jury had sufficient evidence to find a violation of the ADEA. *Hazen Paper Co. v. Biggins*, 507 U.S. 604, 113 S.Ct. 1701, 123 L.Ed.2d 338 (1993).

◆ An airline company required all cockpit crew members (pilots, copilots and flight engineers) to retire at the age of 60. A Federal Aviation Administration regulation prohibited persons from serving as pilots or copilots after turning 60, but there was no similar provision for flight engineers. A group of flight engineers and pilots who wished to become flight engineers sued the airline in a California federal court, contending that the mandatory retirement provision violated the ADEA. The airline argued that the **age 60 limit was a bona fide occupational qualification** (BFOQ) reasonably necessary to the safe operation of the airline. A jury held for the employees, and the Ninth Circuit affirmed. The U.S. Supreme Court stated that the BFOQ exception to the ADEA's prohibition on age discrimination was intended to be extremely narrow. Thus, even if it was "rational" for the airline to set age 60 as the limit for flight engineers, the airline still had to show that it had reasonable cause to believe that all or substantially all flight engineers over 60 would be unable to safely perform their job duties, or that it would be highly impractical to deal with older employees on an individual basis to determine whether they had the necessary qualifications for the job. Because the airline had not shown this, the Court affirmed the lower court decisions in favor of the employees. *Western Air Lines, Inc. v. Criswell,* 472 U.S. 400, 105 S.Ct. 2743, 86 L.Ed.2d 321 (1985).

B. Layoffs for Economic Reasons

Layoffs and discharges for financial reasons have become common in today's business environment. Generally, such actions do not violate the Age Discrimination in Employment Act (ADEA). However, where they are used to create a younger work force or eliminate higher-paid employees, they can result in liability.

Employers should carefully ascertain whether any layoff or reduction in force is going to result in the release of more older workers than younger workers. The failure to consider age (or race, national origin, religion and sex) can result in liability.

- A 57-year-old salesman for a Michigan company endured "old man" comments from his superior, who then took him off a profitable account because he was "too old" and instead gave him a poorly performing one. The profitable account was given to a 33-year-old salesman. Later, the 57-year-old was laid off because of a financial slowdown and because his new account was not performing well. He sued for discrimination under the ADEA and Michigan law. A federal court granted pretrial judgment to the company, finding that the supervisor did not have the authority to fire the salesman, but the Sixth Circuit reversed. **There was substantial evidence that the biased supervisor participated in the decision to lay off the salesman.** Also, the company had no organized layoff plan to support the reasons it gave for laying off the 57-year-old. And the age-based comments were evidence that the salesman was fired because of his age. A trial was required. *Blair v. Henry Filters, Inc.*, 505 F.3d 517 (6th Cir. 2007).

- A custodian at a private school near Philadelphia also performed security guard responsibilities until the day he closed the school's theater before students were finished and forced them to wait for their rides home in the rain.

He was sent home early because his supervisor wanted to motivate him to improve his performance. Later, he was laid off as part of the outsourcing of the entire custodial department. When he sued for age discrimination, he lost. The Third Circuit found no evidence of age bias. **The school had a legitimate reason for disciplining him (poor performance)** and for laying him off (financial concerns). Plus, six of the eight employees who lost their jobs were under age 40. *Abraham v. Abington Friends School*, 215 Fed.Appx. 83 (3d Cir. 2006).

◆ A 49-year-old Indiana employee who had received satisfactory evaluations was laid off as part of a reduction in force. She sued under the ADEA, citing her overall satisfactory ratings. The company cited the negative comments in her review relating to her rapport with co-workers and her duplicative business practices. It also asserted that a new computer program handled most of her duties. A federal court and the Seventh Circuit ruled for the company. **Even though the employee would have been retained under normal circumstances**, she could be laid off as part of the reduction in force without violating the ADEA. *Merillat v. Metal Spinners, Inc.*, 470 F.3d 685 (7th Cir. 2006).

◆ A 51-year-old engineer with a company in New Mexico was laid off in a reduction in force. He was selected because even though he had good technical skills, he repeatedly second-guessed managers and did not get along well with co-workers. He sued for discrimination under the ADEA and lost. A federal court and the Tenth Circuit held that **the reason for the layoff – that he was a poor team player – was legitimate**, even if the company relied on subjective observations to reach its decision. *Pippin v. Burlington Resources Oil and Gas Co.*, 440 F.3d 1186 (10th Cir. 2006).

◆ A Missouri employee lost her job when she was 50 years old in a RIF. She rejected the offered severance package and sued the company under the ADEA, asserting that it engaged in disparate impact discrimination because 15 of the 16 laid-off employees were over 40. The case reached the Eighth Circuit Court of Appeals, which ruled in favor of the company. Here, the great majority of salaried employees were over 40. Before the RIF, 72% of the salaried employees in the employee's department were over 40. Afterwards, 68% were over 40. Accordingly, **the statistical evidence did not support a finding of discrimination** under the ADEA. *Stidham v. 3M Co.*, 399 F.3d 935 (8th Cir. 2005).

◆ A cab company in Oregon purchased a new insurance policy that did not cover drivers over age 70. However, it was not aware of that fact until the day before it had to provide proof of insurance to city officials or lose its business license. It then temporarily fired a 72-year-old driver until it could resolve the insurance issue. In the meantime it found a job for the driver with a competitor, and the insurer agreed to cover the driver if he passed a physical. He refused to take the physical, instead suing the company for age discrimination. A federal court granted pretrial judgment to the company, but the Ninth Circuit reversed, finding that factual questions existed regarding **whether the company harbored discriminatory motives**. A jury would have to decide the case. *Enlow v. Salem-Keizer Yellow Cab*, 389 F.3d 802 (9th Cir. 2004).

- A 53-year-old mechanical engineer learned that his position was going to be eliminated in a reduction in force. He asked the company if another position could be found for him and was put in touch with the company's engineering career development team. However, he was unable to obtain another position in the company. After he was laid off, he sued the company under the ADEA, asserting that **the company's failure to help him find another job to the same extent that it helped younger employees find jobs** was discriminatory. A Wisconsin federal court ruled for the company, and the Seventh Circuit Court of Appeals affirmed. Here, the engineer failed to show that he was similarly situated to three other employees in his division who had found assignments elsewhere in the company. Also, he failed to show that the company had targeted older engineers for the layoff. *Radue v. Kimberly-Clark Corp.*, 219 F.3d 612 (7th Cir. 2000).

C. Constructive Discharge

Sometimes, employers are reluctant to fire employees and, as a result, they create difficult working conditions in the hope that the employees will quit. But if an employer forces an employee to quit, and a judge or jury determines that a reasonable person in the same situation would also have quit, the resignation is treated like a discharge and the employer becomes liable.

- A company in Alabama instituted a voluntary severance program as part of a two-stage program to reduce its work force. It scored employees on work-related skills. A 52-year-old employee was ranked last in his group and was offered early retirement, the possibility of seeking a transfer or staying put and hoping his job would not be eliminated in the future. He chose the early retirement, then sued under the Age Discrimination in Employment Act (ADEA) when he learned that his job would not have been eliminated. A federal court and the Eleventh Circuit ruled against him. **The voluntary severance program was not a constructive discharge** because his choice was never "quit or be fired." Thus, no adverse action had been taken against him. *Rowell v. BellSouth Corp.*, 433 F.3d 794 (11th Cir. 2005).

- A highly paid executive with a Puerto Rico advertising company was told to hire new creative talent. When he resisted, many of the employees in his office were transferred to another location and he was given new job responsibilities. At one point, he was told that his proposals looked tired and that the company needed new blood. He was also ordered to complete a three-page report by the next morning. He became depressed and took sick leave for a year. He then requested an additional five weeks of paid vacation. When his request was denied, he stayed away from work anyway and was fired. In his ADEA lawsuit, the First Circuit ruled against him. Here, he was unable to show that the company had taken **an adverse action against him** that could be construed as age discrimination. He was not constructively discharged. *Suárez v. Pueblo Int'l, Inc.*, 229 F.3d 49 (1st Cir. 2000).

◆ A 59-year-old employee of a paper mill in Arkansas was responsible for three machines. While preparing a machine for repair, he failed to follow the proper safety procedures, and a younger employee under his supervision filed a union grievance against him. The paper mill's labor relations manager recommended that he be fired, but the mill manager decided instead to suspend him for 120 days. He quit and sued for age discrimination under the ADEA, asserting that the mill had constructively discharged him. A jury awarded him $670,000, which the court doubled to $1.3 million, finding that the ADEA violation was willful. The Eighth Circuit U.S. Court of Appeals reversed, holding that **the employee had not shown that the mill intended to force his resignation by suspending him**. In fact, it chose suspension over termination. As a result, the mill did not violate the ADEA. *Tatom v. Georgia-Pacific Corp.*, 228 F.3d 926 (8th Cir. 2000).

◆ A corporation employed a 60-year-old Texas man as the vice president of one of its divisions. When the new division president and the president of the corporation decided they wanted a younger management team, the employee was given three options, the least offensive of which appeared to be a job as warehouse supervisor at the same salary but with a reduction in benefits. He accepted that position. When he reported for work, however, he was placed in charge of maintenance at the warehouse and spent 75% of his working time sweeping floors and cleaning up the employees' cafeteria. He sued the company under the ADEA. He was awarded $3.4 million. The U.S. Court of Appeals, Fifth Circuit, noted that there was substantial evidence to support the jury's ADEA verdict. The court also noted that the degrading and humiliating way in which the vice president had been stripped of his duties and demoted to a menial position took the case out of the realm of an ordinary employment dispute. Here, **the corporation sought to humiliate the vice president in the hopes that he would quit**. The court affirmed the decision in favor of the employee. *Wilson v. Monarch Paper Co.,* 939 F.2d 1138 (5th Cir. 1991).

D. OWBPA

The Older Workers Benefit Protection Act (OWBPA) is an amendment to the Age Discrimination in Employment Act (ADEA) that prohibits discrimination against older workers in all employee benefits "except when age-based reductions in employee benefit plans are justified by significant cost considerations." This is the <u>equal benefits/equal cost</u> defense.

Specifically, the regulations state that a benefit plan will be considered in compliance with the ADEA where the actual amount of payment made, or cost incurred, on behalf of an older worker is equal to that made or incurred on behalf of a younger worker, even though the older worker receives a lesser amount of benefits or insurance coverage.

Many employers attempt to head off age discrimination lawsuits through the use of waivers that discharged employees sign in exchange for a cash payment. Such waivers are valid only if they are "knowing and voluntary."

- A group of employees over the age of 40 signed a severance agreement provided by IBM when they were laid off in a reduction in force. The agreement stated that it was a release of all claims against IBM, including claims under the ADEA, and later stated that the covenant not to sue did not apply to actions based solely on the ADEA. It used the terms "release" and "covenant not to sue" interchangeably. When **the employees sued, challenging the agreement under the OWBPA** (part of the ADEA), a California federal court dismissed their action, finding the agreement was written in a manner calculated to be understood by an average individual selected for layoff. The Ninth Circuit disagreed, ruling that the language was not clear. The employees could continue their lawsuit. *Syverson v. IBM Corp.*, 472 F.3d 1072 (9th Cir. 2007).

- A 55-year-old Iowa manager was laid off after company officials determined that a new system allowed a coordinator to do his job. He was offered two severance options, consulted with an attorney, and signed one. He then sued for discrimination under the ADEA, claiming that the waiver he'd signed did not comply with the OWBPA because it was not written in a manner calculated to be understood by the individual signing it. A federal court and the Eighth Circuit ruled against him. **The provisions in question complied with Department of Labor regulations** that made certain exceptions for ADEA claims. *Parsons v. Pioneer Seed Hi-Bred Int'l, Inc.*, 447 F.3d 1102 (8th Cir. 2006).

- A long-time engineer for a company in Minnesota received a waiver agreement in which he agreed not to sue the company for any claims, including under the ADEA, in exchange for a sum of money. The waiver also contained a covenant not to sue in which he was informed that he would not be liable for the company's attorney fees if he sued it under the ADEA. He did not understand the language and asked for a clarification, but the company did not provide one. When he later sued under the ADEA, a federal court granted pretrial judgment to the company, but the Eighth Circuit reversed. Here, the waiver used unexplained legal terms of art (General Release and Covenant Not to Sue). This ambiguity meant that **the waiver was not "knowing and voluntary" under the OWBPA**. *Thomforde v. IBM Corp.*, 406 F.3d 500 (8th Cir. 2005).

- The 57-year-old chief administrator of the psychiatric department of a Pennsylvania health network was fired for improperly handling lease negotiations for a new office. He signed a separation and release agreement in which he agreed not to file a charge, complaint or lawsuit against the company. In return, he received a guarantee of 36 weeks of salary. If he accepted a lower-paying job during that time, the company would make up the salary difference until the 36 weeks ended. Later, he learned that a 44-year-old had replaced him. He filed EEOC charges that were dismissed as untimely and then sued under the ADEA. A federal court ruled for the company, and the Third Circuit affirmed. **The waiver barred the administrator from pursuing his claim.** Its language was clearly written so that he could understand it; he was given 21 days to sign the waiver and was advised to consult an attorney; and the waiver was supported by adequate consideration. It complied with the OWBPA. *Wastak v. Lehigh Valley Health Network*, 333 F.3d 120 (3d Cir. 2003).

E. Procedural Issues

In many cases, whether an employer will be held liable for age discrimination depends on evidentiary issues like hearsay statements from supervisors. Comments like: "We need new blood around here" and "You're 10 years behind the times" can be real trouble, especially if they're made by a decision-maker.

◆ A 56-year-old Arkansas purchasing supervisor was fired after she altered a previously approved purchase order without authorization, adding a bicycle to the order at a cost of $563 and charging it to the wrong cost center. She did so to assist her husband, who also worked at the company, and who had been denied a replacement bicycle (used to transport materials and tools around the plant). She sued for age and sex discrimination but lost because she could not show that other similarly situated employees had not been fired for similar wrongdoing. **Although other employees who violated company rules had not been fired, they had not violated the same rule she had.** *Bearden v. Int'l Paper Co.*, 529 F.3d 828 (8th Cir. 2008).

◆ A vice president for a company in Iowa was reassigned to a director position during a reorganization. During another shakeup, the director, then 55, was reassigned to a project coordinator position with the same salary and benefits. He sued under the ADEA, and a jury awarded him $46,945. However, the Eighth Circuit reversed the award and sent the case back for a retrial because he failed to provide any direct evidence of discrimination. Therefore, **the company should not have been required to prove that age was not a factor in its decision**. Instead, he would have to prove that the legitimate reason the company gave for his reassignment – co-worker complaints – was a pretext for discrimination. *Gross v. FBL Financial Services*, 526 F.3d 356 (8th Cir. 2008).

◆ The EEOC issued a proposed rule that would allow employers to reduce retirees' health benefits when the retirees became eligible for Medicare. The proposed rule **exempted from the ADEA employer efforts to coordinate retirees' health care benefits when the retirees reach 65**. The AARP sued, challenging the proposed rule, and a Pennsylvania federal court found the rule valid. The Third Circuit Court of Appeals agreed, noting that the ADEA grants the EEOC the authority to provide narrow exemptions that are reasonable and necessary and "proper in the public interest." Here, the EEOC issued the rule in response to the fact that employer-sponsored retiree health benefits were decreasing. The proposed rule would permit employers to offer retirees benefits to the greatest extent possible. *AARP v. EEOC*, 489 F.3d 558 (3d Cir. 2007).

◆ A 49-year-old pharmacist applied for an entry-level job with a drug store chain. He met the qualifications for the job, but was not offered a position. Instead, the hiring manager offered the job to a 42-year-old pharmacist. The applicant then sued under the ADEA. A New York federal court granted pretrial judgment to the drug store, but the Second Circuit reversed, finding issues of fact as to the true reason the drug store did not offer the applicant a job. **It did not matter that the position was offered to someone within the protected class because the age difference was sufficient to allow for an inference of discrimination.** *D'Cunha v. Genovese/Eckerd Corp.*, 479 F.3d 193 (2d Cir. 2007).

◆ A female aircraft mechanic endured comments from a safety inspector about her sex and age. She complained about his comments, and he then reported valid safety infractions that led to reprimands and a suspension. After she was fired, she sued the company under Title VII and the ADEA. A South Carolina federal court ruled for the company, and the Fourth Circuit ultimately affirmed. The court noted that **even though the safety inspector may have had some influence on the termination decision, he was not the actual decision-maker**. And the officials who made the termination decision never demonstrated any discriminatory bias toward the mechanic. *Hill v. Lockheed Martin Logistics Management, Inc.*, 354 F.3d 277 (4th Cir. 2004).

◆ When a 69-year-old employee was fired in what was deemed to be a reduction in force, he sued under the ADEA, claiming that the real reason for the termination was not a drop in available work but age discrimination. A co-worker allegedly heard the president's secretary say that the employee was being fired because he was too old, and the president nodded his head as she said it. A New Jersey court dismissed the case, but the state supreme court reversed, finding that **the head nod could constitute a party admission** and thus be admissible under an exception to the hearsay rule. If so, it could be considered direct evidence of age discrimination so as to shift the burden of persuasion, thereby requiring the company to show that it would have made the same decision absent any discriminatory motive. The court remanded the case for further proceedings. *McDevitt v. Bill Good Builders, Inc.*, 816 A.2d 164 (N.J. 2003).

◆ A Colorado man worked for a company for 29 years, eventually becoming the manager of the company's Denver division. At the age of 52, a little more than two years shy of vesting for the company's supplemental executive pension plan, he was fired. The company claimed he was a poor merchandiser and that sales in his division had flattened or declined. When he sued under the ADEA, a jury awarded him $6.7 million, including **$4.4 million for unrealized stock option appreciation**. The Tenth Circuit affirmed the award, stating that the ADEA gives courts broad discretion to grant relief. Here, by firing the manager, the company forced him to exercise his stock options two years sooner than he otherwise would have. By awarding him that difference, the jury put him in the same position he would have been in absent the discrimination. *Greene v. Safeway Stores, Inc.*, 210 F.3d 1237 (10th Cir. 2000).

F. Other Age Discrimination Cases

Age discrimination claims tend to increase when the economy worsens and employers engage in downsizing. Thus, age should always be considered before any final action is taken to lay off or discharge employees.

Also, state laws are sometimes more protective than the Age Discrimination in Employment Act (ADEA). For example, some states bar discrimination on the basis of age without setting a minimum age. Thus, a 25-year-old employee who is not promoted because she is deemed to be too young might be able to sue for age discrimination under state law.

◆ Ten days after a Howard University employee complained about an ageist remark made by her supervisor, she received a written warning for taking 87 hours of unscheduled leave, most of it on a Monday or Friday. Shortly thereafter, she used another 16 hours of unscheduled leave and received a second warning. Two months after that, she failed to show up for work on Memorial Day or the day after and did not call in to report her absence. Her supervisor recommended a five-day suspension. The university HR office gave her a hearing, after which the suspension was approved. The employee then sued for age discrimination, retaliation and a hostile work environment. A D.C. jury awarded her $15,000 in compensatory damages and $100,000 in punitive damages, but the D.C. Court of Appeals vacated the award and entered judgment for the university. Here, **even if the supervisor's recommendation was vindictive or discriminatory, the university's review process ensured that the discipline was legitimate**. *Furline v. Morrison*, 953 A.2d 344 (D.C. 2008).

◆ A 48-year-old information services program manager at a Best Buy location in Minnesota asked if he could help out on a new project the company was working on – a store-within-a-store for home theater products. He helped develop and launch the new project, then was informed that he would no longer be needed once the development phase ended and the rollout began. He was given 60 days to find another job within the company. His old job had been eliminated and he failed to find anything else. After his termination, he sued under the ADEA. A federal court and the Eighth Circuit ruled against him. Here, his managers thought he wouldn't be interested in the nuts-and-bolts phase of implementing the project, and also believed he didn't have the skills necessary for it. **The youthful culture – starting each morning with a huddle and cheer – did not suggest a pretext for age discrimination.** *Loeb v. Best Buy Co.*, 537 F.3d 867 (8th Cir. 2008).

◆ An Illinois Sears store manager was placed on a performance improvement plan because her district manager thought she was disorganized and did not properly train or lead her employees. She was removed from the plan the following year, but a new district manager arrived a few months later and put her on a second performance improvement plan. At that time, the district's stores performed the worst among the 63 districts nationwide. At the age of 50, she was fired. She sued under the ADEA and lost. The Seventh Circuit agreed with Sears that its reasons for terminating her – consistently poor performance and poor execution of marketing events – were not a pretext for discrimination. *Faas v. Sears, Roebuck & Co.*, 532 F.3d 633 (7th Cir. 2008).

◆ The supervisor of a 42-year-old Minnesota sales director suspected that the director might be working for another company. The supervisor and a vice president took precautionary steps, reassigning six of the 13 states the director covered to other people and copying his laptop files to the company's computer system. During the investigation of the company's suspicions, the director learned that the vice president had stated that he wanted to hire some "young studs." The director was then fired for failing to meet sales revenue goals. His territory was reassigned to a new hire (age 41) and a current salesperson (age 37). When he sued for age discrimination, he lost. The Eighth Circuit held that **the comments were not related to the termination**, and noted that the people who took over his territory were not significantly younger. *Ramlet v. E.F. Johnson Co.*, 507 F.3d 1149 (8th Cir. 2007).

◆ A 56-year-old executive recruiter for Target was told that the recruiting office was going to be decentralized and that if he wanted to stay with the company, he would have to move from Minnesota to Texas. He originally decided not to move, then met with his superior and stated that he was interested in relocating. She allegedly offered him a severance, relocation or a different position in Minneapolis. However, he claimed she only discussed severance options. He failed to report to work or contact his supervisor and was fired. When he sued for age discrimination, he lost. The Eighth Circuit ruled that he failed to prove the discharge (for not showing up for work) was pretextual. *Carraher v. Target Corp.*, 503 F.3d 714 (8th Cir. 2007).

◆ A bank in Texas shut down a four-person unit and eliminated the jobs held by the two oldest people (54 and 58) while transferring the younger two (39 and 41) to another location. The 58-year-old accepted a job with another department, but the 54-year-old chose not to look for another job within the bank. He sued under the ADEA, claiming his new manager had made comments about attracting younger talent. The case reached the Fifth Circuit, which ruled against him. Here, the manager made the single comment nine months before the firing. Also, **the employee was not similarly situated to the younger workers**, whose jobs were different. Finally, he chose not to seek another job within the bank. *Berquist v. Washington Mutual Bank*, 500 F.3d 344 (5th Cir. 2007).

◆ An investment firm offered older employees a voluntary severance incentive plan as the first phase of an overall plan to reduce costs. The firm told employees they might be subject to involuntary termination if they didn't quit early, but informed them it was not pressuring them to quit. It gave them 45 days to decide whether to participate and seven days after signing the agreement to change their minds. A 59-year-old regional manager chose not to participate, then was demoted after not being prepared for a meeting. He stopped coming to work and was fired. When he sued for discrimination under the ADEA, an

Arkansas federal court and the Eighth Circuit ruled against him. **The voluntary early retirement plan was not a "quit or be fired" proposition**, and the firm offered legitimate reasons for its actions. Further, it replaced him with a 63-year-old. *Morgan v. A.G. Edwards & Sons, Inc.*, 486 F.3d 1034 (8th Cir. 2007).

◆ An apartment management company employee in her 60s was subjected to age-related comments by her supervisor once every couple of months. Although he gave her several raises, he eventually fired her after hearing that she wasn't able to keep up with the challenges of relocating various tenants after an apartment explosion. She sued for discrimination under the ADEA. A New York federal court granted pretrial judgment to the company, but the Second Circuit reversed. It found issues of fact that required a trial. In addition to the comments by the supervisor who ultimately fired the employee, there was evidence that the company was **trying to attract young professionals** as tenants and hiring younger people to achieve that end. *Tomassi v. Insignia Financial Group, Inc.*, 478 F.3d 111 (2d Cir. 2007).

◆ Shortly after the 28-year-old stepson of a company's founder took over as president, he concluded that a 73-year-old manager wasn't managing his department properly. He decided not to pay the manager a bonus for the first time in 30 years. Then, needing to cut costs, the president laid off the manager, who sued for age discrimination. The Pennsylvania Commonwealth Court ruled in favor of the company. Here, just because the manager had always received bonuses in the past, he was not necessarily entitled to them under a new supervisor. Also, there was evidence that the manager failed to follow an order to clean up a warehouse floor. Finally, **a statement the president made that the manager, at 74, ought to consider retiring, wasn't coercive**. *Associated Rubber, Inc. v. Pennsylvania Human Relations Comm'n*, 915 A.2d 689 (Pa. Commw. Ct. 2007).

◆ An Illinois company hired a new vice president (VP) of technology and planning, who made comments about wanting to get rid of the "good old boys" and bring an end to the "old boys" club. Two years after the new VP was hired, a 52-year-old manager was fired by his supervisor because he was taking too long to get assignments to his team and wasn't keeping the request database current. He claimed age discrimination and sued. A federal court and the Seventh Circuit ruled against him. **He failed to show that the VP was involved in the decision to fire him or that the comments indicated age animus.** *Luks v. Baxter Healthcare Corp.*, 467 F.3d 1049 (7th Cir. 2006).

◆ An over-40 assistant manager in New Mexico sought a promotion to store manager on numerous occasions, but was told no positions were available. During that same time, the company promoted three younger assistant managers. When he sued for age discrimination, a jury ruled in his favor, rejecting the company's assertion that he was not qualified for the promotion because of a "coaching" letter in his file. The Tenth Circuit upheld the jury's decision, noting that **the company's promotion process was not as objective as it argued**. The coaching letter itself might have been the result of age bias by the supervisor, whom the jury believed made age-based comments to the employee. *Cortez v. Wal-Mart Stores,* 460 F.3d 1268 (10th Cir. 2005).

◆ The operations manager for a company in Maine gave a 61-year-old business unit manager lower performance review scores than six of his colleagues even though the unit manager decreased production lead times (a company objective) and decreased defects by 68%. Two managers who were ranked higher experienced 70% increases in defects. When the unit manager was laid off in a reduction in force, he sued for age discrimination and a jury awarded him $376,000. The First Circuit upheld the award. Here, the performance review categories were subjective, and **the operations manager's explanation for why he ranked the unit manager so low was vague**. The jury permissibly found it to be a pretext for discrimination. *Currier v. United Technologies Corp.*, 393 F.3d 246 (1st Cir. 2004).

◆ A supervisor wanted to fire a 60-year-old branch manager at an equipment rental company in Massachusetts. Three company executives decided to fire the manager after the supervisor told them about an improper payment authorization. However, the supervisor did not tell the executives that he had instructed the manager to authorize the payment. The supervisor replaced the manager with an employee younger than 40. The manager sued for age discrimination under state law, and a federal court granted pretrial judgment to the company. The First Circuit Court of Appeals reversed, finding an issue of fact as to whether **the company could be held liable for the discrimination even though the supervisor was not involved in the termination decision**. The executives should have given the manager the chance to address the allegations against him. *Cariglia v. Hertz Equipment Rental Corp.*, 363 F.3d 77 (1st Cir. 2004).

◆ A New Jersey bank hired a vice president for credit card operations at an annual salary of $70,000. Prior to his starting date, the bank's chairman asked him his age. According to the vice president, the chairman appeared shocked when he stated that he was only 25 years old, and he was then instructed not to disclose his age to anyone. Within days of his hiring, bank officials expressed dissatisfaction with his work, and he was discharged less than five months later. The bank sued him for removing, downloading and deleting some of its computer files, and he counterclaimed for breach of contract and violation of the state Law Against Discrimination (LAD). The court granted the bank pretrial judgment on the LAD claim, ruling that the LAD does not protect persons under the age of 40. The Superior Court of New Jersey, Appellate Division, reversed, observing that, **unlike the federal ADEA, the LAD applies to persons who have reached the age of 18**. *Bergen Commercial Bank v. Sisler*, 307 N.J.Super. 333, 704 A.2d 1017 (N.J. Super. Ct. App. Div. 1998).

IV. DISABILITY DISCRIMINATION

The Americans with Disabilities Act (ADA), 42 U.S.C. § 12101 *et seq.*, prohibits discrimination against qualified individuals with disabilities with respect to job application procedures, hiring, advancement, discharge, compensation, training, and other terms and conditions of employment.

The language of the ADA is based on Section 504 of the Rehabilitation Act of 1973, which applies only to programs or activities receiving federal funds. The ADA expands Section 504's limited scope to most employers with at least 15 employees. Many states have enacted similar legislation on behalf of individuals with disabilities. These laws generally are based on the language of the ADA and Section 504.

The ADA Amendments Act, effective January 1, 2009, expands the definition of "disability" under the ADA, rejecting the holdings in several Supreme Court decisions and portions of the EEOC's regulations. It states that mitigating measures, other than ordinary eyeglasses or contacts, can't be considered in determining whether an individual is disabled.

The ADA Amendments Act also expands the definition of "major life activities" to include such activities as bending, reading and communicating and adds in "major bodily functions" like normal cell growth, digestive and reproductive functions.

A. The ADA and the Rehabilitation Act

The ADA requires employers to make reasonable accommodations for employees (and applicants) with disabilities. However, employers need not make the specific accommodation requested by the employee. As long as they offer an accommodation that is reasonable, they can avoid liability.

Note that the employee who is disabled must be able to perform the essential functions of the job (either with or without a reasonable accommodation). If the employee cannot meet that standard, he will not qualify for ADA protection.

Also, to be disabled under the ADA, the employee must have more than an impairment – he must have an impairment that substantially limits one or more major life activities. In other words, the impairment must substantially limit the individual's ability to perform tasks of central importance to most people's daily lives. The inability to perform one particular job generally will not be sufficient to demonstrate that an individual is disabled under the ADA.

Drug and alcohol users have some protections under the ADA. However, they can be held to the same standards of conduct as other employees. Homosexuality, transvestism and transsexuality are not considered impairments under the ADA.

Section 504 of the Rehabilitation Act (29 U.S.C. § 794) provides that no otherwise qualified individual with a disability shall, solely by reason of his or her disabilities, be excluded from the participation in, be denied the benefit of, or be subjected to discrimination under any program or activity receiving federal financial assistance.

Since most employers do not receive federal financial assistance, most cases of disability discrimination will be brought under the ADA or state law rather than the Rehabilitation Act.

1. Supreme Court Cases

- An Arizona employee tested positive for cocaine during a drug test at work and was allowed to resign rather than face termination. Two years later, the employee sought to be rehired to the same position. He attached to his application glowing reference letters from his pastor and his Alcoholics Anonymous counselor. The company refused to rehire him, and he sued under the ADA. He asserted that the no-rehire policy violated the ADA by discriminating against him **because of a record of a disability or because he was regarded as disabled**. A federal court granted pretrial judgment to the company, but the Ninth Circuit reversed. It stated that the no-rehire policy violated the ADA as applied to former employees whose only work-related offense was testing positive because of their addiction. On further appeal, the U.S. Supreme Court held that the employer could legitimately refuse to rehire an employee who was discharged for violating workplace conduct rules. The employer's neutral no-rehire policy satisfied its obligation under *McDonnell Douglas* to provide a legitimate, nondiscriminatory reason for refusing to rehire the employee. The only remaining question was whether the stated reason for the refusal to rehire was in fact the real reason. The Court remanded the case. *Raytheon Co. v. Hernandez*, 540 U.S. 44, 124 S.Ct. 513, 157 L.Ed.2d 357 (2003).

  On remand, the Ninth Circuit held that a trial was required because the company gave inconsistent reasons for why it refused to rehire the employee. *Hernandez v. Hughes Missile Systems Co. (Raytheon)*, 362 F.3d 564 (9th Cir. 2004).

- A bookkeeper at a medical clinic in Oregon sued the clinic under the ADA after she was fired. The clinic sought to have the case dismissed, alleging that it did not have **the necessary 15 employees to qualify it as a covered employer under the ADA** because the four physician-shareholders who owned the clinic could not be counted as employees. A federal court agreed with the clinic and dismissed the case, but the Ninth Circuit reversed. The case reached the U.S. Supreme Court, which adopted the Equal Employment Opportunity Commission's standard for determining when a director-shareholder should be counted as an employee under the ADA. The standard provides six factors for ascertaining whether the organization has control over the individual. The Court reversed and remanded the case for a determination of whether the doctor-shareholders should be counted as employees. *Clackamas Gastroenterology Associates, P.C. v. Wells*, 538 U.S. 440, 123 S.Ct. 1673, 155 L.Ed.2d 615 (2003).

◆ The U.S. Supreme Court held that a gas company could reject an applicant for a position in a California refinery where the applicant suffered from hepatitis C and could die from prolonged exposure to chemicals in the refinery. Here, the gas company made an offer of employment, then conducted a medical exam that found the hepatitis. When it revoked the offer, the applicant sued under the ADA, claiming that since he was not a direct threat to anyone else in the workplace, the company could not refuse to hire him. The Supreme Court stated that **the "direct threat" defense could be applied to prevent harm to the individual seeking a job**. It was not limited to preventing harm to "others" in the workplace. If a person's disability would create a direct threat of harm to himself in the workplace, the employer need not hire the person, even if the individual is willing to take the risk. *Chevron U.S.A. v. Echazabal*, 536 U.S. 73, 122 S.Ct. 2045, 153 L.Ed.2d 82 (2002).

◆ A 10-year customer service employee for an airline was placed in a mail room position after he injured his back handling cargo. He obtained the position by invoking his seniority rights. A few years later, he learned that two senior employees were going to bid on the mail room position. He asked the airline to make an exception to its seniority policy to accommodate his back injury by allowing him to stay in the mail room. After allowing the employee to stay in the mail room for five months, the airline decided not to make an exception to its seniority policy, and the employee lost his job. He sued the airline under the ADA, and a California federal court ruled that requiring the airline to accommodate the employee would cause an undue hardship. The Ninth Circuit reversed, and the airline appealed. The U.S. Supreme Court held that as a general rule, an accommodation under the ADA is not reasonable if it conflicts with an employer's **seniority rules**. However, employees may present evidence of special circumstances that make a "seniority rule exception" reasonable in a particular case. The Court remanded the case. *US Airways, Inc. v. Barnett*, 535 U.S. 391, 122 S.Ct. 1516, 152 L.Ed.2d 589 (2002).

◆ An employee at a Kentucky manufacturing plant had a severe case of carpal tunnel syndrome and tendonitis that prevented her from gripping tools and raising her arms over her head for extended periods of time. She was assigned to modified-duty positions for two years, but she eventually became unable to perform two of the essential functions of the job. She began missing work and was eventually fired for poor attendance. When she sued under the ADA, a federal court found that she was not disabled under the statute. The Sixth Circuit reversed, but the U.S. Supreme Court reversed the court of appeals. It held that the ADA requires a person to be substantially limited in a "major" life activity, and that **the employee's inability to perform a manufacturing job did not qualify her as disabled under the act**. If the employee was substantially limited in the ability to perform the types of tasks that are centrally important to people's daily lives (like household chores, bathing and brushing her teeth), then she would be disabled under the ADA. The Court remanded the case. *Toyota Motor Manufacturing v. Williams*, 534 U.S. 184, 122 S.Ct. 681, 151 L.Ed.2d 615 (2002).

◆ Twin sisters with uncorrected vision of 20/200 or worse, but corrected vision of 20/20 or better, applied to United Air Lines for positions as global airline pilots. United rejected them because they did not meet its minimum requirement of at least 20/100 uncorrected vision. They sued under the ADA. A Colorado federal court dismissed their lawsuit, and the case reached the U.S. Supreme Court, which found that the sisters had not shown they were disabled under the ADA. First, because the ADA defines a disability as an impairment that "substantially limits" a major life activity, and because the sisters, with glasses or contacts, had 20/20 vision, **they were not presently substantially limited**. The sisters also failed to show that they were regarded as disabled by United. Even though it regarded them as unable to perform in the particular position of global airline pilot, it did not regard them as substantially limited in the major life activity of working. Other jobs were still available to them, including jobs such as regional pilots or pilot instructors. *Sutton v. United Air Lines, Inc.*, 527 U.S. 471, 119 S.Ct. 2139, 144 L.Ed.2d 450 (1999).

◆ The U.S. Supreme Court held that a mechanic with high blood pressure that was controllable with medication was not disabled under the ADA, because **his high blood pressure did not substantially limit him in the major life activity of working**. Further, he was not regarded as disabled. Rather, he was regarded as unqualified to work in the single position of United Parcel Service mechanic because he could not obtain a Department of Transportation health certification. *Murphy v. United Parcel Service,* 527 U.S. 516, 119 S.Ct. 2133, 144 L.Ed.2d 484 (1999).

◆ An Oregon truck driver with monocular vision was fired because he did not meet the visual acuity standards of the Federal Motor Carrier Safety Regulations. The U.S. Supreme Court noted that the driver was not necessarily disabled within the meaning of the ADA. Even though he had monocular vision, his brain had developed subconscious mechanisms for coping with his visual impairment. This was a mitigating measure (like glasses or medication) that had to be taken into account when determining whether he was substantially limited in one or more major life activities. An employer who requires as a job qualification that an employee **meet a federal safety regulation** does not have to justify enforcing the regulation simply because the government has waived the safety standard experimentally in an individual case. *Albertsons, Inc. v. Kirkingburg*, 527 U.S. 555, 119 S.Ct. 2162, 144 L.Ed.2d 518 (1999).

◆ A Texas employee suffered a stroke and applied for Social Security benefits, alleging that she was disabled and unable to work. When her condition improved, she returned to work. However, her employer fired her less than a week later. She sued in a Texas federal court under the ADA asserting that a reasonable accommodation would allow her to perform her job. The court ruled that she could not assert she was disabled in her application for and receipt of Social Security benefits, and later claim that she could perform the essential functions of her job. The case reached the U.S. Supreme Court, which held that **the pursuit and receipt of Social Security Disability Insurance benefits does not automatically bar a person from litigating a claim under the ADA**.

However, to survive a motion to dismiss, the person must present a sufficient explanation of the seeming contradiction that she is disabled under the Social Security Act (SSA) while not disabled under the ADA. Because the SSA does not take into account a reasonable accommodation when it determines whether a person is disabled for Social Security purposes, qualifying for such benefits might not bar an ADA claim. *Cleveland v. Policy Management Systems Corp.*, 526 U.S. 795, 119 S.Ct. 1597, 143 L.Ed.2d 966 (1999).

◆ The U.S. Supreme Court held that **asymptomatic HIV is a physical impairment that substantially limits the major life activity of reproduction**. Accordingly, a dentist's patient was disabled within the meaning of the ADA. The question then became whether the patient's HIV infection posed a significant threat to the health and safety of others that might justify the dentist's refusal to treat her in his office. *Bragdon v. Abbott*, 524 U.S. 624, 118 S.Ct. 2196, 141 L.Ed.2d 540 (1998).

◆ A Florida school board fired an elementary school teacher after she suffered three relapses of tuberculosis within two years. She sued for discrimination on the basis of disability under Section 504 of the Rehabilitation Act. The court held that contagious diseases such as tuberculosis were not disabilities within the meaning of Section 504 and determined that the teacher was not a qualified individual with a disability who was entitled to hold her former position. The U.S. Court of Appeals, Eleventh Circuit, reversed the lower court's ruling, and the U.S. Supreme Court agreed to review the case. On appeal, the Court stated that **contagion cannot remove a person from Section 504 coverage**. Because tuberculosis affected the teacher's respiratory system, she qualified as an individual with a disability within the meaning of Section 504. The Supreme Court remanded the case to the district court to determine whether the teacher was "otherwise qualified" for her job and whether the school board could reasonably accommodate her as an employee. *School Board of Nassau County v. Arline*, 480 U.S. 273, 107 S.Ct. 1123, 94 L.Ed.2d 307 (1987).

2. Reasonable Accommodation

Reasonable accommodation may include making facilities readily accessible to individuals with disabilities, job restructuring, job-sharing, reassignment to vacant positions, the acquisition or modification of equipment, provision of readers and interpreters, and the modification of employment tests.

Employers seeking to show that a proposed accommodation is not reasonable must show that providing the accommodation would create an undue hardship.

◆ An Iowa production employee was diagnosed with a form of multiple sclerosis that caused extreme fatigue, numbness and problems standing, sitting and walking. The HR manager told her to take extra breaks if needed, and to let the company know if she needed other accommodations. Although the company required all production employees to work overtime, it did not require the employee to do so for a time after her doctor restricted her hours. Later it fired the employee because she could not work overtime. She sued under the ADA, but a federal court and the Eighth Circuit ruled against her. **The employee could not be reasonably accommodated because there was no position available that did not require overtime.** Also, the company did not violate the ADA by asking the doctor to clarify his report. *Tjernagel v. The Gates Corp.*, 533 F.3d 666 (8th Cir. 2008).

◆ An insurance company employee in Rhode Island suffered from ulcerative colitis. A week before she was to give a presentation, she told her supervisor she needed time off because some of her symptoms might be returning. He told her to take time off after the presentation. She gave the presentation, but failed to shorten it as her supervisor's boss had instructed, then took two weeks at home rather than the one she had agreed upon with her supervisor. He told her she was being reassigned to a less prestigious project. A short time later she was hospitalized and did not return to work. When she sued under the ADA, the First Circuit ruled for the company. **Her vague comments about feeling ill did not put the company on notice that she needed the time off immediately.** And the demotion was justified by her refusal to shorten the presentation as ordered. *Freadman v. Metropolitan Property and Casualty Insurance Co.*, 484 F.3d 91 (1st Cir. 2007).

◆ An Arkansas route sales manager for a company that delivered frozen foods to customers' houses injured his arm when he fell off a customer's porch. Following surgery, he was restricted to carrying no more than 10 pounds and restricted from driving his route because of the heaviness of the truck doors. The company fired him after it was unable to find light-duty assignments for him. When he sued under the ADA, he lost. The Eighth Circuit held that the manager was not disabled under the ADA because he was not substantially limited in his ability to care for himself. Also, **the company had no duty to assign another employee to travel with him** for the purpose of opening and closing doors. *Didier v. Schwan Food Co.*, 465 F.3d 838 (8th Cir. 2006).

◆ A legally blind Wisconsin man was hired to work on an assembly line but was fired three weeks later. He was told that the reason was because his vision impairment interfered with his work and caused safety concerns. However, the company president later acknowledged that the real reasons were his failure to obey direct orders, safety infractions, making personal phone calls and a bad attitude. When he sued under the ADA, he lost. The Seventh Circuit noted that he could not perform the job's essential functions, and the company did not have to make a special accommodation for him. The president should not have given him a false reason for the termination, even to protect the employee, but **the false reasons for the discharge did not turn it into a discriminatory one**. *Hammel v. Eau Galle Cheese Factory*, 407 F.3d 852 (7th Cir. 2005).

◆ A sheet-metal straightener at an Iowa plant sought a promotion to the next job level, which would require her to use four different machines. However, she had previously injured herself on the job and could not use the machines without an accommodation. She rejected the company's suggested accommodation and agreed to obtain a medical evaluation to determine what other accommodations might be available. She never did so and was not promoted. Later, she was demoted as part of a reduction in force. She sued under the ADA and lost. The Eighth Circuit held that **she had impeded the interactive process** prescribed by Section 1630.2(o)(3) of the regulations. *Kratzer v. Rockwell Collins, Inc.*, 398 F.3d 1040 (8th Cir. 2005).

◆ A convenience store employee with epilepsy sought a promotion to a managerial position at her store, but she was repeatedly rejected because of her inability to drive (to make bank deposits). She was notified that she would only be considered for jobs at stores in undesirable neighborhoods, where an armored car would make the deposits for her. When she offered to hire her own driver and suggested that denying her a promotion would be a violation of the ADA, the company president accused her of slander. She filed discrimination charges with the Equal Employment Opportunity Commission and then suffered a seizure at work. Three days later, she was suspended without pay for two weeks. Eventually, she accepted a promotion at one of the undesirable locations. She worked there for four months and then quit and sued the company. A New York federal court granted pretrial judgment to the company, but the Second Circuit reversed, finding issues of material fact regarding whether the company violated the ADA. Here, the evidence seemed to indicate that **other employees were allowed to seek promotions at specific stores**. By failing to allow the epileptic employee to do so, the company may have refused to provide a reasonable accommodation in violation of the ADA. *Lovejoy-Wilson v. NOCO Motor Fuel, Inc.*, 263 F.3d 208 (2d Cir. 2001).

◆ A first-shift employee with three years of seniority began to suffer seizures and was diagnosed with epilepsy. She took medication but still experienced occasional mild seizures. When an employee with 20 years' experience sought to move to the first shift, the company informed her that she could either move to the second or third shifts, be laid off with recall rights for 12 months, or take a severance package. It refused to bypass its normal seniority policy despite a letter from the employee's doctor stating that the change in shifts would aggravate her seizures. She took the severance package and sued under the ADA. A South Carolina federal court ruled for the company, and the Fourth Circuit affirmed. Although the ADA allows an employee to transfer to a vacant position, **employees have no right under the statute to supersede a company's seniority system**. The senior employee could take the disabled employee's job. *EEOC v. Sara Lee Corp.*, 237 F.3d 349 (4th Cir. 2001).

◆ A Florida woman was hired by a department store to work as an area manager. She began to arrive late for work and was issued a documented warning. Subsequently, she received a second documented warning after being late 29 times in the previous year. At that time, she notified store officials that she suffered from obsessive compulsive disorder, which prevented her from coming to work on time. She asked to be allowed to clock in at whatever time she showed up on a particular day, but they refused. They did, however, allow her to work a later shift. When she continued to be late for work, they fired her.

She sued under the ADA, asserting that the store unreasonably failed to accommodate her disability. A federal court ruled for the store, and the Eleventh Circuit affirmed. Here, **arriving at work on time was an essential job function** that she could not perform even with a reasonable accommodation. Her proposed accommodation was not reasonable. *Earl v. Mervyns, Inc.*, 207 F.3d 1361 (11th Cir. 2000).

3. Perceived Disability

Not only does the ADA bar discrimination on the basis of disability, it also bars discrimination on the basis of a perceived disability. Further, it bars discrimination against individuals who have a record of a disability.

- A pharmacy assistant in New York applied for a job with Wal-Mart. He did not disclose that he had cerebral palsy, nor did he ask for any accommodation to do the job. The pharmacy manager told him to stock merchandise and dispense prescriptions, but she feared that he was mismatching prescriptions and customer names. She refused to schedule him for a second week, and he was transferred to a position collecting shopping carts. He was then offered a job in the food department stocking shelves. He quit and sued under the ADA, alleging that the company perceived him as disabled. A jury agreed and awarded him $600,000 in compensatory damages and $300,000 in punitive damages. The Second Circuit upheld the awards. Here, **the employee's disability was obvious, and the company failed to engage in the interactive process** with the employee to determine if a reasonable accommodation was possible. *Brady v. Wal-Mart Stores, Inc.*, 531 F.3d 127 (2d Cir. 2008).

- A Utah administrative assistant worked for a regional vice president who became concerned when he couldn't reach her by phone while he was on business trips. He had a surveillance camera placed in her work area and fired her when she was not there during the time she was supposed to be. She sued under the ADA, claiming that she was perceived as having a disability because an HR rep gave her a workers' compensation form for a work-related injury. A federal court and the Tenth Circuit held that this was not enough to show the company regarded her as disabled. **She could have a work-related injury without being perceived as disabled.** *Bartunek v. Fred Meyer, Inc.*, 271 Fed.Appx. 815 (10th Cir. 2008).

- An Iowa applicant with arthritis and a history of heart problems took the physical exam and was cleared for driving a forklift, an essential job function. However, the doctor reported that a functional capacity exam would be needed if the job required heavy lifting. After initially informing the applicant that he'd passed the exam, the company told him he'd failed. At trial, the company changed its reason for not hiring him, asserting that it had eliminated the shift he'd applied for. A jury awarded the applicant $60,000 in back pay and $100,000 in punitive damages under the ADA and state law. The Eighth Circuit upheld the awards. Here, the company didn't eliminate the shift until weeks after it rejected the applicant. Also, **its assertion that heavy lifting was a job**

requirement was suspect because it didn't include the task of heavy lifting in its job description. The company wrongly regarded the applicant as disabled. *Chalfant v. Titan Distribution*, 475 F.3d 982 (8th Cir. 2007).

◆ The EEOC, on behalf of a Missouri man with cerebral palsy, sued Wal-Mart under the ADA, claiming it refused to hire him because of his disability. It made an initial showing that the applicant could work as a greeter or cashier with accommodations such as a wheelchair or a motorized scooter. Wal-Mart asserted that its hiring manager believed the applicant had a poor job history and couldn't work weekends, though those reasons were ultimately disproved. It also maintained that he couldn't perform the essential functions of the job safely. A federal court granted the company pretrial judgment, but the Eighth Circuit reversed, finding issues of fact that required a trial. Here, there was **no evidence that the applicant posed a direct threat to the safety of customers or employees**, and it was possible that Wal-Mart came up with the reasons given for the non-hiring after the fact. *EEOC v. Wal-Mart Stores, Inc.*, 477 F.3d 561 (8th Cir. 2007).

◆ A truck driver injured his shoulder in a rollover accident and had surgery, then collected workers' compensation benefits. He later applied for a job with another trucking company, stating on his application that he had not been involved in any work-related incidents causing equipment or property damage in the prior 10 years. After he was hired, he told the new company's doctor about his shoulder injury and was told it would not impede his ability to work. Subsequently, his old company contacted his new company and informed it of the accident. The new company **fired him for lying on his application**. He sued under the ADA, claiming the real reason was perceived disability discrimination. A New Mexico federal court and the Tenth Circuit ruled against him. *Endlich v. Yellow Corp.*, 182 Fed.Appx. 825 (10th Cir. 2006).

◆ An administrator for a Tennessee hospital showed up for a meeting with slurred speech and ruddy skin, and slumped in his seat for almost the entire time. **His supervisor believed he was an alcoholic** because she had a brother and father who were alcoholics. She convinced him to enroll in a recovery program and later fired him, telling him the root cause of his problems was his alcoholism. During the ADA lawsuit that followed, she also cited a health commission inspection and a written report by a fire marshal as reasons for his termination. The administrator claimed that he was fired because of a perceived disability, and the Sixth Circuit agreed that he was illegally fired. The inspection and the report were both done after the administrator was fired, and the supervisor's personal bias against alcoholism colored her judgment about how the administrator's alcoholism affected his ability to work. *Moorer v. Baptist Memorial Health Care System*, 398 F.3d 469 (6th Cir. 2005).

◆ A boiler operator with a company in Iowa underwent shoulder surgery and then experienced pain while removing obstructions from the stoker. When he complained of the pain, the plant manager reassigned him to a position that did not require any lifting or repetitive use of his left arm. However, he believed the new position was demeaning because it required him to clean floors and paint pipes. He was later fired for secretly videotaping the inside of the plant. He sued under the ADA, asserting that the company regarded him as disabled. A jury awarded him back pay and punitive damages, but the Eighth Circuit vacated the award. **The company could reassign him to a less desirable job at the same location and same pay** if it regarded him as unable to perform one aspect of a particular job. This did not violate the ADA. *Knutson v. Ag Processing, Inc.*, 394 F.3d 1047 (8th Cir. 2005).

◆ The Equal Employment Opportunity Commission (EEOC) sued a transportation company, alleging that it violated the ADA by withdrawing offers of employment after discovering that the applicants were taking prescription medicines that appeared on a list the company used to screen truck driver applicants. The company asserted that it developed the "drug review list" as a safety-related qualification to avoid potential problems for truck drivers caused by certain medications' side effects. A New York federal court ruled in favor of the company, noting that even if its policy was unfair, the EEOC failed to show that the affected applicants were disabled under the ADA. The Second Circuit affirmed. Here, each of the disqualifying conditions was either explicitly or implicitly prohibited by Transportation Department regulations, making the company's policy reasonable. Further, **the employer only perceived the truck drivers as unable to perform one particular job**. *EEOC v. J.B. Hunt Transport, Inc.*, 321 F.3d 69 (2d Cir. 2003).

◆ A Kentucky employee worked on the assembly line as a welder for a door manufacturer until she injured her back. She spent almost seven months recuperating and returned to work with a doctor's note listing a number of physical restrictions (no stooping or bending; no lifting more than 25 pounds frequently). The plant manager told her she could not return to work because the company required her to be 100% healed. She then wrote the company asking for any work consistent with her medical restrictions and was told there was no light-duty work available. When she sued the company under the ADA, a federal court granted pretrial judgment to the manufacturer. The Sixth Circuit Court of Appeals reversed and remanded the case. Here, she had to be allowed to present her argument that the company's **"100% healed" policy violated the ADA by discriminating against her because of a perceived disability**. *Henderson v. Ardco, Inc.*, 247 F.3d 645 (6th Cir. 2001).

4. Temporary Impairments

Generally, temporary impairments do not count as disabilities under the ADA. However, if the temporary condition is severe enough and lasts long enough, it might be deemed a disability under the act.

◆ A New York employee injured her Achilles tendon on her way to work and went out on sick leave for approximately 25 weeks. After surveillance indicated that she was more mobile than she had led the company to believe, she was fired. She sued under the ADA, the FMLA and other laws. A federal court ruled against her, noting that **her temporary condition did not qualify as a disability** under the ADA, and that she failed to prove a causal connection between her FMLA leave and her firing. Her misuse of sick leave and misrepresentation of her limitations justified her discharge. *O'Reilly v. Consolidated Edison Co. of New York, Inc.*, 374 F.Supp.2d 278 (E.D.N.Y. 2005).

- A UPS worker in Puerto Rico endured an 8-month battle with ovarian cysts. She eventually sued the company for failing to accommodate her disability and for retaliation under the ADA. A federal court and the First Circuit held that she was not disabled under the ADA because her **condition was temporary** and it did not substantially limit her ability to work. Her condition only caused occasional pain and dizziness. *Guzman-Rosario v. United Parcel Service, Inc.*, 397 F.3d 6 (1st Cir. 2005).

- A New York health services employee had complications with her pregnancy and used a vacation day with her employer's consent in order to see him. Her complications persisted and over the next two months she took five more vacation days to see the specialist without objection from her employer. When she returned to work after the last appointment, her supervisor fired her because she had taken too many days off. She sued under the ADA and state and city anti-discrimination laws. The employer sought to dismiss the case, arguing that pregnancy is not a disability under the ADA. Although some courts have agreed with this argument, the court distinguished a normal, uncomplicated pregnancy from a complicated one. **Under certain circumstances, complications from pregnancy can create physical impairments that limit major life activities so as to be considered disabilities under the ADA.** The court refused to dismiss the case. *Cerrato v. Durham*, 941 F.Supp. 388 (S.D.N.Y. 1996).

- After a corporate takeover, a successful Ohio sales rep was left out of sales meetings, as were other female employees. The sales rep then broke her ankle. She could not travel, but she could conduct business by phone, a common practice for the sales staff. Her supervisor, however, constantly raised her broken ankle as an issue, became verbally abusive, and berated her for not being on the road. He stopped giving her any work, citing her broken ankle as the reason. He would also not allow her to work by phone. The sales rep was then fired because of an alleged drop in business and customers. No other employees were laid off, despite a large drop in business at other plants. She sued for sex discrimination under Title VII and disability discrimination under the ADA. The company moved for pretrial judgment. An Ohio federal court held that ordinarily a temporary impairment does not qualify as a disability, but in this case, **the employer regarded it as an impairment that substantially limited major life activities**. The supervisor believed that the rep could not adequately perform her job with a broken ankle. Also, he refused to accommodate her by allowing her to work by phone, even though other salespeople often worked by phone out of their homes. The motion for pretrial judgment was denied. *Spath v. Berry Plastics Corp.*, 900 F.Supp. 893 (N.D. Ohio 1995).

5. Undue Hardship and Direct Threats

An undue hardship is "an action requiring significant difficulty or expense." Thus, an accommodation that costs a lot of money or negatively impacts a large number of employees generally will be considered an undue hardship.

A direct threat is a threat to either the worker or others that arises as a result of the worker's disability. If hiring a worker will result in a direct threat of harm to the worker or others (even with an accommodation), the employer need not hire the worker. See the *Chevron* case, this chapter.

- UPS required all its package car driver applicants to pass a hearing test before being considered for the job, even though some of the applicants would be driving vehicles that were not covered by Department of Transportation regulations. A class of hearing-impaired individuals challenged the test in a California federal court, which required UPS to show that passing the test was a bona fide occupational qualification. On appeal, the Ninth Circuit held that the lower court applied too stringent a standard. Instead, **UPS only had to prove that there was a significant correlation between the hearing requirement and the performance of the job's essential qualifications**. It also had to prove that an accommodation would pose an undue hardship. This "business necessity" defense more closely tracks the language of the ADA. *Bates v. United Parcel Service, Inc.*, 511 F.3d 974 (9th Cir. 2007).

- A patient care technician in Minnesota who suffered from depression, after being repeatedly disciplined for unpredictable absences, told her supervisors that she was having problems with her medication, and that she might miss a day here and there because of it. She was fired after she failed to show up for work one day, and she sued under the ADA and state law. A federal court and the Eighth Circuit ruled against her, noting that she was not a qualified individual with a disability because **she was unable to perform an essential function of her job – regular and reliable attendance**. She never specifically identified how her depression limited her job or her life so as to allow the employer to engage in the interactive process to find an accommodation. *Rask v. Fresenius Medical Care North America*, 509 F.3d 466 (8th Cir. 2007).

- A paraplegic worked as a mold polisher in a Florida plant and was frequently late by about a minute because the time clock was located in a small room and was often blocked by storage boxes or tables he had to navigate his wheelchair around. Whenever he punched in late, he stayed after his normal shift time. He sometimes worked 60 hours a week, and he was considered an excellent performer. However, a new company president instituted a no-fault attendance policy and he was fired for his lateness. When he sued under the ADA, a federal court granted pretrial judgment to the company on the grounds that punctuality was an essential job function. The Eleventh Circuit reversed, finding issues of fact as to whether punctuality was really essential to the job. **The company had failed to show that his tardiness harmed its operations**. *Holly v. Clairson Industries*, 492 F.3d 1247 (11th Cir. 2007).

◆ A trucking company in Wisconsin fired an excellent driver after he was diagnosed with neurocardiogenic syncope – a disorder of the nervous system that causes fainting. Even though the driver took medication to help control his condition, fainting spells were still possible. An employee with the same condition had driven off a bridge to his death two years earlier. Thus, the company adopted a zero-tolerance policy for the condition. The EEOC sued on the driver's behalf, but the Seventh Circuit ruled for the company. Here, the risk of another serious injury was not zero and the company had a right to decide it didn't want to take that risk. It did not regard the driver as unable to perform the job, but rather **decided to implement safety standards higher than the minimum required by the federal government**. *EEOC v. Schneider National, Inc.*, 481 F.3d 507 (7th Cir. 2007).

◆ A manager for General Motors (GM) was diagnosed with multiple sclerosis, which increasingly interfered with his ability to drive – an essential requirement of his job. After making various accommodations, including providing him with a scooter and equipping his car with a lift to get the scooter in, GM asked him to submit to an exam by its doctor, an occupational medicine specialist who concluded that the manager should not be driving. GM then placed the manager on disability leave. He sued under the ADA, but an Illinois federal court and the Seventh Circuit ruled against him. **GM had legitimate concerns about his ability to drive** and did not discriminate against him on the basis of his disability. *Timmons v. General Motors Corp.*, 469 F.3d 1122 (7th Cir. 2006).

◆ A supervisory employee of a New York company was demoted for making disparaging remarks about a subordinate. He then became severely depressed and threatened the supervisor who demoted him. He was immediately placed on paid leave and told to fill out an FMLA form as well as to get medical certification of his ability to return to work. After he failed to get the required certification, and after he refused to apologize for his threat, he was fired. He sued the company under the ADA and lost because the company had a legitimate nondiscriminatory reason for firing him. **It didn't matter if the threat was due to his depression.** *Sista v. CDC Ixis North America*, 445 F.3d 161 (2d Cir. 2006).

◆ **Exxon could establish a policy that imposed across-the-board safety qualification standards**. The standards permanently removed employees who had undergone treatment for substance abuse from safety-sensitive positions. This resulted in the demotions of several employees who had undergone such treatment many years before. When the EEOC sued on their behalf under the ADA, a Texas federal court sent the case to the Fifth Circuit, which held that Exxon could defend the standard as a business necessity. It did not have to show that such employees were a direct threat to the health or safety of others in the workplace. The direct threat standard focuses on the individual employee and examines the specific risk posed by the employee's disability. Business necessity, on the other hand, addresses whether a standard can be justified across the board. Here, the standard was a proper requirement for all safety-sensitive employees. *EEOC v. Exxon Corp.*, 203 F.3d 871 (5th Cir. 2000).

6. Other ADA Cases

The ADA, by its very nature, requires an individualized examination of the employee's disability and any proposed accommodations in order to determine whether the ADA was violated. As a result, litigation under the ADA is often harder to avoid than litigation under other anti-discrimination statutes. So if you know an employee has a disability (and sometimes you won't), try to accommodate.

However, employees with disabilities do not have to be given special consideration; they merely have to be given the same consideration as nondisabled employees. Thus, an employee with a disability who is less productive than one without disabilities can be considered for layoff in a reduction in force under the ADA.

◆ A Missouri janitor with diabetes was fired after his supervisor came into the break room and saw him asleep at a table. The janitor claimed he was just resting his eyes and not sleeping. He sued the company under the ADA, asserting that the proffered reason for his termination was a pretext for discrimination. A federal court and the Eighth Circuit disagreed. Here, **the company had an honest belief that he had violated a company rule against sleeping on the job**. *McNary v. Schreiber Foods, Inc.*, 535 F.3d 765 (8th Cir. 2008).

◆ A Florida phone company technician had diabetes, hypertension, hypothyroidism and some endocrinology disorders that prevented him from losing weight. He weighed 325 pounds and was thus too heavy to work on ladders or buckets because of manufacturer safety policies. Although the company accommodated him for a while by ensuring he was not assigned any jobs that required climbing, eventually he was told to lose weight or apply for another job within the company. He rejected a job offer and failed to lose weight, then was fired. When he sued under the ADA, a federal court and the Eleventh Circuit ruled against him. **His obesity did not amount to a disability under the ADA.** *Greenberg v. BellSouth Telecommunications, Inc.*, 498 F.3d 1258 (11th Cir. 2007).

◆ A drug company employee in Missouri frequently missed work for personal and medical reasons, more than exhausting his FMLA leave in two consecutive years. He took an additional 40 days off in one year and 36 extra days the next. He was then fired. He sued for age and disability discrimination and lost because even though he hadn't been warned about his absenteeism, **the company's published policy clearly allowed for terminations where absences were excessive**. He was unable to perform one of the essential functions of his job – showing up. And finally, his supervisor's comments about his age and health did not prove discrimination because the supervisor did not make the decision to fire him. *Schierhoff v. GlaxoSmithKline Consumer Healthcare, L.P.*, 444 F.3d 961 (8th Cir. 2006).

◆ A Colorado call center manager with multiple sclerosis (MS) was fired one day after taking FMLA leave to treat her fatigue. She sued under the ADA, claiming disability discrimination. A federal court and the Tenth Circuit ruled against her. Here, she had been counseled because she was not using the proper coaching methods to improve her team managers' performance. And the company had made the decision to fire her before she took the leave. Also, even though the company knew of her MS and her fatigue, which she controlled with medication, **she was neither substantially limited in a major life activity nor regarded as disabled** by the company. *Berry v. T-Mobile USA, Inc.*, 490 F.3d 1211 (10th Cir. 2007).

◆ An Arkansas Wal-Mart order filler sustained a permanent injury to her right arm and hand that prevented her from performing the essential functions of her job. She sought reassignment to a router position, which was a vacant and equivalent position under the ADA. However, Wal-Mart required her to compete for the job with other candidates and eventually hired a more qualified non-disabled candidate for the job. It reassigned her to a janitorial position making about half her previous wages. She sued under the ADA and lost. The Eighth Circuit held that **Wal-Mart was not required to hire her over the more qualified candidate just because she was disabled**. *Huber v. Wal-Mart Stores, Inc.*, 486 F.3d 480 (8th Cir. 2007).

◆ A former Wal-Mart employee with a hearing impairment sued under the ADA, claiming that she was not offered a reasonable accommodation and also asserting that she had been harassed because of her disability. However, she did not claim that she was constructively discharged. A Delaware jury awarded her damages for emotional distress and back pay, but the Third Circuit reversed the back pay award. It joined the First, Seventh, Eighth and Tenth Circuits in holding that **an employee is not entitled to back pay if she does not prove constructive discharge** in a harassment case. Since the employee here agreed to resign and wasn't forced to quit, she could not get back pay. *Spencer v. Wal-Mart Stores, Inc.*, 469 F.3d 311 (3d Cir. 2006).

◆ An employee at a Maine company worked as an engineer even though he did not have an engineering degree. He subsequently injured his knee and had knee replacement surgery. Six months later, he was fired in a reduction in force because he did not have an engineering degree. He sued for disability discrimination, claiming that his supervisor had subjected him to cruel comments, and a jury awarded him $3 million. The judge vacated the award, and the First Circuit agreed that he was not entitled to any recovery. Here, **he presented no evidence that similarly situated nondisabled engineers were not laid off**. The company legitimately chose to lay him off because of his limited ability to handle complex projects. *Webber v. Int'l Paper Co.*, 417 F.3d 229 (1st Cir. 2005).

◆ A Neiman Marcus salesman had a history of alcohol problems that did not interfere with his ability to work. However, he was in and out of treatment for alcoholism. He was fired as manager of the gift gallery after a co-worker reported that he drank in the stock room and was abusive, and after a search of the stock room turned up an empty bottle of vodka. He sued the store under the ADA. A Massachusetts federal court ruled for the store, finding that the salesman could not show he was disabled by his alcoholism. The First Circuit affirmed, noting that **the store legitimately fired the salesman because of its rational belief that he possessed and drank alcohol at work**. *Sullivan v. Neiman Marcus Group, Inc.*, 358 F.3d 110 (1st Cir. 2004).

◆ An employee of a Missouri timber mill suffered from nocturnal epilepsy and had an operation in which part of his brain was replaced by a metal plate. After the employee was injured on the job, his supervisor learned about the metal plate and told his co-workers. They then began to tease him, calling him "platehead." When he asked them to stop, only some of his co-workers obliged him. Following an argument with one of his supervisors, he was fired. He sued the timber mill for harassment under the ADA. The case reached the Eighth Circuit, which agreed with the Fourth and Fifth Circuits that an employee can sue for harassment under the ADA. However, **the harassment here was not severe enough to be actionable**. It was not threatening; it was not physical; and it was not severe enough to cause a need for psychological treatment. The court remanded the case for a determination of whether the employee's former supervisor retaliated against him by refusing to recommend him for a job in retaliation for the lawsuit. *Shaver v. Independent Stave Co., d/b/a Salem Wood Products Co.*, 350 F.3d 716 (8th Cir. 2003).

◆ An Illinois bank employee worked as a team leader, responsible for restructuring loans for middle market companies. After being counseled about lack of leadership and her interpersonal skills, she was replaced in the job, but kept her salary and title. She was also given a written warning to improve her performance in 90 days. At that point, she demanded her old job back and revealed she had multiple sclerosis. She was then given a 30-day performance warning, after which she filed charges with the Equal Employment Opportunity Commission. Over a month later, she was fired. She sued for retaliation under the ADA, seeking compensatory and punitive damages. A federal court ruled against her, and the Seventh Circuit affirmed. It noted that **the ADA does not allow compensatory or punitive damages to be awarded in retaliation cases**. It only allows for equitable relief like reinstatement and back pay. Moreover, the employee failed to prove retaliation. *Kramer v. Banc of America Securities, LLC*, 355 F.3d 961 (7th Cir. 2004).

◆ The associate director of a center that provided job training and other services to people with developmental disabilities suffered from anxiety and bipolar disorder. However, neither she nor the center's executive director considered her to be disabled. When she got into a shouting match with a subordinate, who then resigned, the executive director discovered that she had been verbally abusive to other subordinates and had intimidated them into not reporting the incidents to him. He fired her, and she sued for discrimination under the ADA. A New York federal court ruled in favor of the center, and the Second Circuit affirmed. Here, she was not claiming that she suffered from an actual disability. Also, **the ability to get along with subordinates was an**

essential job function, and since she could not do so, she was not qualified to be a supervisor. *Cameron v. Community Aid for Retarded Children, Inc.*, 335 F.3d 60 (2d Cir. 2003).

- A General Electric employee in Louisiana operated heavy machinery. After being diagnosed with chronic pancreatitis, he began to take pain medications that came with warnings not to operate heavy machinery while under their influence. The company doctor learned of the pain medications and told the employee he could not operate heavy machinery. The company allegedly fired him, though it disputed that claim. At any rate, the employee sued for disability discrimination under the ADA. A federal court and the Fifth Circuit ruled against him, finding that although he had an impairment that limited him in the major life activity of eating, **his impairment did not *substantially* limit him**. As a result, he was not disabled under the ADA. Further, he failed to show that the company regarded him as disabled. The company routinely provided sick leave when his condition became too painful. It only became concerned after learning that he was taking central nervous system depressants while operating heavy machinery. *Waldrip v. General Electric Co.*, 325 F.3d 652 (5th Cir. 2003).

- After 25 years with Xerox, an employee assumed a managerial position that required him to oversee the sales accounts of 25 to 35 independent sales agents. Later that year, Xerox eliminated a number of positions, including one of the manager's support personnel. However, Xerox also increased his sales targets 94% from the previous year. The manager complained about the workload as he fell behind his goals. He was then diagnosed with stress-related chest pains and took a three-month leave. Afterwards, he accepted a sales rep position at a lower salary than the managerial position and remained there for two years until he retired. He then sued Xerox under the ADA. A Massachusetts federal court ruled that he was not disabled under the ADA because his stress only prevented him from performing the responsibilities of the managerial job during the time he was without a full complement of support personnel. He was not unable to perform a broad range of jobs or even other sales-related jobs. The First Circuit affirmed the ruling against him. **Being unable to handle a particular workload did not make him disabled under the ADA.** *Carroll v. Xerox Corp.*, 294 F.3d 231 (1st Cir. 2002).

- A systems engineer in South Dakota received only positive performance reviews before he was involved in an automobile accident that caused brain damage. After undergoing work therapy, he asked to return to work and was released to work part time. However, several days after returning to work, he was fired because of client and co-worker complaints. He then became depressed, threatened suicide, and was hospitalized on two occasions. Eventually, he found another job paying two-thirds of what he was earning before. He sued his former employer under the ADA for wrongful termination, and a jury awarded him $46,000 in back pay, $60,000 in compensatory damages, and $200,000 on his claim for intentional infliction of emotional distress. After the court reduced the compensatory damages award to $50,000 to comply with the ADA's statutory cap on damages, the Eighth Circuit Court of Appeals affirmed. **The employer failed to show that it would have fired the engineer even before he suffered brain damage** (which qualified as a "disability"), and the manner of the termination justified the emotional distress award. *Moysis v. DTG Datanet*, 278 F.3d 819 (8th Cir. 2002).

- An Oklahoma man applied for an assembly line job and was offered a position contingent on his passing a medical exam conducted by the company physician. He completed a medical history form on which he lied about some of his physical problems. Although the doctor recommended him for the job, the human resources department obtained past workers' compensation records from the state and withdrew the conditional offer of employment. When he sued the company under the ADA, a jury found that the company had withdrawn its offer partly for illegal reasons and awarded him $3,850 in damages. The judge then issued an injunction ordering the company not to obtain medical or workers' compensation information except to convey it to appropriate medical personnel. The company appealed, and the Tenth Circuit held that the ADA does not prohibit the **review of entering employees' medical or workers' compensation records by non-medical personnel**. Although the ADA requires confidentiality of information, it does not restrict how an employer may use that information. The court struck down the injunction. *Garrison v. Baker Hughes Oilfield Operations, Inc.*, 287 F.3d 955 (10th Cir. 2002).

- A Rhode Island woman who suffered from multiple sclerosis worked for a toy company. With reasonable accommodation, she was able to perform the essential functions of her position. According to the employee, she was subjected to ongoing sexual harassment and disability discrimination by her immediate supervisor. Eventually, her work performance was affected. After her multiple sclerosis worsened, allegedly as a result of her supervisor's misconduct, she quit her job. She sued the company and several supervisors under the ADA. A federal court refused to dismiss the case, noting that the ADA defines employer to include agents of persons engaged in an industry affecting commerce. An agent is defined as any employee exercising supervisory power or control within a company. Thus, **under the plain language of the ADA, supervisory employees are individually liable**. *Iacampo v. Hasbro, Inc.*, 929 F.Supp. 562 (D.R.I. 1996).

B. State Laws

State laws generally follow the wording of the federal laws, and the analysis of state statutes tends to be very similar to that used in deciding cases under Section 504 and the ADA. However, state laws might be more inclusive – that is, they might apply to all employers in the state, regardless of size, and they might cover conditions that are not covered by the ADA (like gender dysphoria).

- A Connecticut liquor company truck driver injured his back lifting a case of liquor and was placed on a light-duty assignment for 60 days. He sought a permanent transfer from his truck driver job to one in the warehouse, which would allow him to avoid lifting cases of liquor. The company refused to consider his bid even though the job was open. Instead, it terminated him based on its policy requiring injured employees to be fully healed to return to their original jobs. When he sued under state law, a court granted pretrial judgment to the company because Connecticut law did not specify that employers had to reasonably accommodate disabled employees. However, the Connecticut Supreme Court reversed and remanded the case, noting that **even though the statute did not mention reasonable accommodation, the employer still had to accommodate** unless it would cause an undue hardship. *Curry v. Allan S. Goodman, Inc.*, 944 A.2d 925 (Conn. 2008).

◆ The president of a clothing division reported to the CEO of the company's western region – a short-tempered manager who yelled and cursed often. **After the president took a leave for breast cancer, she claimed the CEO became even more abusive**. Eventually, because of poor performance by her division, she was demoted as part of a restructuring. She sued for disability discrimination and lost. Even though she suffered a tangible employment action – demotion and salary reduction – the company proffered a legitimate reason for its action: poor sales by her division. Also, she never told anyone at the company that she was being harassed until after she left. *Ferraro v. Kellwood Co.*, 440 F.3d 96 (2d Cir. 2006).

◆ An Oregon millwright took marijuana under the state's medical marijuana program to calm muscle spasms in his legs so he could sleep at night. He was fired after testing positive for marijuana. When he sued for disability discrimination, he lost. The Supreme Court of Oregon held that he was not a disabled person because even though he had spasms that otherwise would have substantially limited his ability to sleep, **the marijuana mitigated his impairment so that it was no longer a substantial limitation** on a major life activity. *Washburn v. Columbia Forest Products, Inc.*, 134 P.3d 161 (Or. 2006).

◆ An employee brought a lawsuit under the ADA and the Pennsylvania Human Relations Act, which is premised on the ADA but does not place a limit on damages. After a jury awarded her $2 million in compensatory damages and $500,000 in punitive damages, the judge reduced the punitive damages award to $300,000 to comply with the statutory cap of 42 U.S.C. § 1981a and assigned the $2 million compensatory damages award to the state law claim. The Third Circuit Court of Appeals upheld the ruling. It joined the Ninth and D.C. Circuits in holding that where employees sue under both federal and state discrimination laws, **courts can allocate damages so as to maximize recovery**, allowing the employees to recover damages under the state law that exceed the statutory cap of 42 U.S.C. § 1981a. *Gagliardo v. Connaught Laboratories, Inc.*, 311 F.3d 565 (3d Cir. 2002).

◆ A delivery route driver for a bakery injured his wrist in a work-related accident and was restricted from repetitively pushing, pulling or lifting more than 35 pounds. As a result, he could no longer perform all the duties of his position. He requested an alternative position, but the bakery was unable to find one for him and eventually removed him from the payroll. He sued under Washington's Law Against Discrimination, and a state court granted pretrial judgment to the bakery. The court of appeals reversed, finding that there were issues of fact as to whether the bakery had attempted to reasonably accommodate the driver. Here, **it failed to analyze the particular tasks of each job description** to determine whether the driver could be accommodated. *Jackson v. Entenmann's, Inc.*, 101 Wash.App. 1073 (Wash. Ct. App. 2000).

- When a bank examiner was diagnosed with HIV, his physician instructed him to change his work conditions and schedule. His employer agreed to allow him to work a 40-hour week over four days and to telecommute one of the days. Two years later, the employer advised him it could no longer allow a regular telecommuting day. He was given the choice of reporting to the office each day or going on part-time status. Believing that the change would threaten his health, the employee quit and applied for state and federal disability benefits. He then sued the employer under the California Fair Employment and Housing Act. The California Court of Appeal observed that the employer had disrupted the status quo by refusing to continue the previously approved accommodations, prompting the employee to file the disability claims. There was evidence that he continued to view himself as unable to perform essential work duties, but this was due to the cessation of the bank's accommodations. There was also evidence that he did not consider himself disabled if accommodations were made. Accordingly, **his statements in the disability applications were not inconsistent with the position he had adopted in the wrongful discharge claim**. *Bell v. Wells Fargo Bank, N.A.*, 73 Cal.Rptr.2d 354 (Cal. Ct. App. 1998).

- A hearing-impaired woman began working as a dietary aide at a nursing home. Her duties consisted of cooking, washing dishes, filling trays, preparing food and delivering snacks. Shortly thereafter, the nursing home fired her. The West Virginia Human Rights Commission found that she had been illegally discriminated against because of her hearing impairment. The Supreme Court of Appeals of West Virginia upheld that decision. The court noted that the employee was able to perform the job in question. No one at the nursing home spoke with the employee about wearing a hearing aid, and no one asked her if there was anything that could be done to enable her to hear more clearly. She was even **denied a very simple accommodation** – when communicating, she needed a person to look at her while speaking loudly. *Morris Nursing Home v. Human Rights Comm'n*, 431 S.E.2d 353 (W. Va. 1993).

- An engineer who worked for a large Washington airplane manufacturer was a biological male at the time of hire. After a number of years, the engineer determined that he was a transsexual. Transsexualism is known as gender dysphoria. The engineer then began treatment by a physician to undergo sex reassignment surgery. To qualify, he had to live full-time for a year in the social role of a female. He approached his employer with his intentions and was informed that he could not use the female restrooms or wear feminine attire while he was still an anatomical male. The manufacturer allowed him to wear unisex clothing but required him to report daily to his manager – who would monitor his attire. The manufacturer fired the engineer for wearing an outfit that included pink pearls. He sued for handicap discrimination. The Supreme Court of Washington stated that although gender dysphoria qualified as an abnormal condition, the employer **discharged the employee for violating the employer's directives on acceptable attire, not for being gender dysphoric**. *Doe v. Boeing Co.*, 846 P.2d 531 (Wash. 1993).

V. RELIGIOUS DISCRIMINATION

Religious discrimination in employment is prohibited by Title VII. Employers who violate the act by intentionally discriminating against employees because of their religion or religious practices may be liable for compensatory and punitive damages, as well as equitable relief. There are, however, some exceptions, such as the one in Section 702 of the Civil Rights Act for religious organizations.

The U.S. Supreme Court has held that an employer must make reasonable accommodations for the religious beliefs of employees. However, Title VII does not require accommodations that impose an undue hardship on the employer.

Also, religion (like sex, national origin and age) might be a bona fide occupational qualification for a particular job. For example, a Lutheran school can legitimately hire only Lutheran teachers, though it probably cannot hire only Lutheran janitors.

- An employee of an airline belonged to a religion known as the Worldwide Church of God. It proscribed work from sunset Friday to sunset Saturday. Because of the employee's seniority, the airline was able to accommodate his religious beliefs until he transferred to a new position with low seniority. The airline agreed to permit the union to seek a change of work assignments, but it was **unwilling to violate the seniority system**. The airline then rejected a proposal that the employee work only four days a week, stating that this would impair critical functions in its operations. Eventually, the employee was discharged for refusing to work on Saturdays. He sued both the union and the airline under Title VII, claiming religious discrimination. A Missouri federal court ruled in favor of the defendants, and the U.S. Court of Appeals affirmed in part. However, it did hold that the airline failed to satisfy its duty to accommodate the employee's religious needs. On appeal to the U.S. Supreme Court, it was held that the airline made reasonable efforts to accommodate the religious beliefs of others. The Court reversed the court of appeals' decision and held in favor of the airline. *Trans World Airlines v. Hardison*, 432 U.S. 63, 97 S.Ct. 2264, 53 L.Ed.2d 113 (1977).

- An employee of a chain of New England retail stores managed a clothing department at a location in Connecticut. When the store began to keep Sunday hours, the employee worked occasional Sundays for two years. He then notified his employer that he would no longer work on that day because it was his

Sabbath. A Connecticut law stated that employers could not require their employees to work on their Sabbath days, and refusal to work on the Sabbath was not grounds for dismissal. The employer demoted the employee to a clerical position. The employee then resigned and filed a grievance administratively. He was found to have been discharged in violation of the statute, and a state trial court upheld that decision. The Connecticut Supreme Court reversed, and the case came before the U.S. Supreme Court, which held that the Connecticut law violated the Establishment Clause of the First Amendment. Essentially, it **imposed on employers an absolute duty to conform their business practices to the particular religious practices of their employees**. Under this law, Sabbath religious concerns automatically controlled all secular interests at the workplace. The primary effect of this law, then, was the advancement of religion, which is forbidden by the Establishment Clause. The Court affirmed the state supreme court's decision. *Estate of Thornton v. Caldor, Inc.*, 472 U.S. 703, 105 S.Ct. 2914, 86 L.Ed.2d 557 (1985).

- A North Carolina employee had to observe a Sabbath from sundown Friday to sundown Saturday. He also had to observe 20 religious days during the year, 14 of which did not coincide with his Sabbath days. He met with HR to discuss possible accommodations, including transferring to a different shift or job, leaving his shift uncovered during his Sabbath, and being excused from the part of his shift that conflicted with his Sabbath. Ultimately, the HR manager decided that those accommodations wouldn't work because he lacked the seniority to transfer, and he needed to be at work during his scheduled shift. He was allowed to use vacation, holiday and 60 hours of unpaid leave under the company's no-fault attendance policy. However, after exhausting all his leave options, he missed 11 days of work and was fired. When he sued for religious discrimination, he lost. The Fourth Circuit held that **Title VII's obligation to reasonably accommodate doesn't require a company to "totally" accommodate a religious request**. *EEOC v. Firestone Fibers & Textiles Co.*, 515 F.3d 307 (4th Cir. 2008).

- A secretary for an Alabama medical center was required to work alternate weekends. However, as a Seventh-Day Adventist, she could not work her Friday or Saturday shifts from 3:00 p.m. to 11:00 p.m. With the center's approval, she managed to swap all her Saturday shifts with co-workers. However, she failed to show up for her scheduled Friday shifts for three months and was placed on an involuntary leave of absence. Rather than immediately firing her, the center offered her a flexible certified nursing assistant position, which would allow her to work on Sundays instead of Fridays and Saturdays. **It offered her the transfer even though she had not been employed for at least 12 months – a requirement the center was willing to waive** in her case. When she never responded to the offers, the center deemed her to have voluntarily resigned. She sued for religious discrimination under Title VII, but a federal court and the Eleventh Circuit ruled against her. The center met Title VII's reasonable accommodation requirement. *Morrissette-Brown v. Mobile Infirmary Medical Center*, 506 F.3d 1317 (11th Cir. 2007).

◆ A software developer for a company in California claimed that she was **passed over for promotion because she did not belong to the same religion** (the Fellowship of Friends) as the hiring manager, who allegedly exercised his decision-making authority in favor of members of the same religion. When she sued for discrimination under Title VII, a federal court granted pretrial judgment to the company, noting that it offered legitimate nondiscriminatory reasons for the non-promotion. However, the Ninth Circuit reversed, finding issues of fact that required a trial. Here, she presented evidence that she was more qualified, that she was paid less than a Fellowship member in the same job and that the hiring manager told other managers she wasn't interested in the job. *Noyes v. Kelly Services*, 488 F.3d 1163 (9th Cir. 2007).

◆ A Home Depot employee in New York could not work Sundays because of his religion. His managers accommodated him for a year until a new store manager took over. She told him he needed to be "fully flexible" and offered him afternoon or evening shifts so he could attend church in the morning. He refused, explaining that he couldn't work on Sundays at all. After he was fired for missing a Sunday shift, he sued for religious discrimination under Title VII. A federal court granted pretrial judgment for Home Depot, but the Second Circuit reversed, finding an issue of fact that required a trial. **The offer to let the employee have Sunday mornings off was no accommodation at all.** *Baker v. The Home Depot*, 445 F.3d 541 (2d Cir. 2006).

◆ An Iowa employee alleged that the woman in the next cubicle propositioned her and then, after becoming religious, sought to convert her. The day before a mediation session to work out these and other problems, the employee took FMLA leave. She was fired when she failed to return to work, and sued under Title VII and state law. A federal court and the Eighth Circuit ruled against her. The claimed sexual harassment was not severe or pervasive enough to alter her working conditions, and the religious harassment stopped when she asked the co-worker to stop proselytizing. **The only continued "offensive" conduct was the posting of religious material in the next cubicle, which management determined did not violate company policy.** *Powell v. Yellow Book USA, Inc.*, 445 F.3d 1074 (8th Cir. 2006).

◆ A Muslim from Afghanistan claimed that he was subjected to continuing harassment by co-workers at the Maine meat plant where he worked. He sued for race, national origin and religious harassment under Title VII, citing a number of incidents. A jury agreed that the company knew or should have known about the harassment, but refused to award damages, finding **no evidence that the employee sought medical treatment for counseling or lost work as a result of the harassment**. The First Circuit Court of Appeals upheld the jury's findings. Although the jury could have awarded damages, it was not compelled to do so. *Azimi v. Jordan's Meats, Inc.*, 456 F.3d 228 (1st Cir. 2006).

◆ A cashier in Massachusetts with multiple body piercings and tattoos claimed that she was **required by her religion – the Church of Body Modification – to display her body piercings** to the public. Her employer had a dress code policy that forbade the wearing of any facial jewelry except earrings. It rejected her suggested accommodation that she cover her eyebrow piercings with a flesh-colored Band-Aid and fired her for unexcused absences as well as failure to comply with the dress code. During Equal Employment Opportunity Commission mediation, the employer offered to let her return to work with her jewelry covered, but she then took the position that she should be exempted from the dress code for religious reasons. When she sued under Title VII, a federal court ruled against her and the First Circuit Court of Appeals affirmed the ruling. Granting such an exemption would be an undue hardship to the employer because it would adversely affect the employer's public image. *Cloutier v. Costco Wholesale Corp.*, 390 F.3d 126 (1st Cir. 2004).

- An evangelical Christian quality assurance manager in Arizona counseled an openly gay female employee to stop dating other women. She also brought up the employee's sexual orientation at the employee's performance review. Subsequently, she was fired for violating the company's harassment policy, which prohibited harassment on the basis of sexual orientation. The policy also subjected the harasser to immediate termination for coercing, intimidating or threatening a co-worker. When she sued the company for religious discrimination under Title VII, a federal court and the Ninth Circuit ruled against her. The termination was not religious discrimination in violation of Title VII. **Her harassment of her subordinate made her discharge legitimate and nondiscriminatory.** *Bodett v. CoxCom, Inc.*, 366 F.3d 736 (9th Cir. 2004).

- A custodial supervisor made lewd sexual comments to a janitor who was a former pastor. Later, the supervisor made religious insults against the janitor, who complained to the company's human resources department on six occasions. He was told there was nothing that could be done about it, and that if he didn't like it, he could quit. The day after the supervisor harassed the janitor about not working overtime on Sundays, the janitor resigned. He then sued the company under Title VII, and a jury ruled in his favor. The First Circuit affirmed, finding that **the religious harassment violated Title VII**. The damage award of $300,000 against the company was upheld. *Johnson v. Spencer Press of Maine, Inc.*, 364 F.3d 368 (1st Cir. 2004).

- An Idaho employee hung anti-homosexual biblical passages in his cubicle in response to the company's diversity campaign, part of which encouraged tolerance for gay rights. The passages were large enough to be visible by co-workers, customers and others who passed through an adjacent corridor. After a supervisor removed them, the employee met with company officials, where he admitted that he intended the passages to be hurtful to gays by condemning gay behavior. He put the passages back up and was fired, then sued under Title VII for religious discrimination. A federal court ruled for the company, and the Ninth Circuit affirmed. Here, **the company did not fire the employee because of his religious beliefs**. Rather, it fired him because his messages were demeaning to co-workers and in conflict with the company's diversity policy. *Peterson v. Hewlett-Packard Co.*, 358 F.3d 599 (9th Cir. 2004).

◆ A Virginia rental car employee wore a scarf in compliance with her religious beliefs. When she refused to stop wearing the scarf despite a management request, she was placed in another location at the facility where she worked – an area where she did not come into frequent contact with customers. She eventually sued the company for religious discrimination under Title VII. The case reached the Fourth Circuit Court of Appeals, which ruled in favor of the company. Here, the employee was neither disciplined nor terminated for wearing the scarf. **Transfer to a position less in the public eye was not an adverse employment action under Title VII.** *Ali v. Alamo Rent-A-Car, Inc.*, 8 Fed.Appx. 156 (4th Cir. 2001).

◆ An employee assistance program counselor at a medical center in Mississippi refused to provide counseling to a gay employee who wanted help in improving her relationship with her partner. She offered to counsel the employee on other matters but stated that homosexual behavior conflicted with her religious beliefs. She later requested that she be excused from counseling employees in both homosexual and extra-marital relationships, but the center denied her request. It offered to place her in another position, but she declined the offer. When she was fired, she sued under Title VII for religious discrimination. A federal court awarded her more than $300,000 in damages, but the Fifth Circuit reversed. Here, **allowing the counselor's accommodation would create an undue hardship on the center** because of its small staff, the travel involved in visiting the employer clients in the two cities it served, and the fact that counseling required the establishment of trust relationships over time. The employee was not flexible in achieving an accommodation, and the center did not violate Title VII. *Bruff v. North Mississippi Health Services*, 244 F.3d 495 (5th Cir. 2001).

◆ An applicant for a position with a trucking company **failed to provide his Social Security number on his employment application**. Instead, he wrote in the blank, "none for religious reasons," and produced his birth certificate and commercial driver's license. He had previously surrendered his social security number because of his belief that it was a reflection of the mark of the beast as described in the Bible. The company refused to hire him without a social security number and did not inquire as to his religious beliefs. The applicant sued for religious discrimination and lost. It was the Department of Transportation and the Internal Revenue Service that required employees to have social security numbers. Thus, the requirement was something imposed by law and not by the company. *Weber v. Leaseway Dedicated Logistics, Inc.*, 5 F.Supp.2d 1219 (D. Kan. 1998).

VI. RETALIATION

Retaliation (disciplining an employee for engaging in activity protected by law) is forbidden by Title VII and other federal statutes, as well as by most state statutes. However, to succeed on a claim of retaliation, the employee must show a connection between the protected activity and the discipline.

Firing an employee is clearly an adverse employment action; so is demoting him. But many actions can be less clear-cut. For example, giving an employee "the silent treatment" probably won't be considered actionable retaliation. However, it still might lead to litigation, and even if you were to win such a lawsuit, it would cost you to defend it. Therefore, **never** retaliate against an employee for action that might be construed as protected under the law.

◆ After a Tennessee female rail worker complained to company officials that her supervisor had repeatedly told her that women shouldn't be working in the yard and made insulting remarks to her in front of co-workers, she was reassigned to a less favorable position. She filed a retaliation charge with the EEOC and was shortly thereafter suspended for insubordination. After she filed a grievance, the company found she had not been insubordinate and reinstated her with back pay. When she sued for retaliation, a jury awarded her $46,750. The U.S. Supreme Court upheld the award, noting that **reassignment of job duties can be retaliation if it is "materially adverse" to an employee**. It defined materially adverse as a harmful action that could dissuade a reasonable worker from making a charge of discrimination. The suspension was also materially adverse even though she was reinstated with back pay because a reasonable employee might choose not to file a discrimination charge knowing she could be out of work indefinitely. *Burlington Northern and Santa Fe Railway Co. v. White*, 548 U.S. 53, 126 S.Ct. 2405, 165 L.Ed.2d 345 (2006).

◆ An oil corporation fired an African-American employee, who then filed a complaint against it with the EEOC. While the charge was pending, the former employee applied for work with another company. When the company contacted the oil corporation for a reference, the corporation gave him a negative reference, which he believed was in retaliation for having filed the EEOC charge. The former employee sued the corporation for retaliatory discrimination under Title VII. A Maryland federal court dismissed the case, ruling that Section 704(a) of Title VII does not protect the rights of former employees. The Fourth Circuit affirmed. The U.S. Supreme Court reversed, finding that Section 704(a) **protects former employees from retaliatory action**. It agreed with the EEOC that to exclude former employees from Section 704(a) protection would undermine Title VII by allowing retaliation against victims of discrimination. This might give an incentive to employers to fire employees who brought EEOC complaints. *Robinson v. Shell Oil Co.*, 519 U.S. 337, 117 S.Ct. 843, 136 L.Ed.2d 808 (1997).

◆ An employee at an Indiana hospital, who had been subjected to a sexual assault before her hire, complained to her supervisor after a male co-worker twice sat on her lap and told her she was pretty. The supervisor agreed to talk to the co-worker, but never informed the employee that she had done so. As a result, the employee feared that no action had been taken. She complained to her supervisor's superiors. Later, **the supervisor restructured the employee's job so that the employee could not work the new hours**. Eventually she was fired for not working enough hours. She sued for retaliation and a federal court granted pretrial judgment to the hospital. The Seventh Circuit reversed, finding questions of fact over the restructuring and the discharge. *Magyar v. Saint Joseph Regional Medical Center*, 544 F.3d 766 (7th Cir. 2008).

◆ A Kentucky manufacturing employee **claimed that he was fired because his fiancée, also an employee of the company, had filed a gender discrimination complaint**. When he sued for retaliation under Title VII, a federal court granted pretrial judgment to the company. However, the Sixth Circuit reversed, citing the Supreme Court's decision in *Burlington Northern and Santa Fe Railway v. White*, 548 U.S. 53 (2006), which held that employers can't take action that would dissuade "reasonable workers" from making discrimination charges. Here, the employee had to be allowed to present evidence connecting his fiancée's complaint and his discharge. *Thompson v. North American Stainless*, 520 F.3d 644 (6th Cir. 2008).

◆ An Illinois employee complained to her supervisor and a rep from HR about what she perceived as a glass ceiling. Shortly thereafter, her supervisor became critical of her failure to meet her work goals. He also began hearing complaints that she was spending a lot of time on personal matters. Another HR rep found that she made 432 personal phone calls and visited non-work-related Internet sites about 3,000 times over 89 days. She was suspended for five days and told not to contact anyone but her supervisor during that time. Instead, she used an outside computer to access the company's e-mail system and send messages to customers. After she was fired, she sued for retaliation. A federal court and the Seventh Circuit ruled against her, noting that the company had a legitimate reason for firing her. *Gates v. Caterpillar, Inc.*, 513 F.3d 680 (7th Cir. 2008).

◆ A telemarketing manager for a Connecticut newspaper agreed to testify for the newspaper when a supervisor under her authority was accused of sexual harassment. Later, the manager observed the supervisor harassing another employee, and heard from a third employee that the supervisor had harassed her. She also discovered that the supervisor had a history of forging numerous checks. After she decided not to testify on behalf of the paper, she was fired, allegedly for receiving a collect call. She sued for retaliation under Title VII, and the paper sought pretrial judgment because the manager never testified. A federal court ruled that the case required a trial. **The manager was protected by Title VII even though she never testified**, and there were questions about the real motivation for her termination. *Tucker v. Journal Register East*, 520 F.Supp.2d 374 (D. Conn. 2007).

◆ A black employee at an Alabama company endured a hostile work environment, where the foreman and several white co-workers made racial slurs in violation of the company's anti-discrimination policy. He complained to management, which told him that was "just the way" the foreman was and that he had to accept it. After he filed an EEOC complaint, the company issued its new dispute resolution policy and **asked him to sign an arbitration agreement for all past, present and future disputes**. He asked to exclude past and present claims against the company, refusing to sign the agreement as it was written. The company fired him, and he filed another EEOC charge, then sued the company for retaliation. A jury awarded him $27,160 in back pay, $27,160 in emotional damages and $500,000 in punitive damages on his retaliation claim. The Eleventh Circuit upheld the award. *Goldsmith v. Bagby Elevator Co.*, 513 F.3d 1261 (11th Cir. 2008).

- A male employee at a New Hampshire store claimed that his male supervisor made offensive sexual remarks about women's bodies and sexual insults about the woman the employee was dating. The employee claimed that he was fired after he complained about the supervisor's conduct. A federal court found that he could not sue for sexual harassment because the supervisor's comments were equally offensive to both men and women. However, there were issues of fact as to whether the employee had been fired in retaliation for his complaints or for falsifying his time sheets. That issue required a trial. *Foss v. Circuit City Stores, Inc.*, 521 F.Supp.2d 99 (D. Me. 2007).

- A Hispanic maintenance mechanic for a company in Illinois sought a promotion to a higher job level. He learned that a white mechanic hired after him had been promoted to a level-4 while he remained at level-3. He then complained to the HR director about the promotion and claimed that he was treated more harshly by his supervisors than the white mechanic was. After he was denied a promotion a second time, he complained to HR again, at which time several unsigned warnings were found in his personnel file. **He claimed the warnings were placed in his file after he complained.** He later received a formal warning for causing a spill and subsequently left work without permission to pick up a co-worker with a flat tire. He was fired and sued for retaliation. A federal court granted pretrial judgment to the company, but the Seventh Circuit reversed, finding issues of fact as to whether the unsigned warnings and the termination were retaliation for his complaints. *Pantoja v. American NTN Bearing Manufacturing Corp.*, 495 F.3d 840 (7th Cir. 2007).

- Outside of work, a technician at a New Mexico company met with an HR supervisor, who allegedly threatened him if he refused to cooperate during an investigation into inappropriate sexual conversations in the workplace. **The next day, he received a written warning regarding sexual harassment and attendance problems.** He then filed EEOC charges over the way he was treated. Shortly thereafter, his supervisor issued him a second written warning based on performance problems. Several months later, he received a third written warning and was fired per company policy. When he sued for retaliation, a state court granted pretrial judgment to the company. But the New Mexico Supreme Court reversed, finding issues of fact over whether he was fired for filing the EEOC charges. A jury trial was required. *Juneau v. Intel Corp.*, 127 P.3d 548 (N.M. 2005).

- A temporary employee and born-again Christian was assigned to a facility, where she was instructed on its harassment procedures. She complained to co-workers about their language and lifestyles, but never approached any manager.

On at least two occasions she was warned about performance problems. After she told two employees they were living in sin and another that he was going to hell, the facility ended her assignment. She sued the company for retaliation under Title VII and lost. A Pennsylvania federal court noted that she failed to follow the procedures put in place by the company; she was warned about her performance; and she made offensive comments to co-workers. Her discharge was not retaliatory under Title VII. *Bell v. Quest Diagnostics*, 2006 WL 305436 (E.D. Pa. 2/7/06).

◆ A manager at a Colorado resort claimed that her supervisor sexually harassed her and even raped her several times, including once on a business trip. She complained to a regional vice president who, together with the harasser, retaliated against her by inventing performance problems. She then sent an e-mail to a corporate vice president and was fired the next day. When she sued for retaliation under Title VII, a jury awarded her more than $300,000 – including $167,000 in punitive damages. The Tenth Circuit upheld the award, finding that **the company's managers maliciously and recklessly retaliated against the employee for reporting the harassment**. *McInnis v. Fairfield Communities, d/b/a Fairfield Resorts, Inc.*, 458 F.3d 1129 (10th Cir. 2006).

◆ When an employee of a Connecticut company sued it for sex discrimination, she named a female co-worker as a witness who would testify on her behalf. The next day, the company removed the co-worker from an assignment that would provide her with the opportunity for advancement. A month later, it took away a company-related side job and allegedly denied her a promised promotion. She sued for retaliation under Title VII, and the Second Circuit held that she could proceed with her lawsuit. **Even though she never testified (because the earlier lawsuit settled) she was still protected** as a participant in a Title VII investigation or proceeding. *Jute v. Hamilton Sunstrand Corp.*, 420 F.3d 166 (2d Cir. 2005).

◆ A regional sales manager for L'Oreal in California was told to fire a female sales associate because she was not attractive enough. The manager repeatedly asked for an adequate justification for the firing but was never given one and therefore she did not fire the associate. Her supervisor then began soliciting negative information about her job performance and warned her she could be fired if she did not improve her communication skills. She sued for retaliation under the state's Fair Employment and Housing Act. The case reached the California Supreme Court, which noted that she could proceed with her lawsuit. A jury could find that she reasonably and in good faith **believed the order to fire the associate was discriminatory because she had never been told to fire a male associate for being unattractive**, and that the general manager knew she refused to obey the order because she thought it was discriminatory. *Yanowitz v. L'Oreal USA, Inc.*, 116 P.3d 1123 (Cal. 2005).

◆ An Arkansas manufacturer changed the work schedule of a turret operator shortly after she complained about a supervisor's harassment. It also investigated the allegations she made and fired the supervisor five days later.

She sued the company under Title VII, asserting retaliation. A federal court ruled against her, and the Eighth Circuit Court of Appeals affirmed that decision. Even though she had told her supervisors she did not want her schedule changed, **she could not show that the schedule change was an adverse employment action**. Further, all the other turret operators on her shift had their schedules changed, too. *Duncan v. Delta Consolidated Industries, Inc.*, 371 F.3d 1020 (8th Cir. 2004).

VII. DISCRIMINATION AGAINST VETERANS

The Uniformed Services Employment and Reemployment Rights Act (USERRA) guarantees the right of military reservists to return to their jobs with their rights of seniority, status, pay and other benefits as if they had not been absent due to reserve obligations. It also prohibits denials of hiring, retention and promotion because of reserve obligations.

◆ Supervisors at a company in Puerto Rico made jokes about a military reservist. One complained about having to schedule shifts around his military leave. After he returned from military service, the company deducted from his pay the amounts necessary to offset his military income for days he received both a military and civilian paycheck. Three weeks after it finished recouping its pay, it fired him without notice. When he sued under USERRA, a federal court granted pretrial judgment to the company. The First Circuit reversed, holding that **the burden of proof was on the employer to show that it would have fired the reservist even if he wasn't in the military**. *Velazquez-Garcia v. Horizon Lines of Puerto Rico, Inc.*, 473 F.3d 11 (1st Cir. 2007).

◆ A computer technician for a Virginia company was formally reprimanded several times prior to her call-up for active military duty. When she returned to work six months later, some of her job duties changed because of the company's contract with an outside federal agency. The change affected all similar employees. Four months later, after being warned again about her performance and attitude, she was fired when she left the office without authorization to attend to a customer at an off-site location. She sued under USERRA, but a federal court and the Fourth Circuit ruled against her. **The employee's refusal to correct her misconduct justified the firing.** *Francis v. Booz, Allen & Hamilton, Inc.*, 452 F.3d 299 (4th Cir. 2006).

◆ An Arkansas employee, who was also a member of the U.S. Army, took 15 military leaves in three years. **Although company policy allowed employees to use accrued leave for emergency military leave, the plant manager where the employee worked claimed to be unaware of the policy.** After the employee returned from an emergency military leave, he asked to have his accrued sick leave applied to the time off. The plant manager suspended him, then fired him for "stealing" sick days. When he sued under USERRA, a federal court granted pretrial judgment to the company. The Eighth Circuit Court of Appeals reversed, finding an issue of fact over the real reason for the termination. Even though the manager claimed to be unaware of the policy allowing sick leave use, a human resources manager testified that all managers had been instructed on it. *Maxfield v. Cintas Corp. No. 2*, 427 F.3d 544 (8th Cir. 2005).

◆ An employee of Circuit City in Texas claimed that he was fired solely because of his status as a Marine Reserve officer. He sued the company under USERRA, and the company sought to compel arbitration. A federal court ruled that USERRA superseded the arbitration agreement, but the Fifth Circuit reversed. It noted that nothing in USERRA prevented a court from enforcing an arbitration agreement (which dealt with procedural, not substantive rights). **The employee had to arbitrate his USERRA claim.** *Garrett v. Circuit City Stores, Inc.*, 449 F.3d 672 (5th Cir. 2006).

◆ A customer support technician for a company in North Dakota took a military leave of 14 months to go overseas. While he was gone, the company lost the account he had been working on, and it sent him a layoff notice. When he returned from overseas, he filled out a job application, indicating that he would not be available to work until May 4, 2004. A human resources manager told him there were no jobs available and that he was not the only one looking for work. The technician's attorney then faxed a letter to the head of the company's compliance office demanding the technician's immediate rehire. Within 48 hours the company notified the technician that he should report to work on May 4. He sued the company for violating USERRA, but a federal court ruled against him. **His reemployment occurred "promptly" under USERRA, which does not require immediate reinstatement following military leave in excess of one year.** *Vander Wal v. Sykes Enterprises, Inc.*, 377 F.Supp.2d 738 (D.N.D. 2005).

◆ When a reservist from Colorado returned home from active duty, the company he worked for as a design consultant gave him a modified assignment because the unit he had previously worked in was in the middle of developing a plan for 2004. Four months later, the company fired him as part of a cost-cutting move. He sued under USERRA, and a federal court ruled in his favor. The company first violated USERRA by assigning him to a position with less responsibilities even though he kept his title, salary and benefits. Secondly, the company **violated USERRA by firing him less than a year after his return**. It could legitimately do so under the act only if it had "cause," which it did not have here. *Duarte v. Agilent Technologies, Inc.*, 366 F.Supp.2d 1039 (D. Colo. 2005).

◆ A provision of USERRA requires a returning military member to notify his employer of the intent to return to work no later than the next first full calendar day of regularly scheduled work after the expiration of eight hours from the return to the person's residence. When a New Jersey reservist stopped at his convenience store employer to pick up his paycheck on the way home from weekend duties, the manager ordered him to work that night's late shift or be fired. The reservist worked the shift, then fell asleep behind the wheel, crashed his car and died. His mother sued under USERRA and lost. The Third Circuit held that **USERRA did not give the reservist the right to an eight-hour rest period between returning from reservist duty and returning to work**. *Gordon v. Wawa, Inc.*, 388 F.3d 78 (3d Cir. 2004).

- A member of the National Guard owned and operated a hot-air balloon with the Guard's insignia on it and attended various events around the country using the balloon as a recruiting and promotional tool for the Guard. He received several written orders to perform temporary active duty in connection with some ballooning events in the summer of 1996, but he also went to a ballooning event in Colorado for which he received no orders, verbal or written. His employer denied his request for a leave of absence for the summer months and fired him when he attended the events anyway. When he sought reemployment at the end of the summer, he was asked to reapply for the job. He refused to do so, instead suing the company under USERRA. An Oregon federal court granted pretrial judgment to the company, but the Ninth Circuit reversed in part. The court of appeals held that the employee raised a genuine issue of fact as to **whether his uniformed service was a "motivating factor" in the decision to fire him**. That part of the case required a trial. However, the employee was not entitled to reemployment benefits under USERRA because he attended the Colorado ballooning event without any Guard orders. The ruling in favor of the company on that claim was proper. *Leisek v. Brightwood Corp.*, 278 F.3d 895 (9th Cir. 2002).

- USERRA entitles employees returning from military services to reemployment rights and benefits if they give advance notice of service to their employers and their service does not exceed five years. However, the law does not define what kind of application for employment the employee must provide to the employer. An Illinois employee who returned from Army service in Bosnia contacted his former supervisor about procedures for getting his job back. The supervisor responded in writing that "The law specifies there are no requirements for reemployment." The note instructed the employee to contact an individual in the HR department and closed with "Look to see you. ..." The employee interpreted this as a refusal to reinstate him and sued under USERRA.

  The U.S. Court of Appeals, Seventh Circuit, refused to formulate a uniform rule for what kind of employment application triggers USERRA applicability. In this case, the supervisor's note had reasonably advised the employee that no special procedure applied and that he should contact a specific person in the company's HR department. A large employer such as the one in this case was not required to train its supervisors in employment law and could legitimately refer such issues to their HR departments for proper handling. **The employee's contact with the supervisor did not constitute an employment application for USERRA purposes** and the case was properly dismissed. *McGuire v. United Parcel Service*, 152 F.3d 673 (7th Cir. 1998).

CHAPTER TWO

Employer Liability

Page

I. EMPLOYEE INJURIES

An employer may be liable for the tortious (wrongful) acts of its employees to fellow employees. However, state workers' compensation laws, designed to provide an employee's exclusive remedy for job-related injuries, preempt many such claims. See Chapter Seven, Section I.

Where the injury is not within the course and scope of employment, and workers' compensation is not available, an employer may be held liable for its negligence in hiring or supervising the employee(s) who caused the injury.

Allowing employees to engage in horseplay, for example, might result in liability if an employee becomes injured. If the injury is deemed not to have arisen out of and in the course of the employment, workers' compensation will not be available. However, the employee could sue for negligent supervision or negligent hiring and might obtain a much larger award than would otherwise be available under workers' compensation.

Even if the employee cannot recover under tort law and has to settle for workers' compensation benefits, the employer will face increased costs as a result (like higher premiums and lost productivity). Thus, it is important to keep tight control over the workplace to minimize the chance for employee injury.

A. Intentional Conduct

Generally, employers will be held liable for their intentional harmful conduct toward their employees. Some actions are deemed to be intentionally harmful despite the lack of any malicious intent. For example, removing safety mechanisms on certain machines to increase productivity might, if an injury results, lead to a ruling that the injury was intentionally inflicted and move the case outside the workers' compensation system.

Employers may also be held liable for the intentional harmful conduct of their employees where the employees act within the scope of their employment or act with apparent authority on behalf of the employer.

Further, employers can be held liable even for the intentional harmful conduct of third parties, where they create an atmosphere that allows for such conduct. For example, telling a female employee to put up with the harassing behavior of an important client can lead to liability, as can refusing to install safety lighting in the parking lot of a workplace that is known to be in a bad area.

- An Ohio manufacturing employee was injured when an 800-pound metal coil fell on her legs while she and a co-worker were balancing it, trying to load it onto her press with a forklift. She sued the employer, alleging that it acted with the intent of causing her injury by making her participate in a dangerous activity without proper safety systems in place. She also asserted that the state's employment intentional tort statute was unconstitutional. A court granted pretrial judgment to the employer, but the Court of Appeals of Ohio reversed. It held that the employment intentional tort statute exceeded the legislature's constitutional authority and that there were **questions of fact as to whether the employer required employees to balance and load heavy loads, knowing that an injury was substantially certain to occur**. The case required a trial. *Kaminski v. Metal & Wire Products Co.*, 886 N.E.2d 262 (Ohio Ct. App. 2008).

- An Arkansas employee endured requests for sex, grabbing of her private parts and cell phone messages from one of the owners of the company she worked for. When she complained to the other owner, he told her not to flirt with his partner. He later threatened to fire her if she didn't sign a memo indicating that any inappropriate behavior between her and his partner was consensual. She refused to sign the memo and left work, then sued under Title VII. A jury found one partner liable for harassment and the other for retaliation. It awarded her $50,000 in compensatory damages, $60,000 in lost wages and $150,000 in punitive damages. The partner who had retaliated against her then filed for bankruptcy and sought to be relieved of the debt. A bankruptcy judge and the Eighth Circuit Bankruptcy Panel ruled that **he could not be discharged of a debt caused by his "willful and malicious" conduct**. *In re Porter*, 375 B.R. 822 (8th Cir. 2007).

- While cutting metal bands to wrap around stacks of wood, a lumber company employee was struck in the left eye by a piece of metal banding, which caused a deep laceration. Despite five surgeries, he became blind in that eye. He sued the company, seeking damages for his injury, and the company asserted that his sole remedy was workers' compensation. A court agreed, granting pretrial judgment to the company, but the Supreme Court of Appeals of West Virginia reversed and remanded the case. Here, the company failed to comply with an OSHA regulation requiring it to perform a hazard evaluation of the worksite to determine if personal protective equipment was necessary. As a result, **the company could not claim it did not know of the hazards of band cutting** and the necessity of safety glasses. *Ryan v. Clonch Industries, Inc.*, 219 W.Va. 664, 639 S.E.2d 756 (W.Va. 2006).

- An employee of Lockheed-Martin harbored extreme racial hatred toward his African-American co-workers. While attending a mandatory training course on company grounds, he retrieved two weapons from his truck, then gunned down a number of co-workers before taking his own life. One employee's estate sued the company for $5 million in compensatory damages (as well as unspecified punitive damages), asserting that the company intentionally failed to provide a safe work environment. The estate claimed the company knew the killer hated blacks and also knew of his violent nature. The company sought pretrial judgment on the grounds that workers' compensation was the estate's exclusive remedy for the loss. A Mississippi federal court held that the estate could pursue its lawsuit against the company. The U.S. Court of Appeals, Fifth Circuit, then ruled that workers' compensation was the exclusive remedy for the estate. Here, the shooter was acting outside the scope of his employment, but **he shot the co-worker because of the co-worker's employment** while the co-worker was on the job. *Tanks v. Lockheed Martin Corp.*, 417 F.3d 456 (5th Cir. 2005).

- After an employee was apparently too slow in performing a task, a co-worker yelled at him. Profanities were exchanged, and the co-worker grabbed the employee by the neck, causing the employee to fall to the floor. He sustained minor injuries. The company fired both men for fighting, and the employee sued the company, seeking recovery for his physical and mental injuries, and past and future lost wages. He asserted that the company was vicariously liable for the co-worker's assault on him. A jury ruled in his favor, and the court awarded him $145,275. The Louisiana Supreme Court noted that the exclusivity provisions of workers' compensation did not bar the employee's suit because the co-worker intentionally attacked the employee. Also, since **the co-worker was acting in the course and scope of his employment when he attacked the employee**, the company was responsible for the damages that resulted. However, the company was not responsible for any damages that resulted from the firing. Because the employee had been hired "at will," he could be fired at any time so long as the reason for the discharge did not violate public policy. The court remanded the case for a redetermination of the damages owed. *Quebedeaux v. Dow Chemical Co.*, 820 So.2d 542 (La. 2002).

- To detect drug use by employees, a trucking company in California installed **video cameras and listening devices behind two-way mirrors in its employee rest rooms**. When the equipment was discovered, a group of employees sued the company for invasion of privacy. The company maintained that it was allowed to install the equipment by the collective bargaining agreement, (CBA) and that the employees' lawsuit was therefore preempted by Section 301 of the Labor Management Relations Act. A federal court ruled for the company, but the Ninth Circuit Court of Appeals reversed. It noted that a state law claim is not preempted under Section 301 unless it "necessarily requires the court to interpret an existing provision of a CBA that can reasonably be said to be relevant to the resolution of the dispute." Here, the claims were based entirely on California constitutional and statutory rights of privacy guaranteed to all persons regardless of whether they were subject to a CBA. Also, even if the CBA allowed for the surveillance equipment, that provision would be void because Section 301 did not permit parties to a bargaining agreement to contract for what is illegal under state law. *Cramer v. Consolidated Freightways, Inc.*, 255 F.3d 683 (9th Cir. 2001).

- A cook at a deli was diagnosed with diabetes and had her left leg amputated below the knee one year later. The following year, she developed an ulcer in her right foot that required hospital treatment three times a week. She then spilled hot gravy on the foot, and a co-worker helped her remove her sock and place burn cream on the exposed part. The cook filled out a workers' compensation form containing a release of medical information but did not file a workers' compensation claim. Shortly thereafter, she developed a staph infection in her right foot and immediately informed two co-workers, who conveyed the information to the store manager. The corporate manager then decided to discharge the cook because Arkansas health regulations prohibit persons infected with a communicable disease from working in the food preparation industry. When the cook applied for unemployment compensation, she stated on the application that she did not have the infection when she was fired. The corporate manager, seeking to resolve the inconsistency, used the cook's workers' compensation release to obtain from her doctor the truth, which was that the cook did have a staph infection. The cook then sued the deli for invasion of privacy and obtained a jury award of $5,000 in compensatory damages and $50,000 in punitive damages. The Eighth Circuit reversed the award, finding that although the corporate manager intruded on the cook's privacy by faxing the cook's release to her doctor, **the cook did not have a reasonable**

expectation of privacy because she told her co-workers about her staph infection. Thus, the intrusion was not highly offensive, and the cook was not entitled to any damages. *Fletcher v. Price Chopper Foods of Trumann, Inc.*, 220 F.3d 871 (8th Cir. 2000).

◆ Three female employees of a KFC in Illinois sued the company and four male co-workers (one of whom was the restaurant manager) who systematically **spied on them through a hole in the ceiling of the women's bathroom**. The spying occurred over a 13-month period, during which time the male co-workers watched the women disrobe and use the toilet, took photos of them through the hole in the ceiling and described their bodies to others. Claims against the company were dismissed. A state judge later conducted a trial against the male employees, ultimately entering judgment for the women. He awarded one woman $15,000, the second $50,000 and the third $30,000. The Appellate Court of Illinois affirmed the awards, noting that the common law invasion of privacy claim could best be categorized as a tort for "intrusion upon the seclusion of another," for which the statute of limitations had not run. *Benitez v. KFC National Management Co.*, 714 N.E.2d 1002 (Ill. App. Ct. 1999).

◆ While two men were visiting a nurse's aide at a nursing home, the aide's supervisor advised her that personal visits were against company policy. The men left, but the aide confronted the supervisor in a belligerent manner and accused her of being racist. The nursing home administrator told the aide to "clock out." The aide then attacked the supervisor, causing a broken nose and serious bruises to her face. The supervisor sued the nursing home for vicarious liability. A state court ruled for the nursing home, and the Louisiana Court of Appeal affirmed. Here, the attack was neither "reasonably incidental to the performance" of the aide's duties of caring for residents nor primarily rooted in the aide's employment. As a result, **the nursing home was not vicariously liable for the attack**. *Hubbard v. Lakeland Nursing Home*, 734 So.2d 1280 (La. Ct. App. 1999).

◆ A West Virginia convenience store employee was assaulted and stabbed during a robbery. The assailant had appeared at the store previously and had observed cash in the store register, which was in plain view of customers and not protected by a barrier or counter. The store had no cash control policy to prevent the accumulation of large amounts of cash in the register. The employee sued the employer for personal injury. The Supreme Court of Appeals of West Virginia noted that **an employer is immune from suit unless it acts with an actual, specific intent to harm an employee**. Here, the employee had presented substantial evidence of the absence of security measures, which constituted unsafe working conditions and overcame employer immunity on the grounds of deliberate intentional conduct. *Blake v. John Skidmore Truck Stop, Inc.*, 493 S.E.2d 887 (W. Va. 1997).

◆ A Connecticut plastic parts manufacturer required machine operators to remove hot plastic from production machines while they were in operation. A foreman chastised an employee for stopping a production cycle to clean out hot plastic and threatened to fire him if he ever stopped the machine during a cycle again. The employee was later injured removing plastic from a machine while it was in operation. He sued the employer, and the state supreme court held that the exclusivity provision of the state workers' compensation act could be overcome by proof that the employer actually intended to injure the employee or intentionally created a dangerous condition that made injury a substantial certainty. A jury then found that the employer had actual intent to cause the employee's injury, but that it did not create dangerous conditions that made injury a substantial certainty. The Supreme Court of Connecticut ruled that **an employer may be held liable for the intentional conduct of a supervisor only where the supervisor has actual or apparent authority to act on its behalf**, which was not true here. Even if the foreman had apparent authority, there was insufficient evidence of his intent to injure the employee. The court reversed and remanded the case. *Suarez v. Dickmont Plastics Corp.*, 242 Conn. 255, 698 A.2d 838 (Conn. 1997).

B. Emotional Distress

Claims for intentional infliction of emotional distress require extreme and outrageous conduct. For negligent infliction of emotional distress, the conduct need not be as severe, but there must be a physical injury that accompanies the emotional distress in order for a recovery to be made.

The possibility of recovery for negligent infliction of emotional distress is much lower than it is for intentional infliction of emotional distress because workers' compensation will often bar recovery for such claims. Thus, most of the cases that follow involve claims for <u>intentional infliction of emotional distress</u>.

- Four California insurance agents alleged that they were forced to use certain practices to place customers into higher band ratings that were, unbeknownst to them, illegal. Later, the California Department of Insurance got involved and the agents informed corporate security that they had moved customers from lower to higher mileage bands using the practices endorsed by the company. The company then fired them for violating company policy regarding mileage bands. The agents sued the company for wrongful termination in violation of public policy and intentional infliction of emotional distress, among other claims. The company sought to dismiss the claims, but a federal court refused to do so. Here, the agents alleged that the company knew the mileage band practices were illegal but advised them that these practices were legitimate. They also alleged that the company told them **they would be fired if they did not engage in these practices,** and after they did so, the company fired them as "scapegoats." *Maffei v. Allstate California Insurance Co.*, 412 F.Supp.2d 1049 (E.D. Cal. 2006).

- A loss prevention officer for a store in Connecticut was fired after he stopped a customer for shoplifting when the customer had in fact stolen nothing. He claimed that he was ordered to turn over his keys and that the phone in his office was ripped from his hand, with a company official telling him it was for employees only. He sued for assault and battery and false imprisonment, among other claims, and the company sought to dismiss the lawsuit. A federal court held that **the assault and battery and false imprisonment claims could proceed to the extent that they were alleging only emotional distress injuries**. *Rosario v. J.C. Penney*, 463 F.Supp.2d 228 (D. Conn. 2006).

◆ An employee of a private correctional company was captured at knifepoint by one of several inmates and was later released. Two other employees escaped the same fate by barricading themselves in a room. The three employees sued the company for failing to implement policies that would protect them from the wrongful conduct of the prison population. They claimed that they had been "terrorized" by the inmates and that they suffered emotional distress as a result. A trial court held that their exclusive remedy was in workers' compensation, but the Court of Civil Appeals of Alabama reversed. Here, **the employees were alleging purely psychological injuries**, which were outside the coverage of the workers' compensation act. They were entitled to a trial on their tort claims. *Bullin v. Correctional Medical Services, Inc.*, 908 So.2d 269 (Ala. Civ. App. 2004).

◆ A security guard in Maryland was threatened by her boyfriend and obtained a protective order against him, which she showed to her project manager. Despite the project manager's orders to her supervisor to assign her only to indoor, locked posts, the supervisor assigned the guard to an unsecured post outside the building. The former boyfriend tracked her down at work, kidnapped her, then assaulted and raped her, releasing her after six hours. The guard sued her employer for intentional infliction of emotional distress. A federal court granted pretrial judgment to the employer, but the Fourth Circuit reversed. It stated that workers' compensation did not bar the lawsuit. **A jury could infer that the supervisor intended to inflict emotional distress on the guard** by ignoring managers' instructions to assign the guard to an indoor post. *Gantt v. Security USA*, 356 F.3d 547 (4th Cir. 2004).

◆ While an employee of a California auto parts store was urinating in the bathroom, two managers broke in and **photographed him in the act**. They then made fun of his penis, calling him "Shorty," "Peewee" and "Splinter," and passed the photo around to other employees. When the employee transferred to another location, the managers sent the photo to that store, and the employee was again subjected to ridicule. He quit and sued the store for intentional infliction of emotional distress and invasion of privacy. After a jury verdict in his favor, the trial court reduced the compensatory damages award to $350,000 and the punitive damages award to $150,000. The California Court of Appeal struck down the punitive damages award but otherwise affirmed. The employee's claims did not fall within the exclusivity provision of workers' compensation. *Fotiades v. Hi-Tech Auto & Collision Painting Services, Inc.*, 2001 WL 1239716 (Cal. Ct. App. 2001) (Unpublished).

◆ The 70-year-old manager of an Oklahoma apartment complex was summarily discharged in front of two employees and given 30 minutes to clear out her office. She sued for age discrimination after she was replaced by a 27-year-old. She also alleged intentional infliction of emotional distress. The jury found against her on the age discrimination complaint but awarded her $50,000 in punitive damages and $159,330 in compensatory damages for emotional distress. The U.S. Court of Appeals, Tenth Circuit, upheld the verdict. Although there were no previous complaints about the manager's services, she received no advance notice of the termination, and when she asked the regional director why she was being fired, she was told no reason was necessary. The regional director immediately changed the locks to her office, intimated that she had stolen from petty cash and ordered her to make an immediate accounting of the fund. The director also sent the local police to her apartment to retrieve the petty cash fund and, in violation of state law, gave her five days to vacate her apartment. Under these circumstances, the jury did not abuse its discretion in awarding compensatory damages. The jury also could have reasonably concluded that **the company's conduct was reckless and malicious** so as to justify the award of punitive damages. *Hill v. Noram Investments*, 182 F.3d 932 (10th Cir. 1999) (Unpublished).

◆ An electronics manufacturer employed a former U.S. Army sergeant as a supervisor in the company's Arkansas facility. While there, he became the subject of several employee grievances accusing him of harassment. The company investigated but took no formal disciplinary action. Instead, it transferred him to one of its smallest facilities in Texas, where he again became the subject of harassment complaints. Over a two-year period, he engaged in grossly abusive, threatening and degrading conduct, using profanity and physical intimidation in a misguided attempt to carry out his duties. The company issued him a letter of reprimand, but the harassment continued. When some employees sued, a jury awarded them more than $300,000. In upholding the award, the Texas Supreme Court noted that the state workers' compensation act did not bar the employees' claim. Although the act allowed recovery for mental trauma traceable to a particular accidental event, it did not provide coverage for **repetitious mental traumatic activity**. The employees therefore could bring a tort claim against the company. Here, the conduct, evaluated as a whole, was clearly outrageous. The supervisor engaged in a regular pattern of abuse, exceeding the necessary leeway to supervise, criticize, demote, transfer and discipline, and created a workplace that was a "den of terror." Also, his actions were committed in the scope of his employment. *GTE Southwest, Inc. v. Bruce*, 998 S.W.2d 605 (Tex. 1999).

◆ An Amtrak employee became involved with a co-worker. She alleged that after planning to marry, she was told by the co-worker that they could not work together at Amtrak if they married. After she resigned, she learned that the co-worker had misrepresented himself and never intended to marry her. Amtrak refused to rehire her. She sued it in a Pennsylvania federal court. The court considered Amtrak's motion to dismiss the case. It noted that although there are times when an employer may have a **duty to warn an employee about another**

worker, this was not one of those times. The co-worker here had simply been insincere in his courtship of the employee. He had not physically assaulted her or demonstrated a violent propensity of which the employer should have known. Because there was no "special relationship" between Amtrak and the employee that would give rise to a duty to warn, the lawsuit had to be dismissed. *Smith v. Amtrak*, 25 F.Supp.2d 578 (E.D. Pa. 1998).

◆ A Washington clothing retailer employed a sales representative who was a Cambodian refugee of Chinese descent. He endured negative comments from co-workers about his ethnicity and short stature. A district manager failed to act when he complained of the harassment. He was also reprimanded by a regional manager who used profanity and grabbed him by the lapels. The employee filed a claim for workers' compensation benefits, claiming mental and emotional injury, but the state Department of Labor and Industries denied the claim, finding no specific injury or occupational disease. The employee then sued the employer for harassment, retaliation, denial of a promotion based on race or national origin and negligent infliction of emotional distress. A jury awarded him damages for racial harassment and emotional distress. The employer appealed to the Court of Appeals of Washington, which found that a **negligent infliction of emotional distress claim is permissible in a workplace lawsuit** and is not barred by the exclusivity provision of state workers' compensation law. The court affirmed the judgment for the employee. *Chea v. Men's Wearhouse, Inc.*, 932 P.2d 1261 (Wash. Ct. App. 1997).

◆ A North Carolina employee complained to her supervisor that a co-worker was sexually harassing her. The supervisor refused to take action, even when the co-worker harassed the employee in his presence. The co-worker eventually admitted the harassment to company officials and was fired. Several other co-workers retaliated against the employee, and she was also fired after a confrontation with the supervisor. She sued the former co-worker and employer for claims related to the sexual harassment, including negligent infliction of emotional distress, negligent supervision and retention of the co-worker, and ratification of the harassment. The court **awarded her $7,000 against the co-worker and $300,000 against the employer** for intentional infliction of emotional distress. The Supreme Court of North Carolina held that under the "thin skull" rule, if the defendants' actions were such that a reasonable person could be injured, then the defendants would be liable for all the injuries suffered by the plaintiff, even if those injuries were unusually extensive because of the plaintiff's abnormal mental condition. The court upheld the damage awards. *Poole v. Copland, Inc.*, 498 S.E.2d 602 (N.C. 1998).

◆ A pregnant California retail store employee was exposed to carbon monoxide due to inadequate ventilation and improper monitoring of her employer's propane-powered machinery. After being hospitalized for carbon monoxide poisoning, she gave birth to a child with cerebral palsy, seizure disorder, abnormal motor function and other conditions. She sued her employer for negligence and infliction of emotional distress. The court dismissed the lawsuit based on the exclusivity provision of workers' compensation, and the employee appealed. The Supreme Court of California noted that the workers' compensation exclusivity rule did not bar the **child's lawsuit for her prenatal injuries**. Nor did it bar the parents' claim for consequential losses due to the child's injuries. Because the child had not been an employee prior to her birth, she was not barred from pursuing a personal injury action against the employer. *Snyder v. Michael's Stores, Inc.*, 68 Cal.Rptr.2d 476 (Cal. 1997).

C. Negligence

Negligence refers to acts or omissions demonstrating a failure to use reasonable or ordinary care. In particular, a claim of negligence requires:

—the existence of a duty (duty of care, duty to supervise, duty of confidentiality, etc.),
—a breach of that duty, and
—a resulting injury which is caused by that breach.

Although many negligence claims brought by employees will be barred by workers' compensation, there are situations where such claims will survive. And even where those lawsuits are ultimately unsuccessful, the costs of litigation are high.

Negligence claims are more likely to succeed when they do not arise exclusively from the employer/employee relationship. In other words, if the employer's negligence causes an injury to an employee, and the injury occurs outside the work environment or because of factors not associated with the employment, the lawsuit is more likely to be allowed under state workers' compensation law.

1. Negligence Generally

◆ A Florida bank manager sued the bank for negligence and an intentional tort after she was shot during a robbery. She asserted that the bank knew of the danger she faced because of previous aggravated assaults at the bank and a prior robbery during which an employee was pistol-whipped. In fact, the bank had hired a security guard after the earlier robbery but had eliminated that position for economic reasons. The bank sought to dismiss her lawsuit, claiming that workers' compensation was her exclusive remedy. A federal court and the Eleventh Circuit agreed with the bank that the manager was bound by the exclusivity of workers' compensation. **The bank's alleged misconduct was not "substantially certain" to result in the manager's injury or death.** *Locke v. SunTrust Bank*, 484 F.3d 1343 (11th Cir. 2007).

◆ A temporary worker was assigned to work as a press operator for a manufacturer in Rhode Island. **He injured his finger after returning from a coffee break when the press came down on his hand.** After collecting workers' compensation benefits from the temp agency, he sued the manufacturer for negligence. The case reached the Supreme Court of Rhode Island, which ruled that the manufacturer was a "special employer" under state law, and that it was immune to a lawsuit because the temp worker was entitled to workers' compensation benefits from the temp agency. Also, the coffee break did not count as an employer-sponsored social activity such that workers' compensation exclusivity could be avoided. *Urena v. Theta Products, d/b/a Sprague Industries*, 899 A.2d 449 (R.I. 2006).

◆ An employee of a family-owned business in New Jersey managed the customer service department until she left the company for a new job. Later, her new employer questioned the professional experiences she had listed on her résumé and called the former employer's customer service supervisor. He stated that the former employee had never been a manager there. She was fired a few days later. She sued the former company for negligent representation, and a trial court dismissed the case. The Superior Court, Appellate Division, reinstated the lawsuit. It noted that **employers can be held liable for providing false information about a former employee's work history** to a prospective or current employer who calls for references. However, there were questions of fact that required a trial here. *Singer v. Beach Trading, Inc.*, 876 A.2d 885 (N.J. Super. Ct. App. Div. 2005).

◆ A bartender at a club in Indiana suffered injuries when she tried to assist a patron who was attacked by several other patrons in the VIP area. She sued the club for **negligently failing to provide security**, and the club sought to have the case dismissed on the grounds that workers' compensation was the bartender's sole remedy. A trial court refused to dismiss the case and later found in favor of the bartender. The Court of Appeals of Indiana affirmed. Here, the club failed to prove the bartender was engaged in an activity that was at least incidental to her employment. Further, the club failed to provide a security officer in the VIP area like it was supposed to do, and it allowed the assailant patrons to enter the club even though they did not comply with its dress code. The lower court properly awarded damages to the bartender. *Eagledale Enterprises, LLC v. Cox*, 816 N.E.2d 917 (Ind. Ct. App. 2004).

◆ An employee of a supermarket in Massachusetts had a conversation with a co-worker in which he mentioned "guns, revenge, life and politics." The co-worker reported the conversation to a manager, allegedly distorting the employee's comments. The supermarket, aware that the employee suffered from depression, immediately suspended him for three days, then fired him pursuant to its "zero tolerance" workplace violence policy. It also contacted the police to report the threats. Two police officers were waiting outside the building as the employee left on his last day, and they allegedly forced him to go to a hospital for evaluation. After he was released, he sued the supermarket under the state civil rights law. A federal court ruled against him, and the First Circuit Court of Appeals affirmed that decision. The civil rights claim failed because the supermarket had a legal privilege to report the threats to the police. Even if the co-worker distorted the conversation, **the supermarket did not violate the employee's civil rights by reporting the alleged threats**. *Andresen v. Diorio*, 349 F.3d 8 (1st Cir. 2003).

◆ When a corporation decided to spin off a subsidiary, the subsidiary's CEO told employees at a facility about the transaction's probable impact. He reported that the facility was profitable, would not close, and that employees would not lose their jobs. Four months later, employees at the facility were informed that the facility would be closing in a couple of months. A number of employees sued the company and the CEO for negligent misrepresentation, but a trial court ruled against them. The North Carolina Court of Appeals affirmed. Here, **the CEO did not have a duty to the employees; he only owed a duty of care to the company**. Further, the employees failed to show that the CEO knew the plant would be closing at the time he made the statement, and they failed to show that they relied on the CEO's statement to their financial detriment (e.g., they did not show that they turned down any job offers as a result). *Jordan v. Earthgrains Co.*, 576 S.E.2d 336 (N.C. Ct. App. 2003).

◆ The Nevada Supreme Court refused to impose liability on an employer based on claims of fraudulent or negligent misrepresentation, among other claims, where a former employee alleged that his supervisor violated a company confidentiality policy when he **revealed the employee's participation in a chemical dependency program to co-workers**. After the employee was discharged for circulating rumors that two co-workers were having an affair, he sued for negligence, wrongful termination, misrepresentation and emotional distress, among other claims. The Supreme Court of Nevada held that the employee failed to show that the employer had fraudulently induced him into accepting employment or seeking treatment for alcoholism. There was a similar failure of proof in his claims for emotional distress. The negligent misrepresentation claim was inapplicable to the supervisor's alleged breach of the confidentiality policy, since the cause of action is available only in the context of business transactions. *Barmettler v. Reno Air, Inc.*, 956 P.2d 1382 (Nev. 1998).

◆ A Utah retail store employee was assaulted and raped in an employee parking lot after leaving work. She sued the employer and shopping center for negligence. The court used the state's comparative negligence statute to apportion damages by comparing the relative fault among multiple parties and apportioning liability according to each party's fault. Since the unknown assailant was liable for a large portion of the damage award, the employer's and center's liability was substantially reduced. The employee appealed to the Supreme Court of Utah, which held that under the comparative negligence statute, **fault could not be attributed to an unknown wrongdoing party**. It had to be apportioned only among known defendants, plaintiffs, and persons immune from suit. The trial court had erroneously ruled that the comparative fault of the assailant had to be included. The court reversed and remanded the case. *Field v. Boyer Co., L.C.*, 952 P.2d 1078 (Utah 1998).

◆ An Indianapolis auto repair shop required its technicians to supply their own tools according to a common trade practice. Because most toolboxes weighed approximately 1,000 pounds, employees typically left their toolboxes on the premises, even though the shop had been burglarized several times in prior years. The shop was burglarized again, and several employees lost their tools and toolboxes. They sued the employer, asserting that it had negligently failed to protect the premises. The court granted pretrial judgment to the employer, and the employees appealed. The Court of Appeals of Indiana stated that the parties reasonably understood that the **employer would assume control over the tools after working hours** and that the employer-employee relationship gave rise to a duty by the employer to take reasonable care to protect employee property. Also, since there had been prior criminal activity at the shop, it was reasonably foreseeable that further burglaries would occur. Because of disputed facts, a trial was required. The case was reversed and remanded. *Kottlowski v. Bridgestone/Firestone, Inc.*, 670 N.E.2d 78 (Ind. Ct. App. 1996).

◆ An oil company worker abused drugs and was hospitalized a number of times for paranoid schizophrenia. He occasionally failed to take his medication and skipped meetings with his psychologist. The company's physician examined the employee and determined that he was disturbed and depressed. His wife later testified that she was assured by the employee's supervisor that she would be advised if termination was imminent. After the company fired him for poor job performance without any warning, the employee committed suicide within two weeks. His wife sued the employer under the Texas Wrongful Death Statute, claiming negligent and wrongful discharge, intentional and negligent infliction of emotional distress and gross negligence. A jury returned a verdict against the employer for gross negligence and awarded the wife $700,000. The employer appealed to the Court of Appeals of Texas, which determined that **a primary factor in determining employer liability was the foreseeability of the risk of danger to the employee**. An employer generally owes no duty of care to employees based on termination decisions. The employer was not negligent in failing to warn the wife of the imminent termination, and it had no duty to undertake his medical care. The suicide was not reasonably foreseeable. The court reversed and remanded the case. *Shell Oil Co. v. Humphrey*, 880 S.W.2d 170 (Tex. Ct. App. 1994).

2. FELA Actions

The Federal Employers' Liability Act (FELA) establishes a cause of action for railroad workers to recover damages for injuries resulting from employer negligence.

The act differs from workers' compensation in that it does not make the railroad "the insurer" for all employee injuries the way workers' compensation does. In other words, where the railroad is not negligent, it will not be liable for the employee's injuries.

◆ A pipefitter employed by a railroad was exposed to asbestos while removing insulation from pipes over a three-year period. He attended an "asbestos awareness" seminar and began to fear that he would develop cancer or another asbestos-related disease. He filed a FELA action against the employer in a New York federal court, seeking damages for emotional distress and his expenses for expected future medical checkups. The employer admitted negligence but denied that the employee had suffered emotional distress or physical harm. The court agreed with the employer and dismissed the action, but the Second Circuit reversed. The case reached the U.S. Supreme Court. The Court discussed the physical impact rule it had previously set forth in FELA decisions, which permits emotional distress claims where the distress accompanies a physical injury. Employees injured as a result of a physical impact due to employer negligence may also recover damages for negligent infliction of emotional distress. However, the Court **refused to extend the physical impact rule to cover simple physical contact with a substance** such as asbestos that threatens some future risk of disease. The Court characterized the employee's contact with asbestos as an exposure, not a physical impact, and it reversed the court of appeals' decision. The employee had advanced no evidence of an emotional injury, and the Court dismissed the claim for the cost of extra medical checkups. *Metro-North Commuter Railroad Co. v. Buckley*, 521 U.S. 424, 117 S.Ct. 2113, 138 L.Ed.2d 560 (1997).

◆ A track laborer and backhoe operator for a railroad in Indiana died of lung cancer. His estate sued the railroad under the FELA, alleging that the cancer was caused by workplace exposure to asbestos fibers, diesel fumes and exhaust, and herbicides. The employee also had a long history of smoking cigarettes. The estate's **expert testified that the employee's exposure to diesel fumes and asbestos played a significant role in his development of cancer**. He also testified that he could not state to any degree of medical certainty that the employee would not have developed lung cancer if he had not been exposed to asbestos and diesel fumes. The railroad sought to exclude the deposition testimony and asked for pretrial judgment. The court denied its requests, and the Indiana Court of Appeals affirmed. A jury would have to determine how much liability, if any, to attach to the railroad. *Norfolk Southern Railway Co. v. Estate of Wagers,* 833 N.E.2d 93 (Ind. Ct. App. 2005).

◆ A railroad company arranged an influenza vaccination program for company employees who worked at a Texas office. The program was voluntary and took place on the employer's premises during work hours. One employee who participated in the program received a flu shot, then collapsed and struck his head upon returning to his office. He filed a FELA action against the employer in a federal court, asserting that he had suffered a permanently disabling injury. The court granted pretrial judgment to the railroad, and the employee appealed to the U.S. Court of Appeals, Fifth Circuit. The crucial issue was whether the employee had been injured in the scope of his employment. Previous decisions by federal courts applied a broad standard when interpreting the scope of employment under FELA. If a jury could reasonably find that the employer's motivation toward the program was a self-interested desire to reduce absenteeism, **the employee might have felt compelled to accept a flu shot for the employer's benefit**. The employer had planned, administered, paid for and promoted the flu shot program, creating factual issues about its motivation that made pretrial judgment inappropriate. The court reversed and remanded the case. *Smith v. Medical and Surgical Clinic Ass'n*, 118 F.3d 416 (5th Cir. 1997).

◆ A welder employed by a New York railroad worked in an area reputed to be a center for illegal drugs. While in an enclosed area that had been broken into by vagrants, he was stabbed by a discarded hypodermic needle hidden in some debris. He immediately went to a hospital, where he was told to get an HIV test and take other precautions. The welder never developed HIV, but he continued to undergo testing. He developed posttraumatic stress symptoms and lost 30 pounds after the incident. He sued the employer under FELA for emotional distress and received a $126,000 damage award. The railroad appealed to the U.S. Court of Appeals, Second Circuit, which stated that FELA created liability for railroads under a lower standard of proximate cause than was generally applicable in employment cases and that **any causal relation between the injury and the railroad's conduct could create potential employer liability**. FELA plaintiffs only had to show that the employer played a part in bringing about the injury. Here, the welder was entitled to past, present and future damages, as there was evidence that he would suffer from posttraumatic stress disorder for the rest of his life. The court affirmed the district court's judgment. *Marchica v. Long Island Railroad Co.*, 31 F.3d 1197 (2d Cir. 1994).

D. Independent Contractors

Whether an employer may be held liable for injuries sustained by an independent contractor requires a determination of the worker's status. If the employer exerts a significant amount of *control* over the worker, the worker's status may change from independent contractor to employee.

In addition to control over the worker, courts look to other factors, such as the skill required, the type of occupation, supplying of tools, length of time employed, and method of payment.

If the worker retains his/her status as an independent contractor, then workers' compensation will not be available and the worker will likely sue for any injuries sustained under the principles of negligence (duty, breach of duty and harm caused by that breach).

◆ A nurse who worked at a home for mentally disabled adult males was injured when she was attacked by a patient. At the time of the attack, she was performing services as a "consulting nurse" under a contract she signed with the home. When she brought a tort action against the home to recover for her injuries, the home first asserted that she was an employee and thus limited to the exclusive remedy of workers' compensation. It also claimed it was not negligent and that the nurse failed to inform officials that the resident required more care than the home could provide. A court granted pretrial judgment to the home, but the Louisiana Court of Appeal reversed. **The nurse was an independent contractor and not an employee, so she was not limited to the exclusive remedy of workers' compensation.** However, questions of fact existed as to whether the home was negligent. That issue required a trial. *Mouton v. We Care Homes, Inc.*, 915 So.2d 971 (La. Ct. App. 2005).

◆ A staffing agency that provided nurses to a Missouri hospital contracted with a male nurse to operate the hospital's acute-care dialysis unit. The nurse accepted employment with the agency on the condition that he be assigned exclusively to the hospital. The agency agreed. After a female patient accused the nurse of raping her while she was receiving dialysis, investigators found nothing conclusive to support the allegation. However, they did find that the nurse had used inappropriate language in violation of hospital policy. Because he had been warned about his language earlier, the hospital told the agency not to assign the nurse to its facility. **The nurse then sued the hospital for tortious interference with his employment relationship**, and his wife sued for loss of consortium. A jury awarded the nurse $250,000 and his wife $50,000. The Missouri Court of Appeals upheld the award. Here, the nurse had a valid business expectancy with respect to his assignment at the hospital. Also, his admission to having conversations about sexual matters was not an admission to sexual harassment. Thus, the hospital did not have an absolute legal justification for taking action against him. *Hensen v. Truman Medical Center*, 62 S.W.3d 549 (Mo. Ct. App. 2001).

◆ An employee of a contractor working on a California housing development was injured when a wall that he and his co-workers were attempting to raise collapsed on him. The employee sought recovery against the contractor under the state workers' compensation act. He also sued the project owner, alleging that raising the wall created a peculiar risk of injury to him. The court entered pretrial judgment for the owner, and this decision was affirmed by the court of appeal. The California Supreme Court held that a general contractor that hired an independent contractor to do inherently dangerous work **could not be held liable for negligence to an employee of the independent contractor**. Although the peculiar risk doctrine allows innocent bystanders and neighbors to be compensated for independent contractor negligence, employees of the contractor are not entitled to the same protections. Since there was no duty by the owner to protect the contractor's employees in this case, the court affirmed the judgment for the owner. *Toland v. Sunland Housing Group, Inc.*, 74 Cal.Rptr.2d 878, 955 P.2d 504 (Cal. 1998).

◆ A Nebraska taxi company entered into lease agreements with its drivers, wherein the company rented cabs to drivers and a lessor-lessee relationship existed between the parties. The agreements also contained terms that limited driver control, including limitations on work hours, contribution to a company self-insurance fund and cab-calling procedures. Drivers were prohibited from subleasing vehicles and were not permitted to use phones or beepers in vehicles. They kept their fares, and the company did not withhold taxes. When an injured driver submitted a claim for workers' compensation benefits, the state workers' compensation court held that he was an independent contractor who was not entitled to benefits. The Supreme Court of Nebraska reversed, stating that **he was an employee because of the employer's exercise of control over his work**. Although control was only one of several factors in determining employee or independent contractor status, it was the most important. Other factors such as the skill required, the type of occupation, supplying of tools, length of time employed, and method of payment also indicated that the driver was an employee. *Hemmerling v. Happy Cab Co.*, 247 Neb. 919, 530 N.W.2d 916 (Neb. 1995).

◆ A Wyoming natural gas processing company hired a well service to rework some oil wells. The parties had an unwritten working agreement and they assumed that the well service was an independent contractor. Nonetheless, gas company employees routinely exercised control and direction of work performed by employees of the independent contractor well service. An employee of the well service was severely injured in an accident resulting in part from violation of Occupational Safety and Health Act safety regulations. He sued the gas processing company and obtained a damage award of over $1.6 million. The company appealed to the Supreme Court of Wyoming, which stated that the gas company had performed an active role in supervising and inspecting the well service's work. Therefore, **the well service lost its independent contractor status**, because it no longer had the ability to manage its own operations and direct its own employees. This resulted in abandonment of the protection of the independent contractor rule, and the gas company became liable for the well service employee's injuries. The court affirmed the trial court's decision. *Natural Gas Processing Co. v. Hull*, 886 P.2d 1181 (Wyo. 1994).

◆ An Alabama man worked in a coal mine that was leased by his employer. He worked as a "trip rider," which involved loading and unloading supplies and materials that were transported through the mine on material cars. While material was being hauled through the mine and the employee was positioned at the back of the car, protruding material from the car hit a low ceiling, striking the roof and causing it to fall on the employee, severely injuring him. He brought a claim against the mine owner and its agent, alleging negligence for unsafe working conditions. A trial court ruled for the owner and its agent.

On appeal, the Supreme Court of Alabama stated that the agreement between the owner and the lessee gave the owner no right to control mining operations. In fact, **the agreement specifically stated that the lessee was an independent contractor**. The employee argued that the owner and its agent were liable for the negligence of the lessee because a master-servant relationship had been created between them. He claimed that employees of the owner's agent had attended safety meetings and issued safety reports, thereby evidencing a reserved right to control mining operations. The court held that this evidence was insufficient to show that a master-servant relationship existed. It affirmed the trial court's decision, holding that the employee failed to present substantial evidence that the owner or its agent owed a duty to the lessee's employee. *Kendrick v. Alabama Power Co.*, 601 So.2d 912 (Ala. 1992).

II. DEFAMATION

Employers enjoy a limited privilege to communicate necessary information about their employees to the police and prospective employers who require employee information. They may also communicate within the company to ensure that managers who need to know about certain employees are made aware of any necessary accommodations or potential problems.

Courts employ a balancing of interests analysis in determining what information must remain confidential. An employer loses its privilege to communicate information and may become liable for defamation where it communicates false information that damages the employee.

Excessive publication may also expose an employer to liability. For example, if you only need to tell one manager about an allegation of sexual harassment, and you tell other managers about it, you could be liable for defamation.

A. Intra-Company

1. Generally

- A vice president of a Virginia company received a job evaluation stating that: 1) she and her team were "significantly off plan" on certain financial targets; 2) she was responsible for certain losses that adversely affected the company; 3) her frequent verbosity and vocal opinions led others to stop participating in open dialogue; 4) she seemed unwilling to accept feedback; and 5) she engaged in inappropriate criticisms of others. After she was fired, she sued for defamation, among other claims. **A jury awarded her $1.5 million in compensatory damages and $2 million in punitive damages.** The Supreme Court of Virginia reversed and remanded the case. Here, the first two statements were actionable as factual statements that could be proved true or false. However, the latter three were essentially opinion and not actionable. Thus, since the jury did not delineate which statements it found defamatory, a new trial had to be conducted. *Raytheon Technical Services Co. v. Hyland*, 641 S.E.2d 84 (Va. 2007).

- A sales manager at an Indiana radio station was fired while he was on paternity leave for failing to meet certain work goals. The station's general manager then learned that pornographic material had been posted on a Web site the station had been trying to procure (with the same call letters). After a meeting, he inaccurately accused the former sales manager of posting the pornography on the site. The sales manager then lost his next two jobs and sued for defamation. A federal court and the Seventh Circuit ruled for the radio station. Here, **the false statements about the sales manager did not relate to his ability to do his job** even though they suggested that he lacked certain qualities desirable in an employee. Conversely, attacking a teacher's integrity would be defamatory because part of a teacher's job is to serve as a role model for students. *Cody v. Harris*, 409 F.3d 853 (7th Cir. 2005).

- A service manager in Amtrak's product line division had his performance evaluated as part of a company-wide decision to lay off the lowest-rated 10% of mid-level managers. His supervisor gave him four sevens and three threes on the one-to-seven scale, but the general manager lowered his score to five threes (meets expectations) and two twos (rarely meets expectations). She also lowered the ratings of four other employees. The lowered rating put the employee in the bottom 10%, and he was fired. He sued Amtrak for defamation in a Minnesota federal court, which ruled in favor of the company. The Eighth Circuit affirmed. Here, the "meets expectations" ratings could not form the basis of a defamation suit. Only the two twos could be considered. Further, Amtrak had implemented a review process to make sure the ratings were consistently applied, and the general manager had reasonable cause to lower the employee's rating. Even if she was wrong in doing so, **the employee could not prove that her statements about his performance were made with "actual malice,"** the standard required to prove defamation here. *Landers v. National Railroad Passenger Corp.*, 345 F.3d 669 (8th Cir. 2003).

- A pharmaceutical company employee alleged that she was subjected to a hostile work environment and that her performance evaluations declined as she continued to reject her supervisor's advances. She also claimed that when she told her supervisor that she intended to file a sexual harassment complaint against him, he drafted a warning letter detailing her alleged professional shortcomings and threatening probation. The letter was approved by the supervisor's superior and the human resources director and was placed in her file. She was fired when she refused to return to work following a leave she took after she was denied a promotion (allegedly because of the warning letter in her file). She sued, **asserting that the company defamed her by retaining the warning letter**. When the company sought to dismiss the lawsuit, the court denied the motion. Issues of fact required a trial. Here, even if the letter was written outside the scope of the supervisor's employment, the company ratified the alleged misconduct by retaining the letter. There was also evidence that the supervisor and his superior knew the letter contained untruths but published it anyway. *Lewis v. Forest Pharmaceuticals, Inc.*, 217 F.Supp.2d 638 (D. Md. 2002).

- A production associate at a North Carolina company was **fired for allegedly using a work computer to access pornographic Internet sites**. The allegation arose after a student worker saw several employees, including a "big, tall muscular woman" viewing sexual material on the Internet on a Wednesday and Thursday night shift. The associate maintained that she wasn't even at work on Thursday night and that she didn't normally work in the area where the student saw the employees using the terminal. The associate was fired after a meeting with other managers at which she was accused of the conduct. She sued for slander and tortious interference with her contractual rights, and a state court dismissed her case. The North Carolina Court of Appeals reversed, noting that the associate had raised material questions of fact over her claims. She had certain contractual rights by virtue of her 11-year tenure with the company and its "open door" policy, and there were questions about whether the company had met its duty to conduct a fair and thorough investigation. *Barker v. Kimberly-Clark Corp.*, 524 S.E.2d 821 (N.C. Ct. App. 2000).

- A senior research department head for a national chemical company ran the company's microbial department in its agricultural products division. He became the subject of sexual harassment accusations after a secretary in his division told a female manager that he had made numerous sexual remarks to her. **The department head sued for defamation when an investigation into those accusations resulted in his demotion** to a position where he had no supervisory responsibilities and where he earned about $8,000 a year less than before. He claimed the investigation was unfair because investigators relied on defamatory comments by other female employees. A court ruled for the company. Finding no evidence that the witnesses had lied; that, in any event, their comments were privileged; and that company officials did not abuse this privilege in conducting the investigation, the Appellate Court of Illinois affirmed. The company followed its internal policies to rid the workplace of sexual harassment and did not demote the department head until the allegations against him had been fully explored. *Vickers v. Abbott Laboratories*, 719 N.E.2d 1101 (Ill. App. Ct. 1999).

◆ Two officers of a Texas bank met with a senior vice president to discuss his written work evaluation. The evaluation document referred to a customer complaint threatening legal action against the bank for violating the Fair Debt Collection Practices Act. The vice president refused to discuss the evaluation further and requested time to make a formal written response. He then rejected any further discussion of the evaluation, and the bank fired him for insubordination. The vice president filed suit against the bank and its president for defamation. The court ruled for the bank, and the vice president appealed to the Court of Appeals of Texas.

The court observed that in a defamation case, a trial court must first consider whether words used in an allegedly defamatory manner are reasonably capable of a defamatory meaning. If they are, it must then find that the statements are communicated to a third party. Regardless of the nature of the statements contained in the employment evaluation here, **the evaluation was never published to any third parties** and was reviewed only by the bank's president and an executive vice president who was the vice president's immediate supervisor. Both individuals had an interest in the evaluation and enjoyed a privilege that could only be overcome by evidence that they had acted with actual malice. Because the employment evaluation was privileged and there was no showing of actual malice, the trial court judgment was affirmed. *Garcia v. Burris*, 961 S.W.2d 603 (Tex. Ct. App. 1997).

◆ The union steward of a telephone crew at an Oregon telecommunications facility suspected that his immediate supervisor abused alcohol. The steward communicated his suspicions to higher-level supervisors during a training seminar. Within a month, the company discharged the supervisor and offered him another position in California. The supervisor rejected the offer and filed a defamation complaint against the steward and his union. The union filed a third-party complaint against the employer for contribution and indemnity. The case reached the Supreme Court of Oregon, which considered arguments by the steward, union and employer that the steward's statements could not constitute defamation based on the common law rule that intra-corporate communications are shielded from liability. The court determined that **the intra-corporate non-**

publication rule should not apply to the steward's statements. Allowing defamation suits to be filed in cases involving intra-corporate communications protected individual interests in personal reputation. There was also no merit to the employer's argument that it was shielded from any liability for contribution based upon a conflict with federal labor law. *Wallulis v. Dymowski*, 323 Or. 337, 918 P.2d 755 (Or. 1996).

◆ A Massachusetts car rental manager experienced difficulty with her supervisor during a training conference. On the final day of the conference, she was escorted to a small room and interrogated concerning the theft of an agency automobile. She became hysterical and cried when another employee accused her of lying. The interrogator also stated that the company had strong evidence that she was involved in the theft. She sued the rental company for slander and violation of the Massachusetts Civil Rights Act. Her husband also sued for loss of consortium. The court held that the only slanderous statement was the one in which the co-worker stated that the company had strong evidence that the manager had been involved in the theft. Also, the civil rights act did not allow employees to sue employers for the actions of other employees. The U.S. Court of Appeals, First Circuit, determined that many of the other statements made by the interrogating employee were slanderous, including the accusation that the manager was a liar. **There was no requirement that the defamatory statement be communicated to a large group of people in order to create liability.** However, the district court had properly held that the civil rights act did not impose liability on the employer based upon its employee's reckless conduct. The court affirmed in part the district court's decision. *Lyons v. National Car Rental Systems, Inc.*, 30 F.3d 240 (1st Cir. 1994).

2. Publication to Co-Workers

Memos, computer bulletin boards and presentations are all potential pitfalls that should be carefully considered before passing on information that could lead to a defamation lawsuit. For example, telling employees that a worker was fired for theft might result in a lawsuit that, even if you win, will be expensive.

Use only facts and not conclusions when addressing sensitive topics (for example, "Joe was fired for removing company property from the premises," not, "Joe was fired for stealing"). Also, remember that you often need not say anything about a sensitive situation. The grapevine will usually take care of getting the information out.

◆ A financial company in Illinois fired an in-house attorney for improper conduct after the attorney's supervisor wrote a memo to his superior claiming that the attorney had used profanity during his performance evaluation. The superior also sent a memo to a vice president, who initiated the termination process. The attorney then sued the company for defamation, asserting that he never used profanity, that the memos were unprivileged communications to third parties (the superior and the vice president), and that he was fired as a result. A jury ruled in favor of the attorney, and the company appealed. The

Appellate Court of Illinois upheld the verdict. The internal memos constituted publication of the defamatory statement, and the jury properly determined that **publication was not privileged**. *Popko v. Continental Casualty Co. and CNA Financial Corp.*, 823 N.E.2d 184 (Ill. App. Ct. 2005).

◆ A supervisor at a company was accused of sexual harassment by a subordinate, who quit and filed a charge with the Ohio Civil Rights Commission (OCRC). The company conducted an investigation, then stated to the OCRC that there was no evidence of a hostile environment. When the former subordinate sued, the company conducted another more detailed investigation, after which it believed there were some grounds for the charge of harassment. It settled the lawsuit and fired the supervisor, then conducted a series of meetings with employees to explain that it fired the supervisor for sexual harassment. He sued the company for defamation, and a jury returned a verdict in his favor for $100,000 in compensatory damages and $500,000 in punitive damages. The Ohio Court of Appeals affirmed, noting that the jury could conclude that the company defamed the supervisor with actual malice. After stating to the OCRC that no evidence of harassment existed, the company conducted a series of meetings at which it named the supervisor and asserted that he committed sexual harassment. *Blatnik v. Avery Dennison Corp.*, 774 N.E.2d 282 (Ohio Ct. App. 2002).

◆ A female pilot brought a sexual harassment lawsuit against an airline, and a federal jury awarded her $875,000. Before the trial, however, the pilot also filed a lawsuit against the airline and seven individual male pilots for retaliatory harassment, infliction of emotional distress and defamation as a result of derogatory comments about her and the sexual harassment lawsuit on the employees' computer bulletin board. Users could only access the bulletin board through the airline's electronic crew management system, which provided pilots and flight attendants with information on schedules, pay and flight pairings. However, management employees were not allowed to use the bulletin board; no airline department was responsible for monitoring its content, and all computer operations were outsourced to another company. The court dismissed the defamation action, and the appellate division affirmed. On further appeal, the New Jersey Supreme Court reversed. It noted that the male pilots could be sued for defamation in New Jersey if they knew their defamatory messages would be published in the state. Also, if the airline had knowledge that the male pilots were engaging in retaliatory harassment, then it had a duty to remedy that harassment. The court remanded the case for further proceedings. *Blakey v. Continental Airlines*, 751 A.2d 538 (N.J. 2000).

◆ A Nevada employee sued her former employer and two supervisors for defamation. A federal court ruled against the employee, finding that she had failed to establish that defamatory information had been conveyed to individuals outside the company, which was a necessary part of a defamation claim under existing Nevada law. The former employee appealed to the U.S. Court of Appeals, Ninth Circuit, which affirmed. The sharing of allegedly defamatory information with a co-worker did not satisfy the publication requirement of Nevada defamation law. *Crowe v. Wiltel Communications Systems*, 103 F.3d 897 (9th Cir. 1996).

◆ Several days after the Ninth Circuit's decision in *Crowe*, above, the Supreme Court of Nevada announced a new standard for employment defamation cases in a case involving an employee who was fired for sexually harassing a female co-worker. The employee sued for wrongful discharge and defamation, among other claims. The supreme court disregarded the notion that intra-corporate communications could never form the basis for a defamation claim. **Intra-corporate communication would only be a defense under which the employer bore the burden of showing that a communication was privileged.** *Simpson v. Mars Inc.*, 929 P.2d 966 (Nev. 1997).

◆ The union representing employees at a West Virginia bakery filed a grievance against the employer concerning sick pay benefits for part-time workers. The employer responded with a letter that was posted in the plant stating its intention to investigate seven named employees who were identified as habitual sick pay users. A full-time employee named in the letter filed a grievance protesting his identification as a sick pay abuser. He then sued for defamation, among other claims. The court held that the action was preempted by federal labor law and granted the employer pretrial judgment. On appeal, the Supreme Court of Appeals of West Virginia noted that the federal Labor Management Relations Act does not divest state courts of jurisdiction over lawsuits concerning violations of collective bargaining agreements, since state courts have concurrent jurisdiction in these cases. Federal law preempts state law claims that require reference to a bargaining agreement, but not those that are independent of the agreement. The defamation, invasion of privacy and intentional infliction of emotional distress claims did not require the interpretation of the bargaining agreement. The employer had taken no disciplinary action against the employee that might require interpretation of the agreement. The trial court's decision was reversed and remanded. *Greenfield v. Schmidt Baking Co., Inc.*, 485 S.E.2d 391 (W. Va. 1997).

◆ A Tennessee automotive parts worker supported the unionization of the plant where he worked. Management employees learned that defective parts were being produced at the plant, and the pro-union employee was fired for sabotaging the production line. In an alleged attempt to limit further sabotage, the plant manager circulated a memo to employees that criticized the union for its unfair tactics and for exploiting the pro-union employee's firing. The discharged employee sued the company for defamation. The court ruled for the employer, and the U.S. Court of Appeals, Sixth Circuit, affirmed. While the substantive law of Tennessee applied to this diversity case, the existence of a labor-management dispute called for the application of federal law concerning the degree of fault. Under that standard, the discharged employee had to show that the memo had been published with actual malice, a standard that required the complaining party to show that the defamatory communication was made with reckless disregard for its truth or falsity. Because there was evidence that the manager believed that the employee had engaged in sabotage, the district court had properly ruled for the company. *Holbrook v. Harman Automotive, Inc.*, 58 F.3d 222 (6th Cir. 1995).

• An Indiana employer fired six employees for dishonesty after an investigation of theft. Because rumors about other terminations persisted after the firings, the company made a slide presentation at a staff meeting that included the names of the discharged employees and the reasons for dismissal. The slide presentation also reaffirmed "core values" of the company, including trust and honesty. Five terminated employees sued for defamation. The case reached the Supreme Court of Indiana, which held that **intracompany communications concerning employee performance were protected by a qualified privilege**. In order to invoke the privilege, the communication must be made in good faith, limited in scope to its purpose, and published to appropriate parties only. A communication motivated by ill will that is excessively published, or published with disregard for the truth, is not privileged. Here, although the statements were made to a large group of employees and were later posted in a place where non-employees could read them, the company had not excessively published the information. The communication was made to quash rumors within the company and to reaffirm core values. *Schrader v. Eli Lilly and Co.*, 639 N.E.2d 258 (Ind. 1994).

• An Alabama hotel manager concluded that an employee had violated several written policies. The employee resigned when the manager confronted him. Subsequently, the employee sued the hotel and two other employees, alleging defamation. The Supreme Court of Alabama held that the defamation claim failed because there had been no publication to a third party of the allegedly defamatory communications. The communications in question were published only to a few of the hotel's employees and only to the extent reasonably necessary to investigate the employee's behavior. These employees were acting in the scope of their duties with the hotel, and thus they could not be considered third parties. *Burks v. Pickwick Hotel*, 607 So.2d 187 (Ala. 1992).

B. Prospective Employers

Talking with prospective employers is a recognized exception under the laws of defamation. However, it still pays to be careful about what you say. Don't make conclusory statements like: "Sally was fired for harassing her assistant." Instead, use more neutral language: "Sally was discharged for touching her assistant inappropriately and for making statements he found offensive."

• A Rhode Island nurse at a rehabilitation center was suspended for three days because her director believed she failed to dispense necessary medication to patients. She disputed the allegation and resigned to avoid working under that shadow. Two years later, she contacted a placement agency, which asked the center for a reference. The director **wrote that she would not rehire the nurse because of "unacceptable work practice habits."** After she discovered the contents of the reference, the nurse sued the director for defamation. The case reached the Rhode Island Supreme Court, which ruled for the director. Here, the statement wasn't defamatory, and even if it was, the director had a qualified privilege because she acted in good faith. *Kevorkian v. Glass*, 913 A.2d 1043 (R.I. 2007).

◆ A former National Security Agency employee took a job as CEO of a technology services company in Virginia, then learned that the company's financial situation was significantly worse than he had been led to believe. The company had lost nearly $3 million before his hiring, partly due to accounting problems and inventory discrepancies. Shortly after discovering the losses, he was fired. He applied for a job with another company, but **the chairman of his old company told hiring officials that the employee had mismanaged the company, losing $3 million**. When the employee failed to get the job, he sued for defamation. A jury awarded him $5 million in compensatory damages and $1 million in punitive damages. The Supreme Court of Virginia upheld the award, finding sufficient evidence that the chairman made the false statement with the intent to defame. Also, the statement was not protected as opinion. *Government Micro Resources, Inc. v. Jackson*, 624 S.E.2d 63 (Va. 2006).

◆ A nurse was diagnosed with panic disorder and agoraphobia, which caused her to fear leaving her home and traveling. Although medication would treat her condition, she refused to take it out of a fear of addiction. Her accommodation requests were ignored, and she filed a disability discrimination claim. Her employer then fired her for "disobeying a direct order and abandoning a vulnerable client," even though her supervisor later testified that she was merely asked if she "would be around for a while" before she left. It informed her that the matter would be reported to the state board of nursing, but it never reported the incident. The nurse felt compelled to disclose the reason for her termination. She sued the employer for discrimination and defamation and was awarded $23,000. The Minnesota Court of Appeals upheld the award, noting that the nurse qualified as disabled under state and federal law and that she was **compelled to self-publish the employer's defamatory statements** because she believed potential employers knew or could find out the reasons for her firing. *Kuechle v. Life's Companion P.C.A. Inc.*, 653 N.W.2d 214 (Minn. Ct. App. 2002).

◆ A stock room clerk with limited English language skills worked for a New York employer. Several employees of Hispanic descent, including the clerk, were administered polygraph tests to determine if any of them were stealing from the company. The test did not reveal that the employee was lying, but he resigned and went to work for a Maryland bank as a teller trainee. The bank then **solicited a reference** from the New York employer, which responded that the employee had been discharged for pilferage. The company later corrected itself, stating that the bad reference was due to human error. The bank nevertheless fired the employee, and he sued the New York employer for defamation. A court awarded him $100,000 in damages, including $75,000 in punitive damages. A state court of special appeals reversed the punitive damage award, and a new trial resulted in an award of $700,000 for the former employee. The Court of Appeals of Maryland held that an employer can be forced to pay **punitive**

damages in a defamation case only when the complaining employee establishes that it had actual knowledge that a defamatory statement was false. The court reversed and remanded the case for a new trial. *Le Marc's Management Corp. v. Valentin*, 349 Md. 645, 709 A.2d 1222 (Md. 1998).

◆ An Oregon employee was fired for dishonesty, mishandling company funds, violating the law, tending to bring discredit to the company and harming employee morale. She believed that the stated reasons were false and that she would be compelled to communicate falsehoods to any prospective employer to explain her reason for leaving her job. She sued the company for defamation. The case reached the Supreme Court of Oregon, which observed that the employee failed to allege that she had ever been compelled to communicate the reasons given for her firing to any prospective employer. Although several courts have recognized the doctrine of compelled self-publication, those courts have required a showing that the employee was actually **compelled to tell a prospective employer false information** generated by a former employer. Because the complaint here failed to make such an allegation, the court withheld recognition of the doctrine of compelled self-publication. *Downs v. Waremart, Inc.*, 324 Or. 307, 926 P.2d 314 (Or. 1996).

C. Third Parties

There are some limited privileges available for making statements about employees to third parties. For example, statements made in judicial proceedings cannot be used in defamation lawsuits. However, unless necessary, negative statements about employees should *never* be made to third parties.

◆ After an Illinois account executive was fired, he sued his former employer for defamation, alleging that one of his supervisors contacted one of his clients to inform the client that the executive had threatened two superiors. He asserted that he never threatened them. He also claimed that an HR representative told his wife, his sister and a friend that he had threatened his superiors, and finally that the company contacted the police to inform them of the threats and have them attend his grandfather's funeral. The former employer sought to dismiss the case. A federal court refused to do so. It noted that the account executive's claims were not barred by the workers' compensation act, which provides the exclusive remedy for accidental injuries in the workplace. **He put forth a valid claim for defamation and intentional infliction of emotional distress** that could not be dismissed at this stage. *Graves v. Man Group USA, Inc.*, 479 F.Supp.2d 850 (N.D. Ill. 2007).

◆ Officials of a nationwide insurance company fired a Texas branch manager after an agent at the branch fraudulently altered the policy value of a life insurance application. The agent claimed that the branch manager was aware of this and other fraudulent practices that were common at the branch. Because the manager was a registered agent of the **National Association of Securities Dealers** (NASD), the company filed a required NASD Form U-5, which explained the cause of employment termination as failure to follow company rules and procedures. The insurer filed an amended Form U-5 stating that the branch manager had been the subject of a customer complaint for condoning forgery. It later amended the forms twice to reflect a settlement with two other customers and the filing of another lawsuit arising from the same agent's fraudulent behavior.

The branch manager sued the insurer for defamation, alleging that company officials had made statements referring to him that were later republished by videotape. He obtained an award of $1.3 million in compensatory damages and $5 million in punitive damages. The insurer appealed to the U.S. Court of Appeals, Seventh Circuit, which held that **an employer enjoys a qualified privilege to tell the NASD its reasons for terminating an agent**. The district court had failed to inform the jury how to define reckless disregard for the manager's rights. Jury instructions concerning NASD rules were also improper, resulting in prejudice to the insurer. The court vacated and remanded the case. *Dawson v. New York Life Insurance Co.*, 135 F.3d 1158 (7th Cir. 1998).

◆ A Pennsylvania laborer filed a complaint with a local human rights commission, alleging that co-workers had used racial slurs against him. The following day, he was fired for tardiness, absenteeism and drug use. The state Department of Labor and Industry found that he had been fired for filing the human rights complaint and awarded him benefits. During unemployment compensation proceedings, the employer sent the department a copy of two documents detailing its reasons for the termination. The employee claimed that the documents falsely stated that he sold and used illegal drugs, was on parole and was repeatedly late or absent from work without excuse. He sued the employer for defamation, but the court dismissed the case, holding that the documentary evidence submitted for unemployment compensation purposes was absolutely privileged. The Superior Court of Pennsylvania affirmed, holding that **all communications made in the course of a judicial proceeding are accorded an absolute privilege** for which there can be no civil liability. *Milliner v. Enck*, 709 A.2d 417 (Pa. Super. Ct. 1998).

◆ The owners of a Montana newspaper filed criminal charges against a former photographer for stealing proof sheets and photographs from their offices. Based on their information, a police officer obtained an arrest warrant leading to criminal charges that were eventually dropped because the statute of limitations had expired. The photographer filed a lawsuit for negligent and intentional infliction of emotional distress and defamation by the newspaper owners. The court granted pretrial judgment to the defendants, and the photographer appealed. The Supreme Court of Montana recognized an independent cause of action where the complaining party alleges serious or severe emotional distress that was reasonably foreseeable due to a negligent or intentional act or omission. **The district court had erroneously ruled that the statements by the newspaper owners were privileged.** The supreme court reversed and remanded the case. *Sacco v. High Country Independent Press, Inc.*, 896 P.2d 411 (Mont. 1995).

III. AUTOMOBILE INCIDENTS

Generally, when an employee is involved in an automobile accident, an employer will be held liable only if the employee was acting in furtherance of the employer's business or if the employee's actions were authorized by the employer.

A. Intoxicated Employees

Obviously, employers never want employees to drive while intoxicated, but liability can arise where employers knowingly allow employees to do so. Holiday parties and summer picnics are potential problems if employees are expected to attend and the employer serves alcohol.

Problems may also arise where supervisors and their employees go out for a few drinks after work, though employers are unlikely to be held liable in such situations.

◆ A railroad company employee in New Mexico who had a history of alcohol problems left a job site near Los Lunas on a Friday afternoon. He was expected at a job site near Grants the following morning. He left for Grants, but then headed to Gallup, where he had family and where he became intoxicated. Later that night, he headed back toward Grant and struck another vehicle, killing both himself and the other driver. The other driver's family sued his employer, asserting that it was negligent and that the employee was acting in the scope and course of his employment at the time of the crash. The Court of Appeals of New Mexico disagreed. **The employee was not acting in the scope and course of his employment, and the company could not be held vicariously liable for the death.** The job did not require him to drive or place him at the scene of the accident, and there was no indication the employee had been drinking on the job. *Ovecka v. Burlington Northern Santa Fe Railway Co.*, 194 P.3d 728 (N.M. Ct. App. 2008).

◆ While driving home from her shift, a New York pub employee struck a construction employee working on an interstate highway. He sued the pub to recover for his injuries, and a court granted pretrial judgment to the pub. He appealed, claiming that the employee was acting in the scope of her employment at the time of the accident because the pub encouraged its employees to drink alcohol with customers to help promote social good will and business for the bar. Thus, it was foreseeable that an employee might become impaired in her ability to operate her vehicle upon leaving the pub. The Supreme Court, Appellate Division, found that the pub was not liable. **Even if the pub encouraged its employees to drink, the employee was driving home from work** and was not acting within the scope of her employment at the time of the accident. *Cunningham v. Petrilla*, 30 A.D.3d 996, 817 N.Y.S.2d 468 (N.Y. App. Div. 2006).

◆ An employee of a tower service company in Texas got in an accident while driving one of his employer's trucks. He was intoxicated at the time.

The man he hit sued the company for vicarious liability and negligently entrusting the vehicle to the employee. The company maintained that the employee did not have permission to drive the truck at the time of the accident, did not have permission to drive while intoxicated, and was not acting in the course and scope of his employment at the time of the accident. The Texas Court of Appeals held that the employee was not acting in the course and scope of his employment, so the company was not vicariously liable. **Company policy did not allow for the use of company vehicles where alcoholic beverages were consumed.** However, the negligent entrustment claim required a trial. *Green v. Ransor, Inc.*, 175 S.W.3d 513 (Tex. Ct. App. 2005).

◆ A Washington employee left a company awards banquet where she had consumed alcohol. She caused a traffic accident that injured the driver of another vehicle. A Breathalyzer test revealed a blood-alcohol level of .17, and a lawsuit resulted against the company. The employee then stated that she had attended a restaurant immediately after leaving the banquet where she had three drinks prior to the accident. The court granted pretrial judgment to the employer based on insufficient evidence that the employee had become intoxicated at the banquet. The Supreme Court of Washington reversed, noting that there was an issue of fact as to whether the employee had been observed to be intoxicated at the banquet. **An employer may be vicariously liable for an intoxicated employee's actions** where the employee attends an event at which attendance is mandatory and becomes intoxicated under circumstances where the employee has knowledge that she will operate a motor vehicle. An employer may also be liable for negligently furnishing alcohol to an employee who is obviously intoxicated. *Fairbanks v. J.B. McLoughlin Co., Inc.*, 929 P.2d 433 (Wash. 1997).

◆ An Arizona radiology technician had a history of drug abuse that was known to her employer. She arrived at work while under the influence of cocaine and ingested more cocaine during the workday. Her supervisor observed her intoxicated condition and ordered her to leave the premises prior to the end of her shift. The technician left work in her car and collided head-on with another vehicle, seriously injuring the other driver. The driver filed a negligence lawsuit against the employer. The court dismissed the lawsuit, and the Court of Appeals of Arizona affirmed. **Employers are not liable for the negligent acts of intoxicated employees occurring off the employer's property**, even though the employer may be aware of the intoxication. The employer was not liable simply because it had ordered the technician to leave the premises. The employer had not directed her to drive a vehicle and had no duty to prevent her from doing so. *Riddle v. Arizona Oncology Services, Inc.*, 924 P.2d 468 (Ariz. Ct. App. 1996).

◆ A North Carolina publishing company held a retirement party for an editor at the home of a company officer. Employees were not required to attend the party and did not receive compensation for spending time there. An employee who attended the party had three or four drinks and left the party after almost three hours. Shortly after leaving, he became involved in an automobile accident in which the driver of another vehicle was seriously injured and later died. The estate sued the employer. A state court ruled for the employer, and the Supreme Court of North Carolina affirmed. Evidence indicated that the employee was not intoxicated upon leaving the party and that the employer lacked knowledge concerning his potentially intoxicated state. There was also insufficient evidence to establish that the employee had been acting within the scope of his employment when he caused the injury. The employer could not be held liable because the party was held at a private home, **attendance was not required, and employees were not compensated for being there**. *Camalier v. Jeffries*, 460 S.E.2d 133 (N.C. 1995).

◆ A major oil company sponsored a Christmas party for its Alaska employees. The company contracted with a hotel to provide all the services associated with the party, including alcohol service. Shortly after midnight, a few employees decided to go to a local tavern. An intoxicated employee was driven to the tavern and back home again by a concerned co-employee. After he arrived home, he left his residence and drove out of town, where he was involved in an accident. The personal representatives of the accident victims sued the oil company and the co-employee who had driven the intoxicated employee home. The court ruled for the oil company and the co-employee. The Supreme Court of Alaska affirmed. Since the oil company did not hold a liquor license, it was not liable as a social host for the injuries resulting from the employee's intoxication. The court **refused to impose a duty on the employer** not only of getting the employee safely home, but of securing the keys or setting up an all-night vigil to make sure the employee did not leave again. Also, the co-employee had conscientiously discharged his duty by driving the employee home. *Mulvihill v. Union Oil Co.*, 859 P.2d 1310 (Alaska 1993).

B. Other Accidents

Where employees are running *errands* for their employers or are combining personal and business errands, a potential for liability exists. With respect to injuries sustained by employees, workers' compensation will generally be available.

However, where third parties are injured, employers can be vicariously liable for the negligence of their employees.

◆ While delivering a charity pledge solicitation package to a local business, a Mississippi bank employee hit another vehicle, injuring the driver and killing her daughter. The driver and her husband sued the bank, which sought pretrial judgment, claiming the employee was not acting within the scope of his employment at the time of the accident. A trial court denied the motion, and the bank appealed. The Supreme Court of Mississippi reversed, holding that the bank was not vicariously liable for the injuries caused by the employee. Even if the bank encouraged the employee to participate in charitable activities, and even if it benefited from those activities, **the bank did not hire the employee to perform that kind of work**. Therefore, liability could not be imputed to the bank under the doctrine of *respondeat superior. Commercial Bank v. Hearn*, 923 So.2d 202 (Miss. 2006).

◆ An Illinois casino forced a manager to work three 12-hour shifts over three consecutive days because other employees failed to show up or were ill. After her third 12-hour shift ended, the manager fell asleep at the wheel while driving home and drove into a ditch, flipping the car and hitting an electric pole. She sued the casino for negligence, claiming it had a duty to ensure that she was able to drive herself home after her last shift ended and that it should have foreseen how fatigued she would be. A trial court found no such duty, and the Appellate Court of Illinois affirmed. **It is the employee's duty to determine whether she is fit to drive home** and ask someone for a ride if she's unable to do so safely. *Behrens v. Harrah's Illinois Corp., d/b/a Harrah's Joliet Casino*, 852 N.E.2d 553 (Ill. App. Ct. 2006).

◆ A Missouri employee delivered shipping documents to a terminal each week while he was off the employer's clock. On one occasion, he drove his own vehicle to the terminal to drop off some paperwork and pick up his paycheck. His vehicle collided with another, forcing it to strike a third vehicle. The couple in the third vehicle sued the employee and his employer for negligence, stating that he was within the course and scope of his employment at the time of the incident. The court granted pretrial judgment to the employer, and the couple appealed to the Missouri Court of Appeals. The employer argued that pretrial judgment had been proper under the going-and-coming rule of employer liability. Under this rule, employers are generally not liable for injuries caused by the negligent operation of a vehicle by an employee who is going to or coming from work. However, an exception exists for special errands. **An exception also exists where an employee has a dual purpose** in performing a simultaneous personal errand in the course of employment. The employee's trip to the terminal included the personal errand of picking up a paycheck and his delivery of paperwork for the employer. These facts created an issue that required a trial. *Tuttle v. Muenks*, 964 S.W.2d 514 (Mo. Ct. App. 1998).

◆ A Wisconsin man worked for a company as an over-the-road truck driver. He and his wife discussed the possibility of her riding as a passenger with him. However, before she could accompany her husband, the company required her to sign a form entitled "Passenger Authorization." In addition to providing authorization to the wife, the form served as a general release of all claims she might have against the company. Subsequently, she was injured while accompanying her husband on a trip. She sued the company to recover for her injuries, and a state court dismissed her complaint. The court of appeals affirmed. The Supreme Court of Wisconsin then held that **the contract releasing her claims against the company was void** as against public policy and listed three factors that led to its conclusion. First, the release should have been conspicuously labeled to put the wife on notice that she was releasing the company from liability. Since it was labeled as a "Passenger Authorization," it did not do so. Second, the release was extremely broad and all-inclusive. It excused intentional, reckless and negligent conduct. Third, the contract was a standardized agreement on the company's printed form that offered little or no opportunity for negotiation or voluntary bargaining. The lawsuit against the company could proceed. *Richards v. Richards*, 513 N.W.2d 118 (Wis. 1994).

◆ A Texas employee left work for the day and drove to a friend's house to pick up her briefcase, which she had left there accidentally. On her way home, she was involved in an accident in which another woman was killed. Her estate sued the employer. The trial court ruled for the employer, and the Court of Appeals of Texas affirmed. Under Texas law, an employee generally is not in the course or scope of employment while driving a vehicle to and from his or her place of work. An exception exists where an employee has undertaken a special mission at the direction of the employer. To be on a special mission, an employee must be under the control of or acting to further the interests of the employer. No evidence showed that the trip was a special mission undertaken at the direction of the employer. Instead, testimony established that **the employee's trip to retrieve her briefcase was not initiated by the employer**, but instead by the fact that she had left her briefcase at her friend's home that morning. *Direkly v. ARA Devcon, Inc.*, 866 S.W.2d 652 (Tex. Ct. App. 1993).

◆ A bank created an educational assistance program by which it agreed to reimburse employees for tuition and book expenses as long as the employees pursued job-related degrees. An employee, who had already been pursuing a business administration degree, entered into the program. After completing her work shift, and while on the way to the university, the employee struck and seriously injured a motorcyclist. He sued the bank for his injuries. The California Court of Appeal noted that the going-and-coming doctrine normally will not make an employer liable for actions by its employees while engaged in the ordinary commute to the place of work. However, if the employee was engaged in a special errand at the request of her employer, the bank would be vicariously liable. Here, since the employee had been under no specific order or direct request to attend college classes, **the special errand exception did not apply to the going-and-coming rule**. Even though the bank was benefiting from the employee's college course work, her schooling had no direct impact on day-to-day banking operations. *Blackman v. Great American First Savings Bank*, 284 Cal.Rptr. 491 (Cal. Ct. App. 1991).

IV. DANGEROUS CONDITIONS

Liability for dangerous workplace conditions and equipment often involves consideration of whether an employer-employee relationship exists between the parties, and may depend upon an employer's ownership of equipment or property. Independent contractors have greater rights to sue for injuries suffered on the job.

Where an employer fails to provide a safe working environment, liability may also depend on state and federal labor laws, such as the Occupational Safety and Health Act (discussed in Chapter Five, Section IV), which requires employers to provide a safe working environment.

Employer liability is generally foreclosed by the exclusive remedy doctrine of workers' compensation laws. See Chapter Seven, Section I. However, liability can arise for intentional injuries to workers. Moreover, if the employer is also a landlord, or a seller of products or services, liability can arise outside of the employer-employee relationship.

A. Dangerous Premises

Where dangerous conditions exist in the workplace, employers can be liable outside of workers' compensation in limited circumstances – for example, where the employer knows that injury is likely to arise as a result of those dangerous conditions.

An exception in workers' compensation law allows workers to sue their employers for intentionally causing injuries. Dangerous conditions (like defective machinery or hazardous chemicals) can be deemed to be intentionally injurious so as to allow for tort liability.

◆ A Missouri hotel employee, being driven to work, was struck by a valet driver coming out of the hotel driveway, which did not have a stop sign. The employee sued the valet and the hotel for his injuries, claiming premises liability based on the lack of a stop sign. A trial court dismissed the lawsuit because of the question of workers' compensation, but the Supreme Court of Missouri reversed. Here, **the employee was not covered by workers' compensation because he was not yet on the job**. He was on a public street outside the hotel when the valet hit him, not on hotel property or its extended premises. Going to or returning from work is a personal act, so the employee could not be said to have been acting in the course of his employment at the time of the accident. The employee's lawsuit was reinstated. *Harris v. Westin Management Co. East*, 230 S.W.3d 1 (Mo. 2007).

◆ A North Carolina deli and bakery manager **tripped on an extension cord that was stretched across a hallway**. She fell, sustaining injuries to her knee, shoulder and back. When she sought a 10% increase in workers' compensation benefits due to the employer's willful failure to comply with a statutory requirement, the employer claimed that no statute specifically disallowed the stretching of an extension cord across a hallway so as to allow for the 10% increase. The Workers' Compensation Commission awarded the 10% increase, and the North Carolina Court of Appeals upheld that ruling. A federal OSHA regulation prohibited obstructions in aisles that could create a hazard, and an OSHA regulation was considered a statutory requirement. *Brown v. Kroger Co.*, 610 S.E.2d 447 (N.C. Ct. App. 2005).

◆ When a New York City modeling agency hired a sales director with asthma, it allegedly promised to do something about secondhand smoke in the office. The director complained that the smoke caused shortness of breath, sinusitis and nausea. The agency allegedly ignored her complaints and fired her only six weeks into the job for incompetence. She sued the agency for violating the city's Smoke-Free Air Act. The agency sought to exclude her expert witness testimony that she was **harmed by secondhand smoke after only six weeks**. A state trial court refused to prohibit the testimony, noting that there was sufficient scientific support for the expert's theory and that whether the length of time of exposure was enough to cause injury was for the jury to decide. *Gallegos v. Elite Model Management Corp.*, 758 N.Y.S.2d 777 (N.Y. Sup. Ct. 2003).

- A Texas manufacturing plant used machines that leaked coolant onto the floor. To lessen the risk of employee injury, the employer instructed machine operators to stand on wooden pallets while working and to occasionally take time to clean off dripping coolant with rags. An absorbent material was also made available for employees to throw on the floor to absorb excess coolant. A machine operator fell or slipped between the wooden pallets near her machine and injured her back. She required surgery and sued the employer for negligence. The employer did not subscribe to the state workers' compensation system and was prohibited from asserting the common law defenses of contributory negligence, assumption of the risk, and fellow servant negligence. After a trial, the court awarded the employee more than $291,000. The employer appealed to the Court of Appeals of Texas.

On appeal, the employer argued that it could not be held liable for the employee's injuries where it had provided at least one safe way for her to perform her assigned tasks. It also alleged that the injuries were not foreseeable. The court held that there was sufficient evidence that an employee could be injured even by following the employer's prescribed safety methods under existing circumstances. The employer had established an hourly quota of pieces to be finished by each employee and did not hold routine safety meetings or give specific safety instructions to employees. **An employer has a non-delegable duty to provide safety rules and instructions to its employees**, and the employer failed to show that it had met this duty. It also failed to show that the injury was unforeseeable. The trial court judgment was affirmed. *Woodlawn Manufacturing, Inc. v. Robinson*, 937 S.W.2d 544 (Tex. Ct. App. 1996).

- An Alabama hospital employee was robbed and shot in her employer's parking lot after leaving work. A co-worker observed the armed assailant after the shooting. The injured employee filed a claim for workers' compensation benefits and received disability and medical payments. She joined the co-worker in a lawsuit against the employer in which they asserted that the employer had negligently failed to provide them with security. A jury found in favor of the employees. The employer appealed to the Supreme Court of Alabama, which held that the injured employee's negligence claim was barred by the exclusivity provision of the state workers' compensation act. The claims based on failure to provide adequate security required proof that injury was foreseeable. The only basis for this finding would be evidence of similar criminal acts in the area that placed the employer on notice of a potential danger to employees. While there were 57 reports of crime in the area during the previous five years, 48 of these involved motor vehicle thefts and none involved an armed assault. This was **insufficient to place the employer on notice of a danger of criminal activity**.

Therefore, the injuries had been unforeseeable. The court reversed and remanded the case. *Baptist Memorial Hospital v. Gosa*, 686 So.2d 1147 (Ala. 1996).

◆ An Idaho employee who was exposed to dangerous chemicals on the job experienced six miscarriages in a five-year period. When she became pregnant a seventh time, she requested her employer's permission to change work locations and later delivered a child without complications. She sued the employer for wrongful death, failure to warn her of dangerous working conditions and battery. A court granted the employer's motion to dismiss the lawsuit, and the U.S. Court of Appeals, Ninth Circuit, affirmed. It observed that **Idaho does not recognize a cause of action for wrongful death involving a nonviable fetus** and that none of the fetuses had been viable at the time of death. *Santana v. Zilog, Inc.*, 95 F.3d 780 (9th Cir. 1996).

◆ An oil company hired a contractor to repair an offshore drilling platform. Most of the handrails on the second level of the platform were in disrepair, and a welder employed by the contractor was assigned the repair job. He had previously repaired handrails with two assistants to hold the rails, but in this case used only one. The rail fell and the assistant was unable to stop it from landing on the welder's back. He underwent surgery for herniated discs and was assigned a 10 to 15% whole body impairment by his treating physician. He was advised not to return to welding work and filed a lawsuit against the oil company and two employees, asserting strict liability and negligence under Louisiana law. The court awarded the welder damages for lost wages and medical expenses. The case reached the Supreme Court of Louisiana, which stated that an employer is not liable for premises liability under strict liability principles unless the **premises present an unreasonable risk of harm** to others. Here, there had been no such showing. The injury was attributable to the manner of repairing the rail with the help of only one assistant rather than to exposure to an unreasonable risk of harm. Although the status of being a welder had a bearing on the determination of the reasonableness of the risk, the court refused to adopt a repairman exception to strict liability. *Celestine v. Union Oil Co. of California*, 652 So.2d 1299 (La. 1995).

◆ A New York railway supply company leased property to a service that maintained rail cars. An employee of the service company was injured when he fell from a ladder that tipped while he was sandblasting a rail car. The employee sued the supply company and rail car owner alleging violation of New York Labor Law Section 240(1), which requires contractors who clean buildings and structures to furnish workers with proper scaffolding, ladders and safety devices. The Court of Appeals of New York held that the rail car was a structure within the meaning of the Labor Law, and the supply company qualified as an owner. The Labor Law imposed absolute liability on owners to provide safe working conditions where there were risks related to elevation differences. Because the ladder did not prevent the employee from falling, the supply company did not meet the objectives of the Labor Law. Its **failure to provide a safe scaffold or ladder** was a substantial cause leading to the fall and injury, irrespective of the allegedly defective sandblaster. Evidence that the employee had been instructed to use a scaffold rather than a ladder did not create a sufficient fact issue to support the supply company's argument that the employee was a recalcitrant worker who had refused to use appropriate safety devices. The court ruled for the employee. *Gordon v. Eastern Railway Supply Inc.*, 82 N.Y.2d 555, 606 N.Y.S.2d 127, 626 N.E.2d 912 (N.Y. 1993).

◆ The Texas Supreme Court held that a parking garage owner could not be held liable for injuries a motorist sustained after being sexually assaulted in the garage by a police officer, because the owner could not reasonably have foreseen that the motorist would be sexually assaulted after being directed to the garage following a traffic stop. *Mellon Mortgage Co. v. Holder*, 5 S.W.3d 654 (Tex. 1999).

B. Defective Equipment

If an employer knows that equipment is defective and likely to cause injury, it can be held liable for the harm that results despite workers' compensation. Courts may treat such conditions as an exception to the exclusivity rule of workers' compensation and allow employees to sue for additional money.

◆ A Kentucky employee sustained a closed head injury and died as a result of a 30-foot fall off a roof where he was working. His estate asserted that it was entitled to a 30% increase in death benefits because of safety violations. Specifically, **the employer did not provide fall protection gear** or fall protection training. The Workers' Compensation Board determined that the estate was entitled to the 30% increase, and the employer appealed. The court of appeals and the Supreme Court of Kentucky affirmed the ruling in favor of the estate. Because the death resulted from the employer's intentional safety violation, the estate was entitled to the increase. *Realty Improvement Co., Inc. v. Raley*, 194 S.W.3d 818 (Ky. 2006).

◆ An Ohio refinery employee noticed a fire while driving behind a plant and informed the dispatcher of the blaze. She then stopped her truck to help another employee attach a hose to a hydrant, rather than return to the shipping department as required by company policy. **She was not wearing protective equipment, which was also a company requirement.** A secondary explosion occurred and she suffered second- and third-degree burns, making her unable to work. She sued the refinery for her injuries, asserting that she was not bound by the exclusivity of workers' compensation, but a federal court and the Sixth Circuit ruled against her. The employee failed to show that she was required to engage in the activity that ultimately injured her without the proper equipment. Rather, she voluntarily placed herself in harm's way. *Harris v. Sunoco, Inc.*, 137 Fed.Appx. 785 (6th Cir. 2005).

◆ After a machine operator was severely burned while steam-cleaning a machine, he sued the company, claiming that his injuries were a direct result of the company's "intentionally tortious conduct" because the equipment had failed in the past and the company knew that someone was substantially certain to be injured if working on it. The trial court dismissed the case on the grounds that he failed to allege facts sufficient to sustain a cause of action under the Ohio "employment intentional tort" statute, but the court of appeals found the statute unconstitutional and reversed. The Ohio Supreme Court affirmed, holding that the legislature had no power to eliminate, under the guise of promoting employee welfare, **the common law right to sue an employer for intentional misconduct**. The statute held employers liable only for any act that deliberately and intentionally injured, caused an occupational disease in, or caused the death of an employee. The statute also required clear and convincing proof that the employer had committed the intentional tort. By establishing these standards, the court said, the legislature created requirements so unreasonable and excessive that the chance of recovery of damages was virtually zero. *Johnson v. BP Chemicals*, 707 N.E.2d 1107 (Ohio 1999).

◆ A temporary laborer operated a winch while working for a North Carolina subcontractor on a sewer line project. He attempted to manually adjust the cable as it was reeled into the winch and suffered severe injuries when his glove caught on the cable and he was pulled into the winch. He filed a personal injury lawsuit against the temporary service, subcontractor, general contractor and other entities, asserting that they had intentionally engaged in misconduct that was substantially certain to cause serious injury or death, thereby avoiding the exclusivity provision of the state workers' compensation act. The court ruled against him, and he appealed to the Court of Appeals of North Carolina, arguing that the equipment lacked safety guards in violation of state and federal safety regulations, creating a substantial certainty of serious injury or death. The court found that many of the regulations cited by the employee did not apply to winch operation and that **violation of the regulations alone would not entitle him to a finding of employer knowledge of substantial certainty to cause serious injury or death**. He could have unplugged the winch before touching the cable but decided not to take this precaution. The employer had used winches for over 25,000 employee days without any injuries or safety violations prior to the employee's injury. The court affirmed the ruling against him. *Tinch v. Video Industrial Services, Inc.*, 497 S.E.2d 295 (N.C. Ct. App. 1998).

◆ An Ohio factory utilized a metal press equipped with safety cables to pull the operator's hands from the press area during operations. The manufacturer's operating manual called for frequent and regular inspection and recommended weekly maintenance checks. The equipment failed, causing serious injury to a press operator. The operator received a workers' compensation award and then applied for additional compensation for violations of a specific safety requirement under a state law requiring pull guards on hydraulic or pneumatic presses. A hearing officer determined that the employer had violated the specific safety requirement by failing to properly inspect the equipment as described in the manufacturer's manual. The court of appeals reversed, and the Supreme Court of Ohio affirmed. Specific safety rule violation penalties could be imposed on an employer having prior notice of noncompliance with specific safety requirements. However, while a manufacturer's manual may be relevant in determining whether a specific safety requirement has been violated, **state**

law does not expressly require an employer to conduct a weekly maintenance inspection of metal presses. *State ex rel. G & S Metal Products, Inc. v. Moore*, 79 Ohio St.3d 471, 683 N.E.2d 1135 (Ohio 1997).

◆ A Missouri worker was killed while operating a machine at a wire rope factory. The worker's survivors sued employees of the company, including its vice president, managers, foremen and engineers. The survivors claimed that the employees had failed to respond to requests for safety systems and switches on the machine. A court dismissed the lawsuit against the employees, and the Missouri Court of Appeals affirmed. An employer has a duty to provide a safe work environment, and the state workers' compensation act gives employers immunity from common law liability for breaches of the duty. Employer immunity under the workers' compensation act extended to employees carrying out company duties, and **a co-worker's failure to perform a delegated duty does not create liability** unless the co-worker took some affirmative action that increased the risk of injury. That was not the case here, so the employees were immune. *Felling v. Ritter*, 876 S.W.2d 2 (Mo. Ct. App. 1994).

◆ An employee of a Michigan manufacturing company witnessed the death of a co-worker from only a few feet away. The co-worker was killed when struck by a metal bar from a defective machine. The employee alleged that he was struck by the victim's flesh and a piece of metal that he had been holding. However, he did not allege that he had been cut or bruised. Even though the employee was unrelated to the victim and not a close friend, he alleged that the incident caused him emotional distress with physical injuries, including aggravation of his asthma and high blood pressure. He stated that the emotional shock of the incident caused him to suffer a stroke more than one year later. He sued the manufacturer of the machine in a Michigan federal court, which noted that the law did not provide a remedy for third-party bystanders who were not immediate family members. It granted pretrial judgment to the employer. The Sixth Circuit reversed and remanded the case. Even though **the employee was precluded from recovering as a bystander because he was not related to the co-worker**, a fact issue existed as to whether the employee's injuries were caused, at least in part, by his fear for his own safety at the time of the accident. If so, he would be entitled to a recovery. There were also fact issues as to whether the employee suffered objective physical injury as a result of that fear and as to whether the manufacturer's actions caused his injuries. *Maldonado v. National Acme Co.*, 73 F.3d 642 (6th Cir. 1995).

◆ A Wisconsin woman was injured when her hand was drawn into a box-making machine. The president and primary owner of the plant had purchased the box-making machine and leased it to the plant. The employee sued the president. A court entered pretrial judgment in favor of the president, but the Court of Appeals of Wisconsin reversed. Although the exclusive remedy provision of the Worker's Compensation Act provides that the right to the recovery of compensation shall be the exclusive remedy against the employer, under the **doctrine of dual capacity**, an employer may be liable to an employee where the employer acts as a third person rather than as an employer. Here, the president, as the owner and lessor of the machine as well as the president and owner of the corporation, constituted two separate legal persons. Personally purchasing and leasing the machine did not allow him to escape potential tort liability because he created a separate legal entity and accepted the personal advantages derived from such an arrangement. *Rauch v. Officine Curioni, S.P.A.*, 508 N.W.2d 12 (Wis. Ct. App. 1993).

C. Other Dangerous Conditions

Most often, liability in cases involving dangerous conditions arises where employers know of conditions that are *unsafe* and allow workers to continue encountering those conditions – for example, where a safety device is turned off to allow for greater productivity.

As long as the employer knows (or should know) about the dangerous condition, the potential for liability exists. Thus, you should patrol the workplace often and ensure that potentially dangerous conditions are eliminated to the greatest extent possible.

◆ A paper mill in Oklahoma had a policy barring employees from possessing firearms on company property. The mill became concerned about substance abuse and called the county sheriff about using dogs to sniff for drugs/firearms. As a part of that search, guns were discovered in a number of vehicles belonging to employees and contractors. The employees and contractors were fired and they sued, **alleging that their right to bear arms was violated by the company's policy**. The case reached the Tenth Circuit, which ruled that the company was within its rights to act as it did. Also, an amendment to state law prohibiting companies from banning guns locked in trunks had not yet taken effect at the time of the firings and so was not applicable. *Bastible v. Weyerhauser Co.*, 437 F.3d 999 (10th Cir. 2006).

◆ An employee of a Texas drive-in attempted to pick up a freezer cover from the floor. It was there because the manager was repairing the freezer. The cover was "razor sharp" and sliced open the employee's hand. She claimed that she lost the use of her hand and that after she returned to work, she was belittled and forced to try to hold a french-fry scooper in her injured hand. She sued for premises liability, assault and emotional distress. A court granted pretrial judgment to the company, but the Texas Court of Appeals reversed. **There was a question about whether the cover posed an unreasonable risk of harm.** Further, the employee did not have to show an intent to injure her to prove the assault claim. Finally, she could proceed with her emotional distress claim. A trial was required. *Hall v. Sonic Drive-In of Angleton, Inc.*, 177 S.W.3d 636 (Tex. Ct. App. 2005).

◆ An Oregon grocery store maintenance clerk, while off duty, was standing outside the front entrance talking to his roommate, who was also an off-duty store employee. The head clerk ran out of the store chasing a shoplifter who had stolen a bottle of wine. He yelled to the employees to assist him, and the clerk did so, running in the direction the head clerk indicated even though he did not see the shoplifter. He left store property and headed into a dark parking lot, where he ran off a small ledge and tore the ACL in his left knee. After the Workers' Compensation Board determined that his injuries were not compensable because they had not occurred in the course of his employment, he sued the store for negligence. A jury ruled in his favor, and the Oregon Court of Appeals upheld the verdict. **There was sufficient evidence that the injury to the maintenance clerk was reasonable and that the head clerk acted unreasonably in asking him to pursue the shoplifter.** *Najjar v. Safeway, Inc.*, 125 P.3d 807 (Or. Ct. App. 2005).

◆ A Louisiana nurse tested positive for HIV after being splashed with blood from an HIV-positive patient who was being shaved for surgery. She claimed that a co-worker and supervisor either negligently or intentionally failed to advise her of the patient's condition, causing her injury. A Louisiana trial court denied her claim under state law and the Court of Appeal of Louisiana, Third Circuit, reviewed her appeal. The court determined that genuine issues of fact existed concerning the actual notice given to the nurse by her supervisor on the **hazards presented by the patient** and the need to take adequate protective measures. The motives and intent of the supervising employee were also in dispute, making the pretrial judgment inappropriate. The case was reversed and remanded. *Juneau v. Humana, Inc.*, 657 So.2d 457 (La. Ct. App. 1995).

◆ An Ohio industrial employee's position required him to periodically test a sulfuric acid solution and to add the correct amount of concentrated sulfuric acid when necessary. After a number of years, the plant decided to install a meter in the sulfuric supply line. The plant supervisor called an equipment supplier and asked for a meter suitable for use with sulfuric acid. After he was told that no such meter existed he asked for a meter for use with water. The supplier said that he had a meter but warned the supervisor that it was not intended for use with sulfuric acid. The supervisor installed the meter. When the employee used the sulfuric acid line, it burst – drenching him with concentrated sulfuric acid. He sued his employer for an intentional tort. The case reached the Court of Appeals of Ohio.

An action brought by an employee for an intentional tort requires proof that the employer either specifically desired to injure the employee or **knew that injury to the employee was substantially certain to result** from the employer's act. Here, the employer had been warned that the meter was unsuitable for its intended use in a process that was already known to be dangerous. The employer installed the device despite this knowledge. Therefore, the employer could be treated as if it desired the harm that resulted from its conduct. The employee had alleged facts that could convince reasonable minds that the defendant knew that injury was substantially certain to occur. The case was allowed to proceed. *Howard v. Columbus Products Co.*, 611 N.E.2d 480 (Ohio Ct. App. 1992).

◆ A North Carolina construction company was hired to perform services at a manufacturing plant. It delivered a welding machine to the job site to be used by its employees. The standard practice was for the construction company to deliver the welding machine without a male-end plug. At the site, the plug was then wired and grounded by an employee of the manufacturer. The manufacturing employees used the welding machine for projects totally unrelated to the construction project. A manufacturing employee was electrocuted when he touched both the welding machine and another piece of grounded equipment. A safety compliance officer issued the construction company a citation for failure to train employees and properly inspect equipment, but the Safety Health and Review Board dismissed the citation. A court reinstated the citation and the Court of Appeals of North Carolina affirmed. **The construction company was aware that the welding machine utilized high voltages of electricity.** It also knew that if improperly grounded, the welding machine was dangerous. The company had a non-delegable duty to inspect the grounding of its welding machine and properly train all employees. *Brooks v. BCF Piping, Inc.*, 426 S.E.2d 282 (N.C. Ct. App. 1993).

V. EMPLOYEE INJURY OF THIRD PARTY

Where an employee injures a third party, workers' compensation law does not bar recovery in a lawsuit against the employer. However, if the employee was not acting in furtherance of the employer's business, the injured party will not be able to recover from the employer on a theory of vicarious liability (also known as *respondeat superior*).

A. Sexual Assaults

Sexual assaults are never in the furtherance of an employer's business. However, employers can still be liable where they are negligent in investigating potential employees, especially where those employees come into regular contact with customers.

The more employees will come into contact with customers and members of the public, the more they should be investigated. For example, you wouldn't want to hire a convicted rapist to deliver furniture to customers' homes.

◆ A FedEx Kinko's employee also had his own computer-repair business. He struck up a conversation with a customer, gave her his card and visited her home to repair her computer. After repeated visits over six months, during which he earned her trust, the customer left him alone with her youngest son and he raped the boy, who then sued FedEx for negligent hiring and supervision, among other claims. The employee had admitted to a conviction for statutory rape when he was 18 and his girlfriend was 17, but a background check failed to reveal that he had felony convictions for sexually abusing boys in another state. Nevertheless, FedEx was found not liable by a Connecticut federal court because **it could not have reasonably foreseen that the employee would gain access to a customer's home and sexually abuse a child while off duty**. *Doe v. Federal Express Corp.*, 571 F.Supp.2d 330 (D. Conn. 2008).

- A steel plant foreman made numerous vulgar comments to a female security guard assigned to provide security at the plant. She complained to the plant manager at least three times. One night, while she was making her rounds, the foreman followed her into an office, then forced her into a restroom and raped her. After his arrest, the security guard sued the plant for negligence, claiming that it failed to take reasonable steps to prevent the rape. The case reached the Michigan Supreme Court, which ruled in favor of the plant. Here, **the rape was not a foreseeable result** of the foreman's comments. Further, he had no prior criminal record and had never touched her or physically threatened her. Accordingly, the plant could not be liable for negligence. *Brown v. Brown*, 478 Mich. 545, 739 N.W.2d 313 (Mich. 2007).

- The general manager of a dry cleaning business in Colorado was accused of sexual harassment by three employees, but the owner of the business did not discipline him after he denied the accusations. Later, the manager took a friend's 12-year-old daughter to the business while it was closed and sexually assaulted her. Her family sued the owner for negligent supervision and lost when the Colorado Supreme Court determined that even though the manager had a propensity for sexual harassment, **his assault of the girl was not foreseeable**. Had the manager assaulted a customer or employee during business hours, the owner likely would have been liable. *Keller v. Koca*, 111 P.3d 445 (Colo. 2005).

- A staffing services company in Virginia hired a man three different times between 1998 and 2001 to perform janitorial services at a university. Each time it **failed to perform a criminal background check** on him even though its contract with the university required it to conduct such checks on any employee assigned to work there. A university student claimed that the janitor assaulted her and sued the company for negligent hiring and retention. She claimed that the company would have discovered a protective order issued against the janitor for assaulting a woman in a restaurant if it had performed the criminal background check. A federal court granted pretrial judgment to the company, but the Fourth Circuit reversed, finding a triable issue of fact about whether the company would have discovered the protective order. *Blair v. Defender Services, Inc.*, 386 F.3d 623 (4th Cir. 2004).

- A Texas company sponsored a banquet that a non-employee attended as a guest. The following night, the non-employee (again as a guest) attended a dinner party thrown by a regional sales manager, at which she passed out – possibly due to a date rape drug. She was sexually assaulted by the host and a company vice president. The company conducted an investigation and fired the two perpetrators. Later, she sued the company for negligence with respect to its sexual harassment policies. She also asserted that the event at which she was assaulted was sufficiently business related to impose a duty on the company to protect her from harm. A jury found that although she was raped, **the perpetrators were not acting within the scope of their employment at the time of the assault**. Thus, the company was not liable. The Texas Court of Appeals affirmed. Even though the dinner party was held the day after the company-sponsored event, the company did not have a duty to protect the non-employee. Also, the plaintiff failed to show that the company should have known of the danger the executives presented to her. Their behavior was not foreseeable. *Capece v. NaviSite Inc.*, 2002 WL 31769032 (Tex. Ct. App. 2002).

- A customer of a Chicago cable company sued the company for negligent hiring after one of its installers pointed a gun at her and sexually assaulted her during a business trip to her home. Employees were required to have a valid driver's license, and the installer lied on his job application that his license was valid when, in fact, it had been suspended. The cable company did not conduct a criminal background or reference check on the installer. Had it done so, it would have learned about the suspended license and several other speeding violations. A state court ruled for the cable company. Because the customer was not able to show that the **failure to investigate the installer's background** was the proximate cause of her injury, the court of appeals affirmed. Here, the company would not have discovered any "unfitness" other than the installer's traffic problems, and that would not have put it on notice of the installer's danger to customers. *Strickland v. Communications and Cable of Chicago, Inc.*, 710 N.E.2d 55 (Ill. App. Ct. 1999).

- An employee of an Indiana phone company (with a 27-year unblemished employment record) entered the home of a customer and engaged in unwanted sexual touching. The customer sued the phone company for negligent hiring, misrepresentation, vicarious liability for its employee's assault, and intentional infliction of emotional distress. The state trial court rejected the customer's argument that the phone company negligently hired the employee and engaged in any misrepresentation to the public. However, it refused to grant pretrial judgment in the company's favor on the issue of whether it could be held accountable for the employee's assault. Instead, it found a question of fact as to whether the employee's unauthorized acts were within the scope of his employment. The Indiana Court of Appeals reversed, finding that the company was entitled to pretrial judgment on the issue of vicarious liability because it **had no duty to foresee the employee's sexual assault**. Even though company employees had committed similar acts in the past, the court rejected the argument that "improper conduct by a few implies the foreseeability of improper conduct by all." *Indiana Bell Telephone Co. v. Maynard*, 705 N.E.2d 513 (Ind. Ct. App. 1999).

- A Kentucky maintenance company employed a worker with an extensive criminal record. The worker's brother-in-law, who was a regional manager for the company, was responsible for hiring him. The worker sexually assaulted a department store employee at a store where he was assigned. The victim sued the maintenance company. The court granted the maintenance company pretrial judgment, and the victim appealed to the Court of Appeals of Kentucky, asserting that the maintenance company could be held directly liable for negligent hiring. The court found that an employer can be held liable when its **failure to exercise ordinary care in the hiring or retention of an employee** creates a foreseeable risk of harm to a third person. There was evidence that the maintenance company knew or should have known of the employee's criminal background and should have conducted a criminal check under both its own established policy and its agreement with the department store. Because of the employer's knowledge that the employee would be locked inside the store with a single store employee, the court reversed and remanded the case for further proceedings. *Oakley v. Flor-Shin, Inc.*, 964 S.W.2d 438 (Ky. Ct. App. 1998).

◆ A Texas trucking company hired a long-haul driver without confirming a statement on his employment application that he had no prior criminal record. The employer also failed to contact the employee's last employer, but it checked his driving record as required by federal regulations. The employee had a history of sexual misconduct that would have been available in military, criminal and previous employment records. While driving through Austin, the employee left his vehicle and sexually assaulted a college student. The student sued the employer, asserting that it was liable for negligent hiring, supervision and retention of the employee. The court ruled for the employer. The Court of Appeals of Texas affirmed, noting that although federal regulations impose a duty on transportation employers to promote highway safety and prevent accidents by requiring them to confirm the competency of drivers, **verification of criminal background information is not required of all job applicants** and is mandatory only where the wrongdoing party is in a special relationship of trust with a vulnerable group of potential victims. The employer had no expectation that hiring the employee created a risk of sexual assault, and thus had no duty to investigate the employee's criminal background. *Guidry v. National Freight, Inc.*, 944 S.W.2d 807 (Tex. Ct. App. 1997).

◆ The same court held that a vacuum cleaner manufacturer could be held liable for failing to warn or require its distributors to perform a background check of prospective **employees who sold products at the homes of customers**. The case could be distinguished from *Guidry*, above, because the door-to-door sales employment situation created a heightened obligation to an employer where a particular risk of harm was foreseeable. *Scott Fetzer Co. v. Read*, 945 S.W.2d 854 (Tex. Ct. App. 1997).

◆ In 1964, a real estate partnership hired an ex-convict who had been convicted of manslaughter nine years earlier. The employee worked as a porter and lived in the building for over 20 years. During that time, he developed a relationship with a woman in the building and became the godfather of her daughter. The woman then discovered that the employee was sexually molesting her daughter. She sued the real estate partnership and its successor for negligent hiring. The New York Supreme Court, Appellate Division, held that the real estate partnership's hiring of the employee could not be considered the proximate cause of an injury years later. His development of a close relationship with the family was an **independent and unforeseeable intervening event** that severed any connection between the hiring and the molestation. The family's claim was based on a theory that would violate an important public policy of the state, which was to encourage employment of ex-convicts. *Ford v. Gildin*, 613 N.Y.S.2d 139 (N.Y. App. Div. 1994).

◆ A security guard firm in Illinois hired an applicant as a security guard. The guard later resigned, stating that he had found a better-paying job. A year later, he reapplied for a job with the firm. His supervisor remembered that he had left in "good standing," and could be rehired. As a result, the firm neglected to conduct the detailed investigation and background check that would ordinarily be conducted and that was required by Illinois law. Thus, it was never discovered that the guard had several misdemeanor convictions and an arrest warrant outstanding. The guard was sent to work at a gas station, where he abducted, raped and murdered a cashier. The cashier's estate sued the firm, alleging that it was negligent in hiring the guard and that the negligent hiring was a proximate cause of the kidnap, rape and murder. A jury ruled in favor of the estate. The firm appealed to the Appellate Court of Illinois.

On appeal, the firm did not contest that it was negligent in hiring the guard, but it maintained that the negligent hiring was not a proximate cause of the cashier's injuries and death as a matter of law. The court agreed. There must be **a tangible connection between the employee's violent tendencies, the particular job he is hired to perform, and the harm to the plaintiff**. No such connection was present here. It was not the fact that the guard was a security guard that got him into the cashier's car and proximately caused her injuries and death; it was the fact that she trusted him because she knew him from work where he happened to be employed as a security guard. The court reversed the decision in favor of the estate and held that the firm was not liable. *Carter v. Skokie Valley Detective Agency*, 628 N.E.2d 602 (Ill. App. Ct. 1993).

◆ After experiencing back pain and bladder problems, a Washington man went to a clinic, where the doctor told him that certain tests were necessary because of irregularities in the prostate exam. He was also told that a sperm sample was required and that the normal procedure was for the doctor to manually obtain it. The doctor stimulated the patient to ejaculation. Approximately two and a half years later, another patient complained to the director of the clinic about inappropriate sexual behavior by the doctor. The clinic determined that the doctor had engaged in improper sexual conduct with more than 100 patients during a period of two and a half years.

The patient then sued the clinic. The trial court ruled for the clinic, and the Court of Appeals of Washington affirmed. In order to hold an employer vicariously liable for the acts of its employees, it must be established that the employee was acting in furtherance of the employer's business and that he was acting within the scope of employment. The patient argued that the doctor's sexual assault happened in conjunction with an authorized examination and therefore, the clinic should be held liable. The court disagreed and determined that the tortious sexual assault should not be attributable to the clinic. The **assault emanated from the doctor's personal motives for sexual gratification**. There was no evidence that the act was done in furtherance of the clinic's business. *Thompson v. Everett Clinic*, 860 P.2d 1054 (Wash. Ct. App. 1993).

B. Other Injuries

Courts will sometimes hold employers liable for injuries caused by employees even though the employees are not furthering their employers' interests. Usually, this occurs when employers are negligent in hiring or supervising their employees. More commonly, the employee is doing something that is partly for the employer's benefit and partly for his own.

◆ A Mississippi restaurant worker thought a customer was hitting on his girlfriend. He clocked out, then tried to provoke the customer into a fight. The manager heard the commotion and ordered the two to take it outside. A group of employees and customers followed the two out to the parking lot, where another employee struck the customer, who fell from the second-floor parking lot to a concrete surface, severing his spine and becoming a quadriplegic. He sued the restaurant for his injuries, and a jury awarded him $20 million for pain and suffering, medical expenses and lost earnings. The Fifth Circuit upheld the award, noting the manager's failure to intervene to break up the fight. The court of appeals also stated that **the restaurant had a duty to control its off-duty employees to protect its patrons from a foreseeable, unreasonable risk of harm**. *Foradori v. Harris*, 523 F.3d 477 (5th Cir. 2008).

◆ The president of a company in Kentucky owned his own plane and often flew it for business purposes. He invited his pastor along on a trip to Indianapolis so the pastor could visit family while the president worked. On the way back, the plane struck a cell phone tower and both men were killed. The pastor's estate sued the company for vicarious liability, but the Supreme Court of Kentucky held that the estate could not recover for the pastor's death. Even if the president acted within the scope of his authority in inviting the pastor along, **the pastor did not join the president on the trip for the purpose of accomplishing work for the company**. *Mid-States Plastics, Inc. v. Estate of Bryant*, 245 S.W.3d 728 (Ky. 2008).

◆ A California employee sent anonymous threats over the Internet using a company computer. Eventually, the messages were traced back to him. He was arrested and fired. The two people he had threatened sued the company for negligence, and the company asserted that it was immune under Section 230 of the Communications Decency Act of 1996 (CDA). The case reached the California Court of Appeal, which ruled for the company. Here, the company was a "provider of interactive computer service" under the CDA's definition; **because it was only the publisher of information provided by the employee and had no knowledge of the threats, it had immunity** under Section 230. *Delfino v. Agilent Technologies, Inc.*, 52 Cal.Rptr.3d 376 (Cal. Ct. App. 2006).

◆ After discovering his wife was having an affair with one of her co-workers, a man divorced his wife and sued her employer for alienation of affection. He asserted that the company negligently and recklessly allowed the illicit relationship to be carried on in its offices and elsewhere. The company sought to dismiss the lawsuit, but the Mississippi Supreme Court refused to do so.

However slim, **there was a possibility the husband could prove that the company intentionally interfered with his marital relationship**. The court allowed the lawsuit to continue to the next stage. *Children's Medical Group v. Phillips*, 940 So.2d 931 (Miss. 2006).

◆ While a clerk at a bookstore was stooped down to retrieve a book from a bottom shelf, a customer touched her or her shirt. He claimed he was trying to help her tuck her shirt in; she claimed he inappropriately touched her buttocks. Her managers and a security guard detained the customer for over an hour, questioning and photographing him, and calling the police. When he later sued for false imprisonment, a Florida federal jury awarded him $117,000. The Eleventh Circuit upheld the award, noting that **the company did not have in place a policy that would have prevented employees from unlawfully detaining customers**. *Johnson v. Barnes & Noble Booksellers, Inc.*, 437 F.3d 1112 (11th Cir. 2006).

◆ An employee of a New Jersey company used his work computer to access pornography in violation of company policy. For two years, several employees, including his supervisor and the company's finance director, knew about his activity. Yet the company made no real efforts to stop him, only warning him to do so without taking any other action. He transmitted nude photos of his wife's 10-year-old daughter to child porn sites and was arrested. His wife sued the company for negligence. A court granted pretrial judgment to the company, but the Superior Court of New Jersey, Appellate Division, reversed. Here, **the employer breached its duty to report and/or take effective action to stop the employee's activities**. However, there was an issue of fact as to whether the company's breach of duty resulted in harm to the daughter. A trial was required. *Jane Doe v. XYZ Corp.*, 887 A.2d 1156 (N.J. Super. Ct. App. Div. 2005).

◆ The California Supreme Court held that the owner of a restaurant could be held liable for the stabbing of a man in the restaurant's parking lot where **restaurant employees failed to call 911 even though they saw the assault**. The victim was a regular patron of the restaurant but was not eating there that night. The attacker ran into the restaurant yelling for a knife, grabbed one, then ran back outside and stabbed the victim. The court said that if the employees failed to call 911 because their illegal immigrant status would be discovered, the owner would be liable. However, if they failed to call because they feared the attacker would hurt them, or that they would be retaliated against later, the owner would not be liable. Since the victim was an invitee of the restaurant, its employees had a duty to take reasonable and minimally burdensome measures to aid him. The case required a trial. *Morris v. De La Torre*, 113 P.3d 1182 (Cal. 2005).

◆ A disgruntled phone services company customer received an e-mail calling him pathetic and "a grumpy, horrible man." The e-mail purported to come from an employee in the Kentucky Attorney General's (AG's) office, but in fact was sent by several customer service employees of the company who forged the origin of the e-mail. The AG employee sued the company and the customer service employees for defamation, negligent supervision and emotional distress. The company sought to dismiss all claims against it, and a federal court granted the request. Here, **the company was not vicariously liable for the employees' conduct** because even though it was in response to a customer complaint and sent on company equipment during working hours, it did not further the company's interest and could not have been expected in view of the employees' duties. Further, the AG employee failed to show that the company knew or should have known that the employees would do what they did. *Booker v. GTE.net LLC*, 214 F.Supp.2d 746 (E.D. Ky. 2002).

- A Tennessee store hired an off-duty police officer as a security guard. When a customer caused a disruption in the store, the officer issued him a misdemeanor citation for disorderly conduct and warned him never to return to the store. A month later, the store manager notified the officer that the customer had returned. The officer then discovered that the customer had failed to appear for the misdemeanor citation and that a bench warrant had been issued for his arrest. The store manager told the officer to serve the warrant, and the officer attempted to do so, accompanied by four or five other police officers. When the customer threatened to shoot the officers, one of them shot and killed him. His family then sued the store for negligence, but a court dismissed the lawsuit and an appellate court affirmed.

The Tennessee Supreme Court reversed. It held that **the store could be held liable for the off-duty officer's negligence**. It rejected three arguments in arriving at its decision. The first was that off-duty officers have an ever-present public duty to preserve the peace and enforce the law such that they are not acting on the employer's behalf. The second was that off-duty officers act to vindicate a public right or to benefit the public in general. The third was that public policy dictates against finding liability because employing off-duty officers as security guards deters crime. Under agency law, the store could be liable for the officer's actions because he was acting as the store's agent when he went to serve the warrant. *White v. Revco Discount Drug Centers, Inc.*, 33 S.W.3d 713 (Tenn. 2000).

- A bellman at a resort in South Carolina also performed delivery services for the company on his day off. He picked up accounting and payroll documents from two affiliated corporate entities and delivered them to the company. One day, he was speeding on a road adjacent to one of the entities when he lost control of the car and hit another vehicle. He died, and a passenger in the other car was severely burned. When she sued the company and the two affiliated entities in a Georgia state court, they asserted that the bellman was acting as an independent contractor at the time of the accident. The court agreed and granted pretrial judgment to the defendants. However, the Georgia Court of Appeals reversed as to the company. Here, there were **questions of material fact as to whether the bellman was acting as an employee on his day off**. Several items might lead a jury to so find: 1) he simply took over delivery responsibilities that the manager of one of the entities had previously performed; 2) the company exercised control over the time, manner and method in which he performed his delivery services; and 3) the delivery of the documents furthered the company's business. There would have to be a trial on this issue. *Thompson v. Club Group Ltd.*, 553 S.E.2d 842 (Ga. Ct. App. 2001).

- An Oklahoma convenience store employee became involved in a fight with a customer over a returned check. The customer sued the employee and employer for battery, asserting that the employer was liable for damages under the doctrine of *respondeat superior* and the theory of negligent hiring and retention. Prior to trial, the parties stipulated that the employee was within the scope of his employment at the time of the incident and that the employer could therefore be held liable under *respondeat superior*. In view of this stipulation, the court dismissed the negligent hiring and retention claim. The court then excluded evidence of past conduct by the employee, which the customer asserted was relevant in determining whether the employee had battered him.

  The court entered judgment for the employer on the remaining *respondeat superior* claim, and the customer appealed. The case reached the Supreme Court of Oklahoma, which observed the distinction between an employer's direct liability for negligent hiring and retention, and its vicarious liability under *respondeat superior*. It agreed with the employer that the stipulation of facts made direct liability under the negligent hiring and retention claim superfluous. This was because **vicarious liability may be remedied by an award of punitive damages**, and a negligent hiring and retention claim could impose no further liability on an employer. The court affirmed the trial court's judgment on this issue and affirmed its decision to exclude evidence of the employee's prior conduct as within the court's discretion. *Jordan v. Cates*, 935 P.2d 289 (Okla. 1997).

- A tractor-trailer driver stopped his truck at a roadside lounge and drank alcohol for three or four hours. He began crossing the highway to return to his truck and allegedly darted in front of a motorcycle, causing a collision that killed both the driver and cyclist. The motorcyclist's estate sued the driver's employer, asserting that it should be held liable for the motorcyclist's death. A North Carolina court ruled that as a matter of law, the employee had been outside the scope of his employment at the time of the collision and that the employer could not be held vicariously liable for damages. The Fourth Circuit disagreed that the employee had left the scope of his employment as soon as he left his truck to enter the lounge. A long-haul trucker is required to take rest stops and a fact issue existed concerning whether a three to four hour break was within the scope of his employment. The district court had also improperly determined that the employee was outside the scope of employment at the time of the collision because of his intoxicated state. There is no authority for determining that an employee otherwise within the scope of employment is deemed **outside the scope of employment due to intoxication**. Because the district court failed to consider whether the employee intended to act for his employer when he returned to the truck, its judgment was vacated and remanded. *McNair v. Lend Lease Trucks, Inc.*, 95 F.3d 325 (4th Cir. 1996).

- An employment broker furnished an employee to General Motors (GM) to work at GM's Arizona proving grounds. The employee drove a delivery car into a parked vehicle, causing severe injuries to a co-worker. The co-worker sued the employment broker and a court ruled for the co-worker. However, the Court of Appeals of Arizona reversed. The co-worker had argued that the employment broker should be held liable for the employee's negligence because it retained the ability to fire him, sign his time records and perform other administrative duties. Under this argument, both employers had concurrent control of his actions and could be held jointly liable for his actions. The court held that the **vicarious liability for the negligence of an employee depends upon the level of control exercised**. Because GM exclusively controlled the service being performed by the employee, the employment broker had surrendered its control over him and could not be held vicariously liable for his negligence. *McDaniel v. Troy Design Services Co.*, 925 P.2d 693 (Ariz. Ct. App. 1996).

- An engineering director at a Utah laboratory was romantically involved with his secretary. She later began a sexual relationship with another employee. After she filed for a divorce, her husband sued the employer and the employees for intentional infliction of emotional and physical injury, and for intentionally interfering with his marital contract. The Supreme Court of Utah noted that an employer may be vicariously liable for wrongful actions of its employees if they are committed within the scope of their employment. The acts must occur during work hours, must be of the general kind the employee is required to perform, and be motivated by service to the employer. Here, the employees' actions were outside the scope of their employment as **neither had been hired to engage in romantic relationships**. An employee's conduct may be outside the scope of employment even when it takes place on the job, if motivated by personal interest. *Jackson v. Righter*, 891 P.2d 1387 (Utah 1995).

VI. CONTINUING VIOLATION DOCTRINE

The continuing violation doctrine can cause an employer to be liable for conduct occurring outside the statute of limitations where it or its supervisory employees have engaged in a <u>continuing course of conduct</u> against an employee, or where the company has knowingly allowed an employee to engage in a continuing course of conduct against a third party.

As long as at least one of the unlawful acts occurs within the statute of limitations, and as long as the acts are related to one another, the continuing violation doctrine allows the whole series of acts to be taken into account when determining liability.

- A black Amtrak worker alleged that he was consistently harassed and disciplined more harshly than other employees because of his race. When he sued, a California federal court dismissed his action, holding that Amtrak could not be liable for conduct occurring outside the 300-day limitations period of Title VII. The case reached the U.S. Supreme Court, which held that a Title VII plaintiff alleging discrete or retaliatory acts must file his charge within the appropriate 180- or 300-day limitations period. However, a charge of a **hostile work environment** (a series of acts that may not be actionable on their own, occurring over a period of time) will not be time-barred if all acts constituting the claim are part of the same unlawful practice and at least one act falls within the filing period. The Court also held that the *Ellerth/Faragher* sexual harassment standard (see Chapter One, Section II.D.1) applies to claims of racial harassment just as much as it does to claims of sexual harassment. *National Railroad Passenger Corp. v. Morgan*, 536 U.S. 101, 122 S.Ct. 2061, 153 L.Ed.2d 106 (2002).

◆ A female employee at an Indiana company claimed that she endured hostile working conditions, including having to look at pornographic images on male team leaders' computer screens. The company maintained that the pornographic images were the sole problem. It suspended 11 men for two weeks and transferred the woman to another team. She claimed that the company's actions had little effect, that the male team leaders continued to view pornography and that they blamed her and other women for their suspensions. When she ultimately sued, the company claimed that no harassment had occurred in the previous 300 days. The court instructed the jury to consider only the working conditions for the past 300 days, and the jury ruled for the company. However, the Seventh Circuit reversed. **The employee should have been allowed to present evidence of the working conditions for all of her time at the company.** *Bright v. Hill's Pet Nutrition, Inc.*, 510 F.3d 766 (7th Cir. 2007).

◆ A female repair technician worked at a garage in Staten Island for nine years. For the last seven years, she was the only female there. When she quit, she asserted that she had endured disparaging treatment every day for the nine years she was there. She also claimed that her supervisors were non-responsive to her complaints, and that the company's ethics hotline was not effective in eliminating the harassment. A New York federal court granted pretrial judgment to the company, but the Second Circuit reversed. Here, a reasonable jury could find that she was subjected to a sexually hostile work environment during her nine years with the company. Also, under the continuing violation doctrine, **all the harassing acts of the prior nine years could be used in determining whether the work environment was hostile** (despite the 300-day statute of limitations normally imposed by Title VII). *Petrosino v. Bell Atlantic*, 385 F.3d 210 (2d Cir. 2004).

◆ An engineer with a California company was diagnosed with multiple sclerosis and allegedly began to experience disability discrimination (failure to accommodate) and harassment as a result. Five years later, she resigned and sued under state law, asserting that the unlawful behavior was part of a pattern of continuing wrongdoing such that all the acts of the past five years should be considered. A court agreed, and a jury awarded her $925,000 in emotional distress damages and $476,000 in economic damages.

The court of appeal held that the jury should only have considered improper behavior from the past year. The California Supreme Court reversed, finding that neither court had applied the proper standard for determining a continuing violation. To succeed on a continuing violation claim, the employee must show that **the actions before and after the limitations period are sufficiently**

similar in kind, that they occur with sufficient frequency, and that they have not acquired a degree of permanence that would put the employee on notice that additional efforts to resolve the problem would be futile. Thus, when a reasonable employee realizes that further efforts to obtain an accommodation or end harassment will be futile, the statute of limitations begins to run. The court remanded the case for further proceedings. *Richards v. CH2M Hill, Inc.*, 111 Cal.Rptr.2d 87 (Cal. 2001).

- A Massachusetts employee was subjected to both verbal and physical sexual harassment by her supervisor and co-workers. However, she did not report it because they acted the same "to everybody." After a number of years, she reported the harassment and the men were disciplined. They then began retaliating against her. She sued the company under state law, and a trial court ruled that she could only assert hostile environment incidents that occurred within the past six months. The Supreme Judicial Court of Massachusetts held that **she might be entitled to the benefit of the continuing violation doctrine**. Unless she knew or reasonably should have known that she was in a pervasively hostile environment that was unlikely to improve (such that she should have filed a timely complaint with the Commission Against Discrimination), she could assert otherwise untimely claims under the continuing violation doctrine. The court remanded the case for further proceedings. *Cuddyer v. Stop & Shop Supermarket Co.*, 750 N.E.2d 928 (Mass. 2001).

CHAPTER THREE

Discipline, Suspension and Termination

I. AT-WILL EMPLOYMENT

At-will employment is what most of us toil under. As at-will employees, we can quit at any time, but we can also be fired at any time for any reason or no reason at all. The at-will presumption has some exceptions, including an employee discharge that violates an important public policy or forces an employee to choose between employment and personal legal rights.

Just-cause employment offers more protections against firing, and it is more common in union workplaces and in the public employment sector. In these relationships, employees can only be fired for just cause (like insubordination or incompetence). However, they can still quit at any time.

- A Connecticut employee received a written offer to become regional sales manager for another company. The offer was for five days hence and stated that employment would be at will, meaning the employee could quit or be fired at any time. He signed and returned the offer, then was asked to provide job references, which he did. He quit his old job and showed up for work at the new company on the designated day. However, due to a problem with his references, he was asked to provide additional references and was sent home. That evening, he was informed that he would not be hired due to a problem with the references. He sued for breach of contract, claiming that he could not be fired until after he began working for the company. The Connecticut Court of Appeals disagreed. It noted that **the at-will doctrine extends to all aspects of the employment relationship, including the job offer**. *Petitte v. DSL.net, Inc.*, 925 A.2d 457 (Conn. App. Ct. 2007).

- An America Online employee was fired from her job in New Mexico as a "coach" for the company's consultants. She sued, claiming AOL breached an implied contract to fire her only for cause. A federal court granted pretrial judgment to AOL, and the Tenth Circuit affirmed. Comments from the employee's supervisors (that employees were not fired without cause) did not countermand the **four written documents she received, each of which expressly stated that her employment was at will**. The application, the job offer letter, a "business and personal conduct" form and the employee handbook all stated that her employment was at will and that she could be fired at any time, with or without cause. As a result, she was entitled to no relief. *Sullivan v. America Online, Inc.*, 219 Fed.Appx. 720 (10th Cir. 2007).

- A doctor worked as the associate medical director of the medical department of the *New York Times*. She claimed she was fired after she refused, on ethical grounds, to provide management with confidential medical records of employees without their knowledge or consent, and also asserted that she was told to misinform employees regarding whether their illnesses and injuries were work related, in order to cut down on workers' compensation claims. The doctor was fired in a restructuring, and she sued for breach of contract. A state court ruled in her favor, and an appellate court affirmed. However, the New York Court of Appeals reversed. It refused to apply a narrow exception to the employment-at-will doctrine involving the ethical obligations of attorneys. Unlike a situation where an attorney is acting only on behalf of her clients, the doctor here was also acting on behalf of the *Times*. Thus, she was **an at-will employee who could be fired for refusing to breach her ethical obligations**. *Horn v. New York Times*, 760 N.Y.S.2d 378 (N.Y. 2003).

◆ A software company sent a recruit a letter offering him a base salary of $125,000 a year to be paid semi-monthly and also indicated that a bonus would be possible. The recruit signed the letter and returned it, then began working for the company. He subsequently signed a standard employment agreement, which stated that his employment was at will. Five months later, he was transferred to a new position, and a month after that he was fired. He sued the company for breach of contract, arguing that the offer letter limited the company's ability to terminate him. A Texas federal court ruled for the company, and the Fifth Circuit affirmed. **The offer letter did not provide a guarantee of employment** for one year, but rather stated the rate of pay the recruit would receive. It did not express a definite intent to be bound to a specific term of employment except for certain specified reasons. The breach of contract claim failed. *Hamilton v. Segue Software, Inc.*, 232 F.3d 473 (5th Cir. 2000).

◆ An Oklahoma regional manager of the corporation that ran Wendy's Restaurants in the state was shot by an employee in a Tulsa restaurant. He underwent brain surgery and then returned to work. However, he later asked to be demoted to store manager so that he could spend more time with his family. The corporation experienced problems with the manager – in particular, he had difficulty getting along with other employees. Further, he had had similar problems before the shooting. The corporation asked him to resign, which he did. He then sued it for breach of an implied contract. A jury awarded him $370,000. The Tenth Circuit Court of Appeals reversed, finding insufficient evidence that the corporation had made an implied promise to follow certain disciplinary procedures before firing him. First, **the handbook explicitly stated that it did not modify the company's "at-will" employment doctrine**, and it did not provide employees with any kind of contractual rights. Also, there was no evidence of separate consideration for an implied promise in a confidentiality agreement the manager had signed or in the length of time he had been employed by the company. *Bowen v. Income Producing Management of Oklahoma, Inc.*, 202 F.3d 1282 (10th Cir. 2000).

◆ An Ohio auto repair shop was legally entitled to discharge an at-will employee after the employee got into a heated argument with one of the shop's customers – an off-duty police officer. The employee argued that public policy prohibited the shop owner from firing him merely because it was afraid of repercussions from the officer and the officer's department. The Ohio Court of Appeals held that even though the shop owner fired the employee to avoid retaliation from the officer and his department, there was **no public policy against firing an at-will employee for angering a customer**. Had the employee been disciplined or discharged for a reason prohibited by statute, he would have been able to sue for wrongful discharge, but that was not the case here. *Sandoz v. Levine*, 1999 WL 179480 (Ohio Ct. App. 1999).

◆ The CEO of an Alabama company agreed to hire a computer specialist on a trial basis for 90 days. The CEO prepared a document detailing the specialist's salary, his bonuses and his benefits. The specialist then sold his house at a $19,000 loss and his furniture at a reduced price. He also incurred $1,800 in moving expenses and notified his clients that he was taking a new job and would no longer be able to work for them. The day before he was to start, he was told by the CEO that he was not getting the job. He sued for fraud and breach of an implied contract, but his lawsuit was dismissed when the CEO denied hiring him. The Alabama Court of Civil Appeals found that in an employment-at-will situation, a person may maintain an action for **fraud in the inducement of employment based on pre-employment representations**. Because of the document detailing the specialist's salary, bonuses and benefits, and because the CEO admitted that he agreed to a 90-day trial sales job, there were factual questions over whether the CEO had engaged in fraud, and that claim could proceed. However, because a prospective employee in an employment-at-will situation may not sue for breach of contract, that claim was dismissed. *Borum v. Alabama Inter-Forest Corp.*, 719 So.2d 851 (Ala. Civ. App. 1998).

◆ An Iowa food-processing company maintained a drug and alcohol policy that prohibited employees from bringing illegal drugs and look-alike substances onto work premises. An employee brought his girlfriend's asthma medication to work and was discharged under the policy. The employee then claimed that some of his former co-workers told him they had heard he was fired for drug possession. He sued the employer for negligent discharge and defamation. The Supreme Court of Iowa held that **negligent discharge was not an exception to the doctrine of employment at will**. The court also determined that there was insufficient evidence that the employer had communicated defamatory statements to the former employee's co-workers. Because publication is a necessary element of defamation and there had been none, the court ruled for the employer. *Huegerich v. IBP, Inc.*, 547 N.W.2d 216 (Iowa 1996).

◆ Goodyear Tire & Rubber Company enforced an anti-nepotism policy precluding any store manager from supervising a family member. One of the company's Texas stores nonetheless hired the brother of an employee, then trained and promoted him to store manager. The company's management was aware of the family relationship, but no attempt was made to enforce the anti-nepotism policy. Approximately 17 years after the brother was employed at his sister's store as her supervisor, the company determined that the arrangement was in violation of the anti-nepotism policy. After offering the sister a transfer, which she refused for personal reasons, the company fired her. She sued the company for wrongful termination. The Supreme Court of Texas noted that although Texas law presumes employment to be at will, **the at-will doctrine is subject to agreements to the contrary**. In this case, the company had fired the employee for the only reason it could not lawfully fire her. It had expressly waived the anti-nepotism policy as it applied to the sister. *Goodyear Tire & Rubber Co. v. Portilla*, 879 S.W.2d 47 (Tex. 1994).

II. EMPLOYEE HANDBOOKS

Employee handbooks and manuals are usually intended only as a guide for both employer and employee. Yet, these documents can modify at-will employment if they do not clearly state that they are nothing more than a guide.

Courts generally require an employer to conspicuously state that the handbook does not create an employment contract to avoid having the handbook construed as a contract. This means that the typeface must be in **bold letters** or CAPITAL LETTERS

or in a separate paragraph

or in some way stand out from the rest of the text of the manual.

Where the handbook is deemed to be a contract, any rights or procedures listed therein become "written" into the contract with the employee. Thus, if the handbook mentions progressive discipline, the employer might be forced to issue warnings and suspensions before firing an employee for misconduct.

A. Layoffs and Seniority

When seniority is addressed in employee handbooks, it should be discussed as a preference and not an entitlement. In other words, don't state that employees will be laid off in reverse order of seniority. Instead, state that seniority will be taken into account and a preference will be granted for senior employees.

◆ After 16 years as a driver for a company in Illinois, an employee was informed that his position was being eliminated due to budgetary issues. The employee sued for breach of contract, alleging he was wrongfully discharged because a less-senior employee was retained. **He asserted that the employee manual's seniority provisions required the company to terminate the other employee first.** The Appellate Court of Illinois disagreed. The manual did not constitute a contract between the parties. It contained a disclaimer stating that the manual was intended to serve as a general outline of company policy, and that it did not create a contract, express or implied. Thus, the seniority provisions of the manual did not require the company to terminate the other employee first. *Ivory v. Specialized Assistance Services, Inc.*, 365 Ill.App.3d 544, 850 N.E.2d 230 (Ill. App. Ct. 2006).

◆ A Massachusetts investment company employee was recruited to be a sales rep for the company, making him eligible for incentive compensation. Company policy at that time did not provide for the loss of incentive compensation upon termination. Later, the company issued a new handbook, which changed that policy, eliminating incentive compensation upon termination. The employee was then let go in a sales group restructuring. He received severance pay of $137,933, including a bonus of over $58,000. He nevertheless sued, claiming he was due incentive compensation after his discharge. The Appeals Court of Massachusetts disagreed. **The new handbook modified the incentive compensation agreement between the parties**, and the company properly fired him as part of a cost-cutting measure because he remained an at-will employee. *York v. Zurich Scudder Investments, Inc.*, 849 N.E.2d 892 (Mass. App. Ct. 2006).

◆ An airline in North Carolina hired a pilot and gave him a handbook addressing seniority, progressive discipline, and other terms and conditions of employment. It provided a three-step warning process for most offenses. When the pilot became unavailable for an assignment, he was not given progressive discipline, but was instead sent a termination letter. He sued the airline for breach of contract, alleging that it should have taken the seniority and progressive discipline provisions of the handbook into account. A federal court ruled for the airline, deciding that the handbook did not modify the at-will employment relationship. The **seniority and progressive discipline provisions did not imply that the airline could not fire the pilot** for an unspecified major infraction. Further, the pilot signed a document acknowledging that the employment was at will. He had been properly fired. *Norman v. Tradewinds Airlines, Inc.*, 286 F.Supp.2d 575 (M.D.N.C. 2003).

◆ A Michigan employer maintained an employment handbook declaring that employees would not be discharged without good cause. The employer later added disclaimer language to the handbook, stating that it did not constitute a contract of employment and that the employment relationship was at will. One longtime human resources employee, who had been hired prior to adoption of the handbook, claimed that her supervisor gave her a poor work evaluation after she refused to wear a dress to a company function. She was eventually laid off in a reduction in force while her male supervisor and several other younger, less senior males were retained. She sued the employer and supervisor for breach of contract and employment discrimination. The case reached the Supreme Court of Michigan, which noted that **the handbook policy did not overcome the presumption of employment at will**. It contained a specific disclaimer that no just-cause employment contract existed. The employee's discrimination claims also failed because she failed to prove that discrimination was a motivating factor in her layoff. The reduction in force had been based on economic factors. *Lytle v. Malady*, 579 N.W.2d 906 (Mich. 1998).

◆ A Wyoming mining company distributed employee handbooks to four supervisors, which stated that they could be terminated only for cause. The handbooks established 90-day probationary periods, after which an employee became "permanent," and stated that layoffs would generally be made in the reverse order of seniority. The employer later issued a series of handbooks that qualified these provisions by specifying that employment remained at will. It laid off the four supervisory employees while retaining some less experienced employees with better performance ratings. The supervisors sued for breach of contract, breach of an implied covenant of good faith and fair dealing and reliance upon the earlier handbooks. A federal court granted pretrial judgment to the employer, and the supervisors appealed.

The Tenth Circuit Court of Appeals observed that while Wyoming law presumes employment is at will, a handbook may alter this presumption if its terms reasonably **create an expectation that the employee will be fired only for just cause**. Here, the handbooks were sufficiently ambiguous to prevent pretrial judgment on the issue of whether they reasonably created an expectation that there would be no dismissals without cause and that the company would perform layoffs by seniority. Later handbooks could not modify a contract implied from an earlier employee handbook, if such a contract existed. The court reversed the pretrial judgment order on the breach of contract claim, but ruled that there was no covenant of good faith and fair dealing in employment under Wyoming law. This claim was dismissed along with the employees' claim for reliance. *McIlravy v. Kerr-McGee Corp.*, 119 F.3d 876 (10th Cir. 1997).

B. Progressive Disciplinary Policies

Progressive discipline should be addressed as an option that the employer reserves. It should not be the only possible way to discipline an employee. Thus, the handbook could state that:

> the employer reserves the right to discipline any employee for violating company rules and policies, and can take disciplinary action up to and including employment termination for any such violation.

◆ A company hired a pension benefits manager as a salaried employee and gave her a copy of the employee handbook, which contained a termination section for hourly and nonexempt employees (which she was not). The handbook noted that warnings normally were given before an employee was fired. When the manager was terminated without warning for what her supervisors perceived was poor performance, she sued for breach of contract, among other claims. The case reached the South Carolina Court of Appeals, which noted that the handbook did not apply to the manager. And even if it did, **nothing in the handbook outlined progressive disciplinary procedures in mandatory terms**. Finally, even if the company gave other salaried employees a warning before firing them, it was not required to do the same for the manager. At-will employment was presumed and no disclaimer was needed in the handbook. *Grant v. Mount Vernon Mills, Inc.*, 370 S.C. 138, 634 S.E.2d 15 (S.C. Ct. App. 2006).

◆ A company in Vermont had a personnel manual that described progressive discipline and just cause termination policies for employee misconduct. It stated that two written warnings would be given before termination. When the company experienced an economic slowdown, it attempted to reorganize, and one employee resisted changes a new manager tried to institute. She received a letter of reprimand from the company's president, but the letter stated that it was not a disciplinary warning. A month later she was fired. She sued, claiming breach of an implied contract that she would only be fired for just cause after progressive discipline. The Vermont Supreme Court held that **the letter of reprimand established the company's intent to abide by its progressive discipline policy**. Even though the employee could have been laid off for economic reasons without progressive discipline, she was fired for insubordination. *Havill v. Woodstock Soapstone Co.*, 865 A.2d 335 (Vt. 2004).

◆ A 55-year-old manager of a company in Massachusetts claimed that he was improperly fired. He asserted that he should have been progressively disciplined under the employee handbook and the "Guide to Corporate Conduct." He claimed that the real reason for the termination was age discrimination. The company argued that the manager attempted to misuse company property for his personal benefit; that he retaliated against another employee who refused to cooperate in that misuse; and that he had an abusive management style. The First Circuit Court of Appeals held that **the manager was not entitled to progressive discipline**. Nothing in the handbook or the guide promised progressive discipline. And even if the company generally applied progressive discipline to its employees, there was never any such policy for management. *Joyal v. Hasbro, Inc.*, 380 F.3d 14 (1st Cir. 2004).

◆ A Michigan hospital fired an ICU nurse for putting other staff in life-threatening danger. It believed she was trying to discharge the current on a defibrillator before telling other members of the hospital's ICU department to stand clear. An arbitrator found that the nurse was not going to discharge the current, but was just attempting to turn the defibrillator on. As such, the arbitrator concluded **her mistake, although negligent, was not "gross neglect,"** as the hospital claimed. The collective bargaining agreement in place identified two levels of discipline, the first warranting suspension for careless conduct and the second warranting discharge for gross neglect or abuse of a patient. In light of a previous reprimand, the arbitrator ordered the nurse to be reinstated with a six-month suspension. The hospital appealed, and the U.S. Court of Appeals, Sixth Circuit, held that the arbitrator did not exceed his authority. Nor did the arbitrator's order violate Michigan's public policy of ensuring safe and competent nursing care. The arbitrator did not order the hospital to reinstate her to the same department but gave it the flexibility of placing her in a less dangerous position and providing whatever training it deemed appropriate. *MidMichigan Regional Medical Center v. Professional Employees Local 79*, 183 F.3d 497 (6th Cir. 1999).

◆ An Iowa health care center administrator had a poor working relationship with her supervisor. She believed that the supervisor wanted her to withhold information from an auditor. The supervisor allegedly told the center's owners that she would quit unless they fired the administrator. The center fired the administrator without warning for lack of leadership and inability to provide continuity. She obtained unemployment compensation benefits and then sued the center and its owners for breach of contract and intentional interference with her employment contract. The court awarded compensatory and punitive damages to the administrator and held that the owners were jointly liable for compensatory damages and individually responsible for punitive damages. The Supreme Court of Iowa affirmed, finding that the language of the center's employee handbook was sufficiently definite to create an employment contract. The administrator had a **right to receive notice of any deficiencies in her performance under the handbook's progressive disciplinary policy**. Because the employer had failed to follow these procedures, the breach of contract action was appropriate. Corporate officers or directors may be held personally liable if they fail to act in good faith to protect the interests of the corporation. Here, the employment contract had been terminated because of the administrator's failure to perform an illegal act in violation of public policy, and the owners were liable for the damage award. *Jones v. Lake Park Care Center, Inc.*, 569 N.W.2d 369 (Iowa 1997).

◆ A New Jersey maintenance mechanic worked for a large manufacturing company that had distributed an employment manual containing a four-step disciplinary policy. The company found some of its property in the mechanic's locker and fired him for theft, one of several grounds listed for immediate dismissal. The mechanic sued the employer, claiming that it had violated the disciplinary procedure in the manual. The court granted the employer pretrial judgment, finding that the manual did not create an implied employment contract. The appeals court reversed. The Supreme Court of New Jersey stated that **an employment manual that fails to include a clear and prominent disclaimer may create an enforceable contract** even when the employment is otherwise terminable at will. If the manual is sufficiently definite to raise the reasonable expectations of employees concerning job security provisions, the provisions may be construed as contractual promises. The case was reversed and remanded to the trial court to decide whether the manual created a reasonable expectation of job security that formed an implied employment contract. The jury was then to determine whether the mechanic was guilty of stealing or unauthorized possession of company property. *Witkowski v. Thomas J. Lipton, Inc.*, 136 N.J. 385, 643 A.2d 546 (N.J. 1994).

◆ A Utah metallurgical engineer worked for over 15 years for a mining company in several different positions. He eventually got a substandard rating and was told that he had one last chance to redeem himself. The company then fired him for inadequate performance without providing progressive discipline, notice, a hearing or other protections. He claimed that the company policy in effect at the time of his hiring was applicable and required a written warning and a suspension or hearing for disciplinary purposes. He claimed that the policy constituted a contract that replaced the presumption of at-will employment. He sued the company in a Utah trial court, which held for the company. The engineer appealed.

The Court of Appeals of Utah observed that employment in the state is presumed to be at will and that overcoming this presumption requires showing a definite communication by the employer to the employee that a contract exists under different terms. The company policy referred to by the engineer had been **replaced with a policy that did not call for progressive discipline or other protections**. The most recent employee policy was applicable, not the original one. The current handbook language called for hearings for disciplinary offenses, but not in cases of insufficient performance, which was the cause of termination here. The court affirmed the decision for the employer. *Sorenson v. Kennecott-Utah Copper Corp.*, 873 P.2d 1141 (Utah App. 1994).

C. Handbook Terms

Disclaimers need to be clearly stated. If you want to ensure that your handbook is not a contract, plainly state that in bold or larger type on the first page of the handbook. Or consider distributing a separate sheet for employees to sign, indicating that they received a copy of the handbook and agreeing that it does not change the at-will nature of the job.

The optimal handbook contains language that is clear and understandable to employees, yet provides the flexibility the employer needs to run the business without constraints on seniority, discipline, etc.

◆ A company in Indiana created an employee handbook with a chapter on family and medical care leave even though it did not have enough employees to be eligible for coverage under the FMLA. The handbook offered similar benefits to those available under the FMLA. When an employee took unpaid leave and was replaced by another employee, he sued the company for violating the FMLA as well as for promissory estoppel (alleging that he reasonably relied, to his detriment, on a promise to provide benefits). A federal court granted pretrial judgment to the company, but the Seventh Circuit reversed. It found questions of fact over whether the handbook created a binding contract, and also determined that **the handbook gave rise to a cause of action for promissory estoppel**. It remanded the case for further proceedings. *Peters v. Gilead Sciences, Inc.*, 533 F.3d 594 (7th Cir. 2008).

◆ A Hispanic field supervisor for a company with an office in Wyoming lost out on a promotion and had a new manager remove from the office some of the equipment he used to provide oilfield services. He suspected his days were numbered and quit, then sued for racial harassment and breach of contract, among other claims. He asserted that the employee manual created a contract that promised continued employment and **cited the job security provision of the manual**, wherein the company stated that it made "every effort to provide continuous employment." It also stated: "An individual employee can increase his job security by increasing his knowledge and skills. The more knowledge and skill you acquire, the more productive you are likely to be, and naturally the more productive, the better your chance for stable employment." However, the Tenth Circuit noted that those provisions did not promise continued employment. The court allowed the racial harassment claim to proceed but not the breach of contract action. *Herrera v. Lufkin Industries, Inc.*, 474 F.3d 675 (10th Cir. 2007).

◆ The director of a shelter for battered women in South Carolina called the executive director to inform her that no one was operating the hotline but refused to tell the executive director who had given her that information. The executive director suspended her for insubordination, doubled her duties, then fired her when she refused to accept them. She sued for breach of contract, claiming the employee handbook altered the at-will nature of the employment and that she had been fired in violation of its nondiscrimination provision. The handbook stated that the shelter reserved the right to terminate an employee at any time if the executive director believed it was in the shelter's best interests. The Supreme Court of South Carolina ruled that **the handbook did not create contractual rights because of the disclaimer**. The director was not fired in violation of the nondiscrimination provision. *Hessenthaler v. Tri-County Sister Help, Inc.*, 616 S.E.2d 694 (S.C. 2005).

◆ A Texas company distributed a handbook stating that employees who tested positive for drugs on a first offense would be referred to rehabilitation. However, the handbook also stated that employment was at will, that employees could be fired for any reason (including use of illicit drugs), and that the handbook was not designed to be a contract. When a supervisor was fired after testing positive for marijuana, he sued the company for wrongful discharge. The Texas Court of Appeals held that his claim could not succeed. The disclaimers in the handbook clearly stated that it did not alter the at-will employment relationship. Also, **the employee could not show that he reasonably relied on a promise to refer him to rehabilitation** because 1) he knew the employment was at will and 2) he admitted to using marijuana. *Murphy v. Gulf States Toyota, Inc.*, 2001 WL 619557 (Tex. Ct. App. 2001).

◆ An Indiana employee of United Parcel Service (UPS) was demoted. He sued for breach of contract, maintaining that the employee handbook stated that company policy was that employees would not be demoted without just cause. The company asserted that it had placed a disclaimer in the handbook stating that the handbook did not create a contract of employment. The disclaimer further stated that the handbook gave the employee no rights. The case reached the Seventh Circuit Court of Appeals, which held in favor of UPS. It rejected the notion (adopted by Oklahoma and Alaska) that in addition to stating that the handbook did not create a contract, it also had to state that the employee could be terminated at the will of the employer. Here, **the disclaimer was sufficient to inform the employee that the handbook did not create a contract**. Nor could the employee use the doctrine of promissory estoppel (detrimental reliance) because it was not reasonable for him to rely on the statement that he would not be demoted without cause. *Workman v. United Parcel Service,* 234 F.3d 998 (7th Cir. 2000).

◆ A nurse who worked in the intensive care unit of a Wisconsin hospital was discharged after telling a supervisor that she was not going to return to work following a lunch-time doctor's appointment. Prior to the appointment, the nurse had received five disciplinary warnings. She sued for wrongful discharge/breach of contract in a state court, which dismissed her claims. The Court of Appeals of Wisconsin affirmed, noting that although the handbook in place at the time the nurse was hired provided that discipline could only be for just cause upon completion of the probationary period, the updated handbook contained a specific disclaimer that it did not create any employment contractual rights. Here, the nurse had signed an acknowledgement form for the earlier handbook, which stated that she understood it to be "a working guide of policies, rights and responsibilities for [hospital] employees." The form also stated that the handbook did not "replace or supercede original hospital policies," and that hospital **policies, practices and procedures were subject to change at the sole discretion of management**. This language did not alter the at-will relationship. Moreover, the updated handbook clearly reserved the hospital's right to amend or delete any provisions at any time, without advance notice. *Helland v. Froedtert Memorial Lutheran Hospital*, 601 N.W.2d 318 (Wis. Ct. App. 1999).

- A hospital implemented a new employee handbook that changed the discipline procedure. Under the old handbook, discharge could only be for cause, and the third reprimand an employee received would result in automatic dismissal. Under the new handbook, a "flexible" progressive disciplinary procedure was established. Shortly after the new handbook was in place, a nurse's supervisor filled out three performance reports based on three different complaints from patients' family members. She then recommended termination, stating that "the third reprimand results in automatic dismissal." The nurse sued for wrongful discharge. A jury ruled for the nurse. The Vermont Supreme Court affirmed. **Because the supervisor's report recommending termination mirrored language used in the old handbook, there was an ambiguity as to which handbook ought to be used.** Further, the new handbook was unclear as to what the progressive disciplinary procedure was. Finally, the new handbook had been in effect only four months when the nurse was fired. *Trombley v. Southwestern Vermont Medical Center*, 738 A.2d 103 (Vt. 1999).

- An Arizona resort distributed an employment manual reciting that it maintained an at-will relationship with its employees. The manual prohibited the use, possession or sale of illegal drugs and called for immediate termination in such a case. Each employee had to sign an acknowledgment of the employer's drug-free workplace policy and agree to take a drug test at any time subject to discipline including discharge. When the employer's general manager learned that five employees had recently used drugs on company grounds, he attempted to transport them to a test site. Four refused to take the test. The manager fired them, and they sued for breach of contract, invasion of privacy, and other alleged legal violations. The court ruled for the employer, and the employees appealed to the Court of Appeals of Arizona, asserting that their firing violated public policy (the state constitution's personal right to privacy). The court disagreed, stating that while the government was required to refrain from invasions of personal privacy, the constitution did not protect individuals from the actions of private actors. The court also rejected the breach of contract claims since **the employment manual conspicuously notified employees that the employment relationship was at will**. The court affirmed the judgment. *Hart v. Seven Resorts Inc.*, 947 P.2d 846 (Ariz. Ct. App. 1997).

- A Tennessee airline maintenance supervisor complained in writing to two corporate officers about alleged unpaid wages. The letters indicated that he was preparing to present information to the media about unidentified company practices, but it failed to specify any actual violations of law. The employer then conducted an unannounced audit of a petty cash fund controlled by the supervisor and found that he had mismanaged it. It fired him, and he sued for retaliatory discharge in violation of a state law prohibiting discharge for refusing to remain silent about illegal activities. The court ruled for the employer. On appeal, the supervisor claimed that the employer's handbook contained a contractual promise to work with employees to help them correct their performance deficiencies. He also asserted that the employer had falsified functional checks of company aircraft oxygen pressure systems and that he had been preparing to report this to the Federal Aviation Administration (FAA). The Court of Appeals of Tennessee held that **the employee handbook contained a specific reservation of the employer's right to discharge employees** and declared that the employment relationship remained at will. There was no support for the supervisor's retaliatory discharge theory, since he made no report to the FAA, his letters mentioned no illegal activity, and the letters focused mainly on his claim for unpaid wages. The court affirmed the ruling for the employer. *Robins v. Flagship Airlines, Inc.*, 956 S.W.2d 4 (Tenn. Ct. App. 1997).

◆ An Iowa grocery store's management received reports that the night stock crew was eating food without paying for it. A private investigator interviewed the employees, and the leader of the night crew wrote out a statement indicating that during his employment he had eaten about $20 worth of food that he would be willing to pay for. He was fired anyway. He then filed a breach of contract lawsuit. The court ruled for the grocery store. The crew leader appealed to the Supreme Court of Iowa, claiming that the employee handbook created an express contract of employment. The grocery store argued that the employment was at will and that the crew leader was subject to discharge at any time for any reason, or no reason at all. Here, **throughout the handbook, the employer had placed clauses that retained its right to terminate the employment relationship at any time**. Further, the crew leader had signed a receipt for a copy of the handbook that stated: "I recognize that either [the store] or I may terminate the employment relationship at any time for any reason." Thus, the handbook did not create a contract and the court upheld the ruling for the store. *French v. Foods, Inc.*, 495 N.W.2d 768 (Iowa 1993).

III. BREACH OF CONTRACT

Breach of contract complaints arise under both oral and written employment contracts, often where the employee claims that an oral promise or language contained in an employee handbook has modified the presumption of employment at will. Resolution of these cases involves an examination of the agreement between the parties.

A. Written Contracts

When a straightforward written employment contract exists, any dispute is generally resolved by looking at the language it contains. However:

—some written contracts are modified by oral agreement,
—some employee handbooks modify the terms of at-will employment, and
—some employment relationships are governed by a writing only in part.

For example, there may be a drug-testing agreement or a non-compete agreement but no other writings to memorialize the employment relationship. In such a case, the writing generally modifies the at-will relationship only to the extent that the situation pertains to the writing.

- An Arkansas employee signed an employment agreement that guaranteed her 36 months of employment. If the company fired her without just cause as set out in the handbook before that time, she would be entitled to $5,000. If she quit before the 36 months, she would have to pay $5,000. The company fired her two months later and she sued it for wrongful discharge. A trial court found no just cause for the termination because the term "insubordination" was not defined in the handbook. He awarded her $5,000, but the Court of Appeals of Arkansas reversed. The employee angrily confronted the president after he asked her to go to the office, get a key out of the safe and put it on her desk for another employee to pick up. A few days later, she grew belligerent when he talked to her and other employees about a form that was supposed to be placed in files. This was **insubordination justifying the discharge**. *Magic Touch Corp. v. Hicks*, 260 S.W.3d 322 (Ark. Ct. App. 2007).

- A Mississippi hospital hired an emergency room doctor under a one-year employment contract. The contract contained a provision allowing either party to terminate the employment without cause upon 60 days' notice. It also allowed the hospital to terminate the doctor's employment at any time for cause (as defined by the hospital). When the hospital fired the doctor because of patient complaints about rude and obnoxious behavior and insensitivity, the doctor sued for wrongful termination and breach of contract. The Court of Appeals of Mississippi held that **the contract between the doctor and hospital, although ostensibly for one year, actually created an at-will employment relationship**. Thus, the breach of contract action failed. *Miranda v. Wesley Health System, LLC*, 949 So.2d 63 (Miss. Ct. App. 2006).

- A regional account director for an advertising agency was offered a management supervisor position in the company's Los Angeles office and received a three-page letter stating the terms of the offer. The letter also explained the 90-day assessment period and explained that the employment was at will, meaning the company could terminate his employment "at any time," just as he could quit at any time. He signed and returned the letter, then was fired two years later. He sued for breach of contract, claiming that by oral representations, conduct and documents, the company had led him to understand that although he could be fired at any time, he could only be fired for cause. The case reached the Supreme Court of California, which held that **even though the letter did not state that the employee could be fired "without cause," it was not ambiguous**. It did not have to state whether cause was required for termination. The breach of contract claim failed. *Dore v. Arnold Worldwide, Inc.*, 39 Cal.4th 384, 139 P.3d 56 (Cal. 2006).

- An applicant for a sales position took detailed notes about salary and bonuses for the next three years at a meeting with the company president and a branch manager. After the meeting, at the top of the page, he and the branch manager wrote the words, "contract with [company]" and they both signed it. The president did not sign the page. When the salesman was fired during the first year of his employment, he sued for breach of contract. A federal court granted pretrial judgment to the company, but the Eighth Circuit Court of Appeal reversed, finding **issues of fact over whether the notes amounted to an enforceable contract**. Here, there was enough ambiguity in the notes (as to whether the company intended to offer three years of employment) such that a jury would have to consider them. *Baum v. Helget Gas Products, Inc.*, 440 F.3d 1019 (8th Cir. 2006).

◆ A doctor in Vermont entered into a written contract with a physicians' group. The contract allowed for termination "with or without cause" 180 days after written notice was provided. The doctor refused to refer patients to certain specialists in the group because he believed they provided substandard or unnecessary care. When the group decided to close the office out of which the doctor worked, it sent him a termination notice. It ultimately kept the office open, retaining a less senior doctor. He sued for breach of contract based on the implied covenant of good faith and fair dealing, as well as wrongful discharge in violation of public policy. The Vermont Supreme Court held that the doctor could proceed with his wrongful discharge claim despite the "with or without cause" provision of the contract. **Public policy could supersede the written termination provision.** *LoPresti v. Rutland Regional Health Services, Inc.*, 865 A.2d 1102 (Vt. 2004).

◆ A married couple entered into a contract with a property management company to act as 24-hour managers of a Wisconsin motel. The contract provided that after the first year, it would become a year-to-year contract and that either party could furnish the other with a 90-day termination notice. The contract also required the company to furnish the couple with health and accident insurance and living quarters. They managed the motel for over two years, at which time the company abruptly terminated the contract. Afterward, the couple moved back to the house they owned, but they went without health insurance for the rest of the year. They sued for breach of contract, and a jury awarded them $14,000 in lost wages and lodging costs for the rest of the year. It did not award them the costs of health insurance. They appealed. The company also appealed, claiming that the damages should have been limited to the 90-day notice period. The Court of Appeals of Wisconsin held that the contract demonstrated **the parties' intent to have a yearlong agreement automatically renewable** unless one of the parties provided a 90-day termination notice. With respect to health insurance, the couple suffered an economic loss when the contract was breached. The court granted the couple health insurance benefits for the rest of the year. *Becker v. Aramia I, Ltd.*, 600 N.W.2d 54 (Wis. Ct. App. 1999) (Unpublished).

◆ A Texas software developer sold his business to a corporation, which agreed to employ him as an officer for five years at a guaranteed annual salary of $80,000. Before the end of the first year, the officer sought a loan of $18,000 from the corporation, which it agreed to after insisting upon an amendment of the employment agreement to include loan default as a ground for termination. The officer failed to pay the loan when it came due and requested an extension. The corporation fired him and refused to pay him over three years of salary still due under the contract. The officer sued the corporation for breach of contract, asserting that the retention of his salary constituted interest on the loan and that the amount was enough to violate state usury law. The corporation counterclaimed for fraud and breach of contract. The court awarded the officer over $1 million in usury penalties plus additional amounts for breach of contract and attorneys' fees. The Supreme Court of Texas found that unpaid salary could not be characterized as interest due to the uncertainty of its value. It rejected the officer's claim that an employer always stands to gain by discharging an employee who will not pay a debt owed to the employer. The loss of the employee's services may exceed the amount of debt. **Because the unpaid salary was not interest, the officer was not entitled to usury penalties**, and the court reversed the judgment. *First USA Management, Inc. v. Esmond*, 960 S.W.2d 625 (Tex. 1997).

- An Oklahoma supervisor was reprimanded for sexually harassing a secretary. He was also instructed to apologize and participate in an alcohol treatment program. When he later made sexual comments to the secretary, she sued the employer for sexual harassment and creation of a hostile work environment. The employer further disciplined the supervisor and later fired him. He began working as an independent contractor and obtained a work assignment involving his former employer. The secretary complained when she learned of the assignment, and he was then removed from the project. He responded by suing his former employer for breach of contract and negligent investigation of the sexual harassment claim.

The court ruled for the employer, and the U.S. Court of Appeals, Tenth Circuit, affirmed. According to the court, the presumption of employment at will cannot be overcome unless an employee demonstrates that the **employer's representations place substantive restrictions on its power to discharge**. The former supervisor was unable to show that certain employment documents, including the disciplinary letter he received, constituted a contract of employment that placed substantive restrictions on the employer's ability to discharge him. The breach of contract claim therefore failed. The court also held for the employer on the claim of negligent investigation of sexual harassment. Negligent investigation is not a recognized legal cause of action in Oklahoma. There also was insufficient evidence that the employer had interfered with his employment as an independent contractor. *Vice v. Conoco, Inc.*, 150 F.3d 1286 (10th Cir. 1998).

- A South Carolina employer hired a sales rep with oral assurances of job security and a guarantee that he would not be fired without just cause. The parties agreed in writing that the sales rep would receive copies of written reprimands and that three or more reprimands could be considered cause for termination. Several years later, he had to sign a new employment agreement establishing a new commission formula and reciting that he was an employee at will. The sales rep's performance became the subject of two meetings, at which he was told to improve his performance or be fired. He received only one written reprimand, which was never placed in his personnel file, and was then fired without further warning. He sued and was awarded over $70,000, including an amount for severance pay. The employer appealed to the Supreme Court of South Carolina, arguing that the sales rep could not rely upon his original employment agreement and that it no longer created a binding contract. The court disagreed. **The employer could not deviate from its promise to follow its own employment procedures.** It had breached the contract by failing to give the sales rep three written warnings and place them in his personnel file. Even if the employer made a valid change in the employment contract, it had modified that contract by providing a first written warning as required by the original contract. The court affirmed the judgment for the sales rep. *King v. PYA/Monarch, Inc.*, 453 S.E.2d 885 (S.C. 1995).

◆ An Illinois executive for a company that was acquired by an international corporation worked under a contract that paid him approximately double what executives of the international corporation were paid. When he was informed of the salary discrepancy, he indicated that he was not willing to renegotiate. **His contract required a three-year notice of termination, unless he was guilty of some misconduct** or breach of contract. The corporation orally informed him of its intent to give him a three-year notice of termination. While the written notice of termination was being prepared, allegations of sexual harassment against the employee surfaced. Upon further investigation, he was fired for "misconduct." He sued for breach of contract, and a federal court ruled for the corporation. The Seventh Circuit Court of Appeals affirmed, holding that the corporation had not breached the employment contract because there was detailed evidence of sexually harassing behavior that was serious enough to be "misconduct" under the contract provisions. *Scherer v. Rockwell Int'l Corp.*, 975 F.2d 356 (7th Cir. 1992).

B. Oral Contracts

In the absence of a written employment contract, the employment relationship is governed by statutory and common law principles, including the presumption of employment at will. Oral statements are less likely to be construed as creating a contract than writings, but where they are sufficiently definite, they can alter the at-will nature of employment.

One problem with oral contracts is the statute of frauds, which states that no oral contract is enforceable if, by its terms, it is not capable of being performed within a year. So an oral contract for three years is not enforceable under the statute of frauds.

Another problem is the likelihood of confusion or disagreement as to the contract's terms. Without a sufficiently clear writing, the contract is subject to the parties' memories. For example, what one party perceives as a guarantee of employment might be perceived by the other side as a mere statement of intent.

◆ A company unilaterally instituted a management security (no-layoff) policy. Four years later, the company notified its managers that industry conditions could force it to discontinue the program. After nearly another two years, the company announced that it was going to discontinue the program in six months. It offered a severance package to managers affected by the new layoff policy. Sixty former managers sued the company for breach of contract, claiming that it could not end the no-layoff policy unless it could show that there had been a change materially affecting its business plan. The California Supreme Court ruled that **because the company had unilaterally instituted the program, it could unilaterally end the program** so long as the termination occurred after a reasonable period of time and the company provided reasonable notice of the change. Here, after the change, the managers continued to work for the company, signifying their acceptance of the change. No further consideration was needed to support the modified contract. *Asmus v. Pacific Bell*, 999 P.2d 71 (Cal. 2000).

1. Oral Representations

Employers often make statements to employees about an intent to keep the employees around for a long period of time, either to reassure the employees or to motivate them. The statements are seldom meant to be construed as enforceable promises. Yet, employees often take them that way.

So if you're going to make those kinds of statements, keep them as vague as possible and make sure your employees know that they continue to be at-will employees.

◆ The principals of a real estate company interviewed a candidate for its presidency and asked if he would be willing to make a long-term commitment to the company. He agreed to make a 10-year commitment and they allegedly agreed to employ him for 10 years. They gave him an offer letter with his salary, starting date and benefits, but which was silent as to the term of employment. He sold his townhouse in Florida and moved to Washington, D.C., where he bought a $1.9 million penthouse to serve as a residence and facility for entertaining clients. Within a year the relationship soured and the president was fired. He sued for breach of contract. A federal court refused to grant pretrial judgment to the company. Although the 10-year oral contract was ostensibly barred by the statute of frauds, the company might be equitably estopped from asserting the statute of frauds as a defense. Here, **the president presented evidence that he reasonably relied on the principals' oral representations to his detriment** by selling his home and purchasing a penthouse. A jury would have to decide the outcome. *Morris v. Buvermo Properties, Inc.*, 510 F.Supp.2d 112 (D.D.C. 2007).

◆ A financial director for a company was contacted by a headhunter for another company and agreed to head up a division devoted to computer fraud and forensic investigation. He was told that he would be employed for as long as it took to build the department and as long as he desired. He took the job and was fired two months later. When he sued for breach of an oral contract, his lawsuit was dismissed. The Appellate Court of Illinois affirmed the ruling for the company. Here, **the promise of employment was not sufficiently clear and definite to overcome the presumption that the employment was at will**. Further, the promises were not unambiguous offers of permanent employment such that the employee could claim promissory estoppel (detrimental reliance on a promise by another). *Robinson v. BDO Seidman, LLP*, 854 N.E.2d 767 (Ill. App. Ct. 2006).

◆ A Connecticut company employed a husband and wife in high-level positions, then underwent a reorganization and fired the husband. The wife expressed concern to an executive vice president (VP) regarding how her employment would be affected if her husband accepted a job with a competitor. **The VP promised that the company would take no adverse action against her if her husband got a job with a competitor.** When the husband landed such a job, the company reduced her duties, limited her client contact, and asked her to agree to restrictive obligations in relation to her husband's job. When she refused, she was fired. She sued, and a jury ruled in her favor, awarding her $850,000. The Connecticut Supreme Court affirmed. Even though the company had not contractually agreed not to take adverse action, it had promised not to do so, and the wife had justifiably relied on that promise. Thus, her promissory estoppel claim was actionable. *Stewart v. Cendant Mobility Services Corp.*, 837 A.2d 736 (Conn. 2003).

◆ The president of an Ohio electronics company told one of his account executives that he was going to be the president's "right-hand guy" for a long, long time. He also indicated that they were going to have many other ventures together and asked the executive to "look at this five, ten years from now." Subsequently, he fired the executive and a colleague following accusations of sexual harassment. They sued for breach of contract, asserting that either an implied or an express contract of employment existed to prevent the firing. The Ohio Court of Appeals found that **the president's statements did not modify the at-will nature of the employment**. The statements he had made were not specific promises but rather sweeping comments about the future. He never represented that the executive and his colleague were secure in their jobs regardless of their workplace conduct, and there was no dispute that misconduct had occurred. Since their employment had been at will, their breach of contract lawsuit failed. *Daup v. Tower Cellular, Inc.*, 737 N.E.2d 128 (Ohio Ct. App. 2000).

◆ A South Carolina telephone company employee was suspended for improperly disposing of company property. He asserted that he had disposed of the property according to the instructions of a company official, but the company fired him for lying. The employee appealed the decision through the company's progressive appeal process until the company's general manager affirmed the discharge. He then sued for breach of contract based on the employee handbook and alleged **statements by company officials that he would be discharged only for good cause such as misconduct**. The Supreme

Court of South Carolina held that the employer's alleged offer stating that the employee would have his job as long as he kept his nose clean and did his job was not sufficiently explicit to constitute an offer to limit termination to just cause. Thus, his at-will employment status was not altered. *Prescott v. Farmers Telephone Co-op., Inc.*, 516 S.E.2d 923 (S.C. 1999).

◆ An Indiana newspaper employee was granted sick leave of up to five months on three separate occasions for knee surgery. His doctor then told him he needed a total knee replacement. He asked for three months leave and allegedly obtained a promise from his supervisor that he could have leave for as long as needed. However, after the surgery, he notified the employer that he would need more than three months. The supervisor advised him that he would be fired if he did not return to work in three months. When the employee did not receive a release from his physician to return to work until six months after the surgery, he was fired. He sued, and an Indiana court dismissed his case, ruling that the alleged oral employment contract was unenforceable and that he could not show detrimental reliance on the promise of indefinite leave. The Supreme Court of Indiana affirmed the **dismissal of the oral contract claim**. With respect to the claim that he reasonably relied on his supervisor's promise, any lost wage claim would be limited to those wages accruing between the date of actual termination and the date of the employee's release to return to work, less any disability benefits received. *Jarboe v. Landmark Community Newspapers of Indiana, Inc.*, 644 N.E.2d 118 (Ind. 1994).

◆ A plastics manufacturer hired an executive under an oral agreement for a fixed first-year salary and bonus, with bonuses in future years to be based on company profits. The parties did not discuss the duration of employment or what constituted just cause for dismissal. Within four months, the relationship between the executive and the owner became so bad that the executive was fired. He sued for breach of contract, wrongful discharge, negligent misrepresentation and several other alleged legal violations. The court awarded over $400,000 for breach of contract and promissory estoppel, a legal doctrine used in the absence of a contract but where the complaining party allegedly relies on promises by the defendant. The court of appeals reversed, and the executive appealed. The Supreme Court of Washington found insufficient evidence to support the executive's claim that the company had promised him employment beyond one year. **Statements made during the interview process did not constitute clear or definite promises of permanent employment** or guarantee against dismissal except for just cause. The executive was, however, entitled to damages for breach of contract and severance pay of approximately $92,000. *Havens v. C & D Plastics, Inc.*, 876 P.2d 435 (Wash. 1994).

2. Covenant of Good Faith and Fair Dealing

In every employment relationship, there is a duty of good faith and fair dealing – even in at-will employment relationships. Employees have a duty of loyalty to the company, and employers have a duty to comply with the terms of the employment contract in good faith.

◆ A lighting products company in Virginia had an employee handbook that notified employees they were not allowed outside employment that conflicted with the company's interests. The handbook also addressed confidential information, although the company did not require employees to sign confidentiality or noncompete agreements. While working for the company, a manager created a competing business and used a company computer to seek legal advice. When he quit, he deleted e-mails, spreadsheets and files from his computer. A forensic computer expert recovered the material on the hard drive. The manager also encouraged two sales reps who were independent contractors to send business to his new company. The old company sued the former manager and two former sales reps for breach of fiduciary duty. A jury awarded the company $1.5 million in compensatory damages and $56,700 in punitive damages. The Supreme Court of Virginia upheld the award for the company, finding that the manager and sales reps breached their duty of loyalty to the company. **Even though the sales reps were independent contractors, they received exclusive territories in exchange for an expectation of loyalty.** *Banks v. Mario Industries of Virginia, Inc.*, 650 S.E.2d 687 (Va. 2007).

◆ An employee of an Illinois-based commercial real estate developer used a company laptop to identify properties to acquire and assist with acquisitions. When he quit to start his own business, he deleted all the data he had collected and also downloaded a secure-erasure program to write over the deleted files to prevent anyone else from recovering them. The company sued him for breach of contract and for violating the Computer Fraud and Abuse Act (CFAA). A federal court dismissed the lawsuit, but the Seventh Circuit reinstated it. **The CFAA prohibits knowingly transmitting a program or command to intentionally damage a protected computer without authorization.** Here, the allegation in the lawsuit was that he had done just that. *Int'l Airport Centers, LLC v. Citrin*, 440 F.3d 418 (7th Cir. 2006).

◆ A food products company employed a salaried traffic manager to arrange for transportation of its products to stores. During the course of his employment, the manager and his wife formed a company through which they arranged for the transportation of goods for various companies, including two of the company's competitors. Although the manager's wife ran the business out of their home, the manager spent about 15 minutes during each workday on his business. The company fired the manager three years later for failing to conduct inspections of its off-site warehouses and negotiate lower freight rates. It then learned of his home business and sued him in state court for conversion (similar to theft) and breach of his duty of loyalty. The trial court dismissed the complaint. The Appellate Division reversed and remanded for a new trial on the breach of duty claim. The New Jersey Supreme Court then held that **the manager's actions in spending 15 minutes a day on his home business might amount to a breach of the duty of loyalty he owed the company**. On remand, the court would have to determine whether the manager's assistance to the company's competitors was substantial. If so, the company would be entitled to relief. *Cameco, Inc. v. Gedicke*, 724 A.2d 783 (N.J. 1999).

◆ A Colorado employer fired a route supervisor for falsifying time cards. The supervisor sued for failing to follow progressive disciplinary policy, breach of an express covenant of good faith and fair dealing, and other claims. The court awarded damages for breach of contract, plus punitive and noneconomic damages. The case reached the Supreme Court of Colorado, which **refused to recognize a tort claim for breach of the covenant of good faith and fair dealing in employment** but found that the breach of contract action was viable due to the employer's misconduct. Thus, economic and noneconomic damages were available, but punitive damages were not. *Decker v. Browning-Ferris Industries of Colorado, Inc.*, 947 P.2d 937 (Colo. 1997).

◆ A medical imaging technologist employed by a Delaware chemical corporation became aware of his supervisor's potential conflict of interest with the employer because of his involvement in another company's medical imaging technology business. After he met with his supervisor to express his concern, the supervisor became angry and prohibited him from visiting other corporate locations or having visitors without permission. The supervisor gave him negative performance evaluations, and the technologist soon quit. He sued the corporation and supervisor for breach of the employment contract and breach of the covenant of good faith and fair dealing in employment relationships. A jury awarded the technologist over $500,000 in damages. The employer appealed to the Supreme Court of Delaware, arguing that the trial court had given the jury improper instructions by allowing them to find liability based on the supervisor's hatred, ill will or intent to injure. The court agreed, finding that the employment relationship of the parties was at will and that in order **to create an exception for breach of the covenant of good faith, there must be a showing of employer malice**, intent to injure, and causation of termination based on falsified grounds. The trial court decision was reversed. *E.I. DuPont de Nemours and Co. v. Pressman*, 679 A.2d 436 (Del. 1996).

◆ A New Mexico healthcare facility hired a nursing coordinator for a 90-day probationary period. Four months later, the employee was promoted to the director of nursing position at another facility owned by the same company. She began a new 90-day probationary period as director of nursing. Although the employee later stated that she had been assured that her job performance was good, the healthcare facility asked for her resignation within 90 days. The employee sued the healthcare corporation and its individual officers for emotional distress and breach of contract, among other claims. On the breach of contract claim, a jury returned a damage award of $2,500 for economic loss as well as $63,500 for emotional distress. The court entered judgment for $2,500 plus interest and costs, but refused to enter judgment on the emotional distress claim. The employee appealed to the Supreme Court of New Mexico, which determined that there was **no substantial evidence to justify damages for emotional distress**. The lower court judgment was affirmed. *Bourgeous v. Horizon Healthcare Corp.*, 872 P.2d 852 (N.M. 1994).

IV. WRONGFUL DISCHARGE

Employers may not discharge employees for engaging in protected activity or asserting rights to which they are legally entitled, such as the filing of a workers' compensation claim. Even if the employment relationship is at will, actions that violate an important public policy may create liability.

Thus, even though at-will employees can be fired at any time for any reason or no reason at all, they cannot be fired for a reason that violates public policy (like discrimination or retaliation for whistleblowing).

A. Public Policy Protections

When an employee engages in activity that is beneficial to society (like jury duty) or is otherwise protected (e.g., as a minority, a disabled person, a person 40 or older), firing that employee is likely to result in a wrongful discharge or discrimination lawsuit. This does not mean you can't fire such employees, but it does mean you should document the reasons for doing so very carefully to protect yourself from litigation.

Of course, you should always document the reasons for firing any employee, even when the employment is at will. Suppose that the reason for the firing is that the employee dyes her hair green and you hate green hair. You should still document this. It may seem stupid to a court, but it is not a reason that violates public policy.

1. Criminal Activities

Employees cannot be fired for refusing to participate in illegal activities. Nor should they be fired for refusing to participate in activities that they, in good faith, believe are illegal.

- A newly hired telecommunications employee with muscle spasms and chronic pain used marijuana on his doctor's recommendation pursuant to California's Compassionate Use Act of 1996, which provides a defense to criminal drug charges. He was fired after flunking the company's preemployment drug test and sued for wrongful discharge in violation of public policy as well as disability discrimination under state law. The case reached the California Supreme Court, which held that **the employer did not have to accommodate the employee's use of marijuana at home** despite the Compassionate Use Act. Nor did the termination violate public policy because marijuana remains an illegal drug under federal law. *Ross v. RagingWire Telecommunications, Inc.*, 42 Cal.4th 920, 174 P.3d 200 (Cal. 2008).

- A Tennessee truck driver refused to drive a truck that had only a copy of the original "cab card" showing registration of the vehicle. The next day he was fired. He sued for retaliatory discharge, claiming that he had been fired for refusing to participate in an illegal activity (a Tennessee Department of

Safety regulation required the truck to carry an original "cab card" showing registration). A jury ruled for the truck driver, but the Court of Appeals of Tennessee reversed. It held that the employee's refusal to perform the assigned work based on the regulation requiring the original cab card, as opposed to a photocopy, did not further important public policy concerns, and therefore would not support a claim of retaliatory discharge. **The illegal activity the employee chooses not to engage in must implicate important public policy concerns for the employee to be able to claim protection** against retaliatory discharge. *Franklin v. Swift Transportation Co., Inc.*, 210 S.W.3d 521 (Tenn. Ct. App. 2006).

- A Virginia woman alleged that her employer violated state criminal laws when he groped her, demanded that she have sex with him and fired her after she rejected his sexual advances. She sued him for wrongful termination, but the court dismissed her case, finding that she was not covered by either federal or state law because the employer had fewer than five employees. The court also stated that Virginia's Human Rights Act was the only state law that could create a public policy allowing her to sue for wrongful termination. Since she was an at-will employee, she could not sue unless there was a public policy allowing her to do so. The Supreme Court of Virginia held that **she could use the state's criminal laws to state a public policy argument that her termination had been wrongful**. It reversed and remanded the case. *Mitchem v. Counts*, 523 S.E.2d 246 (Va. 2000).

- A national child care company wrongfully discharged a regional director after she refused to fire employees who had threatened to sue over their workers' compensation claims. The Washington Court of Appeals held that the order to fire the employees was unlawful. The regional director had received good performance reviews until about two months after she and five other employees were in a work-related car accident. All of them, including the regional director, filed workers' compensation claims. But a week after the accident, the company's operations director ordered the regional director to fire the other five employees. The operations director had heard that two of them were contemplating a lawsuit against the company and "didn't trust either of them not to sue." The operations director also told the regional director that it would be in the company's best interest to dismiss them to avoid any more problems. The regional director refused to do so and received her first poor performance review several days later. She was fired a month later for neglecting her duties and sued. Because **her refusal to unlawfully fire the other employees was a substantial factor in her own termination**, the termination was wrongful. *Lins v. Children's Discovery Center of America, Inc.*, 976 P.2d 168 (Wash. Ct. App. 1999).

- A Utah telecommunications sales rep observed some of her co-workers falsifying their customer accounts to meet sales quotas and earn higher commissions by making existing accounts appear new. She reported the practices to an internal audit unit and was fired less than a week after the unit conducted an investigation. She sued the employer for wrongful termination.

The Supreme Court of Utah was asked to determine whether the termination of a private sector employee in retaliation for the good-faith reporting of co-worker misconduct violated a clear and substantial public policy. The court observed that **an employment discharge is wrongful where there is criminal activity, the reporting of that activity to a public authority, and a discharge that occurs as a result**. However, firing an employee for reporting a criminal violation to an employer, rather than a public authority, does not contravene a clear and substantial public policy. The employer here had not required the sales rep to engage in criminal misconduct. The reported misconduct reflected only dishonesty and not illegal conduct. Because the misconduct did not affect the public interest in any significant way, the wrongful termination claim could not succeed. *Fox v. MCI Communications Corp.*, 931 P.2d 857 (Utah 1997).

◆ The director of security, safety and occupational health for a Colorado brewery engaged in a series of covert drug purchases under the direction and approval of his supervisors to discover whether some employees were using illicit drugs. He was later fired for misusing company funds and engaging in sexual improprieties with a co-worker. He appealed his discharge to an internal appeals panel, asserting that the supervisors had **conspired to discharge him by making the illegal drug purchases appear to be his idea**. The panel affirmed the discharge action, and he sued the employer for wrongful discharge in violation of public policy and intentional infliction of emotional distress. The Colorado Supreme Court held that even if the employee's claims were true, the conduct alleged by the employee (using him as a scapegoat in a criminal conspiracy involving illegal drugs and money laundering) did not rise to the level of outrageousness necessary to sustain a claim of intentional infliction of emotional distress. The court also held that the employee could not succeed on his wrongful discharge claim because he was not fired in retaliation for whistleblowing or for refusing to commit criminal acts. He had already been fired when he blew the whistle on the employer. *Coors Brewing Co. v. Floyd*, 978 P.2d 663 (Colo. 1999).

◆ A supervisor working for a Texas construction company learned that some of his co-workers were involved in a workplace conspiracy including theft, fraud and violations of state and federal regulations involving the construction of a nuclear power plant. He found discrepancies in recordkeeping, including falsified claims for hours worked. He refused to participate in the fraudulent activity and received negative performance ratings. When he took a vacation, the company fired him as part of a work force reduction. He sued the company and a jury awarded him $150,000 for wrongful termination.

The employer appealed to the Court of Appeals of Texas, where it claimed that the evidence of wrongful termination was insufficient to support the judgment, that the relationship between the parties was terminable at the will of either party, and that there was no applicable exception to the at-will doctrine. The court disagreed, finding substantial evidence in the record of a criminal conspiracy among the employee's co-workers. It also observed that **a departure from the employment-at-will doctrine has been recognized in Texas where a discharge action violates a public policy** as expressed in state or federal law. Here, the conspiracy involved falsification of records in violation of federal and state law. Accordingly, although the employment relationship was at will, the wrongful termination action was permissible. The court affirmed the district court judgment. *Ebasco Constructors, Inc. v. Rex*, 923 S.W.2d 694 (Tex. Ct. App. 1996).

2. Unsafe Working Conditions

Employees cannot be fired for reporting unsafe working conditions. Nor should they be fired for refusing, in good faith, to work in such conditions. Employers occasionally win such lawsuits, but the cost of litigating a wrongful discharge lawsuit is high.

Moreover, if the workplace is in fact unsafe, there is a potential for liability (either tort liability or workers' compensation). Thus, when an employee complains of unsafe working conditions, an investigation should be undertaken to ascertain whether a safety threat exists.

- A safety coordinator for an energy company in Iowa openly disagreed with company policies allowing for a one-man line crew and permitting linemen to use a body belt instead of a body harness. When a new supervisor learned of his failure to support the company's safety policies, she fired him. He sued the company for wrongful discharge, and a federal jury awarded him $920,000 in damages. The company appealed. The Eighth Circuit affirmed the award, finding that even though the employee handbook contained a disclaimer that employment was strictly at will (such that the employee could be fired at any time for any reason or no reason at all), a public policy exception modified the employment-at-will doctrine. Under Iowa's Occupational Safety and Health Act, there was an implied cause of action for wrongful discharge where an **employee is fired for trying to institute new or perfect existing safety policies**. *Korht v. MidAmerican Energy Co.*, 364 F.3d 894 (8th Cir. 2004).

- A production worker in the Indiana plant of a national pharmaceutical company claimed that he was protected from retaliatory discharge under Indiana's Occupational Safety and Health Act (IOSHA). The U.S. Court of Appeals for the Seventh Circuit disagreed. The Indiana legislature "created a specific statutory remedy," which forbids the discharge of an employee who files a complaint with state labor department officials within 30 days of the suspected violation. According to the record, the worker **only reported the claimed safety violation to his employer's safety division**. Because he did not pursue the remedy provided by statute, he was not entitled to rely on it for protection. The case arose after the worker engaged in horseplay and insubordinate conduct. He claimed that two co-workers then failed to follow proper safety procedures and deliberately set him up for a "near miss" accident. He reported the incident to the plant's safety department. Ultimately, he was fired for misconduct. In his lawsuit for retaliatory discharge under the IOSHA, the Seventh Circuit found that he had no rights under the act. *Groce v. Eli Lilly & Co.*, 193 F.3d 496 (7th Cir. 1999).

◆ A helicopter manufacturer employed an aircraft maintenance instructor for several years as a member of a nonmilitary project team. However, the employer instructed him to conduct maintenance training at a military base in Bahrain when the U.S. became involved in military action in the Persian Gulf. The instructor refused to travel to Bahrain based on the threat to his personal safety as supported by a U.S. government travel advisory discouraging travel to the area. The employer fired the instructor and removed him from its premises under a security escort. He sued for wrongful discharge and negligent and intentional infliction of emotional distress. The Supreme Court of Connecticut noted the general public policy requiring each employer to provide its employees with a reasonably safe workplace and the limited exception to the presumption of employment at will where an employer sends an employee to work at an unsafe work site. Here, there was evidence that **the employer had directed the employee to work in an unsafe location**. The wrongful discharge claim could continue, but the employer prevailed on the negligent and intentional infliction of emotional distress claims. *Parsons v. United Technologies Corp.*, 243 Conn. 66, 700 A.2d 655 (Conn. 1997).

◆ The Supreme Court of Oklahoma rejected a claim by a discharged private security employee that the Oklahoma Occupational Safety and Health Standards (OSHS) Act provided an underlying public policy that precluded his employer from firing him in retaliation for protesting unsafe working conditions. The case arose when the employee protested a new company security policy by rigging a package with an alarm that sounded during a meeting. The employer fired the employee, who sued for retaliatory discharge. The court observed that the state OSHS Act no longer applied to private employers and could not create a valid public policy exception to the presumption of employment at will for private employers. The federal Occupational Safety and Health Act was also unavailable to provide protection in this case. **No public policy existed under state workplace safety laws that would form the basis for a retaliatory discharge claim** against a private employer. *Griffin v. Mullinix*, 947 P.2d 177 (Okla. 1997).

◆ A group of Missouri employees working at a fireworks factory complained of unsafe working conditions. The employer fired them. They filed a lawsuit against it in a state trial court, alleging violations of the federal Occupational Safety and Health Act, which prohibits employers from discharging employees for exercising OSHA-protected rights. The court dismissed the lawsuit. The Missouri Court of Appeals observed that while the employees were at will, an exception existed to the at-will rule in Missouri law where employees **reported violations of law or public policy**. The employer argued that OSHA provided the employees a complete remedy with which they had failed to comply by not first complaining to the U.S. Secretary of Labor. The court disagreed, finding that their administrative remedy was incomplete and that OSHA did not prohibit a state law complaint for wrongful discharge in violation of public policy. The decision was reversed and the case was remanded. *Shawcross v. Pyro Products, Inc.*, 916 S.W.2d 342 (Mo. Ct. App. 1995).

◆ Two truck drivers alleged that they were fired by their employer because they refused to operate a truck that they had not had time to inspect before driving. They sued the employer. A jury held for the drivers, but the court of appeals reversed, finding that the state Motor Carriers Act did not create a cause of action for retaliatory discharge. The Supreme Court of Tennessee observed that the Motor Carriers Act declared it the public policy of Tennessee to protect the safety and welfare of the public by imposing a number of requirements upon motor vehicle operators. Tolerating the **retaliatory discharge of these employees for observing the safety provisions of the act** would impair the legislature's declared policy of protecting the public. Because the firing violated a clear public policy, the court reinstated the jury verdict. *Reynolds v. Ozark Motor Lines, Inc.*, 887 S.W.2d 822 (Tenn. 1994).

3. Other Public Policy Protections

As a way to avoid potential wrongful discharge liability, make certain that the real reason an employee is being fired is not retaliation for some activity or speech that is protected or that in some way advances public policy.

◆ A nursing home employee reported suspected patient abuse to the Nebraska Department of Health and Human Services. A few days later, her supervisor yelled at her for going over her head, then fired her when she refused to resign. **She sued for retaliatory discharge in contravention of public policy, and a jury awarded her $79,000 for emotional distress.** The nursing home appealed, and the Supreme Court of Nebraska upheld the award for the employee. Here, the evidence showed that the employee was fired for making a report of abuse as mandated by the Adult Protective Services Act, and there was sufficient evidence of emotional distress to support the damage award. *Wendeln v. The Beatrice Manor, Inc.*, 712 N.W.2d 226 (Neb. 2006).

◆ A bank teller in Nebraska attended a public meeting and questioned the propriety of a school board action, asking about the potential tax consequences of a proposed merger with another school district. The superintendent and two school board members then told bank officials they would not deal with the teller when they visited the bank to conduct personal business. Two weeks later, the teller was fired. She sued the bank under 42 U.S.C. § 1983 (Section 1983), **alleging that she was fired for speaking at the public meeting** and that the bank had acted under color of state law by conspiring with the school board members to retaliate against her for her public speech. Although the bank claimed it could not be held liable under Section 1983 because it was not a public entity, the Eighth Circuit held that if a conspiracy was shown, the teller could win. The teller was entitled to a trial on the issue. *Dossett v. First State Bank*, 399 F.3d 940 (8th Cir. 2005).

◆ A security guard for a company that provided security services to an oil refinery in Illinois went on television and talked about a fellow security officer who bragged about being a felon. The guard stated that convicted felons should not be trusted to provide security at oil refineries, which are potential terrorist targets. He was then placed on indefinite suspension, and 11 months later sued for wrongful discharge. The company sought to dismiss the lawsuit because he had agreed (as a condition of employment) to take action within six months of the date a cause of action arose. The Seventh Circuit Court of Appeals refused to dismiss the case because **it was not clear that the company actually fired the guard at the time it placed him on indefinite suspension**. *Thomas v. Guardsmark, Inc.*, 381 F.3d 701 (7th Cir. 2004).

◆ An at-will manager for an Ohio Sears store was **fired for correcting an employee's time card**. He sued the store for wrongful discharge, asserting that Sears had violated a public policy requiring employers to keep accurate employee records. The Ohio Court of Appeals ruled against him, finding that he failed to demonstrate that his discharge jeopardized the public policy of keeping accurate employment records. Through regulatory oversight (including inspections) and civil and criminal penalties, the state and federal government have adequate means to enforce the public policy here. The discharge was not wrongful. *White v. Sears, Roebuck & Co.*, 837 N.E.2d 1275 (Ohio Ct. App. 2005).

◆ A transportation company in Texas required its truck drivers to submit to random drug testing pursuant to Department of Transportation (DOT) regulations. A driver submitted to urinalysis and tested positive for marijuana. However, the company failed to comply with the DOT procedures for collecting a sample. For example, the collection container was unsealed, and it was out of the driver's sight for over a minute after he provided the sample while he was washing his hands. After he was fired, he sued the company for failing to use ordinary care in collecting his urine sample, which he alleged resulted in the positive reading. A jury awarded him over $800,000 in lost wages and mental anguish, as well as $100,000 in exemplary damages. The court of appeals affirmed the award, but the Supreme Court of Texas reversed. It held that **the company did not owe the driver a common-law duty of care when collecting the urine sample** for drug testing pursuant to DOT regulations. *Mission Petroleum Carriers, Inc. v. Solomon*, 106 S.W.3d 705 (Tex. 2003).

◆ An employee of a company in Louisiana submitted to a random drug screen urinalysis and allegedly tested positive for a cocaine metabolyte. After he was fired, he sued the company for breaching its statutory duties to him in firing him for a positive drug test without first allowing him the opportunity to provide information about prescription medication he was taking that could result in a false positive result. The company asserted that because it could fire the employee at any time for any reason or no reason at all, it could not be held liable for wrongful termination. It conceded that it failed to follow the state drug testing statute by failing to have a medical review officer review the results before the termination. The Court of Appeal of Louisiana ruled that even though the company had failed to comply with the statute, it still had the right to fire the employee for testing positive. **The drug testing statute did not provide an exception to the at-will employment doctrine**. *Sanchez v. Georgia Gulf Corp.*, 860 So.2d 277 (La. Ct. App. 2003).

◆ An administrative assistant for a senior care facility in Maryland initially received an "above average" performance evaluation. However, she was later reprimanded for complaining about her shortened workweek, for failing to conform to a new recruiting policy and for refusing assistance in improving her performance. After receiving an employee warning report, she informed her supervisor she would be late in returning it to the company because she wanted to talk with an attorney before formally responding. She thought some of the statements in the report were libelous. The company fired her the same day. She sued for wrongful termination, asserting that the company violated public policy by firing her for expressing an intent to seek legal counsel. The case reached the Maryland Court of Appeals, which dismissed the action. Although Maryland public policy favors access to attorneys, **it does not require employers to retain at-will employees who attempt to seek legal advice on a work-related matter**. The exceptions to the at-will doctrine are few and narrow, and consulting an attorney is not one of them. *Porterfield v. Mascari II, Inc.*, 823 A.2d 590 (Md. 2003).

◆ When a Nevada hospital employee incurred large medical expenses, he tried to negotiate repayment with the hospital. The negotiations failed, and the employee informed the hospital that he intended to file for bankruptcy protection. Before he could file, the hospital fired him. The trustee in bankruptcy sued the hospital under Section 525(b) of the Bankruptcy Code, which prohibits the termination of an employee solely because the employee is or has been a debtor in bankruptcy. The Bankruptcy Court dismissed the claim against the hospital, finding that **the statute did not protect people who had not yet filed for bankruptcy protection**. The Ninth Circuit Court of Appeals affirmed. Because the employee had not yet filed for bankruptcy protection, the hospital did not violate the Bankruptcy Code's prohibition against retaliation, and the wrongful termination action could not succeed. *In re Majewski*, 310 F.3d 653 (9th Cir. 2002).

◆ A provider of electricity in Tennessee had **an exogamy rule, which required that when two permanent-status employees married, one of them had to quit**. When two employees decided to get married, they were informed that one of them would have to quit, but that whichever one did could continue on in a temporary capacity until he or she found a new job. The employees married and returned to work without deciding which one would leave. The husband was then called in to his supervisor's office, where he indicated that he did not agree with the policy. He was fired and he sued under the First Amendment, alleging that the policy violated his constitutional right to marry (freedom of association). He also asserted that he was fired in retaliation for speaking out against the policy. A federal court granted pretrial judgment to the provider, and the U.S. Court of Appeals, Sixth Circuit affirmed in part. The policy did not significantly restrict his ability to marry. However, there was a question of fact as to whether he had been fired for speaking out against the policy. That issue required a trial. *Vaughn v. Lawrenceburg Power System*, 269 F.3d 703 (6th Cir. 2001).

- An employee in the photo processing department at a Nebraska Wal-Mart store saw pictures of a child lying on a newspaper, apparently covered with marijuana leaves and $100 bills. Under store policy, she was supposed to take "questionable pictures of minors" to the store manager. She instead showed the pictures to the department manager, but was dissatisfied with the response she received. She took copies of the pictures to the police. She was then fired for violating the store's customer confidentiality policy and for showing an unwillingness to adhere to company policies in the future. When she sued under the Nebraska Fair Employment Practices Act, a jury found that Wal-Mart did not have a practice of preventing the reporting of child abuse. It also found that **she failed to prove her report to the police was the sole factor in Wal-Mart's decision to fire her**. It returned a verdict for the store. The Eighth Circuit Court of Appeals affirmed. *Gasper v. Wal-Mart Stores,* 270 F.3d 1196 (8th Cir. 2001).

- A nurse practitioner at a Texas nursing home found an 83-year-old resident who had fallen out of a geriatric chair. She took the resident's vital signs and called the home's medical director. When he asked her if she had assessed the resident's condition, she replied that she did not think she could judge the extent of the injuries and sought to call an ambulance. He allegedly told her that if she was not qualified to do an assessment, she should call emergency medical services. She then became upset and told him he was not a good physician. The next day, she was fired for insubordination. She sued the nursing home for wrongful termination, alleging that she had been fired for reporting abuse or neglect in violation of the Texas Health and Safety Code. A trial court ruled in favor of the nursing home, and the Texas Court of Appeals affirmed. Here, the nurse practitioner **did not put the medical director on notice that she was reporting an act of abuse** or neglect as contemplated by the statute. Further, she did not know how or why the resident fell out of the chair or whether neglect had caused the fall. The nursing home was not liable for retaliatory discharge of the nurse practitioner. *Gonzales v. Methodist Retirement Communities*, 33 S.W.3d 882 (Tex. Ct. App. 2000).

- An at-will veterinary assistant at a clinic in Washington began an unpaid maternity leave and was discharged three months later because of an "economic slowdown." The owner of the clinic advertised for the position a year later. When she applied, he refused to rehire her. She sued the owner, asserting that the real reason for the termination was pregnancy discrimination. A state trial court ruled in favor of the owner, finding that even if she was fired because of her gender, the clinic and its owner were excluded from liability because the clinic was a small employer with less than eight workers. The Washington Supreme Court reinstated her claim, holding that **at-will employees can sue for gender-based wrongful discharge under the common law**. So even though the state's law against discrimination exempted employers with less than eight employees, such employers could still be liable for wrongful discharge if they fired employees because of their sex. *Roberts v. Dudley*, 993 P.2d 901 (Wash. 2000).

◆ A quality control inspector for a Virginia poultry processor informed government inspectors about questionable practices regarding sanitation at the processing plant. Her supervisor told her that she would be fired if she ever again brought plant deficiencies to government inspectors. Two months later, the employee and other quality control inspectors condemned some poultry products as adulterated based on improper work on the "wash line." After a government inspector required the employer to reprocess a large quantity of poultry due to contamination, the employer fired the inspector. She sued, claiming she was protected from discharge by a state law requiring governmental inspection of food and poultry plants. The Supreme Court of Virginia disagreed, explaining that **the statute provided her with no public policy rights to evade the employment-at-will doctrine** and that a generalized, common-law "whistleblower" retaliatory discharge claim was not recognized as an exception to the at-will doctrine either. The statute in question established a regulatory mechanism "directed only to government inspectors and industry management." It did not give employees the right to disregard management requirements that they report to company superiors. *Dray v. New Market Poultry Products, Inc.*, 518 S.E.2d 312 (Va. 1999).

◆ A California convenience store employee thought employees could help themselves to free soft drinks and coffee at any time. He agreed to testify at a former employee's unemployment compensation hearing. On the way there, he stopped at the store and helped himself to a soft drink. A regional manager who appeared at the unemployment compensation hearing fired him, allegedly for stealing the soft drink. The employee sued for wrongful discharge in violation of public policy, breach of contract, breach of an implied covenant of good faith and fair dealing, slander and intentional infliction of emotional distress. A court awarded the employee $42,000 in damages plus $300,000 in punitive damages for discharge in violation of public policy. The California Court of Appeal noted that employers may not discharge an employee for a reason that violates a fundamental public policy. **Discharge in retaliation for testifying before an unemployment compensation hearing violates a fundamental policy** deemed by the legislature to be vital to the state's economic interests. Thus, the wrongful discharge award was affirmed. The punitive damages award was also affirmed, since the employee had been discharged by a "managing agent" in a policymaking position with immediate control over the decision to fire the employee. The California Supreme Court affirmed the award of punitive damages. *White v. Ultramar, Inc.*, 981 P.2d 944 (Cal. 1999).

B. Jury Duty

Employees who miss work for jury duty cannot be fired for that reason.

◆ An on-air traffic manager for a local New York television and radio station was fired after he missed a day of work because of jury duty. He had mentioned to his supervisor and some co-workers that he might be out for jury duty but did not submit any written notice. On the day he was directed to report for jury duty, he tried unsuccessfully to contact his supervisor. In his wrongful discharge lawsuit, the trial court held that the judiciary laws did not allow him to sue for damages. An appellate division court agreed. The applicable section of the judiciary law, although prohibiting an employer from discharging or penalizing an employee for complying with a jury duty directive, provides only that employers will be subject to criminal sanctions for violating the law. It does not provide for any civil cause of action against the employer for wrongful discharge, and at the time the law was passed, the governor vetoed such a remedy. Even though the station's actions violated public policy, **the court had no power to fashion a remedy for wrongful discharge**. *DiBlasi v. Traffax Traffic Network*, 681 N.Y.S.2d 147 (N.Y. App. Div. 1998).

◆ A New York employer maintained an employee handbook encouraging its employees to fulfill their jury duty obligations. An employee accepted jury duty but was soon fired. He sued the employer for breach of contract and violation of **a state law making the dismissal of an employee for serving on a jury a misdemeanor**. The court dismissed the case, and the New York Supreme Court, Appellate Division, affirmed. The misdemeanor statute did not create a civil cause of action against an employer for wrongful discharge. Also, even though the employee handbook encouraged employees to fulfill their jury duty obligations, it did not alter the at-will relationship because it contained a prominent disclaimer that it did not create an employment contract. *Gomariz v. Foote, Cone & Belding Communications, Inc.*, 644 N.Y.S.2d 224 (N.Y. App. Div. 1996).

◆ An Oklahoma customer service supervisor received a jury summons that required her to report for one week of service. She gave her supervisor a copy of the summons and reported for jury duty. She was not selected for a jury on either Monday or Tuesday and was released for the afternoon. However, she did not return to work in the afternoon on those days. On Wednesday, the regional supervisor met with her after jury duty had concluded for the day and requested that she obtain a statement from the court that she was not allowed to be on call for jury duty at work. She did not obtain the statement and was fired. She received juror compensation for the entire week and then sued the employer for wrongful discharge. A jury awarded her $175,000 in actual damages and $350,000 in punitive damages. On appeal, the Oklahoma Court of Appeals noted that to establish a *prima facie* case of wrongful discharge under Oklahoma law, **the employee needed to show that she had been absent from work because of the requirement that she serve as a juror**, and that she had been discharged because of this absence. Here, there had been sufficient evidence presented from which the jury could conclude that the discharge had been retaliatory in nature. The court affirmed the jury's verdict but lowered the punitive damages award to $175,000. *Brown v. MFC Finance Co. of Oklahoma*, 838 P.2d 524 (Okla. Ct. App. 1992).

◆ A secretary at a Texas company was selected as a juror and served on a jury for six days. Three days after her selection, she was fired. She sued. A federal court awarded her six months' compensation, which was the maximum amount allowed under the Texas Juror Reemployment Statute (TJRS). She appealed to the U.S. Court of Appeals, Fifth Circuit, asserting that she should have received punitive damages also. The court noted that the TJRS did not seem to contemplate punitive damages. However, by analogizing the statute to the Texas Workers' Compensation Retaliation Statute, the court found that the term "damages" **allowed punitive damages** according to the Texas Supreme Court. Nevertheless, even though punitive damages could be recovered, the maximum amount recoverable was six months' compensation. *Fuchs v. Lifetime Doors, Inc.*, 939 F.2d 1275 (5th Cir. 1991).

C. Workers' Compensation

Employees injured on the job who file claims for workers' compensation and then are discharged often file lawsuits for retaliatory discharge, alleging that their employers have discharged them for filing the workers' compensation claims.

Employees who return to work after filing workers' compensation claims may be required to pass a fitness-for-duty exam to ensure that they can perform the job safely.

For cases dealing with workers' compensation generally, refer to Chapter Seven.

- An Illinois woman was allegedly injured on the job. She notified her employer and requested compensation for her medical expenses under the Illinois Workers' Compensation Act. Shortly thereafter, her employer fired her for filing a "false" workers' compensation claim. Her union filed a grievance, and an arbitrator found in the employee's favor and ordered her reinstated with full back pay. Meanwhile, she brought a retaliatory discharge claim against her employer. The case reached the U.S. Supreme Court, which examined whether the employee's claim was preempted by Section 301 of the Labor Management Relations Act. The Supreme Court held that it was not. Therefore, **if the employee could show that she had been discharged to deter her from exercising her rights under the workers' compensation act, she could win her suit**. No interpretation of the parties' collective bargaining agreement would have to be made. Since the inquiries were purely factual, the claim was independent of the agreement and Section 301 did not preempt it. The employee could continue with her claim. *Lingle v. Norge Division of Magic Chef, Inc.*, 486 U.S. 399, 108 S.Ct. 1877, 100 L.Ed.2d 410 (1988).

- A hotel maintenance employee in Iowa filed three workers' compensation claims in three years. The first claim was for a neck injury from lifting wet carpet; the second claim was made three days after a supervisor criticized him for not finishing his work. He asserted that he had hurt his back while moving a TV. On the third claim, he asserted that he slipped and fell near the loading dock, then changed his story to aver that he hurt his back on a stairway. However, videotapes from a security camera showed that he was not on the stairs at all on the morning he claimed the injury occurred. The hotel fired him, and he sued for wrongful discharge. The Eighth Circuit ruled against him, noting that **he had no public policy right to file a false workers' compensation claim**. *Napreljac v. John Q. Hammons Hotels, Inc.*, 505 F.3d 800 (8th Cir. 2007).

◆ The owner of a Pennsylvania car dealership fired his brother, who was also the body shop manager, after the brother refused to convince a mechanic to waive his workers' compensation claim against the company. The mechanic had injured himself while unloading heavy computer equipment for the dealership. The brother sued the dealership for wrongful discharge and a jury awarded him compensatory damages in the amount of $192,000. The case reached the Supreme Court of Pennsylvania, which upheld the award. The same public policy that prohibits firing an employee for seeking workers' compensation applies to situations where an **employee is fired for refusing to force a subordinate not to seek workers' compensation**. *Rothrock v. Rothrock Motor Sales, Inc.*, 883 A.2d 511 (Pa. 2005).

◆ A Wal-Mart employee in Indiana got into a fight with a co-worker and suffered injuries that required him to go to the hospital. While Wal-Mart conducted an investigation into the fight, he inquired about workers' compensation benefits. Five days later, he and the co-worker were fired for fighting. He sued for retaliation, claiming that he had been fired for asking about workers' compensation. A federal court and the Seventh Circuit Court of Appeals ruled against him. **Wal-Mart had a legitimate reason for firing him: he violated its workplace violence policy.** *Hudson v. Wal-Mart Stores*, 412 F.3d 781 (7th Cir. 2005).

◆ An employee of a lawn and landscaping services company in Florida injured his shoulder and got treatment at a workers' compensation clinic. He was put on lifting restrictions and was fired a month later. He sued to recover workers' compensation benefits and for retaliatory discharge. The company settled the workers' compensation claim by paying him $8,300 and having him sign a general release waiving "any and all rights" to past, present or future benefits as well as to any claims, demands or causes of action he might have against the company. It then sought to dismiss the retaliatory discharge claim because of the waiver. The Eleventh Circuit held that **he could pursue his retaliatory discharge claim because it was not clear from the language of the general release that he was waiving his right to do so**. *Borque v. Trugreen, Inc.*, 389 F.3d 1354 (11th Cir. 2004).

◆ A maintenance worker at a school district in Illinois injured his back and obtained workers' compensation benefits for chiropractic treatments. While receiving benefits, he applied for a job with a manufacturer and lied about ever having a work-related back injury on the health history questionnaire that was part of the application process. He agreed that any misrepresentation would be cause for termination. He then injured his back again and sought further chiropractic treatment. The manufacturer fired him after its insurer denied the workers' compensation claim, and he sued for wrongful discharge. An Illinois federal court and the Seventh Circuit Court of Appeals ruled against him. Here,

he was not fired for filing a workers' compensation claim, but for falsifying his answers on the health history questionnaire. *Carter v. Tennant Co.*, 383 F.3d 673 (7th Cir. 2004).

◆ To control workers' compensation costs, a company that operated a Kansas meatpacking plant had an accident-free incentive program and certain "cost-per-injury" goals. While doing his job, one of the plant workers injured his back and was put on light duty. Never having been disciplined before, the worker began receiving disciplinary notices once he was assigned to light duty. The company's personnel manager, who knew about the worker's injury, eventually fired him. The worker sued in federal court, **claiming that he was fired in retaliation for being injured on the job**. A jury found in his favor and awarded him more than $39,000. The company appealed to the U.S. Court of Appeals, Tenth Circuit, arguing that the district court should have thrown out the award because the jury was allowed to hear evidence that the company's personnel director frequently heard complaints from other plant workers that it mistreated injured workers. The Tenth Circuit agreed. The workers' complaints were hearsay and therefore inadmissible. A new trial had to be conducted. *Sanjuan v. IBP, Inc.*, 160 F.3d 1291 (10th Cir. 1998).

◆ A Texas employee was injured at work and took a medical leave of absence. The employer placed her on indefinite medical layoff status, informing her that she had recall rights and would be called back for the next available job. The employer never called her back to work. She sued it for violating the state workers' compensation act, which prohibits discrimination against an employee for filing a workers' compensation claim. She also sued for fraud and breach of contract. A court dismissed the action as barred by the compensation act's two-year statute of limitations and granted the employer's post-trial motion to overturn a jury verdict of $275,000 on the fraud claim. The Supreme Court of Texas determined that the employer had failed to unequivocally notify the employee of her termination. The evidence indicated that the employer's personnel manager had created an unwritten, indefinite category called medical layoff that did not comply with the collective bargaining agreement of the parties but was in practice indistinguishable from a layoff or termination. **Because the employer never notified the employee of a definite employment separation, the workers' compensation act claim was not barred by the statute of limitations.** However, the trial court correctly dismissed the fraud claim. *Johnson & Johnson Medical, Inc. v. Sanchez*, 924 S.W.2d 925 (Tex. 1996).

◆ A Vermont forest products employee was fired after an on-the-job injury for which she had sought workers' compensation benefits. The employer had previously distributed an employee handbook with an attendance policy that allowed 10 unexcused absences per year. However, the handbook contained a broad disclaimer stating that the employer could disregard any policy in the manual when management determined it to be in the best interest of the company. The employee sued for retaliatory discharge in violation of the state workers' compensation act. A federal court dismissed the case. The Second Circuit affirmed, and the U.S. Supreme Court denied further appeal. The

Vermont Supreme Court subsequently ruled in an unrelated case that **a private right of action may exist for retaliatory discharge in violation of an employee's rights under the state workers' compensation act**. The court of appeals then held that the employee had to be allowed to pursue the matter further. Failure to reconsider the matter in view of the state law change would be unfair to the employee, as she had originally filed the matter in state court. *Sargent v. Columbia Forest Products, Inc.*, 75 F.3d 86 (2d Cir. 1996).

◆ A Kentucky steelworker claimed that he was **laid off by his employer because of his workers' compensation claims history with previous employers**. The employer justified the layoff on economic grounds, and the employee sued. The Supreme Court of Kentucky analyzed the case under state workers' compensation law, which prohibited the retaliatory discharge of an employee for filing a valid workers' compensation claim. The court distinguished the discharge in this case from retaliatory discharge complaints based on firings motivated by the desire to punish an employee for exercising legal rights. Here, the discharge was not retaliatory in nature, but had an economic basis in reducing the employer's cost of workers' compensation insurance premiums. The court rejected the employee's argument that it should adopt case law from Michigan and Illinois that expanded retaliatory discharge claims to include discharges based on claims filed against prior employers. *Nelson Steel Corp. v. McDaniel*, 898 S.W.2d 66 (Ky. 1995).

D. State Whistleblower Statutes

Reporting violations or suspected violations of law to state agencies qualifies employees for protection under state whistleblower acts. However, reporting violations or suspected violations of law to supervisors within the company may not.

◆ A nurse at a Minnesota clinic received an unfavorable performance review that, among other things, criticized her failure to follow proper sterile procedures during a surgery. She was placed on probation for 90 days. In response, she wrote a letter to the clinic's owners, addressing many of the concerns in her review and informing them that she refused to comply with the clinic's policy of attaching a previously used syringe with a new needle to a multi-dose vial of medication and then using the vial with other patients because doing so violated Minnesota law. Thirty minutes later, she was forcibly removed from the premises for insubordination.

Although she was not fired, she refused to return to work and sued for retaliation under the state's Whistleblower Act. The Eighth Circuit ruled against her because **she did not write the letter for the purpose of exposing an unknown illegality; the clinic was aware of the alleged violation before she wrote the letter**. Also, she did not raise the issue, before the trial court, of refusing to perform an act she believed violated the law, and she could not do so for the first time on appeal. *Fjelsta v. Zogg Dermatology, PLC*, 488 F.3d 804 (8th Cir. 2007).

◆ The co-CEO of a Minnesota company was suspected by the board of directors of having an affair with a subordinate. He denied having a sexual affair with her. The board began a formal investigation. That same day, the co-CEO told board members their mileage reimbursement policy might be in violation of federal tax laws. Two weeks later, the co-CEO admitted to having a sexual affair with the subordinate and using a company credit card to buy Viagra and personal cell phones so he could continue to carry on the affair. The board fired him and he sued, claiming whistleblower protection. A federal court and the Eighth Circuit ruled against him. **The only evidence he presented was the short time span between bringing up the mileage problem and his termination**, while the board presented a legitimate reason for firing him. *Freeman v. Ace Telephone Ass'n*, 467 F.3d 695 (8th Cir. 2006).

◆ An engineer at an Ohio facility lost his job in a reduction in force. He sued the company, claiming that the real reason was retaliation for whistle-blowing activity. He had been assigned to look into air quality issues at the facility and had stated to a supervisor that there were still issues to look into even after the air conditioning system had been cleaned and purified. He had also offered to conduct more research into the problem of mold and had suggested that the company buy an air filter that would remove mold spores from the air. The company claimed that he was fired because of excessive absenteeism and belligerence to co-workers. The Sixth Circuit determined that he did not qualify for whistleblower protection because **his statements were not sufficient to put the company on notice that it was violating any governmental policy** concerning workplace safety. *Jermer v. Siemens Energy & Automation, Inc.*, 395 F.3d 655 (6th Cir. 2005).

◆ A company in North Dakota provided respiratory therapy and medical equipment to home-bound patients. The Fargo office manager questioned the regional manager about the company's practice of having technicians set up the equipment and educate customers on it. She believed this violated state law. He maintained that the practice was legal and told her to address personality conflicts and other personnel problems in the office. When she complained to him about the practice again, she was fired. She sued under the state's whistleblower protection law and a court dismissed the lawsuit. The North Dakota Supreme Court reversed, noting that **she did not have to report the wrongdoing to a law enforcement or government agency** to enjoy the protections of the act. She only had to act in good faith. And even if she was concerned that employees were being "hung out to dry," this did not mean she acted in bad faith. *Heng v. Rotech Medical Corp. d/b/a/ Arrowhealth Medical Supply*, 688 N.W.2d 389 (N.D. 2004).

◆ Xerox had a fixed-price contract with a Tennessee company to implement a software program, but sought additional funds after unauthorized persons at the company broke the software code, necessitating repairs. Xerox shut down the company's computer system during the dispute over additional payments. It also fired an employee for performance problems. He sued Xerox, alleging that the real reason for his termination was his refusal to keep Xerox's misconduct a secret. A federal court ruled against him, and the Sixth Circuit affirmed. Here, Xerox's risking of a breach of contract action did not give rise to a common law whistleblower claim so as to support his allegation of wrongful termination. If Xerox indeed breached the contract by shutting down the computer system, this was not "illegal" activity that jeopardized the public good. Thus, **the employee could not claim that his firing violated a public policy**. *Fleming v. Xerox Connect Inc.*, 50 Fed.Appx. 211 (6th Cir. 2002).

◆ A supervisor at General Motors (GM) was warned on several occasions about time sheet errors, but was not disciplined. Subsequently, he had a run-in with a co-worker who was a member of the union committee. He claimed that the co-worker shoved him when he refused to leave a room where the committee was meeting. He informed plant security of the incident, as well as two superiors. He also filed a police report. Later, he was prohibited from working overtime because of his time sheet errors and, after claiming two hours' overtime that company investigators determined he did not work, he was fired. He sued under the Michigan Whistleblowers' Protection Act. A trial court ruled for GM, and the Supreme Court of Michigan ultimately concurred. **He had to show more than that he was disciplined after he filed the assault report**; he had to show that he was disciplined because of it. He failed to do so because evidence indicated he had repeatedly falsified his time sheets. *West v. General Motors Corp.*, 665 N.W.2d 468 (Mich. 2003).

◆ A longtime private security guard employed by Sears also had a job as a sheriff's deputy. On a number of occasions, he observed the store manager taking merchandise into his office, which violated company rules. As a result, the security guard decided to install a camera in the manager's office. He also reported the manager's suspicious activities to company officials. Two months later, he was fired for a security problem that occurred at the store a month earlier. He sued Sears for wrongful termination, claiming that the real reason for his firing was his report of suspicious activity by the store manager. A jury ruled in his favor, but an appellate court reversed the decision. The Maryland Court of Appeals affirmed, noting that the security guard was **not entitled to whistleblower protection because he did not report suspected criminal activity to the police**. He merely reported it to company officials. This was not enough to invoke the public policy exception to at-will employment. *Wholey v. Sears Roebuck & Co.*, 803 A.2d 482 (Md. 2002).

◆ After reporting instances of suspected resident abuse to state investigators, a nursing home social services director was fired. She filed suit under the state's whistleblower protection act, and a jury ruled in her favor. The Michigan Court of Appeals affirmed, noting that a reasonable juror could find that the director had been **fired in retaliation for reporting suspected violations of law.** Even though the nursing home had presented some legitimate reasons for the discharge, the jury could conclude that those reasons were a pretext for retaliation, especially since the director had been fired within hours of telling a nursing home official that she had reported her suspicions to the authorities. *Roulston v. Tendercare, Inc.*, 608 N.W.2d 525 (Mich. Ct. App. 2000).

◆ A part-time nurse in the Mobile Intensive Care Unit (MICU) of a New Jersey hospital reported two instances of misconduct by fellow employees, including an instance where a paramedic took a patient's medication and put it in his pocket. After an investigation revealed no wrongdoing, she was taken off the MICU and had her hours reduced. She sued the hospital under the state whistleblower law. The case reached the Supreme Court of New Jersey, which held that the law protects an employee from retaliation for objecting to "any activity, policy or practice" the employee reasonably believes 1) violates the law; 2) is fraudulent or criminal; or 3) violates public policy concerning public health, safety or welfare. A paramedic's theft of patient medication, whether or not condoned by the hospital, clearly violates public health and safety. As a result, the nurse was entitled to recover for the hospital's retaliation against her, even if it did not condone the alleged theft of the medication and subsequent cover-up investigation, because **the basis for her complaint was reasonable**. *Higgins v. Pascack Valley Hospital*, 730 A.2d 327 (N.J. 1999).

◆ The Michigan Department of Transportation cited an employer for transporting a prohibited substance in a trailer that was not properly certified for that purpose. A supervisor sought the identity of the person reporting the violation and questioned an employee about it. The employee denied making the report, but the supervisor fired him. The employee then sued under the state Whistleblowers' Protection Act (WPA). The court dismissed the case, and the Supreme Court of Michigan affirmed. In order to prevail in a WPA action, the complaining party must demonstrate that he was engaged in protected activity. Protected activity under the WPA consists of reporting a violation of a law, regulation or rule to a public body, preparing to report such a violation to a public body, or being asked to participate in an investigation by a public body. **Since the employee had denied reporting an employer violation to the state transportation department, he was not protected** by the WPA. He was not protected simply because he was perceived to be the reporting employee. *Chandler v. Dowell Schlumberger Inc.*, 572 N.W.2d 210 (Mich. 1998).

E. Federal Statutory Protections

1. ERISA

The Employee Retirement Income Security Act (ERISA), at Section 510, prohibits employers from taking adverse action against employees who assert their rights under the act (29 U.S.C. § 1140).

◆ An employee of an Illinois hospital received an evaluation describing her as an outstanding manager. However, the hospital faced financial troubles and the employee's husband suffered from prostate cancer, which cost the hospital thousands of dollars in insurance payments. The hospital fired the employee, who sued it for discrimination because of her association with a disabled person. The hospital then asserted for the first time that the reason for her firing was insubordination. She sought to amend her lawsuit to claim retaliation under ERISA, but a federal court granted pretrial judgment to the hospital. The

Seventh Circuit reversed, finding issues of fact that required a trial. It also held that **she could amend her complaint to allege retaliation under ERISA**. *Dewitt v. Proctor Hospital*, 517 F.3d 944 (7th Cir. 2008).

◆ A New York human resources (HR) director discovered that a payroll discrepancy resulted in the **under-funding of her company's 401(k) plan**. She told the company's chief financial officer (CFO), who advised her to drop the matter, and the controller, who refused to address the problem. Finally she contacted the company's outside attorney, who confirmed her findings and set up a meeting with her and the company's president. Afterwards, the HR director was demoted. A year later she was fired. She sued the company under Section 510 of ERISA, alleging retaliation. A federal court dismissed the case, but the Second Circuit reinstated it. The HR director did not have to go as far as filing an official complaint with the government to be protected as a whistleblower. She only had to respond to an inquiry about the matter from company officials. *Nicolaou v. Horizon Media, Inc.*, 402 F.3d 325 (2d Cir. 2005).

◆ The manager of the Chicago office of a Georgia-based manufacturer allowed an employee to conduct personal business on the job and let employees take an unauthorized extra week of holiday time without notifying the Georgia office. At about the same time, the company failed to make required 401(k) contributions. The manager contacted the Illinois Department of Labor concerning the failure to make contributions and made a written complaint to the company's chief financial officer and plan trustee. The company then made appropriate distributions with interest. It later confirmed reports of the extra holiday leave and fired the manager for misuse of company property. He sued, and an Illinois federal court ruled for the employer. The U.S. Court of Appeals, Seventh Circuit, affirmed. This was not a case of an employer taking adverse employment action against an employee to interfere with his pension rights. The reasons given by the employer were not pretextual, and there had been no ERISA violation. **The discharge was justified by misuse of company time and property.** *Grottkau v. Sky Climber, Inc.*, 79 F.3d 70 (7th Cir. 1996).

◆ A Massachusetts engineer's supervisor suspected that the engineer was abusing alcohol. The supervisor suggested that the engineer take a medical leave of absence under the company's short-term disability benefits plan. The plan required a physician's certification of disability within 10 days of the commencement of disability leave. The engineer obtained the certification form from the company and stopped going to work. He submitted the form 30 days later and listed hypertension, rather than alcoholism, as the cause of disability. The company notified the engineer that it considered him as having voluntarily quit and rejected the certification of disability. The engineer sued the company, claiming that it had violated Section 510 of ERISA by terminating his employment to deprive him of disability benefits. A federal court dismissed the case, and the engineer appealed.

The U.S. Court of Appeals, First Circuit stated that a retaliatory discharge complaint under ERISA requires proof of an employer's specific intent to interfere with employee benefits. Deprivation of employee benefits must be a motivating factor for the employment termination action, not a mere consequence. In this case, the district court had properly dismissed the case because no reasonable employee would have taken 30 days to return the certification form. The court rejected the engineer's argument that the company had discriminated against him because other employees had not been denied plan participation for failure to return a timely certification. **Inconsistent application of the terms of a health plan did not demonstrate a specific intent to interfere with plan benefits.** *Barbour v. Dynamics Research Corp.*, 63 F.3d 32 (1st Cir. 1995).

◆ A Pennsylvania packaging employee underwent relatively minor foot surgery and received full medical benefits from her employer's short-term disability plan. A year later, she took a second leave of absence for additional surgery and again received full medical benefits. During the second leave of absence, the company's HR manager hired a private investigator to determine whether the employee was disabled and entitled to continue receiving benefits. The investigator prepared a report, which stated that the employee operated a cleaning service during her leave, despite never actually observing her perform these services. In reliance on the report, the employer fired the employee. She sued in a New Jersey federal court, claiming that the discharge violated ERISA. The court granted pretrial judgment to the employer. On appeal, the Third Circuit, rejected the employer's argument that ERISA claims for wrongful discharge were prohibited in cases where benefits were not withheld and were actually paid. **ERISA provides a cause of action to challenge a discharge where the employee presents evidence of retaliation for exercising ERISA rights.** The district court had improperly awarded pretrial judgment to the employer in view of evidence that the company did not have a regular practice of investigating employees on disability leave. *Kowalski v. L & F Products*, 82 F.3d 1283 (3d Cir. 1996).

◆ An Ohio physician formed a pension plan for which he served as administrator and trustee on behalf of himself and his employees. Some plan funds were invested with a commodities investor who embezzled the funds, resulting in a substantial loss of plan assets. An employee whose lost share of plan funds was almost $20,000 demanded reimbursement and rejected the physician's offer to repay the amount in the form of taxable bonuses. She sued for reimbursement despite the physician's threats of discharge or reduced work hours. Within a month, the physician fired her, stating that he was reducing the extent of his practice. A federal court awarded the employee the entire amount of claimed plan benefits with interest. It also awarded over $100,000 in back pay and front pay for wrongful discharge in violation of ERISA, plus $33,000 in attorneys' fees. The U.S. Court of Appeals, Sixth Circuit, affirmed. Although ERISA prohibits damage awards that are characterized as legal damages, **the award of back pay here was considered an equitable remedy because it was restitutive**. The front pay award was also an equitable remedy that was not prohibited by ERISA. The court rejected the physician's argument that he should not be liable for plan losses that had been suffered long before the employee's discharge. *Schwartz v. Gregori*, 45 F.3d 1017 (6th Cir. 1995).

2. False Claims Act

The False Claims Act prohibits employers from taking adverse action against employees who assert their rights under the act.

◆ The president of a Rhode Island company that did contract work for the government wrote a letter to the owner stating his belief that the owner's nephew was fraudulently collecting two salaries. He also confronted the nephew, who told him to mind his own business or he would be fired. A month later, the president was fired. He brought a False Claims Act lawsuit against the company. The First Circuit ruled against him. Here, his job required him to warn of possible billing violations. Thus, **to be entitled to False Claims Act protections, he would have had to do more than just send a letter to the owner**; he would have had to make clear that he was alerting her to a possible False Claims Act problem. Also, the nephew's threat was not relevant because he never told the owner about the conversation. *Maturi v. McLaughlin Research Corp.*, 413 F.3d 166 (1st Cir. 2005).

◆ The federal False Claims Act (FCA) allows private citizens to bring an action on behalf of the U.S. government against anyone committing a fraud upon the government. A prevailing party in an FCA action may receive up to 30% of the amount recovered, and the FCA protects employees from retaliatory discharge, demotion or other discrimination for reporting fraudulent activities. A longtime Tennessee telephone company dispatcher observed that service reports were being falsified to avoid the necessity of providing refunds to customers, some of which were government agencies. She showed her supervisor a newspaper article describing a similar fraud being perpetrated in Florida. Afterward, the dispatcher alleged that she was harassed and threatened with discharge. She took a permanent disability leave and sued the employer under the FCA. The court dismissed the complaint. The dispatcher appealed to the U.S. Court of Appeals, Sixth Circuit, which held that **an FCA lawsuit must be based upon public disclosure of allegations of fraud**. The complaining party must be the original source of the disclosure. Here, the employee had based part of her allegations on information already reported by the press and made public in two separate lawsuits. She could not prevail, since she was not the original source of the information. The whistleblower portion of her complaint had been properly dismissed, but the court reversed and remanded the retaliatory discharge portion of the claim. *U.S. ex rel. McKenzie v. BellSouth Telecommunications, Inc.*, 123 F.3d 935 (6th Cir. 1997).

◆ The U.S. Court of Appeals, Fourth Circuit, affirmed a pretrial judgment order for a Maryland employer in an action brought by a former employee who claimed he had been discharged in violation of a public policy stated in the federal False Claims Act. The court ruled that the act contains its own remedy for public policy violations, prohibiting an abusive discharge claim on the basis of public policy. The False Claims Act cause of action failed because **the employee had not told the employer during his tenure that he was pursing an action under the act**. The employer was entitled to dismissal of the breach of contract claim and to judgment on its counterclaim for breach of certain nondisclosure agreements. *Zahodnick v. IBM Corp.*, 135 F.3d 911 (4th Cir. 1997).

◆ A Pennsylvania woman worked as the bookkeeper-accountant for a home-health service. The service was a nonprofit corporation that provided skilled nursing care, home health aids, and other services to individuals, some of whom were covered by Medicare. The bookkeeper's duties included providing information and documents used to prepare cost reports to be submitted to a Medicare intermediary. In 1991, the service received a letter from the intermediary requesting additional information concerning the 1990 fiscal year cost report. The service asked the bookkeeper to recreate documents to provide a fictitious account of the services provided by the service. After she refused, she was fired. She then sued the employer for violating the federal False Claims Act. A court noted that the act makes it unlawful for an employer to discharge an employee because the employee refuses to participate in submitting false claims under the Medicare program. The court found for the bookkeeper. The act provides for **reinstatement with the same seniority status the employee would have had but for the discrimination**, two times the amount of back pay, and interest on the back pay. Therefore, the bookkeeper was entitled to receive twice her lost wages, reinstatement, and attorneys' fees. *Godwin v. Visiting Nurse Ass'n Home Health Service*, 831 F.Supp. 449 (E.D. Pa. 1993).

◆ A Missouri physician operated a clinic that employed four workers. He fired a lab technician who had reported Medicare and Medicaid fraud by the clinic to federal agencies. When the technician sued the physician and clinic in a Missouri circuit court for wrongful discharge, the physician denied any knowledge of the technician's reports prior to the discharge, and the court ruled for the physician. The Missouri Court of Appeals affirmed, finding substantial evidence that the physician and the other employees of the clinic lacked knowledge of the federal agency reports. Accordingly, **there was no basis for the wrongful discharge claim on the ground of violation of public policy**. *Williams v. Thomas*, 961 S.W.2d 869 (Mo. Ct. App. 1998).

3. Surface Transportation Assistance Act

The Surface Transportation Assistance Act prohibits employers from taking adverse action against employees who assert their rights under the act.

◆ A trucking company discharged one of its drivers, alleging that he had disabled several lights on his assigned truck in order to obtain extra pay while awaiting repairs. The driver filed a grievance, asserting that the discharge had been in retaliation for having complained of safety violations. He also filed a complaint with the Department of Labor, alleging that his firing violated Section 405 of the federal Surface Transportation Assistance Act. A field investigator obtained statements substantiating the driver's claim and offered the company the opportunity to submit a written statement detailing the basis for the employee's discharge, but it was not allowed to examine the substance of the investigator's evidence. A preliminary administrative order called for the employee's reinstatement. The company filed suit in a Georgia federal court, arguing that reinstatement prior to an evidentiary hearing violated its due process rights. The court ruled for the company. The U.S. Supreme Court affirmed in part and reversed in part. **Due process required pre-reinstatement notice of the employee's allegations, notice of the substance of the relevant supporting evidence, an opportunity to submit a written response, and an opportunity to meet with the investigator** and present statements from rebuttal witnesses. Due process did not require employer confrontation and cross-examination before preliminary reinstatement if a prompt post-reinstatement evidentiary hearing was available. *Brock v. Roadway Express, Inc.,* 481 U.S. 252, 107 S.Ct. 1740, 95 L.Ed.2d 239 (1987).

◆ A Florida employee complained of gasoline fumes in his truck at an employee "speak-out session," a periodic meeting of employees to solicit grievances. Later, the employer fired him after he refused to take a scheduled run, first offering to let him use another truck or use a portable radio set. He filed an administrative action against the employer for Surface Transportation Assistance Act (STAA) violations. The U.S. Department of Labor found that the employee had no reasonable apprehension of serious injury to himself or the public arising from use of the truck and held that the employer did not violate the STAA. An administrative law judge affirmed, but the U.S. Secretary of Labor remanded the case. The parties reached a partial settlement but the employer appealed the liability issue to the U.S. Court of Appeals. The Second Circuit observed that **the employer had attempted to remedy the employee's safety concerns**, yet the employee had refused to perform his assigned task. The STAA does not require portable radios in vehicles. The speak-out session complaint about gas fumes was not reasonably linked to the firing, since the employee had not mentioned it at the time of the incident leading to discharge. Because the employer had offered to correct the situation, the court ruled in its favor. *Brink's Inc. v. Herman*, 148 F.3d 175 (2d Cir. 1998).

◆ An environmental services employer transported, stored, treated and disposed of hazardous waste. It instituted a policy of charging customers for extra time spent by drivers to bring drums of hazardous waste into compliance with federal regulations. A driver drove trucks from a Connecticut service center and was the subject of many customer complaints for taking too much time at their facilities. After receiving numerous complaints, the driver's supervisor told him to leave each customer's premises without extra time regardless of the condition of the drums. The driver responded that accepting improperly sealed and labeled drums was illegal and could result in his own liability. The employer fired him for being rude to customers, but it reinstated him on the condition that he remain under strict supervision and abide by a strict chain of command.

The employer assigned the driver to haul material between company-owned facilities in order to remove him from customer contact. However, it fired him again for his continuing regulatory compliance concerns, which included a report to the Massachusetts Department of Environmental Protection. The driver filed an administrative action with the U.S. Department of Labor, asserting violation of the STAA. An administrative review board ruled for the driver, and the employer appealed. The First Circuit Court of Appeals rejected the employer's claim that STAA protection was unavailable to employees who make only internal complaints and do not commence formal agency or court proceedings. **The driver had effectively communicated his safety and compliance concerns prior to the first discharge**, and the employer had sufficient notice that he believed the company risked regulatory violations. There was a link between the activity and the discharge, and the court upheld the decision reinstating the driver. *Clean Harbors Environmental Services, Inc. v. Herman*, 146 F.3d 12 (1st Cir. 1998).

4. Other Federal Statutes

Most federal statutes that protect employees contain provisions barring employers from retaliating against employees who exercise their rights under the statutes.

- The president and CEO of a Florida insurance holding company discovered that other officers and directors of the company were diverting corporate funds for personal use and submitting false financial statements to government regulators, shareholders and creditors. He contacted the regulators about the statements, causing the directors and officers involved in producing them to orchestrate a scheme to remove him from the company. After his termination, he sued them under the Racketeer Influenced and Corrupt Organizations Act (RICO). A federal court dismissed his lawsuit, and the Eleventh Circuit affirmed. The U.S. Supreme Court also affirmed. It stated that because **the termination was not an act of racketeering and was not independently wrongful** under any substantive provision of RICO, the president could not sue under the statute. *Beck v. Prupis*, 529 U.S. 494, 120 S.Ct. 1608, 146 L.Ed.2d 561 (2000).

- An at-will employee of a Georgia-based health care company cooperated with federal agents investigating the company for Medicare fraud. The employee had been subpoenaed to testify before the grand jury but never did. After the company was indicted, the employee was expected to appear as a witness in a subsequent criminal trial. He was fired and sued under 42 U.S.C. § 1985(2), alleging that three of the company's officers conspired to intimidate him and to retaliate against him for attending the grand jury proceedings and to keep him from testifying at the criminal trial. Section 1985(2) prohibits people from entering into conspiracies to "deter, by force, intimidation or threat," any witness from testifying in court. It provides a cause of action when parties to a conspiracy cause the witness to be "injured in his person or property."

  The district court dismissed the lawsuit, finding that an at-will employee has no constitutionally protected property interest in continued employment. The Eleventh Circuit affirmed, but the U.S. Supreme Court reversed. The sort of harm alleged by the employee – essentially third-party interference with at-will employment relationships – stated a claim for relief under Section 1985(2).

Even though at-will employment is not "property" for purposes of the Due Process Clause, **an at-will employee who loses his job suffers injury to his "person or property" as contemplated by Section 1985(2)**. *Haddle v. Garrison*, 525 U.S. 121, 119 S.Ct. 489, 142 L.Ed.2d 502 (1998).

◆ A Kentucky husband and wife worked for the same company. The husband also bought a welding shop, which forced him and his wife to file for bankruptcy protection under Chapter 7 of the Bankruptcy Code. After he lost his car, he approached two company officials and offered to falsify their income tax returns if they would give him a company car. He and his wife were fired the next day. They sued the company for firing them in violation of federal bankruptcy law. The case reached the Sixth Circuit Court of Appeals, which ruled against them. Here, **their bankruptcy was not the sole reason they were fired**. Rather, the company cited sloppy bookkeeping, rudeness to customers and the car issue as additional reasons for the discharge. Since the Bankruptcy Code only prohibits firing employees "solely" because of their bankruptcy, the company did not violate the law. *White v. Kentuckiana Livestock Market, Inc.*, 397 F.3d 420 (6th Cir. 2005).

◆ A Florida carpenter worked for a contractor at a nuclear power plant. He was transferred to a crew working on a temporary project and began experiencing disagreements with his foreman concerning safety procedures for contaminated tools. The foreman learned that the carpenter went over his head to make a complaint concerning the handling of contaminated tools. The carpenter was then laid off before less experienced crew members. Within 30 days, the entire crew was laid off. The carpenter filed an administrative complaint with the U.S. Department of Labor, claiming that the employer had violated the whistleblower protection provision of the Energy Reorganization Act. An administrative law judge held for the carpenter but only awarded back wages for one month and refused to order reinstatement. The secretary affirmed the final administrative decision, and the U.S. Court of Appeals, Eleventh Circuit, agreed with the secretary that the carpenter had made out a valid claim for discrimination. He showed that the Energy Reorganization Act applied and that **he had been engaged in protected activity that adversely affected the terms and conditions of his employment**. The carpenter's initiation of an internal complaint constituted a protected activity. *Bechtel Construction Co. v. Secretary of Labor*, 50 F.3d 926 (11th Cir. 1995).

◆ An Oklahoma personnel director was responsible for monitoring her employer's compliance with state and federal wage and hour laws. She learned that the employer's overtime compensation policies conflicted with these requirements and met with the company attorney and president. The president fired her within a month for releasing confidential information and for misconduct. She filed a wrongful discharge lawsuit against the employer, and also alleged that her discharge violated the Fair Labor Standards Act (FLSA) and state wage and hour laws. The court dismissed the wrongful discharge claim prior to trial, and it granted the employer's post-trial motion to set aside a jury award of over $325,000 in damages for her FLSA claim. The U.S. Court of Appeals, Tenth Circuit, affirmed, finding no clear statement of Oklahoma law that required an employer to pay overtime. Thus, there was no public policy protecting the employee from an at-will discharge. The court disagreed with the district court's justification for dismissing the FLSA complaint. Nevertheless, **the FLSA did not protect the employee's activity here because she failed to assert her own rights under the act**. Her reporting of the company's potential FLSA violations took place in her capacity as a personnel manager and was not an assertion of her own FLSA rights. *McKenzie v. Renberg's Inc.*, 94 F.3d 1478 (10th Cir. 1996).

- A Missouri shoe company employee was exposed to a chemical spray used in a machine. She questioned the safety of the chemical and inquired about safety protection methods. After contacting the local Occupational Safety and Health Administration (OSHA) office, she filed a formal complaint alleging hazardous conditions at her workplace. An OSHA compliance officer conducted an on-site investigation, which infuriated the company president. Within five weeks of the investigation, the company fired the employee under a relatively new tardiness policy. The employee was the first person ever prosecuted under the policy, and there was evidence that other employees had similar or worse attendance records. She sued in a Missouri federal court, which granted the employer's motion for pretrial judgment.

The Eighth Circuit Court of Appeals held that the district court had incorrectly required the employee to prove that the manufacturer had actual knowledge of her identity as the complaining employee. Even though the OSHA inspector had not revealed the employee's identity, evidence indicated that the president was aware of it. To escape dismissal in a retaliatory discharge case, an employee must show that she engaged in a protected activity and that **a causal connection existed between the protected activity and the adverse employment action**. Because the district court had applied a higher standard of inquiry that ignored evidence of the causal connection, pretrial judgment was inappropriate and the district court decision was reversed. *Reich v. Hoy Shoe Co., Inc.*, 32 F.3d 361 (8th Cir. 1994).

V. CONSTRUCTIVE DISCHARGE

Sometimes, employers will seek to get an employee to quit by making work conditions intolerable. Where such actions force an employee to quit, and where a court determines that the employer's action would make a reasonable employee quit, an employer will generally be found to have constructively discharged the employee.

Generally, constructive discharge lawsuits only arise where the employee is protected (e.g., by being a minority or a disabled person or a member of a particular religion).

A constructive discharge will be deemed to be the same as firing the employee. Any damages the employee could recover for wrongful discharge will also be available to the employee who quits under a constructive discharge.

See also Chapter One for cases involving discrimination.

◆ A communications operator for the Pennsylvania State Police claimed that three of her supervisors subjected her to sexually harassing comments and gestures. She told the EEO officer about the harassment but never filed a complaint. Shortly thereafter, she was arrested for theft in the workplace and was interrogated. She was allowed to resign and then sued under Title VII. **The question of constructive discharge reached the U.S. Supreme Court**, which held that if the constructive discharge was not the result of an official act by the police, but instead the misconduct of a rogue supervisor, then the police could assert the *Faragher/Ellerth* defense. However, if the police sanctioned the actions leading to the constructive discharge, then a tangible employment action would have occurred so as to make the defense unavailable. The Court remanded the case for further proceedings. *Pennsylvania State Police v. Suders*, 542 U.S. 129, 124 S.Ct. 2342, 159 L.Ed.2d 204 (2004).

◆ A 53-year-old Kansas news photographer **claimed that he was constructively discharged based on his age** when the TV station he worked for began to emphasize live, on-site reporting. He claimed his shift was changed, he was denied necessary training, he was denied vacation time, and he was issued verbal and written reprimands that forced him to quit. The case reached the Tenth Circuit, which ruled against him. Although his working conditions, and particularly the night shifts, were unpleasant, they were not objectively intolerable such that a reasonable person would have had no other choice but to quit. As for the reprimands, they did not indicate that he faced either discipline or termination. Further, the photographer never formally requested that he be allowed to take owed vacation time. Instead, he asked to sit down to discuss his vacation plans, and management never responded to that request. *DeWalt v. Meredith Corp.*, 288 Fed. Appx. 484 (10th Cir. 2008).

◆ During a job interview for a New Hampshire nonprofit, the agency's food services director told a prospective employee that if she encountered anything she disliked about employees, she made it miserable enough for them to quit so she didn't have to fire them. She hired the applicant as an assistant director and had a good working relationship with her until the assistant director refused to submit time sheets for the director's daughters (who also worked there) because she had questions about whether they worked the hours they reported. For the next two weeks, the director then yelled at her for minor things and gave her a less than satisfactory evaluation. The assistant director quit and sued for wrongful termination. The New Hampshire Supreme Court held that her claim deserved a trial and that **she could use the director's statements at the interview to prove she was constructively discharged**. *Lacasse v. Spaulding Youth Center*, 910 A.2d 1262 (N.H. 2006).

◆ An African-American aircraft cleaning supervisor was confronted about being off base during his designated shift. He resigned in lieu of being fired, then sued under Title VII, claiming that he had been constructively discharged because of race-based harassment, asserting that his supervisor had made four derogatory comments about blacks in the past year. An Oklahoma federal court ruled against him, finding that he was not constructively discharged. **His working conditions were not so severe as to force him to quit**, and his decision to resign in lieu of being fired did not meet the conditions for a constructive discharge. *McGriff v. American Airlines, Inc.*, 431 F.Supp.2d 1145 (N.D. Okla. 2006).

◆ A black human resources (HR) director complained to the corporate attorney that the head of recruiting refused to promote African-Americans to senior-level positions. The month before, the company had eliminated the HR director's position when it combined his department with another and created a new position. It offered him a consulting contract with full salary and benefits for two months, followed by a six-month consulting contract, but informed him he would not be hired for the new job. He quit and sued for wrongful termination and retaliation under 42 U.S.C. § 1981, claiming that he had been constructively discharged. A Virginia federal court and the Fourth Circuit ruled against him. Even though he found the **work environment miserable and professionally unfulfilling**, this was not enough to show a constructive discharge. Also, informing him he would not be hired for the new position did not amount to a termination. *Honor v. Booz-Allen & Hamilton, Inc.*, 383 F.3d 180 (4th Cir. 2004).

◆ A maitre d' for an Ohio country club provided deposition testimony against the club in an age discrimination lawsuit. The club president later sent the maitre d' a letter assuring him that retaliation would not occur and that the club would investigate his concerns regarding his manager's retaliatory conduct. A few months before, the club's food and beverage operations had begun slipping. The club manager, the maitre d's direct supervisor, yelled at his staff and threatened that if he lost his job, others would "go down" with him. The club manager increased the staff's work hours and required the maitre d' to work six days a week. The club manager also told the staff that the maitre d' was using Valium, took away his scheduling duties and allegedly excluded him from two meetings. After the maitre d' resigned and sued for constructive discharge, the Ohio Court of Appeals held that **the maitre d' could not establish constructive discharge**. Despite being pressured by his manager to work long hours and improve service, his working conditions were not so severe that they would force a reasonable person to quit. *Mayo v. Kenwood Country Club*, 731 N.E.2d 190 (Ohio Ct. App. 1999).

VI. COLLECTIVE BARGAINING AGREEMENTS

Where a collective bargaining agreement exists, the agreement governs employment termination issues, as permitted or supplemented by federal labor law. Most of these cases fall within the jurisdiction of the National Labor Relations Board.

Generally, collective bargaining agreements bestow greater rights on employees, making it harder for companies to fire them. They also provide a grievance process so discharged or disciplined employees can challenge the actions taken against them without having to resort to lawsuits.

For further cases involving union and employer obligations under federal law, see Chapter Five.

◆ A Michigan garbage truck driver, while substituting on another driver's route, hooked a low-hanging overhead wire and pulled it down from a house while backing up on the wrong side of a dead-end residential street. He immediately informed dispatch, and supervisors arrived on the scene. They determined that the driver violated the company's zero-tolerance safety guidelines and safe driving practices. The driver was suspended without pay and was fired the next day. He filed a grievance with his union, which contended on his behalf that he should have been given a warning and should not have been immediately discharged. **An arbitrator examined the collective bargaining agreement and determined that the offense was one demanding a warning prior to termination.** The arbitrator ordered the driver reinstated with back pay, and the company appealed. A federal court ruled for the company, but the Sixth Circuit reversed, finding that the arbitrator did not operate outside the scope of his authority, and that he was arguably construing and applying the collective bargaining agreement when he ordered reinstatement. *Truck Drivers Local No. 164 v. Allied Waste Systems, Inc.*, 512 F.3d 211 (6th Cir. 2008).

◆ A company fired a Pennsylvania employee for attempting to steal meat from the company by using a stolen credit card. When a security guard told the employee he was being fired, the employee allegedly attacked the guard and broke two ribs. The employee's union filed a grievance, and an arbitrator ruled that the company did not have just cause to fire the employee. The arbitrator ordered the employee to be reinstated. The company notified the employee that it would pay him back pay, but also informed him he was fired for attacking the security guard. The union sued and the Third Circuit ruled that **the second firing was proper**. It was for a different offense. Also, the back pay satisfied the arbitrator's order to reinstate the employee. *United Food & Commercial Workers, Local 1776 v. Excel Corp.*, 470 F.3d 143 (3d Cir. 2006).

◆ A manufacturing company in Tennessee fired a union employee for accumulating too many absenteeism points. Three weeks later, it notified him that it had an alternative reason for firing him – that he had falsified his time card. The union filed grievances with respect to both reasons, but the company denied both. The union then proceeded to arbitration with respect to the absenteeism reason, and an arbitrator determined that the employee should not have been fired because he had not accumulated enough points to warrant a discharge. The arbitrator ordered the employee reinstated. When the company refused, a lawsuit resulted. The Sixth Circuit ultimately determined that the union's failure to challenge the alternative reason for the discharge prevented the employee from getting his job back. *Int'l Brotherhood of Boilermakers, Local No. S-251 v. Thyssenkrupp Elevator Manufacturing, Inc.*, 365 F.3d 523 (6th Cir. 2004).

◆ A bakery employee in Michigan was fired for violating a company's anti-harassment policy when he said, "Relax, Sambo" to an African-American co-worker. He filed a grievance, and an arbitrator determined that he should be suspended and then placed on probation for five years. When the bakery sued, a federal court ruled for the employee and union. The Sixth Circuit affirmed. Here, the employee had no prior disciplinary record, and **the collective bargaining agreement provided for progressive discipline**. The arbitrator did not exceed his authority in finding that the employee should have been afforded progressive discipline based on both the bargaining agreement and the anti-harassment policy. *Way Bakery v. Truck Drivers Local No. 164*, 363 F.3d 590 (6th Cir. 2004).

◆ A company fired a truck driver for gross insubordination and fighting on the job with his supervisor. Under the collective bargaining agreement, the company had the right to discharge employees for just cause and without warning for either reason. However, when the truck driver's union challenged the discharge, an arbitrator found that **the company had to establish by clear and convincing evidence that the truck driver had started the fight**. He determined that the company failed to meet this standard and ordered it to reinstate the driver. A Massachusetts federal court held that the arbitrator had exceeded his authority, but the First Circuit Court of Appeals reversed, stating that the arbitrator was free to set the standard for the burden of proof where the bargaining agreement was silent on the issue. As a result, the driver had to be reinstated. *Keebler v. Truck Drivers, Local 170*, 247 F.3d 8 (1st Cir. 2001).

◆ A union representing employees at a Japanese-controlled Alaska pulp mill called a strike when their collective bargaining agreement expired and a new agreement could not be reached. The employer hired permanent replacement workers and resumed mill operations, and union members later voted to de-certify their union. During the strike, a millwright who was a union member signed an anti-Japanese letter to the editor of a local newspaper and gave testimony before a Congressional committee that was unfavorable to the employer. He was not rehired after the strike but was reinstated after a successful hearing before the NLRB. The millwright then sued the employer for wrongful termination, infliction of emotional distress and tortious interference with his contractual rights. A trial court ruled for the employer, and the Supreme Court of Alaska affirmed. **Any contractual rights to employment under the collective bargaining agreement lapsed when it expired prior to the strike.** The employer's refusal to reinstate him had occurred after the expiration of the contract, and the trial court had properly rejected the violation of public policy claim. Since the employer had no duty to rehire the millwright, the tort-based claims also failed. *Sever v. Alaska Pulp Corp.*, 931 P.2d 354 (Alaska 1996).

◆ Drivers employed by a Denver concrete manufacturer de-certified their union. Several years later, a driver began unionization efforts. The employer suspended and then discharged the employee for failing to report an on-the-job accident, failing to wear his hard hat and having a bad attitude. The driver complained to the National Labor Relations Board (NLRB), which charged the employer with violating federal labor laws. An administrative law judge determined that the firing had been motivated in part by protected union conduct and ordered the driver reinstated with back pay. The NLRB adopted this decision, and the U.S. Court of Appeals, Tenth Circuit, enforced the NLRB order. The court stated that it is an unfair labor practice to interfere with, restrain or coerce an employee's right to form, join or assist a labor organization, or to discourage membership in a labor organization. There was sufficient evidence to support the NLRB finding that the driver had been engaged in union activities at the time of the discharge and that the employer was aware of his activities. There was also evidence that no other employee had been subjected to similar discipline for similar violations of company rules. Because there was evidence of anti-union sentiment by the employer, **the NLRB could have reasonably found that the discharge was improperly motivated**. *Ready Mixed Concrete Co. v. NLRB*, 81 F.3d 1546 (10th Cir. 1996).

◆ The collective bargaining agreement between employees of a Minnesota paper mill and their employer expired, and the parties were unable to reach a new agreement. The employer gave the union notice that it would unilaterally impose new employment terms. The employer then fired an assistant power plant operator suspected of sabotaging computer discs. The employee, who was also president of the local union, sued the employer under Section 301 of the Labor Management Relations Act for wrongful discharge. A federal court awarded the employee over $600,000 in damages. The Eighth Circuit determined that after the expiration of a collective bargaining agreement, an employer may unilaterally change terms and conditions of employment if there is a bargaining impasse. The National Labor Relations Act did not create a wrongful discharge cause of action, and there could be no implied contract right under state law in this case. **The unilateral implementation of employment conditions pursuant to a bargaining impasse did not provide a contractual basis under Section 301.** Because the jury instructions suggested that a contract was formed when the employees agreed to continue working for the employer, they erroneously infringed upon the employer's NLRA rights. The court ordered a new trial. *United Paperworkers Int'l Union, AFL-CIO, Local 274 v. Champion Int'l Corp.*, 81 F.3d 798 (8th Cir. 1996).

◆ A copper refinery employed a unionized work force at a Texas plant and generally had peaceful labor relations with the unions. Employees were not typically disciplined for horseplay incidents. However, an employee who served as president of one of the unions representing plant employees was fired after throwing a sandwich bag filled with water at another employee. The employer also barred the employee from attending a meeting and an Occupational Health and Safety Administration inspection. His union filed an unlawful labor practice charge with the NLRB. An administrative law judge held that the employer's actions violated the National Labor Relations Act (NLRA). The NLRB upheld the decision. The Fifth Circuit rejected the union's theory that the timing of the discharge was sufficient evidence of anti-union sentiment so as to demonstrate a violation of the NLRA. There was evidence that the employee had violated safety rules, lied to management and neglected his job duties twice in two months. There was no evidence that the employee had been disciplined differently than others because of his union activity. **The NLRA does not prohibit employers from disciplining employees, including union presidents.** Mere suspicion of unlawful motivation did not establish an NLRA violation. *Asarco, Inc. v. NLRB*, 86 F.3d 1401 (5th Cir. 1996).

◆ A Louisiana man worked for a company as a machine operator on a hazardous machine. Company rules provided that the use or bringing of controlled substances onto the premises would result in discharge. Police officers found the employee in another person's vehicle on company premises where marijuana was present. They also found traces of marijuana in the employee's car. The company learned of the first incident and fired the employee. He filed a grievance seeking arbitration under the collective bargaining agreement. Shortly before the arbitration hearing, the company learned of the marijuana found in the employee's car. However, the arbitrator then held for the employee because there was insufficient proof that the employee had used marijuana on the premises. The company appealed to a federal court, which overturned the arbitrator's decision. The Fifth Circuit affirmed. The case then reached the U.S. Supreme Court, which noted that the lower courts had erred in overturning the arbitrator's decision because of public policy concerns. Here, **the arbitrator's refusal to consider the later evidence was not bad faith or affirmative misconduct**. Further, arbitrators have wide discretion in formulating remedies, and it was error for the courts to overturn the arbitrator's decision because they viewed discharge as the proper remedy. The Court reversed the lower courts' holdings and upheld the arbitrator's decision. *United Paperworkers Int'l Union v. Misco, Inc.*, 484 U.S. 29, 108 S.Ct. 364, 98 L.Ed.2d 286 (1987).

◆ Caterpillar Tractor Company hired a group of employees to work at a California facility under a collective bargaining agreement. These employees all reached managerial or weekly salaried positions, outside the coverage of the agreement. They held their positions for a number of years and alleged that the employer made oral and written representations that "they could look forward to indefinite and lasting employment." The company then downgraded them to unionized positions that were supposedly only temporary. Thereafter, the company notified them that it was closing the California facility and that they would be laid off. The employees sued for breach of contract, and the case was dismissed for failure to state a claim under Section 301 of the Labor Management Relations Act. The Ninth Circuit Court of Appeals reversed, holding that the case must be heard in state court, and the case reached the U.S. Supreme Court.

The Supreme Court agreed that the state law contract claims were not preempted by Section 301. Here, even though the employees could have brought suit under Section 301, they chose to sue under state law on their individual contracts. **No interpretation or application of the collective bargaining agreement was necessary to decide their claims.** Further, even though the employees were covered by the collective bargaining agreement, their individual contracts were not necessarily subsumed into it. The Court affirmed the court of appeals and held that the state law claims should be heard in state court. *Caterpillar, Inc. v. Williams*, 482 U.S. 386, 107 S.Ct. 2425, 96 L.Ed.2d 318 (1987).

VII. PROCEDURAL CONSIDERATIONS

Prior to taking disciplinary action against an employee, you should consider the consequences of doing so. There may be reasons for avoiding such action. First, are you being consistent? In other words, have you disciplined other employees for similar misbehavior?

Second, even if the employee is at will, should you offer him/her due process? That is, should you give notice of the offense committed and an opportunity to respond? You don't need to provide a full-fledged hearing, but you probably want to get the employee's side before disciplining or firing.

Third, is there some protected activity the employee has engaged in that would make disciplining him/her less attractive? Or is there an employment contract that requires you to follow certain steps?

A. Termination Agreements

Employers often agree to a monetary settlement with a fired employee in exchange for a promise not to sue. If executed properly, these agreements (waivers) can minimize liability and the costs of litigation.

- A longtime General Motors (GM) employee who worked on fuel line designs frequently testified for GM in product liability cases. In one Georgia case, he testified that a GM truck fuel system was an inferior product. He was then fired, and he sued GM in a Michigan court for wrongful discharge. GM counterclaimed for breach of a fiduciary duty not to disclose privileged and confidential information and for misappropriating documents. The parties reached a settlement agreement under which the former employee received payment in return for a permanent injunction prohibiting him from testifying as an expert witness in other GM product liability cases without prior written consent. However, the order did not affect the still-pending Georgia litigation. A separate agreement permitted the employee to testify in other cases if another tribunal ordered his appearance.

  Six years later, the former employee was subpoenaed to testify in a Missouri wrongful death action involving a GM vehicle fire. GM resisted his appearance, asserting that the Michigan court order barred his testimony. A federal court allowed the employee to testify, and a jury awarded the victim's estate over $11 million in damages. The U.S. Court of Appeals, Eighth Circuit, reversed the judgment under the Full Faith and Credit Clause of the Constitution. The U.S. Supreme Court then found no public policy exception permitting a state court to resist the recognition of a foreign state court judgment. However, the Michigan court order could not control the Missouri action and **could not prevent the employee from testifying**. Moreover, the parties' agreement allowed the employee to testify where ordered by another court. The Court reversed and remanded the case. *Baker v. General Motors Corp.*, 522 U.S. 222, 118 S.Ct. 657, 139 L.Ed.2d 580 (1998).

- The vice president of a Tennessee company was fired after she was accused of sexually harassing a former hourly employee. She signed an agreement with the company releasing any employment-related claims she might have had against it under state or federal law as of the date the agreement was signed. As of that date, the former hourly employee had filed a lawsuit against her, and she had hired an attorney. After that date, the former hourly employee settled with the company and then dropped his lawsuit against the vice president. When she sought indemnification from the company for the expenses she incurred in defending the lawsuit, the Tennessee Court of Appeals ruled in her favor. **Since the indemnification claim did not exist at the time the release was signed, the release did not bar the claim.** Also, since her defense of the lawsuit was wholly successful, and since the lawsuit was brought against her because she was a director of the company, the company had to indemnify her under the state's Revised Model Business Corporation Act. *Sherman v. American Water Heater Co., Inc.*, 50 S.W.3d 455 (Tenn. Ct. App. 2001).

- A Missouri employee resigned from his job of 30 years under a written agreement calling for a retirement benefit package and an assurance that he was "welcome to approach" the company as a vendor or buyer in the future. The agreement also provided monetary benefits in exchange for dismissal of age discrimination and retaliation claims. He then negotiated a $1.7 million sale involving his former employer. After arranging the details of the sale, the former employer canceled it, and he sued for breach of the resignation agreement and other claims. The court granted the former employer's pretrial judgment motion, and he appealed to the Missouri Court of Appeals.

The court held that the settlement agreement foreclosed the employee's claim for an additional $330 per month in further retirement benefits. The lower court had correctly granted pretrial judgment on that claim and on the employee's claim for tortious interference with a business expectancy. However, the court had improperly granted pretrial judgment on the employee's claim for breach of contract and fraud because of evidence in the record that the sale had been rejected in violation of the negotiated agreement. **The "welcome to approach" language was not insufficiently vague and uncertain to be unenforceable**, and the employee should have received an opportunity to show whether the former employer had breached its contract and defrauded him in the process of negotiating the agreement. *Maupin v. Hallmark Cards, Inc.*, 894 S.W.2d 688 (Mo. Ct. App. 1995).

B. After-Acquired Evidence

After-acquired evidence refers to situations where an employee is fired for an improper reason but the employer then learns that it could have legitimately fired the employee for other misconduct.

Some courts will deny all recovery to employees who have, for example, lied on their applications. Others will just limit the recovery available (usually, back pay from the date of the wrongful termination to the date the employer discovered the misconduct).

◆ After an unplanned forced outage shut down both nuclear reactor units at a Michigan nuclear plant, a test engineer informed the night-shift engineer that he believed he had reached or exceeded the work hour limitations set by the Nuclear Regulatory Commission and that he planned to take the next day off. However, the next day, he was told he had to come in for a meeting. He demanded written authorization before going to work. He then left before a fellow engineer completed crucial documentation with respect to tolerance data. He was suspended and then fired. When he sued for wrongful discharge, a federal court and the Sixth Circuit held that he engaged in protected conduct when he complained about working excessive hours and required written authorization. The nuclear plant maintained that it had found **after-acquired evidence of personal or objectionable e-mails** in his mailbox and that it should not have to pay the front pay award. The Sixth Circuit disagreed. Other employees had received or forwarded the same or similar e-mails without being disciplined. Therefore, the nuclear plant could not use that information to deny the front pay award. *Indiana Michigan Power Co. v. U.S. Dep't of Labor*, 278 Fed.Appx. 597 (6th Cir. 2008).

◆ A doctor signed an employment agreement with a Florida hospital and noted that the reason for leaving his previous position was a change in administration. He worked as the chief medical officer for over two years, and was discharged along with other management personnel upon the replacement of the hospital's top management. He sued for breach of contract, seeking severance pay and other accrued benefits. The hospital defended by stating that he had committed prior acts of moral turpitude, including lying about the circumstances of leaving his previous job and the taking of a bonus he did not earn. When he sought pretrial judgment in his favor, a federal court granted it in part, noting that **the hospital could not use the after-acquired evidence to avoid paying severance to the doctor**. Further, the hospital offered no evidence that he had lied about why he left the previous job. However, there were questions about the bonus that required a trial. *Tomasini v. Mount Sinai Medical Center of Florida, Inc.*, 315 F.Supp.2d 1252 (S.D. Fla. 2004).

◆ The president and 10% owner of a company that sold water purifiers refused to illegally copy a supplier's patented process so that the company's equipment could be manufactured in China. He was then fired. He sued for wrongful termination in violation of public policy and breach of contract, among other claims. The company moved for pretrial judgment, asserting that after-acquired evidence justified its decision to fire him – namely, that **he had contacted a law firm to review the patent without disclosing that fact to his superiors and thus was dishonest**. It also claimed that refusing to violate a patent was not a public policy reason that would warrant a wrongful discharge lawsuit. A Colorado federal court refused to grant the company pretrial judgment. It found issues of fact as to whether the company acted in good faith when it fired him, and also ruled that the after-acquired evidence doctrine did not bar the wrongful discharge claim. *Ziegler v. Inabata of America, Inc.*, 316 F.Supp.2d 908 (D. Colo. 2004).

- A clerical worker used a false employment reference on her job application for a Colorado employer and omitted listing a former employer who had fired her. The employer's handbook allowed termination for misrepresentations. When the employee took an unexcused absence from work, the employer fired her. She sued, asserting that her termination had come in retaliation for her prior complaint to a state agency concerning rest breaks. During pretrial activity, the employer learned of the misrepresentations on her employment application and moved for dismissal on that basis. The case reached the Supreme Court of Colorado, which adopted the **after-acquired evidence rule, permitting an employer to retroactively rely on evidence of employee fraud** in a wrongful discharge action if it can prove that the fraud undermines the basis upon which the employee was hired. An employer may justifiably fire an employee who commits résumé8 fraud since the misrepresentation fraudulently induces the employer to enter into the contract. *Crawford Rehabilitation Services, Inc. v. Weissman*, 938 P.2d 540 (Colo. 1997).

- A Kansas nursing home employee removed and copied a videotape of a company meeting and later returned the original tape. She was fired for inconsiderate treatment of residents and sued, claiming that the discharge breached an implied employment contract. During pretrial activity, the employer learned that she had taken the videotape and stated that this action justified her firing. The employee responded that she had viewed the tape in the course of her employment and that her actions complied with company policy. The court agreed with the employer and granted its motion for pretrial judgment. The court of appeals reversed, finding issues of fact that required a trial. **If the employer could establish after-acquired evidence sufficient to justify termination, the employee would not be entitled to any relief.** The Supreme Court of Kansas agreed with the lower courts that the after-acquired evidence doctrine should be recognized in a wrongful discharge case based on breach of an implied contract that raises no public policy issues. It also agreed that material issues of fact remained to be resolved. *Gassmann v. Evangelical Lutheran Good Samaritan Society, Inc.*, 933 P.2d 743 (Kan. 1997).

C. Damage Awards

When employees are fired, they have a duty to try to find other work to mitigate their damages. If they do not try to find other work, their claim for damages will suffer. Thus, even if they were wrongfully discharged, any recovery they obtain may be limited.

Damages can be awarded for breach of contract where one party (usually, the employer) terminates the contract early. Generally, with breach of contract, there are no punitive damages or equitable damages awarded.

Equitable damages (like front and back pay) can be awarded where necessary to make one party (usually, the employee) whole. Front pay is often awarded where it would be counterproductive to reinstate the wrongfully fired employee in the job.

Compensatory and punitive damages can be awarded where the employee brings a tort action against the employer. (A tort is a civil wrong other than breach of contract.) Compensatory damages can include money for emotional distress, and pain and suffering. Punitive damages are awarded to punish one party (usually, the employer) for acting inappropriately.

◆ A New York consultant worked under a contract that allowed his termination upon his "absolute failure to perform the contract's specification." Four months after he signed the contract, he was fired. He sued for breach of contract and the company countersued for breach of contract, negligence and fraud. The case reached the Supreme Court, Appellate Division, which held that no reasonable view of the evidence would establish that the consultant "absolutely" failed to perform under the contract. During his four months with the company, he was paid $33,000 in salary and bonuses, and the company paid out $116,000 in marketing and advertising costs at his direction. Accordingly, the counterclaims were dismissed and **the consultant was entitled to recoup the base salary he would have earned ($5,000 per month for over 18 months) plus interest** from the date he was fired. However, on remand, the lower court would have to determine whether that amount should be reduced because of questions over whether the consultant met his duty to mitigate damages. *Mitchell v. Fidelity Borrowing LLC*, 40 A.D.3d 557, 837 N.Y.S.2d 78 (N.Y. App. Div. 2007).

◆ An Arizona ex-employee sued his former company for wrongful termination and discrimination. The parties reached a settlement agreement, under which the company would pay him $40,000, "less all lawfully required withholdings." The company then issued him a check for $25,140, retaining $14,860 in federal income tax, FICA and state income tax. After he cashed the check, the company sought to dismiss the lawsuit. He opposed the motion, arguing that taxes should not have been withheld, but the court and the Ninth Circuit disagreed with him. **He never claimed that the settlement award was for physical injuries, so as to make it not taxable.** *Rivera v. Baker West*, 430 F.3d 1253 (9th Cir. 2005).

◆ A Colorado hotel distributed an employee manual allowing medical leaves of absence and granting employees preference for a similar position upon return. Failure to advise the hotel of the availability for return to work upon a doctor's release or a continued absence was deemed voluntary termination. A hotel employee was injured in a non-work-related traffic accident and missed several weeks of work. When her medical leave was to expire, she requested more time off. The request was granted, but the employer later fired her, asserting that she had failed to provide a full medical release and that her former position was unavailable. After she sought reinstatement with restrictions, she was offered her former position. She rejected the offer and sued for breach of contract. The court awarded her damages for loss of salary plus interest accrued after the offer of reinstatement.

The Court of Appeals of Colorado ruled that the award was limited to damages incurred before the offer of reinstatement. The employee appealed to the Supreme Court of Colorado, which affirmed, finding that **an employee may be required to accept a reinstatement offer as part of the general duty to mitigate damages**, absent special circumstances. In this case, the employee had identified no special circumstances that would relieve her of her duty to mitigate her damages. The employer was not required to offer her a position with more favorable terms than she had originally enjoyed, and her rejection of the reinstatement offer was a failure to mitigate her damages. *Fair v. Red Lion Inn*, 943 P.2d 431 (Colo. 1997).

◆ A Michigan employee injured her wrist on the job and claimed that her employer fired her before the end of her probationary period in retaliation for filing a workers' compensation claim. A trial court awarded her damages despite the employer's argument that her at-will employment status barred the claim. The court of appeals ruled that the employee was not entitled to punitive damages or damages for mental or emotional distress, but that she was entitled to nominal damages. The Supreme Court of Michigan then held that despite the at-will status of the employment relationship, the employer had a duty not to retaliate against the employee for filing a workers' compensation claim. The cause of action for violating the workers' compensation act was independent of the employment contract. Although the court had previously declined to recognize a cause of action for bad faith breach of an employment contract, it authorized a cause of action for mental and emotional distress apart from the breach of contract in appropriate cases. Here, **the employee was entitled to recover her lost wages because she had a reasonable expectation that she would not be fired for filing a workers' compensation claim**. An award of nominal damages would not compensate the employee for the employer's violation of public policy, and the case was therefore reversed and remanded. *Phillips v. Butterball Farms Co., Inc.*, 531 N.W.2d 144 (Mich. 1995).

CHAPTER FOUR

Employee Benefits

I. RETIREMENT BENEFITS

ERISA, the Employee Retirement Income Security Act of 1974, 29 U.S.C. § 1001 *et seq.*, is a comprehensive federal statute that imposes uniform rules and standards upon private pension and welfare benefit plans. It describes the fiduciary responsibilities of plan administrators and specifies rules for pension participation, funding, vesting and financial reporting.

ERISA preempts all state laws "as they may now or hereafter relate to any employee benefit plan described in section 1003(a) of this title…." Because the question of ERISA applicability frequently determines the outcome of pension litigation, a substantial body of law has developed concerning whether a particular state law "relates to" a plan described by ERISA.

Defined benefit plans consist of a general pool of assets rather than individual dedicated accounts. Under these plans, employees are entitled to a fixed periodic payment upon retirement, and employers generally bear the risk of investment. If there is under-funding of plan assets, the employer must make up the difference. On the other hand, if there is a surplus of plan assets, the employer may reduce or suspend its contributions.

Defined contribution plans are more common. Under these plans, the employer's contribution is fixed, and the employee receives whatever level of benefits the amount contributed on his or her behalf will provide. Each beneficiary is entitled to whatever assets are dedicated to his or her individual account. Employees bear the risk of loss and reap the rewards of high returns.

A. ERISA in General

ERISA requires each pension plan to provide that an employee's right to normal pension benefits is "non-forfeitable" if the employee meets the statutory age and years of service requirements. ERISA does not create the same requirement with respect to welfare benefits (like vacation benefits).

ERISA also sets certain limits on lawsuits for money damages. It permits ERISA plans (but not individual beneficiaries) to bring such lawsuits against fiduciaries in certain circumstances, and it defines as fiduciaries not only those persons named as fiduciaries by a benefit plan, but also anyone else who exercises discretionary control or authority over the plan's management, administration or assets.

Non-fiduciaries cannot be sued for money damages, but they can be sued for equitable relief (like injunctions and restitution).

ERISA fiduciaries have a number of duties and responsibilities, including: "the proper management, administration, and investment of [plan] assets, the maintenance of proper records, the disclosure of specified information, and the avoidance of conflicts of interest."

1. Supreme Court Cases

- A former employee sued his ex-employer, alleging that he had asked the company to make certain changes to his 401(k) investments and that it had never made the changes. He asserted that this failure "depleted" his interest in the plan by approximately $150,000 and amounted to a breach of fiduciary duty under ERISA. A South Carolina federal court granted pretrial judgment to the company, and the Fourth Circuit affirmed. The U.S. Supreme Court vacated and remanded the case, holding that although Section 502(a)(2) of ERISA does not provide a remedy for individual injuries distinct from plan injuries, **ERISA does authorize recovery for fiduciary breaches that impair the value of plan assets in a participant's individual account**. Here, the misconduct alleged by the employee fell squarely within the statutory duties imposed by ERISA. This was a different situation than a defined benefit plan, where participants are entitled to a fixed payment (like from a pension). Here, fiduciary misconduct could reduce a participant's benefits below the amount he would otherwise receive. Further proceedings were necessary. *LaRue v. DeWolff, Boberg & Associates, Inc.*, 128 S.Ct. 1020, 169 L.Ed.2d 847 (U.S. 2008).

◆ Participants in a multiemployer pension plan in Illinois retired after accruing enough pension credits to qualify for early retirement payments under a "service only" pension scheme that paid them the same monthly benefit they would have received had they retired at the usual age. They were only 39 at the time. The plan prohibited them from taking jobs as construction workers (but not as supervisors) if they wanted to continue receiving pension payments. They took supervisory construction jobs so as to be able to receive pension benefits in addition to their salaries. The plan then expanded its definition of barred employment to include any construction industry job, and stopped payments when the participants did not leave their supervisory jobs. They sued to recover the suspended benefits, claiming that the suspension violated the "anti-cutback" rule of ERISA, which prohibits any pension plan amendment that would reduce a participant's "accrued benefit."

A federal court ruled for the plan, but the Seventh Circuit reversed, holding that imposing new conditions on rights to benefits already accrued violated the anti-cutback rule. The U.S. Supreme Court affirmed, holding that ERISA Section 204(g) prohibits an amendment expanding the categories of barred post-retirement employment so as to suspend payment of early retirement benefits already accrued. Here, the suspension of benefits allowed by **the plan amendment had the effect of reducing an early retirement benefit that had been promised**. *Cent. Laborers' Pension Fund v. Heinz*, 541 U.S. 739, 124 S.Ct. 2230, 159 L.Ed.2d 46 (2004).

◆ A Washington state law automatically revoked, upon divorce, the designation of a spouse as beneficiary to a life insurance policy or employee benefit plan. When a divorced employee died in a car accident, his children sought the proceeds of his life insurance policy and his pension plan, even though his ex-wife was still named on both documents. Also, both documents were governed by ERISA. A question arose as to whether ERISA preempted the state law, making the children the recipients of the proceeds. The U.S. Supreme Court ruled that **ERISA preempted the state law**. To rule otherwise would require plan administrators to familiarize themselves with the statutes of all 50 states. ERISA allowed them to pay out proceeds per the plan documents. Thus, the ex-wife was entitled to the proceeds. *Egelhoff v. Egelhoff*, 532 U.S. 141, 121 S.Ct. 1322, 149 L.Ed.2d 264 (2001).

◆ The Retirement Equity Act of 1984 allows participants in survivor's annuity plans to designate a beneficiary other than their spouse only with the spouse's consent. A Louisiana telecommunications employee with a wife and three sons participated in several ERISA-qualified retirement plans. Following the death of his wife, the employee remarried. When he died several years later, his sons submitted claims against his estate based upon the first wife's will for his undistributed retirement benefits, including a savings plan, an employee stock ownership plan, and a survivor's annuity. A federal court held that the sons were entitled to a share of the retirement benefits under Louisiana community property law. The Fifth Circuit affirmed. The U.S. Supreme Court held that ERISA preempted the state law that allowed the first wife to transfer (upon her death) an interest in undistributed pension plan benefits. **The surviving spouse was entitled to receive the survivor's annuity since she had not waived her rights or consented to the designation of the sons as beneficiaries.** She was also entitled to the stock shares and the savings plan proceeds, since the claims of the sons were based on community property law and were inconsistent with ERISA's anti-alienation provision. *Boggs v. Boggs*, 520 U.S. 833, 117 S.Ct. 1754, 138 L.Ed.2d 45 (1997).

◆ A class of former employees of the Kaiser Steel Corporation, who participated in the company's ERISA-qualified retirement plan, brought suit for the plan's losses against an actuary employed by the company. They alleged that the actuary had knowingly participated in misfeasance by plan fiduciaries. Kaiser had hired the actuary when it began to phase out its steel-making operations, prompting early retirement by a large number of plan participants. The actuary failed to change the plan's actuarial assumptions to reflect the additional costs imposed by the retirements. As a result, Kaiser did not adequately fund the plan, and its assets became insufficient to satisfy its obligations. When the plan was terminated, the former employees began receiving only the benefits guaranteed by ERISA, which were substantially lower than the fully vested pensions due them under the plan. After a California federal court and the Ninth Circuit dismissed the complaint, the U.S. Supreme Court affirmed. ERISA Section 502(a)(3) permits plan participants to bring civil actions to obtain "appropriate equitable relief" to redress violations of the plan. The Court determined that **requiring the actuary to make the plan whole for the losses it sustained would not constitute "appropriate equitable relief."** What the employees were seeking here was compensatory damages, not "equitable relief." *Mertens v. Hewitt Associates*, 508 U.S. 248, 113 S.Ct. 2063, 124 L.Ed.2d 161 (1993).

◆ One of the trustees of a sheet metal workers' pension fund embezzled over $375,000 from the union. Two pension plans contended that the trustee had forfeited his right to receive benefits as a result. They also asserted that even if he had not forfeited his benefits, those benefits should be paid to the union and not to him. A Colorado federal court held that because there was a judgment against the trustee for $275,000, a constructive trust should be imposed on the trustee's benefits until the judgment was paid off. The Tenth Circuit affirmed. The U.S. Supreme Court held that the constructive trust violated the prohibition on assignment or alienation of pension benefits called for by ERISA. Here, although the trustee had stolen money from the union, he had not stolen money from the pension funds. Even if the Labor-Management Reporting and Disclosure Act authorized the imposition of a constructive trust when a union officer breached his fiduciary duties, that did not override ERISA's anti-alienation provision. ERISA reflected a congressional policy choice to **safeguard a stream of income for pensioners even if that prevented others from obtaining relief for the wrongs done them**. The Court reversed and remanded the case. *Guidry v. Sheet Metal Workers National Pension Fund,* 493 U.S. 365, 110 S.Ct. 680, 107 L.Ed.2d 782 (1990).

On remand, the union and the trustee agreed that the trustee's monthly pension payments would be made to a bank account opened specifically to receive the pension funds, and that the funds would then be subject to garnishment by the union. The Tenth Circuit noted that Section 206(d)(1) protection did not extend to the funds once the plan participant asserted dominion over them. Since the garnishment action was not "against the plan," it was not prohibited by ERISA. *Guidry v. Sheet Metal Workers Local No. 9,* 10 F.3d 700 (10th Cir. 1993).

- In an ERISA lawsuit, the issue of who constitutes an employee came before the U.S. Supreme Court. The case involved a North Carolina insurance agent who sold insurance for competitors after his relationship with an insurer was terminated. When the insurer sought to avoid paying his retirement benefits on the grounds that he violated a non-compete clause, he sued. The Supreme Court noted that the agent's ERISA claim could succeed only if he was an employee. Because ERISA's definition of "employee" as "any individual employed by an employer" was not helpful, the Court suggested **assessing and weighing all the elements of an employment relationship**, including: the location of the work, the duration of the relationship between the parties, the method of payment, and the provision of employee benefits, among others. The Court reversed and remanded the case for a determination of whether the agent qualified as an employee under traditional agency law. *Nationwide Mutual Insurance Co. v. Darden*, 503 U.S. 318, 112 S.Ct. 1344, 117 L.Ed.2d 581 (1992).

2. Preemption

ERISA preempts state laws that affect employee benefit plans. However, if a state law of general applicability has only a minor connection with covered ERISA plans, it will not be expressly preempted.

The preemption issue is important because if a state law and ERISA both address employee benefit plans, courts need to know whether to apply state or federal law to resolve any conflict.

With large companies, there might be employees in several different states, each with its own laws relating to employee benefit plans. The application of ERISA ensures uniformity of enforceability that makes it easier for ERISA fiduciaries to properly administer their plans.

◆ A Massachusetts engineer worked for a company and one of its subsidiaries over his career. At one point, his pension benefits from his earlier work with the company were transferred to another pension trust without notification to his then-current employer. As a result, both the company and the subsidiary included his total service time in their respective pension calculations. Relying on the company's estimate of his pension benefit, he retired. Later, the company notified him that it had overstated his pension benefits and that he was actually entitled to less than half of what he had been receiving – although he was entitled to benefits from the other pension trust to cover his earlier time with the company. He sued the company for negligence and misrepresentation, but the First Circuit held that his claims were preempted by ERISA. **They related to a retirement plan and to the company's recordkeeping responsibilities under that plan.** *Zipperer v. Raytheon Co.*, Inc., 493 F.3d 50 (1st Cir. 2007).

◆ A California employer sponsored a self-funded employee benefit plan covered by ERISA. The employer contracted with a third party to provide administrative services for the plan, but it retained management control as the plan administrator with final discretion over claims decisions. It also contracted with an insurer for excess loss coverage to reimburse it for payments above a specified deductible amount. The third-party administrator failed to timely process and submit a claim by a plan beneficiary to the excess insurer. As a result, the excess insurer failed to reimburse the employer for benefits it paid the beneficiary through the plan. The employer sued the third-party administrator and excess insurer for breach of contract. The administrator and insurer asserted that the case was preempted by ERISA. The court agreed and dismissed the complaint. The U.S. Court of Appeals, Ninth Circuit, reversed, holding that **ERISA does not preempt regulation of the relationships between the plan and its employees, insurers or creditors**. The state laws at issue here did not directly regulate an ERISA plan. They were laws of general application that did not depend upon the interpretation of ERISA. *Geweke Ford v. St. Joseph's Omni Preferred Care, Inc.*, 130 F.3d 1355 (9th Cir. 1997).

◆ A Hawaii subcontractor breached an agreement to pay hourly pension contributions to employees working on two golf courses. The Hawaii Laborers' Trust Funds sued the subcontractor on the employees' behalf to recover unpaid trust fund contributions. The funds obtained a default judgment and then sued to enforce the judgment. The golf course owners were named as parties under the state mechanic's and materialmen's lien law because labor and improvements had been furnished on their property. The owners got the lawsuit dismissed on the grounds that ERISA preempts state law claims relating to employee pension plans. The Supreme Court of Hawaii noted that **state laws of general applicability were not expressly preempted by ERISA if they had only a tenuous or remote connection with a covered plan**. ERISA did not preempt general creditor rights created by state law such as the mechanic's and materialmen's lien law. Creditor remedies were necessary for trust funds to enforce their rights under ERISA, and preemption was not warranted under any other ground. The trial court decision was vacated and remanded. *Hawaii Laborers' Trust Funds v. Maui Prince Hotel Corp.*, 918 P.2d 1143 (Haw. 1996).

3. Interference With Benefits/New Plan Offers

ERISA prohibits interfering with employees' benefit rights. For example, it is a violation of ERISA for a company to fire employees to prevent them from seeking medical benefits.

Companies also must provide employees with information about new plan offers. For example, where a company has a new pension plan offer under "serious consideration" and employees have been asked to contemplate early retirement, that new plan offer must be made known to the eligible employees.

If the new plan being contemplated is not under serious consideration (that is, if it is just one of several potential offers being discussed and no firm timetable has been put in place for instituting it), then there is no fiduciary duty to divulge that information to eligible employees.

◆ A company regularly monitored employees' compliance with its expense policies by hiring an independent contractor to conduct a scan for red flags – patterns of irregular or inaccurate reporting. During one of these monitoring sweeps, several employees were identified as having repeatedly violated company policy by submitting false or improper expense account reports. After the company fired them, they sued, alleging that the real reason for the termination was to deprive them of benefits in violation of ERISA. A Pennsylvania federal court ruled against them. Despite their argument that many of their expenses (like visits to gentlemen's clubs) were tolerated and even approved by their superiors, the company had a good-faith belief that they engaged in inappropriate conduct. *Balmat v. CertainTeed Corp.*, 2007 WL 4570928 (E.D. Pa. 12/28/07).

◆ A retired group of middle managers sued AT&T, claiming that it breached its fiduciary duties under ERISA by modifying its traditional defined benefit pension plan with a new cash balance plan and creating a "Special Update" plan for older employees that froze their benefits. They claimed that AT&T lured them into retirement with the "Special Update" as a means of reducing the workforce prior to instituting a voluntary retirement plan that they were no longer eligible for. A New Jersey federal court and the Third Circuit ruled in favor of AT&T. **The retirees failed to show that the voluntary retirement plan was under serious consideration at the time they retired.** In order to be under "serious consideration," a change to an employee benefit plan must meet three requirements: 1) there must be a specific proposal; 2) it must be being discussed for the purpose of implementation; and 3) it must be discussed by senior management who have the authority to implement the change. Here, the earliest the company began seriously considering the plan was after all the retirees had retired. *Peterson v. American Telephone and Telegraph Co.*, 127 Fed.Appx. 67 (3d Cir. 2005).

◆ Employees of a company in South Carolina brought a lawsuit alleging that company officials used their healthcare contributions deducted from their paychecks for other business debts in violation of ERISA. A federal court granted pretrial judgment to the company, but the Fourth Circuit reversed. Funding the employees' health plan was a fiduciary function, not a business function, and there was a material question of fact as to whether the company deducted money from the employees' checks and then failed to pay it to the health plan's claims administrator. **Assets of ERISA-covered plans cannot inure to the benefit of employers.** A trial would determine whether the company had violated ERISA. *Phelps v. C.T. Enterprises*, 394 F.3d 213 (4th Cir. 2005).

◆ A technician on an offshore oil-drilling rig became eligible for retirement. He began to hear rumors that, in addition to regular retirement benefits, the company was going to be offering a lump-sum retirement incentive under a special ERISA welfare plan designed to induce employees to retire early. He asked several company officials about the incentive, and they told him truthfully that they knew nothing about it. A company attorney also told him that she could not confirm the rumors. Shortly thereafter, a vice president reviewed a proposal to provide an early retirement incentive, but no one told the technician. Two weeks after he retired, the company announced the incentive. He sued under ERISA, and a California federal court granted pretrial judgment to Exxon. The Ninth Circuit reversed and remanded, finding issues of fact that required a trial. If the incentive was under "serious consideration" when the technician tried to confirm the rumors, then the company had a fiduciary duty to provide him with complete and truthful information. **A plan is under serious consideration when it is specific and it is being discussed for purposes of implementation by senior management** who can implement it. However, if the plan was not under serious consideration at that time, then the company owed him no duty to follow up with information about the plan unless the officials promised to do so. *Bins v. Exxon Co.*, 220 F.3d 1042 (9th Cir. 2000).

◆ A division head for a Kentucky company told a manager that he wanted to reduce salaries and cut medical costs. He asked the manager to put together information on employee birth dates, hire dates, smoking habits and benefits. Another supervisory employee prepared a reduction in work force memorandum entitled "High Risk," which flagged employees by salary, age, disability, premature births of children, surgeries, and exemption status. Two older employees, ages 60 and 59, were among the workers who were laid off. They sued the company under the Age Discrimination in Employment Act (ADEA) and ERISA, asserting that the company fired them due to their age and to interfere with their pension rights. A jury ruled against them on their ADEA claim, but ruled in their favor on the ERISA claim, awarding one employee $135,000 and the other $348,000. The Sixth Circuit Court of Appeals affirmed. The evidence indicated that the reasons the company had given for terminating the employees were false. The employees' supervisors had testified that their work was either "above quality" or excellent. The jury had properly found that **the company had fired the employees to interfere with their retirement benefits**. *Pennington v. Western Atlas, Inc.*, 202 F.3d 902 (6th Cir. 2000).

◆ When an employee of a Colorado doctor asked to participate in his Simplified Employee Pension (SEP) plan, he gave her a choice of making $21,000 with a 15% contribution or making $24,000 with no contribution. The $21,000 was less than her annual compensation for the prior two years, and the doctor conceded that he was asking her to take a pay cut to fund the plan. She sued, alleging that the doctor violated the anti-discrimination provision (Section 510) of ERISA. The Tenth Circuit Court of Appeals noted that although the employee lacked a present right to the contribution, she was still **protected against unilateral changes designed to interfere with future contributions** and could sue to protect those contributions. Further, although an employer may make fundamental decisions about employee compensation and about whether and how much to contribute to an SEP plan, Section 510 places limits on using the plan as a device to adjust employee compensation. The doctor was prohibited from making *ad hoc* changes to the plan's allocation formula for a particular employee to avoid his cost of contribution. *Garratt v. Walker*, 164 F.3d 1249 (10th Cir. 1998).

◆ Following a heart attack, the interim plant manager at a Texas plant went on medical leave to undergo open heart surgery. He was fired the day after he returned to work. He claimed the company fired him so it wouldn't have to restore him to his previous position, in violation of the Family and Medical Leave Act (FMLA), and so it wouldn't have to pay his medical benefits, in violation of ERISA. The company argued that it had decided to terminate him for substandard performance the day before he suffered the heart attack. A federal jury found that **the termination decision did not take place until after the manager returned to work and was made to keep him from staying in his position and to avoid paying medical benefits**. It awarded him more than $41,000 in past lost wages and employee benefits; $11,000 for mental anguish; and $5,166 in out-of-pocket expenses. The district court entered judgment for more than $119,000, which included liquidated (double) damages. The Fifth Circuit Court of Appeals upheld the verdict, but reversed the award of out-of-pocket expenses and damages for mental anguish. Damages under the FMLA and ERISA do not include out-of-pocket expenses or damages for mental anguish. *Nero v. Industrial Molding Corp.*, 167 F.3d 921 (5th Cir. 1999).

◆ An Oklahoma petroleum company manager discussed early retirement with a vice president. Although the vice president was aware of an impending work force reduction, he did not inform the manager of the possibility of obtaining better retirement packages that were then under consideration. The manager retired. Within two months, the company announced a downsizing and the availability of a new voluntary retirement program with substantially better benefits than those he had accepted. He sued it for breach of fiduciary duties under ERISA and wrongful denial of participation in the new plan. A federal court found the employer liable for breach of fiduciary duty, but it held that the manager was not entitled to participate in the new plan. The U.S. Court of Appeals, Tenth Circuit, affirmed the ruling that the manager was not entitled to participate in the new plan. It reversed the breach of fiduciary duty ruling, observing that an employer is under no duty to disclose a future retirement plan offering until it is under "serious consideration." Here, **senior management employees had not met to discuss the plan until nearly two months after the manager retired**. *Hockett v. Sun Co., Inc.*, 109 F.3d 1515 (10th Cir. 1997).

4. Other Retirement Benefits Issues

The following cases address other issues that can arise in the retirement benefits area.

◆ Three former Home Depot employees brought a lawsuit against the company under ERISA, asserting that it allowed a company-appointed investment committee to invest in corporate stock even though **corporate officials were backdating stock options and making fraudulent transactions that artificially inflated the stocks' value**. The employees claimed that Home Depot and the investment committee breached their fiduciary duty. A Georgia federal court dismissed the case, ruling that the employees were seeking "damages" rather than "benefits" because they were not seeking a "readily ascertainable amount that could directly affect a payment" to them. However, the Eleventh Circuit ruled that they were seeking benefits. Nevertheless, the lawsuit was premature. The employees first had to exhaust their administrative remedies. *Lanfear v. Home Depot, Inc.*, 536 F.3d 1217 (11th Cir. 2008).

◆ Two companies converted the pension plans they offered employees to cash balance plans. Under a cash balance (or hybrid) plan, a hypothetical account is established in each participant's name. Benefits are credited to that "account" over time, driven by two variables: (1) the employer's hypothetical "contributions," and (2) hypothetical earnings expressed as interest credits. Employer "contributions" are usually expressed as a percentage of salary, the rate of which may vary with employee tenure. Interest credits are usually tied to an extrinsic index, like Treasury bills. Each year an employee receives a statement of her "account" balance. These features are designed to mimic the simplicity of a defined contribution plan. However, under hybrid plans, employers bear the market risks. When participants challenged the two companies' plans, asserting that they violated ERISA's rule against age-based reductions in the rate of benefit accrual, federal courts in New York held that the plans did not violate ERISA. The Second Circuit affirmed, noting that the plans did not inherently result in an age-based reduction in the rate of benefit accrual even though **younger employees might achieve greater growth because of the longer time they had until retirement**. *Hirt v. Equitable Retirement Plan for Employees, Managers, and Agents*, 533 F.3d 102 (2d Cir. 2008).

◆ A New Jersey employee participated in his company's 401(k) plan and directed that his money be put into a stock fund composed entirely of company stock. In March 2004, the stock traded at a 52-week high of $7.42 per share. By October 4, the stock was trading at $1.70 per share, and the employee voluntarily cashed out. The employee claimed the stock price plummeted because of a risky and failed merger. He sued the company for breaching its fiduciary duties to him and other plan participants by offering the stock as an investment option despite knowing it wasn't a prudent investment. He also asserted that plan administrators made misleading statements about the merger that caused him to invest in the plan. A federal court ruled that he was not a "participant" for purposes of ERISA because he had already cashed out of the plan. However, the Third Circuit reversed. It ruled that **he could sue the plan administrator for mismanaging the plan before he cashed out**, causing him to have less than he was entitled to. *Graden v. Conexant Systems, Inc.*, 496 F.3d 291 (3d Cir. 2007).

◆ An Indiana retiree chose a lump-sum distribution rather than an annuity from his company's defined benefit pension plan. Several years later, he discovered that Cost of Living Adjustments (COLAs) were available only to those retirees who chose annuities. On behalf of himself and all others similarly situated, he sued the pension plan under ERISA, asserting that COLAs were an accrued benefit to which retirees were entitled regardless of whether they took their pensions in one lump sum or via annuity. A federal court granted class certification and agreed that COLAs were an accrued benefit. The Seventh Circuit affirmed the ruling. Although the plan excluded COLAs from participants' accrued benefits, ERISA requires any lump-sum substitute for an accrued pension benefit to be the actuarial equivalent of that benefit. **By giving annuitants COLAs, the plan had to give that actuarial equivalent to participants who chose to receive lump-sum distributions.** *Williams v. Rohm and Haas Pension Plan*, 497 F.3d 710 (7th Cir. 2007).

◆ A new manager at a window plant in Minnesota told the engineers that he had higher performance expectations than his predecessor. An engineer began to receive poor evaluations and was told that he was going to be put on a Performance Improvement Plan (PIP). If he failed to improve in defined areas within 30 days, he would be fired. He then learned that a co-worker had avoided getting placed on a PIP by announcing his retirement. The engineer did the same, then sued the company under ERISA, asserting that he had been constructively discharged because the PIP set goals that could not be achieved. A federal court and the Eighth Circuit ruled against him. Here, **he presented no evidence that the company forced him to retire to avoid paying health benefits**, nor could he prove that the PIP set impossible goals. In fact, he conceded that the plan conformed with what one would expect from an engineer. *Fischer v. Andersen Corp.*, 483 F.3d 553 (8th Cir. 2007).

◆ While in Chapter 11 bankruptcy, a company in Ohio discovered that 295 retirees had received overpayments totaling about $1 million, and 145 retirees had been underpaid about $500,000. It entered into a voluntary compliance program with the Internal Revenue Service and began correcting the payment mistakes. Six retirees brought a lawsuit seeking a temporary restraining order, hoping to prevent the company from reducing their overpayments. They claimed the company negligently misrepresented how much they could expect to receive in monthly retirement benefits. The case reached the Sixth Circuit Court of Appeals, which ruled in favor of the company. **ERISA did not provide**

for continued overpayments. Here, the retirees were really seeking money damages rather than the equitable relief allowed by ERISA. *Ramsey v. Formica Corp.*, 398 F.3d 421 (6th Cir. 2005).

- In response to financial difficulties, a Texas insurance company implemented a reduction-in-force and amended its retirement plan to allow certain participants enhanced retirement benefits. The company was then placed under the control of a conservator. By the time the eligibility period for enhanced benefits expired, 90% of the company's eligible employees were terminated (so as to make them eligible), including almost every officer. However, 25 otherwise eligible employees who requested termination were not fired by the conservator and thus were not eligible for enhanced benefits. They sued under ERISA's anti-retaliation provision (Section 510), asserting that the company and the conservator breached a fiduciary duty to terminate them. A federal court ruled against them, and the Fifth Circuit affirmed. The failure to fire the employees was not a prohibited adverse action that was taken to interfere with protected rights; **the offer of enhanced benefits was not a promise that created ERISA entitlements**; and the conservator did not discriminate against them even though eligible officers were terminated before the company went into receivership. *Bodine v. Employers Casualty Co.*, 352 F.3d 245 (5th Cir. 2003).

- Newspaper haulers for a publishing company in Delaware sent a letter to the company in 1988, citing a Third Circuit decision holding that newspaper haulers were common-law employees and thus employees under the National Labor Relations Act. They wanted to have the company treat them as employees for purposes of pension benefits, while the company had asserted since 1976 that they were independent contractors who were not entitled to pension benefits. The company answered that it was going to continue treating the haulers as independent contractors. In 1999, the haulers sued under ERISA, but a Delaware federal court held that **their claims were barred by ERISA's three-year statute of limitations**. The Third Circuit affirmed. The company's 1988 letter put them on notice that they had some sort of claim, and they failed to act on that notice for 11 years. *Tinley v. Gannett Co.*, 55 Fed.Appx. 74 (3d Cir. 2003).

B. Vesting Rights and Plan Amendment Issues

1. Vesting Rights

Where employees work the minimum number of years to vest their pension rights, they are entitled to benefits. Where there is a break in service (like where an employee is laid off and has to find another job), plans usually spell out the kind of employment that can be taken to stay on course for vesting.

- Participants in a New Jersey company's pension plan sued the company, alleging that it violated ERISA by 1) illegally ceasing benefit accrual by reason of age; 2) backloading pension accruals; and 3) providing a benefit at normal retirement age that was less than the early retirement amount. A federal court dismissed the lawsuit, finding that the participants failed to show any of the claims they asserted were true. Their calculations on the issue of ceasing benefit accrual failed to take into account one step. They also failed to prove that pension accruals were backloaded by the plan or that someone retiring at normal retirement age would receive less than someone who retired early. Without specific facts to back up their claims, their lawsuit could not proceed. *Haesler v. Novartis Consumer Health, Inc.*, 426 F.Supp.2d 227 (D.N.J. 2006).

◆ An employee of a steel company with 14 years, 11 months, and 11 days of service had his continuous service terminated for pension purposes because he had been absent from work for two years with a heart condition. He was 19 days short of eligibility for the company's 70/80 pension. He claimed that he did not learn of the service being broken until eight years later. The benefits plan administrator had determined that since his disability had not been incurred during the course of his employment, his continuous service stopped after two years away from the job. He sued under Section 502(a)(3) of ERISA, asserting that he was entitled to the 70/80 pension and that, at the very least, the plan administrator had breached a fiduciary duty to notify him of how it was interpreting his disability and that it was about to break his service. A Pennsylvania federal court granted pretrial judgment to the company, and the employee appealed. The Third Circuit Court of Appeals vacated the decision in part, finding that **the administrator had breached its fiduciary duty to him by failing to notify him of the break in service**. Had he known his service was broken earlier, he could have taken certain steps to protect himself from a total loss of his pension. The court remanded the case for further proceedings. *Harte v. Bethlehem Steel Corp.*, 214 F.3d 446 (3d Cir. 2000).

◆ A pension plan provided three retirement options, including enhanced benefits for employees who retired at any age with over 25 years of current service. Plan trustees amended the early retirement provision for the class of 25-year employees who retired at any age by incorporating a break-in-service exclusion. However, the trustees did not amend an alternate retirement option providing for enhanced benefits for employees over the age of 55 with 25 years of service who retired with at least 15 years of current service. The trustees denied enhanced retirement benefits to a 58-year-old retiring plan participant on the basis of a break in his service, applying the language from the provision allowing for enhanced benefits when retiring at any age. The retiree claimed he was still entitled to enhanced benefits under the alternate (over-55 with 25 years of service) provision and sued the trustees under ERISA. A New York federal court ruled for the retiree, and the Second Circuit affirmed. **The trustees had arbitrarily and capriciously imported the break-in-service requirement from the any-age retirement provision** to the section providing for enhanced benefits to those employees retiring after 55 with 25 years of service and at least 15 years of current service. The trustees could not take language from one plan option and graft it into another in contravention of the plan's explicit language. *Gallo v. Madera*, 136 F.3d 326 (2d Cir. 1998).

◆ A Colorado-based communications company leased employees from a leasing company. Eleven of the leased employees asserted that they were performing the same or similar functions as the communications company's own workers and were therefore entitled to participate in its employee pension and welfare benefit plans. They sued the communications company under ERISA. The case reached the Tenth Circuit Court of Appeals, which observed that ERISA does not create substantive rights such as those asserted by the leased employees. **ERISA makes no reference to leased employees and does not prohibit employers from distinguishing among various groups or classes of employees.** It only prohibits distinctions based on age or length of service. The leased employees were not entitled to participate in either the pension or the welfare benefit plans. *Bronk v. Mountain States Telephone and Telegraph, Inc.*, 140 F.3d 1335 (10th Cir. 1998).

◆ A Chicago steel plant supervisor requested a two-year leave of absence to accommodate her husband's health problems. The employer accepted her request but issued a written memorandum stating that she would be rehired only if she was needed and that a company reorganization was already planned. When she requested reinstatement less than two years later, the employer stated that no position was available in her former department and that she would be discharged at the expiration of her leave. Although she was entitled to a deferred vested pension, she sought a comprehensive pension supplement available to participants whose employment termination resulted from a permanent plant shutdown or job elimination. The company refused to award the supplement, stating that the separation had been caused by the leave of absence. The U.S. Court of Appeals, Seventh Circuit, found the administrator's interpretation of the plan reasonable. **The discharge had been due to the lack of an available position at the time she returned from her scheduled leave of absence.** Plan language could reasonably be read as requiring a direct cause and effect between job elimination and employment termination, a condition that was not satisfied where the employee initiated the separation. *Brehmer v. Inland Steel Industries Pension Plan*, 114 F.3d 656 (7th Cir. 1997).

◆ A California construction worker became permanently disabled at age 56. He was erroneously advised by union officials that he was two months short of the 15-year eligibility requirement for the normal retirement benefit from the Construction Laborers Pension Trust (CLPT) for Southern California. Thus, he did not apply for pension benefits when he turned 62, even though he had actually accrued 23 years of service. Plan trustees then lowered the eligibility requirement to 10 years. The laborer applied for pension benefits, but the plan awarded retroactive benefits covering only the time period after he had turned 65. He was denied benefits retroactive to the age of 62 because he had failed to apply for them. He sued, asserting violations of ERISA. The U.S. Court of Appeals, Ninth Circuit, stated that the CLPT plan had **only three requirements for eligibility**: the completion of the credited service requirement, the attainment of age 62, and the performance of a minimal requirement of covered service. Plan trustees had been arbitrary and capricious in adding further requirements for eligibility. The administrative requirement of applying for benefits was not a prerequisite to eligibility. *Canseco v. Construction Laborers Pension Trust for Southern California*, 93 F.3d 600 (9th Cir. 1996).

2. Plan Amendment Issues

Employers can generally adopt, modify or terminate pension plans just as they can welfare benefit plans. Where employers amend plans in their capacity as employers (and not as fiduciaries), they will not have liability under ERISA as long as they act consistently with ERISA, its regulations and the plans' requirements.

◆ An aircraft manufacturer doing business in Arizona and California established a "defined benefit" pension plan for its employees in 1951. By 1986, plan assets exceeded the value of accrued plan benefits by almost $1 billion. Even though the plan was funded by both employer and employee contributions, the employer ceased its contributions to the plan and used part of the surplus to fund a separate early retirement plan for current employees. A group of retired participants in the pension plan filed a California federal court action against the employer and plan, asserting violations of ERISA. The court dismissed the lawsuit, and the participants appealed. The U.S. Court of Appeals, Ninth Circuit, held that the employer's actions violated ERISA.

The case then came before the U.S. Supreme Court, which noted that **the retirees, as members of a *defined benefit plan*, had no interest in the plan's surplus**. This was so despite the fact that the plan surplus was partially attributable to the investment growth of the retirees' contributions. Defined benefit plan members have a non-forfeitable right to accrued benefits, and the employer is responsible for any shortages. By the same token, the employer is entitled to any windfall produced by the plan. Had this been a *defined contribution plan*, the retirees would have been entitled to whatever assets were dedicated to their accounts, and the employer could not have used the plan surplus to provide early retirement benefits to current employees. Because no fiduciary duty existed to prohibit the plan's amendment, the Court reversed the court of appeals' decision and held for the employer. *Hughes Aircraft Co. v. Jacobson*, 525 U.S. 432, 119 S.Ct. 755, 142 L.Ed.2d 881 (1999).

◆ An aircraft manufacturer rehired an employee who had left to work for a competitor earlier in his career. He was 61 years old at the time of reemployment and was excluded from participation in the employer's retirement plan because of his age. Congress amended ERISA to disallow age-based exclusions in 1979, and the manufacturer amended the plan. Employees previously excluded on the basis of age were allowed to participate, but without credit for service prior to plan enrollment. The manufacturer then offered two programs encouraging early retirement. Acceptance of early retirement benefits was expressly conditioned on the waiver of any employment-related claims. The employee retired without seeking such benefits. Instead, he sued the employer and plan in a California federal court, seeking a declaration that they violated their duty of care under ERISA and engaged in a prohibited transaction by funding the early retirement plan with surplus plan assets. The case reached the U.S. Supreme Court, which held that **the inducement of early retirement through waivers such as that used here did not violate ERISA**. Plan sponsors who amend plans in their capacity as employers are not fiduciaries under ERISA. Because the plan amendments were enacted in an employer capacity, the manufacturer was under no ERISA fiduciary duty. *Lockheed Corp. v. Spink*, 517 U.S. 882, 116 S.Ct. 1783, 135 L.Ed.2d 153 (1996).

On remand, the court of appeals observed that because the employer was not acting in a fiduciary capacity when amending the plan, the employee could not recover on his ERISA claims. However, he had alleged sufficient facts that he had relied upon the employer's promises of his entitlement to participate in the retirement plan as an inducement to return to work to support his claim for detrimental reliance. He was thus entitled to pursue his claim for benefits for the first four years of his reemployment, and the court reversed this portion of the judgment. *Spink v. Lockheed Corp.*, 125 F.3d 1257 (9th Cir. 1997).

◆ IBM amended its defined benefit pension plan by adopting a new way to calculate how benefits would accrue to the plan – the pension credit formula. Under the formula, an employee who began working for IBM at 35 and earned an annual salary of $60,000 until his employment ended at 50 would have an age-65 accrued benefit equal to $15,110 per year, while an employee who began working at age 50 (also making $60,000) would be left with an age 65 accrued benefit of $13,189 per year. Later, IBM amended the plan again, adopting a cash balance formula for determining benefits. Under this formula, a 49-year-old employee with 20 years' service would accrue an age-65 annuity of $8,093 in the year 2000. The following year, he would accrue an additional $622, and by 2010 his additional accrual would be $282. A court held that **the plan amendments violated ERISA because they provided lesser benefits for older employees**. *Cooper v. IBM Personal Pension Plan*, 274 F.Supp.2d 1010 (S.D. Ill. 2003).

◆ A pension committee made up of employer representatives and union representatives voted to increase union members' benefits after learning that the employer's contributions to the plan might result in a surplus. The employer contended that **the committee did not have the authority to increase union members' benefits**. A lawsuit resulted, and a Vermont federal court ruled for the employer. The Second Circuit Court of Appeals affirmed, noting that the collective bargaining agreement (CBA) did not give the committee power to increase benefits. Nor did employees have an automatic interest in a surplus that occurs when employer contributions turn out to be more than the amount needed to fund the plan at current levels. The CBA reserved to the company the right to amend the plan, including the right to increase benefits. *Bozetarnik v. Mahland*, 195 F.3d 77 (2d Cir. 1999).

◆ The Omnibus Budget Reconciliation Act (OBRA) of 1986 amended ERISA by prohibiting age-based employee benefit accruals effective January 1, 1988 and requiring plans to bring themselves into compliance with OBRA by the end of 1993. During the interim "remedial amendment period," employers had to be in operational compliance with OBRA. A Connecticut employer maintained an

ERISA plan that provided monthly pension benefits based on a participant's average monthly compensation, excluding the last five calendar years preceding the normal retirement date, which was defined as age 65. The plan was amended in 1990 to eliminate the age-based exclusion. A new provision was added excluding the last five years of service regardless of the age of the employee. Two employees who retired in 1988 asserted that they were entitled to include the last five years of their earnings in their benefit calculations. They asserted that the plan had not been in operational compliance with OBRA due to impermissible age-based calculations. A federal court held that the plan complied with OBRA and did not violate ERISA. The Second Circuit Court of Appeals affirmed, holding that OBRA permitted retroactive plan amendments such as those made here. Since the plan had amended its benefit calculation method to eliminate age discrimination within the appropriate time frame, it was in operational compliance with the OBRA amendments. **The plan was not required to consider the last five years of service when calculating pension benefits.** *Greenlaugh v. Putnam Savings Bank*, 140 F.3d 427 (2d Cir. 1998).

◆ A corporation amended its pension plan to change the definition of "normal retirement age" from 65 to 67. Several retirees elected to take early retirement and received a lower benefit under the new plan. Whereas the old plan included a subsidy to raise the amount of early retirement benefits, the new plan eliminated their opportunity for further accrual of retirement subsidies. The retirees sued the corporation and plan in a Utah federal court, which ruled for the employer and plan. The retirees appealed, asserting that ERISA requires a plan to define normal retirement age only as age 65 or earlier. The Tenth Circuit Court of Appeals, however, stated that ERISA permits normal retirement to be defined as an age over 65 where an employee has participated in a plan for less than five years. ERISA does not require normal retirement age to be defined in a plan the same way it is defined in the statute. Although the amended plan established age 67 as the benchmark for determining plan benefits, 65 was maintained as the age for benefit accrual and vesting requirements as per the language of ERISA. As a result, employees retiring at age 65 received only 86.7% of the accrued benefit as calculated by the plans. Since these benefits were protected against elimination by plan amendment, **the plan complied with ERISA even though the early retirement subsidy eliminated the further accrual of early retirement benefits**. *Lindsay v. Thiokol Corp.*, 112 F.3d 1068 (10th Cir. 1997).

◆ An American Motors Corporation (AMC) early retirement incentive program provided for a dollar-for-dollar reduction in retirement benefits whenever a recipient's additional income exceeded a specified ceiling. The provision was not enforced by AMC, but when the company merged with Chrysler in 1987, Chrysler stated its intention to enforce the excess earnings policy by imposing a two-dollar penalty for each dollar of excess income earned by a participant. It further stated that if the entire excess amount could not be recovered within a single calendar year, it would carry over the balance of the penalty to following years. Plan participants sued under ERISA. A Wisconsin federal court ruled for the plan. The Seventh Circuit affirmed, noting that the participants had not been harmed by the two-dollar penalty for each excess dollar earned, as Chrysler had quickly withdrawn this intention after reviewing the matter. **No plan language limited recovery of the penalty to a single calendar year, and the plan authorized the imposition of a dollar-for-dollar penalty.** The court also held that ERISA does not impose liability upon an employer or plan for incorrectly conveying plan information to a participant. Technical violations of ERISA notification requirements do not create a cause of action in the absence of bad faith, active concealment or detrimental reliance by a participant. *Andersen v. Chrysler Corp.*, 99 F.3d 846 (7th Cir. 1996).

◆ A labor union sponsored a pension fund whose trustees were vested with broad powers. The trustees served on boards for both the union's pension and welfare funds. Although the pension fund had a surplus, the welfare fund was forced to require participants to pay an additional $100 each month for coverage. The trustees voted to amend the pension plan by paying participants who also participated in the welfare fund an additional $100 each month to fund the new coverage expense. A group of pension fund members who did not participate in the welfare fund due to lack of sufficient years of service sued the plan trustees in a Delaware federal court, asserting ERISA violations. The court granted pretrial judgment to the participants, but the U.S. Court of Appeals, Third Circuit, reversed. The district court had improperly imposed a fiduciary duty on the trustees with respect to their action to amend the pension plan. **Plan sponsors, including employers and labor organizations, are not fiduciaries when they act to amend a plan and are free to take actions that are not inconsistent with ERISA and its regulations.** Plan sponsors have fiduciary duties to plan participants when acting as administrators, but are not bound by such obligations when amending or terminating a plan. *Walling v. Brady*, 125 F.3d 114 (3d Cir. 1997).

C. Coordination of Benefits

Coordination of benefits refers to a procedure whereby an employee receiving one type of benefit (like workers' compensation) is prevented from receiving another kind of benefit (like pension benefits) at the same time. These benefits are sometimes coordinated (offsetting one against the other) to prevent employees from receiving a windfall.

◆ Three employees of Xerox received lump sum payments when they retired. They returned a few years later and did not repay any of the retirement money they had received. When they later retired again, Xerox reduced their final retirement benefits to account for the earlier distribution by calculating the amount they had received plus any increase the distribution would have earned had it remained in the plan. By doing so, it drastically reduced the monthly payments due the three employees (from $1,600 to $83, from $2,000 to $260, and from $2,800 to $550). The employees challenged the offset, and a California federal court ruled for Xerox. The Ninth Circuit reversed and remanded the case, noting that **the method of accounting Xerox used for calculating the prior accrued benefit distributions used to offset the final**

retirement amounts owed violated the actuarial equivalency requirements of ERISA. *Miller v. Xerox Corp. Retirement Income Guarantee Plan*, 464 F.3d 871 (9th Cir. 2006).

- A New Jersey employee retired at the age of 69 and, as a highly compensated former employee, was a participant in three separate retirement plans. He ultimately sued the plan administrator, challenging the calculation of his benefits under one of the plans. A federal court and the Third Circuit ruled against him. The plan at issue was a "top hat" plan maintained for the purpose of providing deferred compensation to a select group of top managers. It contained a Social Security benefits offset. **The employee asserted that the offset ought to be only the amount he would receive if he retired at 65 rather than the greater amount he actually received for retiring at 69.** The courts instead noted that the plan administrator acted within its discretion in selecting the greater offset amount. Since there was no showing of bad faith, the plan administrator's decision was entitled to deference. *Ahearn v. Marsh & McLennan Companies, Inc.*, 124 Fed.Appx. 118 (3d Cir. 2005).

- Two longtime Michigan brewery employees were laid off in a plant closing. Both were inactive due to work injuries at the time of the closing and were receiving workers' compensation. Before the actual closing, the employer's pension plan administrator presented plant employees with the option of either receiving a lump sum of their pension benefits or transferring their retirement funds into an insurance annuity trust. Both employees opted to take a lump sum. They applied for and were granted continuation workers' compensation benefits. The state Worker's Compensation Appeal Board held in one case that lump sum pension distributions and workers' compensation benefits could not be coordinated. A contrary result was reached in the other case. The cases reached the Supreme Court of Michigan, which observed that **employees should be limited to the receipt of one wage loss benefit at any one time**. The coordination of workers' compensation benefits with lump sum pension distributions properly prevented duplicate wage loss benefits. *Drouillard v. Stroh Brewery Co.*, 449 Mich. 293, 536 N.W.2d 530 (Mich. 1995).

- Three Maryland steelworkers were laid off when a mill was permanently closed. Each had over 35 years of service and elected to retire and collect pension benefits rather than accept lower-paying jobs or go on layoff status. The company pension plan called for a special payment equal to 13 weeks of vacation pay, less any regular vacation pay disbursed during the year of retirement. The state Department of Economic and Employment Development (DEED) denied the retirees' claims for unemployment benefits under a statute that disallowed benefits where monthly pension benefits exceeded the amount of unemployment claimed. The DEED board of appeals held that the special payment was not a lump sum payment and thus disqualified the applicants from benefits during the first 13 weeks of unemployment. The board allowed compensation only to the extent that the special payment represented vacation pay (four weeks in the case of one employee and three weeks for the other two). A trial court disallowed benefits entirely, and the Court of Special Appeals of

Maryland affirmed. **The special payment was part of a periodic pension compensation package and not a lump sum** because it was an advance on the first three months of retirement compensation. Accordingly, the special payments did not constitute a lump sum due to a plant closing or layoff that would be exempt from the deductibility provisions of state unemployment compensation law. The trial court had correctly refused to deduct the amount of vacation pay from the gross value of the special payment. *Facello v. Dep't of Economic and Employment Development*, 104 Md. App. 575, 657 A.2d 363 (Md. Ct. Spec. App. 1995).

II. WELFARE AND HEALTH BENEFIT PLANS

ERISA also covers employee welfare benefit plans. ERISA participation, vesting and funding requirements do not apply to welfare benefit plans, but such plans may create vested rights by an agreement of the parties.

Employers generally can adopt, modify or terminate welfare benefit plans as long as they act consistently with ERISA, its regulations and the plans' requirements.

A. ERISA Applicability and Compliance

ERISA, at 29 U.S.C. § 1002(1), defines an employee welfare benefit plan as:

[A]ny plan, fund, or program which was heretofore or is hereafter established or maintained by an employer or by an employee organization, or by both, to the extent that such plan, fund, or program was established or is maintained for the purpose of providing for its participants or their beneficiaries, through the purchase of insurance or otherwise, (A) medical, surgical, or hospital care or benefits, or benefits in the event of sickness, accident, disability, death or unemployment, or vacation benefits, apprenticeship or other training programs, or day care centers, scholarship funds, or prepaid legal services, or (B) any benefit described in section 186(c) of this title (other than pensions on retirement or death, and insurance to provide such pensions).

ERISA applies to an employee benefits plan if it is established or maintained by an employer or an employee organization engaged in commerce or in any industry or activity affecting commerce [29 U.S.C. § 1003(a)]. This section applies to both pension benefit plans and welfare benefit plans.

However, group or group-type insurance programs are not employee welfare benefit plans for purposes of ERISA:

1) where they are offered by an insurer under which the employer does not contribute any funds,
2) where participation is voluntary,
3) where the employer does not endorse the program but merely collects premiums, and

4) where the employer receives no compensation in connection with the program.

See 29 C.F.R. § 2510.3-1(j).

1. Supreme Court Cases

◆ A Sears employee was diagnosed with a heart condition that prevented her from performing her job. She received disability benefits under the company's plan for 24 months, and applied for Social Security benefits as well. An administrative law judge found her eligible for benefits, which Sears' insurer took by right of offset. Sears' insurer then found her ineligible for long-term disability benefits on the ground that she could do sedentary work. She sued under ERISA. An Ohio federal court ruled for the insurer, the Sixth Circuit reversed, and the U.S. Supreme Court affirmed the ruling for the employee. The Court noted **the conflict of interest where an insurer decides if an employee is eligible for benefits and is also responsible for paying the claim**. *Metropolitan Life Insurance Co. v. Glenn*, 128 S.Ct. 2343, 171 L.Ed.2d 299 (U.S. 2008).

◆ After a Maryland employee and her husband were injured in an automobile accident, the employee's ERISA-covered health insurance plan paid the couple's medical expenses. They then sued several third parties for injuries they suffered as a result of the accident. The health plan administrator sent them a letter asserting a lien on any proceeds from the lawsuit. After the lawsuit settled for $750,000, the plan administrator sued to recover the medical expenses it had paid. A federal court ordered the couple to reimburse the plan administrator for the medical expenses, and the Fourth Circuit affirmed in part. The U.S. Supreme Court also affirmed, noting that **the plan properly provided for beneficiaries to reimburse the plan from any recovery from outside sources**. This was a claim for equitable relief that could be brought under ERISA. The couple had to reimburse the plan. *Sereboff v. Mid Atlantic Medical Services, Inc.*, 547 U.S. 356, 126 S.Ct. 1869, 164 L.Ed.2d 612 (U.S. 2006).

◆ Two Texas employees sued their health plan administrators when their respective HMOs refused to cover their physicians' recommended medical treatment and they suffered medical setbacks as a result. Federal courts dismissed the cases as preempted by ERISA, but the Fifth Circuit reversed. On further appeal, the U.S. Supreme Court reversed the Fifth Circuit, noting that **ERISA preempted their state law claims for medical negligence**. The employees' claims fell squarely within the parameters of Section 502(a), which has extraordinary preemptive power and which allows plan participants to sue to enforce rights or recover benefits under their plans. Here, contrary to the employees' argument, the plan administrators were making eligibility decisions, not treatment decisions. Also, the failure of the plans to cover the requested treatment was the proximate cause of the employees' injuries, not the denial of coverage. *Aetna Health Care v. Davila*, 542 U.S. 200, 124 S.Ct. 2488, 159 L.Ed.2d 312 (2004).

◆ A Black & Decker employee alleged that a mild degenerative disk condition made him eligible for long-term disability benefits under ERISA. Although his personal physician backed up his claim, a separate neurologist recommended by Black & Decker concluded that he could perform "sedentary work" if aided by pain medication. Based on this opinion and the recommendation of its insurer, Black & Decker denied the employee's claim. He sued in a California federal court to overturn this determination. The judge ruled in favor of Black & Decker, but the U.S. Court of Appeals for the Ninth Circuit reversed, holding that the company had not come up with adequate reasons for rejecting the opinion of the employee's treating physician. The Supreme Court, however, disagreed. It held that **plan administrators are not obliged to accord special deference to the opinions of treating physicians** when making benefit determinations under ERISA. The statute and its regulations "require 'full and fair' assessment of claims and clear communication to the claimant of the 'specific reasons' for benefit denials," the Court explained. "But these measures do not command plan administrators to credit the opinions of treating physicians over other evidence relevant to the claimant's medical condition." *Black & Decker Disability Plan v. Nord*, 538 U.S. 822, 123 S.Ct. 1965, 155 L.Ed.2d 1034 (2003).

◆ Employees of a railway subsidiary were entitled to railroad retirement benefits and pension, health and welfare benefits under collective bargaining agreements covered by ERISA. When the contract between the railway and the subsidiary was terminated, the railway hired another service to do the work. The new contractor retained some of the subsidiary's employees; however, it was not required to make railroad retirement contributions and its welfare plan was inferior to the subsidiary's plan. Employees who continued to work for the new contractor sued the railroad, the subsidiary and the new contractor in a California federal court, asserting that the manner of the discharge interfered with their pension and welfare benefits. The court dismissed the ERISA claims. The Ninth Circuit reinstated the claim for interference with pension benefits, but agreed that ERISA did not protect employees from elimination of welfare benefits that did not vest.

The U.S. Supreme Court found that Section 510 of ERISA prevents an employer from discharging a plan participant or beneficiary for the purpose of interfering with the attainment of any right to which the participant might be entitled. Section 510 draws no distinction between those rights that vest under ERISA and those that do not. Further, **although an employer has the right to unilaterally amend or eliminate a welfare benefit plan, Section 510 requires the employer to follow the plan's formal amendment process**. The Court vacated the judgment and remanded the case for further proceedings. *Inter-Modal Rail Employees Ass'n v. Atchison, Topeka and Santa Fe Railway Co.*, 520 U.S. 510, 117 S.Ct. 1513, 137 L.Ed.2d 763 (1997).

◆ A manufacturer transferred its money-losing divisions to a new subsidiary and told employees in these divisions that their benefits and salaries would remain the same if they transferred. Many employees transferred to the subsidiary, which went into receivership within two years. Employees and retirees who participated in the subsidiary's welfare benefit plan asserted that the manufacturer was aware that the subsidiary was insolvent at its creation and that they had been fraudulently induced to accept the transfers. They sued the manufacturer in an Iowa federal court, which held that the manufacturer violated its obligation under ERISA to administer the plan in the employees' interest. The court awarded damages to the participants and ruled that they had a right to appropriate equitable relief including reinstatement into the manufacturer's plan. The U.S. Court of Appeals, Eighth Circuit, affirmed much of the district court decision but disallowed a $46 million damage award.

The manufacturer appealed to the U.S. Supreme Court, arguing that it was acting in its capacity as an employer when it decided to transfer employees to the new subsidiary, appropriately exercising business judgment. It also claimed that ERISA does not permit individual claims but only authorizes remedies that benefit the plan as a whole. The Court found that the manufacturer had been **acting as both a plan fiduciary and an employer when it promised to preserve employee benefits and salaries after the transfer**. Accordingly, its actions were held to the standard of fiduciary care that subjected it to potential ERISA liability. The Court rejected the argument that ERISA did not allow individual equitable relief, and affirmed the lower court decisions. *Varity Corp. v. Howe*, 516 U.S. 489, 116 S.Ct. 1065, 134 L.Ed.2d 130 (1996).

- A corporation maintained and administered a single-employer health plan for its employees. After closing a New Jersey facility, the corporation's executive vice president notified retirees of the facility by letter that their post-retirement health benefits were being terminated. The retirees sued the corporation, alleging that the termination of benefits violated Section 402(b)(3) of ERISA, 29 U.S.C. § 1102(b)(3), which required employee benefit plans to have "a procedure for amending such plan, and for identifying the persons who have authority to amend the plan." The retirees claimed that the company's summary plan description lacked a valid amendment procedure and that the action constituted a plan amendment. The court agreed with the retirees and ordered the corporation to pay them over $2.6 million in benefits. The Third Circuit affirmed, and the corporation appealed.

The U.S. Supreme Court agreed with the corporation that the minimal language in its summary plan description satisfied the amendment procedure requirement of ERISA Section 402(b)(3). Under the plan description, the corporation "reserve[d] the right at any time to amend the plan. ..." ERISA creates no substantive entitlement to employer-provided welfare benefits and employers are allowed to freely modify, amend or terminate welfare plans under most circumstances. **A plan that simply identified the person or persons having authority to amend a plan necessarily indicated the amendment procedure.** The Court reversed and remanded the case. *Curtiss-Wright Corp. v. Schoonejongen*, 514 U.S. 73, 115 S.Ct. 1223, 131 L.Ed.2d 94 (1995).

- A corporation operated a self-funded health care plan under which plan members agreed to reimburse it for benefits paid if the member recovered on a claim in a liability action against a third party. The daughter of a plan member was seriously injured in an automobile accident, and the plan paid part of her medical expenses. A negligence action against the driver of the vehicle settled, and the plan member refused to reimburse the plan, asserting that Pennsylvania law precluded subrogation by the plan. A federal court held that the state statute prohibited the plan from enforcing the subrogation provision. The case reached the U.S. Supreme Court, which stated that ERISA preempted the application of the Pennsylvania law, and that the plan could seek subrogation. State laws that directly regulate insurance are "saved" from preemption, but this does not apply to **self-funded employee benefit plans** because they are not insurance for purposes of such laws. *FMC Corp. v. Holliday*, 498 U.S. 52, 111 S.Ct. 403, 112 L.Ed.2d 356 (1990).

◆ A District of Columbia workers' compensation statute required employers who provided health insurance for their employees to furnish equivalent health insurance coverage for injured employees eligible for workers' compensation benefits. An employer sued the district and its mayor, claiming that the act was preempted by ERISA. The U.S. Supreme Court stated that a law "relates to" a covered employee benefit plan if it has a connection with or reference to such a plan. ERISA preempts any state law that refers to or has a connection with covered benefit plans that do not fall within its exceptions – even if: 1) the law is not specifically designed to affect such plans, 2) the effect is only indirect, and 3) the law is consistent with ERISA's substantive requirements. The Court held that **employer-sponsored health insurance programs are subject to ERISA regulation**, and any state law imposing requirements by reference to such covered programs is preempted by ERISA. ERISA superseded the workers' compensation act because the act related to a covered plan. The district could not require employers to provide equivalent health insurance coverage for injured employees eligible for workers' compensation. *District of Columbia v. Greater Washington Board of Trade*, 506 U.S. 125, 113 S.Ct. 580, 121 L.Ed.2d 513 (1992).

2. Preemption Cases

The same rationale for preemption used in retirement cases is applied here: namely, that it is better to have a single, federal law applied uniformly than different laws for each state. If a state law and ERISA both address employee benefit plans, courts will preempt the state law with ERISA to resolve any conflict.

◆ Through payroll deductions, an Oregon employee obtained life insurance from a group plan. After she was diagnosed with terminal cancer and went on disability leave, her employer canceled the group plan and changed to a new plan for insurance. Under the new plan, the employee was not eligible for benefits because of her condition. The company offered employees the option of converting old policies to individual policies, but under the conversion provision, the employee would only have been eligible for $5,000 in coverage. When she died, her children sued the company, claiming that company officials had told the employee and her daughter that the employee was covered by a $150,000 insurance policy. They sought the benefits. A federal court dismissed the case, finding that ERISA preempted it. However, the Ninth Circuit reversed, holding that the children could pursue a breach of contract and negligence claim against the company. **ERISA did not preempt the lawsuit because the employee was not covered by an ERISA plan at the time of her death.** *Miller v. Rite Aid Corp.*, 504 F.3d 1102 (9th Cir. 2007).

◆ Maryland passed a law requiring employers with 10,000 or more employees that spend less than 8% of total wages on health insurance to pay the state the difference. A trade association filed a lawsuit to challenge the law, and the case reached the Fourth Circuit. The court of appeals held that the law was preempted by ERISA. A state law has an impermissible "connection with" an ERISA plan if it directly regulates or effectively mandates some element of the structure or administration of employers' ERISA plans. Here, **the law essentially mandated that employers provide a certain level of benefits, thus bringing it within the scope of ERISA**. The law was not enforceable. *Retail Industry Leaders Ass'n v. Fielder*, 475 F.3d 180 (4th Cir. 2007).

◆ A Georgia company allowed an insurer to publicize a disability plan to its employees. The company collected premiums through payroll deductions and remitted the payments to the insurer (satisfying the safe harbor exemption from ERISA). However, it also decided on the 90-day eligibility period, identified the plan as a benefit in its handbook and allowed the insurer to distribute booklets stating that the plan was covered by ERISA. When an employee with rectal cancer was denied benefits he thought he deserved under the plan, he sued the employer under state law. A federal court and the Eleventh Circuit ruled that the plan was governed by ERISA, which preempted the employee's state law claims. **Even though the company's involvement in the plan was minimal, it was enough that the plan did not qualify under the safe harbor exemption of ERISA.** The employee had to pursue his claim using ERISA's procedures. *Moorman v. UnumProvident Corp.*, 464 F.3d 1260 (11th Cir. 2006).

◆ A marketing specialist for a Massachusetts company was offered a position 100 miles from her home. After commuting for several weeks, she experienced increasing back pain and applied for relocation benefits. The company denied her request, and she went on disability leave. Later, the company decided that she was no longer disabled under its policy and required her to return to work. She worked intermittently for three days and was fired on the fourth day as part of a work force reduction. Instead of following the company's procedure for appealing a denial of short-term benefits or for requesting an application for long-term benefits, the employee sued the company for breach of contract, negligence, and violations of ERISA. The First Circuit held that **the company's short-term disability plan qualified as an ERISA plan**. Accordingly, ERISA preempted her state law claims because they were dependent on the ERISA plan. Further, because the employee failed to follow the company's appeals procedure, she was barred from bringing the ERISA claim. *McMahon v. Digital Equipment Corp.*, 162 F.3d 28 (1st Cir. 1998).

◆ A Delaware resident who worked for a Pennsylvania employer died after he fell in his home while intoxicated. The death occurred a few days after a dispute with his employer's insurer in which coverage for alcoholism treatment was denied under the employer's group health plan. Pennsylvania law requires employee benefit plans to provide alcoholism treatment for a minimum of 30 days per year, while Delaware law contains no such requirement. The employee's estate sued the insurer in a Delaware court, asserting breach of contract, wrongful death, unfair claims settlement and intentional infliction of emotional distress. The court held that the case was barred by ERISA, which preempts state laws governing employee benefit plans. The lack of uniformity in the state laws at issue in this case illustrated the policy reasons underlying ERISA preemption of state laws. The employee had never undergone treatment and **the breach of contract action was preempted**. Punitive damages were unavailable under ERISA, and the remaining claims were not brought on the employee's behalf but were for the benefit of his survivors. The court dismissed the case. *Yardley v. U.S. Healthcare, Inc.*, 698 A.2d 979 (Del. Super. Ct. 1996), *aff'd,* 693 A.2d 1083 (Del. 1997).

3. Amending Welfare Benefit Plans

Employers can generally adopt, modify or terminate welfare benefit plans. Where employers amend plans in their capacity as employers (and not as fiduciaries), they will not have liability under ERISA as long as they act consistently with ERISA, its regulations and the plans' requirements.

With the astronomical increase in medical care costs, many companies have amended their health care plans to eliminate or reduce such benefits, particularly for retirees. Generally, unless the employer has contractually agreed not to amend the plan, this is permissible.

- A real estate investment company offered an ERISA plan with a reservation of rights that allowed it to terminate the plan at any time. When two Iowa employees left the company, they each received a letter informing them that the company would continue to provide medical and life insurance benefits. After the company closed its U.S. operations, it terminated the ERISA plan. The two employees sued, claiming the letters they received constituted separate ERISA plans that offered lifetime benefits which could not be terminated by the company. A federal court and the Eighth Circuit disagreed. The letters merely stated that the employees would continue to receive benefits the same as their current coverage and instructed them to complete and return a "continuation of insurance upon retirement form" if they wanted the continued coverage. **Since the letters were not freestanding ERISA plans, the employees were not entitled to continuing coverage.** *Johnson v. Lend Lease Real Estate Investment*, 467 F.3d 1131 (8th Cir. 2006).

- An employee at an Ohio assembly plant took a promotion into a nonunion management position but then asked to return to her old job. Her request was denied. After an employee accused her of harassment and threatening behavior, an investigation determined that the accusations were exaggerated. She took a leave for stress and sought short-term disability benefits through the company's disability absence plan. The company denied her claim and she sued under ERISA, **claiming the company was now improperly requiring her to be 100% disabled**. A federal court held that she was not entitled to benefits. Here, the plan was paid out of the company's general fund. Thus, it met the definition of a "payroll practice" that was excluded from ERISA's coverage. Further, the company's decision to deny benefits was not arbitrary and capricious. It reasonably determined that she was not unable to perform all her duties. *Langley v. DaimlerChrysler Corp.*, 407 F.3d 897 (N.D. Ohio 2005).

◆ From 1974 until a 1993 collective bargaining agreement (CBA) went into effect, a Pennsylvania manufacturer agreed to pay all of its hourly retirees' health care benefits. In 1991, industry-wide accounting guidelines for reporting employee benefits changed. As a result, the manufacturer reduced the benefits it provided active employees. After the terms of the 1993 CBA were agreed upon, the manufacturer retroactively eliminated or modified health and life insurance benefits for retirees, so employees who retired before the CBA became effective were no longer eligible for those benefits. The union sued, alleging violations of Section 301 of the Labor Management Relations Act and ERISA. The district court ruled for the manufacturer, and the Third Circuit affirmed. Because ERISA did not require automatic vesting of employee welfare benefit plans, an employer's commitment to vest such benefits had to be stated in clear and express language. Contract phrases stating that the company would continue to provide certain coverage **did not explicitly indicate that the benefits would continue indefinitely**, and a more reasonable interpretation was that the benefits would continue for the life of the CBA. *Int'l Union v. Skinner Engine Co.*, 188 F.3d 130 (3d Cir. 1999).

◆ A collective bargaining agreement (CBA) between a Michigan manufacturer and the machinists' union provided lifetime health care benefits to members who retired between 1985 and 1988. In the negotiations for the 1988-1991 contract, the parties made some significant changes to the insurance agreement, increasing, among other things, the amount of paid-up life insurance by $1,000. However, the later contract did not include language found in the 1985-88 agreement continuing retirees' benefits until death. When the company sold its assets, closed its Michigan plant and terminated its employees, it notified the employees who had retired after 1988 that they would no longer receive health care benefits to which they had been entitled under the CBAs. The union sued, and the case reached the Sixth Circuit, which rejected the company's argument that benefits had not vested because the parties agreed to time limits on them as a trade-off for increased benefits.

The court noted that whether benefits survive the termination of a CBA depends on the intent of the parties. Retiree benefits "are in a sense 'status' benefits which ... carry with them an inference ... that the parties intended those benefits to continue as long as the beneficiary remains a retiree." This conflicted with the Third Circuit's decision in *Int'l Union v. Skinner Engine*, above, where the Third Circuit held that retired workers' health benefits ended with the expiration of their contract. Since the language of the contract was unclear as to the intent of the parties, the court looked to affidavit testimony that supported the union's assertion that **time limits were not proposed as a trade-off for increased benefits during CBA negotiations**. *Int'l Union, UAAAIWA v. BVR Liquidating, Inc.*, 190 F.3d 768 (6th Cir. 1999).

◆ A series of collective bargaining agreements between an employer and several unions provided that the employer would pay full medical insurance premiums for company retirees. The employer amended the medical plan so that retirees would pay a portion of the premium if costs increased at a rate higher than the annual increase in the consumer price index. The unions and retirees sued in a New York federal court, asserting violations of the Labor Management Relations Act (LMRA) and ERISA, arguing that the bargaining agreements had promised lifetime medical benefits. The court ruled that the benefits were not vested under either plan documents or the bargaining agreements, which had by then expired. The Second Circuit affirmed. Under ERISA, welfare benefits are not vested in the absence of a promise. An employer can generally give notice to amend or terminate a welfare plan at any time. Under the LMRA, **an employer may modify or terminate employee medical benefits after the expiration of a bargaining agreement**. The bargaining agreements in this case specifically limited benefits to the term of each agreement and the benefits did not vest. The summary plan documents contained an express reservation of the employer's right to terminate the plan, which alerted retirees to that right. *American Federation of Grain Millers, AFL-CIO v. Int'l Multifoods Corp.,* 116 F.3d 976 (2d Cir. 1997).

◆ An Illinois manufacturer laid off most of its employees at one plant. The plant shutdown agreement stated that all employees who retired prior to the termination date of the company retirement plan would be entitled to lifetime life, hospitalization, medical and surgical benefits as described in earlier collective bargaining agreements. The most recent agreement contained a disclaimer that the employer reserved the right to amend the group health plan. The employer changed health insurance carriers several years later, increasing participant deductible rates and decreasing company contributions. A group of retirees and their union reps sued the employer under the LMRA and ERISA. The Seventh Circuit noted that the shutdown agreement unambiguously promised retirees lifetime benefits. Although the bargaining agreement referred to the reservation of rights, the reservation of rights could not take precedence over the later promise of lifetime benefits. The employer was not prohibited from imposing cost-saving measures that did not substantially reduce benefits or contravene its earlier promise. **The shutdown agreement required the employer to make reasonable efforts to obtain the expected level of coverage.** The case was remanded for a determination of whether the proposed changes would significantly reduce the general level of benefits for the retirees. *Diehl v. Twin Disc, Inc.*, 102 F.3d 301 (7th Cir. 1996).

4. Notice Issues

ERISA establishes notice requirements for denying benefit claims. According to regulation 29 C.F.R. § 2560.503-1(f), the initial notice must contain:

1) The specific reason or reasons for the denial,
2) Specific reference to pertinent plan provisions on which the denial is based,
3) A description of any additional material or information necessary, and
4) Appropriate information as to the steps to be taken if the participant or beneficiary wishes to submit his or her claim for review.

Employers also have a duty to provide notice with respect to plan terminations or modifications.

◆ An employee of a company in Michigan became disabled by depression and received short-term disability benefits. She applied for long-term disability benefits and was informed that payment of future benefits was dependent on her continuing disability, requiring her to visit her doctor once a month and attend therapy on the same day. After the company learned that she missed multiple sessions, it terminated her benefits because of her failure to comply with the terms of her treatment plan. She sued for ERISA violations, including failure to give notice that one of the reasons it was terminating benefits was because she was no longer disabled. A federal court and the Sixth Circuit ruled against her. Since she had missed her sessions, there was no continuing medical evidence that she was still disabled. **Even though the company failed to give proper notice of all its reasons for denying benefits, it still provided a reasonable basis for denying benefits** – her refusal to comply with her treatment plan. *McCartha v. National City Corp.*, 419 F.3d 437 (6th Cir. 2005).

◆ An Indiana clinical supervisor was diagnosed with fatigue syndrome and fibromyalgia and received disability benefits under her employer's employee welfare benefit plan. The plan discontinued disability payments and sought further information (including an independent medical examination) concerning her application for long-term disability benefits when it learned that she had regularly been attending sales shows throughout the Midwest to sell jewelry she had made. The employee sued the plan administrator and provider under ERISA. The court ruled for the administrator and provider. The employee appealed, claiming that the plan had failed to provide her with adequate notice of its review process and that she was excused from exhausting the plan's internal appeal procedure. The Seventh Circuit Court of Appeals disagreed, observing that while ERISA establishes minimum notice and procedure requirements when a plan administrator denies a claim, **these safeguards do not apply until a claim is actually denied**. The plan had not denied the claim here, but had only discontinued payments while seeking further information about the employee's condition. The administrator and provider did not violate ERISA, and the district court had properly ruled in their favor. *Robyns v. Reliance Standard Life Insurance Co.*, 130 F.3d 1231 (7th Cir. 1997).

◆ A small Indiana manufacturer maintained an employee health insurance plan under which it contributed two-thirds of each participant's monthly premium and withheld the remaining amount from wages. When the company was faced with serious financial difficulties, it suspended its health insurance premium payments, using withheld employee contributions to fund its daily operating expenses. An employee learned that her coverage had been canceled for failure to pay premiums. She threatened a lawsuit, and the employer presented participants with a reinstatement form from the health insurer. The employee refused to sign the form and walked off the job. Although the insurer then paid her outstanding claims, she refused to complete the reinstatement form and sued the employer under ERISA. The court dismissed the lawsuit, and the Seventh Circuit affirmed. Although the employer's misappropriation of employee withholding for its operating expenses was inexcusable and its failure to inform employees of the lapse of insurance coverage violated its ERISA fiduciary duties, **the employee failed to show any economic loss** as a result. There had been no use of plan assets for the employer's personal gain. *Mira v. Nuclear Measurements Corp.*, 107 F.3d 466 (7th Cir. 1997).

- A Maryland arms manufacturer hired a supervisor under a written employment offer by which it promised to pay disability benefits based upon 60% of salary until the age of 70. The supervisor was instead enrolled in a life and disability plan issued by an insurer. The plan excluded coverage for disabilities caused by preexisting conditions. The summary plan description did not mention the exclusion. The employee suffered a heart attack arising out of a preexisting condition. Although the insurer denied the claim for benefits based on the exclusion, the employer continued to voluntarily pay the employee's premiums and salary until he began receiving social security disability benefits. The employee sued the employer for long-term disability benefits in a Maryland federal court, which ruled for the employer. On appeal, the Fourth Circuit Court of Appeals found that **the employee was not entitled to relief based on the employment offer letter, as it did not qualify as an ERISA plan**. Further, the employee had not relied upon summary plan documents issued by the employer and was thus not entitled to relief for that claim. ERISA does not protect employees from the revocation of gratuitous benefits. *Stiltner v. Beretta USA Corp.*, 74 F.3d 1473 (4th Cir. 1996).

- A Georgia clinic provided group health insurance to its employees without cost. The employer then purchased a different policy that excluded coverage for preexisting employee medical conditions that were evident during the 12 months immediately preceding the date of coverage. An employee who was unaware of the exclusionary clause had surgery on her knee shortly after the change in policies, and both carriers denied coverage. When the hospital sued for her treatment costs, the employee filed a third-party complaint against her employer, alleging that it had breached her employment contract by failing to inform her of the effective termination of her coverage when it changed policies. A state court granted pretrial judgment to the employer. The Court of Appeals of Georgia reversed, noting that **an employer acts as the agent of its employees when changing group insurance policies and has a duty to notify employees of the differences**. Employers must advise employees of their rights to continuation coverage under existing policies when they purchase new insurance policies. Here, factual issues remained concerning whether anyone had notified the employee of the change in coverage. This and other fact questions made pretrial dismissal of the lawsuit inappropriate. *Brandon v. Mayfield*, 452 S.E.2d 181 (Ga. Ct. App. 1994).

5. Other Applicability and Compliance Cases

ERISA protects against actions taken by employers to either prevent the use of benefits or retaliate against employees for asserting rights under the act.

ERISA does not apply to independent contractors.

ERISA does not protect employee rights to job benefits that are provided solely at the discretion of the employer. Only where the employee has an entitlement to certain benefits can ERISA be used to protect those benefits.

◆ An Iowa employee was diagnosed with multiple sclerosis shortly after she began working for a convention center. She was fired five years later for poor performance. The general manager cited her failure to request menus in a timely fashion, selling more rooms than were available and not charging the correct amount for events. She later met with the company's CEO and **claimed that he told her he couldn't afford her health benefits**. He disputed her version of events. When she sued under the ADA and ERISA, the Eighth Circuit rejected her claims. Here, her poor performance was well documented, and she could not show that the manager who fired her was simply being used as a conduit for the CEO's alleged bias. *Libel v. Adventure Lands of America*, 482 F.3d 1028 (8th Cir. 2007).

◆ A Kentucky plant manager was suspended for three days without pay because he took too long to respond to a malfunction in a conveyor belt. The year before, he was suspended for negligently operating a forklift. While he was on suspension, his doctor diagnosed him with a heart condition and determined he was unable to work. He was not allowed to return to the job, and was fired for violating company policy regarding plant safety. When he sought short-term disability benefits, they were denied. He sued under ERISA, but the Sixth Circuit ruled against him, noting that **he was not actively at work when he notified his employer of his disability**. The plan defined "actively at work" as being actually at work on the day immediately preceding an excused leave of absence. The court rejected the manager's argument that a suspension was the same as an excused leave of absence. *Pollett v. Rinker Materials Corp.*, 477 F.3d 376 (6th Cir. 2007).

◆ Mobil Oil Corporation contracted with other companies for services it wished to outsource. An electronics technician for one of the outsourcing companies worked at a Mobil Oil facility in Louisiana for 12 years, doing work similar or identical to work performed by Mobil employees. When the technician was discharged, he filed a claim with Mobil for retroactive employment benefits on the ground that he was a "common law employee" of Mobil. Mobil's plan administrator determined that the technician was not entitled to benefits because he had never been a Mobil employee. The technician sued Mobil under ERISA, claiming that he was entitled to the same benefits as employees of Mobil. A federal court ruled against him, and the Fifth Circuit affirmed. The employee had signed a contract with the outsourcing company, which had in turn signed a contract with Mobil, agreeing that all its employees worked solely for it. **Since the technician was never a "regular employee" of Mobil, he was not entitled to employment benefits.** *MacLachlan v. ExxonMobil Corp.*, 350 F.3d 472 (5th Cir. 2003).

◆ The benefits administrator at a Philadelphia law firm was also a member of the HMO that provided health care to firm employees. The HMO sent her a letter advising her that she could request information about physician compensation. Instead, she sued, claiming that the HMO had a fiduciary duty to disclose detailed information about its physician incentive plan. A federal court ruled against her, and the Third Circuit affirmed. It ruled that **ERISA does not impose a duty on an HMO to disclose physician incentive information** unless the employee requests the information, the HMO has notice that the employee needs the information to prevent her from making a harmful decision about her health care, and the employee suffers some harm. Here, the employee never requested the information, and the employee suffered no harm because the law firm offered only the HMO plan to employees. It offered no alternatives. *Horvath v. Keystone Health Plan East, Inc.*, 333 F.3d 450 (3d Cir. 2003).

◆ A customer service representative was fired after 11 months on the job, allegedly for poor work performance. However, she claimed that she was really fired in violation of ERISA because the company wanted to avoid the increased health insurance costs it would have incurred because of her son's hydrocephalus (water on the brain). An Ohio federal court granted pretrial judgment to the company, but the Sixth Circuit reversed. Here, **the employee did not have to show that the sole purpose in firing her was to interfere with her right to receive benefits under ERISA**; she only had to show that the interference was a motivating factor. She was entitled to a trial because she presented evidence that: 1) she was fired just two weeks after her supervisor learned of her son's condition, 2) all the customer complaints cited by the company for her poor performance dated from that two-week period, 3) a company official stated that families like hers were the cause of rising insurance costs and were a drain on the company, and 4) she received an 8% pay raise six weeks before she was fired. *Smith v. Hinkle Manufacturing, Inc.*, 36 Fed. Appx. 825 (6th Cir. 2002).

◆ In a collective bargaining agreement, a union negotiated changes to its members' health insurance benefits. The new plan provided specific claims procedures. When a lawsuit arose over disputes in payment for certain individuals' claims, a Kentucky federal court held that the employer did not have to submit to binding arbitration. The Sixth Circuit Court of Appeals affirmed, holding that although changes to the group health insurance plan were incorporated into the bargaining agreement, **disputes over individual members' benefits were not subject to arbitration**. The plan provided for a separate benefit claims procedure, and by incorporating that procedure into the agreement, the parties intended that the claims would not be subject to arbitration. *United Steelworkers of America v. Comwlth. Aluminum Corp.*, 162 F.3d 447 (6th Cir. 1998).

◆ Microsoft hired independent contractors to work for periods sometimes exceeding two years. It did not withhold federal and state taxes from their compensation and did not allow them to participate in its ERISA-qualified stock purchase plan or its non-qualified savings plan. The Internal Revenue Service determined by applying common law principles that the workers were actually employees, and Microsoft agreed to treat them as employees by deducting taxes from their earnings. However, some of the workers were laid off and referred to a temporary employment agency through which they could do the same work on an as-needed basis. A number of workers rejected the offer and sued Microsoft in a Washington federal court for violations of ERISA, seeking benefits under the savings and stock purchase plans. The court granted pretrial judgment to Microsoft. The Ninth Circuit Court of Appeals emphasized that Microsoft now recognized the workers as **employees who were eligible for benefits, rather than independent contractors**, and had changed its treatment of them as soon as the erroneous classification had been discovered. It characterized as a mutual mistake the agreement of the parties to classify the workers as independent contractors. Therefore, the plan administrator should have received the first opportunity to determine what benefits the claimants were entitled to receive. The court remanded the issue of an appropriate remedy to the district court. *Vizcaino v. Microsoft Corp.*, 120 F.3d 1006 (9th Cir. 1997).

◆ The U.S. Court of Appeals, Seventh Circuit, held that **ERISA does not prevent the discharge of an employee for excessive absenteeism** unless the employee can demonstrate a specific intent by the employer to either prevent the use of benefits or retaliate against her. The case arose from the discharge of an Illinois inventory control analyst for violating her employer's no-fault attendance policy. Some of the absences were considered excused for the purposes of the company's short-term disability plan, but the company counted all absences, whether excused or unexcused, under the no-fault policy. The employer fired the employee, and she sued, asserting a violation of ERISA Section 510 (29 U.S.C. § 1140), which prohibits the discharge or discipline of plan participants and beneficiaries for exercising rights under the plan. The court ruled for the employer. The Seventh Circuit affirmed, holding that the employee presented no evidence of the employer's specific intent to interfere with her ERISA rights. Excessive absenteeism is a legitimate reason for termination, as long as there is no connection between the discharge and any entitlement to benefits. *Lindemann v. Mobil Oil Corp.*, 141 F.3d 290 (7th Cir. 1998).

◆ A Colorado accounts receivable specialist had a poor relationship with his supervisor and claimed that it caused him severe depression. He rejected a transfer to work under a different supervisor, since the job remained in the same supervisory chain. The employee received benefits under the company's sickness disability benefits plan, which limited benefits to 52 weeks. The employer rejected his request to continue his benefits under the plan's accident disability benefits plan, which made benefits available indefinitely for work-related, on-the-job accidents. The employer also maintained an "other benefit payment" plan that allowed a payment of up to $1,000 to employees who demonstrated severe financial hardship. After the employer rejected the employee's application for an "other benefit payment," he sued. The Tenth Circuit ruled for the employer. The employee failed to show that his disability had been caused by an accident or was directly connected with his job duties. Also, he was not entitled to benefits under the "other benefit payment" plan, since **its vague language created no employee entitlement and was not an ERISA plan**. *Siemon v. AT&T Corp.*, 117 F.3d 1173 (10th Cir. 1997).

B. Coverage Issues

Many of the ERISA cases that arise have to do with either the denial of benefits or the improper administration of plans (for example, failing to notify a departing employee of his or her COBRA continuation coverage rights). Where an employer, rather than an outside entity, acts as the plan administrator, its actions will be more closely scrutinized for self-dealing.

1. COBRA Cases

The Consolidated Omnibus Budget Reconciliation Act of 1985 (COBRA) was enacted as an amendment to ERISA (among other statutes) and requires employers who sponsor group health plans to give the plans' qualified beneficiaries the opportunity to elect continuation coverage under the plans when the beneficiaries might otherwise lose coverage upon the occurrence of certain qualifying events (like the termination or death of an employee).

When the qualifying event is termination or reduced hours (so as to make the employee no longer eligible under the company health plan), the maximum period of coverage is generally 18 months. The benefits offered must be the same, but the employee is now the party responsible for paying for that coverage.

COBRA coverage can stop when the qualified beneficiary "first becomes, after the date of the election … covered under any other health plan … which does not contain any exclusion or limitation with respect to any preexisting condition of such beneficiary."

- COBRA amended ERISA by authorizing qualified beneficiaries of employer group health plans to obtain continuation coverage in specified circumstances, including employment termination. A Missouri medical corporation discharged an employee with cancer who was covered under its group health plan. It informed the employee that he had COBRA continuation coverage rights, and he participated in the plan for six months. At that time, the employer notified him that he was not entitled to COBRA benefits because he was already covered by a group health plan supplied by his wife's employer as of his election date. The former employee sued for wrongful denial of coverage. The case reached the U.S. Supreme Court.

The Court stated that the COBRA amendments to ERISA require group health plan sponsors, including employers, to provide continuation coverage when plan beneficiaries might otherwise lose coverage upon the occurrence of a qualifying event, such as employment termination or divorce. COBRA coverage may cease on the date on which the qualified beneficiary first becomes covered, after the date of election, under any other group health plan that does not limit or exclude a beneficiary's preexisting health conditions. The employer and plan argued that the former employee was "first" covered by his wife's plan after the time of the election. The Court disagreed, finding that **the former employee had been continuously covered by his wife's group health plan and did not "first become" covered under the wife's plan after the date of election**. The employer could not cut off the former employee's COBRA coverage. *Geissal v. Moore Medical Corp.*, 524 U.S. 74, 118 S.Ct. 1869, 141 L.Ed.2d 64 (1998).

◆ Along with his wife, a Nebraska employee who was severely injured when he fell from a railcar sued the Professional Employer Organization (PEO) that had entered into a staff servicing agreement to provide employment and HR services for another company. The couple claimed that the PEO violated ERISA by failing to give proper COBRA notice after firing the employee, and that it wrongfully denied health insurance benefits. They also asserted a claim for breach of fiduciary duty. The PEO claimed that he was never covered by insurance and thus was not entitled to COBRA coverage, but that it had sent a COBRA notice anyway. A federal court held that the PEO breached its fiduciary duty and that since **the PEO had wrongfully denied health insurance coverage while the employee was still working, it would have been futile for the couple to elect COBRA coverage upon his termination**. The ex-employee and his wife were entitled to the medical expenses they would have received had they elected COBRA coverage. However, the Eighth Circuit limited the time period in which the couple could claim unreimbursed medical expenses and denied them statutory penalties of $110 per day. *Delcastillo v. Odyssey Resource Management, Inc.*, 292 Fed.Appx. 519 (8th Cir. 2008).

◆ A Michigan cemetery fired an employee and discontinued her health insurance coverage at that time. However, the employee did not learn of the discontinuation until two months later. She sued the cemetery for violating COBRA. The cemetery asserted that it did not have to comply with COBRA's requirements because it did not have at least 20 employees. A federal court and the Sixth Circuit agreed with the cemetery. Further, equitable estoppel (a legal doctrine barring a party from using its misrepresentation to another party for the purpose of gaining an advantage) did not apply here because the cemetery never misrepresented to the employee that she had any COBRA rights. *Thomas v. Miller*, 489 F.3d 293 (6th Cir. 2007).

◆ A South Dakota employee worked for an oil company until the retail location where she was assigned closed. She then developed health problems that required surgery. Three months after her job ended, she received a letter stating that she was no longer eligible for continuing COBRA benefits. She sued, claiming that the company had failed to appropriately notify her of her COBRA rights. A federal court ruled for the company, but the Eighth Circuit reversed. **It was not enough for the company to show that a notification letter had been generated and that it had a mailing process for letters.** The company also had to show that the notice was sent by means reasonably calculated to reach the employee. Among the ways it could do this were: photocopying a letter addressed to the employee or providing a report showing the date the notice was mailed. *Crotty v. Dakotacare Administrative Services, Inc.*, 455 F.3d 828 (8th Cir. 2006).

◆ The wife of an Oklahoma employee filed for divorce and obtained three protective orders requiring him to stay away from her. She sent a letter to the company asking that her "estranged husband" not be informed of any medical services she received. The company then determined that the couple had legally separated, which would be a qualifying event under COBRA, and notified the wife of her right to elect continuing health insurance coverage. She did not pay the premiums. When the divorce became final, she asked for COBRA coverage and the company refused to reinstate the policy. She sued and won. The Tenth Circuit ruled that **the company violated COBRA by sending out the notice prematurely**. Divorce proceedings did not amount to a legal separation (qualifying event) under COBRA. *Simpson v. T.D. Williamson*, 414 F.3d 1203 (10th Cir. 2005).

◆ An employee who had enrolled himself, his wife and his children in his employer's group health insurance plan told his employer that he had divorced his wife and that he wanted to drop her from his medical coverage. Because a divorce is a qualifying event under COBRA, the employer gave the employee the necessary paperwork so he could give it to his wife. He apparently failed to give it to her. When she underwent medical treatment and discovered that she no longer had health insurance, she sued the employer to recover the money she had spent for her treatment. A New York federal court dismissed the case, ruling that because the employee's divorce had actually been invalid under state law, there was no "qualifying event" under COBRA. The Second Circuit reversed. Here, **the employer should have notified the wife that she had been dropped from her husband's coverage**, rather than relying on him to notify her. Further, the act of telling the employer about the divorce (a qualifying event) triggered the employer's COBRA obligations, regardless of the validity of the divorce. *Phillips v. Saratoga Harness Racing, Inc.*, 240 F.3d 174 (2d Cir. 2001).

◆ A Wal-Mart employee resigned and sought continuing medical coverage under COBRA. She was rehired a month later. When she returned to work, she asked about the status of her COBRA premiums because she had become pregnant while she was not an employee. An in-store contact for the health plan administrator told her that she would be covered under the original health plan and that she would not need COBRA coverage. As a result, she did not pay the COBRA premium for the month she was not employed. After the plan administrator refused to pay her pregnancy-related medical expenses, she sued. An Indiana federal court ruled in her favor, and the Seventh Circuit affirmed.

Because of misleading statements and the unclear wording of Wal-Mart's health plan (particularly the Summary Plan Description), **she was entitled to coverage for her pregnancy-related medical expenses** as long as she paid the premium for the month she was not an employee. *Bowerman v. Wal-Mart Stores,* 226 F.3d 574 (7th Cir. 2000).

◆ Under COBRA, employers must notify plan administrators of a qualifying event, including termination, within 30 days, and the plan administrator is then responsible for notifying employees of their continuation rights within 14 days of receiving the employer's notice. An Illinois retail manager claimed that she was not provided with a COBRA notice upon her resignation. She sued the employer and plan administrator. The employer presented evidence that it had supplied the administrator with three separate notices of the employee's separation within the statutory period. The plan administrator submitted evidence that it had followed its usual internal procedures by generating a timely notice to the employee, then sending a follow-up letter when no response was received. The court held that employers and plan administrators can prevail when they show that they have made good-faith attempts to comply with COBRA. **Notice by first class mail sent to a former employee's last known address is an acceptable method of COBRA notification.** Here, the employer and plan administrator presented unrefuted evidence that they had satisfied the good-faith standard for compliance with COBRA notice requirements. *Keegan v. Bloomingdale's, Inc.*, 992 F.Supp. 974 (N.D. Ill. 1998).

2. Denial of Benefits

Where an employer self-administers an employee welfare benefit plan, there is a conflict of interest between the employer's interest and the employees.' As a result, the denial of benefits is more likely to be construed as arbitrary and capricious in such cases.

◆ On the way home from a company meeting that included a boat cruise, a Rhode Island employee drove his car into a tree and died. He had stopped off at a bar on the way home and had also consumed a few drinks on the cruise. His blood alcohol level was three times the legal limit. His widow sought to recover accidental death benefits from the company's insurer, but the insurer offered to pay only the basic life insurance policy proceeds. The widow then sued under ERISA, and a federal court ruled against her. The First Circuit affirmed, noting that the ERISA plan granted the insurer discretionary authority to make benefit determinations, and that the decision here was not arbitrary and capricious or an abuse of discretion. **Alcohol-related deaths and injuries are not "accidental" under insurance contracts governed by ERISA.** *Stamp v. Metropolitan Life Insurance Co.*, 531 F.3d 84 (1st Cir. 2008).

◆ A Wisconsin employee had health insurance through work. When his three-year-old son was diagnosed with brain cancer, the company's insurer paid for the surgery to remove the tumor. Following the surgery, the doctor recommended high-dose chemotherapy with stem cell rescue because it had a higher cure rate and was less risky for a young child. The insurer then terminated coverage, finding that the treatment was experimental. An independent doctor reviewed the case and agreed that the treatment was experimental. However, the doctor recommended approving the treatment because it was standard for a young child with brain cancer. Also, because there were no alternatives with superior or proven results, the doctor considered the treatment to be medically necessary. The insurer denied coverage and the boy received the treatment anyway. His father then sued under ERISA. The Wisconsin Supreme Court ordered the insurer to resume coverage. It noted that **the insurer acted arbitrarily when it stopped coverage by failing to give specific reasons for its decision**, and by failing to refer to the specific plan provision that precluded coverage. *Summers v. Touchpoint Health Plan, Inc.*, 749 N.W.2d 182 (Wis. 2008).

◆ A Massachusetts employee became disabled as a result of a work-related hand injury. She received workers' compensation benefits. When those benefits ended, she applied for long-term disability benefits. She asserted that it was not the work-related hand injury that caused the disability but rather her worsening diabetes. The company's group disability plan allowed employees who were no longer active to receive benefits if the disability that led to the leave of absence was caused by a non-occupational injury or sickness. Her application for benefits was denied, and she sued the employer and its insurer. A federal court dismissed the lawsuit, and the First Circuit Court of Appeals affirmed. Here, the employee first became disabled as a result of her hand injury, not her non-occupational sickness. Thus, since she was not rendered disabled as a result of her diabetes, **she was not entitled to long-term disability benefits**. *Perry v. New England Business Service*, 347 F.3d 343 (1st Cir. 2003).

◆ A District of Columbia man lost his left eye in an explosion and required brain surgery. Over 30 years later, he was hired by a hospital. Before starting work, he was required to receive an MMR vaccination. Two days later, he began to have seizures that caused him to lose consciousness. Within the next six years, he had 39 such seizures. The Department of Employment Services granted him temporary total disability benefits, and the hospital appealed. The D.C. Court of Appeals affirmed. Even though the vaccination occurred before the insured reported for work, the insured had been hired at the time of the inoculation, which was administered by and at the behest of the employer. Therefore, **there was an employer-employee relationship at the time of the vaccination**. The fact that the requirement of vaccination was imposed by law did not alter this conclusion. In receiving the vaccination, the insured furthered the interests of the employer in avoiding liability and absenteeism. Also, the insured had suffered no seizures in the 32 years between his accident and the vaccination. *Washington Hospital Center v. D.C. Dep't of Employment Services*, 821 A.2d 898 (D.C. 2003).

◆ A Massachusetts man worked on a part-time basis as an addiction counselor for a hospital. He later became a full-time employee, then went back to part time because of a heart condition. During these switches the hospital never informed him that only full-time employees were entitled to long-term disability benefits. After several years as a part-time employee, he again went to full time. However, he lasted only a month before his heart condition rendered him totally disabled. When he sought long-term disability benefits, the hospital and its insurer denied them on the grounds that his heart problem was a preexisting condition. He sued under ERISA, asserting that the hospital, the insurer and the plan administrator breached their fiduciary duties by failing to inform him about his eligibility for long-term disability benefits. A federal court ruled for the defendants, and the First Circuit Court of Appeals affirmed. Here, although the hospital had a duty to provide the counselor with certain benefits information, **it did not have a duty to inform individual employees of their eligibility for benefits each time their employment status changed**. Since the hospital made no misrepresentations to the counselor and did not refuse to provide requested information, the counselor's lawsuit could not succeed. *Watson v. Deaconess Waltham Hospital*, 298 F.3d 102 (1st Cir. 2002).

- An employee sustained injuries while riding his motorcycle under the influence of alcohol and was charged with DUI. He sought payment of more than $81,000 in medical claims through the company health and welfare plan. The company refused payment under a provision that excluded coverage for care or services caused by illegal activity. While the claim was pending, the company amended the plan to give itself (as the administrator) discretionary authority in making benefit determinations. When the employee sued under ERISA, a Pennsylvania federal court granted pretrial judgment to the company, finding that the decision to deny benefits was not "arbitrary and capricious." The Third Circuit Court of Appeals reversed, noting that the lower court had applied an incorrect standard of review. Here, since the company both funded and administered the ERISA plan, **a conflict of interest existed that required a somewhat heightened arbitrary and capricious standard of review**. The court also noted that the amended version of the plan should be used to determine whether the administrator's decision to deny benefits was proper. The court remanded the case. *Smathers v. Multi-Tool, Inc./Multi Plastics, Inc. Employee Health and Welfare Plan*, 298 F.3d 191 (3d Cir. 2002).

- The executive director of a California law firm suffered from debilitating migraines and applied for long-term disability benefits. The law firm's insurer began paying him $11,500 per month but then investigated his condition. One of its investigators impersonated a bank lender to get information about his business contacts, and the insurer determined that he might be working for another company. In fact, he was a minority owner of the business. When the insurer suspended his payments, he sued it under ERISA, as well as for invasion of privacy. The case reached the Ninth Circuit, which held that the insurer had improperly terminated the employee's benefits. This was not a case where the employee stonewalled the insurer by refusing to provide information; rather, **the insurer stopped paying benefits and then asked for information that would restart them**. The court also held that the employee's invasion of privacy claim could proceed. It was not preempted by ERISA. *Dishman v. UNUM Life Insurance Co. of America*, 269 F.3d 974 (9th Cir. 2001).

◆ A Virginia bank branch manager participated in her employer's long-term disability plan, which was governed by ERISA. She developed a number of symptoms following a dental procedure, including chronic pain, balance and vision problems. Although she underwent many examinations, medical opinions remained inconclusive. Her employer's health care insurer denied her long-term disability claim based on findings that she was not unable to perform her work duties and was therefore not disabled under the plan. The employee sued the insurer, stating that it had failed to give her adequate written notice of the reasons for denial of the claim and that she had been deprived of a full and fair opportunity for review of her claim under ERISA. The court ruled for the insurer, and the Fourth Circuit affirmed. Here, **the insurer had reasonably found no incompatibility between the employee's functional capabilities and her job requirements**. Although the denial letter did not state the specific reasons for denying the claim, the employee had not been prejudiced in pursuing her appeal of the insurer's decision. *Ellis v. Metropolitan Life Insurance Co.*, 126 F.3d 228 (4th Cir. 1997).

◆ A Connecticut employee (a hemophiliac who contracted AIDS from a blood transfusion) participated in an ERISA group health and life insurance plan. When he was hospitalized for an AIDS-related infection that causes blindness, he was given a drug that decreased his white blood cell count, causing neutropenia. His physician prescribed two drugs to counteract the neutropenia for which the hospital was subsequently reimbursed by the plan. When the employee was released, he continued to receive the drugs through home therapy treatments administered by a home intravenous drug therapy provider. The plan denied the provider's claim for the cost of the drugs, stating that, although approved for other uses, they were experimental and not approved by the Food and Drug Administration (FDA) for treating neutropenia in AIDS patients to counteract the effects of another drug.

A federal court granted pretrial judgment to the plan, and the home therapy provider appealed to the Second Circuit. The provider argued that **the plan's language should be broadly construed to allow coverage for any FDA-approved drug** so long as it is used for treating the same condition for which FDA approval has been given. The court agreed, finding the plan language ambiguous. The ambiguity was sufficient to raise factual issues, which made pretrial judgment inappropriate. The court reversed and remanded the case. *I.V. Services of America, Inc. v. Trustees of American Consulting Engineers Council Insurance Trust Fund*, 136 F.3d 114 (2d Cir. 1998).

◆ An Alabama employee developed illnesses including fibromyalgia and lumbar disc syndrome. Her physician prescribed several drugs that caused drowsiness. The employee submitted a claim for benefits under the employer's sickness and accident disability plan. The employer, which self-administered plan benefits from its operating expenses, ordered the employee to return to work or be discharged. The employee resumed work but was frequently absent due to pain. Eventually, she was disciplined for absenteeism and disqualified from the company's long-term disability plan. The employee sued under ERISA. A federal court found that she was disabled under the sickness and disability benefit plan, and it ordered the employer to pay her $58,300 in benefits. The U.S. Court of Appeals, Eleventh Circuit, affirmed, observing that the employer's self-administration of the plan created a conflict of interest. **The denial of benefits here was contrary to clear medical evidence and was arbitrary and capricious.** The employer had unlawfully acted to prevent the employee's receipt of benefits under both plans. *Godfrey v. BellSouth Telecommunications, Inc.*, 89 F.3d 755 (11th Cir. 1996).

- A South Carolina warehouse employee was covered under his employer's ERISA qualified health care plan, which excluded medical claims for losses occurring while the claimant was intoxicated. The employee was shot in the hand after fighting with a friend while drunk. The employer denied the $38,000 claim based on the exclusion, and the employee sued the employer and its claims administrator. A federal court relied upon South Carolina law in finding the exclusion inapplicable because there was no causal connection between intoxication and the injury. The court awarded judgment to the employee, and the U.S. Court of Appeals, Fourth Circuit, affirmed. While ERISA creates a federal employee benefit plan regulatory system, **courts are allowed to adopt and apply state law if compatible with underlying national policies**. The application of South Carolina law to the exclusion did not conflict with ERISA because there was no ERISA language on the matter and it was not otherwise precluded. *Jenkins v. Montgomery Industries, Inc.*, 77 F.3d 740 (4th Cir. 1996).

3. Intentionally Harmful Conduct

Employers can be liable under ERISA where they engage in intentionally harmful conduct toward eligible employees. They may not retaliate against employees for availing themselves of their ERISA rights, nor may they interfere with the attainment of ERISA rights.

- A husband and wife who had worked for a utility company for many years were fired for falsifying their time sheets shortly after their son suffered a relapse of his brain cancer. The couple asserted that the real reason for the termination was the company's desire to avoid the insurance costs. They sued under the ADA and ERISA. A Wyoming federal court granted pretrial judgment to the company, but the Tenth Circuit reversed, finding issues of fact that required a trial. Besides the timing of the firings, the investigation itself was suspicious. **The company relied on logs that were known to be inaccurate, and also fired the employees while docking the pay of and using progressive discipline on other employees** who had been accused of falsifying time sheets in the past. The company may have illegally discriminated against the couple based on their association with a disabled person, and also may have violated Section 510 of ERISA, which bars employers from discriminating against employees who exercise their rights under an employer-provided health plan. *Trujillo v. PacifiCorp.*, 524 F.3d 1149 (10th Cir. 2008).

- An Ohio refinery employee was allowed to retire in lieu of being fired after a number of incidents, including the contamination of two fuel tanks. The employee sued the refinery, claiming it did so to interfere with his ability to attain his full pension, and asserting that the incidents had not been his fault. A federal court ruled in favor of the refinery, noting that **the employee failed to prove a causal connection between his "forced" resignation and his entitlement to a full pension**. He still had 13 years to go until that event, and the refinery did not force him to retire. It would have been happy to fire him for potentially dangerous performance of duties. *Zbuka v. Marathon Ashland Petroleum, LLC*, 447 F.Supp.2d 845 (N.D. Ohio 2006).

◆ An Illinois sales employee had a bad relationship with his manager. His physician called the manager and stated that the employee suffered from severe job-related stress and should not return to work before seeing a psychiatrist. Although a psychiatric appointment was made for the following week, the manager fired the employee the day before the appointment, which was coincidentally the first day the employee would have been eligible to participate in the company's short-term disability benefits plan. The manager back-dated the action to the previous day. The action was justified as being pursuant to a longstanding, unwritten policy applicable to employees who failed to report to work for three consecutive days without calling the office. The employee sued, asserting that he had been discharged to deny his participation in the short-term disability plan in violation of ERISA. The court held for the employee, and the Seventh Circuit affirmed. **The manager's action of back-dating termination documents provided the necessary inference of intent to interfere with benefits.** The employer's assertion that it maintained a well-established employment abandonment policy was contradicted by the testimony of a former human resources administrator. *Salus v. GTE Directories Service Corp.*, 104 F.3d 131 (7th Cir. 1997).

◆ A health and welfare fund created under collective bargaining agreements between a local and international union and several employers was fully insured during the first 16 years of its existence. The plan administrator caused the cancellation of insurance due to late payments. The plan became self-insured but was later terminated due to inability to pay its claims. Plan trustees then transferred the plan's remaining assets to another plan which refused to assume liability for existing claims. The trustees offered to settle these claims for 25 cents on each dollar claimed. A participant in the plan underwent kidney dialysis, incurring over $66,000 in medical expenses that were not covered due to the plan's insolvency. When a medical provider sued him for unpaid bills, he sued the plan in federal court, seeking damages and restitution. The court refused to grant pretrial judgment to the plan on the claim for restitution because there was evidence that plan trustees had breached their fiduciary duties by causing the plan to default in its obligations. ERISA confers equitable powers upon courts to protect participants from fiduciary breaches by plan trustees and administrators. **There was also evidence that plan trustees and administrators had misrepresented the financial health of the plan.** Accordingly, the case had to proceed to trial. However, the employee was not entitled to a monetary damage award under ERISA. *Jackson v. Truck Drivers' Union Local 42 Health and Welfare Fund*, 933 F.Supp. 1124 (D. Mass. 1996).

◆ An Alabama marketing manager participated in his employer's medical, life, and disability insurance plans, for which he authorized payment by payroll deduction. The plan's underwriter claimed that the employee's premiums were delinquent. When the employee had a heart attack requiring hospitalization, the plan issued a letter retroactively canceling coverage due to nonpayment. The employee sued the underwriter and employer under ERISA. He also sought payment of his medical expenses and brought other state law claims. The court held that ERISA foreclosed any state law claims and did not authorize extra-contractual or punitive damages. The Supreme Court of Alabama ruled that the state law claims for fraud and breach of contract were barred by ERISA. However, the U.S. Supreme Court has construed ERISA as allowing state and federal courts **authority to develop remedies beyond those expressly stated in ERISA**. This included claims for extra-contractual and punitive damages if the facts of a case required such remedies. Because the employee had stated a valid ERISA complaint, the trial court had improperly foreclosed the possibility of a punitive damage award. The ERISA claims were reversed and remanded for reconsideration. *Weems v. Jefferson-Pilot Life Insurance Co., Inc.*, 663 So.2d 905 (Ala. 1995).

4. Other Coverage Issues

ERISA does not provide a statute of limitations. Thus, courts must borrow the most applicable state statute of limitations in cases brought under the act.

ERISA generally does not allow for money damages (except when the plan is suing a fiduciary for breach of duty). Only equitable remedies are available for individuals asserting violations of the act. This is because ERISA was enacted to protect whole employee benefit plans rather than the rights of individual employees.

◆ After a car accident, a California woman became a quadriplegic. Her husband's employee benefit plan paid over $411,000 in medical expenses. The plan included a reimbursement provision that permitted the plan to recover from the beneficiary any third-party payments made to her, up to the amount of benefits paid out by the plan. When the woman sued various third parties to recover for her injuries, she reached a settlement of $650,000. A court ordered her to pay the plan $13,828 as her share of the medical costs, but the plan sought to be reimbursed for the full amount of benefits it had paid out. It sued the beneficiary under ERISA, and the case reached the U.S. Supreme Court. The Court held that the plan was not entitled to impose personal liability on the beneficiary for the contractual obligation. **Under Section 502(a)(3), only equitable relief is available, and the plan here was seeking a legal remedy** – the payment of money damages. The plan was not entitled to reimbursement of the $411,000 it had paid out. *Great-West Life & Annuity Insurance Co. v. Knudson*, 534 U.S. 204, 122 S.Ct. 708, 151 L.Ed.2d 635 (2002).

◆ A co-worker caused an Arkansas employee to fall, aggravating a pre-existing back and shoulder injury. The employee tried to file an accident report, but was told that the accident would be taken care of "informally." A few days after he informed his supervisor that he needed time off for shoulder surgery, he was laid off due to a "lack of work." He obtained unemployment benefits, then alleged ERISA and ADEA violations, claiming he was really fired so the company could avoid paying his insurance benefits. When the EEOC sought information, **the company claimed it fired him for disciplinary reasons, despite the fact that it did not follow its own policies for a disciplinary termination**. In the lawsuit that resulted, the Eighth Circuit reversed pretrial judgment for the company on the ERISA claim, noting that questions of fact existed as to the real reason for the firing. *Fitzgerald v. Action, Inc.*, 521 F.3d 867 (8th Cir. 2008).

- A company in Illinois had a "Sickness and Accident Disability Benefit Plan" covered by ERISA, which provided disability benefits for accidents that arose out of and in the course of employment. Compensable injuries had to arise solely from an accident during and in direct connection with the performance of the employee's duties. When an employee slipped and fell in a restroom, suffering disabling injuries, she collected workers' compensation, then sought benefits under the plan. **The plan administrator granted sickness benefits (with a maximum 52 weeks of coverage)** but not potentially unlimited accident benefits. She sued, and the Seventh Circuit ruled against her. It refused to find the administrator's decision arbitrary and capricious. *Sisto v. Ameritech Sickness and Accident Disability Benefit Plan*, 429 F.3d 698 (7th Cir. 2005).

- A chemical operator in Delaware suffered back injuries as a result of an on-the-job accident. Two months later, he was laid off in a reduction in force but managed to obtain long-term disability benefits for two years under the company's "Income Protection Plan." After an independent medical evaluation determined that he was able to perform sedentary or light work, the insurer cut off his benefits. Fifteen months later, he sued the company in its capacity as the plan administrator under ERISA, alleging that his benefits had been improperly terminated. A federal court held that **the statute of limitations prevented him from pursuing his claim**, and the Third Circuit affirmed. Because ERISA did not have a limitations period of its own, the Delaware (one-year) limitations period for actions involving wage or benefit claims applied. *Syed v. Hercules, Inc.*, 214 F.3d 155 (3d Cir. 2000).

- Four part-time grocery store employees were covered under a self-funded group health insurance plan containing coordination of benefits provisions purporting to provide coverage only after all other sources of insurance had been exhausted. The plan denied claims by the employees for medical expenses because the employees were dependents of participants in another self-funded group health plan containing a similar coordination of benefits clause. The other plan also denied primary coverage for the claims. The employer plan paid the claims under a reservation of rights and sued in a New Jersey federal court, seeking a declaration that the dependent plan was primarily liable for the claims and seeking reimbursement. The court **adopted the "employer first" rule** recommended by the Model Regulations of the National Association of

Insurance Commissioners, which imposes primary liability for coverage on plans that cover claimants as employees. The Third Circuit affirmed. Assigning primary liability to an employer-supplied plan provided certainty and uniformity and would best further the ERISA's goals. Thirty-nine states, including New Jersey, had adopted the employer first rule, instead of the pro-rata rule advocated by the employer plan. *McGurl v. Trucking Employees of North Jersey Welfare Fund, Inc.*, 124 F.3d 471 (3d Cir. 1997).

- A Pennsylvania-based company maintained an employee health plan that provided benefits 60 days after the commencement of active, full-time employment (defined as regularly working 30 or more hours per week). An employee handbook additionally described 30 hours each week as the minimum requirement for coverage. However, the company's president utilized an informal classification system which allowed him to designate an employee as full time, temporary or part time. An employee worked for the company almost nine months before the president agreed to cover him under the plan. He was instructed to fly to company headquarters to complete enrollment forms but was injured in an off-the-job accident the day before the flight. His claim for coverage was denied. The Third Circuit Court of Appeals noted that **ERISA plans must be in writing, and a consistent pattern of improper plan interpretation by an employer or administrator cannot convert written plan language**. The employee had worked more than 30 hours per week for over 60 days, which satisfied plan language for coverage. The employer and plan were liable for benefits. *Epright v. Environmental Resources Management, Inc. Health and Welfare Plan*, 81 F.3d 335 (3d Cir. 1996).

- An employee welfare benefits plan paid for the medical expenses of a covered employee's daughter after a train accident. When the employee's plant was sold to another company, the successor company promised the plant employees insurance benefits under the same terms as the predecessor's plan. It continued paying medical expenses on behalf of the employee's daughter. When the plan administrator learned that the family had obtained a $7 million settlement from the railroad and engineer, it sought reimbursement for benefits paid on her behalf under the plan's third-party exclusion, which required covered persons who received third-party judgments or settlements to reimburse the plan for any amounts advanced. The employee refused to reimburse the plan, and sued it and the successor company in an Illinois federal court. The court ruled for the company and plan. The U.S. Court of Appeals, Seventh Circuit, affirmed, holding that **the successor company was entitled to restitution**. *Harris Trust and Savings Bank v. Provident Life and Accident Insurance Co.*, 57 F.3d 608 (7th Cir. 1995).

III. EMPLOYER LIABILITY AND RECOUPMENT

A plan may incur liability not only by failing to pay benefits that are due participants, but also by withdrawing from a multi-employer plan. Under the Multi-employer Pension Plan Amendments Act, employers who withdraw from under-funded multi-employer pension plans must pay a withdrawal liability.

However, employers may also recoup excess funds from terminated defined benefit plans if the funds do not have to be paid out as accrued benefits (nonforfeitable benefits) or as other benefits under the plans.

A. Supreme Court Cases

◆ A paper company and its parent entity employed 2,600 people in seven paper mills. A union represented employees covered by 17 of the companies' defined benefit pension plans. When the companies filed for bankruptcy, they considered, as ERISA allows, terminating the plans through the purchase of annuities. The union proposed that the companies merge the plans with its multiemployer pension plan, conveying the plans' assets to the union's plan, which would then assume the liabilities of the companies' plans. However, the companies discovered that by purchasing annuities, they could satisfy their obligations to plan participants and retain a $5 million surplus. They rejected the union's proposal and purchased the annuities. A California bankruptcy court ruled that the companies breached a fiduciary duty to fully consider the union's proposal, and the Ninth Circuit agreed. The U.S. Supreme Court reversed. It noted that the Pension Benefit Guaranty Corporation (PBGC) – the entity administering the federal insurance program that protects plan benefits – took the position that **ERISA did not permit merger as a method of terminating a defined benefits plan because the statute provides for merger as an alternative to plan termination**. Since the PBGC's interpretation was reasonable, the Court upheld it. *Beck v. PACE Int'l Union*, 127 S.Ct. 2310, 168 L.Ed.2d 1 (U.S. 2007).

◆ The Multi-employer Pension Plan Amendments Act of 1980 (MPPAA), 29 U.S.C. §§ 1381-1461, requires employers who withdraw from under-funded multi-employer pension plans to pay a withdrawal liability. Employers may contest an assessed liability but are required to make payments pending appeal. An employer made contributions to a multi-employer pension fund for laundry workers in the San Francisco Bay area for several years and then ceased making contributions. The fund's trustees demanded payment of a withdrawal liability and notified the employer of its payment options. The employer refused to make payments. However, the fund did not sue the employer until eight years after it withdrew from the fund and over six years after missing its first scheduled payment. A federal court dismissed the case as barred by the MPPAA's six-year statute of limitations, and the Ninth Circuit affirmed.

The fund appealed to the U.S. Supreme Court, which rejected the employer's claim that its withdrawal commenced the statute of limitations, because the MPPAA does not require a withdrawing employer to pay anything until the plan demands payment. **The cause of action did not accrue until the employer was assessed a liability, notified of the amount and means of payment, and failed to make a required payment.** Although over six years had passed from the employer's failure to pay the first installment, the fund was entitled to recover all but the first of the installment payments. The Court reversed and remanded the lower court decisions. *Bay Area Laundry and Dry Cleaning Pension Trust Fund v. Ferbar Corp. of California, Inc.*, 522 U.S. 192, 118 S.Ct. 542, 139 L.Ed.2d 553 (1997).

◆ The MPPAA requires employers who withdraw from under-funded multiemployer pension plans to pay a fair share of the plan's unfunded liabilities. It gives withdrawing employers the option to pay their withdrawal liability in a lump sum, or to amortize the amount in level annual payments "calculated as if the first payment were made on the first day of the plan year following the plan year in which the withdrawal occurs and as if each subsequent payment were made on the first day of each subsequent plan year." A Wisconsin brewing company withdrew from an under-funded plan with a withdrawal charge of $23.3 million. Although the plan and the brewery agreed on the amount of withdrawal liability, the parties disagreed on the amount of interest that had accrued during the withdrawal year. The case reached the U.S. Supreme Court, which stated that **nothing in the MPPAA required withdrawing employers to pay an actuarially perfect fair share of withdrawal liability**. The MPPAA provision describing withdrawing employer liability did not cause interest to start accruing during the withdrawal year itself. Rather, it called for calculation as if the first payment were made on the first day of the plan year following the plan year in which withdrawal occurs. Because a withdrawing employer owed nothing to a plan until the plan demanded payment as set forth by the MPPAA, the employer was unable to determine its liability until sometime after the beginning of the withdrawal year. The Court affirmed the decision for the brewery. *Milwaukee Brewery Workers' Pension Plan v. Jos. Schlitz Brewing Co.*, 513 U.S. 414, 115 S.Ct. 981, 130 L.Ed.2d 932 (1995).

◆ A former employee of a closely held corporation claimed that the corporation and a corporate officer/shareholder violated ERISA by failing to properly administer the corporation's employee pension plan. The former employee sued the corporation and the officer/shareholder, obtaining a judgment of $187,000 against the corporation. The former employee was unable to collect on his judgment, even though the shareholder/officer continued to take cash out of the corporation as a favored creditor. The former employee then sued the corporate officer for engaging in a civil conspiracy to siphon assets from the corporation to prevent satisfaction of the ERISA judgment. The court allowed the employee to collect his judgment from the officer. The Fourth Circuit, affirmed, but the Supreme Court reversed. **ERISA contains no authority for imposing liability for an existing ERISA judgment against a third party**. There were no independent grounds for a federal court to exercise jurisdiction in this case under a corporate veil-piercing argument. There was also no merit to the former employee's argument that a federal court could exercise jurisdiction over the matter as factually interdependent with and related to the prior lawsuit. Because the case was based on theories of relief that did not exist, the district court lacked jurisdiction to hear it. *Peacock v. Thomas*, 516 U.S. 349, 116 S.Ct. 862, 133 L.Ed.2d 817 (1996).

◆ The U.S. Supreme Court held that the **Coal Industry Retiree Health Benefit Act of 1992 (Coal Act) unconstitutionally deprived a Massachusetts employer of property** by requiring it to fund healthcare benefits for retired coal miners and their dependents, which created a severe, disproportionate and retroactive burden on the employer. The Court found that the Coal Act imposed severe retroactive liability on a class of employers that could not have anticipated it, and that the liability was substantially disproportionate to the experience of the parties. The employer's cumulative liability under the act was estimated at $50 to $100 million, even though it had employed no miners since before 1965, when the retirement and health care benefits offered were far less extensive. The act retroactively divested the employer of property long after it believed its liabilities were settled. *Eastern Enterprises v. Apfel*, 524 U.S. 498, 118 S.Ct. 2131, 141 L.Ed.2d 451 (1998).

◆ A corporation sold a subsidiary and terminated the ERISA retirement plan it funded. As a single-employer plan, all accrued benefits automatically vested. The corporation paid out the benefits that had vested, including non-reduced early retirement benefits to those employees who met both the age (62) and years of service (30) requirements. A group of employees who did not meet both requirements sued the corporation because it recouped nearly $11 million. They maintained that it was first required to distribute contingent early retirement benefits, even if unaccrued, before recouping plan assets. A Virginia federal court ruled for the corporation, and the Fourth Circuit reversed. The case reached the U.S. Supreme Court, which held that **the section of ERISA under which this lawsuit was brought did not create benefit entitlements** but merely provided for the orderly distribution of plan assets. However, since there were two alternative sections of ERISA, which could potentially lead to a recovery by the employees, the Court remanded the case. *Mead Corp. v. Tilley*, 490 U.S. 714, 109 S.Ct. 2156, 104 L.Ed.2d 796 (1989).

◆ A New York corporation filed for Chapter 11 bankruptcy (reorganization). At that time, it was the sponsor of three defined benefit pension plans covered by Title IV of ERISA that were chronically under-funded. At the corporation's request, the Pension Benefit Guaranty Corporation (PBGC) terminated the plans. The corporation and its employees then **negotiated new pension arrangements that provided substantially the same benefits as before**. The PBGC then issued a notice of restoration to undo the termination because the new "follow-on" plans were abusive of the insurance program. When the corporation refused to comply with the restoration, a lawsuit followed. The U.S. Supreme Court found that the PBGC's restoration decision was not arbitrary or capricious. As such, the corporation had to restore the plans that had been terminated. *Pension Benefit Guaranty Corp. v. LTV Corp.*, 496 U.S. 633, 110 S.Ct. 2668, 110 L.Ed.2d 579 (1990).

B. Other Employer Liability Cases

As more employers move toward 401(k) plans and away from defined benefit plans, the number of employer liability cases should decrease. However, employers can still be liable for improper conduct of supervisory employees who serve as plan administrators.

◆ The owner of an Illinois company was also the 401(k) plan and the profit-sharing plan trustee for his 100 employees. After the profit-sharing plan lost

$400,000 and the 401(k) plan lost $700,000 from 2000 to 2002, an employee sued the company and its owner for breach of fiduciary duty under ERISA. A federal court granted pretrial judgment to the defendants, but the Seventh Circuit reversed in part. Although the owner did not owe employees a fiduciary duty under the 401(k) plan to investigate each participant's investments, **he might have improperly delegated his responsibilities to manage the profit-sharing plan**. *Jenkins v. Yager*, 444 F.3d 916 (7th Cir. 2006).

◆ A couple with a construction company in Oklahoma made payments to a multi-employer fund for employee benefits under a collective bargaining agreement. When their business worsened, they stopped making contributions to the fund. After they filed for Chapter 7 bankruptcy protection, an audit determined that they owed more than $121,000 to the fund. The fund's trustees sought the unpaid contributions and the case reached the Tenth Circuit. The court of appeals held that the couple's decision to pay other business expenses rather than make contributions was a business decision and not a breach of fiduciary duty. Accordingly, **they were entitled to discharge the pension fund debt in bankruptcy** and were not personally liable for the unpaid amount. *In re Luna*, 406 F.3d 1192 (10th Cir. 2005).

◆ Two family-owned Massachusetts construction companies operated from the same building, shared employees, worked on the same projects and were managed by the same persons. One of the companies entered into a collective bargaining agreement with its employees and signed a state-wide agreement with a carpenters' union requiring it to make pension contributions for each hour of work performed by its employees. However, it did not make all required contributions, and the union collection agency sued both businesses for failing to make required contributions under ERISA. It sought unpaid contributions from the non-signatory business under the theory that it was the alter ego of the signatory business. The court ruled for the collection agency, awarding damages and penalties in excess of $121,000. The First Circuit affirmed. The alter ego theory of entity liability may apply to ERISA cases. It may also apply to parallel companies such as those involved here. Courts must consider factors including continuity of ownership, similarity of business purposes, management relations, operations, equipment, customers, supervisors, and anti-union sentiment. Although there was no finding of anti-union sentiment here, enough other factors demonstrated that **the non-signatory entity was the alter ego of the signatory business and both were liable**. *Massachusetts Carpenters Cent. Collection Agency v. Belmont Concrete Corp.*, 139 F.3d 304 (1st Cir. 1998).

◆ A Connecticut employer maintained an ERISA-qualified employee benefits plan. The employer contracted with a private company to provide administrative case management services. An employee who received inpatient treatment at a psychiatric hospital sought benefits for her hospitalization costs from the plan. When they were denied, she sued the employer. A federal court held that the employer had control over the plan's administration and could therefore be sued and held liable for benefits. However, the Second Circuit rejected the employee's assertion that an **employer acting as a co-administrator of an**

ERISA plan is always jointly liable with the named plan administrator. The employer was entitled to dismissal of the claims against it because it was neither the designated plan administrator nor a plan trustee. *Crocco v. Xerox Corp.*, 137 F.3d 105 (2d Cir. 1998).

- A corporation with three subsidiaries in California sponsored an ERISA-qualified retirement plan. Two subsidiaries closed and the corporation made contributions to the plan through the third subsidiary. It later sold the third subsidiary and discontinued making contributions for all three subsidiaries. The retirement fund assessed a withdrawal liability against the corporation for withdrawing from the two closed subsidiaries, but not for the sold subsidiary, as its purchaser continued making contributions. The selling corporation argued that it could not be liable for withdrawing from the retirement plan because the cessation of contributions came as a result of a changed corporate structure as defined by the Multi-employer Pension Plan Amendments Act of 1980 (MPPAA). A California federal court held for the fund, and the Ninth Circuit Court of Appeals affirmed. **The corporation's withdrawal liability for the two closed subsidiaries had been shielded from assessment because the third subsidiary had continued making contributions to the plan.** However, upon the sale of the third subsidiary, the corporation was no longer shielded from liability under the MPPAA, and the district court had properly awarded judgment to the pension fund. *Penn Cent. Corp. v. Western Conference of Teamsters Pension Trust Fund*, 75 F.3d 529 (9th Cir. 1996).

IV. SEVERANCE BENEFITS

Employee severance pay or retirement incentive plans may be qualified under ERISA, if they are part of a written employee benefit plan that creates a reasonable expectation for the payment of benefits. One-time-only lump sum payments that are not subject to an ongoing administrative program are typically not covered by ERISA.

- A packaging and processing company discontinued operations at a plant, laying off almost all its employees. Some of the former employees then filed suit against the company, seeking severance pay under Maine law. The company asserted that ERISA preempted the plant-closing statute (which required the company to provide severance pay). The Supreme Judicial Court of Maine held that the company was liable for severance pay because ERISA only preempted state laws that relate to benefit plans created by employers or employee organizations. The U.S. Supreme Court held that the Maine statute was not subject to ERISA preemption. **The state law merely required a one-time lump-sum payment triggered by a single event** (the plant closing). There was no ongoing administrative program the employer had to meet. Thus, there was no potential problem of multiple regulation by state and federal statutes. Also, the Maine statute was not preempted by the National Labor Relations Act because it did not impermissibly intrude upon the collective bargaining process. *Fort Halifax Packing Co. v. Coyne*, 482 U.S. 1, 107 S.Ct. 2211, 96 L.Ed.2d 1 (1987).

◆ An insurance company in Illinois, anticipating the sale of a business unit, decided to revoke severance benefits for employees who sold life and long-term health care insurance. The company posted the change on its intranet but did not highlight, underline or otherwise draw attention to the newly added language. Over six months later, and four days before it terminated its life and long-term health care insurance sales people, it sent them written copies of the change. The employees sued under ERISA, claiming they were not given "reasonable" notice as required by the severance plan's summary plan description. The company sought pretrial judgment, but a federal court refused to grant it. A trial was required because **the intranet posting did not amount to an "alert" to the sales people that the severance plan had changed**. Department of Labor guidelines clearly stated that the mere placement of material in a location frequented by participants was insufficient for electronic notice. *Rosenberg v. CNA Financial Corp.*, 2007 WL 2126085 (N.D. Ill. 7/23/07).

◆ A bank developed a severance plan that disallowed benefits for covered employees who were fired "for cause." The plan defined "cause" as "gross and willful misconduct" including acts or omissions that violated the bank's policies. A Minnesota employee working as a financial analyst accessed a personnel salary file and allegedly told two subordinates that he had information about personnel changes in two divisions. **After he was fired for violating company policy on confidentiality, he sought severance benefits, which were denied.** He then sued under ERISA and lost. Even though he claimed he had accessed the file for business reasons, he did not state what those reasons were. Benefits were properly denied. *Anderson v. U.S. Bancorp*, 484 F.3d 1027 (8th Cir. 2007).

◆ As part of a company-wide layoff, a vice president was told that he would be offered a severance package. At that time, the company's severance plan provided up to 26 weeks of salary, conditioned on the employee signing a release of claims. However, the next day, the company offered the vice president a new severance plan calling for 32 weeks of pay if the vice president would sign a non-compete clause. A week later, the company formally adopted this amendment to the severance plan. The vice president's last day of work came the following week. Without signing the non-compete agreement, the vice president sought severance benefits. The company denied them and a lawsuit resulted. A Texas federal court and the Fifth Circuit ruled that the vice president's lawsuit under ERISA could not succeed. **The company had the right to amend its severance plan, and the vice president was not entitled to benefits because he didn't sign the non-compete agreement.** *Chacko v. Sabre, Inc.*, 473 F.3d 604 (5th Cir. 2006).

◆ In accepting a job with a Michigan company, a vice president signed a contract that provided a financial penalty if he quit within the first year, and also offered to pay him a separation allowance (representing the difference between his first year's compensation and the payments he'd already received) if he was fired other than for cause. This second clause did not specifically state that it applied only to the first year of employment, but it immediately followed the preceding clause, which did. Six years later he was laid off and offered a severance package of nine months' pay plus continued health insurance coverage. He refused to sign the release offered by the company and sued, claiming he was owed his compensation for the six years he'd worked for the company, minus his first year's compensation. A federal court and the Sixth Circuit ruled for the company. Here, the two clauses in the contract had to be read together. They offered reciprocal obligations and were only meant to apply to the first year of the contract. *Reardon v. Kelly Services, Inc.*, 210 Fed.Appx. 456 (6th Cir. 2006).

- An employee of a company in South Carolina resigned after 17 years when he was transferred to a new position. Several months later, he returned to the company and worked for the next two years until he was laid off for economic reasons. The company gave him severance benefits for the two years he worked after being rehired. He appealed to the plan administrator, seeking benefits for 19 years of service. When they were denied, he sued under ERISA. The case reached the Fourth Circuit, which noted that **the plan administrator reasonably interpreted the phrase "employment commencement date" to mean the date at which the employee had been rehired**. The employee was only entitled to severance benefits based on two years' employment. *Colucci v. Agfa Corp. Severance Pay Plan*, 431 F.3d 170 (4th Cir. 2005).

- After rumors circulated that a division of a company was going to be sold, a company official read a letter to employees indicating that if there were a change of control or sale of a business unit resulting in job loss, employees would receive a severance package. Eventually the company folded the division and paid employees severance benefits and cooperation bonuses as it had for earlier internal consolidations. However, that amount was less than it would have been if the division had been sold to an outside party. A number of terminated employees sued under ERISA, claiming that the letter served as a summary plan description (SPD) and that the company owed them the larger benefits promised therein. An Iowa federal court held that the letter was a faulty SPD that conflicted with the severance plan. It awarded the employees an additional $1.6 million in benefits. The Eighth Circuit reversed. Here, **although the letter was confusing and deceiving, it was not an SPD because it did not contain the information required by ERISA regulations**. Thus, the employees could not use the letter to obtain extra benefits. *Antolik v. Saks, Inc.*, 463 F.3d 796 (8th Cir. 2006).

- An Illinois company hired an employee under a written contract that required it to pay her one year's base salary as severance if she was terminated "for reasons other than cause." Later, the company fired the employee for failing to meet a $380,000 billing quota. It claimed this was a "for cause" reason under the contract and refused to pay severance. The employee sued and a federal court granted pretrial judgment to the company. The Seventh Circuit reversed and remanded the case, noting that **there can be a difference between cause for discharge and cause for the denial of severance benefits**. Here, the employee's performance was deemed unsatisfactory based on criteria selected after she began working, and was not specified in the contract. Thus, a factual issue existed as to whether there was cause to deny severance benefits. *Joy v. Hay Group, Inc.*, 403 F.3d 875 (7th Cir. 2005).

◆ An insurance company in Maryland hired an employee under a written contract that required it to pay him one year's base salary as severance if he was terminated "without cause." Subsequently, the company sold his division to another insurer and arranged for his transfer to the new company. He sought severance benefits after the sale, claiming that he had been "terminated" without cause even though he continued to perform the same job for a new employer. The case reached the Fourth Circuit, which held that he was entitled to severance pay. Most courts agree that **when a company sells a business unit, that unit's employees are terminated, even if they continue working for the buyer**. Such terminations are not "for cause." *Gresham v. Lumbermen's Mutual Casualty Co.*, 404 F.3d 253 (4th Cir. 2005).

◆ An employee of a risk management and insurance company in Massachusetts forwarded seven internal e-mails containing confidential information to a former co-worker who had become a senior official with a direct competitor. When the company learned of the e-mails, it fired him. He asked for severance benefits, which the company denied, noting that **severance pay was barred for employees who were fired for just cause**. Rather than make a written claim for benefits or appeal internally, he sued, claiming ERISA violations. The First Circuit ruled against him, holding that he had to exhaust his administrative remedies before filing suit. He could not just assume that an internal appeal would be futile. Further, the company's decision to fire him was reasonable. *Madera v. Marsh USA, Inc.*, 426 F.3d 56 (1st Cir. 2005).

◆ A company in Minnesota laid off an employee while it had a severance plan in place. By the time it actually terminated him, however, it had replaced its severance plan with a new one that paid less benefits. When the employee attempted to collect his benefits from the human resources department, he was informed that he was only entitled to benefits under the new plan, and that he had to sign a waiver of any rights under the old plan to get any benefits at all. He instead sued the company. A federal court held that ERISA governed the situation, and that the company had to pay the employee his severance benefits under the new plan even though he did not sign the waiver. The Eighth Circuit reversed, holding that the employee could be required to sign a waiver as a condition of receiving benefits under the new plan. Since **the company had no legal obligation to pay any severance benefits**, there was no ERISA violation in requiring a waiver. The employee was not entitled to severance pay. *Petersen v. E.F. Johnson*, 366 F.3d 676 (8th Cir. 2004).

◆ The head of security for a pharmaceutical company in Missouri learned that his job was going to be cut as a result of corporate restructuring. Rather than relocate to New Jersey, he decided to participate in the company's ERISA-qualified severance plan. He began to pursue a real estate career and charged more than 3,000 minutes on his company cell phone in violation of company policy. He also misused a confidential employee list by mailing real estate notices to the employees. When the company fired him for misconduct, he became ineligible for severance pay. He objected to the disqualification, asserting that other employees committed misconduct without being similarly punished. A federal court ruled in favor of the company, and the Eighth Circuit affirmed. It did not matter if the company inconsistently disciplined its employees as long as **it did not intentionally interfere with his severance benefits**. Since he could not prove that the termination was designed to interfere with his ERISA-protected rights, he was not entitled to severance pay. *Koons v. Aventis Pharmaceuticals*, 367 F.3d 768 (8th Cir. 2004).

◆ A chef in Rhode Island received an employee handbook that described the company's severance policy, which was based on tenure and salary. The handbook also contained a disclaimer stating that it was not intended to be a contract, and that the company reserved the right to revise any or all policies contained therein, even without notice. The company then abandoned the severance policy and told the chef about the company's new completely subjective, or arbitrary, severance approach. A month later, **the chef was fired without severance for planning to open a competing restaurant nearby**. He sued for severance benefits, but the Supreme Court of Rhode Island ruled against him. The only document he produced to support his claim of entitlement to severance pay was the employee handbook, which clearly stated that it was not a contract and that it could be modified at any time. *D'Oliveira v. Rare Hospitality Int'l, Inc.*, 840 A.2d 538 (R.I. 2004).

◆ Sixteen utility company employees in Washington, D.C., asked company officials whether the company was considering a retirement incentive program. After being informed that no such plan was being considered, they retired between January and June. In fact, the company implemented such a program at the end of June, **offering employees in their classification a one-time opportunity to receive specified severance benefits if they would retire early**. They sued the utility under ERISA, asserting that it had breached its fiduciary obligations as a plan administrator by failing to inform them of the program. A federal court dismissed the lawsuit, and the U.S. Court of Appeals, D.C. Circuit, affirmed. It noted that the retirement incentive program was not covered by ERISA because it could be implemented with a straightforward factual determination of whether an employee qualified for it. The program was based on a one-time triggering event. Since this was not the kind of administrative decision that required the protection of ERISA, the federal court had no jurisdiction to hear the retirees' claims. *Young v. Washington Gas Light Co.*, 206 F.3d 1200 (D.C. Cir. 2000).

◆ An Indiana woman worked for a General Motors (GM) facility for 19 years, at which time the facility was sold to another company. She continued working there. Less than three years later, the facility was sold again, this time to a GM subsidiary. She was offered a job but refused it, instead seeking severance benefits under GM's employee welfare plan, which was covered by ERISA. The U.S. Court of Appeals, Seventh Circuit, held that the woman had quit her job voluntarily when she chose not to continue her employment after the sale of the facility. Because the employee handbook clearly explained that **refusing a suitable offer of employment amounted to quitting** the job, the woman was not entitled to severance benefits. *James v. General Motors Corp.*, 230 F.3d 315 (7th Cir. 2000).

◆ A New York severance plan required its administrators to apply their discretion and analyze each employment termination on a case-by-case basis. The payment of benefits required numerous managerial decisions that made the plan as a whole an ongoing one. When an employee was discharged for sexually harassing his subordinates, he alleged that the termination was really about saving money. A jury agreed and awarded him $364,000. However, the U.S. Court of Appeals, Second Circuit, held that the state law claim was preempted by ERISA because **the severance plan required ongoing administration**. *Tischmann v. ITT/Sheraton Corp.*, 145 F.3d 561 (2d Cir. 1998).

◆ A Wisconsin paper manufacturer established a severance package for certain employees prior to a hostile takeover. The plan called for the payment of a lump sum to employees who suffered a material reduction in compensation or authority. The successor's health plan offered less favorable benefits than the manufacturer's plan, prompting many employees to select the severance package. Several employees retired and claimed that because the new employer's health package was less favorable, they were entitled to severance benefits. The plan administrator denied the claims, and the retirees sued the plan, administrator, and both employers under ERISA. The court ruled against the retirees on all claims, and the Seventh Circuit Court of Appeals affirmed. Here, **the anticipated reduction in benefits did not trigger the severance package eligibility clause** because the employees had retired instead of switching to the new plan. The court of appeals rejected the retirees' argument that the plan and employers had a fiduciary duty to fully advise them that selecting early retirement would make them ineligible for the severance package since ERISA does not require a plan administrator to prepare an advisory opinion for each plan participant. *Chojnacki v. Georgia-Pacific Corp.*, 108 F.3d 810 (7th Cir. 1997).

◆ A multi-employer plan that provided retirement benefits for grocery employees required participating employers to include a standard clause in all collective bargaining agreements under which the employers agreed to make retirement contributions based on severance pay. Despite the obligation, one participating employer negotiated a bargaining agreement with its employees exempting the employer from doing so. When the employer began reducing its workforce, it paid severance pay to laid off employees but failed to make retirement contributions under the standard clause. The plan's trust fund sued the employer in a Maryland federal court, seeking to collect severance pay contributions. The court ruled for the employer, but the U.S. Court of Appeals, Fourth Circuit, reversed. **The collective bargaining provision excluding pension contributions for severance pay was ineffective** against the trust fund since the standard clause governed the relationship between employer and fund.

The employer had agreed to incorporate the standard clause in all its collective bargaining agreements, and the fund was entitled to rely on this representation. *Bakery and Confectionery Union Pension Fund v. Ralph's Grocery Co.*, 118 F.3d 1018 (4th Cir. 1997).

◆ A retailer notified its workers that an Arizona facility was closing permanently and that they would soon be laid off. However, it offered 25 employees a bonus for continuing to work through the windup of operations. The bonus included four weeks of pay plus a severance payment based on time of service. After a number of employees accepted the offer, the facility was sold to another retailer and remained open. The purchaser retained many of the employees in their former job capacities, and the former employer refused to pay the bonus or severance payment. The employees filed a breach of contract lawsuit against the former employer in an Arizona federal court. The court ruled for the employees, and the U.S. Court of Appeals, Ninth Circuit, affirmed. The breach of contract action was not preempted by ERISA because **the plan required no ongoing administration**; it simply required employees to work in a satisfactory manner until a stated date. *Velarde v. Pace Membership Warehouse, Inc.*, 105 F.3d 1313 (9th Cir. 1997).

◆ A Washington employer operated a hazardous waste-testing facility where employees were entitled to participate in a severance plan that provided benefits in the event of a work force reduction. The plan did not define "work force reduction." When the employer sold the facility it announced that the purchaser offered them continued employment at the facility. Most of the employees stayed on. A number of them filed a lawsuit against the former employer, claiming that they were entitled to benefits under the severance package. The court ruled for the former employer, and the Court of Appeals of Washington affirmed. Here, **the plan contained no language governing the entitlement to benefits after the sale of the business**. Its language limited severance pay to a work force reduction. While the former employer had technically eliminated positions within the company when it sold the plant, there had been no work force reduction because jobs at the facility remained intact. *Lardy v. U.S. Testing Co., Inc.*, 930 P.2d 347 (Wash. Ct. App. 1997).

V. VACATION AND SICK LEAVE BENEFITS

Vacation and sick benefits are generally a matter of contract interpretation and require an examination of the employment contract. No federal or state law requires an employer to offer paid sick leave or vacation leave.

In recent years, many employers have lumped vacation and sick leave benefits into one unified bank of hours, generally called personal leave. For example, an employee with 18 days (or 144 hours) of personal leave could use any portion of that time for sickness or vacation.

The U.S. Supreme Court has held that a policy of paying discharged employees a lump sum out of corporate general assets does not constitute an employee welfare benefit plan under ERISA.

A. Vacation Benefits

◆ A Massachusetts bank discharged two vice presidents and allegedly failed to compensate them for vacation time they had accrued but not used. The state charged the bank president with criminal violation of a state law that prohibited this. The bank president moved to dismiss the case against him on the ground that ERISA preempted all state laws relating to an "employee welfare benefit plan." The question of whether payments for unused vacation time constitutes an employee welfare benefit plan came before the U.S. Supreme Court. The Court noted that **the creation of a separate fund to pay employees vacation benefits would bring the plan under ERISA coverage**. However, the employer here had a policy of paying vacation benefits out of its general assets. Because ERISA had been enacted to prevent mismanagement of accumulated plan funds and to prevent failure to pay benefits from such funds, it did not apply to the situation involved here. The vacation pay owed in this case was fixed, payable from general assets, and not dependent on contingencies outside the employee's control. Accordingly, the criminal action against the bank president was not preempted by ERISA. *Massachusetts v. Morash*, 490 U.S. 107, 109 S.Ct. 1668, 104 L.Ed.2d 98 (1989).

◆ A collection agency obtained money judgments against 25 people who were participants in an employee welfare benefit plan covered by ERISA. The covered workers drew their vacation benefits from the plan annually. The collection agency sought to garnish the debtors' plan benefits to collect the money judgments. A state court allowed the garnishment, but the court of appeals reversed, holding that a Georgia statute barred the garnishment of funds of an employee benefit plan subject to ERISA. The Georgia Supreme Court reversed, deciding that ERISA preempted the Georgia statute. The case reached the U.S. Supreme Court, which first noted that ERISA preempted the state law because it related to a pension plan described under ERISA. It then stated that Congress did not intend to preempt state-law garnishment of ERISA welfare benefit plans, even where the purpose was to collect judgments against plan participants. ERISA only placed a ban on alienation or assignment of *pension* benefits. Here, **the vacation benefits could be garnished because they were not part of a pension plan**. The Court affirmed the decision in favor of the collection agency. *Mackey v. Lanier Collections Agency & Service,* 486 U.S. 825, 108 S.Ct. 2182, 100 L.Ed.2d 836 (1988).

◆ A Minnesota clinic employed a dialysis patient care technician and issued her a copy of the employee handbook, which explained the Paid Time Off (PTO) policy. The handbook also provided that an employee who resigned would be paid for earned but unused paid time off if she gave proper notice, but specified that an employee who resigned without giving proper notice or who was terminated for misconduct would not be eligible for payment of earned but unused PTO. The clinic fired the technician for a "pattern of behavior" that resulted in "performance and patient safety issues." She sued the clinic to recover her unused vacation time, alleging that she had 181 hours of PTO worth over $3,000. The case reached the Minnesota Supreme Court, which noted that the handbook constituted a valid contract between the clinic and the technician. **The clinic could set conditions that the technician would have to meet to become eligible for paid vacation** because nothing in state law mandated the terms on which PTO must be offered, or that it be offered at all. The clinic's decision not to offer the benefit of payment in lieu of paid time off to employees terminated for misconduct did not violate state law. *Lee v. Fresenius Medical Care, Inc.*, 741 N.W.2d 117 (Minn. 2007).

- Four employees of a company voluntarily resigned and submitted requests for accrued vacation time. The company refused to pay them and they sued under the Nebraska Wage Payment and Collection Act. The handbook stated that, upon termination, employees would not be paid for unused vacation time. The dispute reached the Supreme Court of Nebraska, which held that the employee handbook conflicted with the wage payment act and was thus unenforceable. The act stated that vacation pay was a fringe benefit that was included in the definition of wages under the act, and that an employee was entitled to payment for any accrued vacation time provided for in the employment agreement. Here, **vacation pay was an agreed-to benefit between the company and the employees, and the company could not refuse to disburse the pay simply because the employees had quit**. The employees were entitled to their accrued vacation pay. *Roseland v. Strategic Staff Management, Inc.*, 272 Neb. 434, 722 N.W.2d 499 (Neb. 2006).

- Two Indiana employers published handbooks that contained policies regarding the payment of vacation time upon termination of employment. The handbooks did not constitute a contract. Two employees were involuntarily terminated by the employers. Both employees had accrued vacation time prior to termination, and both employers refused to pay the employees for the unused vacation time. The question that arose before the Court of Appeals of Indiana was whether, as a matter of law, the non-contractual published policies in the employee handbooks relieved the employers of any obligation to pay the employees for the accrued, but unused, vacation time. The court held that **the handbooks properly relieved the employers of the obligation to pay the unused vacation time**. The problem for the employees was that they were claiming they were entitled to accrued vacation pay granted by the handbooks while at the same time repudiating the terms of the handbooks that took away their right to the pay. *Mitchell v. Universal Solutions of North Carolina, Inc.*, 853 N.E.2d 953 (Ind. Ct. App. 2006).

- A Louisiana long-term acute care hospital maintained a written employment policy calling for the forfeiture of all accrued benefits when an employee abandoned a position. A licensed practical nurse employed by the hospital twice threatened to leave work but was reminded by the hospital's director of nursing that quitting without notice violated company policy. She later walked off the job without notice, and her employment was deemed terminated by the hospital. It confiscated her accrued vacation pay in compliance with hospital policy. She sued, asserting violations of state wage law. The case reached the Supreme Court of Louisiana, which noted that **the employee's accrued vacation pay constituted "wages" under state law**. Quitting a job abruptly without notice to the employer does not justify the withholding of earned wages. The court also stated that the employer's reliance on an unlawful company policy did not provide it with a good-faith defense to the imposition of penalty wages. *Beard v. Summit Institute of Pulmonary Medicine and Rehabilitation*, 707 So.2d 1233 (La. 1998).

◆ A Montana employer adopted a personnel manual providing employees with two weeks of paid vacation per year after completion of the second year of employment. The policy required employees to work the shift before and after their vacation days and to provide a 30-day notice for taking vacation. Just after completing her second year of work, an employee quit, giving a two-week notice that coincided with the start of her scheduled vacation. The employer denied vacation pay because the employee did not work her shifts before or after her scheduled vacation. She filed a wage claim against the employer with the state department of Labor and Industry. The department's appeals board held that she was not entitled to the pay. The Supreme Court of Montana found that the employee was entitled to two weeks of pay as described in the personnel manual. **Although an employer has no legal obligation to provide a paid vacation, once vacation benefits are granted, the employer must pay them.** After an employee has accrued paid vacation, the employer may not impose conditions that might operate to deny the employee of the benefits. Accordingly, the employer could not divest the employee of her vacation pay because of her failure to work the shifts before and after her scheduled vacation. *Langager v. Crazy Creek Products, Inc.*, 954 P.2d 1169 (Mont. 1998).

◆ To reduce its work force size, a Missouri employer offered a severance package to employees who accepted voluntary retirement or separation. Acceptance of the severance benefits required separation on the last day of the current fiscal year – the date when earned vacation benefits ordinarily became available for use during the following year. Employees accepting severance benefits were required to waive all claims against the employer. A number of employees who accepted benefits claimed that they were entitled to the vacation benefits that had vested on the day they accepted the severance packages. After they sued the employer to recover vacation benefits, a federal court ruled for the employer. The U.S. Court of Appeals, Eighth Circuit, affirmed. **The severance waiver barred the claims against the employer**, since the waiver encompassed any claim related to employment. *Mange v. Petrolite Corp.*, 135 F.3d 570 (8th Cir. 1998).

◆ The Appellate Court of Illinois determined that three longtime management employees who lost their jobs due to a reduction in force were not entitled to compensation for claimed vacation pay. The company's vacation policy allotted qualified employees their full vacation allowance for the year on January 1st. If an employee left the company prior to the end of a calendar year and had remaining vacation days available, the company paid the employee for the unused time. In the case of the three employees, each had received payment for their unused vacation days, but claimed further entitlement to vacation benefits because each had been discharged in September. They argued that they would have received vacation benefits for the following year had they been on the payroll at the close of the calendar year and that they were **entitled to *pro rata* benefits through September**. The appellate court disagreed. *Prettyman v. Comwlth. Edison Co.*, 653 N.E.2d 65 (Ill. App. Ct. 1995).

B. Sick Leave Benefits

Many of the issues that arise with respect to sick leave are issues that also arise under the *Family and Medical Leave Act* (FMLA). Although leave under the FMLA is unpaid, employees can request (and employers can require) that paid leave run concurrently with FMLA leave. For cases involving the FMLA, please see Chapter Six, Section V.

◆ An Indiana not-for-profit penal facility hired a corrections officer as an at-will employee making $9.25 an hour. Its handbook provided that after 90 days, she would be eligible for benefits, including sick time. It also stated that the company did not pay employees for unused sick time upon termination. Moreover, the handbook described the vacation time policy and stated that employees would not be paid for unused vacation time if they were fired or gave less than two weeks' notice. The officer was fired 45 days later, and was paid only minimum wage for her final pay period. She sued under the state's Wage Claims Statute, asserting that she was entitled to 7.4 hours of accrued sick pay, 14.76 hours of vacation pay and the difference between $9.25 per hour and $5.15 per hour for her final pay period. The case reached the Court of Appeals of Indiana, which held that she was entitled to the difference between her agreed-upon salary and minimum wage, but that she was not entitled to her accrued but unused sick pay or vacation. She never met the requirements for vacation pay because she did not work at least 90 days. **As for the sick pay, the handbook clearly limited its use and did not allow it to be converted or otherwise made available to the employee.** Further, even if the sick pay were analogous to vacation pay, she was still not eligible for it because she did not meet the handbook's requirements for eligibility. *Williams v. Riverside Community Corrections Corp.*, 846 N.E.2d 738 (Ind. Ct. App. 2006).

◆ An accountant in Nebraska gave his employer 90 days' notice as required by his contract, stating that he intended to open a competing accounting firm. The company fired him on the spot, not letting him work out the remainder of the 90 days. It also sued him for breach of the non-compete agreement. A trial court ruled that the non-compete agreement was more restrictive than was reasonably necessary to protect the company's rights and was therefore unenforceable. However, the company properly fired the accountant for malfeasance after he gave his 90-day notice. The court also held that the accountant was entitled to 32 hours of unused vacation pay and 72 hours of unused sick leave under the employment handbook. The Nebraska Supreme Court affirmed. The non-compete clause was overly restrictive. And although the accountant was entitled to his earned but unused vacation and sick leave pay as of the day he gave notice, **he was not entitled to the vacation and sick leave he would have accrued during the 90-day notice period**. *Professional Business Services Co. v. Rosno*, 680 N.W.2d 176 (Neb. 2004).

◆ An airline paid employees for sick leave during their own illnesses, but it did not permit the use of sick leave for parental leave. Employees received sick pay at the same time they received their regular pay during the period when leave was taken. The airline denied use of paid sick leave to two Oregon-based employees for parental leave. The employees contended that Oregon's parental leave law required the airline to allow the use of accrued sick leave for this purpose and filed complaints against the airline with the state Bureau of Labor and Industries. The bureau issued cease and desist orders against the airline, and it brought a federal court action against the bureau, seeking declaratory and injunctive relief from the orders. The court granted pretrial judgment to the bureau, and the airline appealed to the U.S. Court of Appeals, Ninth Circuit.

The airline argued that the state law claims were preempted by ERISA, but the court noted that **ERISA regulations exempt certain payments as payroll practices** where the compensation is normal, paid out of an employer's general assets and payable on account of time during which the employee is physically or mentally unable to perform job duties. The sick leave payments in this case satisfied these elements. The compensation system utilized by the employer had the characteristics of an unfunded payment, rather than an ERISA trust fund payment. The sick pay plan was not subject to ERISA preemption, and the court affirmed the district court judgment. *Alaska Airlines, Inc. v. Oregon Bureau of Labor*, 122 F.3d 812 (9th Cir. 1997).

◆ A Utah bank required employees to sign an agreement that called for them to submit written requests to their supervisors for sick leave. One department manager announced a no-leave policy during the bank's acquisition of another bank and conversion to a new computer system. The manager repeatedly denied an employee's request for a full day off to have a lump removed from her lip. After four months, she was allowed a day off for surgery. She was diagnosed as having an aggressive, malignant form of melanoma. She sued the bank for breach of contract and breach of an implied covenant of good faith and fair dealing to use sick leave. The court granted the bank's motion for pretrial judgment, finding no employment contract between the parties. The Court of Appeals of Utah observed that even though the employment relationship was at will, there was still an employment contract. And the at-will relationship did not negate the sick leave contract between the parties. The court remanded the case for a determination of **whether the bank had breached the contract by denying permission to use sick leave** and whether it had acted unreasonably and in violation of its obligation of good faith and fair dealing. *Cook v. Zions First National Bank*, 919 P.2d 56 (Utah App. 1996).

◆ An Illinois hospital employee with 20 years of experience was fired for taking a $25 gift certificate a few weeks before they were scheduled to be given out to employees. Because the employee was qualified to participate in the hospital pension plan, she requested her pension benefits on the same day she was fired. However, the hospital denied her request for payment of accumulated unused sick days, stating that she had been fired and had not retired. The employee filed a lawsuit against the hospital in an Illinois circuit court, which granted the hospital's pretrial judgment motion. On appeal, the Appellate Court of Illinois observed that the hospital's employee handbook stated that employees who retired became immediately eligible to receive payment for their unused sick time. **The handbook was sufficiently definite to create a binding contract to pay for sick time** and failed to distinguish between voluntary retirement and retirement caused by firing. The employee was over 55 years of age and had five years of service, which were the only requirements for payment of accrued sick time. The employee was entitled to an award of over $9,000 plus interest. *Dow v. Columbus-Cabrini Medical Center*, 655 N.E.2d 1 (Ill. App. Ct. 1995).

CHAPTER FIVE

Labor Relations

I. WAGE AND HOUR LAWS

The Fair Labor Standards Act of 1938 (FLSA), 29 U.S.C. § 201 *et seq.*, is a comprehensive federal statute that mandates the payment of minimum wage and overtime compensation to covered employees.

States have laws that are similar to the FLSA. Most employees are covered under these laws, but there are some exceptions (such as disabled workers, full-time students and tipped employees, among others).

The FLSA prohibits employment of any covered employee in excess of 40 hours per week unless the employee is paid at least time-and-a-half. The FLSA also requires employers to pay at least the minimum wage ($6.55 per hour until July July 24, 2009, then $7.25 per hour).

State laws generally provide similar requirements, though the minimum wage may be slightly higher or lower. If your state's minimum wage requirement is higher than that of the FLSA, you will have to comply with the higher state minimum wage requirement.

A. The Fair Labor Standards Act (FLSA)

The FLSA applies where there is an employer/employee relationship (it does not apply to independent contractors). Although the FLSA sets minimum wage and overtime requirements, it does not require employers to provide sick leave, vacation time, holiday pay or severance pay.

The FLSA is enforced by the Wage and Hour Division of the federal Department of Labor, which conducts investigations, usually in response to complaints by employees or former employees. It is a violation of the FLSA to retaliate against an employee for making a complaint or participating in an investigation (or other legal proceeding) under the FLSA.

If an employer is found to have violated the minimum wage or overtime provisions of the FLSA:

1) the Wage and Hour Division may supervise the payment of back wages
2) the Secretary of Labor may sue for back wages and an equal amount as liquidated damages
3) the employee may sue for back pay, liquidated damages, attorneys' fees and costs, or
4) the Secretary of Labor may obtain an injunction against the employer.

1. Covered Employment

In addition to the students and disabled workers discussed above, there are other exceptions to covered employment. These include executives, bona fide administrative employees and professional employees paid on a salaried basis.

On-call time is considered to be working time if the employee is sufficiently restricted in the ability to pursue non-work activities. In other words, if the employee is called often and required to give repeated assistance, she is probably going to have to be paid for such on-call time.

Break time is not compensable under the FLSA if the employee has no job responsibilities during the break. If the employee is expected to help out during a break (for example, where a store or restaurant is extremely busy), then the break time is compensable under the FLSA.

- The FLSA was amended in 1974 to exempt from minimum wage and maximum hours rules persons "employed in domestic service employment to provide companionship services for individuals ... unable to care for themselves." A Department of Labor regulation includes in the exemption companionship workers employed by an agency other than the family or household using the services. A domestic worker in New York who provided companionship services sued her former employer (a third-party agency) for minimum and overtime wages. The case reached the U.S. Supreme Court, which held that the third-party regulation was valid and binding, meaning **the worker was not entitled to minimum or overtime wages**. *Long Island Care at Home, Ltd. v. Coke*, 127 S.Ct. 2339, 168 L.Ed.2d 54 (2007).

- Employees of meat and poultry processing plants in Washington and Maine brought class action lawsuits against the company who owned the plants, alleging FLSA violations. They asserted that the company owed them for the time they spent waiting to change into and out of required specialized clothing and safety gear, and that it owed them for the time it took to walk between the locker room and the production floor. The case reached the U.S. Supreme Court, which determined that **the time spent walking between the locker room and the production floor was compensable**. The Portal-to-Portal Act does not exclude such time from the FLSA's coverage. Further, the time spent waiting to doff the protective gear was covered by the FLSA. However, the time spent waiting to don the protective gear before the start of each shift was not compensable. Donning and doffing gear that is integral and indispensable to employees' work is a "principal activity" under the Portal-to-Portal Act, but waiting to don the first piece of gear is two steps removed from the productive activity on the assembly line. *IBP, Inc. v. Alvarez*, 546 U.S. 21, 126 S.Ct. 514, 163 L.Ed.2d 288 (2005).

- A nonprofit religious organization derived most of its income from the operation of commercial businesses staffed by its "associates." These people, former drug addicts and criminals, received no cash salaries, but were provided with food, clothing, shelter and other benefits. The Secretary of Labor sued the organization and its officers for violating the FLSA. An Arkansas federal court held that the organization was an "enterprise" within the meaning of the FLSA, and that the associates were employees protected by the FLSA. The case reached the U.S. Supreme Court, which affirmed, noting that the FLSA contained no express or implied exception for commercial activities conducted by religious or other nonprofit organizations. Further, even though the associates claimed that they were not employees, they did expect compensation of a sort; thus, **the economic reality was that they were employees under the FLSA**. Finally, the Court held that application of the FLSA did not violate the Free Exercise Clause or the Establishment Clause of the First Amendment. The FLSA did not require the payment of cash wages, so the employees could still be paid in the form of benefits. Also, they could return any payments made to them if they so wished, and provided it was voluntary, this would not violate the FLSA. Nor did the FLSA's recordkeeping requirements inhibit religious activities undertaken with a business purpose. The FLSA applied to the organization. *Tony & Susan Alamo Foundation v. Secretary of Labor,* 471 U.S. 290, 105 S.Ct. 1953, 85 L.Ed.2d 278 (1985).

◆ A satellite dish company in Texas decided to change its technicians' schedules to eliminate overlapping time. It went from two four-day shifts of 10 hours to a four-day shift and a three-day shift of 12 hours. Under the old schedule, technicians earned a considerable amount of overtime pay. A manager believed that under the new schedule, technicians would earn less overtime even though he was assured that that was not the case. He was told to assure subordinates about the positive features of the change. Instead, he told them it would likely lead to less overtime and that they should find out from an HR manager. When he was then fired for poor performance and insubordination, he sued under the FLSA, asserting retaliation for protected activity. A federal court and the Fifth Circuit ruled against him, noting that **his personal objections to the new schedule did not amount to protected activity**. And asking the HR manager to answer his subordinates' questions about the schedule did not amount to protected activity either. *Hagan v. Echostar Satellite, L.L.C.*, 529 F.3d 617 (5th Cir. 2008).

◆ An Ohio gas and convenience store manager, who was expected to work 50 hours a week, received a salary of $522 per week, with a bonus of up to 5% of the store's gross profit margin on the sale of certain products, up to $2,500 per month. She spent 60% of her time performing non-managerial tasks like stocking shelves, cleaning restrooms and operating the cash register. She also hired employees, trained them, set schedules, wrote formal evaluations and frequently recommended terminations to her district manager. After she was fired, she sued for overtime under the FLSA, claiming she was not exempt as a bona fide executive employee. A federal court and the Sixth Circuit ruled against her. **Even though she spent 60% of her time in nonexempt tasks, she exercised discretion every day**; her district manager adopted a largely hands-off approach; and her "primary" duties were those inherent to the management of the business. *Thomas v. Speedway SuperAmerica*, 506 F.3d 496 (6th Cir. 2007).

◆ After a vice president of sales in Virginia lost his job, he sued for unpaid overtime under the FLSA. Two weeks later, the company sued the vice president for fraud for failing to tell it a sales contract had been terminated (preserving his $50,000 annual bonus). The vice president then amended his lawsuit to claim retaliation. A federal court granted pretrial judgment to the company on both the FLSA and retaliation claims, but the Fourth Circuit reversed as to the retaliation claim. Here, the vice president was an exempt employee under the FLSA because he made $150,000 a year and his duties involved the exercise of discretion and independent judgment directly related to general business operations. However, **he could pursue his retaliation claim after the company sued him for fraud because he had a reasonable belief that his employer violated the FLSA**. *Darveau v. Detecon, Inc.*, 515 F.3d 334 (4th Cir. 2008).

◆ Two Utah employees worked for a private company that contracted with the Army and the Army Reserves to provide recruiting services. The company was paid when a recruit enlisted in either branch. The two employees received a salary of $600 per week under the "fluctuating workweek" method. One employee worked 480 overtime hours; the other worked 596. The company didn't pay either employee overtime. When they sued under the FLSA, **the company asserted that they were "outside salespersons" and thus were exempt from overtime**. A federal court and the Tenth Circuit disagreed and awarded them overtime. Here, the employees did not have the authority to actually enlist recruits. Their job was more akin to promotional work, paving the way for the Army to "make the sale." The court ordered the company to pay for their overtime at the "half-time" rate. *Clements v. Serco, Inc.*, 530 F.3d 1224 (10th Cir. 2008).

◆ A customer relations manager for a motorcycle dealership coordinated with various departments to ensure that customers were satisfied with their purchases, and he exercised discretion in reacting to the unique needs of the dealership's customers. He also attended management meetings to give status reports on previously ordered motorcycles and their delivery dates. He was paid $1,153.85 a week ($60,000 a year), except for two paychecks of $769.24 and $961.55. He also frequently worked more than 40 hours a week. After he was fired, he sued for overtime under the FLSA. A Massachusetts federal court ruled for the dealership, and the First Circuit affirmed. Here, **the manager was an exempt administrative employee within the meaning of the FLSA because his primary duties related to management** and included the exercise of discretion. Also, the two aberrant paychecks out of approximately 50 received were not enough to show an actual practice of making improper deductions by the employer. No overtime was due. *Cash v. Cycle Craft Co., Inc.*, 508 F.3d 680 (1st Cir. 2007).

◆ A company that drilled and serviced oil and gas wells in New Mexico distributed a travel policy informing employees that it did not require them to travel to the drilling rigs with their crew supervisors. However, as a practical matter, employees met their foremen at a convenience store near company headquarters, then drove together to the drilling rigs. Bad roads, limited parking, permits and gate keys, as well as pressure on foremen to arrive with a full crew drove the decision to commute together. **When a group of employees brought a collective action under the FLSA to be paid for their travel time,**

the Tenth Circuit ruled against them. The Portal-to-Portal Act (which states that the FLSA does not require employers to compensate an employee for time spent traveling to or from work) barred the employees' claims. *Smith v. Aztec Well Servicing Co.*, 462 F.3d 1274 (10th Cir. 2006).

◆ A Virginia man created a software integration system and entered into an agreement with a company, giving it exclusive rights to market his system for 15 months, with an option to buy it for $1.5 million. He became an employee and was paid $7.00 an hour, but was told not to report hours in excess of 40 per week. When the sale fell through and he was fired, he sued under the FLSA, seeking overtime for 300 hours of unreported work. A federal court ruled in his favor, finding that he was not an exempt employee. The company appealed, and the Fourth Circuit affirmed. Here, the company claimed he was exempt under the "administrative" and "outside sales" classifications. However, **to take advantage of the combination exemption, the company had to meet each individual exemption's requirements under the FLSA**. Here, the employee did not satisfy the administrative exemption's "salary basis" test because he was not paid a salary of at least $455 per week (only receiving $280). *IntraComm, Inc. v. Bajaj*, 492 F.3d 285 (4th Cir. 2007).

◆ A Maryland nonprofit corporation operated community living facilities for disabled residents and employed community living assistants (CLAs) to check on the residents every two hours around the clock. A Department of Labor (DOL) investigator determined that the weekend CLAs, who worked 48 hours straight over the weekend, but were only paid for 40 hours, were entitled to be paid for their full shifts (as well as overtime). **The unpaid four-hour break periods the CLAs received each day amounted to work because the CLAs could not leave the premises during the breaks, and their breaks were frequently interrupted.** A federal court and the Fourth Circuit agreed with the DOL that the CLAs were entitled to be paid for the break time as well as for overtime. However, since the violation of the FLSA was not willful, the company's liability reached back only two years instead of three. Damages were assessed at $527,900. *Chao v. Self Pride, Inc.*, 232 Fed.Appx. 280 (4th Cir. 2007).

◆ A manager in the District of Columbia claimed that he was fired because he sought overtime wages for his subordinates. His former employer asserted that he could not claim retaliation because he never filed a formal complaint under the FLSA. When he sued under the statute, a federal court joined the First, Third, Sixth, Eighth, Ninth, Tenth and Eleventh Circuits in holding that **the FLSA protects informal complaints**. If a court were to provide protection only against retaliation for formal complaints, employees would be discouraged from reporting violations of the FLSA to their employers. *Haile-Iyanu v. Cent. Parking System of Virginia, Inc.*, 2007 WL 1954325 (D.D.C. 7/5/07).

◆ An employee of an electric cooperative in North Dakota was the head of a stand-alone department and was an exempt employee under the FLSA. When she asked about getting overtime pay, the manager told her that her job would have to be reconfigured into a less responsible position in another department and possibly with a demotion or reduction in pay. She then had a disagreement with the manager that resulted in her termination for insubordination. When she sued for retaliation under the FLSA, she lost. A federal court and the Eighth Circuit held that **the cooperative was merely trying to comply with the FLSA when it explained to her why she might have to take a cut in pay if she wanted to be covered by the act**. *Humann v. KEM Electric Cooperative, Inc.*, 497 F.3d 810 (8th Cir. 2007).

◆ A Michigan company paid all its employees, whether salaried or hourly, under a single payroll system. Because some salaried employees worked 36 hours one week and 48 hours the next, the company told them to report 40 hours in the weeks they worked 36. This would insure that they received 1/26th of their annual salary biweekly. When some exempt employees accidentally underreported their hours, they were underpaid. They sued under the FLSA, claiming they had been misclassified as exempt. A federal court and the Sixth Circuit disagreed. **The company allowed them to report hours in excess of what they worked to generate their full pay for each biweekly period.** Even though the company paid the employees on an hourly basis, they were still salaried employees. *Acs v. Detroit Edison Co.*, 444 F.3d 763 (6th Cir. 2006).

◆ A Delaware-based farm corporation considered its crew leaders to be exempt from overtime as executive employees. It converted them from hourly to salaried employees but did not change their duties. Five crew leaders sued to collect overtime, **asserting that they were not really executive employees because the company gave their hiring and disciplinary recommendations little consideration**. A federal court granted pretrial judgment to the company, but the Third Circuit reversed, finding issues of fact that required a trial. Although the crew leaders did have the responsibility for keeping a full crew at all times, there was a question as to how much weight was given their hiring and firing recommendations. *Davis v. Mountainaire Farms, Inc.*, 453 F.3d 554 (3d Cir. 2006).

◆ After a merger, a company in Maine assigned a salesman accounts with chronic service problems. Although those accounts would not generate new sales opportunities, the salesman was still required to handle their service requests. As a result, he spent 70% of his time in the office receiving customer calls instead of out in the field generating new sales. When the company quintupled his sales quota, then fired him, he sued for unpaid overtime under the FLSA and the Maine Prompt Pay Act. A federal court and the First Circuit ruled against him. **Even though the Prompt Pay Act allows commissioned salespeople to earn overtime where their employer exerts substantial control over hours and work location, the company here did not do so.** It merely required the salesman to answer customers' service calls without detailing how that should be done. *Palmieri v. Nynex Long Distance Co., d/b/a Verizon Enterprise Solutions*, 437 F.3d 111 (1st Cir. 2006).

◆ Finance and insurance managers at two car dealerships in Oregon claimed that they were entitled to overtime under the FLSA and brought lawsuits against their respective employers. The cases reached the Ninth Circuit, which held that the managers were exempt employees under Section 207(i). That section **exempts retail employees in "big ticket" departments who are paid wholly or in large part by commission**. The court held that the provision was not limited to commissions on goods and services but also applied to other commission-earning employees who make more than one-and-a-half times the minimum wage. *Gieg v. DDR, Inc.*, 407 F.3d 1038 (9th Cir. 2005).

◆ Pharmacists in Colorado brought a collective action against Wal-Mart under the FLSA, **asserting that Wal-Mart violated the FLSA by prospectively reducing their salaries during the slow summer months**, effectively turning them into hourly employees who were entitled to overtime. The case reached the Tenth Circuit, which ruled that the practice of prospectively reducing salaries does not convert a salaried employee into an hourly employee unless the company does it so often that the purported salary becomes the functional equivalent of an hourly wage. Here, Wal-Mart had 4,000 pharmacists at 2,000 stores and only a few of them allegedly had their salaries reduced. Accordingly, the collective action could not survive. However, the court remanded the case for a determination of whether the individual pharmacists who had their salaries reduced had it happen so frequently that they were in effect hourly employees entitled to overtime. *In re Wal-Mart Stores,* 395 F.3d 1177 (10th Cir. 2005).

◆ An IT support specialist for the same company fixed problems on fellow employees' PCs and also installed hardware and cable for the local area network (LAN). He was not involved in designing how the cables or hardware would be configured, and he did not install programs on the LAN. When he claimed that the company violated the FLSA by failing to pay him overtime, the Sixth Circuit agreed. It rejected the company's argument that he fell within the "computer professional" or "administrative" exemptions to the FLSA. **He did not perform the highly specialized system analyst tasks that the computer professional exemption requires**; he merely performed tasks to pre-determined specifications in a system design created by others. Also, his work could not be considered of "substantial importance to the management or operation of the business" so as to make him exempt under the FLSA's administrative exemption. He was entitled to overtime. *Martin v. Indiana Michigan Power Co.*, 381 F.3d 574 (6th Cir. 2004).

◆ The Eleventh Circuit ruled that six Allstate **insurance agents** in Florida were not entitled to overtime under the FLSA. Even if they were employees and not independent contractors, they were paid on a salary basis, making a minimum monthly compensation regardless of the number of policies they sold. Also, they were primarily responsible for promoting sales, advising customers, adapting policies to fit customers' needs, deciding on advertising budgets, and hiring and training staff. Finally, they exercised discretion and independent judgment despite the fact that Allstate closely regulated what products they sold and how they sold them. They were exempt as administrative employees. *Hogan v. Allstate Insurance Co.*, 361 F.3d 621 (11th Cir. 2004).

◆ A Manhattan garment manufacturer used a subcontractor to perform assembly line stitching and sewing. When 26 of the subcontractor's workers sued the manufacturer as a joint employer under the FLSA – alleging that the manufacturer allowed the subcontractor to avoid paying minimum wage and overtime – a New York federal court granted pretrial judgment to the manufacturer. The Second Circuit reversed, finding that the lower court had used an improper test for determining **whether the manufacturer was a joint employer under the FLSA**. The court of appeals remanded the case for a determination of the "joint" status under a six-part test: 1) shared premises and equipment; 2) whether workers shift from one putative employer to another as a unit; 3) whether the work is integral to the putative employer's operations; 4) whether responsibility could pass from one subcontractor to another without material change; 5) the degree of supervision; and 6) whether the employees worked exclusively for the putative employer. Under this standard, the district court would have to determine whether the manufacturer "suffer[ed] or permit[ted]" the employees to work so as to be liable as a joint employer. *Zheng v. Liberty Apparel Co., Inc.*, 355 F.3d 61 (2d Cir. 2003).

◆ A company that leased workers to construction contractors on an as-needed basis informed job candidates during the pre-hire interview of its prerequisite that field employees complete a 10-hour Occupational Safety and Health Administration general construction safety course. Employees were required to complete the class within 60 days of being hired or they would be fired. The company did not pay the employees for taking the class. When the DOL determined that attendance at the class was involuntary, such that overtime compensation had to be paid under the FLSA, an Ohio federal court agreed. However, the Sixth Circuit Court of Appeals reversed the lower court's decision. It held that attendance at the class (after hours, unrelated to the employees' jobs, where no productive work was being performed for the company) was in fact voluntary. **Even though employees would be fired if they did not attend, that did not make attendance at the classes involuntary** under the FLSA. *Chao v. Tradesmen Int'l Inc.*, 310 F.3d 904 (6th Cir. 2002).

◆ A company that owned a number of KFC restaurants in Mississippi paid its managers a salary of $300 a week, plus a monthly bonus of 2% of the gross sales of the restaurant they managed. It deducted cash register shortages from the managers' monthly bonuses. However, the company then began deducting cash register shortages from managers' weekly salaries. After its attorneys advised it to stop, it resumed its policy of deducting shortages from bonuses and eventually repaid the improper deductions with interest. A number of managers sued the company for violating the FLSA, asserting that the improper deductions turned them into nonexempt employees who were entitled to overtime. A Mississippi federal court ruled for the managers, finding that they were not exempt executive employees for the four-month period when the improper deductions were made, and that the company could not avail itself of the FLSA's "window of correction" because it had a policy of improper deductions. The Fifth Circuit Court of Appeals reversed, holding that **the**

company could assert the "window of correction" defense because it returned the improper deductions with interest and changed the offending policy. *Moore v. Hannon Food Service Inc.*, 317 F.3d 489 (5th Cir. 2003).

2. Recordkeeping

In addition to minimum wage and overtime requirements, the FLSA has certain recordkeeping requirements. The basic information that must be kept is:

1) Employee's full name and Social Security number
2) Address, including zip code
3) Birth date, if younger than 19
4) Sex and occupation
5) Time and day of week when employee's workweek begins
6) Hours worked each day
7) Total hours worked each workweek
8) Basis on which employee's wages are paid (hourly, weekly, piecework)
9) Regular hourly pay rate
10) Total daily or weekly straight-time earnings
11) Total overtime earnings for the workweek
12) All additions to or deductions from the employee's wages
13) Total wages paid each pay period
14) Date of payment and the pay period covered by the payment

◆ A cashier at an Indiana store was quickly promoted to assistant store manager and, after the store manager was fired, she took on some of the manager's responsibilities while still remaining an hourly employee. Six weeks later she was promoted to store manager and held that position for four months until she requested a transfer. The following month she was fired. She then sued for overtime under the FLSA. A federal court noted that she couldn't specifically identify the hours or even days she worked overtime without pay. The court granted pretrial judgment to the store. However, the Seventh Circuit reversed, noting that **when an employer fails to keep proper records required by the FLSA, an employee can still proceed with her claim**. Here, although employees submitted accurate time sheets, the company could and apparently did use a computer to alter the hours employees said they worked. The store even showed the manager clocking out before closing time on several occasions even though she was the only employee who could lock up. *Brown v. Family Dollar Stores of Indiana, LP*, 534 F.3d 593 (7th Cir. 2008).

◆ After a Texas husband and wife were fired, they sued their former employer under the FLSA, asserting that they were entitled to unpaid wages. They put together records documenting their hours worked. The employer submitted her own records, which were not fully complete. Nevertheless, the court used the employer's records because **the employees' records were a reconstruction after the fact and were insufficient to allow a "just and reasonable inference" of hours worked**. Also, witness testimony supported the employer's version. The Fifth Circuit U.S. Court of Appeals ruled that the employer's records had properly been used to determine hours worked. *Rosales v. Lore*, 149 Fed.Appx. 245 (5th Cir. 2005).

- A husband and wife took a job with a Virginia storage facility. They lived on the premises and agreed to be paid for 40 hours a week each as a reasonable estimate of the time they would have to work. If unusual circumstances caused them to exceed a 40-hour week, they were supposed to notify the owner within 24 hours. They submitted only one such notification and were paid accordingly. Four years later they were fired. They sued under the FLSA, seeking overtime for many other weeks, but a federal court and the Fourth Circuit ruled against them. The agreement they had signed was reasonable under 29 CFR § 785.23 – a regulation applying to situations where employees reside on the owner's premises – and they chose not to adhere to it. *Garofolo v. Donald B. Heslep Associates, Inc.*, 405 F.3d 194 (4th Cir. 2005).

- Waiters at a chain of Tennessee steakhouses filed a lawsuit under the FLSA, claiming that they were entitled to unpaid minimum wages for a three-year period when they were assigned during some shifts to make salads instead of waiting on tables. They claimed they were not "tipped" employees under the FLSA when they worked in this capacity because they performed exclusively behind-the-scenes food preparation. As such, they argued that they were entitled to recoup the 50% of the $4.25 per hour minimum wage that the employer claimed for itself under the FLSA as a tip credit.

The Sixth Circuit Court of Appeals agreed that the waiters were not "tipped" employees when they worked as salad makers. However, although each waiter was entitled to payment of the full $4.25 per hour for all work time logged during those shifts, ultimately they could not legally recoup the payment because they failed to disclose the precise hours of each salad-making shift worked. The burden was on them to prove their salad-making hours, because the restaurant's records were in proper order. **Thus, the waiters failed to prove the specific amount they were owed.** Nor did the restaurant forfeit its entitlement to a tip credit for any of the waiters' work hours because it habitually deducted a 3% service charge from each tip when a customer charged the tip to a credit card. The practice is not necessarily inconsistent with Section 203(m) of the FLSA, which commands that a tipped employee be permitted to retain all tips, except tips shared in a pooling arrangement. When tips are charged to credit cards, the employer can deduct the amount the credit card company charges without violating the FLSA. *Myers v. Copper Cellar Corp.*, 192 F.3d 546 (6th Cir. 1999).

- The U.S. Department of Labor (DOL) investigated a Michigan care facility for violations of the FLSA and determined that it owed employees over $1,000 in unpaid wages and had failed to keep required records. Two years later, the department renewed its investigation based on information that employees at the facility were not paid for the whole time they worked during some shifts when they were required to remain on the employer's premises for 24 hours at a time. The employer imposed an eight-hour sleep deduction for these shifts, regardless of the number of hours actually worked during the sleep period. The employees submitted evidence that the employer's failure to pay them regardless of the number of hours actually worked during these shifts resulted in violations of the minimum wage and overtime requirements of the FLSA. Because the employees submitted evidence that they remained alert, checked on residents and performed safety measures, they were paid at a rate below the minimum wage. **The employer had failed to keep statutorily required records and was not entitled to any defense for good-faith action.** The DOL was awarded judgment on behalf of the employees for unpaid back wages of over $60,000 plus an equal amount of liquidated statutory damages and the costs of litigation. *Herman v. Palo Group Foster Home, Inc.*, 183 F.3d 468 (6th Cir. 1999).

◆ A janitorial service in Maryland and Washington, D.C., failed to pay its workers overtime. The employer kept records for total hours worked per shift rather than on a workweek basis as required by FLSA regulations. This recordkeeping method made it extremely difficult to determine whether overtime pay was due. A group of employees sued, claiming violations of the FLSA. The court rejected evidence prepared by the employees' attorney designed to show that each claimant was owed unpaid overtime wages. It determined that the methodology was improper and that the employer's policy of issuing make-up checks for overtime wages adequately compensated employees. The U.S. Court of Appeals, D.C. Circuit, found that the district court had erroneously placed the burden on the employees to prove their overtime hours and wages. **Where employer records are inadequate or inaccurate, courts may not penalize employees by denying them recovery based on inability to precisely prove their damages.** Because the employer failed to maintain accurate records, the evidence presented by the employees was sufficient to establish damages. The court vacated and remanded the case. *Arias v. United States Service Industries, Inc.*, 80 F.3d 509 (D.C. Cir. 1996).

◆ A small Arkansas corporation operated a marina that was managed by one of its three corporate shareholders. The manager's wife assisted him for three years during which they were on call 365 days a year, 24 hours a day. When the manager injured himself, his wife ran the facility until the two other shareholders voted to remove him without notice. The manager and his wife sued the other shareholders for wrongful discharge and unpaid wages. A court found that the shareholders had unlawfully discharged the manager by failing to give him three days' written notice of a special board meeting to remove him as required by corporate bylaws and Arkansas law. The court also **allowed the wife's claim for back wages, even though she failed to keep appropriate records** and her proof rested only on testimony from her own recollection of working approximately 60 hours per week for three years. The Supreme Court of Arkansas agreed with the trial court that the discharge without notice of a shareholder meeting violated state corporate law. It also agreed that under the FLSA, a court may rely upon employee recollection in determining an unpaid wage claim because employers had a duty to keep proper records. *Marine Services Unlimited, Inc. v. Rakes*, 918 S.W.2d 132 (Ark. 1996).

◆ Employees of an award-winning New Hampshire daily newspaper claimed that their supervisors discouraged them from reporting overtime and falsified time records to avoid payment for overtime work. The U.S. Secretary of Labor (Secretary) brought an administrative action on their behalf, claiming that the newspaper willfully violated FLSA overtime and recordkeeping provisions. Federal regulations under the FLSA classify most newspaper employees as entitled to overtime, unless they primarily perform duties that require them to use invention, imagination, or talent. The Secretary sought a permanent injunction against future FLSA violations plus an award of back pay, interest and liquidated damages. A federal court held that while **the employees were entitled to overtime compensation because they were not engaged in primarily artistic or creative endeavors**, it would not grant an injunction against future FLSA violations and refused to award compensation for a willful violation of the FLSA. On appeal, the First Circuit affirmed. *Reich v. Newspapers of New England, Inc.*, 44 F.3d 1060 (1st Cir. 1995).

B. State Laws

State wage and hour laws are similar to the FLSA. They may apply to more employers than the FLSA, and they may cover more employees. They may also have a higher minimum wage. If a state's minimum wage is less than the FLSA, and if the FLSA applies to the employer, then the employer must pay the higher federal rate.

1. Federal Preemption

Preemption occurs when a state and federal law address the same subject matter. In such cases, the federal law takes precedence over the state law by virtue of the Supremacy Clause (U.S. Constitution, Article VI, clause 2).

◆ California's prevailing wage law is based on the federal Davis-Bacon Act. It requires contractors working on public works projects to pay their employees at least the general prevailing wage rate for similar work being performed in the locality. Both laws allow public works contractors to pay apprentices less than the prevailing journeyman wage where they participate in approved programs complying with the National Apprenticeship Act. The California Apprenticeship Council charged a subcontractor working on a county construction project with improperly paying apprentices in a non-approved program the apprentice wage rather than the appropriate journeyman wage. It ordered the county to withhold payments to the contractor for the violation. The contractor sued, claiming that the prevailing wage act was preempted by the Employee Retirement Income Security Act (ERISA). The court agreed with the contractor that the apprenticeship training system under which the apprentices worked was an employee welfare benefit plan under ERISA and that the prevailing wage statute related to it. However, it held that the state wage act was not preempted. The U.S. Supreme Court affirmed, noting that **the California prevailing wage act was not preempted because it referred to approved apprenticeship programs that did not necessarily have to be ERISA plans.**

Here, the prevailing wage statute merely offered economic incentives to apprenticeship programs to comport with the state's requirements. *California Division of Labor Standards Enforcement v. Dillingham Construction*, 519 U.S. 316, 117 S.Ct 832, 136 L.Ed.2d 791 (1997).

- Undocumented aliens who worked for a contractor on construction projects with the New York City School Construction Authority and the New York City Housing Authority filed a lawsuit claiming that the contractor failed to pay them the prevailing wage as required by law. The contractor asserted that the Immigration Reform and Control Act (IRCA) preempted the lawsuit and sought to have the case dismissed. A New York trial court refused to dismiss the lawsuit. It noted that **IRCA did not preempt New York law with respect to paying prevailing wages**. The court also held that the undocumented workers could seek wages for work they had already performed even if they allegedly offered fraudulent documents to obtain employment. *Pineda v. Kel-Tech Construction, Inc.*, 832 N.Y.S.2d 386 (N.Y. Sup. Ct. 2007).

- A Massachusetts pavement contractor received an administrative ruling by the state Commissioner of Labor and Industries that it was required to comply with a state prevailing wage law that covered the construction of public works. The contractor argued that the law was inapplicable to its activities because its work was limited to maintenance and repair work and was not "construction." It also asserted that the act was preempted by ERISA, since the contractor was bound by collective bargaining agreements to make contributions to ERISA plans and the statute credited amounts placed in the plans for each hour an employee worked against the employee's hourly wage as determined by the commissioner. The Supreme Judicial Court of Massachusetts found that **the prevailing wage law was applicable to the contractor's employees despite the claim that its work was limited to repairs**. The commissioner's interpretation of the act concerning road work was permissible. ERISA does not preempt state wage laws that have a minimal effect on an ERISA plan, and the state prevailing wage law did not "relate to any [ERISA] plan" by listing ERISA benefits as an example to be factored into the prevailing wage. The prevailing wage law applied to the contractor. *Marino Co., Inc. v. Commissioner of Labor and Industries*, 426 Mass. 458, 689 N.E.2d 495 (Mass. 1998).

- A Washington driver-salesperson worked under a collective bargaining agreement that guaranteed employees 40 hours of pay per week. However, no overtime wages were paid under a long-term understanding between the company and its employees that longer hours worked during the busy summer season would be offset by shorter hours during the winter. The driver-salesperson claimed that he never finished his workday in less than eight hours. He failed to pursue a grievance under the bargaining agreement, quit his job, and sued his former employer for unpaid overtime wages. The court determined that the employee's failure to file a grievance with the union barred the complaint. The Court of Appeals of Washington observed that federal law requires employees claiming violation of a labor contract to use the bargaining agreement's grievance procedure prior to seeking relief from a court. However,

the state minimum wage act was not preempted by federal labor law. The employee's rights under state law existed independent of the bargaining agreement. Union members are not deprived of the protections afforded to all workers in the state. The withholding of overtime compensation in lieu of seasonal variations was insufficient to establish an agreement with individual employees, and the trial court would have to reconsider the former employee's claim that he never received overtime pay or compensatory time off. *Ervin v. Columbia Distributing, Inc.*, 930 P.2d 947 (Wash. Ct. App. 1997).

2. Applicability

The following cases address the applicability of state wage and hour laws to various situations.

- A Pennsylvania borough maintained that a street resurfacing project was "maintenance" and not "construction, reconstruction, demolition, alteration and/or repair work." The state Department of Labor and Industry determined that the resurfacing was not maintenance and that the borough had to pay prevailing wages for the project. The borough appealed and the case reached the Pennsylvania Supreme Court, which ruled that **the resurfacing was principally a reconstruction project and not mere maintenance**. Accordingly, the borough had to pay prevailing wages. *Borough of Youngwood v. Pennsylvania Prevailing Wage Appeals Board*, 947 A.2d 724 (Pa. 2008).

- A company in New Mexico paid an employee under an agreement that provided a fluctuating rate of pay. She received a basic salary each week that didn't change regardless of the number of hours worked. However, if she worked more than 40 hours in a week, her overtime was calculated by taking her weekly pay and dividing the number of hours worked to reach her regular hourly rate. This meant that **the more hours she worked, the smaller her regular hourly rate became, giving her diminishing overtime wages**. She filed a wage claim under the state's minimum wage law. The case reached the Court of Appeals of New Mexico, which ruled that the agreement violated the law because in extreme cases, overtime wages would be less than minimum wage. *New Mexico Dep't of Labor v. Echostar Communications Corp.*, 134 P.3d 780 (N.M. Ct. App. 2006).

- When a Montana pawnshop employee was hired, he was told he would receive a monthly wage based on an hourly rate. For about a year, besides working Monday to Friday, he worked two eight-hour Saturdays a month. He was paid the same amount regardless of how many hours he worked each day, although he was compensated for the two extra Saturdays he worked each month. After he began working only one Saturday a month, he continued to be paid the same monthly wage, calculating overtime for the Saturdays and not taking out for sick days missed. A few years later, after the employee received his last paycheck, he filed a claim for unpaid overtime with the state department of labor. A state court dismissed the claim because the employee failed to notify the pawnshop about the overtime before he filed with the state. The Montana

Supreme Court reversed, noting that the Montana statute governing overtime had no advance notice requirement. An employee may not waive by silence his or her right to overtime, because such a waiver would be contrary to public policy. Therefore, **the employee's failure here to assert his right to overtime while still working did not bar him from pursuing his claim.** *Lewis v. B&B Pawnbrokers, Inc.*, 968 P.2d 1145 (Mont. 1998).

- A food distributor employed route salespersons to make deliveries to retail establishments and collect payments. Salespersons remitted collections to the company and received their wages without regard to account deficiencies. However, the employer required salespersons to reimburse it for any cash shortages. The New York Commissioner of Labor filed a complaint against the employer under a state law prohibiting unauthorized wage deductions. The case reached the Court of Appeals of New York, which noted that the salespersons accepted funds from retail purchasers, converted them to their own accounts, then accepted an obligation to make corresponding payments to the employer. **Funds collected from retailers were not wages, and the transaction was entirely separate from the payment of wages.** *Hudacs v. Frito-Lay, Inc.*, 90 N.Y.2d 342, 660 N.Y.S.2d 700, 683 N.E.2d 322 (N.Y. 1997).

- A West Virginia employer hired two employees under contracts stating that each would receive a 15% raise per year. The employer failed to award the raises, and the employees quit. They sued the employer for **unpaid annual raises** under the state wage payment and collection act. The court ruled against the employer's principal owner, who appealed to the Supreme Court of Appeals of West Virginia. The owner argued that the contracts had been modified by the agreement to defer raises until the company became profitable. The court found the annual raises to be within the definition of wages under state law since they were accrued benefits capable of calculation that were payable directly to an employee. The court rejected the owner's assertion that he should have received the opportunity to demonstrate that he had not knowingly violated the act. *Britner v. Medical Security Card, Inc.*, 489 S.E.2d 734 (W.Va. 1997).

- The president of a Connecticut corporation required a bookkeeper to work over 40 hours per week. However, the bookkeeper was not paid overtime wages. The state labor commissioner sued the employer on the employee's behalf to collect unpaid overtime wages, asserting that the president was personally liable for the award due to his exclusive authority to determine the hours and wages of his employees. A trial court agreed with the commissioner and found the president personally liable for the wages, doubling the damage award as allowed by state law. The Supreme Court of Connecticut affirmed, observing that individuals may be held liable as employers under the law. **Because the president could require employees to work overtime, he was appropriately considered an employer under the act and was personally liable for the wage award.** The doubling of the damage award had been appropriate since there was evidence of bad faith by the president. *Butler v. Hartford Technical Institute, Inc.*, 243 Conn. 454, 704 A.2d 222 (Conn. 1997).

◆ An Idaho corporation apparently experienced financial difficulties and repeatedly fell behind in wage payments. **Its president unilaterally modified two employees' payment schedules**, claiming that the employees were no longer paid by the hour, as had been understood at the time of their hiring. The employees sued the corporation and president for unpaid wages. The trial court awarded them wages plus treble damages under the state wage collection act, and the court of appeals affirmed. It found substantial evidence that there was a unity of interest in corporate ownership that required disregarding the corporate entity and holding the president personally liable. The court rejected the president's assertion that the employees had accepted the modification in their payment terms and refused to award him a credit for insurance benefits, cash and property payments to the employees that had been intended as bonuses. *Hutchison v. Anderson*, 950 P.2d 1275 (Idaho Ct. App. 1997).

◆ An Iowa employer fired a probationary claims examiner for insubordination, which had the effect of excluding him from the company's profit-sharing plan. The employee consequently received no profit share for the months prior to his firing. He sued the employer for breach of contract, wrongful discharge, breach of an implied covenant of good faith and fair dealing and violation of the state wage payment collection law. The Supreme Court of Iowa found that although the profit share was a wage under the state wage law, **the employee's claim for wages was not valid because he had been appropriately placed on probation** for violating company policy. The firing did not violate any public policy that was sufficient to defeat the presumption of employment at will, and there was no cause of action in Iowa for breach of an implied covenant of good faith and fair dealing in employment. *Phipps v. IASD Health Services Corp.*, 558 N.W.2d 198 (Iowa 1997).

◆ A wage regulation issued by the Washington Department of Labor and Industries required contractors to pay prevailing local wages to employees delivering materials to public works project sites where they performed spreading, leveling, rolling and any other incorporation of materials into a project. **An asphalt contractor argued that the regulation unlawfully amended the state prevailing wage statute.** The court of appeals found that the reference to workers upon all public works in the prevailing wage act was sufficiently broad to encompass contract workers delivering materials to a public work site for asphalt spreading and related activities. The regulation was consistent with the prevailing wage law and was not an unconstitutional amendment as the contractor had asserted. *Superior Asphalt and Concrete Co. v. DOLI (Washington)*, 929 P.2d 1120 (Wash. Ct. App. 1997).

II. THE NATIONAL LABOR RELATIONS ACT

The National Labor Relations Act (NLRA) guarantees employees "the right to self-organization, to form, join, or assist labor organizations, to bargain collectively through representatives of their own choosing, and to engage in other concerted activities for the purpose of collective bargaining or other mutual aid or protection." [29 U.S.C. § 157]

Employees also have "the right to refrain from any or all of such activities except to the extent that such right may be affected by an agreement requiring membership in a labor organization as a condition of employment." [29 U.S.C. § 157]

The NLRA makes it an unfair labor practice for an employer "to interfere with, restrain, or coerce employees" in the exercise of their Section 157 rights [29 U.S.C. § 158(a)(1)]. The NLRA also prohibits employers from refusing to bargain collectively with the employees' representatives.

A. Applicability

Not all employees of a company qualify as "employees" under the NLRA. For example, any individual employed as a "supervisor" is not considered an employee for purposes of the NLRA.

A supervisor is an employee who has the authority to use independent judgment to "hire, transfer, suspend, lay off, recall, promote, discharge, assign, reward, or discipline other employees, or responsibly to direct them, or to adjust their grievances, or effectively to recommend such action," and the employee holds that authority "in the interest of the employer."

◆ The U.S. Chamber of Commerce sued the state of California to challenge a law that barred private employers who received more than $10,000 in state funds in a year from using those funds "to assist, promote, or deter union organizing." It claimed that the law illegally **required employers to take a neutral position with regard to unions**, that it was preempted by the NLRA and that it violated the First Amendment. A federal court agreed, but the Ninth Circuit reversed. On further appeal, the U.S. Supreme Court reversed, holding that the NLRA preempted the state statutes. Here, the statutes attempted to regulate within a zone protected and reserved for market freedom. *Chamber of Commerce of U.S. v. Brown*, 128 S.Ct. 2408 (U.S. 2008).

◆ The U.S. Supreme Court overturned a decision by the National Labor Relations Board (NLRB) awarding back pay to an undocumented alien worker who was laid off in retaliation for his role in union organization activities. The Court held that the award exceeded NLRB powers, trivialized immigration laws and encouraged future violations. Here, the employer laid off a worker who supported a union organization campaign and distributed authorization cards to co-workers. The NLRB imposed sanctions and ordered the employer to offer to reinstate the laid-off worker. However, the worker admitted that he used fraudulent documents to get the job. An administrative law judge found that an award of back pay would be contrary to Supreme Court precedent and the Immigration Reform and Control Act of 1986 (IRCA), but the NLRB held that the worker was entitled to almost $67,000 in back pay and interest. The case reached the Supreme Court, which held that **the NLRB had no power or authority to award back pay to the illegal alien**, since to do so was contrary to policies underlying the IRCA. The employer was still subject to other sanctions imposed by the NLRB. *Hoffman Plastic Compounds, Inc. v. NLRB*, 535 U.S. 137, 122 S.Ct. 1275, 152 L.Ed.2d 271 (2002).

◆ A Minnesota electrical contractor refused to grant employment interviews to 10 job applicants who were union members. The only union applicant accepted for employment was fired after a few days on the job. The union members filed a complaint against the contractor with the NLRB, asserting that the contractor had failed to hire or retain them because of their union affiliation in violation of the NLRA. An administrative law judge held for the union members, and a panel of the NLRB affirmed. The U.S. Court of Appeals, Eighth Circuit, reversed the NLRB's decision, finding that the job applicants were not "employees" for the purposes of the NLRA because they were being paid by the union to organize the company. They were therefore not protected from anti-union discrimination.

The U.S. Supreme Court stated that the NLRB's broad, literal interpretation of the statutory term "employee" was consistent with NLRA purposes, one of which was to protect the right of workers to organize for mutual aid without employer interference. The contractor argued that common law agency principles prohibited this interpretation, and that the applicants were paid union organizers who could only serve the union's interest. The Court noted that common law agency principles did not prohibit workers from accepting employment from more than one employer. **Union organizing was equivalent to performing work for another employer during non-work hours, which no employer had a legal right to prevent.** The Court held that the NLRB's interpretation of the term "employee" was correct. *NLRB v. Town & Country Electric, Inc.*, 516 U.S. 85, 116 S.Ct. 450, 133 L.Ed.2d 371 (1995).

On remand, the Eighth Circuit found that substantial evidence supported the NLRB's ruling that the firing of the union electrician had been retaliatory and motivated by the contractor's anti-union sentiment. It enforced the NLRB order. *Town & Country Electric, Inc. v. NLRB*, 106 F.3d 816 (8th Cir. 1997).

◆ A poultry processing corporation purchased a company that operated a production plant in North Carolina. The plant employed crews of workers who collected live chickens for slaughter from independent contractor farmers. Before the sale was completed, a labor organization filed a petition to represent crew workers who worked out of the plant. The NLRB approved the crew workers as a bargaining unit that was protected by the NLRA and determined that **they were not excluded from coverage as agricultural laborers**. It ordered the corporation to recognize the union and bargain with it. The U.S. Supreme Court upheld the NLRB's ruling. The NLRB had properly focused on the status of the corporate employer, which was not a farmer, and noted that despite doing their work at farm locations, the employees began and ended each workday at the production plant. *Holly Farms Corp. v. NLRB*, 517 U.S. 392, 116 S.Ct. 1396, 134 L.Ed.2d 593 (1996).

◆ "Supervisors" are not covered under the NLRA if they have the authority to use independent judgment to "hire, transfer, suspend, lay off, recall, promote, discharge, assign, reward, or discipline other employees, or responsibly to direct them, or to adjust their grievances, or effectively to recommend such action," and they hold that authority "in the interest of the employer." The NLRB issued a complaint against the owner and operator of an Ohio nursing home, alleging that unfair labor practices had been committed in the disciplining of four licensed practical nurses. It determined that the nurses were not supervisors. The U.S. Supreme Court held that the NLRB's test for determining whether nurses were supervisors was inconsistent with the NLRA. Here, **the NLRB had erroneously concluded that the nurses were not supervisors because their focus was on the well-being of the nursing home residents**, not on the interests of the employer. The Court noted that because patient care is a nursing home's business, attending to residents' needs is in the employer's interests. Thus, the nurses were supervisors outside the coverage of the NLRA. *NLRB v. Health Care & Retirement Corp.*, 511 U.S. 571, 114 S.Ct. 1778, 128 L.Ed.2d 586 (1994).

- A Massachusetts corporation that operated a textile dyeing and finishing plant laid off all its employees and went out of business. One of its officers then teamed up with a former customer, acquired the plant, and began to operate a similar business. The new company hired many ex-employees of the old corporation. The union that had represented those employees asked the new company to recognize it as the collective bargaining agent for the new company's employees. The company refused. The union then filed an unfair labor practice charge with the NLRB. An administrative law judge found that the new company was a "successor" to the old corporation and that its refusal to bargain was an unfair labor practice. The U.S. Supreme Court agreed, holding that **there was "substantial continuity" between the two enterprises since the employees' jobs remained essentially unaltered**. Further, at the time one full shift of workers had been hired, a majority were ex-employees of the old corporation. Accordingly, even though the union's demand for bargaining had been premature, the new company was under an obligation to bargain once it had a "substantial and representative complement" of its work force in place. *Fall River Dyeing & Finishing Corp. v. NLRB*, 482 U.S. 27, 107 S.Ct. 2225, 96 L.Ed.2d 22 (1987).

- After employees of two small Illinois leather processing firms elected a union as their collective bargaining representative, the firms challenged the election on the ground that six of the seven eligible voters were illegal aliens. When the NLRB denied the challenge, the firms sent a letter to the Immigration and Naturalization Service (INS), asking it to check into the status of a number of employees. The NLRB determined that the firms had committed an unfair labor practice by reporting the employees to the INS in retaliation for their union activities, and ordered reinstatement with back pay. The U.S. Court of Appeals, Seventh Circuit, modified the NLRB's order, keeping the reinstatement offers open for four years and requiring the offers to be written in Spanish. It also held that even though the employees were not entitled to back pay when they were not legally entitled to be present in the United States, an award of six months' back pay would be appropriate.

On further appeal, the U.S. Supreme Court held that **the NLRA applied to**

undocumented aliens with respect to unfair labor practices committed against them. Accordingly, the firms had committed an unfair labor practice against the illegal aliens by constructively discharging them (by reporting them to the INS). However, back pay can only reimburse for actual, not speculative, consequences of an unfair labor practice. The court of appeals exceeded its authority by keeping the offers open for four years and by requiring them to be written in Spanish. The Court remanded the case to the NLRB so appropriate relief could be determined. *Sure-Tan, Inc. v. NLRB,* 467 U.S. 883, 104 S.Ct. 2803, 81 L.Ed.2d 732 (1984).

◆ A condominium association in Florida provided maintenance and security services to individual condo owners. A union sought to bargain for the maintenance employees after they voted for representation, but the association refused to bargain, claiming that the employees were domestic employees who were excluded by the NLRA. The National Labor Relations Board ruled that the employees were not domestic employees and ordered the association to bargain with the union. The Eleventh Circuit enforced the board's order. **The maintenance employees were not employed by the individual homeowners but rather by the condominium association. They were thus not exempt domestic employees.** *Shore Club Condominium Ass'n, Inc. v. NLRB*, 400 F.3d 1336 (11th Cir. 2005).

◆ A supervisor of maintenance employees for a Missouri company claimed that he was asked by company management to create "false and misleading" disciplinary reports and employee evaluations for maintenance employees who were engaged in union-organizing activities. When he refused to do as management asked, he was fired. He sued the company for wrongful termination, seeking $1.5 million. The company moved to have the case dismissed on the grounds that the lawsuit could only be brought under the NLRA. The trial court agreed, and the Missouri Court of Appeals affirmed. Even though the supervisor was not covered by the NLRA, he was essentially asserting that **his discharge interfered with the rights of protected employees** under the act. An employer violates the NLRA if it fires a supervisor because the supervisor refuses to engage in unfair labor practices against protected employees. Here, because the NLRB had primary jurisdiction over the case, the lower court had properly dismissed it. *Hinton v. Sigma-Aldrich Corp.*, 93 S.W.3d 755 (Mo. Ct. App. 2002).

◆ A Colorado gas and electric company considered transmission employees responsible for monitoring and directing the flow of electricity over the company's high-voltage transmission network to be supervisory. The NLRB then issued a ruling that such employees were not statutory supervisors under the NLRA, and a union sought to represent the employees. When the company refused to bargain with the union, the NLRB ordered it to do so and then petitioned the Tenth Circuit for an enforcement order. The court of appeals denied enforcement. It noted that the NLRA defines a supervisor as someone who has the authority, in the interest of the employer, to responsibly direct employees, if the exercise of that authority requires the use of independent judgment. Here, **the employees at issue used their professional, technical knowledge to direct less-skilled employees in performing their work**. As a result, they used independent judgment and exercised authority that was not merely routine or clerical in nature. Because the employees were supervisors under the NLRA, the company did not have to bargain with the union. *Public Service Co. of Colorado v. NLRB*, 271 F.3d 1213 (10th Cir. 2001).

B. Handbilling and Picketing

As a general rule, employers do not have to allow non-employee organizers on their property for the purpose of distributing union literature. However, where the employees are beyond the reach of reasonable union efforts to communicate with them, employers may have to allow handbilling on company property.

However, the burden is on the union to show that no other reasonable means of communicating its organizational message to the employees exists. Off site, employers do not have the right to prevent the distribution of union literature.

Employees have the right to peacefully picket an employer during a strike. As long as the employees can lawfully assemble in a place (usually a sidewalk area), employers cannot prevent them from doing so.

1. Handbilling

Handbilling is the distribution of union literature for the purpose of unionizing a workplace. Sometimes such information is distributed to employees; however, it is often targeted to customers.

- A food and commercial workers union attempted to organize employees at a Connecticut retail store. When the employer refused to allow the union on store property to distribute handbills, the union filed a complaint with the NLRB, which ordered the employer to cease and desist barring the union from the parking lot. The Fifth Circuit affirmed the NLRB's decision, but the U.S. Supreme Court reversed, noting that "the right to distribute [handbills] is not absolute, but must be accommodated to the circumstances." If it is unreasonable for a union to distribute literature to employees entirely off the employer's premises, distribution in parking lots or other common areas may be warranted. The Court concluded that there were no "unique obstacles" hindering the union from reaching the employees because it had access to the list of names and addresses. Therefore, **the employer did not violate the NLRA by preventing union organizers from distributing handbills in the parking lot**. *Lechmere, Inc. v. NLRB*, 502 U.S. 527, 112 S.Ct. 841, 117 L.Ed.2d 79 (1992).

- A grocery store manager in California called the police when union organizers handed out flyers to customers in the parking lot and refused to leave. The store had a no-solicitation policy prohibiting solicitors from operating on store premises. The NLRB determined that the store violated Section 8(a)(1) of the NLRA by calling the police, but the U.S. Court of Appeals, District of

Columbia Circuit, held that the store did not commit an unfair labor practice. The NLRB had relied on a California Supreme Court case that had a labor-picketing exception to the trespass laws, but that had since been discredited. Here, **the store's policy clearly prohibited all picketers, regardless of the content of their speech**, and this did not violate the First Amendment or the NLRA. *Waremart Foods v. NLRB*, 354 F.3d 870 (D.C. Cir. 2004).

- A Nevada casino leased space to a restaurant company to provide food service facilities inside its hotel and casino complex. When employees of the restaurant company sought to unionize, they distributed handbills on casino property. Casino security told the employees they could not distribute literature on casino property, but the employees refused to leave. The police were called, and the employees were cited for trespassing. The union then filed unfair labor practice charges against the casino, asserting that the restaurant employees could handbill in non-work areas during non-work times. **The casino asserted that the restaurant employees were not casino employees and thus had no Section 7 organizing rights** under the NLRA. The NLRB ruled in favor of the employees, but the U.S. Court of Appeals, D.C. Circuit, refused to enforce its order. It remanded the case for a determination of whether the restaurant employees enjoyed the same Section 7 rights as casino employees. *New York New York, LLC v. NLRB*, 313 F.3d 585 (D.C. Cir. 2002).

- A Pennsylvania contractor began work on a condominium project using union carpenters who were paid at prevailing wage rates. However, the contractor began employing nonunion carpenters, and a labor organization distributed handbills stating that the contractor employed foreign and immigrant workers at less than prevailing wages. The contractor ejected the union representatives from its property. The U.S. Court of Appeals, Third Circuit, noted that the dispute involved general property rights under state law as well as interpretation of the NLRA. The court stated the NLRA confers rights upon employees, not upon unions or their non-employee organizers. **Employers cannot be compelled to allow non-employee organizers to distribute union literature on their property.** The non-employees did not have any right of access to the employer's property. *Metropolitan Dist. Council of Philadelphia United Brotherhood of Carpenters v. NLRB*, 68 F.3d 71 (3d Cir. 1995).

- A contractor was hired to build a department store in a Florida mall. A union believed the contractor was paying substandard wages and fringe benefits. It thus engaged in **peaceful handbilling of the businesses in the mall**, asking customers not to shop there until the mall's owner publicly promised that all construction at the mall would be done using contractors who paid fair wages. The mall owner, after failing to convince the union to alter the handbills to state that the dispute was not with the owner, filed a complaint with the NLRB, charging the union with engaging in unfair labor practices under Section 8(b)(4) of the NLRA. The NLRB dismissed the complaint, concluding that the handbilling was protected by Section 8(b)(4)'s proviso exempting non-picketing publicity intended to truthfully advise the public that products are produced by an employer with whom the union is involved in a labor dispute.

The Eleventh Circuit affirmed, but the U.S. Supreme Court reversed on the ground that the mall owner and its other tenants did not distribute the contractor's products. *Edward J. DeBartolo Corp. v. NLRB,* 463 U.S. 147, 103 S.Ct. 2926, 77 L.Ed.2d 535 (1983).

On remand, the NLRB ordered the union to stop distributing the handbills because the handbilling was an attempt to inflict economic harm on secondary employers. This constituted economic retaliation and was therefore a form of coercion prohibited by Section 8(b)(4)(ii)(B). The Eleventh Circuit refused to enforce the NLRB's order, holding that there was no clear congressional intent to proscribe such handbilling in the NLRA. The U.S. Supreme Court then held that **Section 8(b)(4) did not contain any clear expression of congressional intent to prohibit this kind of handbilling**. Further, since there were serious constitutional problems, including First Amendment free speech concerns, with the NLRB's construction, a clear expression that that was Congress' purpose would be required before such an interpretation would be adopted. The Court affirmed the decision denying enforcement of the NLRB's order. *Edward J. DeBartolo Corp. v. Florida Gulf Coast Building & Construction Trades Council,* 485 U.S. 568, 108 S.Ct. 1392, 99 L.Ed.2d 645 (1988).

2. Secondary Picketing

Secondary picketing is picketing targeted at entities that are not the employees' direct employer – for example, a union may picket the largest customer of a non-unionized employer to pressure the employer to unionize.

A union cannot threaten, coerce, or restrain an entity that is not a party to a labor dispute "where … an object thereof is … forcing or requiring [the entity] to cease using, selling, handling, transporting, or otherwise dealing in the products of any other producer … or to cease doing business with any other person …" [29 U.S.C. § 158(b)(4)(ii)(B)]

Not all peaceful picketing at secondary sites is prohibited. Where such picketing is designed only to persuade the picketed entity's customers not to buy the struck product, it is allowed.

- After contract negotiations between a title insurance company and its employees' union reached an impasse, the employees went on strike. They also picketed five local title companies who derived over 90% of their gross incomes from the sale of the insurer's policies. The U.S. Supreme Court held that **the secondary picketing amounted to coercion of neutral parties** with the object of forcing them to cease dealing in the primary party's product. Successful secondary picketing would force the local title companies to choose between survival and cutting their ties with the insurer. Section 8(b)(4)(ii)(B) of the NLRA barred such coercive activity, and its application to the picketing involved here did not violate the First Amendment. The NLRB's order to stop the picketing had to be enforced, held the Court. *NLRB v. Retail Store Employees Union, Local 1001,* 447 U.S. 607, 100 S.Ct. 2372, 65 L.Ed.2d 377 (1980).

◆ A union had a dispute with a railroad over the renewal of a collective bargaining agreement. The union struck the railroad and then extended its picketing to other railroads that interchanged traffic with the struck railroad. These railroads sued to enjoin the picketing, and an Illinois federal court issued an injunction against the picketing. The court found that the case did not "grow out of a labor dispute" as defined by the Norris-LaGuardia Act, and that none of the picketed railroads were "substantially aligned" with the struck railroad. The court of appeals reversed, and the U.S. Supreme Court affirmed that decision. It held that **the district court did not have jurisdiction to enjoin the secondary picketing in the railway labor dispute**. The Norris-LaGuardia Act was enacted to preclude courts from enjoining secondary as well as primary activity. Railroads were to be treated no differently than other industries in this regard. Because the definition of "labor dispute" is broad, the adoption of the "substantial alignment" test (which would narrow that definition) would defeat Congress' intent by requiring courts to second-guess which activities are truly in the union's interest. Further, there was nothing in the Railway Labor Act to indicate that Congress intended to permit federal courts to enjoin secondary activity as a means of settling strikes and avoiding interruptions to commerce. *Burlington Northern Railroad Co. v. Brotherhood of Maintenance of Way Employees,* 481 U.S. 429, 107 S.Ct. 1841, 95 L.Ed.2d 381 (1987).

◆ Members of a local union in Georgia began picketing a resort to protest a construction company the resort had hired. The union members believed the construction company was violating its collective bargaining agreement by hiring employees represented by another union to work on the project. The picketers gathered adjacent to a highway that was a major artery for traffic in the county. The resort became concerned about a potential safety hazard and called the police, who informed the picketers they needed to obtain an assembly permit. The picketers left peaceably. When they later decided not to wait a week for the permit and resumed picketing, the police again asked them to leave. However, the city attorney, after conferring with the police, allowed them to stay. They then filed an unfair labor practice charge with the NLRB, which determined that the resort had violated the NLRA by calling the police. The case reached the Fourth Circuit, which disagreed. **The resort did not interfere with the union members' Section 8(a)(1) rights under the NLRA by calling the police because of the potential safety hazard** created by the picketers. *CSX Hotels, Inc. v. NLRB*, 377 F.3d 394 (4th Cir. 2004).

◆ A national railway carrier with a major hub in Seattle terminated its contract with a subcontractor that provided loading and unloading services to the carrier. The union representing the subcontractor's employees threatened to picket after the carrier entered into an agreement with another company to provide those same services. The carrier sued and a Washington federal court granted it an injunction to prevent the picketing. The Ninth Circuit reversed, finding the dispute covered by the Norris-LaGuardia Act because it centered on who would perform work at the hub, which union would represent employees of the carrier's subcontractors, and the terms of the workers' employment. Even though there was no employer-employee relationship between the carrier and the union, the "matrix" of the dispute was the employer-employee relationship. Thus, **the Norris-LaGuardia Act (which deprives federal courts of jurisdiction to enjoin peaceful picketing in any case involving or growing out of any labor dispute) applied** to prevent the court from stopping the picketing. *Burlington Northern & Santa Fe Railway v. Int'l Brotherhood of Teamsters Local 174*, 203 F.3d 703 (9th Cir. 2000).

- A labor organization called a strike against a Louisiana store that was located in a strip mall. The owners of an adjoining store claimed that picket lines from the primary employer's store blocked its entrance and that their customers were harassed, threatened and coerced not to enter the store. They requested a temporary restraining order to stop the secondary picketing, and they sought damages. They also filed an unfair labor practice charge against the union with the NLRB, which was dismissed. One of the owners committed suicide, and his estate claimed that the union was responsible for causing his financial ruin and depression. When the strike ended, the court dismissed the restraining order issues as moot. The estate pursued the damages issue.

  The Court of Appeal of Louisiana stated that the NLRA prohibits a secondary boycott of a neutral employer, but allows activity surrounding a primary strike that may indirectly affect a secondary employer. A union's intent is determinative of whether secondary activity exists at a common picketing site, and the challenged conduct must seek to force a neutral business to cease doing business with another through threats, coercion or other restrictive activity. In this case, no business relationship existed between the stores, and the union had no intent to coerce secondary employees to support the strike against the primary employer. **Because the case did not involve a secondary boycott, the court had no jurisdiction to award damages.** *Foxe Lady, Inc. v. National Tea Co.*, 701 So.2d 761 (La. Ct. App. 1997).

- An unincorporated association of affiliated labor organizations representing Pennsylvania workers engaged in a course of illegal secondary boycotts and picketed work sites to exert pressure on nonunion employers. The NLRB entered into a consent judgment with the association and its business agent prohibiting further secondary boycotts, but the association continued the practice. Over the next 15 years, the NLRB entered four contempt adjudications against the association for repeated violations of the consent decrees. By 1989, the NLRB had increased the fine against the association to $250,000 for past noncompliance and increased prospective fines to $100,000 per violation as well as $10,000 per day. For six years the association discontinued its picketing and then filed a motion to vacate the prior contempt adjudication based upon alleged hardship and its changed behavior. The Third Circuit held that **the passage of time did not constitute a change in circumstances that justified lifting the injunction**. Compliance with prior orders was also insufficient to trigger a change in circumstances, especially given the association's history of noncompliance. Because the association failed to identify a significant hardship caused by the decrees, the court refused to dissolve the consent judgments or the contempt adjudications. *Building & Construction Trades Council of Philadelphia v. NLRB*, 64 F.3d 880 (3d Cir. 1995).

◆ Washington's "Little Norris LaGuardia Act," patterned after federal labor law, protects workers who engage in "self organization or in other concerted activities for the purpose of collective bargaining or for mutual aid or protections." Ten unrepresented dairy workers claimed that their employer retaliated against them for attempting to negotiate better wages, medical coverage and working conditions. The workers went on strike, and shortly thereafter, managers advised them that if they did not return to work they would be fired. Managers also videotaped employees on the picket line and eventually fired those who participated in the strike. The former employees sued, claiming the employer violated their rights to engage in concerted activities and wrongfully discharged them in violation of public policy. The court dismissed the lawsuit.

On appeal, the former employees argued that they had been engaged in activity that required the protection of the act. The Supreme Court of Washington agreed. **It rejected the employer's argument that the state law did not create rights for nonunion workers.** Nothing in the statute limited its application to union workers. It observed that federal courts interpreting the NLRA did not require union membership to establish claims. Because the state labor act was not limited to unionized workers, the former employees had also stated a claim for wrongful discharge in violation of public policy. The court reversed and remanded the case. *Bravo v. Dolsen Companies*, 888 P.2d 147 (Wash. 1995).

◆ Members of a Pennsylvania grocery workers' union called a strike and began picketing grocery stores. The workers allegedly engaged in mass picketing, violence, harassment and intimidation against customers and employees who failed to respect the picket line. On the second day of the strike, a grocery store applied to a state court for an injunction against mass picketing, violence and harassment. The court granted the order based on the testimony of several witnesses that union officers had organized, participated and abetted mass picketing with the intention of intimidating customers, vendors and employees. The parties settled the labor dispute within six weeks, and the strike ended. However, the union appealed the trial court's decision. The Pennsylvania Superior Court determined that the injunction had been granted erroneously and remanded the case for an award of attorneys' fees and costs. The employer appealed.

The Supreme Court of Pennsylvania held that reasonable cause existed for granting an injunction against mass picketing and violence. The state Labor Anti-Injunction Act **generally prohibits courts from issuing injunctions involving labor disputes**, but allows courts to do so where striking employees "seize" an employer's property. Mass picketing constitutes a seizure under the act when it forcibly denies free access to the employer's property. Since the trial court had found a consistent pattern of forcible denial of access to the employer's property, a seizure had occurred. Accordingly, it was irrelevant that union representatives were not directly involved in the violence or harassment, and that the acts committed were not in furtherance of express union policies. *Giant Eagle Markets Co. v. United Food and Commercial Workers Union*, 652 A.2d 1286 (Pa. 1995).

C. Strikes and Strike Replacement Workers

Where a strike is determined to be an unfair labor practices strike (a strike caused in whole or in part by an employer's unfair labor practices), employers cannot permanently replace the striking workers.

In an unfair labor practices strike, employers cannot refuse to reinstate striking workers upon their unconditional offer to return to work (unless they can show "legitimate and substantial business justifications" for their refusal).

Where a strike is an economic strike, employers can hire permanent replacement workers and refuse to immediately reinstate strikers who offer to return to work. The employer only has to reinstate strikers as vacancies arise (unless the union can force the employer to discharge the replacement workers as a condition for ending the strike).

- After collective bargaining between a union and a company in Tennessee broke down, 53 of the 75 employees in the bargaining unit went on strike. The company hired "permanent" replacement workers, though it stated that it reserved the right to terminate the replacement workers when the strike ended. Several months later, the union, on behalf of the striking employees, made an unconditional offer to return to work. The company refused to immediately reinstate the striking workers, but offered to put them on a preferential recall list. About a month later, the company offered reinstatement to 47 strikers, and 18 accepted. The union then filed charges against the company over its refusal to reinstate the strikers. It **argued that the replacement workers were in fact temporary and not permanent**. The NLRB disagreed, and the union appealed to the Seventh Circuit, which upheld the NLRB's decision. The company offered legitimate and substantial business justifications for retaining the permanent replacement workers following the unconditional offer to return to work. *United Steel, Paper and Forestry, Rubber, Manufacturing, Energy, Allied Industrial and Service Workers Int'l Union v. NLRB*, 544 F.3d 841 (7th Cir. 2008).

- A health care provider in Kentucky operated a rehabilitation center that employed therapists and rehabilitation technicians. It announced a wage cut for its rehabilitation employees, who discussed what actions to take to reverse that decision. Five of them wrote a grievance letter and decided to stop seeing patients until upper management met with them to discuss issues. They instead would perform necessary paperwork. Their manager, after speaking with upper management, sent them home. They chose not to picket, instead demanding a meeting. The company fired them for insubordination and they filed an unfair labor practice charge. The case reached the Sixth Circuit, which ruled that **the employees' actions were not protected because they amounted to a partial strike**. To be protected, they would have had to completely stop work. They could not simultaneously walk off the job and retain the benefits of working. *Vencare Ancillary Services, Inc. v. NLRB*, 352 F.3d 318 (6th Cir. 2003).

◆ During negotiations for a new collective bargaining agreement, a newspaper publisher in Pennsylvania hired stringers to perform night/weekend photography assignments without first notifying the union or giving it the chance to bargain over the issue. The union filed an unfair labor practice complaint with the NLRB. Shortly thereafter, the union and publisher failed to come to terms on the bargaining agreement, and the publisher's employees voted to strike. The publisher hired temporary replacement workers and later informed the union that it considered the strike to be an economic strike such that it could permanently replace the strikers. **The strikers then made an unconditional offer to return to work, but the publisher refused to let them.** The NLRB ruled that the publisher had engaged in an unfair labor practice, and the Third Circuit upheld the NLRB's order. The unilateral subcontracting of the night/weekend work during negotiations was an unfair labor practice; the strike was not an economic one; and even if it was, the publisher's efforts to prevent the strikers from making the unconditional offer to return to work (by sending the union a letter stating that the replacement workers were permanent) violated the NLRA. *Citizens Publishing and Printing Co. v. NLRB*, 263 F.3d 224 (3d Cir. 2001).

◆ A food processor and the union representing its employees reached a collective bargaining impasse. The union organized a strike that lasted over two years and resulted in the loss of two recertification elections. The employer used replacement workers, and the strike was characterized by violence. A group of strikers sought reemployment prior to the second election, and **the employer rehired them in positions that were less desirable and lower paying** than those they had formerly held. The employer feared that reemployment in their former positions created the possibility of industrial sabotage and more violence that could affect plant security. After losing the second reelection, the union filed an unfair labor practices complaint against the employer with the NLRB, which agreed that the employer had discriminated against the returning strikers. The U.S. Court of Appeals, D.C. Circuit, held that the NLRB could not have reasonably found a risk of industrial sabotage with regard to one returning striker who operated a forklift. However, there were valid safety concerns with respect to an employee in a quality control position. *Diamond Walnut Growers, Inc. v. NLRB*, 113 F.3d 1259 (D.C. Cir. 1997).

◆ A union successfully organized many electrical workers employed by an Indiana industrial contractor. The contractor then transferred almost all union supporters to a single job site and employed an "expediter" with no electrical work experience to enforce company rules. Five union members at the site commenced a week-long unfair labor practice strike to protest this tactic. They then approached a supervisor and indicated their willingness to return to work but were advised that the contractor considered them to have quit. Although the union provided the contractor three written notices of their willingness to return to work, the contractor refused to reinstate the employees, and the union filed an unfair labor practice complaint with the NLRB. The NLRB ordered the contractor to reinstate the employees. The U.S. Court of Appeals, Seventh Circuit, enforced the board's order, holding that **unfair labor practice strikers**

are entitled to reinstatement upon making an unconditional offer to return to work and that an employer violates the NLRA by failing to offer immediate reinstatement. The resumption or continuance of picketing is not inconsistent with an offer to return to work. *Dilling Mechanical Contractors, Inc. v. NLRB*, 107 F.3d 521 (7th Cir. 1997).

◆ A labor organization filed numerous unfair labor practice charges against a Michigan employer for coercing, intimidating and discriminating against union supporters and refusing to bargain with the union in good faith. The charges included retaliation against returning strikers who protested unfair labor practices. The employer claimed that the strikers had not been engaged in an unfair labor practice strike and asserted that replacement workers had been hired in their place. The NLRB ruled that the employer had violated the NLRA by failing to reinstate some of the strikers but had properly refused to reinstate one striker for failing to communicate his unconditional offer to return to work. The Sixth Circuit found substantial evidence that the employees had engaged in protected conduct. **A strike caused in whole or in part by unfair labor practices is an unfair labor practice strike**, and the employer must reinstate striking employees unless there is a legitimate and substantial business justification for refusing to do so. The court enforced the NLRB order. *Allied Mechanical Services, Inc. v. NLRB*, 113 F.3d 623 (6th Cir. 1997).

◆ A union representing 700 Maryland nursing professionals employed by health care facilities declared two 10-day strikes within six months due to the inability of the parties to renegotiate a new collective bargaining agreement. The employer obtained replacement nurses from a company that regularly furnished replacement nurses during strikes. The union sued the employment service, asserting that it violated a Maryland statute prohibiting persons not directly interested in a strike from providing, obtaining, recruiting or referring for employment any individual who customarily and repeatedly replaced strikers. The court found that the case should be dismissed due to federal preemption of state law. The Court of Special Appeals of Maryland affirmed. Although the employment service's conduct violated state law and could form the basis of a complaint for contractual interference, **the state law impermissibly limited the right of the employer to obtain replacement workers**. Because the state law unfairly interfered with the relative economic powers of management and labor and limited the employer's resort to a peaceful response to a strike, the state law was preempted by federal labor law. *Professional Staff Nurses Ass'n v. Dimensions Health Corp.*, 110 Md. App. 270, 677 A.2d 87 (Md. Ct. Spec. App. 1996).

◆ Employees of a jewelry manufacturer declared an economic strike. Two managers told some bargaining unit employees that they could resign from the union and keep their jobs. Managers also threatened to set back employment anniversary dates one week for each week an employee stayed out on strike. After the employees had been on strike for some time, the union filed an unfair labor practice charge with the NLRB. An administrative law judge determined that the company had violated the NLRA by demanding union resignation and threatening to push back anniversary dates but rejected the union's argument that these actions prolonged the strike and converted it from an economic strike into an unfair labor practice strike. The NLRB found that the strike had been converted into an unfair labor practice strike, but the Eighth Circuit observed that **the commission of unfair labor practices by an employer during a strike does not automatically convert an economic strike into an unfair labor practice strike**. In such cases, the NLRB must prove that unlawful employer conduct prolonged the work stoppage. Here, the strike had been continued solely to obtain a more favorable collective bargaining agreement. *F.L. Thorpe & Co., Inc. v. NLRB*, 71 F.3d 282 (8th Cir. 1995).

◆ In a Texas case, employees called an economic strike after a collective bargaining agreement expired. The employer hired permanent replacement employees. When the union attempted to accept the employer's previous offer, the employer informed it that the offer was no longer available. It then withdrew recognition from the union, refusing to further bargain with it. The employer felt that the union was no longer supported by a majority of the employees in the unit. The union then filed an unfair labor practice charge with the NLRB, asserting that the employer had violated the NLRA. The NLRB found that the employer's evidence of its replacements' union sentiments was not sufficient to rebut the presumption of the union's majority support. The Fifth Circuit held that the NLRB had to presume that strike replacements opposed the union. The case then came before the U.S. Supreme Court, which held that **the NLRB did not have to presume opposition to the union by the replacements**. A replacement who otherwise supports the union may be forced by economic concerns to work for a struck employer. The Court thus reversed the court of appeals' ruling and remanded the case. *NLRB v. Curtin Matheson Scientific, Inc.*, 494 U.S. 775, 110 S.Ct. 1542, 108 L.Ed.2d 801 (1990).

◆ Some local labor unions engaged in a number of unauthorized, "wildcat" strikes at several West Virginia coal mines in violation of the collective bargaining agreements in place between the employer and the international union. The regional subdivision of the international was unsuccessful in attempting to persuade the miners not to strike and to return to work. The employer then sued the international, the regional subdivision, and the local unions under Section 301 of the Labor Management Relations Act. A federal court granted injunctive relief and damages against all the defendants, but the U.S. Court of Appeals reversed as to the international and the regional subdivision because they did not instigate, support, ratify, or encourage the strikes. On further appeal, the U.S. Supreme Court affirmed, holding that **neither the international nor the regional subdivision could be held liable for the unauthorized strikes**. There was no obligation implied in law on their part to use all reasonable means to prevent and end unauthorized strikes. If the strike had been authorized (and in violation of the collective bargaining agreements), then the international would have been liable under Section 301, but such was not the case here. *Carbon Fuel Co. v. United Mine Workers of America,* 444 U.S. 212, 100 S.Ct. 410, 62 L.Ed.2d 394 (1979).

◆ A Massachusetts linen supply company was a member of an association formed to negotiate collective bargaining agreements with a truck drivers' union as a multi-employer unit. During negotiations for a proposed agreement, an impasse was reached, and the union began a selective strike against the company. The company hired permanent replacements and notified both the union and the association that it was withdrawing from the association. When a collective bargaining agreement was later executed, the company refused to sign it. The U.S. Supreme Court held that **the bargaining impasse did not justify the company's withdrawal from the multi-employer bargaining unit**. Here, there was no unusual circumstance to justify the unilateral withdrawal. To permit withdrawal at an impasse would undermine the utility of multi-employer bargaining as a practical matter. The Court required the company to implement the new agreement. *Charles D. Bonanno Linen Service v. NLRB,* 454 U.S. 404, 102 S.Ct. 720, 70 L.Ed.2d 656 (1982).

D. Unfair Labor Practices

The NLRA makes it an unfair labor practice for an employer "to interfere with, restrain, or coerce employees" in the exercise of their organizational rights under Section 157 [29 U.S.C. § 158(a)(1)]. The NLRA also prohibits employers from refusing to bargain collectively with the employees' representatives.

Because of the greater protections available for unfair labor practice strikers, workers will generally seek to find some element of an unfair labor practice so that a strike will not be deemed an economic strike.

1. Terms and Conditions of Employment

It is an unfair labor practice to refuse to bargain over terms and conditions of employment. A plant closure or partial closure (or consolidation) is not a term or condition of employment; nor is a relocation. Although such a decision can affect employees' tenure, it does not affect their terms and conditions of employment.

If an employer bargains to impasse over terms and conditions of employment, it may effect a unilateral change in such terms or conditions without committing an unfair labor practice.

◆ A company purchased a circuit board manufacturing facility in New York and laid off 200 employees. The union contacted an employee about speaking to a newspaper, which the employee did, stating that the layoffs would hurt the company over the long term, and that there were gaping holes in the business. A vice president of IBM then called one of the owners to determine if the company was still viable. The owner later met with the employee and threatened to fire him if he disparaged the company again. The employee then posted a message on a newspaper's Web site stating that the business was being "tanked" by a group of people who did not have the ability to manage it. He was then fired. The NLRB found that the threat and the firing violated Section 8(a)(1) of the NLRA, but the U.S. Court of Appeals, D.C. Circuit, held that **the employee's disloyal, disparaging and injurious attacks on the company deprived him of the protection of Section 8(a)(1)**. The company did not commit an unfair labor practice by firing the employee. *Endicott Interconnect Technologies, Inc. v. NLRB*, 453 F.3d 532 (D.C. Cir. 2006).

- Lead care aides at an assisted living facility in Ohio circulated a petition criticizing work conditions and planning a day-long strike. Managers interviewed all the aides to determine who had spearheaded the effort, then fired one lead care aide and demoted another. The strike never happened. After an unfair labor practices charge was filed, the NLRB ruled in favor of the employees, ordering reinstatement and full back pay. The Fourth Circuit enforced the order, finding that **the drafting of the petition was protected as a concerted activity under the NLRA**. Also, the managers committed an unfair labor practice by coercively interviewing the aides about the strike and the petition without assuring the aides that there would be no reprisals. *Sunrise Senior Living, Inc. v. NLRB*, 183 Fed.Appx. 326 (4th Cir. 2006).

- A newspaper employee in North Carolina was also the president of his union's local bargaining unit. He called his supervisor a racist and stated that the newspaper was a racist place to work. His supervisor told him such behavior was unacceptable and threatened to suspend him if it did not stop. He nevertheless again called the supervisor and newspaper racist and also cursed at the supervisor. After an investigation, he was fired. He filed a complaint with the NLRB, claiming that he was fired in retaliation for engaging in protected union activity under Section 7 of the NLRA. The case reached the Fourth Circuit Court of Appeals, which held that **his behavior could not be deemed to be protected activity**, and that his discharge for insubordination was lawful. *Media General Operations, Inc. v. NLRB*, 394 F.3d 207 (4th Cir. 2005).

- A company in New York had a decades-old tradition of giving employees paid time off to donate blood. Twice a year during blood drives, employees could receive up to four hours of paid time to travel to the site, give blood, recover, and return to their jobs. In 2001, the company decided to stop paying employees for time off to give blood because of the disruption it caused in the workplace. The union filed a grievance, and the NLRB found that the company violated Section 8(a)(5) of the NLRA by failing to give the union a chance to bargain over the change to employees' wages and hours as established by longstanding company policy. The U.S. Court of Appeals affirmed. Even if the company established the policy for charitable reasons, it had an effect on employees' hours and wages the same as if the company had given them four hours' paid time off twice a year. As a result, the company had to bargain before changing the policy. *Verizon New York v. NLRB*, 360 F.3d 206 (D.C. Cir. 2004).

- An Illinois steel plant used more than 100 "plain view" video cameras to monitor areas of the plant, and it also used hidden cameras at various times over the years to investigate specific cases of theft, vandalism and other kinds of wrongdoing. Using a hidden camera, the plant ascertained that an employee was using a manager's office to make unauthorized long-distance phone calls. It fired him. During the grievance process that followed, the local union president learned that the NLRB had concluded in another case that the use of hidden surveillance cameras was a mandatory subject of collective bargaining. The union asked the company for information about the hidden cameras, and the company refused to provide it. The union filed unfair labor practice charges, and **the NLRB determined that the company had to bargain over the use of the hidden cameras**. The Seventh Circuit Court of Appeals enforced the NLRB's order. It noted that the use of hidden cameras was analogous to physical exams, drug testing and polygraphs. The NLRB's order did not strip the company of the right to use the cameras; it attempted to preserve the confidentiality necessary for the company to effectively use the hidden cameras. *National Steel Corp. v. NLRB*, 324 F.3d 928 (7th Cir. 2003).

◆ A production operator at a New York brewery allegedly obstructed an independent contractor doing work at the brewery. The following morning, two senior managers approached the operator and began questioning him. He promptly requested the assistance of a shop steward in his department, who was aware of the facts underlying the incident. The managers denied the request because the shop steward was at lunch. They called for another steward, who arrived 15 minutes later. The employee refused to talk and was sent home for the day. The next day, he again requested the shop steward be there for the investigation, and the request was again denied. He was disciplined for the incident. The union then filed an unfair labor practices complaint, and the administrative law judge found that **he should have been allowed the representative of his choice**. The NLRB agreed, and so did the Fourth Circuit Court of Appeals. This "Representation Rule" furthers workers' ability to seek mutual aid and protection under the NLRA. *Anheuser-Busch v. NLRB*, 338 F.3d 267 (4th Cir. 2003).

◆ Two nonunion employees were asked to attend a disciplinary meeting after criticizing their boss in a memo to his supervisor. One of the employees refused to attend the meeting without the other and was fired. The other employee agreed to meet, received a warning about gross insubordination, and was fired three months later for refusing to sign performance objectives. The employees filed an unfair labor practices complaint with the NLRB, and an administrative law judge found no NLRA violation. The NLRB reversed, extending the *Weingarten* rule to nonunion workers. (In *NLRB v. Weingarten*, 420 U.S. 251 (1975), the Supreme Court held that employees in a unionized workplace may request the presence of a union representative at an investigatory interview that the employee reasonably believes might result in disciplinary action.)

The case reached the U.S. Court of Appeals, D.C. Circuit, which upheld the NLRB's decision. Section 7 of the NLRA (29 U.S.C. § 157) gives employees the right "to engage in other concerted activities for the purpose of collective bargaining or other mutual aid or protection." Here, **even though the workers did not belong to a union, they had the right to have a co-worker present at the investigatory interview**. *Epilepsy Foundation of Northeast Ohio v. NLRB*, 268 F.3d 1095 (D.C. Cir. 2001).

On June 9, 2004, the NLRB reversed itself and ruled that nonunion employees do not have the right to demand that a co-worker be present during investigatory interviews.

◆ A manufacturer of trailers in Pennsylvania began to negotiate with its employees' union over a new collective bargaining agreement. Negotiations became heated, and the company instituted a new attendance policy, reducing the number of unexcused absences allowed before an employee could be fired. After the employees went on strike, the company decided to purchase a new plant in Georgia. The employees then unconditionally offered to return to work. However, the company rehired only some of them. A few months later, it closed the Pennsylvania plant and fired all the employees. The NLRB charged the company with violating Sections 8(a)(1), 8(a)(3) and 8(a)(5) of the NLRA. The company was found to have violated Section 8(a)(1) (unfair labor practice to interfere with employee rights to organize and bargain collectively), **Section 8(a)(3) (unfair labor practice to discriminate with respect to hiring, or length or term of employment to discourage union membership),** and Section 8(a)(5) (unfair labor practice to refuse to bargain collectively with the employees' representatives) as well as Section 8(d) (unfair labor practice to refuse to bargain over terms and conditions of employment).

The company appealed the NLRB's ruling to the Fourth Circuit Court of Appeals, which affirmed in part and reversed in part. Here, the company violated Sections 8(a)(1) and 8(a)(5) by unilaterally instituting the new attendance policy. It also violated Sections 8(a)(1) and 8(a)(3) by refusing to reinstate some of the employees after the unconditional offer to return to work. However, it did not violate Section 8(a)(3) by closing the plant. Nor did it violate Section 8(a)(5) by refusing to bargain to impasse over the plant's relocation. Because economic reasons largely drove the decision to relocate, that decision was not a term or condition of employment over which the company had to bargain. *Dorsey Trailers, Inc. v. NLRB*, 233 F.3d 831 (4th Cir. 2000).

◆ Two unions negotiating over contracts with an Illinois utility company failed to reach an agreement nine months after the previous contracts expired. Rather than strike, they decided to initiate an "inside game" strategy wherein their members would refuse to work voluntary overtime and generally "work to rule," strictly adhering to all company safety and other rules, doing exactly and only what they were told, reporting to work precisely on time, and parking work trucks at company facilities at the end of the day, which would prevent the company from responding to after-hours emergencies. Union members also agreed to present all grievances as a group and to advise non-employees to report unsafe conditions. Two months later, the company instituted a lockout that lasted for three months. The unions eventually reached an agreement with the company. However, they filed unfair labor practice charges with the NLRB. The U.S. Court of Appeals, D.C. Circuit, noted that lockouts are not inherently anti-union. **The lockout here was not an unfair labor practice.** It was supported by a legitimate business interest in stopping the "inside game" and in getting the unions to place the company's offer before their memberships. *Local 702, IBEW v. NLRB*, 215 F.3d 11 (D.C. Cir. 2000).

◆ A California manufacturer purchased the assets of a bankrupt company and notified employees that they were being discharged because of the sale. However, the employees were also told that some of them would be hired back immediately and that others would be hired as needed. All of the initial employees hired to run the new business had worked for the bankrupt company. The manufacturer set the terms of employment without bargaining with the employees' former union. It also stated that there would be no union in its workplace. A lawsuit resulted. The case reached the Ninth Circuit Court of Appeals, which held that **a successor employer has a duty to bargain with an incumbent union** before imposing terms when it hires an essentially intact bargaining unit from its predecessor. However, it has no obligation to accept the predecessor's labor agreement. Therefore, if it bargained to impasse, it could then set the initial terms of employment. Here, because the employees all came from the predecessor, it was clear that the union represented a majority of the employees hired by the manufacturer. The manufacturer had violated its duty to bargain with the union, and a court would have to determine whether the manufacturer would have bargained to impasse, thus giving it the right to impose terms like pay rate. *NLRB v. Advanced Stretchforming Int'l*, 233 F.3d 1176 (9th Cir. 2000).

◆ An Illinois company engaged in an unfair labor practice by refusing to hire union organizers who applied for advertised jobs. The organizers were engaged in "salting," which refers to the practice of applying for jobs at a nonunion company in an effort to unionize the employer's work force. The company did repair work for petrochemical refineries. Some of its work was done on turnaround projects, which caused the company's labor needs to soar. In 1994, after it was hired for two such projects, the company advertised for workers, and 80 organizers for the boilermakers union mailed applications. After they were told to apply in person, some of the 80 showed up, identifying themselves with VUO (voluntary union organizer) buttons, but only two were hired. The union filed an unfair labor practice with the NLRB, which issued an order requiring the company to hire and pay back pay to the 80 organizers. The Seventh Circuit found **substantial evidence that the company's actions were motivated by an anti-union animus**. Thus, the part of the order prohibiting the company from similar behavior in the future was proper. But the part of the order requiring the company to hire the 80 organizers and pay them back wages was invalid because the company never hired 80 workers for the project and probably would not have hired all the union organizers, even if it hadn't known of their status. *Starcon, Inc. v. NLRB*, 176 F.3d 948 (7th Cir. 1999).

◆ The union representing employees at a Mississippi facility filed unfair labor practice charges against the employer for unilaterally adopting and enforcing a ban on employee use of tobacco products at the facility. The NLRB found that the ban violated federal labor law and ordered the employer to post rescission notices. The employer then engaged in several anti-union activities, including firing an employee for wearing a pro-union T-shirt, refusing to hire a pro-union job applicant and honoring a worker as employee of the month after she supported a pending de-certification election. When a majority of the facility's employees returned union de-certification cards, the employer withdrew recognition of the union and announced a wage increase. It also declared a bargaining impasse and refused to rescind the tobacco ban.

The NLRB found that the employer had violated federal labor law by failing to bargain in good faith over the tobacco ban. It also found that the employer had committed numerous unfair labor practices, including the withdrawal of recognition of the union. The Fifth Circuit disagreed with the NLRB's decision concerning rescission of the tobacco ban. In general, an employer may unilaterally implement a term or condition of employment when a bargaining impasse is reached, so long as the term has been the subject of collective bargaining. However, substantial evidence supported the remaining part of the order. There was evidence that **the employer's practices had tainted the de-certification process**, in particular its promise of rewards for voting against the union. The court affirmed this portion of the NLRB's order. *NLRB v. Hi-Tech Cable Corp.*, 128 F.3d 271 (5th Cir. 1997).

◆ An electrical subcontractor, whose employees were represented by a union, performed installation work at a Texas petroleum plant. The union initiated a recognitional strike, during which the project's general contractor issued a safety directive to all subcontractors requiring all workers to remain in their work areas unless they obtained permits. During the strike, the union employed a paid informant whose union membership remained a secret from the subcontractor's management. He reported to the union that the safety directive was being enforced in a discriminatory manner against union members. He stated that he was never disciplined for violating the directive, whereas the subcontractor discharged 15 union employees for violating it. The union filed an unfair labor practices petition with the NLRB, which determined that the subcontractor had unlawfully applied the safety directive against union members. Before the Fifth Circuit, the subcontractor asserted that it was not in violation of federal law because the employees who were responsible for enforcing the safety directive were not supervisors. The court, however, deemed such employees to be agents of the subcontractor, which was sufficient to make the subcontractor responsible under agency principles. Even though the safety directive was legitimate, there was strong evidence that **the subcontractor had enforced it in an anti-union manner** that violated federal law. *NLRB v. Thermon Heat Tracing Services, Inc.*, 143 F.3d 181 (5th Cir. 1998).

◆ A manufacturer assigned salaried, nonunion employees to work the third shift at an Ohio plant. A union representing nonsalaried plant employees filed a grievance claiming that the collective bargaining agreement required the assignment of union employees to perform the work. Union representatives met with a company HR manager, who asserted that the grievance could lead to the elimination of the entire shift. The employer later eliminated the shift for economic reasons. The union filed a complaint with the NLRB, and an administrative law judge (ALJ) agreed that the employer had violated the NLRA by failing to provide prior notice and an opportunity to bargain before eliminating the shift. The Sixth Circuit noted that the decision to lay off employees is a mandatory subject of bargaining but disagreed with the administrative rulings that the decision to abolish the third shift had to be negotiated. **The bargaining agreement reserved scheduling, assignment, hiring and layoff decisions to the employer**, which satisfied the NLRB's notice requirement. Also, since there were legitimate business reasons for the layoffs, this portion of the decision was remanded for further consideration. *Uforma/Shelby Business Forms, Inc. v. NLRB*, 111 F.3d 1284 (6th Cir. 1997).

◆ A union representing production and maintenance workers at a Michigan paper mill objected when the employer introduced certain initiatives. The union encouraged members to wear buttons and T-shirts declaring opposition to the initiatives. The employer formally declared an impasse and unilaterally implemented some of the initiatives before a new bargaining agreement went into effect. When the union members continued wearing buttons and T-shirts, the employer announced a formal ban against expressive clothing and buttons. The union filed an unfair labor practice charge against the employer, claiming violations of the NLRA. An administrative law judge found that wearing expressive buttons and T-shirts was protected under the NLRA. The NLRB affirmed the decision and the employer appealed to the U.S. Court of Appeals, Sixth Circuit, which stated that **the NLRA protects employee rights to wear union-related insignia at work**. It rejected the employer's argument that the restriction was necessary to maintain workplace discipline and prevent negative public perceptions of the employer's products. The court enforced the NLRB's order. *NLRB v. Mead Corp.*, 73 F.3d 74 (6th Cir. 1996).

◆ A New Mexico trucking company employed a casual dock worker under a contract that required him to be available prior to a shift in case he was needed. The company fired the employee in a dispute over the contract provision, but he was reinstated after filing a grievance and an unfair labor practice charge. He was fired a second time for allegedly failing to respond to a call and was again reinstated after a successful grievance. The company then instituted a new policy calling for discharge of employees who were late for work twice without good cause. The employee was late for work twice within six days, and on the second occasion called to explain that his car had broken down. The company determined that he had been lying and fired him again. He filed a second unfair labor practice charge against the company and repeated his false story at a hearing. An administrative law judge determined that the third discharge had been based upon good cause. The NLRB reversed the ruling. Even though the employee had lied about his reason for being late, the company had not actually discharged him for lying. The company had instituted a retroactive policy and had used it as a pretext to discharge him. Accordingly, the discharge was unlawful and the board reinstated the employee with back pay. The Tenth Circuit affirmed, and the U.S. Supreme Court also affirmed. **Because the NLRB's authority to order reinstatement was not restricted, it was not required to adopt a strict rule barring reinstatement with back pay for an employee who falsely testified.** *ABF Freight System, Inc. v. NLRB*, 510 U.S. 317, 114 S.Ct. 835, 127 L.Ed.2d 152 (1994).

2. Organization Issues

It is an unfair labor practice for an employer to interfere with employees' rights to organize and bargain collectively. Thus, if employees engage in organizing activity, they cannot be threatened, disciplined, transferred or fired.

Employers can explain the predicted negative effects that will result from unionization. However, such statements are often deemed to be threats, so any such statement should be cleared with an attorney before being made to ensure that it will not be found unlawful.

If an employee would have been otherwise disciplined for legitimate reasons, the employee may still be disciplined. However, any action taken is likely to be heavily scrutinized. Thus, it is important to be consistent with any action taken. Don't just discipline the union organizer for being late if you don't discipline others for tardiness.

Where employees seek to de-certify their union, only ministerial aid can be offered.

- Two employees of a Las Vegas casino also served as union organizers. They approached some co-workers during lunch to ask if the co-workers wanted to sign union cards. After watching this for a moment, a vice president of HR walked over to their table and said she wanted to make sure they had all the facts before they signed the cards. She pointed out that signing the cards was "legal and binding," and also stated that the cards authorized the union to start taking dues out of the employees' paychecks. She further told the employees that union dues were $32.50 a month. This interruption lasted about eight minutes. The vice president then walked away. When the union filed unfair labor practice charges with the NLRB, the case reached the Ninth Circuit. The court of appeals held that **the vice president did not violate the NLRA because her statements to the employees were not coercive or threatening**. Thus, she did not interfere with the employees' right to organize. *Local Joint Executive Board of Las Vegas v. NLRB*, 515 F.3d 942 (9th Cir. 2008).

- A company operated several hospitals and related facilities in Ohio. When a union began organizing efforts at several of those facilities, the company hired consultants to provide labor relations training to managers and supervisors. A few months later, the union filed unfair labor practice charges with the NLRB, asserting that **the company selectively enforced its "no solicitation/no distribution" policy**, disciplined employees based on their union activities, created the impression of surveillance among its employees, and unlawfully threatened its employees. The NLRB ordered the company to take various remedial measures, which it refused to do. The Sixth Circuit held that the "coachings" (warnings) given to employees involved in organizing activities amounted to disciplinary action in violation of the NLRA. Also, the company selectively enforced its no-solicitation policy only against union organizing material. Further, it improperly gave the impression that employees' union activities were under surveillance. Finally, a warning to an employee not to talk to other employees about the union while on the job amounted to an implied coercive threat. The court ordered enforcement of the NLRB's order in part. *NLRB v. Promedica Health Systems, Inc.*, 206 Fed.Appx. 405 (6th Cir. 2006).

◆ A nonunion company in Nebraska advertised for electricians. Eight union employees who applied for the job were not hired. A ninth union employee was hired, but he went on strike because he was not being paid union wages. The company's president told him that he viewed the action as a "voluntary quit." He then told employees that the electrician's recruiting efforts could cost them their jobs, and denigrated the union and its members. The union filed an unfair labor practice charge, and the NLRB found that **the company violated the NLRA by threatening employees with plant closure and job loss**. It ordered various remedies. The U.S. Court of Appeals, DC Circuit, granted the NLRB's petition for enforcement, ruling that the president's comments violated the NLRA. *Progressive Electric, Inc. v. NLRB*, 453 F.3d 538 (D.C. Cir. 2006).

◆ A man jumped into a Puerto Rico bakery truck and demanded that the driver take him to the next light. The driver did so and a supervisor saw the incident. The driver was then fired for violating a policy against letting non-employees ride in company vehicles. The driver filed an unfair labor practices complaint with the NLRB, **claiming that the real reason for his firing was retaliation for his attempts to organize his co-workers**. The NLRB agreed, noting that another driver had transported his cousin around all day without being fired. On further appeal, the First Circuit upheld and enforced the NLRB's order. The driver had to be reinstated to his job. *Holsum de Puerto Rico v. NLRB*, 456 F.3d 265 (1st Cir. 2006).

◆ A driver for a trucking company in Florida had three separate incidents in less than a month in which a client's merchandise was damaged. On the day of the third incident, he faxed a letter to his supervisors stating that he intended to form a union. He was fired three days later. He then filed unfair labor charges with the NLRB. An administrative law judge and the NLRB ordered his reinstatement, but the Fourth Circuit reversed. Here, the driver was fired because of his pattern of negligence, which cost the company over $2,000. **Even though he engaged in protected activity, he was not shielded from termination for his poor performance.** *TNT Logistics of North America, Inc. v. NLRB*, 413 F.3d 402 (4th Cir. 2005).

◆ A Wal-Mart employee in Oklahoma wore a pro-union T-shirt into the store during off-duty time but did not discuss union matters with fellow employees. Store managers nonetheless escorted him out. The next day, he invited several co-workers to a union meeting and told one co-worker he wanted her to sign a union authorization card. He was then subjected to a written "coaching session" – the first step in Wal-Mart's progressive disciplinary process. The union filed an unfair labor practice charge with the NLRB, which held that Wal-Mart violated Section 8(a)(1) and (3) of the NLRA. The Eighth Circuit upheld that decision in part. **Wal-Mart should not have escorted the employee out of the**

store, and disciplining him for inviting others to a union meeting was improper. However, Wal-Mart could, in keeping with its anti-solicitation policy, discipline him for asking the co-worker to sign the union authorization card. *Wal-Mart Stores v. NLRB*, 400 F.3d 1093 (8th Cir. 2005).

◆ A maintenance mechanic for a company in Arizona had a perfect attendance record and no disciplinary problems. He became a vocal supporter of a union that had begun a campaign to organize the company's workers. When he was temporarily assigned to work the night shift for a co-worker on special assignment, he left work early on two consecutive days after day shift maintenance mechanics arrived and told him the floor was covered. The company decided to treat his actions as job abandonment under the code of conduct rather than an attendance problem. It fired him, and the union filed an unfair labor practice charge with the NLRB. The NLRB ruled against the company, citing four incidents that demonstrated its anti-union animus: 1) making the employee remove a union button because of a ban on jewelry, but not requiring anyone else to remove their jewelry; 2) barring talk about the union because of a so-called ban on non-work conversations that never existed; 3) forcing the employee to cover up his union T-shirt while walking through the shop to collect his personal belongings after being fired; and 4) commenting to the employee about his bad attitude. The Seventh Circuit Court of Appeals upheld the NLRB's order, finding that **the company's inconsistency in enforcing its policies justified the ruling against it**. *SCA Tissue North America LLC v. NLRB*, 371 F.3d 983 (7th Cir. 2004).

◆ Bowling Transportation had a single client: AK Steel. AK Steel awarded safety bonuses to Bowling of up to $1 for each employee-hour of injury-free work. It encouraged Bowling to pass the entire bonus on to its employees, but Bowling kept half the money for a Christmas party and some safety equipment. When two Bowling employees complained to an AK Steel manager about not receiving the entire bonus, AK Steel instructed Bowling to remove the employees from its premises. Bowling fired the employees, who then filed a complaint with the NLRB. An administrative law judge determined that the employees had engaged in "protected concerted activity" under the NLRA, and that Bowling had violated their rights when it fired them. The Sixth Circuit agreed with that assessment. Even though the employees' complaints about the safety bonuses had nothing to do with union activity, **their actions qualified as protected concerted activity**. Despite the difficult position Bowling was in, it could have sued AK Steel for breach of contract or sued under federal labor laws if AK Steel had thrown it off site for noncompliance. *Bowling Transportation, Inc. v. NLRB*, 352 F.3d 274 (6th Cir. 2003).

◆ An HR manager at a Tennessee plant overheard two stockroom employees talking about paying union dues. The HR manager talked with a stockroom team leader, who promised to reprimand employees for punching in early even though the company had tolerated punching in early in the past. The stockroom team leader then told an employee that the HR manager was on the warpath and that the "union stuff" had management "stirred." A few days before union elections, the division president held a series of meetings at which he warned employees that the plant might have to shut down if they voted for the union. When the union lost the election, it filed charges with the NLRB. An administrative law judge found that **the stockroom team leader was properly considered part of management** for NLRA purposes when he threatened to impose more stringent working conditions on employees because of their union activity, and also determined that the division president had improperly threatened to close the plant. However, the company did not violate the NLRA when it removed union flyers from the bulletin board because it had a consistently enforced policy of allowing only personal postings. The Seventh Circuit upheld that ruling. *Fleming Companies, Inc. v. NLRB*, 349 F.3d 968 (7th Cir. 2003).

◆ A distributor of food products operated a warehouse in Arizona, at which a union began an organizing campaign. Four months after filing a petition for a representation election, the union charged the company with committing unfair labor practices in connection with the organizing campaign by firing the leader of the organization effort. The company fired the employee after two co-workers accused him of threatening them while soliciting union authorization cards. The company claimed it had a good-faith belief that the threats had occurred. During the hearing, the fired employee testified that he did not even know one of his accusers, and another employee testified that he was the one who had actually solicited that worker's card and that the fired employee had not been present. The administrative law judge found the accusers' testimony not credible and ruled that the fired employee had not committed misconduct. The NLRB upheld that ruling, and the U.S. Court of Appeals, D.C. Circuit, sustained the board's petition for enforcement. **The company's good-faith belief was not relevant where the misconduct simply did not occur.** The firing violated the NLRA. *Shamrock Foods Co. v. NLRB*, 346 F.3d 1130 (D.C. Cir. 2003).

◆ A Louisiana man and his wife owned all the shares of an electrical company that provided residential and commercial contracting services. The man agreed to recognize a union as the collective bargaining agent of the company's employees and paid union wages to employees working on commercial jobs. The company, with the knowledge of the union's business manager, followed a longstanding industry practice of using nonunion labor at nonunion wages for residential projects. When a new business manager later complained about that practice, a payment was made to the union's apprentice fund to resolve the matter. However, the man then resigned as president of the company and opened another business with his wife, providing the same services and using the old company's employees, building and three of its five trucks. The stock of the old company was transferred to the man's father without compensation. The new business did not pay union wages. When the union complained, the NLRB concluded that **the man had violated the NLRA by forming a new company that was the alter ego of the first company** in order to avoid his collective bargaining obligations. The Fifth Circuit upheld the board's order in favor of the union. *Vallery Electric, Inc. v. NLRB*, 337 F.3d 446 (5th Cir. 2003).

◆ A nonunion company "lent" several thousand temporary construction workers a year to contractors on the West Coast. The company implemented a 30% rule with respect to wages (refusing to hire applicants whose recent wages were 30% higher or lower than its starting wages), and it also began a better screening process in an effort to retain more employees. When a union targeted the company as part of a "salting" campaign, two union employees obtained jobs with the company. When their projects were completed, they were let go and were not offered any further positions because the company knew that they were pro-union. An unfair labor practices charge was filed, and the NLRB determined that the 30% rule was discriminatory under the NLRA. It also found that the two employees should be reinstated with make-whole damages. The U.S. Court of Appeals, D.C. Circuit, enforced the NLRB's order only in part. It noted that **the 30% rule was not discriminatory against union employees** because the rule was motivated by legitimate business objectives. *Contractors' Labor Pool, Inc. v. NLRB*, 323 F.3d 1051 (D.C. Cir. 2003).

◆ A majority of an Illinois company's employees signed a petition seeking de-certification of the union. The company assisted them in taking the petition to the NLRB regional office and refused to bargain with the union over a new collective bargaining agreement. This resulted in unfair labor practice charges. The company then bargained for five sessions, until the parties were close to a new agreement, at which time it refused to bargain further (after receiving another petition stating that employees wanted to de-certify the union). It withdrew its recognition of the union and made unilateral changes to terms and conditions of employment. New unfair labor practice charges were filed, and the NLRB ruled that where an employer refuses to bargain with an incumbent union and the union loses support, there is a presumption that the loss of support was the result of the employer's unlawful conduct. The presumption can be rebutted by showing that the employees' disaffection with the union occurred after the company resumed recognition of the union; and **the company had to bargain for a reasonable period of time (at least six months, but not more than one year)** without committing additional unfair labor practices before the union's majority status could be challenged. The NLRB ordered the company to "cease and desist from further unlawful refusals to bargain." The U.S. Court of Appeals, D.C. Circuit, enforced the NLRB's order, finding that it was neither arbitrary nor unsupported by substantial evidence. *Lee Lumber and Building Material Corp. v. NLRB*, 310 F.3d 209 (D.C. Cir. 2002).

◆ A full-time union organizer applied for a job with a Florida nonunion contractor. He informed the interviewer of his intention to try to unionize the work force if he was hired, and the contractor refused to hire him. Five years later, the NLRB determined that the contractor's refusal to hire the organizer was an unfair labor practice under the NLRA. It ordered that the organizer be "made whole." The contractor then offered the organizer a job, which he left after five weeks during an unfair labor practices strike. He never offered to return to work and did not seek reinstatement. After a compliance hearing on the issue of back pay for the organizer, an administrative law judge awarded only five weeks of back pay. The NLRB reversed, ordering five years' worth of back pay. The Fourth Circuit Court of Appeals held that **the NLRB had abused its discretion in making such a large award** in light of evidence that the organizer would not have stayed in the job for five years. He would only have stayed long enough to determine if the prospects for organizing were good. The court remanded the case for the NLRB to fashion a more appropriate remedy. *Aneco, Inc. v. NLRB*, 285 F.3d 326 (4th Cir. 2002).

- After a company solicited employees to appear in an anti-union video, the union filed charges with the NLRB, alleging unfair labor practices and objectionable conduct. A question then arose as to **how companies can go about soliciting employees to appear in anti-union videos**. The NLRB came up with five requirements that companies need to follow: 1) solicit through a general announcement disclosing the purpose of the video, and assure that non-participation will not result in reprisal and that participation will not be rewarded, 2) don't pressure employees in the presence of a supervisor, 3) don't engage in coercive conduct when making the announcement, 4) don't create a coercive atmosphere, and 5) don't seek information that might violate an employee's rights under the NLRA. The Third Circuit upheld the NLRB's test and ruled that the company failed the test because it forced employees to make an observable choice demonstrating their support for or rejection of the union, and it failed to assure employees that there would be no reprisals or benefits. Even though the company did not intend to "poll" employees about their union sentiments, its subjective intent was not an element of the definition of "polling" under the NLRA. *Allegheny Ludlum Corp. v. NLRB*, 301 F.3d 167 (3d Cir. 2002).

- A company operated a manufacturing plant in Oklahoma that made and distributed steel tubing. **The plant employed about 400 nonunion workers and had a no-solicitation policy that it did not enforce uniformly.** For example, it allowed employees to sell candy for their children or to solicit co-workers to join the football pool during working hours. However, when several employees allegedly solicited co-workers to join a union during working hours, the plant manager disciplined them. Unfair labor practice charges were filed, and the NLRB found that the company had violated Sections 8(a)(1) and (3) of the NLRA. The Tenth Circuit affirmed, noting that it did not matter whether the company believed it was acting in good faith by enforcing the no-solicitation policy. Further, the company's assertions that it had acted in good faith were not convincing. Also, the company president had given a plant-wide speech that was anti-union after disciplining the employees for their alleged union activity. *WEBCO Industries, Inc. v. NLRB*, 217 F.3d 1306 (10th Cir. 2000).

- A food-processing company resisted organization efforts by employees at a Wisconsin plant. Its president made an anti-union speech and promised employees a general wage increase about one month prior to a union election. The employer made changes in its overtime and attendance policies that were favorable to employees, and a shift supervisor discouraged an employee from speaking out in favor of the union. After the union lost the election, it filed an unfair labor practice charge with the NLRB. While the action was still pending, the employer granted a 5% wage increase to production employees, far more than had ever been granted in the 10 previous years. The NLRB held in favor of the union and ordered a new election. The Seventh Circuit observed that **the award of economic benefits had occurred at a critical time during an election period in a manner that violated federal labor law**. The promise of a pay raise during an organizational campaign qualified as an unfair labor practice, and the promised wage increase was inconsistent with prior plant history. The court upheld the NLRB's order. *NLRB v. Wis-Pak Foods, Inc.*, 125 F.3d 518 (7th Cir. 1997).

◆ A Massachusetts employer recognized a union as the collective bargaining representative of its employees and negotiated a series of agreements with it over an 11-year period. Contract negotiations for a new agreement were unsuccessful, and employees struck for over a month. The employer then made an acceptable contract offer. The union accepted by telegraph. The following day, the employer disavowed the agreement and denied any duty to continue bargaining with the union, claiming that 13 of the 23 bargaining unit employees had resigned from the union and that nine of them had crossed the picket line during the strike. The union filed a complaint with the NLRB, which determined that a contract existed between the parties and that the employer's action violated the NLRA. It ordered the employer to reduce the agreement to writing. The First Circuit enforced the NLRB order, and the U.S. Supreme Court affirmed. Under prior NLRB decisions, **collective bargaining organizations were entitled to a presumption of majority status for one year following certification and for up to three years during the term of any bargaining agreement**. The employer could not raise the issue of majority support after the acceptance of a collective bargaining agreement because to do so would give the employer an unfair advantage in contract negotiations. The Court required the employer to bargain. *Auciello Iron Works, Inc. v. NLRB*, 517 U.S. 781, 116 S.Ct. 1754, 135 L.Ed.2d 64 (1996).

E. Union Elections

The NLRB has wide discretion in establishing procedures to ensure the fair and free choice of bargaining representatives by employees. However, it cannot act arbitrarily and capriciously in doing so.

Employers can withdraw recognition from a union, or conduct an internal poll of employee support for a union, only where they have a good-faith reasonable doubt about the union's majority support. They may also request a formal, NLRB-supervised election where they doubt a union enjoys majority support.

◆ The managers of a Pennsylvania truck parts and service factory branch purchased the branch and began operating it. They hired 32 of the 45 branch employees and learned that eight of them had expressed doubt about support for their existing union. The new employer rejected the union's request for recognition as the employees' bargaining representative and then conducted a poll that resulted in a 19-13 loss by the union. The NLRB determined that the employer had inherited the branch's bargaining obligation under the presumption of continuing majority support. The poll was unlawful because the employer had no objective reasonable doubt about continuing majority support for the union. It ordered the employer to recognize and bargain with the union. The U.S. Court of Appeals enforced the order.

The U.S. Supreme Court upheld the NLRB's standard for reviewing employer polling, even though it resembled the high standard required for evaluating an employer's withdrawal of recognition. However, the NLRB's decision in this case was contrary to the standard since at least 20% of the employees had expressed doubt about continuing support for the union. The NLRB had disregarded important statements by two employees who had stated that the union would not win an election, supporting the inference of reasonable uncertainty by the employer. Because **the employer had a reasonable, good-faith ground to doubt the union's majority support**, the Court reversed the judgment and remanded the case with instructions to deny enforcement of the NLRB's order. *Allentown Mack Sales and Service, Inc. v. NLRB*, 522 U.S. 359, 118 S.Ct. 818, 139 L.Ed.2d 797 (1998).

- The NLRB certified a local union in Washington as the collective bargaining representative of a bank's employees. Eight years later, in an election in which only union members were allowed to vote, the local voted to affiliate with an international labor organization. It then petitioned the NLRB to amend its certification to reflect this change. The NLRB initially granted the petition, finding that the bank had committed an unfair labor practice by refusing to bargain with the new entity. Eventually it decided that, because nonunion employees had not been allowed to vote in the affiliation election, the election did not meet minimal due process standards. It found the affiliation invalid. The U.S. Court of Appeals, Ninth Circuit, remanded the case because it deemed the NLRB's requirement that nonunion employees be allowed to vote on affiliation questions inconsistent with the NLRA. The U.S. Supreme Court affirmed the Ninth Circuit's decision, holding that **the NLRB had exceeded its authority in requiring that nonunion employees be allowed to vote for affiliation** before it would order the employer to bargain with the affiliated union. *NLRB v. Financial Institution Employees of America Local 1182,* 475 U.S. 192, 106 S.Ct. 1007, 89 L.Ed.2d 151 (1986).

- After 57 of 91 union-eligible employees of a California company signed union authorization cards, the company disciplined and fired two employees because of their support for the union. It also disciplined a third employee and threatened a fourth. When the election was held, only 37 of 79 votes cast were in favor of representation by the union. The union filed an unfair labor practice charge with the NLRB, and an administrative law judge (ALJ) found that the company had violated the NLRA. The ALJ recommended a number of remedies, including reinstatement of the fired workers and a *Gissel* order requiring the company to recognize and bargain with the union. The NLRB affirmed the ALJ's recommendations except for the *Gissel* order. Instead, the NLRB determined that the other remedies would enable the union to get a fair rerun election, and satisfactorily protect and restore employees' section 7 rights. The case reached the Ninth Circuit, which held that **the NLRB did not abuse its discretion in refusing to impose the extreme remedy of a *Gissel* order on the company**. *United Steel Workers of America AFL-CIO-CLC v. NLRB*, 482 F.3d 1112 (9th Cir. 2007).

◆ Shortly before a union election at a Virginia plant, a union circulated a "vote yes" petition, after a voluntary meeting where a union representative told employees that everyone should sign the petition. After several employees complained that they felt intimidated by the union's actions, the company sent out a memo in which it characterized the "vote yes" petition as a straw vote, and emphasized that regardless of whether employees felt pressured to sign the petition, they should not feel pressured to vote for the union. The memo told employees they had an "absolute right to vote NO" in the election. When employees voted for union representation, the company refused to bargain with the local, and the international union filed an unfair labor practices charge. The NLRB found in favor of the union, and the Fourth Circuit Court of Appeals granted its request for an enforcement order. Although employers cannot poll employees prior to a union election, unions can – provided their actions are not coercive. Here, a reasonable employee would not have felt "intimidated, threatened or coerced" because **the company sent out a memo countering the union's allegedly coercive actions**. *NLRB v. Media General Operations*, 360 F.3d 434 (4th Cir. 2004).

◆ Prior to a union election, an organizer for the Communications Workers of America invited the employees of a Michigan cable company to Chicago for a two-hour meeting on cable industry issues. The meeting was to take place on the weekend after the election and the union promised to pick up all the expenses for the weekend (about $50 per person). After the employees voted 31 to 17 in favor of the union, the company refused to bargain. The union filed an unfair labor practice charge with the NLRB, which ruled in its favor. The Sixth Circuit Court of Appeals reversed the ruling and invalidated the election. It found that **the offer of a free weekend in Chicago had the potential to influence employees' votes**. Earlier cases had invalidated elections where unions had given away benefits that were far less substantial. *Comcast Cablevision-Taylor v. NLRB*, 232 F.3d 490 (6th Cir. 2000).

◆ After a California concrete manufacturer's contract with a local teamsters bargaining unit expired, the unit went on strike. The manufacturer hired replacement workers who signed a de-certification petition. The company then withdrew its recognition of the union. The union filed unfair labor charges with the NLRB, asserting that the company's requirement that replacement employees list their union affiliation on the job application form illegally coerced them into signing the union de-certification petition. An administrative law judge (ALJ) held that the inquiry into union membership of replacement applicants and a manager's later interrogation of a replacement driver each violated Section 8(a)(1) of the NLRA. The ALJ concluded, however, that neither violation tainted the signatures supporting de-certification. The Board reversed, and the company appealed to the D.C. Circuit Court of Appeals. Finding **no causal connection between the application form and the decertification petition**, the court held for the company. Nothing about the way the request for union information in the form was presented would draw attention to it or suggest that it would leave a memorable impression. *Mathews Readymix, Inc. v. NLRB*, 165 F.3d 74 (D.C. Cir. 1999).

◆ A union local won an election at an Atlanta transportation service center by a wide margin. However, the employer refused to bargain with the union, accusing it of unlawfully conducting video and photographic surveillance of employees within the election area. The employer stated that the union had intimidated and coerced employees by conducting a raucous rally within the hearing of a polling station and within sight of employees waiting to vote. The union stated that it had only conducted a cookout that was not characterized by electioneering. The NLRB found that the employer unlawfully refused to bargain with the union and certified the union as the exclusive bargaining representative for the employees. The employer appealed to the U.S. Court of Appeals, D.C. Circuit, arguing that the video and photo surveillance had interfered with the election and required setting it aside. The union stated that the activity was not attributable to it but rather to certain union-supporting employees and that a lower standard for third-party conduct applied, requiring enforcement of its order. The court stated that **misconduct attributable to third parties may result in the setting aside of a union election only where it is so aggravated as to create a general atmosphere of fear and reprisal**. The alleged misconduct did not create an atmosphere of fear and reprisal so as to require setting aside the election. The court enforced the NLRB's order. *Overnite Transportation Co. v. NLRB*, 140 F.3d 259 (D.C. Cir. 1998).

◆ A Pennsylvania employer complained of **pro-union songs blaring from a truck loudspeaker parked at a plant on the day of a union election**. It refused to negotiate with the union after the election. An administrative law judge found that the employer did not commit an unfair labor practice by doing so. The NLRB disagreed, finding that the campaign songs did not constitute campaign speech because the songs were void of specific campaign promises. The U.S. Court of Appeals, Third Circuit, reversed the decision of the NLRB, holding that it was inconsistent with earlier NLRB determinations. The court observed that music might appeal to the visceral emotions of workers and have a potentially larger impact upon them than an actual speech. The court refused to enforce the NLRB's order requiring the employer to bargain with the union. *Bro-Tech Corp. v. NLRB*, 105 F.3d 890 (3d Cir. 1997).

◆ An election was held to determine whether a union should represent certain employees of a Pennsylvania manufacturer. One employee voting in the election had been absent from work for five months due to a work-related injury. The union won the election by only one vote, and the NLRB certified the result. The employer refused to bargain, stating that the certification was invalid because of the injured employee's participation. The union filed an unfair labor practice charge against the employer, and the NLRB ruled for the union. The employer appealed to the Third Circuit, arguing that it had sent the injured employee a notice of termination of medical benefits pursuant to COBRA, removed him from the payroll and replaced him with another employee. It asserted that the NLRB's test for laid-off employees should be applied, based on the lack of a reasonable expectation of his return to work. The court found that the COBRA notice and replacement action were insufficient to indicate formal termination. There was contrary evidence that the employee expected to return to work and had never been notified of his discharge. The reasonable expectation test used by the NLRB in layoff cases was not proper. **The NLRB used a separate test for employees who were absent from work due to medical reasons.** That test imposes a presumption of voting eligibility until the employer affirmatively shows that the employee has been discharged or has resigned. The court affirmed the NLRB's order. *Cavert Acquisition Co. v. NLRB*, 83 F.3d 598 (3d Cir. 1996).

- A management employee of a New England pharmaceutical distributor gave speeches discouraging unionization and referred to possible closure of the warehouse, loss of jobs and loss of benefits should the union win an election. The union won the election by three votes; however, the vote of regular employees was evenly split. The distributor contested votes cast by temporary employees, asserting that they had no community of interest with regular employees sufficient to allow them to vote in the election. When the distributor refused to bargain, the NLRB issued a bargaining order to recognize the union. The Second Circuit stated that a bargaining order is a rare administrative remedy that is to be used only when other remedies cannot eliminate an employer's unfair labor practices. Here, the management employee had a right to tell employees his opinion of the economic consequences of unionization. The only unfair labor practice of the employer was a threat of discharge that had later been retracted. Because of this mitigating factor, the NLRB had inappropriately issued a bargaining order. There was a genuine fact issue concerning **whether some of the temporary employees had a community of interest sufficient to allow them to vote**. The NLRB was required to either order a new election or reconsider the validity of the temporary employees' ballots. *Kinney Drugs, Inc. v. NLRB*, 74 F.3d 1419 (2d Cir. 1996).

- A paper manufacturer and two unions representing employees of a Maine paper mill were unable to renegotiate their collective bargaining agreement, and union members engaged in an economic strike. The company hired replacement workers and laid off 151 striking union employees. Some of the union employees petitioned the NLRB to hold an election to de-certify the union. Prior to the election, the unions ended the strike with an unconditional offer to return to work. The parties entered into an agreement to recall former strikers when positions occupied by replacement workers became available. The union members then voted for de-certification. The manufacturer advised the unions and some of the laid off employees that they no longer had recall rights under the agreement. The unions sued in a Maine federal court, arguing that the recall agreement had survived the de-certification election and remained binding. The court held for the manufacturer, and the First Circuit affirmed. It found **no**

evidence that the parties had contemplated the survival of the recall agreement in the event of de-certification. *United Paperworkers Int'l, Local 14 v. Int'l Paper Co.*, 64 F.3d 28 (1st Cir. 1995).

F. Arbitration

This section addresses arbitration in the context of labor relations. For cases involving arbitration with respect to other employment issues, see Chapter Six, Section VI.

The Supreme Court has found a presumption of arbitrability with respect to collective bargaining agreements (CBAs) in Section 301 of the Labor Management Relations Act (LMRA), noting that arbitrators are in a better position than courts to interpret the terms of a CBA.

However, where the question is not one of interpreting a CBA but rather a federal statute, the presumption in favor of arbitrability fails.

- The U.S. Supreme Court held that **a collective bargaining agreement's general arbitration clause did not require a covered employee to use arbitration to redress alleged violations of the Americans with Disabilities Act (ADA)**. The Court left open the question of whether such a clause would be enforceable if it provided a clear and unmistakable waiver to redress those rights in federal court. The case involved a longshoreman who brought suit under the ADA. A South Carolina federal court dismissed the case because the longshoreman had failed to pursue his administrative remedies. However, the Supreme Court held that the general arbitration clause was not specific enough to require arbitration. The Court also refused to reconcile two earlier Supreme Court cases on arbitration: *Alexander v. Gardner-Denver Co.*, 415 U.S. 36 (1974), where the Court held that an individual subject to a collective bargaining agreement's arbitration clause does not forfeit his or her right to sue in court for discriminatory discharge under Title VII, and *Gilmer v. Interstate/Johnson Lane Corp.*, 500 U.S. 20 (1991), where the Court held that a security broker's federal age discrimination claim could be subject to compulsory arbitration under a clause in the security registration form that the broker had to sign in order to work. *Wright v. Universal Maritime Service Corp*, 525 U.S. 70, 119 S.Ct. 391, 142 L.Ed.2d 361 (1998).

- The collective bargaining agreement between an airline and a union included an agency shop clause, under which nonunion pilots had to pay a monthly agency fee of 81% of union dues. The fee was based only on expenditures attributable to collective bargaining. A number of nonunion pilots sued the union, asserting that the agency fee overstated collective bargaining expenses. Union policies and procedures provided for the arbitration of fee calculations, but the bargaining agreement did not specify arbitration. The union treated objections to the fee calculation as requests for arbitration and referred them to an arbitrator, who consolidated the cases and recalculated the agency fee. The union then moved for pretrial judgment, asserting that the pilots were required to exhaust their arbitral remedies before filing suit. The court agreed, finding that 62 pilots who had not joined the arbitration were bound by the decision. The U.S. Court of Appeals, D.C. Circuit, reversed.

The U.S. Supreme Court noted that *Chicago Teachers Union v. Hudson*, 475 U.S. 292 (1986), required public employee unions to provide objecting employees a reasonably prompt opportunity to challenge the amount of an agency fee by appeal to an impartial decision maker. This rule did not require a party to accept arbitration where no arbitration agreement existed, since arbitration is a matter of contract. The requirement of an impartial decision maker did not bar the dissenting pilots' immediate resort to federal court. **The Court rejected the union's assertion that arbitration was necessary to assure a prompt decision by an impartial decision maker.** The Court affirmed the court of appeals. *Air Line Pilots Ass'n v. Miller*, 523 U.S. 866, 118 S.Ct. 1761, 140 L.Ed.2d 1070 (1998).

- A Michigan company discharged two employees for "just cause," and the employees disputed this. They believed there had been no just cause as required by the collective bargaining agreement. They invoked the agreement's grievance procedures without success and then filed suit against the company under Section 301 of the Labor Management Relations Act. A federal court granted pretrial judgment to the company, and the Sixth Circuit affirmed, holding that a strike or other job action is the proper remedy for failure to successfully resolve a grievance where arbitration is not required. The U.S. Supreme Court reversed the appellate court's ruling. It noted that Section 301 provides a federal remedy for breach of a labor agreement and that there was **a strong presumption that the federal courts would provide access for the peaceful resolution of labor disputes**. Here, since the parties had not agreed to arbitration, a neutral forum would be provided. Even though the collective bargaining agreement allowed strikes or lockouts upon exhaustion of the grievance process, this did not mean that the employees had to resort to such economic weapons as strikes. The Court remanded the case for further proceedings. *Groves v. Ring Screw Works*, 498 U.S. 168, 111 S.Ct. 498, 112 L.Ed.2d 508 (1990).

- A carman, employed by a railroad, brought a lawsuit against the railroad under the Federal Employers' Liability Act (FELA). He claimed that fellow employees had harassed, threatened and intimidated him, causing him emotional injury, and that the railroad had condoned these acts. The railroad asserted that the employee's sole remedy was through the National Railroad Adjustment Board, according to the Railway Labor Act (RLA). The U.S. Supreme Court held that **although the injury at issue might have been subject to arbitration under the RLA** (a dispute arising out of workplace conditions which was similar to a "minor" labor dispute), it was also possibly the type of injury that the FELA was enacted to address. The Court remanded the case for a determination of whether emotional injury was cognizable under the FELA. *Atchison, Topeka and Santa Fe Railway Co. v. Buell,* 480 U.S. 557, 107 S.Ct. 1410, 94 L.Ed.2d 563 (1987).

◆ A California grocery clerk worked under a collective bargaining agreement that called for binding arbitration to resolve disputes arising from termination or suspension. After the employer fired the clerk, it refused to comply with her demand for the immediate payment of wages owed. Full payment was made by mail three days later. When the clerk filed a claim for a penalty, the California Division of Labor Standards Enforcement (DLSE) refused to take action to enforce the claim, advising her by letter that it did not resolve disputes arising from bargaining agreements that contained arbitration clauses. The clerk sued under 42 U.S.C. § 1983, claiming that the DLSE's policy violated her rights under the NLRA. The U.S. Supreme Court held that **the issue of whether the employer had willfully failed to pay the clerk's wages was independent of the bargaining agreement** and was a matter of state law. It was unnecessary to look to the bargaining agreement except to compute damages. Therefore, there was no federal preemption of the state law claim. The employee was entitled to relief under Section 1983 for violation of her rights under the NLRA. *Livadas v. Bradshaw*, 512 U.S. 107, 114 S.Ct. 2068, 129 L.Ed.2d 93 (1994).

◆ A corporation operated a check-printing plant in California. After the collective bargaining agreement expired, 10 of the plant's employees were laid off. The union filed grievances, claiming a violation of the agreement. The corporation refused to process the grievances or submit to arbitration. The NLRB determined that the corporation had violated the NLRA and ordered it to process the grievances and to bargain with the union over the layoffs, but it refused to order arbitration. The Ninth Circuit enforced the NLRB's order except that it found the layoff grievance arbitrable. The corporation appealed to the U.S. Supreme Court, which held that the layoff dispute was not arbitrable. It refused to impose a statutory duty on the corporation to arbitrate a post-expiration dispute. **Arbitration will not be imposed if to do so would go beyond the scope of the parties' consent.** Further, since the layoff dispute did not arise under the collective bargaining agreement, its arbitration provisions could not be used to force arbitration. *Litton Financial Printing v. NLRB*, 501 U.S. 190, 111 S.Ct. 2215, 115 L.Ed.2d 177 (1991).

◆ A union entered into an agreement with a healthcare company setting forth rules governing the parties' conduct during a union organizational drive. One of the promises the company made was that it would not imply that employees would lose benefits, wages or be subject to less favorable working conditions by unionizing. After the union lost the election, it sent a letter to the company, charging it with engaging in 18 incidents that violated the pre-election agreement, including granting more favorable working conditions to employees on the hospital's "Vote No" committee. When it sought to arbitrate the dispute, the company denied the request. The union sued to compel arbitration, and a California federal court dismissed the case.

The Ninth Circuit Court of Appeals reversed, noting that **arbitration should have been ordered because the heart of the case was contractual** and not representational. Under Section 301 of the LMRA, federal courts have jurisdiction over cases involving the violation of private labor agreements. Since the agreement called for arbitration, the district court should have compelled arbitration. *Service Employees Int'l Union v. St. Vincent Medical Center*, 344 F.3d 977 (9th Cir. 2003).

◆ A manufacturer employed a unionized work force at an Illinois engine plant. A plant employee who was fired filed a grievance under the collective bargaining agreement. He then requested an arbitration hearing to challenge the action. A plant manager testified at the arbitration hearing that the employee slept on the job and falsified employment records. When the employee sued the manager and former employer for defamation, the court dismissed the case, ruling that the manager and former employer were protected by absolute immunity for their statements in the arbitration proceeding. The employee appealed to the Appellate Court of Illinois, which followed the majority of jurisdictions and held that **absolute immunity protects witnesses testifying before grievance and arbitration hearings**. The prospect of criminal prosecution for perjury acted as a check against false statements before an arbitrator. The court affirmed the dismissal of the case. *Bushell v. Caterpillar, Inc.*, 683 N.E.2d 1286 (Ill. App. Ct. 1997).

◆ The union representing steelworkers at a Missouri plant negotiated a collective bargaining agreement containing a "contracting out" prohibition. Under the agreement, the employer was forbidden from contracting out work that was normally performed by employees where there was appropriate equipment and time, and enough qualified employees to perform the work. The employer nonetheless transferred work from the Missouri plant to a nonunion Illinois facility that it operated, resulting in layoffs and other adverse effects for 60 employees. The union sought arbitration, and the arbitrator agreed that intra-corporate transfers of work violated the contracting out prohibition. The U.S. Court of Appeals, Eighth Circuit, observed **that an arbitrator's interpretation of a collective bargaining agreement is entitled to extreme judicial deference** so long as it is not unlawful and draws its essence from the bargaining agreement. Because the arbitrator's decision drew its essence from the bargaining agreement, the court upheld it. *American National Can Co. v. United Steelworkers of America*, 120 F.3d 886 (8th Cir. 1997).

◆ The U.S. Court of Appeals, Second Circuit, held that a federal court had improperly refused to enforce an arbitration order requiring the conditional reinstatement of a New York nuclear power employee who adulterated a urine sample and then tested positive for cocaine use. The conditional reinstatement did not violate public policy, as the lower court had held. **The public policy exception to the finality of arbitration awards is limited**, the Supreme Court has held, to cases where a labor contract or arbitration award actually violates laws or legal precedent. This was not such a case, since federal nuclear regulations do not require the discharge of employees who adulterate a drug test or submit a single positive test. The regulations specify a two-week suspension, encouraging employee retention and rehabilitation. The employer had never discharged an employee for a single positive drug test, and the award did not conflict with nuclear safety goals. *Int'l Brotherhood of Electrical Workers v. Niagara Mohawk Power Corp.*, 143 F.3d 704 (2d Cir. 1998).

◆ An Alabama employer established a peer review panel to review management actions for compliance with corporate policy. However, a management board had the power to overturn its decisions. A truck operator whose job was classified as safety critical violated a substance abuse screening policy twice and was discharged in accordance with company rules. He appealed his termination to the company's peer review panel, which determined that the cutoff level for the substance abuse policy was set too low and that he should be reinstated with back wages if he passed another drug test. The panel's decision was set aside by the management board as an abuse of power, and the employee sued. The Supreme Court of Alabama **rejected the employee's argument that the peer review panel was a form of arbitration that was entitled to judicial deference**. An internal grievance procedure is not arbitration, and the panel's decision was not entitled to deference. The peer review panel exceeded the scope of its authority by challenging the employer's substance abuse policy. *Hobson v. American Cast Iron Pipe Co.*, 690 So.2d 341 (Ala. 1997).

◆ A Texas power company laid off 1,100 workers. A laid-off heavy equipment operator filed a grievance through his union, asserting that the employer had violated the seniority provision of the parties' collective bargaining agreement by retaining less-senior employees. The matter went to arbitration, where the union challenged the evaluation process used by the employer as arbitrary and unreasonable. The arbitrator determined that the employer had unreasonably applied the evaluation procedure to the employee by giving him low rankings. The arbitrator reevaluated the employee and ordered him reinstated with back pay and seniority. The U.S. Court of Appeals, Fifth Circuit, found that the company retained the right to evaluate employee performance under the bargaining agreement, subject to an employee's right to assert a grievance. **The arbitrator had exceeded his authority by reevaluating the employee.** *Houston Lighting & Power Co. v. Int'l Brotherhood of Electrical Workers*, 71 F.3d 179 (5th Cir. 1995).

III. LABOR ASSOCIATIONS AND COLLECTIVE BARGAINING AGREEMENTS

Labor associations may be liable to their members for unfair labor practices under the National Labor Relations Act (NLRA) and may also be liable for violating the Labor Management Relations Act (LMRA), which requires labor associations (unions) to act on behalf of their members in good faith and to fairly represent them.

A labor association that engages in conduct that is arbitrary, discriminatory, or in bad faith may be liable for breach of the duty of good faith and fair representation of its membership. Unions also have a duty, when collecting fees from nonmembers, to use those fees only for collective bargaining.

A. Agency Fees and Union Security Agreements

The NLRA permits parties to a collective bargaining agreement to include union shop clauses under which the employer agrees to condition employment in a bargaining unit upon union membership. However, the U.S. Supreme Court has held that employers may not compel employees to support a union's political activities through their union dues.

Dissenting employees may avoid union membership by paying an agency fee, which is the portion of union dues representing only union expenditures for collective bargaining activities.

◆ The U.S. Supreme Court held that **a union does not breach its duty of fair representation by negotiating as part of its collective bargaining agreement a union security clause that tracks the language of Section 8(a)(3) of the NLRA**. A union cannot be said to be acting arbitrarily or in bad faith by failing to explain in the clause that membership is required only insofar as the "member" is required to pay fees used to support the union's collective bargaining activities. The case involved a part-time actress who obtained a one-line role in a television series. After she accepted the part, the Screen Actors Guild required her to pay the $500 union fees before she could start working. When she failed to pay the amount by the first day, she was replaced. She sued the Screen Actors Guild for violating its duty of fair representation. The Supreme Court held that her claim could not succeed. By tracking the statutory language, the clause incorporated all of the judicial fine-tuning that has been associated with it in cases like *Beck*, below. *Marquez v. Screen Actors Guild*, 525 U.S. 33, 119 S.Ct. 292, 142 L.Ed.2d 242 (1998).

◆ Employees of a Maryland company, who chose not to become union members, were required to pay the union agency fees under the applicable collective bargaining agreement. A group of these employees sued the union, challenging its use of agency fees for purposes other than collective bargaining. A federal court found that such expenditures violated the First Amendment rights of nonmembers and enjoined the collection of fees for purposes other than collective bargaining. The U.S. Court of Appeals, Fourth Circuit, agreed that the **agency fees could not be used for non-representational purposes**, but based its ruling on Section 8(a)(3) of the NLRA. The U.S. Supreme Court affirmed, finding that Section 8(a)(3) did not permit a union to expend funds collected from nonmember employees, over objection, on activities unrelated to collective bargaining. *Communications Workers of America v. Beck*, 487 U.S. 735, 108 S.Ct. 2641, 101 L.Ed.2d 634 (1988).

◆ A mechanic for TWA was subject to the collective bargaining agreement's union security clause, meaning he had to either join the union or pay an agency service fee (under which he would not be paying for any political activities of the union). After initially joining the union and having his union dues deducted from his paycheck, the mechanic requested that he be placed on agency fee payer status. The union complied, and TWA stopped deducting his union dues from his paycheck. However, he then stated that he would only pay the agency fees if they were deducted from his paycheck; he would not write a separate check to the union to cover his agency fees. He was fired for violating the bargaining agreement and sued under the Railway Labor Act (RLA) and the First Amendment. A Missouri federal court ruled against him, and the Eighth Circuit affirmed. Here, the RLA allowed TWA and the union to negotiate a check-off procedure that best suited their interests, and **nothing in the bargaining agreement required TWA to deduct agency fees**. Also, there was no First Amendment violation because the refusal to offer payroll deduction did not infringe on the mechanic's speech or association rights. *Conrad v. Int'l Ass'n of Machinists*, 338 F.3d 908 (8th Cir. 2003).

◆ A clerical worker in Virginia was employed by a company that withheld union dues and initiation fees from his paycheck without his authorization. The collective bargaining agreement required employees to become and remain union members in good standing under a security clause that required full union membership. When the worker requested a breakdown of how his union dues were being spent, he was not told that he could object to the withholding of fees for non-representational activities and could only be compelled to pay the amount spent on representational activities. He was instead threatened with employment termination if he failed to become a union member. He filed an unfair labor practices charge against the employer and union with the NLRB. The employer and union settled the matter with the NLRB, and the U.S. Court of Appeals, Eighth Circuit, held that the settlement was proper. **A security clause can track the language of Section 8(a)(3) of the NLRA, using terms of art that employees may not understand without further explanation.** *Bloom v. NLRB*, 209 F.3d 1060 (8th Cir. 2000).

◆ A number of nonunion machinists whose bargaining units were represented by a union filed a complaint with the National Labor Relations Board (NLRB), challenging the union's assessment of dues. They claimed that the union should not be allowed to pool expenditures among all workers in the union, arguing that the agency fee should be limited to expenses from their own bargaining unit. They also claimed that audits should be performed by certified public accountants rather than union employees, and that the union had failed to properly notify them of their right to avoid union membership. The NLRB issued an order specifying procedures by which the union had to protect the dissenting employees' rights but upholding the union's pooling of expenditures, audit method and notification of rights through a union newsletter. It agreed with the dissenting machinists that the union could not require the payment of full union dues for the rest of the year for union members who quit after the "window" period. The U.S. Court of Appeals, Seventh Circuit, found a reasonable basis for the NLRB's decision as to each issue. **It was appropriate to allow the pooling of expenditures given the interdependence of each bargaining unit in the union**, and the notice to employees was reasonably calculated to notify employees of their rights. The court enforced the order. *Int'l Ass'n of Machinists and Aerospace Workers v. NLRB*, 133 F.3d 1012 (7th Cir. 1998).

- An employee of a New York aircraft manufacturer decided to resign from the union after more than 20 years of membership. Because union membership was a condition of continued employment under the union security clause, he had to pay almost 80% of normal union dues as "membership" dues despite resigning from the union. The dues deduction authorization he originally signed provided for a 10-day window each year during which he could revoke it. He attempted to revoke the payroll deduction authorization despite the passage of the revocation window period for that year. The company honored his demand, and the union filed a grievance against the company. The employee filed a complaint with the NLRB, asserting that the union had committed an unfair labor practice in violation of the NLRA, which prohibits unions from causing an employer to discriminate against an employee. The NLRB determined that the union action did not constitute an unfair labor practice, and the U.S. Court of Appeals, Second Circuit, agreed that **the employee's fee should be deducted from his wages by the employer until he made a timely revocation**. *Williams v. NLRB*, 105 F.3d 787 (2d Cir. 1997).

- An employee who worked in a unionized facility complained that the union security agreement in place violated the NLRA by ambiguously requiring bargaining unit employees to become union members "in good standing." The NLRB agreed with the employee, stating that the union's failure to disclose that employees could not be required to participate in a union beyond the payment of dues and fees constituted an unfair labor practice. The U.S. Court of Appeals, D.C. Circuit, observed that **the NLRB's decision had reversed a longstanding policy of tolerating such ambiguous notices to employees**. There was also a complete lack of evidence that the union had acted in bad faith, which was a requirement of any unfair labor practice charge. Although the NLRB was free to adopt a new policy, it could only have prospective application and could not constitute grounds to support the unfair representation complaint in this case. *Int'l Union of Electronic, Electrical, Salaried, Machine and Furniture Workers v. NLRB*, 41 F.3d 1532 (D.C. Cir. 1994).

B. Union Representational Duties

The Supreme court has held that Section 301(a) of the Labor Management Relations Act (LMRA), 29 U.S.C. § 185, authorizes lawsuits by and against individual employees as well as between unions and employers, including actions against employers for wrongful discharge.

Unions have a <u>duty of fair representation</u>, which is inferred from their exclusive authority under the NLRA to represent all employees in a bargaining unit. This duty requires unions "to serve the interests of all members without hostility or discrimination toward any [individual member], to exercise [their] discretion with complete good faith and honesty, and to avoid arbitrary conduct." *Vaca v. Sipes*, 386 U.S. 171, 87 S.Ct. 903, 17 L.Ed.2d 842 (1967).

Hybrid lawsuits brought under Section 301 of the LMRA assert breach of contract against the employer and breach of the duty of fair representation against the union. In such actions, employees need to show not only that the employer breached the collective bargaining agreement, but also that the union breached its duty of fair representation to the employee.

1. Unfair Labor Practices

It is an unfair labor practice for a union to restrain or coerce an employer in the selection of its representatives for the purposes of collective bargaining or the adjustment of grievances. A union also cannot restrict the right of employees to resign from the union.

◆ A union representing employees at a Pennsylvania manufacturing plant claimed that their employer fraudulently induced them to enter into a bargaining agreement that prohibited strikes for any reason. According to the union, absent the employer's fraud, it would not have entered into either the bargaining agreement or a separate memorandum agreement requiring the employer to give the union a seven-day notice prior to subcontracting out work. The union made the assertion after the employer announced its intention to contract out work, which would cause many union members to lose their jobs. A federal court dismissed the complaint as not arising under the LMRA since it alleged no violation of a labor contract. The U.S. Supreme Court agreed, noting that **the LMRA limits federal court jurisdiction to lawsuits for violations of labor contracts, not claims asserting that a contract is invalid**. This case had no purpose or object of demonstrating a violation of any contract, as the union argued. The bargaining agreement had already expired. *Textron Lycoming, AVCO Corp. v. United Automobile, Aerospace and AI Workers of America*, 523 U.S. 653, 118 S.Ct. 1626, 140 L.Ed.2d 863 (1998).

◆ A labor union fined two of its members who worked as supervisors for violating its constitution by working for employers who did not have collective bargaining agreements with the union. The employers then filed unfair labor practice charges with the NLRB, alleging that the union had violated Section 8(b)(1)(B) of the NLRA by restraining or coercing an employer in the selection of its representatives for the purposes of collective bargaining or the adjustment of grievances. An administrative law judge agreed with the employers, and the board entered an order against the union. However, the U.S. Court of Appeals reversed. The U.S. Supreme Court held that **discipline of a supervisor union member is prohibited under Section 8(b)(1)(B) only when that member is engaged in Section 8(b)(1)(B) activities**, like collective bargaining and grievance adjustment, or some other closely related activity. Since neither supervisor had such responsibilities, the union discipline was not an unfair labor practice. Further, the absence of a bargaining relationship between the union and the employers made the possibility of employer coercion too attenuated to form the basis of an unfair labor practice charge. Finally, the employers were not coerced by reason of the supervisors being fined by the union. The Court affirmed the ruling for the union. *NLRB v. Int'l Brotherhood of Electrical Workers, Local 340,* 481 U.S. 573, 107 S.Ct. 2002, 95 L.Ed.2d 557 (1987).

◆ A national union amended its constitution to provide that resignations or withdrawals from the national or its locals would not be permitted during a strike or lockout, or at a time when either appeared imminent. Ten Illinois union members violated this provision by resigning during a strike and returning to work. After the strike ended and a new bargaining agreement was signed, the union fined the 10 employees. The employers' representative then filed charges with the NLRB against the union, claiming that the imposition of fines was an unfair labor practice. The board agreed that it was unfair – in violation of Section 8(b)(1)(A) of the NLRA – and the U.S. Supreme Court upheld that decision. The levying of fines against the employees here violated their Section 7 rights because it coerced or restrained them from choosing not to engage in "concerted activities." Further, the board had justifiably concluded that **by restricting the right of employees to resign from the union, the provision in question impaired the policy of voluntary unionism implicit in Section 8(a)(3) of the NLRA**. Finally, Congress' intent to preserve for unions the control over their own "internal affairs" did not suggest an intent to authorize restrictions on the right to resign. *Pattern Makers' League of North America v. NLRB,* 473 U.S. 95, 105 S.Ct. 3064, 87 L.Ed.2d 68 (1985).

◆ An Ohio company fired an employee because of her excessive absenteeism and prior disciplinary history. The union filed a grievance for her, but chose not to take the grievance to arbitration and notified her that it would take no further action on her behalf. She brought a hybrid suit under Section 301 of the LMRA, claiming that the employer violated the collective bargaining agreement by firing her and that the union breached its duty of fair representation. A federal court held that her lawsuit was untimely, but that even if she had filed it in time, she could not prove that the firing had been in violation of the bargaining agreement. **The company had taken numerous disciplinary actions against her prior to her termination.** Further, she failed to provide the company or the union with medical documentation to support her absences. Also, the union's decision not to arbitrate her grievance was not arbitrary or discriminatory. The hybrid lawsuit failed. *Burrell v. Henderson,* 504 F.Supp.2d 330 (S.D. Ohio 2007).

◆ A trailer manufacturer experienced a backlog of work orders at a Pennsylvania plant due to increasing customer demand. Without notifying the employees' collective bargaining representative, the manufacturer entered into a subcontracting agreement under which it shipped materials to the subcontractor for assembly. The union filed an unfair labor practices complaint against the employer for unilaterally implementing new job duties and wages and for subcontracting bargaining unit work. The NLRB ordered the employer to rescind the agreement. The Third Circuit Court of Appeals held that a decision to subcontract bargaining unit work must be evaluated to determine the underlying management reasons for the agreement. Here, **the employer entered into the agreement for economic reasons**. There was substantial evidence that it was unable to meet customer demand at its Pennsylvania plant and would lose business if it did not subcontract the work. The court also held that the employer's motivation for the changes in wages and job duties was based on a desire to fill orders and not to eliminate overtime at the plant. The court denied enforcement of the NLRB's order. *Dorsey Trailers, Inc. v. NLRB*, 134 F.3d 125 (3d Cir. 1998).

◆ A California publishing company proposed a new wage system to its employees when the collective bargaining agreement of the parties expired. The parties deadlocked over wage terms, and, following an impasse, the employer awarded wage increases to employees based upon merit without consulting the union. The union filed an unfair labor practice complaint with the NLRB. The NLRB held that the employer was obligated to bargain with the union prior to changing any employee's pay and that the unilateral merit increases constituted an unfair labor practice. The union had not waived its right to be consulted about wage changes as contained in the bargaining agreement. The NLRB then determined that while **an employer generally satisfies its statutory duty by bargaining to impasse over a discretionary pay proposal**, the facts of this case presented an exception due to the lack of a waiver by the union as to its right to be consulted about wage changes. The U.S. Court of Appeals, D.C. Circuit, found that the NLRB could permissibly create an exception to the bargaining to impasse rule, since the employer's wage action was inherently destructive of fundamental principles of collective bargaining and allowed it to circumvent its statutory bargaining obligation. The court affirmed the NLRB's decision concerning implementation of the merit increase. *McClatchy Newspapers, Inc. v. NLRB*, 131 F.3d 1026 (D.C. Cir. 1997).

2. Breach of Duty

A union breaches its duty of fair representation if it acts in an irrational, arbitrary fashion that fails to provide its members with fair and adequate representation.

The <u>arbitrary, discriminatory or bad faith</u> standard applies to all union activity – not just contract negotiation – and the behavior must be so far outside a "wide range of reasonableness" as to be irrational.

◆ An Arizona union employee was suspended and warned after a former lover alleged that she used profanity in the parking lot before work. She asked the union to file a grievance on her behalf and a field representative promised to do so but never did. She was fired after another incident of alleged profanity during an argument over a pay error. The union filed a grievance over the termination but refused to arbitrate it. **The employee then sued the union for sex discrimination and breach of the duty to represent her.** A federal court ruled in her favor and the Ninth Circuit affirmed. Here, the employee presented evidence that the union aggressively represented two male employees who had been involved in tussles with co-workers, including one who threatened a fellow employee with a knife. She also presented evidence that the union did not aggressively represent another female employee who allegedly extended the expiration date on some meat, even though two male employees who allegedly engaged in the same behavior were not fired. The employee was entitled to her award of $16,304 in lost wages, $125,000 in compensatory damages and $50,000 in punitive damages. *Beck v. United Food and Commercial Workers Union, Local 99*, 506 F.3d 874 (9th Cir. 2007).

◆ United Parcel Service (UPS) fired two Kansas and Missouri employees for job abandonment. Their union filed grievances on their behalf and represented them. UPS nevertheless upheld the terminations. The two employees then filed hybrid suits against UPS and the union under Section 301 of the LMRA, claiming UPS breached the collective bargaining agreement, and that the union breached its duty of fair representation. They also asserted a claim under the Labor Management Reporting and Disclosure Act (LMRDA), arguing that the new union leadership retaliated against them for supporting the opposition slate of candidates. The case reached the Eighth Circuit, which ruled that **the union did not breach its duty of representation to the employees**. Thus, it did not even have to decide whether UPS breached the collective bargaining agreement because both claims had to be proved to prevail in a hybrid lawsuit. The union represented both employees adequately. For the same reason, the LMRDA claim failed. *Jones v. United Parcel Service,* 461 F.3d 982 (8th Cir. 2006).

◆ The union representing passenger service employees of US Airways negotiated a collective bargaining agreement that changed the system for business-necessitated layoffs. Under the agreement, the most senior employee would displace the most junior employee, the second most senior would displace the second most junior, etc. Under the older system, the most senior employee bumped a less senior employee, who in turn bumped a less senior employee, etc. After the September 11 attacks, the airline had to close operations at 10 small locations, and it attempted to reduce its work force under the old system. Instead, the union forced it to use the displacement system in the bargaining agreement, which resulted in certain senior employees being left without jobs or in less desirable assignments, but reduced by more than 100 the number of displacements system-wide. A number of senior employees adversely affected by the bargaining agreement sued the union for breaching its duty of fair representation. A Virginia federal court ruled for the union, and the Fourth Circuit affirmed. **The union's conduct in forcing the airline to adopt the bargaining agreement was not arbitrary, discriminatory or in bad faith**, and did not breach its duty to the employees. *Jeffreys v. Communications Workers of America, AFL-CIO*, 354 F.3d 270 (4th Cir. 2003).

◆ An employee of a Massachusetts sporting goods company was accused of spreading false rumors that a female co-worker and a male co-worker were having an affair. Not only did the employee tell the female co-worker's husband, but he also told his supervisor and another employee. He was fired for violating the company's sexual harassment policy. The union initially filed a grievance on his behalf, but when the company refused to resolve the complaint, the union accepted the company's response and failed to pursue the matter. The employee sued the company and the union under Section 301 of the LMRA, alleging that the company fired him without proper cause (as required by the collective bargaining agreement) and that the union breached its duty of fair representation by failing to pursue the grievance. A federal court ruled for the defendants, and the First Circuit Court of Appeals affirmed. Since there was substantial evidence to support the discharge decision, the company had proper cause to fire the employee. He could not have thought he was reasonably justified in discussing the alleged affair with third parties who had no legitimate interest in the subject matter. **Because the firing was proper, the union did not breach its duty of fair representation, and the Section 301 claim failed.** *Mulvihill v. The Top Flite Golf Co.*, 335 F.3d 15 (1st Cir. 2003).

- An Ohio truck driver was fired for intentionally destroying the brake pedal of a tractor he was instructed to drive. He was suspected of deliberately damaging the vehicle, which he had earlier referred to as a "piece of junk." However, another driver corroborated the driver's statement that the brakes had failed at an intersection. The union filed a grievance against the employer, but an arbitration panel upheld the discharge. The driver sued the employer and union under Section 301 of the LMRA. The jury returned an $850,000 verdict for the driver, which the court apportioned between the employer and union. The Sixth Circuit affirmed. **Evidence indicated that the union had failed in its duty to fairly represent the driver**, since it did not call an expert witness who might have contradicted the testimony of the employer's expert. There was strong circumstantial evidence in the driver's favor suggesting that the employer had "set him up." In Section 301 cases, the focus is on whether the employer has breached the contract and the union has contributed to the erroneous outcome of contractual proceedings. Here, the union's conduct had tainted the arbitration, and the employee was entitled to judgment. *Schoonover v. Consolidated Freightways Corp. of Delaware*, 147 F.3d 492 (6th Cir. 1998).

- A teamsters local maintained a written policy forbidding members from harming one another. The policy was construed as prohibiting members from releasing negative information about co-workers to management. An employer threatened to fire an African-American employee if he did not reveal the names of other employees involved in thefts. The employee revealed names of three co-workers, in violation of the union's policy. The company fired the identified employees, who filed grievances. Union members began harassing the African-American employee, and he quit after several months. After he quit, a union officer drove by his home at least 30 times during a three-week period. The African-American employee sued the union, the officer and the union business agent. The case reached the U.S. Court of Appeals, First Circuit, which observed that **the officer's conduct was intentional and met the necessary standard of proof for extreme and outrageous conduct**. A reasonable jury could have found that the union knowingly tolerated and encouraged harassment of the employee as punishment for identifying the three co-workers. *Johnson v. Teamsters Local 559*, 102 F.3d 21 (1st Cir. 1996).

- A meatpacking company and a union negotiated a master agreement restricting the company's right to close a Kansas packing plant. The company closed the plant three years later, but to facilitate negotiations at a South Dakota plant, the union entered into two secret side-letter agreements with the company that would allow reopening of the Kansas plant without the master agreement restrictions. The union failed to notify its membership of the side-letter agreements, and the plant reopened as a nonunion facility. Union members sued it for breach of the duty of fair representation. A Kansas federal court found breach of contract by the company and bad faith by the union. The union members and company settled, and the court awarded the union members $4.7 million against the union. The Tenth Circuit reversed and remanded the case for inclusion of additional damages. On remand, the district court rejected an argument by the union that the company would have been forced by market factors to lay off the entire group of workers. Instead, it held that the plant would have employed a similar number to that employed by the non-unionized facility, and that less senior employees would have been laid off. It approved a $13.7 million damage award based on this analysis. The Tenth Circuit found no error in the district court's damage calculation. It had been based on reasonable findings of fact that **all class members would have been retained for some time at a higher wage than that which was actually paid when the facility was non-unionized**. The court granted a $1 million reduction for damages that should have been set off for pension benefit netting. *Aguinaga v. United Food and Commercial Workers Int'l Union*, 58 F.3d 513 (10th Cir. 1995).

◆ Continental Airlines filed a petition for reorganization under Chapter 11 of the Bankruptcy Code. It then repudiated its collective bargaining agreement with the pilots' union and cut pilots' salaries and benefits by more than half. This resulted in a strike that lasted for more than two years. During the strike, Continental set up a system of bidding for vacancies and assigned all the positions to working pilots, effectively ending the strike. The union then entered into an agreement with Continental to allow striking pilots to participate in the bidding allocation. Thereafter, a group of pilots sued their union, alleging that it had breached its duty of fair representation by negotiating an agreement that arbitrarily discriminated against striking pilots. A Texas federal court ruled for the union, but the Fifth Circuit reversed.

The U.S. Supreme Court held that the rule announced in *Vaca v. Sipes*, 386 U.S. 171, 87 S.Ct. 903, 17 L.Ed.2d 842 (1967) – that a union breaches its duty of fair representation if its actions are either "arbitrary, discriminatory, or in bad faith" – applies to *all* union activity, including contract negotiation. The Court then stated that a union's actions would be arbitrary only if the union's behavior was so far outside a "wide range of reasonableness" as to be irrational. This issue had to be considered in light of the factual and legal landscape at the time of the union's actions. Here, **even if the union made a bad settlement, its actions at the time of the settlement were not irrational**. Thus, it did not breach its duty to the pilots. The Court reversed the court of appeals' decision. *Air Line Pilots Ass'n Int'l v. O'Neill*, 499 U.S. 65, 111 S.Ct. 1127, 113 L.Ed.2d 51 (1991).

3. Federal Law Preemption

When a state law claim is based on an analysis of the terms of a collective bargaining agreement (CBA), the state law claim will be preempted by Section

301 of the Labor Management Relations Act (LMRA). However, where the state law claim can be resolved without reference to the CBA (or independently of the CBA), the LMRA will not preempt the state law claim.

◆ After an underground fire at an Idaho mine, the survivors of four miners filed a state-law wrongful death action against the miners' union, alleging that, based on a collective bargaining agreement, it had negligently conducted safety inspections. The Idaho Supreme Court eventually determined that the survivors had stated a valid claim under state law that was not preempted by Section 301 of the LMRA. The U.S. Supreme Court reversed, holding that the survivors' claims (that the union had been negligent in its safety inspections) were not independent of the collective bargaining agreement. Here, the union's representatives were participating in the inspection process according to the provisions of the agreement. Thus, **any duty owed the miners arose out of the agreement, and the state-law tort claim was preempted by Section 301**. Also, the Section 301 claim could not succeed against the union because the complaint had alleged only negligence. More than mere negligence was needed for liability under Section 301. *United Steelworkers of America v. Rawson,* 495 U.S. 362, 110 S.Ct. 1904, 109 L.Ed.2d 362 (1990).

◆ An electrical apprentice, who was a member of a union, worked for a Florida power company. She was assigned to a job in an electrical substation and was injured when she came into contact with some highly energized components. Two years later, she sued her union, alleging that it had a duty to ensure that she was provided safety in her workplace and that she not be required to take undue risks while performing her duties – risks that were beyond her training and experience. She claimed that the tasks she had been performing at the time of her injury were beyond the scope of her training and experience. The union removed the case to a federal court, which dismissed the suit as untimely, but the U.S. Court of Appeals reversed. The U.S. Supreme Court noted that **the LMRA preempted any state-law action she might have had because interpretation of the collective bargaining agreement would be necessary**. Under federal law, the court of appeals would be required to determine whether the apprentice's claim was time-barred by the six-month limitations period of the National Labor Relations Act, or whether some other period should be used. The Court vacated the court of appeals' decision and remanded the case. *Int'l Brotherhood of Electrical Workers, AFL-CIO v. Hechler,* 481 U.S. 851, 107 S.Ct. 2161, 95 L.Ed.2d 791 (1987).

◆ Three gas company employees in Atlanta were bumped out of their positions by employees with more seniority during a statewide reduction in force. They refused offers to transfer to other locations and were laid off. The company denied their grievances and the union chose not to take the matter to arbitration. They then sued the company for breach of contract and emotional distress, and also raised other claims. A Georgia federal court granted pretrial judgment to the company, and the Eleventh Circuit largely affirmed. Here, the breach of contract claims were preempted by the LMRA because they were substantially dependent on analyzing the terms of the collective bargaining agreement between the company and the union. Also, the emotional distress claims were preempted because they revolved around the alleged failure to provide proper notice of termination or the meaningful opportunity to consider transfers. As such, those claims also required analysis of the bargaining agreement. Finally, the court noted that the employees could not proceed under the LMRA because their claims were properly considered hybrid Section 301 claims, and they waited more than the allowed six months to file suit. *Bartholomew v. AGL Resources, Inc.*, 361 F.3d 1333 (11th Cir. 2004).

- A California employer installed video cameras and listening devices behind two-way mirrors in its employee restrooms, ostensibly to detect drug use by employees. After the equipment was discovered, employees filed two class action lawsuits against the company for invasion of privacy and infliction of emotional distress. They sought injunctive relief to end the use of the surveillance devices. The company asserted that the lawsuits were preempted by Section 301 of the LMRA because the claims required interpretation of the collective bargaining agreement (CBA) to determine the employees' reasonable expectations of privacy. A federal court dismissed one of the lawsuits and found the other one preempted by Section 301. The Ninth Circuit Court of Appeals reversed, holding that **a state law claim is not preempted by Section 301 unless it requires a court to interpret part of a CBA that is relevant to the resolution of the dispute**. Here, the invasion of privacy claims were based on California constitutional and statutory rights of privacy guaranteed to all persons, whether or not they happen to work subject to a CBA. And even if the CBA allowed the use of two-way mirrors to detect drug use, that provision would be illegal under California law and thus unenforceable. Also, the emotional distress claims were not preempted by Section 301 because the conduct alleged violated California penal law and therefore was per se outrageous. *Cramer v. Consolidated Freightways, Inc.*, 255 F.3d 683 (9th Cir. 2001) *cert. denied*, 534 U.S. 1078 (2002).

- A mechanic at a New Mexico facility also served as a union steward. His supervisor confronted him about leaving his post to conduct union business, and he asserted that he had the right to do so under the collective bargaining agreement. Management then conducted surveillance on him, allegedly to catch him misusing his time card. Based on this surveillance, the company terminated him. After a hearing, an arbitrator found that there was not just cause for the termination and ordered reinstatement. The mechanic claimed that the company then stripped him of a security clearance that would have allowed him to be promoted or eligible for other career opportunities. He sued the company, but the case was dismissed on the ground that Section 301 of the LMRA preempted his lawsuit. The Tenth Circuit reversed, finding that he could pursue his retaliation claim against the company. **His lawsuit was not about interpreting a collective bargaining agreement**, but rather about the motivation behind the company's actions. *Garley v. Sandia Corp.*, 236 F.3d 1200 (10th Cir. 2001).

- A California tire plant hired strike replacement workers and promised a number of them that they would not be laid off when the strikers returned. When the strikers returned to work, 207 replacement workers were laid off, but not those replacement workers who were promised they would not be. The company and the union then entered into a new collective bargaining agreement (CBA), and the retained replacement workers became members of the union. Subsequently, diminished sales forced the layoff of 175 more employees, including the replacement workers who had been promised no layoffs when the strikers returned. The laid-off workers sued the company for fraud and breach of contract under state law, but a federal court ruled in favor of the company. The Ninth Circuit affirmed, holding that **Section 301 of the LMRA preempted the lawsuit because the workers had become part of the bargaining unit** covered by the CBA, and because the CBA dictated how seniority-driven layoffs would take place. The lawsuit could not be resolved without interpreting the CBA's layoff and seniority provisions. *Aguilera v. Pirelli Armstrong Tire Corp.*, 223 F.3d 1010 (9th Cir. 2000).

◆ Meter readers for a gas company in California were paid according to a collective bargaining agreement that set forth a complex arrangement. The meter readers were paid a flat sum that was calculated by multiplying a standard rate ($16.56 per hour) by the amount of time the company expected them to complete their routes. Meter readers who worked more than eight hours in a day received an adjustment to the flat sum. They sued the company under state law, asserting that under the formula in place, they were actually being paid less than $16.56 per hour for overtime. The Ninth Circuit held that **their lawsuit was preempted by Section 301 of the LMRA** because resolution of their claim depended on an interpretation of the bargaining agreement. *Firestone v. Southern California Gas Co.*, 219 F.3d 1063 (9th Cir. 2000).

◆ After a female longshore worker sued the local union and an association of employers, asserting that she had been denied entry into a higher classification of workers because of her gender, the parties entered into a settlement agreement whereby the association agreed not to deny the worker entry into the higher classification the next time classifications were organized. However, when the association refused to register any workers into the higher classification, a number of workers sued under the LMRA. A Washington federal court dismissed the suit because it was filed after the six-month statute of limitations had passed. When the workers then sued under state law, the case was again dismissed. The Ninth Circuit affirmed, finding that **the LMRA preempted the state law action** because resolving whether the settlement agreement had been breached required interpreting the bargaining agreement. As a result, Section 301 of the LMRA was the appropriate mechanism to be used. And since the statute of limitations had passed on their LMRA cause of action, the workers' lawsuit had to be dismissed. *Audette v. Int'l Longshoremen's and Warehousemen's Union*, 195 F.3d 1107 (9th Cir. 1999).

◆ A claims processor for a service center worked under a collective bargaining agreement that contained a nondiscrimination clause prohibiting discrimination on the basis of sexual orientation. The employee's supervisor allegedly began to harass him after learning of his homosexuality, and the employee was later laid off. His union filed grievances against the employer on his behalf. While the grievances were pending, the employee sued the employer and supervisor for breach of contract and intentional infliction of emotional distress. A federal court dismissed the action as preempted by LMRA Section 301, finding that resolution of the claims depended upon analysis of the collective bargaining agreement. The Eighth Circuit affirmed, observing that the contract alleged to have been breached in this action was the bargaining agreement. Because **the claims alleged by the employee were inextricably intertwined with the consideration of the bargaining agreement**, they were preempted by the LMRA. This was also true of the emotional distress claim, which was also grounded in the bargaining agreement. *Oberkramer v. IBEW-NECA Service Center, Inc.*, 151 F.3d 752 (8th Cir. 1998).

- A South Carolina electric company foreman was a union member for 38 years. The union constitution prohibited members from "working for any company declared in difficulty" with the union. When the union and company were unable to renegotiate a collective bargaining agreement, the union called a strike. The foreman resigned from his union executive board post and stopped paying membership dues. The union terminated his membership for failure to pay dues and filed internal charges against him for continuing to work for the employer after the union declared a strike. The union also declared him ineligible for his union pension. The foreman sued the union for violating the state Right-to-Work Act, which prohibits employer-labor agreements that make union membership a condition of employment. The court awarded the foreman over $100,000 in damages. The Court of Appeals of South Carolina held that **the LMRA preempted the Right-to-Work Act because reference to the union constitution was necessary to determine whether the foreman had a property interest in his union pension**. The state supreme court affirmed. *Lewis v. Local 382, IBEW*, 518 S.E.2d 583 (S.C. 1999).

- A Texas petroleum company utilized an employee absenteeism program under which it sent "letters of concern" to employees injured on the job who had filed workers' compensation claims. A list of employees who received the letters was published and distributed to other employees working at the plant. The injured employees stated that the reason for publishing the list was to embarrass and humiliate them, and they sued the employer for intentional infliction of emotional distress and invasion of privacy. A federal court held that **because the terms of the parties' bargaining agreement were relevant to resolving the claims, they were preempted by the LMRA**. Employee expectations of privacy in the workplace depended upon powers and duties described in the CBA; thus, the invasion of privacy claim was preempted. The intentional infliction of emotional distress claim was also preempted, since examination of the employer's conduct required interpretation of the CBA. *Dancy v. Fina Oil & Chemical Co.*, 921 F.Supp. 1532 (E.D. Tex. 1996).

- A Montana grocery employee was discharged after 25 years of employment for allegedly violating work rules regarding the proper procedure for recording customer sales. After meeting with two security personnel during an investigation, the employee signed a letter in which she admitted that she failed on occasion to record customer transactions. She was then fired. She filed a grievance with the union, but when the company denied the grievance, the union did not seek arbitration as provided for in the collective bargaining agreement. The employee later sued the company and the two security officers, alleging that she had been coerced into writing the confession. A state court granted pretrial judgment to the defendants, finding that the claims brought by the employee were preempted by Section 301 of the LMRA. The Supreme Court of Montana reversed, holding that **a decision could be reached without reference to or interpretation of the collective bargaining agreement** because the employee was suing for damages resulting from false imprisonment, emotional distress, unlawful restraint, intimidation, employer misconduct, and slander. *Hanley v. Safeway Stores, Inc.*, 838 P.2d 408 (Mont. 1992).

C. The Labor-Management Reporting and Disclosure Act (LMRDA)

The LMRDA was enacted to guarantee union members equal voting rights, rights of free speech and assembly, and the right to sue to protect those rights. It aims to ensure that unions are democratically governed and responsive to the will of their memberships.

The LMRDA makes it unlawful for a union to "fine, suspend, expel or otherwise discipline" any of its members for exercising rights secured by the LMRDA. Thus, for example, it is unlawful for a union to refuse to refer union members for jobs in retaliation for those members' opposition to union policies.

◆ An auto company employee worked full-time in an elected union position. When he learned that local union leaders had agreed silently to end a production process that would have resulted in the loss of several hundred jobs, he refused to sign a settlement agreement and told the media that the union had sold out its membership. Problems erupted between the employee and the union's leaders. They urged acceptance of the agreement and allegedly disparaged him in doing so, while he urged the agreement's defeat. After the agreement passed, he claimed that the union cancelled a meeting to discuss his charges against union leadership and ignored his charges against union leaders. He retired early, then sued under the LMRDA. A Michigan federal court ruled against him and the Sixth Circuit affirmed. Here, **he failed to show that he was "disciplined" for exercising his legal rights**. He also failed to show that union leaders defamed him or intentionally caused him emotional distress. *Webster v. United Auto Workers, Local 51*, 394 F.3d 436 (6th Cir. 2005).

◆ Two union members in New York violated their union constitution by being disruptive at union meetings. After hearings, both were suspended and fined by the union. They sued under the LMRDA, asserting that the union violated their speech rights under the law. A federal court held for the union, and the Second Circuit affirmed. Here, **the employees had been suspended for their**

disruptive and abusive actions, not their words. Further, even though the union constitution did not specifically allow for suspensions, it did allow for discretionary discipline as well as greater punishments than they received. The suspensions did not violate the LMRDA. *Hughes v. Bricklayers and Allied Craftworkers Local #45*, 386 F.3d 101 (2d Cir. 2004).

◆ An international labor organization imposed a trusteeship on a local union representing Tennessee office workers because of a paralyzing division in the local's executive board. The division resulted from the activities of a business agent who questioned the local's election processes, selection of delegates, membership dues increases and failure to process grievances. The union trustee reprimanded the business agent for his continuing criticism of the union and then fired him and revoked his union membership without notice or a hearing. Union reform candidates who supported the business agent eventually won election to the local board, and the trusteeship was lifted. The new board reinstated the agent, and he sued the international. The court denied relief based upon claims that the trusteeship had been improperly imposed, but awarded compensatory and punitive damages to the business agent for the international's violation of the LMRDA. The Sixth Circuit considered the international's argument that the business agent was not entitled to protection under the LMRDA because he was a union employee and was not required to be a union member. The LMRDA was enacted to ensure that unions were democratically governed and responsive to their memberships. **Because the agent was a voluntary union member who was subjected to retaliatory action and deprived of his union membership, he was entitled to LMRDA protection.** The jury properly considered the appropriateness of the trusteeship as it had a direct bearing on the claim for damages. There was also substantial evidence supporting the award of damages. *Thompson v. Office and Professional Employees Int'l Union, AFL-CIO*, 74 F.3d 1492 (6th Cir. 1996).

◆ A member of a local electrical union sued the union and its officers in an Ohio federal court. He asserted that, because of his opposition to proposed union actions, they had discriminated against him with respect to certain job referrals in violation of the LMRDA. He also alleged that their conduct breached Section 301 of the LMRDA by violating the union's constitution and bylaws. The district court dismissed all the claims, and the Sixth Circuit Court of Appeals affirmed in part, reversing the dismissal of the LMRDA claim. The U.S. Supreme Court then held that **the union member was entitled to a jury trial on the LMRDA claim**. Even though he sought injunctive relief as well as damages, the court compared an LMRDA action to a personal injury action for which a jury trial right existed. Further, federal courts have jurisdiction to hear suits brought against unions by individual members under the LMRA. Here, even though the union member's suit under the LMRA was a third-party suit seeking to enforce a contract between the local and international union, Section 301 of the LMRA did not limit itself to suits by the contracting parties. His suit was governed by federal law. The Court remanded the case. *Wooddell v. Int'l Brotherhood of Electrical Workers, Local 71,* 502 U.S. 93, 112 S.Ct. 494, 116 L.Ed.2d 419 (1991).

◆ A local union in the midst of a financial crisis asked its international union for help. A trustee was sent to put the local back on sound economic ground. At a special meeting set up to vote on a dues increase, one of the local's officials voiced opposition to the increase because the trustee would not commit to lowering expenditures. After the vote for a dues increase failed, the trustee removed the elected official because of his outspoken opposition to the increase in union dues. In a California federal court, the official challenged his removal as violative of his free speech rights under the LMRDA. The court ruled for the international, but the court of appeals reversed. On further appeal, the U.S. Supreme Court held that **the removal of the elected union official, in retaliation for the statements he made at the dues meeting, violated the LMRDA**. It not only interfered with his Title I rights – which protected him if he spoke out against the union leadership – but it also denied the members who voted for him the representative of their choice, chilling their Title I free speech rights as well. The Court affirmed the court of appeals' decision, holding that the official's statements were entitled to protection. His removal was invalid even though it was carried out during a trusteeship that was lawfully imposed. *Sheet Metal Workers' Int'l Ass'n v. Lynn,* 488 U.S. 347, 109 S.Ct. 639, 102 L.Ed.2d 700 (1989).

◆ A local union operated a hiring hall through which it referred both members and nonmembers for construction work. A union member brought suit against the union for violating its duty of fair representation by passing him over in making job referrals and in refusing to honor employer requests for his services – all because he supported a rival business manager candidate. He also alleged that the union's actions violated the LMRDA. An Ohio federal court dismissed the suit as outside its jurisdiction, and the Sixth Circuit affirmed. The U.S. Supreme Court granted review and held that the union member had stated a valid claim for breach of the duty of fair representation. However, the failure of the business manager and business agent to refer him for employment could not be attributed to the union for the purpose of maintaining a claim under Sections 101(a)(5) and 609 of the LMRDA. Here, **the union was not attempting to discipline the member for his political convictions; it was only individual officers who allegedly did so**. Also, the fair representation claim did not require a concomitant claim against an employer for breach of contract; whatever an employer's liability, the union member would still have a legal claim against the union. The Court reversed in part and remanded the case. *Breininger v. Sheet Metal Workers Int'l Ass'n Local Union No. 6,* 493 U.S. 67, 110 S.Ct. 424, 107 L.Ed.2d 388 (1989).

IV. OSHA AND OTHER SAFETY REGULATIONS

The Occupational Safety and Health Act of 1970, 29 U.S.C. § 651 *et seq.,* (OSH Act), requires employers to provide a place of employment that is "free from recognized hazards that are causing or are likely to cause death or serious physical harm."

Employers' duties are of two kinds:

—first is the general duty to provide a safe work environment, and
—second is the specific duty to conform to particular health and safety standards that are promulgated by the Secretary of Labor and the Occupational Safety and Health Administration (OSHA).

It is important for employers to know which OSHA standards apply to their workplaces. The standards are published and are organized by industry. Also, a great deal of information about OSHA standards and procedures is available from the OSHA Web site at *www.osha.gov/.*

A. Regulatory Interpretations

OSHA can set safety standards on its own initiative or as a result of petitions from other parties, including the Secretary of Health and Human Services. Problems arise when those standards exceed the requirements of the Occupational Safety and Health (OSH) Act.

◆ A Colorado steel corporation equipped 28 of its employees with respirators that failed an "atmospheric test" designed to ascertain whether such respirators would protect the wearers from carcinogenic emissions. As a result, some employees were exposed to coke-oven emissions exceeding the regulatory limit. A compliance officer, under the direction of the U.S. Secretary of Labor (Secretary), issued a citation to the steel company for violating an OSH Act regulation. The company contested the citation, and the Occupational Safety and Health Review Commission (Commission) vacated the citation because the officer had cited the wrong regulation. The Secretary appealed to the U.S. Court of Appeals, Tenth Circuit, which affirmed the Commission's order. The U.S. Supreme Court then examined to whom a reviewing court should defer when **the Secretary and the Commission have reasonable but conflicting interpretations** of an ambiguous Department of Labor regulation. The Court decided that it would defer to the Secretary, who is more likely to develop the expertise relevant to assessing the effect of a particular regulatory interpretation. The Court thus reversed the court of appeals' decision and remanded the case for a determination of whether the Secretary's interpretation was reasonable. *Martin v. OSHRC*, 499 U.S. 144, 111 S.Ct. 1171, 113 L.Ed.2d 117 (1991).

◆ Two employees of an Ohio corporation refused to perform their usual maintenance duties on a suspended wire-mesh screen that hung about 20 feet above the plant floor. They believed the screen was unsafe (and in fact, one fatality had already resulted from an employee's fall through an old part of the screen). The corporation suspended the employees and placed written reprimands in their files. The U.S. Secretary of Labor then sued the corporation for discriminating against its employees in violation of the OSH Act. A federal court held for the corporation, but the Sixth Circuit Court of Appeals reversed. The U.S. Supreme Court affirmed, holding that the regulation, which allowed an employee to choose not to perform an assigned task because of a reasonable apprehension of death or serious injury (coupled with a reasonable belief that no less drastic alternative was available), was valid. **Here, the employees had exercised their rights under the OSH Act, and the corporation had taken adverse actions against them.** The regulation helped effectuate the general duty clause of the act, which requires employers to provide a place of employment free from recognized hazards that are likely to cause serious injury or death. The corporation had to pay the employees for the period of time they were suspended and remove the reprimands from their files. *Whirlpool Corp. v. Marshall,* 445 U.S. 1, 100 S.Ct. 883, 63 L.Ed.2d 154 (1980).

- The OSH Act gives the U.S. Secretary of Labor (Secretary) broad authority to establish standards to ensure safe and healthy working conditions. With respect to carcinogens, the Secretary stated that no safe exposure level could be determined, and that the OSH Act required the exposure limit to be set at the lowest technologically feasible level that would not impair the viability of the industries regulated. The Secretary then lowered the benzene exposure limit to one part per million, prompting Texas benzene producers to challenge the standard. The Fifth Circuit held the standard invalid, and the U.S. Supreme Court affirmed. The Secretary had not made a finding that the workplace was "unsafe" before creating the standard. The Court noted that "safe" is not the equivalent of "risk-free." There must be a significant risk of harm before a workplace can be termed "unsafe." Even though certain assumptions indicated that the number of leukemia cases might be reduced by lowering the exposure level, there had never been a finding that leukemia was caused by exposure to low levels of benzene. **The Secretary had exceeded his power in setting the new standard.** *Industrial Union Dep't v. American Petroleum Institute,* 448 U.S. 607, 100 S.Ct. 2844, 65 L.Ed.2d 1010 (1980).

- UPS contracted with a consultant to conduct a study of its aircraft facilities throughout the country to determine what hazards were present in those work environments and the personal protective equipment necessary to protect workers from those hazards. The consultant determined that UPS could satisfy its obligations under OSHA by conducting a single representative assessment at its central hub in Louisville. Targeting two Michigan facilities, a union complained to the state's occupational safety and health administration, which found no safety violations but issued citations after determining that UPS's safety assessment was inadequate. UPS appealed, and the Michigan Court of Appeals held that **the state's OSHA rule did not require employers with multiple similar workplaces to perform a separate hazard assessment at each workplace**. Rather, it allows for representative assessment. The citations were vacated. *UPS v. Bureau of Safety and Regulation*, 745 N.W.2d 125 (Mich. Ct. App. 2007).

- Under the OSH Act, parties adversely affected by an occupational safety or health standard may file a petition for review "at any time prior to the sixtieth day after such standard is promulgated." In 1983, OSHA promulgated the Hazard Communication Standard (HCS), which imposed obligations on manufacturers based on the "latest edition" of a list of dangerous chemicals published by a private group of industrial hygienists. When the hygienists added several chemicals to the list in 2006, industry groups filed a petition for review, alleging that publication of the privately created list effectively amended the standard without notice and comment. The U.S. Court of Appeals, D.C. Circuit, disagreed. The HCS provisions referencing the list were promulgated in 1983. Thus, the groups were about two decades too late in filing their challenge. The conditions required of the regulated parties did not change at all in 2006. **Both before and after publication of the new list, regulated parties were required to treat as hazardous any chemical listed in the then-current version of the list.** Since the new additions to the list did not modify the HCS, the challenge to the HCS was untimely. *National Ass'n of Manufacturers v. OSHA*, 485 F.3d 1201 (D.C. Cir. 2007).

◆ The owner of a stucco company contested a citation issued by a Department of Labor inspector for violating the OSH Act. He claimed that he was not involved in a business affecting interstate commerce and that he had no employees. The case reached the Tenth Circuit Court of Appeals, which ruled in favor of OSHA. First, the stucco company, as part of the construction business, was in a "class of activity that affects interstate commerce" even if it did not have a specific impact on interstate commerce. Second, the owner was paying a helper $8 an hour to assist in the project. He controlled the scope of the helper's work and provided all the materials. Accordingly, **he was an employer for purposes of the OSH Act**. *Slingluff v. Occupational Safety & Health Review Comm'n*, 425 F.3d 861 (10th Cir. 2005).

◆ A water and sewer company in Wisconsin was excavating along a public street when an OSHA compliance officer drove by. He noticed the excavation, stopped his car and walked up to the trench. He saw an employee in the trench while a supervisor worked up above. This was a violation of OSHA regulations. He began videotaping the scene and identified himself to the project superintendent. The superintendent let him continue his inspection. Based on soil samples and measurements of the trench, as well as the video, OSHA issued the company three citations. The company claimed that the citations should not be enforced because the OSHA officer violated its Fourth Amendment right to be free of unreasonable searches and seizures. The Seventh Circuit disagreed. Here, **the excavation occurred along a public street, and the superintendent did not object to the inspection or demand a warrant** before letting the officer proceed. Thus, the evidence collected against the company was admissible. *Lakeland Enterprises of Rhineland, Inc. v. Chao*, 402 F.3d 739 (7th Cir. 2005).

◆ A company purchased a gas grill with a 20-pound propane tank for an outdoor barbecue at its bread-baking plant in Denver. A plant official determined that the 20-pound tank was not big enough to handle the barbecue and ordered a 40-pound tank. The 40-pound tank came with a warning that it was not to be used with a grill equipped for a 20-pound tank. The plant superintendent ignored the warning and directed a plant engineer to install the 40-pound tank. When the flow of gas was insufficient to cook the meat, the superintendent asked the engineer to reposition the tank. A fire erupted when some fuel escaped, and the engineer was burned. An OSHA investigator issued the company a citation, charging it with violating the OSH Act's general duty clause. The Tenth Circuit upheld that decision. Here, **the hazard was obvious and recognizable; it was likely to cause death or serious injury; and it could have been avoided**. The court of appeals also rejected the company's assertion that the improper installation of the 40-pound tank was not a "condition with respect to work." Even though this was a barbecue, the engineer was "working" when he was instructed to improve the flow of fuel to the grill. *Safeway, Inc. v. OSHRC*, 382 F.3d 1189 (10th Cir. 2004).

◆ While a four-man crew for an excavation company in North Dakota replaced a main water pipe in Fargo, an OSHA compliance officer conducted an unscheduled inspection of the site. On his recommendation, the Labor Department cited the company for four OSHA violations and assessed penalties. An administrative law judge affirmed three of the four citations. The Tenth Circuit then upheld two of the citations, the first of which involved the company's failure to abide by the "ladder" regulation (requiring workers to have a safe means out of an excavation trench) and the second of which involved employee protection from cave-ins. The company asserted that it should have been cited and fined for only one violation, but the court disagreed. **Because the two violations required different solutions, individual penalties were permissible**, even though the penalties combined exceeded the statutory maximum for a single violation. Further, the company had a history of related violations under the OSH Act that justified the assessment of penalties. *Dakota Underground v. Secretary of Labor*, 200 F.3d 564 (8th Cir. 2000).

◆ A compliance officer for OSHA videotaped construction activities at a Florida work site from a rooftop adjacent to the site. He taped two employees who were working about 80 feet above the ground without adequate safety cables. OSHA held an evidentiary hearing to determine whether a violation of its regulations had occurred. An administrative law judge determined that one of the employees was a foreman and imputed his knowledge of safety violations to the employer based on his supervisory authority. The employer appealed the imposition of a $7,000 fine to the Fourth Circuit, which rejected the employer's privacy claim. The employer had no reasonable expectation of privacy in the work site since it was a public place and the surveillance did not create an unreasonable intrusion into it. **The surveillance did not violate the OSH Act, which allows reasonable entry by OSHA officials to inspect and investigate work sites** during an employer's regular work hours, provided that the OSHA inspector presents his credentials before any inspection. The long distance observation by the inspector did not constitute an entry onto the work site. However, the foreman's knowledge of the violation could not be imputed to the employer. *L.R. Willson and Sons, Inc. v. OSHRC*, 134 F.3d 1235 (4th Cir. 1998).

◆ An OSHA compliance officer observed a New York power company employee using a jack hammer without protective eye and foot wear. The U.S. Secretary of Labor issued a citation against the company for safety violations and filed a complaint with the OSH Review Commission. An administrative law judge determined that the company had constructive knowledge of employee safety violations and had failed to provide employees with adequate supervision. In reaching its decision, the Commission placed the burden on the employer. The Second Circuit stated that an employer's defense on the basis of employee misconduct may be shown by establishing that the misconduct was unforeseeable. The Commission had improperly allocated the burden of proof to the employer. Instead, the Secretary of Labor should have been required to show that the employer had constructive knowledge of the violation. **The Commission had also improperly subjected the company to absolute liability without the opportunity to present evidence of an adequate safety policy.** The safety policy was not inadequate simply because employees were not constantly monitored. The Commission's order was remanded. *New York State Electric & Gas Corp. v. Secretary of Labor*, 88 F.3d 98 (2d Cir. 1996).

B. Willful Violations

—Repeat and willful violations of OSHA standards may have penalties as high as $70,000.
—Serious violations may have penalties of up to $7,000.
—Where a violation is deemed "other than serious," there will often be no monetary penalties, though such penalties can be imposed up to $7,000.

◆ An administrative law judge (ALJ) with the Occupational Safety and Health (OSH) Review Commission found that two related companies in Texas committed 59 willful violations of the recordkeeping regulation by intentionally and knowingly failing to record certain work-related accidents or illnesses. The Secretary of Labor sought a penalty of $9,000 per violation for one company and $8,000 per violation for the other. The ALJ instead treated the companies as if they had each committed only one willful violation and assessed a penalty of $70,000 each. The case came before the Fifth Circuit, which held that although the OSH Review Commission had the authority to assess all civil penalties, and could assess a penalty anywhere between $5,000 and $70,000 for each willful violation, the commission could not group separately charged and proven willful offenses for the purposes of assessing a penalty. On remand, the ALJ would have to assess penalties based on the number of proven willful violations. *Chao v. Occupational Safety and Health Review Comm'n*, 480 F.3d 320 (5th Cir. 2007).

◆ A Pennsylvania foundry doing work on a furnace believed that any asbestos had been removed. It also believed that any new insulation added would be asbestos-free. Therefore, it did not conduct tests to determine if asbestos was present. However, an employee noticed that some insulation in a dumpster appeared to contain asbestos. Testing revealed that it contained 5% asbestos, and **OSHA issued a citation for failure to determine the presence, location and quantity of asbestos** at the worksite and for failing to notify employers whose employees might be working there that they could be exposed to asbestos. OSHA characterized these violations as "serious." The OSH Review Commission upheld the two violations but reclassified them as "non-serious."

The Secretary of Labor contended that the commission erred in reclassifying the violations, and the Third Circuit agreed. Under the OSH Act, when the violation of a regulation makes the occurrence of an accident with a substantial probability of death or serious physical harm possible, the employer has committed a serious violation. The substantial probability part of the act refers not to the probability that an accident will occur but to the probability that, an accident having occurred, death or serious injury could result. *Secretary of Labor v. Trinity Industries, Inc.*, 504 F.3d 397 (3d Cir. 2007).

◆ A Nevada company was cited for willfully violating the federal fall protection regulations of the state Occupational Safety and Health Review Board after a worker fell 90 feet to his death. The company was fined $56,000 for failing to ensure that a proper fall protection system was in place and utilized by employees. The company asserted that its violations, if any, were only "serious" and not "willful." The case reached the Supreme Court of Nevada, which noted that state law essentially mirrored federal law on willful violations. Thus, **the court relied on federal case law standards to define a willful violation**. Under those standards, there was substantial evidence to support the willful violation. In addition to the employee who was killed, two other employees were observed working without fall protection one day and one week after the fatal fall. *Century Steel, Inc. v. State, Division of Industrial Relations*, 137 P.3d 1155 (Nev. 2006).

◆ An OSHA compliance officer visited a Wal-Mart store in Alabama to investigate a complaint about dangerous conditions in the store's stockroom. She found that **an emergency exit was blocked by a knee-high rail conveyor system and a stack of boxes**. The Department of Labor issued a citation, characterized it as a repeat violation (because of an incident in Georgia where shopping carts blocked an exit) and recommended a $25,000 fine. An administrative law judge assessed a penalty of $5,000, which the U.S. Court of Appeals, DC Circuit, upheld. Even though the conveyor system could be taken apart easily and the boxes could be moved, the regulation requires emergency exits to be "continuously maintained free of obstructions." *Wal-Mart Stores v. Secretary of Labor*, 406 F.3d 731 (D.C. Cir. 2005).

◆ OSHA cited a manufacturing plant in Illinois for violating safety regulations. One of the manufacturer's machines (a "track press") had an exposed hole that could impede the machine's operations if debris fell into it. A worker who failed to stop the machine before removing the debris could get his or her fingers crushed. The manufacturer had placed a cover over the hole, but when it became damaged it was removed. The investigation revealed that workers had disabled an electric eye on the press. The "eye" automatically stopped the press when someone put his or her hand near the hole. Two years earlier, the manufacturer had been cited for failing to provide another press with a barrier guard for its hole.

The OSH Review Commission (Commission) fined the manufacturer $10,000 for engaging in a "willful" violation of the OSH Act and $12,000 for a "repeat" violation of the act. The U.S. Court of Appeals, Seventh Circuit, sustained the order. With respect to a willful violation, there was substantial evidence for the Commission to find that the manufacturer knew the cover had come off the press machine and failed to fix the problem in conscious disregard of the regulations. With respect to a repeat violation, the Seventh Circuit rejected an interpretation adopted by the Third Circuit in *Bethlehem Steel Corp. v. OSHRC*, 540 F.2d 157 (3d Cir. 1998), that the term implies more than two violations but not necessarily of a similar character. Instead, it examined **whether the first violation was "substantially similar" to the second one so as to alert the employer to the condition that brought about the later violation**. Here, even though the first problem was mechanical and the second was electrical, they both involved "interchangeable methods of protecting the operator's hands from moving machinery" and were substantially similar. *Caterpillar, Inc., v. Herman*, 154 F.3d 400 (7th Cir. 1998).

◆ OSHA conducted an investigation into a workplace accident at a South Dakota car dealership that resulted in an employee's death. The employee habitually used the facility's freight elevator instead of its stairs because he had bad knees. The elevator was three-sided; there was no door, gate, or interlock safety device on the open side. Controls were located on each floor outside the elevator and could be reached from inside once the elevator stopped, but when the elevator was moving, there were no controls inside it to stop it or reverse its movement. The employee was killed when his head was caught in a shear as the elevator ceiling lowered past the floor of the second floor. The Eighth Circuit Court of Appeals found substantial evidence to support a ruling that **the dealership knew the elevator's unprotected shear points posed a safety hazard**. The configuration of the elevator and its lack of safety features made the risk plainly obvious. The court also affirmed a finding that the safety violation was "willful." The fact that the dealership had no meaningful safety program, that another employee had been injured in a similar accident, and that the dealership continued to let employees ride the elevator demonstrated that the dealership was "plainly indifferent" to the hazard. *McKie Ford v. Secretary of Labor*, 191 F.3d 853 (8th Cir. 1999).

◆ Three employees of a Milwaukee contractor were killed by a methane gas explosion in a sewage tunnel. OSHA performed an investigation and cited the contractor for 68 willful violations of OSHA standards. The case was referred to the U.S. Department of Justice for criminal prosecution while OSHA proceedings were stayed. The prosecution resulted in criminal fines of $750,000 for 49 OSHA violations. The Department of Labor then resumed administrative hearings on the civil OSHA claims. The parties settled claims arising from the 19 violations not prosecuted in the criminal proceeding, and the contractor asserted that further review of the previously adjudicated 49 violations would violate the Double Jeopardy Clause of the Fifth Amendment. An administrative law judge imposed additional fines in excess of $300,000. The Seventh Circuit enforced the OSHA order, noting that under a recent Supreme Court decision, **the Double Jeopardy Clause does not forbid OSHA sanctions following criminal punishment for the same conduct**. *S.A. Healy Co. v. Occupational Safety and Health Review Comm'n*, 138 F.3d 686 (7th Cir. 1998).

◆ A heavy equipment manufacturer utilized a forging press to make track links for earth-moving equipment. Regular maintenance procedures for the press involved removing the hub of the press by placing great pressure on it. During these maintenance operations, metal fragments were sometimes thrown for long distances, and in some cases came close to hitting employees. In one maintenance procedure, pressure propelled a nine-pound metal fragment 121 feet, causing serious injury when it struck an employee. The manufacturer had placed warning markers 90 to 100 feet from the press but had not employed recommended safety precautions. The OSH Review Commission affirmed a citation against the manufacturer for willful violation of the general duty clause of the OSH Act. In doing so, it increased the penalty from $30,000 to $49,000. The manufacturer appealed to the U.S. Court of Appeals, Seventh Circuit, where it argued that it had taken appropriate precautions for the foreseeable hazards of the operation. The court observed that a violation of the OSH Act is established where a hazard is likely to cause death or serious physical harm, and the employer, aware of the hazard, fails to implement known feasible abatements. In this case, the manufacturer **had a heightened awareness of the risk of flying metal fragments and failed to employ recommended safety precautions**. This evidenced a plain indifference to employee safety. The penalty was appropriate, and the court affirmed the Commission's order. *Caterpillar, Inc. v. Occupational Safety and Health Review Comm'n*, 122 F.3d 437 (7th Cir. 1997).

◆ A North Carolina employer was cited for several serious violations of the OSH Act, including failure to provide machine guards on an assembly line. The employer obtained a time extension for abatement of the violations. Before the extension ended, an employee was severely injured when emergency cutoff switches malfunctioned on the equipment. The employee sued the employer and two supervisors for negligence. The Court of Appeals of North Carolina held that where an employer intentionally engages in misconduct substantially certain to cause serious injury or death and an employee is injured or killed by the misconduct, workers' compensation exclusivity does not bar a negligence action. Here, although the employer had been aware of the OSH Act violation, **it did not operate the equipment with substantial certainty of causing serious injury or death**. The employer had received permission to continue operations without abating the hazard, and there was no evidence that the supervisors had engaged in reckless or willful conduct. *Regan v. Amerimark Building Products, Inc.*, 489 S.E.2d 421 (N.C. Ct. App. 1997).

◆ Employees working at a Maryland steel plant placed a toaster oven in the employee break room. The toaster was placed on a floor-mounted air conditioner for several years and became dilapidated. An employee was then killed during his break when he placed his arm on the toaster and was electrocuted. The Maryland Occupational Safety and Health Administration cited the employer for violating state and federal employment safety laws and fined it for violating a federal regulation requiring employers to maintain electrical equipment in a condition that is free from recognized hazards likely to cause death or serious physical harm. The penalty was based on willful or repeated violations of safety laws. The Court of Appeals of Maryland reviewed the federal regulation and found that the employer could be held responsible for electrical hazards caused by equipment brought to a work site by employees. The regulation obligated employers to abate electrical hazards and maintain worker safety without regard to the source of the risk. The court also upheld administrative findings that **the outer condition of the oven, which was in an obvious state of deterioration, put the employer on notice of the risk of electrocution**. The court remanded the case for further consideration of whether the employer was guilty of repeated violations. *Commissioner of Labor and Industry v. Bethlehem Steel Corp.*, 344 Md. 17, 684 A.2d 845 (Md. 1996).

◆ An OSHA regulation prohibits workers from riding on a load suspended from a crane except where the use of a conventional personnel platform or scaffold would be more hazardous. A contractor demolished a bridge in West Virginia using a backhoe suspended by a crane. An OSHA compliance officer determined that the backhoe was a load, not a personnel platform, and that the arrangement violated the regulation. The employer disregarded the officer's instruction to discontinue the operation, and the work was completed without incident. OSHA cited the employer for a willful violation. An administrative law judge found that the backhoe arrangement was a personnel platform, not a load, and did not violate the regulation.

The OSH Review Commission (Commission) reversed the administrative ruling, and the employer appealed, arguing that under the OSH Act, the backhoe was a non-conforming personnel platform, and that a non-conforming platform did not warrant a citation. The court of appeals agreed with the employer, finding no merit to the Commission's argument that the use of the backhoe as a personnel platform converted it into a load. **The regulation did not prohibit the conversion of equipment designed for one function to other purposes.** The court vacated and set aside the Commission's order. *S.G. Loewendick & Sons, Inc. v. Reich*, 70 F.3d 1291 (D.C. Cir. 1995).

C. Federal Law Preemption

Generally, the OSH Act preempts state safety laws that address the same area.

◆ While working on a boat in Louisiana, a contractor's employee fell down a manhole as he descended into the rudder room. Although he had safely negotiated the angle iron steps several times previously, this time he slipped and fell as a result of some anti-corrosive material. He sued the boat owner for negligence, seeking to recover for his injuries. The boat owner sought pretrial judgment, asserting that it did not violate its duties under the LHWCA, and also maintaining that **Coast Guard regulations preempted OSHA regulations as they related to inspected vessels**. The court agreed with the boat owner, noting that it was not liable for failing to warn the contractor's employee of the hazard, and that the presence of the anti-corrosive material was open and obvious. *Romero v. Cajun Stabilizing Boats, Inc.*, 501 F.Supp.2d 816 (W.D. La. 2007).

◆ A mechanic who worked for a Kansas paper manufacturer was disciplined for arguing with his supervisor about the safety of a piece of machinery. He filed a complaint about the machinery's safety with OSHA, which conducted a surprise investigation and found that some of the mechanic's complaints were valid. The mechanic was fired a month later, and he sued, claiming wrongful discharge under Kansas common law and retaliatory discharge pursuant to Section11(c) of the OSH Act. He withdrew the OSH Act claim after an OSHA employee told him that the claim was no longer valid because the machinery had been fixed. The Kansas Supreme Court determined that **the remedy provided by the OSH Act for retaliatory discharge was not sufficiently adequate to prevent fired employees from suing for wrongful discharge** under state law. Using the "adequate remedy" standard, the court found that the mechanic could pursue his state law claim because the remedies provided by the OSH Act limited his rights of redress to filing a complaint with the Secretary of Labor (Secretary). Under the OSH Act, the mechanic could not file a lawsuit himself, and he was afforded no right of appeal if the Secretary declined to do so. *Flenker v. Willamette Industries*, 967 P.2d 295 (Kan. 1998).

◆ A Houston pipe and tubing company vice president was killed while unloading a truck after regular working hours when no appropriate help was available. The Workers' Health and Safety Division of the state Workers' Compensation Commission identified the company as an extra-hazardous employer under its regulatory guidelines. The company was able to escape the designation after six months of compliance with the accident prevention plan developed for it. However, it challenged the designation in state court, asserting that the regulatory basis for the designation was preempted by the OSH Act. The court dismissed the case as moot, and the employer appealed. The Court of Appeals of Texas held that the case was not moot because the designation could affect the company in the future. The OSH Act generally preempts state workplace safety regulations unless they fall within the act's savings clause. This includes federally approved state regulatory regimes under which the state agrees to enforce the act. Another area of state authority that is not preempted is a state workers' compensation system. Here, although the state extra-hazardous designation arose under a program closely related to the state workers' compensation system, it did not affect any award or amount of compensation and focused on accident prevention and safety. Because **this was the exact area of OSHA application, and the state program was not a federally approved OSHA enforcement regime**, the state program was preempted by OSHA. *Ben Robinson Co. v. Texas Workers' Compensation Comm'n*, 934 S.W.2d 149 (Tex. Ct. App. 1996).

◆ A building subcontractor's employee was injured when he fell from the second floor of a building that was under construction. He filed a lawsuit against another subcontractor at the work site, claiming that it was liable for his injuries because it had control of the unfinished staircase from which he had fallen. He also alleged that state and federal OSHA standards imposed a duty of care upon the subcontractor and added claims based on alternate theories. A Delaware trial court determined that **state Occupational Safety and Health standards were**

inapplicable because they were preempted by the federal OSH Act as concerning identical areas of workplace safety regulation. Federal OSHA standards did not create a private cause of action for injured workers by establishing a duty of care on the part of subcontractors. Even though the employee was deprived of this cause of action, OSHA workplace regulations served as a guide for a standard of conduct that bound the subcontractor. The negligence action against the subcontractor could not be dismissed. *Figgs v. Bellevue Holding Co.*, 652 A.2d 1084 (Del. Super. Ct. 1994).

◆ A laboratory technician at a nuclear fuels production facility complained to management and to the Nuclear Regulatory Commission about perceived violations of nuclear safety standards. When the company did not adequately address her concerns, she deliberately failed to clean some contamination left by a previous work shift. She outlined the contaminated areas with red tape and then pointed them out to her supervisor a few days later (when they still had not been cleaned). Her employer discharged her for her knowing failure to clean up radioactive contamination. After unsuccessfully pursuing an administrative remedy, the technician sued the employer in a North Carolina federal court for intentional infliction of emotional distress. The court dismissed her claim as conflicting with Section 210 of the Energy Reorganization Act. The U.S. Court of Appeals, Fourth Circuit, affirmed. The U.S. Supreme Court held that **the technician's claim was not preempted by Section 210**. This section was primarily intended to protect employees even though it did bear some relation to the field of nuclear safety. Accordingly, not all state law claims arising from the section were included in the field (nuclear safety) that Congress intended to preempt. The Court reversed the court of appeals' decision and remanded the case for a trial on the merits. *English v. General Electric Co.*, 496 U.S. 72, 110 S.Ct. 2270, 110 L.Ed.2d 65 (1990).

V. OTHER LABOR REGULATIONS

There are many federal and state statutes and regulations that affect labor relations and employment. The FLSA, the NLRA and the OSH Act are among the most litigated. The cases below involve some of the other labor statutes and regulations with which employers must contend.

A. The Railway Labor Act

The Railway Labor Act (RLA) governs labor relations in the railroad and airline industries by imposing a comprehensive scheme for dispute resolution. The federal goal of keeping labor disputes in these areas out of lengthy court proceedings is reflected in the relegation of "minor disputes" to compulsory arbitration, and the requirement of bargaining and mediation for "major disputes," with arbitration of a major dispute if mediation fails.

Minor disputes are defined as those arising out of the interpretation of collective bargaining agreements concerning rates of pay, rules, or working conditions.

Major disputes relate to the formation of collective bargaining agreements or efforts to secure them, and concern rates of pay, rules or working conditions.

◆ A Hawaii aircraft mechanic recommended replacement of a part during an inspection of an aircraft. His supervisor refused to replace the part. At the end of the shift, the mechanic refused to sign a maintenance record approving the plane for flight. The supervisor suspended the mechanic pending a termination hearing, and the mechanic reported the incident to the Federal Aviation Administration. The mechanic filed a grievance under the collective bargaining agreement, which prohibited discharge without just cause and prohibited discipline for refusing to perform work in violation of safety laws. The hearing officer recommended termination for insubordination, and the employee sued for violation of the Hawaii Whistleblower Protection Act, among other claims. His claims were dismissed as preempted by the RLA. The Supreme Court of Hawaii held that the state tort actions were not preempted by the RLA.

The U.S. Supreme Court affirmed. The RLA and other federal labor statutes promoted stability in labor-management relations by offering comprehensive frameworks for resolving labor disputes. **Although the RLA preempted minor disputes under collective bargaining agreements, it did not preempt substantive protections under state laws.** Here, the mechanic alleged that the airline had a state law obligation not to fire him in violation of public policy or in retaliation for whistleblowing. The RLA and other similar federal labor statutes did not preempt such claims. *Hawaiian Airlines, Inc. v. Norris*, 512 U.S. 246, 114 S.Ct. 2239, 129 L.Ed.2d 203 (1994).

◆ A railroad with operations in Pennsylvania agreed to sell its assets to a newly formed subsidiary of another railroad (buyer). The buyer did not intend to assume the seller's collective bargaining contracts, needing only 250 of the 750 employees then working for the seller. The Railway Labor Executives' Association sued to determine the seller's obligations under the RLA and to enjoin the sale until those obligations could be met. The unions representing the seller's employees filed RLA Section 156 notices proposing extensive changes in existing agreements and went on strike. The buyer obtained an exemption from the ICC, which essentially amounted to an approval of the sale, and a federal court enjoined the work stoppage. The court also issued an injunction against the sale, and the Third Circuit affirmed in part but set aside the injunction against the strike. The U.S. Supreme Court held that the RLA did not require or authorize an injunction against the sale of the seller's assets to the buyer. Also, the Section 156 notices did not obligate the seller to postpone the sale beyond the approval date set by the ICC. However, the seller did have a limited duty to bargain regarding the effects of the sale. This obligation ceased on the date for closing the sale. The Court remanded the case for a determination as to **whether the RLA created a duty not to strike while its dispute resolution mechanisms were under way**. *Pittsburgh & Lake Erie Railroad Co. v. RLEA*, 491 U.S. 490, 109 S.Ct. 2584, 105 L.Ed.2d 415 (1989).

◆ A union representing flight attendants declared a strike after reaching a collective bargaining impasse over wages and working conditions, and after pursuing the required dispute resolution mechanisms of the RLA. The airline hired permanent replacements to help those who had not gone out on strike or who had abandoned the strike. After the strike ended, an agreement was entered into whereby strikers who returned to work would be reinstated with their seniority rights intact. The union then sued, contending that even if the strike was economic, the full-term strikers were entitled to displace junior crossover attendants. A Missouri federal court denied relief to the union, but the U.S. Court of Appeals, Eighth Circuit, held that the less senior crossovers could be displaced. Further appeal was taken to the U.S. Supreme Court, which held that **the RLA did not require the airline to lay off the junior crossovers**. Since new hires could not be displaced after an economic strike, it would be unfair to differentiate between them and junior crossovers. The airline had lawfully exercised its economic power during the strike. *Trans World Airlines v. Independent Federation of Flight Attendants*, 489 U.S. 426, 109 S.Ct. 1225, 103 L.Ed.2d 456 (1989).

◆ While Northwest Airlines was in Chapter 11, a bankruptcy court gave it the right to reject its collective bargaining agreement with the union representing its flight attendants. The union characterized this as unilateral action allowing it to strike. Northwest petitioned the bankruptcy court to enjoin the flight attendants from striking, but the court denied the motion for injunctive relief. Northwest then asked a New York federal court to issue a preliminary injunction to prevent the strike. The court issued the injunction, finding that **the rejection of the bargaining agreement did not automatically terminate the dispute resolution process under the Railway Labor Act**. Here, the rejection of the bargaining agreement did not constitute an act of bad faith, or an arbitrary or unilateral change in the status quo so as to give the union the right to strike. The union was required to exert every reasonable effort to resolve the dispute before striking so as not to disrupt commerce. The flight attendants were not allowed to strike. *In re Northwest Airlines Corp.*, 349 B.R. 338 (S.D.N.Y. 2006).

◆ An airline required its pilot trainees to agree to compulsory arbitration of statutory claims as a condition of employment. The pilots' union, which did not represent the trainees, sued the airline under the RLA, asserting that the arbitration clause was a mandatory subject of bargaining that could not be enforced because the airline had not bargained over it. The U.S. Court of Appeals, D.C. Circuit, ruled in favor of the airline, noting that unions cannot use an individual's statutory right to a judicial forum in the collective bargaining process. In other words, a union cannot lawfully agree to binding arbitration. As a necessary consequence of this ruling, **the arbitration clause could not be a mandatory subject of bargaining**, and the airline could require its pilots to agree to arbitration without bargaining over the issue. *Airline Pilots Ass'n Int'l v. Northwest Airlines, Inc.*, 199 F.3d 477 (D.C. Cir. 1999).

◆ A New York commuter railroad dispatcher was accused of drug use by her supervisor in the presence of two other supervisors. She requested a grievance hearing under the applicable collective bargaining agreement and also commenced a defamation lawsuit against the supervisor in state court. A jury awarded her $1.2 million. The court refused to set aside the verdict on the grounds of preemption by the RLA. The New York Court of Appeals held that **state law actions for retaliatory discharge do not involve minor disputes and are not preempted by the RLA** because they do not involve the interpretation of a bargaining agreement. Although the state law claim involved some factual consideration of the bargaining agreement, it required no construction of contractual terms so as to be preempted by the RLA. *Harris v. Hirsh*, 86 N.Y.2d 207, 654 N.E.2d 975 (N.Y. 1995).

- An association was certified as the representative of the flight attendants of an airline with operations in Oregon. However, over a year and a half later, negotiations between the union and the airline were still unproductive, despite the intervention of the National Mediation Board. The union sued the airline under the RLA, asserting that it had violated its statutory duty to "exert every reasonable effort" to reach an agreement. A federal court held that the airline had violated the RLA. The U.S. Court of Appeals, Ninth Circuit, noted that it is proper for federal courts to consult NLRA cases for assistance in construing the RLA. The U.S. Supreme Court has held that **"the duty to exert every reasonable effort imposed by the RLA requires at least the avoidance of bad faith** as defined under the NLRA, that is, going through the motions with a desire not to reach an agreement." Here, the district court had relied on the NLRA cases solely to impose on the airline the duty which the Supreme Court had held to be common to both statutes. Since the district court had merely ordered the airline to perform its existing duty under the RLA (without imposing upon it any duties derived from the NLRA) the court of appeals affirmed the district court's decision. *Ass'n of Flight Attendants v. Horizon Air Industries, Inc.*, 976 F.2d 541 (9th Cir. 1992).

B. The Worker Adjustment and Retraining Notification Act

The Worker Adjustment and Retraining Notification (WARN) Act, 29 U.S.C. § 2101 *et seq.*, requires large companies to serve written notice upon employees or their representatives 60 days in advance of a plant closing or mass layoff where a third of the work force at a single site and 50 or more employees lose their jobs during a 30-day period, or where 500 or more employees lose their jobs.

Where an employer violates the notice requirement, it becomes liable for back pay for each day of the violation, as well as lost benefits, civil penalties and attorneys' fees. The statute does not contain a limitation on actions.

1. Notice Requirements

Although the WARN Act generally requires a 60-day advance notice in cases of mass layoffs and plant closings, it contains an exception for:

—unforeseeable business circumstances (sudden, dramatic and unexpected actions outside the employer's control), and

—situations where the employer is pursuing a reasonable possibility of future business that would avoid the plant closing or mass layoff, and the giving of notice would jeopardize the possibility of acquiring that business.

◆ When a New York mortgage company could not fund its continued operations, it retained money owed to a creditor by falsifying certain data. Eventually, the creditor discovered the misappropriations. It refused to do business with the individuals responsible for the fraud. Those people resigned, and a new manager was brought in. The creditor worked with the business, but eventually the business failed and the creditor issued a default notice. Two days later the business closed. **Employees who were let go filed a WARN Act suit against the creditor, alleging that it was the employer for WARN Act purposes** and failed to give proper notice before closing it down. A federal court and the Second Circuit ruled for the creditor, finding that it was not liable as an employer under the WARN Act because it was not operating the business as a going concern at the time it closed. Instead, it acted to shore up the business in the short term to facilitate the sale of the business and recover the $5.6 million in loans that had been misappropriated. It did not exercise control over the business beyond that which was necessary to recoup some or all of what was owed it, and it took no long-term control over the business. *Coppola v. Bear Stearns & Co., Inc.*, 499 F.3d 144 (2d Cir. 2007).

◆ A Texas-based company provided personnel management, payroll and other administrative services for a New Jersey-based manufacturer of men's clothing, essentially acting as an off-site human resource department. When the manufacturer closed its plant without providing 60 days' advance notice as required by the WARN Act, the union representing the manufacturer's employees demanded that the human resources (HR) company compensate each member of the bargaining unit for 60 days' pay plus benefits. The HR company refused to pay, and a Texas federal court ruled in its favor. The Fifth Circuit U.S. Court of Appeals affirmed, noting that the HR company played no role in the closing of the plant, and did not even know of the closing until after the fact. Further, even though it was a co-employer for purposes of providing group medical benefits and workers' compensation, it did not employ the workers in the normal business sense. **The HR company could not be held liable as a joint employer under the WARN Act.** *Administaff Companies, Inc. v. New York Joint Board*, 337 F.3d 454 (5th Cir. 2003).

◆ A school bus transportation company notified its seasonal and year-round employees in July 1995 that it would be closing its local terminal because it had not been assigned any transportation routes for the upcoming school year. In the same notice, the employees were advised that they would not be rehired in September. The union and eight nonunion employees sued, alleging that the employer violated the WARN Act by failing to provide its seasonal and non-seasonal employees with 60 days' notice of an impending plant closing. A Missouri federal court found that the seasonal workers received adequate notice but that the non-seasonal employees did not. Both sides appealed. The Eighth Circuit Court of Appeals affirmed, holding that although the seasonal employees on temporary layoff were "employees" under the act, **they did not suffer an "employment loss"** so as to be entitled to damages. Despite evidence that the employer knew it would probably close the terminal sometime before September 1995, the seasonal employees would have been laid off in June of that year anyway. At most, they lost the immediate expectation of being rehired, and a loss of an expectation is not an "employment loss" under the act. *Teamsters Local 838 v. Laidlaw Transit*, 156 F.3d 854 (8th Cir. 1998).

- The WARN Act allocates the notice responsibility in the case of a sale of an employer's assets to the party actually making the decision that creates an employment loss. A business seller is responsible for giving the notice up to and including the effective date of sale. After the effective date of sale, the purchaser is responsible for any required notice. A Nebraska optical company negotiated with another business to sell the company. The parties contemplated the continuing operation of the seller's plant until several days before the sale, when the purchaser suddenly determined that it would only buy the seller's equipment, tools, supplies and inventory. Two days after the parties signed a purchase agreement, the seller announced the plant closing to employees. The purchaser hired some of the seller's former employees, and several of the others sued the buyer and seller, asserting WARN Act violations. The court held for the buyer and seller, and the employees appealed. The U.S. Court of Appeals, Eighth Circuit, found that **the responsibility for giving notice had never passed to the purchaser** and that the seller became obligated to provide notice two days prior to the plant closing, when it learned of the sale of assets. The seller was liable for damages resulting from the violation. *Burnsides v. MJ Optical, Inc.*, 128 F.3d 700 (8th Cir. 1997).

- An Ohio barge company purchased the assets of a Kentucky barge and towing company and offered to rehire the seller's employees. It circulated job applications to most of the seller's employees and eventually hired 49 of 160 affected workers. Some former employees of the seller filed a lawsuit against both companies in a Kentucky federal court for WARN Act violations. The court granted pretrial judgment to the employers, and the former employees appealed. The U.S. Court of Appeals, Sixth Circuit, found that the district court had improperly held that each of the barges utilized by the seller constituted a single site of employment for WARN Act purposes. Because the employees all reported to a single site in Kentucky, the boats were based there and all work assignments originated there, it constituted a single site for WARN Act purposes. However, there was **no employment loss under the WARN Act because all but 24 of the 160 affected employees had received an opportunity to continue employment** with the purchaser. *Wiltz v. M/G Transport Services, Inc.*, 128 F.3d 957 (6th Cir. 1997).

- A mining company sold the entire annual coal output from a particular Virginia mine to a Canadian steelmaker under annual contracts that were renegotiated each year. After 30 years, the parties were unable to reach an agreement, and the coal company closed the mine, giving employees only a one-day notice. The employees' union sued under the WARN Act. A federal court ruled for the employer, and the Fourth Circuit affirmed. One of the exceptions to the general WARN Act requirement for a 60-day advance notice of a plant closing or mass layoff is a closing caused by business circumstances that are not reasonably foreseeable as of the time that notice would have normally been required. In those situations, an employer must give as much notice as is practicable and explain the reason for reducing the notification period. Here, **the loss of the contract was not reasonably foreseeable in view of the previous 30 years of successful contract negotiations**. The employer had made an economic decision that could not have been made at a prior time. *Local Union 7107, UAW v. Clinchfield Coal Co.*, 124 F.3d 639 (4th Cir. 1997).

◆ The U.S. Navy canceled the contract of a defense contractor involved in production of the A-12 Avenger fighter-bomber, resulting in the loss of thousands of jobs in the St. Louis area. Although the contractor was aware of the government's unhappiness with its failure to meet production timetables and costs, the cancellation announcement was abrupt and unexpected. As a consequence, the contractor failed to give advance layoff notices to many of its employees. Two employees who received notices of two weeks or less sued the employer under the WARN Act. The court held for the employer, and the U.S. Court of Appeals, Eighth Circuit, affirmed. Here, the contract termination had not been reasonably foreseeable until the date it was announced. **The employer had given layoff notices as promptly as possible under the circumstances** and was not required to give conditional notices as the employees argued. *Loehrer v. McDonnell Douglas Corp.*, 98 F.3d 1056 (8th Cir. 1996).

◆ A manufacturing company advised the labor union representing employees working at a Missouri plant that a permanent layoff of 277 employees would occur 60 days later. The union charged that the manufacturer had already begun the layoff in violation of the WARN Act. An employer violating the notice requirement of the act must pay each employee wages for each day of the violation, and unions are specifically authorized to file suit on behalf of injured employees. The union sued, but the court dismissed the lawsuit, finding that the union could not recover monetary damages on behalf of individual union members without their participation in the lawsuit. The Eighth Circuit affirmed, but the U.S. Supreme Court reversed. **The WARN Act explicitly allows unions to recover damages on behalf of individual union members.** The Constitution did not prohibit Congress from conferring legal standing upon labor organizations to sue for damages on behalf of their individual members. Earlier decisions of the Court restricting monetary damage claims by representative organizations prohibited such claims as a matter of judicial convenience, and not as a constitutional prohibition. *United Food and Commercial Workers Union Local 751 v. Brown Group, Inc.*, 517 U.S. 544, 116 S.Ct. 1529, 134 L.Ed.2d 758 (1996).

◆ In a case involving the statute of limitations under the WARN Act, the U.S. Supreme Court observed that where Congress fails to specify a limitations period in a federal law, the appropriate **statute of limitations** is drawn from the state in which the case is venued. Since 1830, state laws have supplied the appropriate limitations period for such claims under federal law, except where to do so would frustrate an important Congressional purpose. In this case, it was entirely appropriate to apply Pennsylvania law as the limitations period for WARN Act actions. The employers had set forth no reason to deviate from the general rule, and the court of appeals' decision was affirmed. *North Star Steel Co. v. Thomas,* 515 U.S. 29, 115 S.Ct. 1927, 132 L.Ed.2d 27 (1995).

2. Number of Employees

A mass layoff includes any employment loss at a single site of employment that involves one-third of the employees at that site and at least 50 employees, or alternatively, at least 500 employees.

◆ An Arkansas employer laid off 62 employees, most of whom then sued the company for violating the WARN Act by failing to give proper notice. They sought 60 days of back pay and lost benefits. A federal court ruled that there was no WARN Act violation because the company had 202 qualified employees at the time of the layoff, not the 191 claimed by the plaintiffs. The 11 employees at issue had been hired more than six months prior to the layoffs and were thus not part-time employees for WARN Act purposes. Also, four employees resigned prior to the layoffs because they knew a layoff was inevitable. So instead of 66 employees being laid off, only 62 were. And **the four employees who resigned did not count for purposes of the WARN Act**. Since 33% (or 66) employees had to be laid off to reach the mass layoff trigger requirements, the 62 who were laid off had no claim. *Guinn v. Timco Aviation Services, Inc.*, 317 F.Supp.2d 888 (W.D. Ark. 2004).

◆ A Louisiana grocery retailer operated three stores in a metropolitan area. Although about 30% of its employees had been permanently or temporary transferred between stores on at least one occasion, the stores maintained separate payroll records, and no employee was paid at his or her base store when working at another. The retailer announced that it was closing the three stores due to decreased sales, and those employees who did not accept transfers to other stores were discharged. A number of former employees sued, arguing that the three area stores constituted a "single site of employment" under the WARN Act. The court held that because none of the individual stores employed the statutory minimum 50 full-time employees, the WARN Act was inapplicable. The Fifth Circuit Court of Appeals affirmed. WARN Act regulations state that **non-contiguous sites in the same geographic area that do not share the same staff should not be considered a single site**. The retailer had taken steps to ensure that transferred employees were paid by their temporary store rather than their base store and stores did not routinely share employees and equipment. Because occasional transfers of employees did not establish the necessary connection for a single site, the WARN Act claims failed. *Viator v. Delchamps, Inc.*, 109 F.3d 1124 (5th Cir. 1997).

◆ An Ohio plant superintendent announced the permanent closing of the facility, providing employees with only 10 days written notice. Employees were offered tentative positions with a facility located in another city, but only 17 of over 100 employees accepted employment there. Fifty-one separated employees sued the company under the WARN Act. The court held for the employees, finding that the factory was subject to WARN Act coverage since it employed over 100 workers at the relevant time, and that the employer had failed to make them a reasonable transfer offer. It awarded damages to the employees for 60 calendar days of pay and attorneys' fees. The U.S. Court of Appeals, Sixth Circuit, found that the employer had over 100 employees at the plant during the relevant time period, despite employment fluctuations due to leave, vacation and temporary layoffs. It agreed with the employer, however, that the district court had improperly awarded damages based on calendar days, rather than work days. **WARN Act damages should be equal to wages that would have been received** had employees remained on the job during the violation period. The district court had also erroneously failed to credit from the damage award the 10 days of actual notice given by the employer. The court affirmed the finding of liability and vacated and remanded the damage award for reconsideration. *Saxion v. Titan-C-Manufacturing, Inc.*, 86 F.3d 553 (6th Cir. 1996).

◆ A California videotape business was acquired by a holding company, with only a few days notice to employees. Most of the company's employees accepted employment with the new entity, but many suffered a pay cut and loss of fringe benefits under collectively bargained-for union health and pension plans. The new employer refused to recognize the union's representation of approximately one-third of the transferred employees, and the union sued the selling company for damages under the WARN Act. A federal court held that there had been no employment loss under the WARN Act because fewer than 50 employees lost their jobs. The union appealed to the Ninth Circuit.

The union argued that the definition of "employment loss" under the WARN Act should encompass a reduction in pay and benefits resulting from a business sale. It also claimed that the sale had been a sham and that the new entity was the alter ego of the former employer. The court found no WARN Act violation, accepting the U.S. Department of Labor's interpretation that a business seller is liable for violations of the act only up to the date of sale. The buyer is responsible thereafter. Also, the WARN Act applied only to employees who actually experienced a covered employment loss and not a technical termination through sale. The WARN Act did not apply to modifications of the terms of employment, such as compensation and benefits. **The sale in this case was not an event that triggered the coverage of WARN**, and the district court had properly held for the former employer. *Int'l Alliance v. Compact Video Services, Inc.*, 50 F.3d 1464 (9th Cir. 1995).

◆ An industrial products manufacturer closed a department and laid off 41 employees there. It also laid off 15 employees who worked in the same division in departments related to the one that had been dissolved. The employees sued under the WARN Act. A federal magistrate judge found that the corporation did not order a "mass layoff" under the statute but that it had ordered a "plant closing" without providing the required 60-day notice. A Rhode Island federal court agreed, finding that the department was an "operating unit" for purposes of the WARN Act. The corporation considered the department to be a separate organizational unit, and it planned and executed a shutdown of that unit. Even though some of the department's work was picked up by other departments, **the department was a distinct organizational and production entity that was closed by the corporation**. Also, more than 50 employees lost their jobs within a 30-day period. Even though the general downturn in the economy was the reason the additional 15 employees were not reassigned to other groups, the employment loss was caused by the closure of the department. *Pavao v. Brown & Sharpe Manufacturing Co.*, 844 F.Supp. 890 (D.R.I. 1994).

C. Other Statutes

The following cases address the Hours of Service Act and the Immigration Reform and Control Act.

◆ The federal Hours of Service Act (HSA) states that railroad employees can work shifts of up to 12 consecutive hours. The employer must then allow the employee at least 10 consecutive hours off or face considerable penalties. The HSA states that time spent in transportation to a duty assignment is on-duty time, but time spent in transportation from a duty assignment at the end of a shift is neither time on duty nor off duty. Because many railroad workers spend considerable time periods being transported from work sites, the HSA recognizes a category, known as limbo time, which applies to employees who are not working but are being transported from a work site. This time is not assessed against the 12-hour limitation.

The Federal Railroad Administration (FRA) then declared time spent waiting to travel to be on-duty time that counted against the 12-hour prohibition. Nine major railroads filed a lawsuit in the U.S. Court of Appeals, Seventh Circuit, for review of the FRA's changed interpretation. The court agreed with the railroads and held that time spent waiting for transportation is limbo time.

The U.S. Supreme Court stated that the HSA treats time spent in transit to a work site as on-duty time because this time contributes to worker fatigue. However, the HSA does not treat time spent traveling from a work site at the end of a shift as on-duty time because there is no similar safety concern in transporting an employee to an eventual point of release from work. For the same reason, **time spent waiting to be transported to a work site should be regarded as on-duty time** (to be assessed against the 12-hour limitation) while time spent waiting for transportation at the end of a shift should be treated as limbo time, which did not count against the 12-hour limit. Because this interpretation supported HSA safety goals and granted the railroads a necessary measure of flexibility, the Court affirmed the Seventh Circuit decision. *Brotherhood of Locomotive Engineers v. Atchison, Topeka & Santa Fe Railroad Co.*, 516 U.S. 152, 116 S.Ct. 595, 133 L.Ed.2d 535 (1996).

◆ A group of businesses and civil rights organizations brought a lawsuit challenging the Legal Arizona Workers Act (LAWA), asserting that it was preempted by the Immigration Reform and Control Act of 1986 (IRCA) and by the Illegal Immigration Reform and Immigrant Responsibility Act of 1996. The LAWA allows the state to revoke businesses' licenses if they don't fire all unauthorized workers, and it requires businesses to use the e-verify system to check the work-authorization status of employees. A federal court held that the state law was not preempted, and the Ninth Circuit affirmed. The court of appeals noted that IRCA allows for state licensing laws, and that LAWA is such a law. Further, **even though the e-verify system was enacted as a voluntary system, that did not mean Congress intended to prevent states from making participation mandatory**. *Chicanos Por La Causa, Inc. v. Napolitano*, 544 F.3d 976 (9th Cir. 2008).

◆ A company in California was notified by the Social Security Administration (SSA) that information the company reported about 48 employees did not match what the SSA had on file. In response to the "no-match" letter, the company gave the employees three days to provide proof that they had applied for new Social Security cards. It then fired 33 employees who didn't provide the proof after seven days. The employees' union filed a grievance. The case reached the Ninth Circuit, which held that **a "no-match" letter, by itself, does not put a company on constructive notice that the employees named in the letter are undocumented**. Further, the short turnaround time the company gave the employees to provide documentation did not allow the company to draw the inference that the employees were undocumented. Since the arbitrator who heard the union's grievance found no convincing evidence that any of the employees were undocumented, the employees were entitled to be reinstated with back pay. *Aramark Facility Services v. Service Employees Int'l Union*, 530 F.3d 817 (9th Cir. 2008).

◆ A Kansas restaurant manager agreed to pay an illegal immigrant $6 an hour for work as a cook. The cook worked 50 to 60 hours a week but was paid $50 or $60 per week on top of his rent for six months ($100/month). He sought to be paid the agreed-upon amount and a hearing officer determined that the restaurant owed him $3,720 in wages, $217 in interest, and $3,720 in penalties for the willful withholding of his wages. A federal court then held that the cook could only receive the minimum wage because he was an undocumented worker. However, the Kansas Supreme Court disagreed and reinstated the award for the cook. Here, **the Immigration Reform and Control Act (IRCA) did not bar his recovery because he did not obtain the work by fraudulent means or fake documents**. The court held that enforcing state wage laws actually furthers IRCA's goals by creating disincentives for employers to hire illegal immigrants and pay them low or no wages. *Coma Corp. d/b/a Burrito Express v. Kansas Dep't of Labor*, 154 P.3d 1080 (Kan. 2007).

CHAPTER SIX

Employment Practices

I. HIRING PRACTICES

Employers use various pre-employment measures to ensure that applicants will be suited for the positions available. Among the options most frequently used are physical and mental tests, psychological examinations, and of course the interview process, during which the applicant's intelligence and personality are gauged (even through such clues as dress and mannerisms).

Generally, the problem isn't choosing between a qualified and a non-qualified candidate. More often, the problem is in choosing between two or more seemingly equal candidates. Here are several potential solutions:

1) having each qualified candidate work a week or a pay period for an amount not less than minimum wage to see who is most qualified – any candidate refusing to participate can be eliminated,
2) obtaining more information through the use of additional tests or reference and background checks – some candidates may withdraw during this process, making your job easier, and
3) adding an additional interview stage with the employees the candidate will be working with to see which one is most compatible with the group.

Part of what employers do in the hiring process is discriminate against applicants who are perceived to be less qualified or less easy to work with. This is <u>not</u> against the law.

However, employers must be careful not to discriminate or otherwise refuse to hire applicants for reasons that violate public policy. For discrimination cases involving race, sex, religion, national origin, age and disability, please see Chapter One.

Employers also have to be careful not to let information about prior workers' compensation claims, union activity, National Guard duty, lawsuits against former employers, marital status, children and (in some states) sexual orientation color their decision-making process.

Employers should also try to keep as much objectivity in the hiring process as possible to avoid charges of unfairness.

◆ On August 15, 2007, the Department of Homeland Security (DHS) issued a **final rule on how employers must handle no-match letters** they receive while determining whether a new hire is authorized to work in the United States. No-match letters are notices from the Social Security Administration (SSA) that the employee's Social Security number doesn't match the SSA's records. Because the rule created stiff new penalties for employers who did not comply within 90 days of receiving a no-match letter, a group of unions and businesses sought a preliminary injunction to prevent the rule from taking effect. A California federal court granted the injunction, finding serious questions about whether the rule violated the Administrative Procedure Act and the Regulatory Flexibility Act. There were also questions about whether the DHS had the authority to enforce the rule. *American Federation of Labor v. Chertoff*, 552 F.Supp.2d 999 (N.D. Cal. 2007).

A. Negligent Misrepresentation

Occasionally, lawsuits will arise when employees or applicants claim that certain representations were made to them that never materialized. These cases tend to be for negligent, as opposed to intentional, misrepresentation. Often, they arise because of casual or careless statements by company managers, or because a company official asserted an opinion that was taken as more than an opinion.

◆ A New Mexico physician's assistant resigned from a hospital and sued for constructive discharge, alleging that mismanagement in the ER compromised patient care, forcing him to resign. He was then provisionally hired by another hospital, pending receipt of information from his former employers. He signed several releases of liability during the application process, discharging third parties from liability for providing answers to the new hospital's questions about his prior employment. After the old hospital provided responses, some of which were negative, the physician's assistant was not hired at the new hospital. He sued the old hospital for intentional interference with contractual relations and intentional infliction of emotional distress. The Court of Appeals of New Mexico ruled for the old hospital. Here, it had a duty of care to **third parties who could be physically injured by the physician's assistant if the information provided in its reference was a negligent misrepresentation** of the employee's work history. The physician's assistant failed to prove that the old hospital abused its conditional privilege to provide information about him to his new employer. *DiMarco v. Presbyterian Healthcare Services, Inc.*, 141 N.M. 735, 160 P.3d 916 (N.M. Ct. App. 2007).

◆ An executive at a venture capital firm that invested in Internet start-up companies offered a high-level job to a prospective employee, indicating that the firm was close to raising a $40 million venture capital fund. The prospective employee accepted the job, turning down an offer from another Internet company. When the funding fell through, the firm exercised its option to fire the employee. He sued the firm and the executive for negligent representation. A New York federal court ruled in favor of the defendants, noting that they made efforts toward raising the money. **They did not lure the employee into a job while never intending to raise the capital needed**; they merely were unable to obtain it. Thus, there was no negligent misrepresentation. *Elliot v. Nelson*, 301 F.Supp.2d 284 (S.D.N.Y. 2004).

◆ An Illinois employer solicited applications for a marketing manager position. It hired an applicant who later asserted that the company's vice president told him during his employment interview that the company's size was going to double over the next few years and that it had impressive sales figures. Shortly after he started, he learned that the company was in a deteriorating financial condition and he was soon fired as part of a restructuring. He sued for negligent misrepresentation, breach of fiduciary duty and breach of contract. The Supreme Court of Illinois held for the employer, stating that there is no duty to avoid misrepresentations that cause only emotional harm. In order **to state a claim for negligent misrepresentation, there must be a communication of false information that results in physical injury or harm to property**. While other states have recognized a duty to avoid negligent misrepresentations in employment cases, the court refused to expand the scope of employer liability for negligent misrepresentation in Illinois. *Brogan v. Mitchell Int'l, Inc.*, 181 Ill.2d 178, 692 N.E.2d 276 (Ill. 1998).

◆ A prospective employee in New York turned down an offer with another company because a vice president assured her that she would get a job offer. Ultimately, the offer did not materialize. She sued for breach of contract and negligent misrepresentation. The trial court ruled for the employer. The New York Supreme Court, Appellate Division, affirmed. Even if the employer's representations could be construed as an offer, there was no agreement regarding duration; therefore, she could have been terminated at any time and for any or no reason without eliciting a breach of contract action. Also, **the negligent misrepresentation claim could not stand**. The employer's assurance was not false information, but rather an expression of future expectation, which she could not reasonably rely on. *Bower v. Atlis Systems, Inc.*, 582 N.Y.S.2d 542 (N.Y. App. Div. 1992).

B. Mental and Physical Tests

As mentioned above, employers often require prospective employees to undergo psychological and/or physical examinations prior to employment. As long as such requirements apply to all prospective employees (and not just those who seem disabled, for example), the testing requirements will be upheld.

For pre-employment drug screening tests, please see Section II.

◆ An Indiana manufacturer of mineral wool insulation hired an applicant on the condition that he pass a physical examination. The applicant suffered from type I diabetes and was insulin dependent. A doctor examined the applicant, administering a urine glucose test and interviewing him. The doctor determined that his diabetes was not under control and that he was not capable of performing the physical requirements of the job. When the manufacturer withdrew its employment offer, he sued it under the ADA. He claimed that the manufacturer unreasonably relied on the doctor's opinion because the doctor did not perform an adequate, individualized assessment of his ability to do the job. A federal court and the Seventh Circuit ruled for the employer. Here, **the manufacturer reasonably relied on the doctor's opinion** because the applicant admitted to the doctor that he had a history of poor compliance and failure to seek medical attention. He even became angry when the doctor suggested he could do better at controlling his blood sugar levels. Thus, the doctor did not need to do more testing. The evidence also suggested that the applicant posed a direct threat to the safety of the workplace because of the environment where he would be working. *Darnell v. Thermafiber, Inc.*, 417 F.3d 657 (7th Cir. 2005).

- An employee began work at a company in Minnesota but was told that he would have to pass a pre-employment examination that took place a week later. **Although he had had an MRI on his back, he did not mention that to the doctor.** He passed the exam, then injured his back and went on short-term disability leave. After 26 weeks, when the leave expired, he got a note from his doctor stating that he could return to work. However, the company believed he could not perform the essential functions of the job and fired him. He sued for discrimination, claiming the real reason was his race, but a federal court ruled against him. Here, the company legitimately believed he could not do the job, based in part on statements he had made while on leave. *Lavela v. S.B. Foot Tanning Co.*, 2005 WL 1430302 (D. Minn. 3/7/05).

- Four candidates for firefighter positions in the District of Columbia were required to complete certain pre-employment mental examinations, including the Minnesota Multiphasic Personality Inventory-2, a sentence completion test, a figure drawing test and a clinical interview. Based on their test results, they were referred to psychologists for further evaluation. They were **denied employment on the grounds that they were "psychiatrically disqualified,"** and they sued under the Rehabilitation Act and 42 U.S.C. § 1983. The District of Columbia moved for pretrial judgment, asserting that it did not regard the applicants as disabled and that, even if it did, it did not consider their impairments to substantially limit their ability to work. A federal court held that there was a genuine issue of fact as to whether the employer regarded them as individuals with mental impairments that substantially limited them in the major life activity of working. The motion for pretrial judgment was denied. *Does I-IV v. District of Columbia*, 962 F.Supp. 202 (D.D.C. 1997).

- A taconite mining company required prospective employees to participate in a pre-employment physical examination because the jobs involved physically demanding work. The company relied upon the medical recommendation of the doctors performing the physicals to reject or disqualify applicants. A group of prospective employees, rejected because their back conditions indicated their lack of employability, filed a complaint with the Department of Human Rights. The company again consulted with the doctors regarding the accuracy of the examinations, particularly the back x-rays. Obtaining reassurance from the doctors, the company continued its policy of pre-employment screening. An administrative law judge concluded that the rejected applicants were unlawfully discriminated against under the state Human Rights Act. The Minnesota Court of Appeals held that an employer can rely upon competent medical advice that there exists a reasonably probable risk of serious harm should the applicant be hired. **The court upheld the employer's policy of relying on medical advice before hiring applicants.** *State of Minnesota, Dep't of Human Rights v. Hibbing Taconite Co.*, 482 N.W.2d 504 (Minn. Ct. App. 1992).

C. Employment Agencies

Employment agencies provide employers with prospective employees for a fee. Lawsuits arise when employers hire employees without paying the employment agency fee or otherwise violate the agency agreement.

- **A Minnesota nursing home contracted with a recruiting service to bring in foreign registered nurses.** The nursing home retained final discretion on whether to accept an individual nurse as an employee, and was not required to accept a specific number of nurses under the contract. The contract also allowed either party to terminate it on 30 days' notice, and stated that all applications already submitted to the Immigration and Naturalization Service would be considered valid and carried in accordance with the terms of the agreement. When the nursing home terminated the contract, and wrote to the Justice Department, withdrawing the I-140 (Immigrant Petition for Alien Worker) petitions pending for 34 foreign nurses recruited by the service, the service sued it for the fees on those 34 nurses. It claimed that the nursing home had to pay those fees under the "Duration of Agreement" clause. A federal court and the Eighth Circuit ruled for the nursing home. The "Duration of Agreement" clause was subordinate to the "Final Discretion" clause, which stated that the nursing home was not required to hire a specific number of nurses. *Team Nursing Services, Inc. v. Evangelical Lutheran Good Samaritan Society*, 433 F.3d 637 (8th Cir. 2006).

- A Texas company sought to hire an operations manager and asked its accountant for help. The accountant contacted a personnel firm, which referred several candidates to him. He in turn referred one to the company, which hired the candidate. When the personnel firm billed the company, it refused to pay. A lawsuit resulted, and the case reached the Court of Appeals of Texas. The court ruled that the company had to pay the personnel firm. **Since the accountant was acting as the company's agent, there was a valid contract between the company and the personnel firm.** The company owed 25% of the employee's starting salary – $18,500. It also owed the personnel firm its attorneys' fees. *Burnside Air Conditioning and Heating, Inc. v. T.S. Young Corp.*, 113 S.W.3d 889 (Tex. Ct. App. 2003).

- An Illinois company contacted several employment recruiters, seeking a new controller. A recruiter found a candidate for the company, but he lived in

Iowa and made more than the company wanted to pay. The company informed the recruiter that it would not consider the candidate. Two weeks later, another recruiter gave the company the same candidate's name, location and salary information. The company now needed to hire someone quickly, and its CFO did not remember seeing the candidate's name earlier. After discussions among the second recruiter, the candidate and the company, the candidate accepted the job. The company paid the second recruiter, and the first recruiter sued for its fee as well. The Appellate Court of Illinois held that **although the first recruiter did discuss the candidate with the company, it did not follow up after the company rejected the candidate**. The second recruiter did the work in putting the two sides together. The first recruiter was not entitled to its fee. *Vinzenz v. Hintzsche Fertilizer, Inc.*, 783 N.E.2d 1087 (Ill. App. Ct. 2003).

◆ A New York company asked an employment referral agency to find it an assistant comptroller. The referral agency referred two applicants, one of whom was hired. The other applicant was offered a job as a financial manager and assistant vice president. Although she initially turned down the company's offer, she accepted a similar offer 10 months later. The company refused to pay the fee for the second applicant, and the referral agency sued, claiming it had earned the fee by referring the employee for the assistant comptroller position. The Civil Court, City of New York, held that **the agency was entitled to the fee because the agency had introduced the employee to the company and she was ultimately hired by it even though for a different position**. The company had to pay the agency $35,000. *Macro Group, Inc. v. Swiss Re Life Co. America*, 681 N.Y.S.2d 186 (N.Y. City Civ. Ct. 1998).

II. DRUG TESTING

Challenges to drug testing in the private sector are less likely to succeed than their counterparts in the public sector. For instance, the Fourth Amendment only prohibits unreasonable searches and seizures by the government. It does not prohibit unreasonable searches by private employers.

However, discriminatory drug testing is illegal, so any drug testing plan must target all employees and not just a select few. Further, privacy issues may arise, so any drug testing plan should provide for confidentiality of information obtained.

For cases involving drug testing and unemployment benefits, please see Chapter Eight.

A. Pre-Employment Testing

Employers often present job applicants with conditional offers of employment, contingent upon the successful completion of a drug screening test. This is perfectly legal as long as it is not done as a pretext to discriminate against certain applicants.

◆ A North Carolina applicant with depression, bipolar disorder and ADHD received a conditional offer of employment, contingent on passing a drug test. He did not mention that he was taking medication for his condition and tested positive for amphetamines. When the job offer was withdrawn, he did not contact the company's medical review officer to provide proof that he was taking legal medication. Instead, he sued under the ADA. A federal court ruled for the company, noting that **its drug-free workplace policy did not improperly prohibit employees' use of prescription drugs**. In fact, several other applicants had contacted the medical review officer after testing positive for amphetamines, and provided documentation that they were taking prescription medication. They were subsequently hired. Thus, the company did not discriminate against the applicant. *Meyer v. Qualex, Inc.*, 388 F.Supp.2d 630 (E.D.N.C. 2005).

◆ After Wal-Mart offered a West Virginia applicant a job, it required her to give a urine sample. The test came back negative for drugs and the employee began working. She later quit and sued the company for invasion of privacy. The case reached the Supreme Court of Appeals of West Virginia, which noted that an employer may not require an employee to submit to drug testing unless it has a reasonable good-faith suspicion of drug use, or the employee's job responsibilities involve public safety or the safety of others. However, **in the pre-employment context, the individual has a lower expectation of privacy**. Background checks, references and medical examinations all contribute to that lower expectation. The urine sample requirement did not violate the employee's privacy rights. *Baughman v. Wal-Mart Stores,* 592 S.E.2d 824 (W.Va. 2003).

◆ A manager accepted a conditional offer of employment that required him to pass a drug test prior to beginning the job. He succeeded in delaying the test until four days after his eventual date of hire and then submitted a test indicating marijuana use. The employer withdrew its offer of employment, and the manager sued, claiming that he could not be tested for drugs without individualized suspicion of drug use. The Court of Appeal of California noted that the state **approved of drug testing without individualized suspicion for job applicants**. Suspicionless testing is appropriate in such cases, because prospective employers have not had the opportunity to observe them and may have a need to evaluate their drug usage. In contrast, an employer generally should not have to resort to suspicionless testing of current employees. In this case, the manager had not performed any work for the new employer and was properly viewed as a job applicant. An applicant could not avoid drug testing by delaying a test beyond the date of hire. *Pilkington Barnes Hind v. Superior Court (Visbal)*, 77 Cal.Rptr.2d 596 (Cal. Ct. App. 1998).

◆ An electrical contractor hired employees for construction projects in North and South Carolina. A labor organization charged that the contractor violated federal labor law at the North Carolina site by refusing to hire, threatening and interrogating union-affiliated applicants, and for devising and enforcing a drug testing policy to discourage union activities. The union also claimed that the contractor failed to offer work to 16 union-affiliated employees at the South

Carolina site based on their union activities or sympathies. The National Labor Relations Board (NLRB) affirmed the findings of an administrative law judge (ALJ) in favor of the union and ordered the contractor to reinstate two union-affiliated employees who had been fired for refusing to take a drug test. The contractor appealed. The Fourth Circuit rejected the contractor's claim that the ALJ was biased and held that the contractor had committed unfair labor practices. However, the drug testing policy had been **legitimately enacted in response to information that employees of other contractors at the two work sites were using drugs**. The drug testing policy had been uniformly applied to all new employees. The court reversed the NLRB's decision concerning the drug testing policy. *Eldeco, Inc. v. NLRB*, 132 F.3d 1007 (4th Cir. 1997).

B. Employee Testing

Employees may also remain subject to drug testing throughout their employment. Some employer policies rely on random testing (usually for "safety-sensitive" positions), while other policies require reasonable cause or suspicion before testing an employee.

Where an employee has a history of drug use or alcohol abuse but is currently clean and sober, that past history generally cannot be used against the employee.

Absent a last chance agreement (an agreement wherein an employee who has tested positive agrees to be tested in the future in order to save his or her job, with any further positive result allowing the employer to fire him or her), testing targeted to employees with only a past history of drug or alcohol use can be a violation of the Americans with Disabilities Act.

- When a railway engineer reported for work in Indiana, he was informed that he had been selected for random drug testing. He was unable to provide a sample and was given a second opportunity some time later. On the second try, he provided an insufficient sample. According to then-existing Federal Railroad Administration regulations, he was to be afforded two hours to produce an adequate sample. Failure to produce would result in dismissal, unless the failure was medically excusable. When he again **failed to produce a sample**, he was removed from service. A doctor's exam found no medical explanation for his failure to provide a sample. An arbitration panel upheld his dismissal, finding that the railway's actions were not "unjust." A federal court and the Seventh Circuit affirmed. A court's role is not to judge whether the arbitrator's contract interpretation is right or wrong but solely to review whether the arbitrator interpreted the contract at all. If so, that interpretation is conclusive. *Lyons v. Norfolk & Western Railway Co.*, 163 F.3d 466 (7th Cir. 1999).

1. Privacy Claims

It is not uncommon for invasion of privacy and defamation claims to arise as a result of drug testing policies. Although such claims usually fail, they can succeed where the employer goes out of its way to publicize the results of a test, or where it breaches its own policy of confidentiality.

- A temporary employee of a nonprofit agency in New Jersey was taking six different medications for degenerative disc disease. When he applied for a permanent job with the agency, he was required to provide a urine sample, which came back positive for morphine. After the agency fired him, he sued for invasion of privacy, negligence and wrongful discharge. The case reached the Superior Court of New Jersey, Appellate Division, which ruled in favor of the agency. **The employee had no reasonable expectation of privacy with regard to the drug testing**, and the actions taken by the agency and its laboratory did not amount to negligence even though it used an older opiate cutoff level that might pick up on innocent activity, like eating a poppy seed muffin. Here, the employee's level was above what might be expected from such an occurrence. Also, it was not unlawful for the agency to perceive that the employee was taking illegal drugs. *Vargo v. National Exchange Carriers Ass'n, Inc.*, 870 A.2d 679 (N.J. Super. Ct. App. Div. 2005).

- A Texas employer periodically tested its employees for use of illegal controlled substances and randomly tested an employee who yielded a positive result for a cocaine metabolite. He told his supervisor that the result was due to his consumption of herbal teas and offered to have the teas tested by an independent laboratory. A doctor hired by the employer stated that tea could not have caused a positive drug test, and the employee was fired. He sued the employer and physician for discrimination, false light invasion of privacy, negligence, and intentional infliction of emotional distress. The court stated that **Texas does not recognize claims for false light invasion of privacy** because of concerns that doing so would duplicate other claims, including defamation. It dismissed the negligence claims since the employee had sought to impose upon the employer a duty of good faith and fair dealing, which was nonexistent in Texas. In the absence of any evidence of outrageous conduct by the employer, there was also no basis for the intentional infliction of emotional distress claim, and the court granted a partial dismissal of the case. Only the discrimination claims remained. *Quintanilla v. K-Bin, Inc.*, 993 F.Supp. 560 (S.D. Tex. 1998).

- A hotel employee signed a consent form required by her employer under which she agreed to participate in a random drug and alcohol testing program. She tested positive for illegal drug use and requested another test from a different laboratory. The employer declined the request but offered to retest the original sample, which the employee refused. The employer then discharged her, and she sued it for wrongful discharge and invasion of privacy. A state court dismissed her lawsuit, and the court of appeals affirmed. The employee appealed to the Supreme Court of Tennessee, arguing that Tennessee public policy protected her against wrongful discharge because the employer had violated a clear mandate of public policy. The court **rejected her claim that the state constitutional guarantee of privacy restricted the right of a private employer to fire an at-will employee who tested positive for drug use**. Privacy standards applicable to public employers were inapplicable in private employment cases and to the extent that public policy existed concerning drug screening, it favored drug-free workplaces. The court affirmed the ruling for the employer. *Stein v. Davidson Hotel Co.*, 945 S.W.2d 714 (Tenn. 1997).

◆ A Texas employer required its employees to participate in random drug testing. The testing laboratory informed the employer's vice president that one employee tested positive for drug use, and the vice president told the employee's supervisors not to assign him hazardous work. The confirming test result was negative, and the supervisors apologized to the employee for telling him he had failed the drug test. The employee was fired the next year for an unrelated matter, and he sued the employer for negligent and intentional infliction of emotional distress, breach of contract, defamation and invasion of privacy. The court ruled for the employer, and the Court of Appeals of Texas affirmed. Although it agreed with the employee that the employer had breached its own policy of confidentiality in reporting lab results, its report was not false. **Truth was a complete defense to the slander cause of action.** The employee's breach of contract claim also failed, because the employment relationship was at will. The employee was unable to show that the employer's conduct had been intentional, reckless, extreme or outrageous. Accordingly, it did not support a claim for emotional distress. *Washington v. Naylor Industrial Services, Inc.*, 893 S.W.2d 309 (Tex. Ct. App. 1995).

◆ A Massachusetts tool grinder was never under any reasonable suspicion that she ingested illegal drugs. However, one of the company's owners became concerned about drug use by employees and decided to initiate a drug testing policy. When the tool grinder refused to take the test because she found the testing procedure degrading, the company fired her. She sued, alleging a violation of her statutory right to privacy and wrongful termination in violation of public policy. The Supreme Judicial Court of Massachusetts ruled for the employer. Although submission to urinalysis involves a significant invasion of privacy, especially when employees are required to submit to a visual inspection to ensure that they are not concealing vials of urine, the company had a legitimate business interest in protecting its employees and customers, and the owner had a strong basis for suspecting that employees were using drugs. Further, the owner had promised that anyone who tested positive would not be fired, but would be retested in 30 days and given an opportunity to undergo counseling at company expense. Thus, **the drug testing policy was reasonable and did not violate the tool grinder's right to privacy**. *Folmsbee v. Tech Tool Grinding & Supply, Inc.*, 630 N.E.2d 586 (Mass. 1994).

2. Consent

Employees can be required to consent to drug testing as a condition of employment.

◆ A full-time warehouse employee for a Minnesota company also served as a part-time driver. When he was selected for random drug testing, he refused to take the test. After he was suspended and fired, he sued under state and federal drug testing laws. A federal court ruled for the company, and the Eighth Circuit Court of Appeals affirmed. **Even though the employee was only a part-time driver, he was still subject to random testing under the federal law**, and the refusal to take that test could be treated as a positive test justifying his discharge. Also, state law did not prevent the company from firing him for refusing to take a federally mandated test. *Belde v. Ferguson Enterprises, Inc.*, 460 F.3d 976 (8th Cir. 2006).

◆ An employee attempted to steal a surge protector and made several misrepresentations to different employees in his effort to conceal the theft. His behavior prompted the employer to conduct a fitness-for-duty evaluation, which included a drug test. He tested positive and was offered enrollment in an employee assistance plan. However, he was fired after submitting another positive result in a random drug test. He sued for violations of the state workplace drug testing law. The court found that the employer lacked probable cause to suspect the employee of drug use. It also refused to include testimony suggesting that the employer could have fired the employee solely on the basis of the theft incident. The employer appealed. The Supreme Court of Connecticut held that **private sector employees could waive their statutory rights by giving their consent to be tested**. Waiver rights were necessary to ensure that employees maintained the option of entering employee assistance programs and retaining their employment, and to remove an employer's incentive to simply fire employees in response to their drug problems. The trial court had improperly excluded testimony concerning the employee's state of mind at the time of the waiver, and a new trial was required at which evidence concerning the theft incident would be considered. *Poulos v. Pfizer, Inc.*, 244 Conn. 598, 711 A.2d 688 (Conn. 1998).

◆ Georgia workers' compensation law, as affected by the Drug-Free Workplace Programs Act, creates a presumption that a workplace injury has been caused by alcohol or drug use when an employee unjustifiably refuses to submit to testing after a workplace injury. An employee sought workers' compensation benefits for a workplace injury after refusing to submit to drug testing. An administrative law judge applied the presumption and denied benefits, even though the employer had failed to provide the required statutory notice of the consequences of failing to submit to testing. The Supreme Court of Georgia noted that the workers' compensation law incorporated only the drug testing procedures of the drug-free act, and did not incorporate the notice provisions. Since the employer in this case was not alleged to have violated the applicable drug testing procedures of state law, it was entitled to rely upon the presumption that the injury was caused by drug or alcohol use. The state law created no constitutional issues since the presumption could be overcome by evidence and **did not conclusively presume drug use**. *Georgia Self-Insurers Guaranty Trust Fund v. Thomas*, 501 S.E.2d 818 (Ga. 1998).

◆ A California employer maintained a drug testing policy under which employees could be tested where reasonable cause or suspicion of drug or alcohol use was present. **Employees consented in writing to testing as a**

condition of employment. The policy stated that disciplinary action, including discharge, could be imposed for refusing to consent to a test. The employer hired an executive secretary, then discharged her eight months later when she refused to take a drug test after two co-workers observed her slumping over her desk. She sued the employer for wrongful discharge, intentional infliction of emotional distress and violation of the California Constitution, which has been interpreted by state courts as creating a right of action against private employers for invasion of privacy. The Court of Appeal of California stated that employee drug testing claims under the state constitution required balancing the employee's reasonable privacy expectations against the employer's legitimate business interests. The employee had presented evidence that the employer had no reasonable cause to suspect her of drug abuse, and had offered an alternative explanation for the discharge (retaliation against her for refusing to work uncompensated overtime). A trial was required on the wrongful discharge and invasion of privacy claims. However, the trial court had properly dismissed the claim for intentional infliction of emotional distress. *Kraslawsky v. Upper Deck Co.*, 65 Cal.Rptr.2d 297 (Cal. Ct. App. 1997).

3. Adequacy of Testing

The employer should put in place procedures that ensure the testing will be accurate so that any challenge to the procedures will be unsuccessful. The lab used to test the samples should comply with the guidelines of the U.S. Department of Health and Human Services.

◆ An Oklahoma UPS driver was subject to the federal Omnibus Transportation Employee Testing Act, which requires drug and alcohol testing of employees in "safety sensitive" jobs in various transportation industries. After he swerved onto the shoulder of a highway, overturning the two trailers he was pulling, he was ordered to submit to a drug test. When his tests came back positive, he was fired. He sued under Oklahoma's drug testing law, **claiming he did not receive proper notice of the first test as required by federal DOT regulations**. He sought reinstatement, back pay and lost benefits – remedies not available under the federal law. The Tenth Circuit ruled against him, noting that he was not entitled to his job back or any monetary compensation. Here, the driver was required to be tested by federal law; therefore, the Oklahoma statute exempted him from its protections. *Williams v. United Parcel Service, Inc.*, 527 F.3d 1135 (10th Cir. 2008).

◆ A Kentucky truck driver was fired after testing positive for drugs. However, **the testing was not conducted in a manner required by federal regulations** and the results were inaccurate due to the improper handling of the sample and the driver's use of legal over-the-counter medications. He submitted to a later, more accurate test, which demonstrated that the earlier test had indicated a false positive. After he had trouble finding another job due to disclosures by his former employer that he had tested positive for drugs, he sued for wrongful termination and defamation. A trial court dismissed the lawsuit, and the Kentucky Court of Appeals agreed that his wrongful discharge claim could not stand because he was an at-will employee and there was no public policy against firing someone based on a violation of federal regulations. However, he did state a claim for defamation based on the release of the drug test information. That part of the lawsuit required a trial. *Shrout v. The TFE Group*, 161 S.W.3d 351 (Ky. Ct. App. 2005).

◆ A Texas truck driver was required to submit to random drug testing pursuant to Department of Transportation (DOT) regulations. He tested positive for THC (marijuana) in two different urine samples and was fired after the second test. He sued the company for violating five of the DOT collection protocols. A jury found that the company was negligent in collecting his urine sample and awarded him more than $800,000 in damages, as well as exemplary damages of $100,000 after finding that the company acted with malice. The court of appeals affirmed, but the Supreme Court of Texas reversed. It found no basis for holding an employer liable for firing an at-will employee for a positive drug test. Under the at-will employment doctrine, an employer does not have to determine if a termination was based on correct information. **The court refused to adopt a new theory of negligent drug testing.** *Mission Petroleum Carriers, Inc. v. Solomon*, 106 S.W.3d 705 (Tex. 2003).

◆ A North Carolina employer asked an employee to submit to random drug screening. The employee tested positive for drug use and was fired. He filed a wrongful discharge action against the employer, asserting that the laboratory used for the testing was not approved by the state as required by law. The court granted pretrial judgment to the employer, but the court of appeals reversed, holding that state law established procedures required of employers to conduct drug screening on employees to protect them from unreliable or inadequate testing. It agreed with the employee that the law was an express policy declaration by the state and that any discharge inconsistent with the law violated a public policy exception to the presumption of employment at will. The employer here had violated public policy by utilizing an unapproved laboratory. On further appeal, the North Carolina Supreme Court reversed, holding that **the employer's failure to use an approved laboratory for the drug testing did not give rise to a claim for wrongful discharge**. There must be more than a statutory violation; there must also be an unlawful reason or purpose that violates public policy. Here, there was no evidence of such a purpose. *Garner v. Rentenbach Constructors, Inc.*, 515 S.E.2d 438 (N.C. 1999).

4. Collective Bargaining Agreements

In unionized workplaces, collective bargaining agreements generally define the nature of drug testing policies and limits. They also generally provide a disciplinary procedure and a grievance process for employees who wish to challenge positive test results.

◆ A New Jersey brewery worker submitted a hair for drug testing and was fired when a positive result came back. He and his wife sued the brewery, alleging that although the drug test reading was below the "minimum detection level," and thus was not reliable, the brewery nonetheless discharged him. They asserted breach of contract and intentional infliction of emotional distress, among other claims. A federal court ruled against them, noting that the breach of contract action was preempted by Section 301 of the LMRA because a collective bargaining agreement was in place at the time of the firing and any resolution of the claim would demand the interpretation of the agreement. Further, the emotional distress claim could not survive because the brewery's action in firing the worker was not so extreme and outrageous that it went beyond all possible bounds of decency. *Brandt v. Anheuser-Busch, Inc.*, 2007 WL 1175751 (D.N.J. 2007).

◆ An employee of an aircraft manufacturing corporation was fired after his second positive drug test. He sued the company and the union under Section 301 of the LMRA, alleging wrongful discharge by the company and breach of the duty of fair representation by the union. A Connecticut federal court and the Second Circuit ruled against him. **Firing the employee for the second positive drug test did not violate the collective bargaining agreement.** Further, the union's decision not to arbitrate the employee's claim was not irrational or arbitrary so as to constitute a breach of the duty of fair representation. *Verrilli v. Sikorsky Aircraft Corp.*, 221 Fed.Appx. 8 (2d Cir. 2007).

◆ A West Virginia truck driver, subject to Department of Transportation regulations requiring random drug testing for workers engaged in "safety-sensitive" tasks, tested positive for marijuana on two occasions. Both times, his employer sought to discharge him, but the union went to arbitration on both occasions and obtained awards that ordered his reinstatement. The employer then sued to nullify the arbitrator's award. A federal court enforced the award, and the Fourth Circuit affirmed. The U.S. Supreme Court also affirmed. It held that **public policy did not require the courts to prevent the driver's reinstatement despite the positive drug tests**. Federal law encourages rehabilitation where possible. Here, the arbitration award did not condone the driver's conduct or ignore the risk to public safety that drug use by truck drivers may pose, but punished the driver by placing conditions on his reinstatement. He had to pay both parties' arbitration costs, undergo further substance abuse treatment and testing, and provide a signed letter of resignation in the event he failed any more drug tests. *Eastern Associated Coal Corp. v. UMW of America*, 531 U.S. 57, 121 S.Ct. 462, 148 L.Ed.2d 354 (2000).

◆ An electrical contractor in Illinois agreed to abide by the collective bargaining agreement between a contractors association and the International Brotherhood of Electrical Workers. **The bargaining agreement contained a drug testing provision for all employees of each participating firm.** When the contractor refused to implement the drug testing rule for employees other than electricians represented by the union, an arbitration board ordered the electricians' union not to refer any of its members to the contractor for employment. The contractor sued, and a federal court held the board's order invalid, but the Seventh Circuit Court of Appeals reversed. It held that the contractor had agreed to be bound by the bargaining agreement, and that federal labor law allowed bargaining agreements to reach beyond the certified unit of workers. Thus, the contractor could not test only the electricians. However, if the separate bargaining agreement between the contractor and the operating engineers' union had its own drug testing rules, the contractor would have to abide by those rules for those employees. *Lid Electric, Inc. v. IBEW, Local 134*, 362 F.3d 940 (7th Cir. 2004).

◆ A bus driver for the New York City Transit Authority was randomly called to the office for a drug test. She was unable to provide an adequate sample of at least 45 ml of urine and was required to drink 40 ounces of liquid within a three-hour period. She still could not provide an adequate sample and was referred to a doctor, who could find no medical reason for the failure. This was deemed a "refusal" to provide a sample and resulted in the employee's suspension. The transit authority also told her it intended to fire her. Doctors later found that she had slow urine flow and urgency incontinence, but that she should have been able to provide a sample within the three-hour period. Her union filed a grievance, and an arbitration panel determined that she should not be disciplined. The Supreme Court, Appellate Division, held that **Department of Transportation regulations specified removal from a safety-sensitive position (like driving a bus) where an employee "refuses" to provide a sample**. However, the Court of Appeals reversed, ruling that the appellate division improperly substituted its factual finding for that of a majority of the arbitration panel. *Dowleyne v. NYCTA*, 816 N.E.2d 191 (N.Y. 2004).

◆ A collective bargaining agreement provided that where a company had reasonable cause to believe that an employee was working while under the influence of drugs, the employee would be required to submit to a blood or urine test or be fired. After the company received anonymous phone calls accusing an employee of drug trafficking, it used a machine to sweep the employee's car and work area for drug residue. Cocaine was detected in both places. The company asked the employee to take a drug test. He refused and was fired. The union took the case to arbitration, where the arbitrator determined that the company **could require the drug test only if there was reasonable cause to believe the employee was on drugs at the time** he was asked to submit to the test. Since the company did not believe the employee was on drugs at the moment it asked him to take the drug test, it could not fire him for refusing to submit. The Seventh Circuit Court of Appeals affirmed the arbitrator's order that the employee be reinstated. Although it would not have read the bargaining agreement so literally, it refused to overturn the ruling because the ruling was not arbitrary and capricious. *Int'l Truck and Engine Corp. v. United Steel Workers of America, Local 3740*, 294 F.3d 860 (7th Cir. 2002).

III. NON-COMPETITION AGREEMENTS AND TRADE SECRETS

Employers, particularly in specialized areas (like broadcasting), often require employees to enter into non-compete agreements that prohibit employees from leaving their employment and competing against their former employer.

Non-compete agreements are generally valid if supported by consideration. In other words, if both sides give something of value, they will be upheld. This means they should be signed prior to employment (as a condition of employment) wherever possible.

However, non-compete agreements must also be reasonable in scope, geographic area and duration. A non-compete agreement that lasts for three years will likely be struck down as too harsh, as will one that includes too great a geographical area.

Agreements that prevent an employee from soliciting all potential customers, even those who are not currently customers of the employer, may also be struck down as too broad in scope.

Although non-compete agreements are not appropriate for many employees, trade secret and confidentiality agreements should be used more frequently – first, to protect confidential information, and second, to establish that the employer considers certain information confidential.

A. Non-Compete Agreements

The key to restrictive covenants and covenants not to compete is that they must be reasonable or courts will not uphold them. There is no automatically reasonable agreement; each agreement will be examined in light of the individual facts pertinent to it.

Courts look to the scope, duration and geographic limitations of "no compete" clauses to test their validity.

- The manager of a trucking company in St. Louis made plans to leave the company and join a competitor. She let the renewal deadline for the company's lease of its premises pass without informing company officials, then **gave confidential information about the company to the competitor**. When the company sued her for breach of the duty of loyalty (and sued the competitor for conspiracy), she claimed that as an at-will employee who had never signed a non-compete agreement, she could not be held liable. A jury and the Missouri Supreme Court disagreed. However, the verdict ($54,000 against the manager and $254,000 against the competitor) could not stand because it included preparations the manager made. Instead, the jury could only consider actions taken beyond the preparation stage. The case had to be re-tried. *Scanwell Freight Express STL, Inc. v. Chan*, 162 S.W.3d 477 (Mo. 2005).

- A North Carolina publisher of internal company magazines hired a general manager to oversee the production of several magazines, including one for a furniture company's employees. The general manager hired an assistant to help him. Neither employee signed a non-compete agreement. Later, when the publisher, general manager and assistant entered into discussions with the furniture company about renewing the contract, the assistant quit. She formed a competing business with the general manager and contracted with the furniture company to publish the magazine. The general manager then resigned. The publisher sued the general manager and the assistant for breach of the duty of loyalty as well as deceptive trade practices. A trial court dismissed the case, but the court of appeals reversed in part, finding that the general manager may have breached a duty of loyalty to the employer. On further appeal, the Supreme Court of North Carolina ruled that **the general manager was not in a fiduciary relationship with the employer such that he could be held liable for breach of duty**, and the employer failed to show that he engaged in unfair or deceptive trade practices. *Dalton v. Camp*, 548 S.E.2d 704 (N.C. 2001).

1. Enforceability of Agreements

Where a non-compete agreement is not supported by valid consideration (usually, where all the burden is on the employee and there is no cost or burden on the employer), it will not be enforceable. Thus, where possible, an employer should condition employment on the signing of the agreement.

However, if an employer wishes to ask a current employee to sign such an agreement, it should provide extra benefits (independent consideration) to support the contract. Such benefits should only be given to employees who sign the agreement.

If the benefits are provided to other employees who do not sign (or who are not asked to sign), the contract will not be enforced.

- The manager of a company in Michigan had an employment agreement that prohibited the company from firing her without just cause. The agreement also contained a non-compete provision preventing her from working for a competitor for a year after leaving the job, regardless of the reason. The company then fired her without just cause and she went to work for a competitor. In the lawsuits that arose, the Michigan Court of Appeals noted that **the company could enforce the non-compete clause even though it breached the contract first by improperly firing the manager**. Here, the non-compete clause stated that it was effective "regardless of the reason" for the termination. As a result, even though the company breached the contract first, it was entitled to damages for the ex-manager's violation of the non-compete clause. *Coates v. Bastian Brothers, Inc.*, 741 N.W.2d 539 (Mich. Ct. App. 2007).

- A Pennsylvania salesman working in a three-state area signed a non-compete agreement that prevented him from working for a competitor for 12 months following his departure. **The agreement covered a 10-state area as well as any area in which the company's products were sold, and it listed nine competitors by name as prohibited employers** during that time. When the employee went to work for one of the competitors in the 10-state area (but outside the three-state area where he had worked), he and his new employer sued for a declaration that the non-compete agreement was invalid. A federal court dismissed the case on the pleadings, finding the agreement unenforceable. However, the Third Circuit vacated and remanded the case, finding that the district court should have considered the fact that the agreement only restricted the salesman from working for nine named competitors. It also should have considered that the 10-state limitation might be reasonable. The case should not have been dismissed on the pleadings. *Victaulic Co. v. Tieman*, 499 F.3d 227 (3d Cir. 2007).

- A company required an employee to sign a non-compete agreement in order to continue in his job. It also promised to provide him with special training on its business methods and confidential information about current and prospective customers. It subsequently provided that training and information. When the employee left to join a competitor, the company sued to enforce the non-compete agreement. The case reached the Texas Supreme Court, which noted that an employer cannot enforce a stand-alone promise from an employee not to compete unless it provides new consideration. Here, **the non-compete agreement, although originally unenforceable, became enforceable when the employer performed the future promise to provide training and information**. *Alex Sheshunoff Management Services, L.P. v. Johnson*, 209 S.W.3d 644 (Tex. 2006).

- A housekeeping company in Indiana required its office manager to sign a non-compete clause restricting her from "owning, managing or materially participating" in any substantially similar business within a 25-mile radius for two years after leaving the company. When the manager quit and began offering housekeeping services of her own, the company sued to enforce the non-compete clause. A trial court ruled for the company, but the Court of Appeals of Indiana reversed. Here, **the non-compete clause was unreasonably broad because it prevented the manager from working for a competing business in any capacity**, rather than just in positions similar to the one she held. Although the company had a legitimate interest worth protecting, its overbroad non-compete clause went too far and thus was not enforceable. *MacGill v. Reid*, 850 N.E.2d 926 (Ind. Ct. App. 2006).

- A global brand manager for a cosmetics company signed a non-compete agreement, then resigned and sued in a California court to have the non-compete agreement declared unenforceable so he could take a position with a skin care products company. The cosmetics company sued in a New York court to enforce the agreement. The New York court noted that the agreement contained an international geographic restriction for one year. However, it also provided that **the company would pay his $375,000 salary for the duration of the restriction**. The company also offered to reduce the term of the non-compete agreement to four months. The court held that New York law applied and granted the temporary injunction to enforce the agreement. *Estee Lauder Companies, Inc. v. Batra*, 430 F.Supp.2d 158 (S.D.N.Y. 2006).

- An at-will bank employee in Texas signed a series of stock option agreements that contained non-compete and confidentiality clauses. After exercising his stock options, the employee left the bank and sought to have the non-compete and confidentiality provisions declared unenforceable. The case reached the Fifth Circuit Court of Appeals, which ruled that the non-compete and confidentiality provisions were unenforceable because they were based on an illusory promise – i.e., the bank could fire the employee at any time and make the stock options disappear, so in effect the bank was promising nothing. However, because the non-compete and confidentiality provisions were unenforceable, and because the stock options were tied to those provisions, the employee had to return his profits from exercising his stock options. *Olander v. Compass Bank*, 363 F.3d 560 (5th Cir. 2004).

◆ An employee in Oregon was promoted to regional sales manager. Before receiving the official written offer, he began performing some of the job's duties. Three weeks later, he signed the official written offer, as well as the non-compete agreement that the company required him to accept as a condition of the promotion. When he quit to take a position with a competitor, the company sought to enforce the one-year non-compete agreement. He argued that the agreement was not enforceable because it was not supported by consideration, since he had begun performing the job's duties before signing the non-compete clause. The Ninth Circuit disagreed, noting that **the signing of the non-compete agreement came as part of the promotion**; it did not come after the fact. Further, the company had a legally protected interest in the confidential information he acquired while in the position. The one-year non-compete clause was enforceable. *Nike v. McCarthy*, 379 F.3d 576 (9th Cir. 2004).

◆ An at-will employee of a company in Ohio signed a non-compete agreement after a couple years on the job, and continued working for another 10 years. He then began a competing venture, and the company sued him. The case reached the Supreme Court of Ohio, which noted that **employers do not have to provide extra consideration to an at-will employee (other than continued employment) to enforce a non-compete agreement**. If the employee is not satisfied with the agreement, he is always free to quit and look for work elsewhere. By consenting to the terms of the non-compete agreement and continuing employment under the new terms, the employee receives consideration (something of value) to support the new contract. The court remanded the case for a determination of whether the terms of the non-compete agreement were reasonable. *Lake Land Employment Group of Akron v. Columber*, 804 N.E.2d 27 (Ohio 2004).

◆ After signing a confidentiality agreement, the vice president of sales of a lock manufacturer went to work for a competitor. He maintained that he could take the job because the company never asked him to sign a non-compete agreement. The company sued to prevent him from taking the job, and he sued for a declaration that he was allowed to do so. The company invoked the "inevitable disclosure" doctrine, which holds that an employee can be prevented from working for a competitor if the new position would inevitably cause the employee to rely on knowledge of the former employer's proprietary information. Under the doctrine, an employer need not prove that the employee has misappropriated or threatened to misappropriate trade secrets. The

California Court of Appeal rejected the doctrine in holding for the employee. It noted that **the "inevitable disclosure" doctrine rewrites the employee's relationship with the employer**, in effect turning a confidentiality agreement into a non-compete agreement. *Whyte v. Schlage Lock Co.*, 125 Cal.Rptr.2d 277 (Cal. Ct. App. 2002).

◆ An Arizona woman worked for a commercial property management firm for two years. Subsequently, she submitted her resignation and stated that she intended to start her own commercial property management firm. On the same day, she notified her commercial clients that she was resigning and gave the effective date. She expressly stated that she was not soliciting their business for her new firm, but only thanked them for their kindness and support during their business relationship. Her employer sued and alleged, among other things, a breach of fiduciary duty. The trial court ruled for the former employee, and the Arizona Court of Appeals affirmed, stating that before the end of the employment relationship, an employee can properly purchase a rival business and upon termination of employment immediately compete. The employee is not, however, entitled to solicit customers before the end of her employment, and she cannot directly compete with the employer's business. Here, no evidence existed to indicate that the employee acted improperly. **An employee making preparations to compete after leaving her job can advise current customers that she is leaving.** *McCallister Co. v. Kastella,* 825 P.2d 980 (Ariz. Ct. App. 1992).

2. Terms and Conditions

The terms and conditions of non-compete agreements must be reasonable to be enforced. Where parts of the agreement are not reasonable, some courts will strike down the entire agreement. Other courts will strike down only those elements that are unreasonable. Still other courts will strike down the unreasonable elements and substitute their judgment of what is reasonable.

◆ A company with its headquarters in Ohio required a sales rep to sign a non-compete clause when it promoted him to account manager for its Illinois and Indiana regions. While working for the company, the manager was contacted by a competitor's HR director. He submitted his résumé to the competitor and eventually accepted an offer to become a vice president of sales. After resigning and going to work for the competitor, he was sued by the company for breaching the agreement. A federal court held that although he had violated the agreement, **the agreement was overbroad because it did not contain a geographic limitation**. The court refused to rewrite the non-compete clause to make it enforceable, and the Seventh Circuit upheld that decision. Under Ohio law, the court had the discretion to decide whether to modify the agreement. *Cintas Corp. v. Perry*, 517 F.3d 459 (7th Cir. 2008).

◆ A company in Michigan asked an employee to sign a non-compete agreement that prohibited him from "directly or indirectly" engaging in the operation of a competing business, except for a county in which the employee already owned a competing business. After the employee signed the agreement, he allegedly carried out some sales and deliveries in the prohibited area. The company sued him for violating the non-compete agreement, and a federal court ruled in favor of the employee. The Sixth Circuit affirmed, reading the non-compete agreement narrowly. It stated that **the transactions the employee engaged in did not amount to management or oversight of the competing business**. It was the mere soliciting of customers or selling of products, which was technically not the same thing as "operating a business." *United Rentals (North America), Inc. v. Keizer*, 355 F.3d 399 (6th Cir. 2004).

◆ An insurance agent signed an employment contract in which he agreed not to disclose proprietary information or to compete with the company within a 25-mile radius for five years. The restrictive covenants contained no information concerning assignability. Later, the company sold its insurance business assets, and the buyer told the agent it was going to eliminate his position. The agent sought employment with a competitor and also sought to obtain the business of one of the buyer's largest clients. The buyer and seller objected, and the competitor refused to hire the agent. When the agent sued, a state court held that the non-compete agreement was assignable to the buyer but modified its terms because it was not reasonable as to time and distance. The Supreme Court of Pennsylvania reversed, holding that **the non-compete agreement was not assignable without the employee's consent**. Further, the non-compete agreement could not be enforced by the seller because the seller did not have a legitimate interest that needed protecting. The seller was no longer in the insurance business. *Hess v. Gebhard & Co.*, 808 A.2d 912 (Pa. 2002).

◆ A Missouri employee signed a non-compete agreement that prohibited him from soliciting business from the company's clients and from soliciting or encouraging its employees to terminate their employment. He later went to work for a competitor and had lunch with a former co-worker (still employed by the company). During the lunch, he explained that the competitor was looking for people with the co-worker's experience and skills and that the job would be a good opportunity for the co-worker. When the co-worker reported the conversation to the company, it sued the former employee for breach of contract. The Missouri Court of Appeals ruled against the company. It noted that the agreement here was **a restrictive covenant limiting the employee's ability to pursue his occupation**, and therefore a restraint of trade that violated Missouri law. A restrictive covenant cannot be used to maintain a stable workforce. They are allowed only to protect trade secrets or customer contacts. The company did not have a proprietary interest in its at-will employees or their skills that would justify such an agreement. *Schmersahl, Treloar & Co. v. McHugh*, 28 S.W.3d 345 (Mo. Ct. App. 2000).

◆ A North Carolina man worked for a company that provided individuals with orthotics and prosthetics. He signed an employment agreement containing a "confidential information" provision that barred him from working for a competitor for two years after "the date of termination of [his] employment by the Employer or any other member of the Company Group." When he resigned and went to work for a competitor, the company sued him seeking a preliminary injunction to prevent him from doing so. The case reached the North Carolina Court of Appeals, which noted that **the language of the confidential information provision was ambiguous** and that it had to be construed against the company because the company had drafted the agreement. The court also noted that the company could not claim trade secret protection because it failed to show that it took any special precautions to ensure the confidentiality of its customer information. Although the company was entitled to seek arbitration over the employment agreement, it was not entitled to an injunction to keep the employee from working for the competitor. *Novacare Orthotics & Prosthetics East, Inc. v. Speelman*, 528 S.E.2d 918 (N.C. Ct. App. 2000).

- A New York title insurance company's highest paid salesman, represented by his lawyer, agreed to a non-compete provision that prohibited him from selling title insurance in New York for six months after he left the company. A direct competitor subsequently offered him a job and agreed to pay him a salary during that six-month period. Before he resigned, the salesman spoke to 20 of the company's customers, informing them of his interest in joining a competitor and expressly asking one to follow him. The company applied for an injunction to have the agreement enforced, and a federal court ordered him to abide by the terms of the agreement. The Second Circuit upheld the order. First, **the agreement was reasonable in time (six months) and in its geographic scope (the state of New York)**. Second, the salesperson's services were unique, making the agreement valid, for three reasons: 1) the title insurance business relies heavily on personal relationships; 2) because potential clients are limited, maintaining current clients from this group is crucial; and 3) the salesman negotiated the agreement with the assistance of counsel. *Ticor Title Insurance Co. v. Cohen*, 173 F.3d 63 (2d Cir. 1999).

- An analyst for a Connecticut software company had access to confidential sales and marketing information. He was employed under a confidentiality agreement and a restrictive covenant in which he agreed not to compete against the employer in the event of his termination by refraining from soliciting business opportunities from any customer or from rendering his services to a competing venture for one year. However, the employee resigned and accepted a marketing position with a competitor. The former employer sued him and the competitor in federal court, seeking to enforce the non-compete and confidentiality agreements. The court found that the covenant not to compete was reasonable. It examined the duration of the restriction, its geographical scope, fairness to the parties and the public interest. **The restrictive covenant lasted only one year and was not overly broad** in view of the company's nationwide business presence. The company had made reasonable efforts to maintain the secrecy of its confidential information and was thus entitled to enforce the confidentiality agreement. Although there was no evidence that the employee had disclosed confidential information, the possibility of such a disclosure was likely, and the court enjoined him from working for the competitor for at least six months. *Weseley Software Development Corp. v. Burdette*, 977 F.Supp. 137 (D. Conn. 1997).

◆ A Georgia veterinarian signed a contract agreeing to forgo employment at any other veterinary clinic within five miles of her employer's clinic for two years following the termination of her employment. The contract prohibited solicitation of all persons in the area, not just customers of the clinic. She purchased another practice located within five miles of the clinic, and her former employer sued her to enjoin her from managing or providing services at the clinic she had purchased. The court granted the former employer's request for a permanent order, and the veterinarian appealed. The Court of Appeals of Georgia stated that where a **territorial limitation is specific, narrow, and limited to the area actually worked**, it is reasonable and enforceable even though it prohibits the provision of services to all persons in the area. Here, the contract was enforceable, and the court affirmed the judgment. *Chaichimansour v. Pets Are People Too, No. 2, Inc.*, 485 S.E.2d 248 (Ga. Ct. App. 1997).

◆ A telecommunications service company employed salespersons under written contracts that included non-compete covenants and protected the company's confidential information. A salesperson in the company's Indianapolis office was one of three employees who quit to join a competitor. She used confidential information from her former employer's business records to solicit customers for her new employer. The former employer sought a preliminary order from an Indiana federal court to restrain the solicitation of its customers and to protect its confidential customer information. The court held that the customer limitation in this case was not reasonable concerning new customers with whom the former employees had no previous relationship. **The covenant was enforceable as to existing customers of the former employer,** and the employees were restrained from misusing the former employer's confidential information. However, the court refused to enforce the covenant concerning new customers. *Frontier Corp. v. Telco Communications Group, Inc.*, 965 F.Supp. 1200 (S.D. Ind. 1997).

◆ A Florida floor care maintenance employee signed an employment and non-competition agreement with his employer that prohibited him from competing with the employer for five years within 100 miles of the employer's branch offices. He later assisted a competitor in obtaining an account and went to work for the competitor. The former employer sued to enforce the agreement. The District Court of Appeal of Florida held that an employer's **legitimate business interests include trade secrets, confidential business lists, records, customer goodwill and specialized training** provided to employees. The employer here had a legitimate interest in prohibiting direct solicitation of its existing customers. Also, the geographic restrictions were reasonable. However, the former employer had given no specialized training to the employee that justified an injunction to prevent employment with the competitor. *Dyer v. Pioneer Concepts, Inc.*, 667 So.2d 961 (Fla. Dist. Ct. App. 1996).

B. Trade Secrets

Most states have enacted the Uniform Trade Secrets Act, which states that trade secrets must be subject to efforts that are reasonable to maintain their secrecy. If information is readily available, or if the employer does not take reasonable steps to protect it, it will not be given trade secret protection.

Following are a few ways to demonstrate that an employer is making reasonable efforts to keep information secret:

1) Require every employee to sign trade secret or confidentiality agreements,
2) Restrict visitor access to sensitive areas of the workplace,
3) Separate sensitive departments or processes from the main workplace,
4) Keep secret documents in locked file cabinets or safes, and
5) Distribute confidential information on a strictly need-to-know basis.

Note that customer lists can be trade secrets if they are properly protected, and if they cannot be obtained by other (legal) methods.

1. Defining "Trade Secrets"

Generally, a trade secret is "information" that derives independent economic value (actual or potential) from not being generally known and not being generally ascertainable (by legal means) by competitors.

◆ An Illinois manufacturer of tubes used in filtration devices hired an employee and required him to sign two non-compete agreements during his tenure with the company. He later left, formed his own business and began to compete with his old company. The company sued him for misappropriating trade secrets and violating the non-compete agreements. An Illinois court determined that the company's customer information was protected as a trade secret. The Appellate Court of Illinois disagreed. The company **failed to take reasonable steps to protect the customer information as a trade secret**. All it did was require its employees to sign a confidentiality agreement. Thus, the customer information was not protected. Further, the non-compete agreements were invalid because they were blanket prohibitions on competition. *Arcor, Inc. v. Haas*, 842 N.E.2d 265 (Ill. App. Ct. 2005).

◆ A Texas company performed high performance upgrades on motor vehicles. An employee who gained substantial knowledge of the business began competing with the company after resigning without notice. A state court granted temporary injunctive relief to the employer, forbidding the new venture from performing a variety of acts including disclosing information and servicing motor vehicles of the type that the company upgraded. The former employee appealed the adverse decision to the Court of Appeals of Texas, asserting that the relief granted was excessive. The court held that **the employer's information was protectable as a trade secret**. The employee had a duty arising from the employment relationship not to use confidential or proprietary information in a manner adverse to the employer. The court modified the scope of the trial court order. Here, the employer had argued that its sales might drop $2 million in the absence of such protection, and injunctive relief was appropriate. The parties settled after an appeal to the state supreme court. *T-N-T Motorsports, Inc. v. Hennessey Motorsports, Inc.*, 965 S.W.2d 18 (Tex. Ct. App. 1998).

◆ A Georgia computer software developer hired two employees under written agreements to develop programs for tracking assets. The employees breached a restrictive covenant in their employment agreements by forming a competing venture and offering to sell similar software to the employer's customers. The employer sued them for breach of contract, seeking an injunction against violation of the covenants. The court found that the former employees had misappropriated the employer's trade secrets and were currently using them in violation of the covenants. However, it found that the former employees had not been unjustly enriched and should not pay any damages. Instead, it imposed a 7% royalty upon them for four months for use of the trade secrets and enjoined them from soliciting the former employer's customers according to the terms of the covenants, which were to expire in three days.

The Supreme Court of Georgia found that **computer software constituted trade secrets** that were a proper subject of the covenants. The evidence sufficiently detailed the existence of trade secrets and the trial court had permissibly imposed a royalty payment for their improper use. The trial court had also properly enjoined the former employees from soliciting customers for the duration of the covenants, even though they were set to expire only three days beyond its order. The court refused to extend the duration of the covenants by excluding the time of the litigation from the two-year period contained in them, noting that the parties could have included a tolling provision. *Electronic Data Systems Corp. v. Heinemann*, 493 S.E.2d 132 (Ga. 1997).

◆ A marketing representative solicited customers for a Florida healthcare management consulting firm. The company offered seminars that provided information on Medicare reimbursement and management information. After four years, the representative formed his own company for presenting seminars in related areas, and quit working for the consulting firm. He signed a release agreement with his former employer under which he agreed not to solicit the consulting firm's current clients and agreed not to compete against it for one year. When the firm discovered that the representative's new company was advertising a home healthcare seminar, it sued him, seeking to prohibit his use of trade secrets and forbidding him from direct solicitation of its clients. The court issued a temporary injunction against the representative, but later determined that he was not in competition with the consulting firm and dissolved the injunction. The consulting firm appealed to the District Court of Appeal of Florida, which noted that **a trade secret is defined under Florida law as something of independent economic value that is not readily ascertainable by ordinary means**. Here, the consulting firm's information was readily ascertainable, but the solicitation of the consulting firm's customers was presumed to be subject to an injunction. The court reversed and remanded the trial court's decision. *Health Care Management Consulting, Inc. v. McCombes,* 661 So.2d 1223 (Fla. Dist. Ct. App. 1995).

2. Employer Protections

Generally, employers wish to protect themselves by obtaining injunctive relief (usually in the form of a court order prohibiting a competitor from using trade secrets to its advantage) in addition to money damages and attachment of future royalties. However, courts will generally not issue an injunction unless there is more than a suspicion of injury.

- Two managers of a Dallas consulting firm's claims office were approached by a competitor about selling off the claims practice. The managers prepared a detailed proposal without informing their employer of the competitor's interest in buying the practice. When the deal fell through, they continued to try to sell the claims practice to other competitors, hoping to route the transaction through a company they owned. They eventually left to work for one of the competitors, and the firm sued them for breach of contract, breach of fiduciary duty and misappropriation of trade secrets. A jury awarded the firm over $2 million in damages, including punitive damages, and the Fifth Circuit upheld the award. The jury had properly determined that **the managers breached their fiduciary duty, breached the contract, and misappropriated trade secrets** by disclosing confidential information to the firm's competitors. *Navigant Consulting, Inc. v. Wilkinson*, 508 F.3d 277 (5th Cir. 2007).

- A chiropractor, while working for a clinic, began looking for another job and agreed to work for a nearby clinic that would pay her $3,800 per month plus a $100 bonus for every new client. The chiropractor appropriated the confidential client list from the first clinic over the next few months, then urged clients to switch to the nearby clinic. The chiropractor who owned the first clinic **sued the former employee as well as the owner of the nearby clinic for violating the Uniform Trade Secrets Act (UTSA)**. A jury awarded $89,000 against the defendants, and the trial judge doubled the damages award on the grounds that the former employee acted willfully. The Washington Court of Appeals held that the nearby clinic could be vicariously liable for the UTSA violation. However, it did not clearly establish at trial that the former employee had been acting as the nearby clinic's agent when she stole the confidential list. The nearby clinic claimed to be unaware of the theft until the lawsuit. Thus, the case had to be retried. *Thola v. Henschell*, 164 P.3d 524 (Wash. Ct. App. 2007).

- Two salesmen for a Missouri medical devices company signed confidentiality agreements, pledging not to disclose or use any confidential information acquired during their employment. While with the company, the salesmen decided to create a competing product. They hired the engineer who had built the company's device to create a similar product. He did so using spare parts from the company and with the assistance of a company employee. The salesmen then used sales information acquired while with the company to compete with it. When the company sued, a jury awarded it over $2 million in damages. The Eighth Circuit upheld the award. Here, **the employees violated the confidentiality agreement and misappropriated the company's trade secrets**. *Synergetics, Inc. v. Hurst*, 477 F.3d 949 (8th Cir. 2007).

◆ A Minnesota insurance agency hired a salesman from a competitor after checking the non-compete agreement that the salesman had signed. The agreement stated that the salesman could solicit business from his close family and friends even if they were on the competitor's list of policyholders. The agency gave the salesman stationery and other supplies, and he proceeded to solicit approximately 250 people from the competitor's list, which was about 200 more than he was entitled to solicit. A lawsuit arose under the Minnesota Trade Secrets Act, and a trial court found that the salesman had violated the act but that the agency was not liable because the salesman had been acting outside the scope of his employment when he violated the non-compete agreement. The court of appeals held that the agency was liable because it should have supervised the salesman, but the Minnesota Supreme Court held that the agency was not vicariously liable. Here, although vicarious liability was possible under the act, **the competitor failed to show it was foreseeable that the salesman would misappropriate trade secrets**. *Hagen v. Burmeister & Associates, Inc.*, 633 N.W.2d 497 (Minn. 2001).

◆ An auto leasing company hired a senior manager to work in its Phoenix office and required him to sign a non-disclosure and non-compete agreement. After he was fired, he took 45 confidential documents comprising strategic plans, programs, methods and approaches. When the company demanded that he return the documents, he returned only photocopies, asserting that he had destroyed the originals. However, he then used the originals in his own competing business until the company obtained a temporary restraining order and a preliminary injunction against him. He subsequently went to work for another competitor, and the company sued him again, this time to obtain a permanent injunction preventing him from disclosing and using the information in the stolen documents. A state court determined that the information was no longer a trade secret and refused to grant the injunction. The Arizona Court of Appeals reversed, noting that **even though the information was not fresh, it was still protected by the Uniform Trade Secrets Act**, which Arizona had adopted. The company had made reasonable efforts to maintain the secrecy of the information. Thus, it was entitled to trade secret protection. *Enterprise Leasing Co. v. Ehmke*, 3 P.3d 1064 (Ariz. Ct. App. 1999).

◆ A roofing repair company employed sales reps who signed agreements promising not to use, duplicate or disclose customer information in the event of termination. Two employees resigned, took customer business cards with them and began soliciting customers whom they had contacted when they worked for the company. The company sued them for misappropriation of confidential customer information in violation of the state civil code. The court ruled for the company, and the Court of Appeal affirmed, observing that California and 40 other states have enacted the Uniform Trade Secrets Act (UTSA). **A trade secret is information having independent economic value, not generally known to the public, which the employer takes reasonable steps to protect.** Here, the written employment agreements constituted a reasonable step to protect the customer information, and the information had independent economic value. Because the former employees had misappropriated the customer lists and used them in a manner that violated the UTSA, the court ordered the former employees not to do business with customers of the company. It also awarded the company over $39,000 for trade secret violations. *Morlife, Inc. v. Perry*, 66 Cal.Rptr.2d 731 (Cal. Ct. App. 1997).

◆ A biomedical supply employee worked under a non-compete agreement. After he resigned to work for a competitor, he returned to his office to copy confidential files and erase business records from the former employer's computer. The former employer sued the employee and competitor for trespass, conversion, criminal mischief and misappropriation of trade secrets. The Court of Appeals of Ohio agreed with the trial court that the trespass complaint against the competitor had to be dismissed. It could not be liable for the employee's action. The trial court also properly dismissed the misappropriation of trade secrets claim because **the former employer had failed to guard the secrecy of its customer lists, inventory reports and other information** that it now sought to protect. Finally, the trial court had properly dismissed the breach of contract claim because the former employer had failed to demonstrate that the non-compete agreement was valid. *Biomedical Innovations, Inc. v. McLaughlin*, 103 Ohio App.3d 122, 658 N.E.2d 1084 (Ohio Ct. App. 1995).

◆ A Virginia man began to operate a business selling hair replacement units. His employees attached the units to customers' hair. Two employees quit without notice. They had never entered into a covenant not to compete. When they left, they did not take any supplies, equipment, or products with them; nor did they take any written customer lists or documents. They then began a competing business and solicited 100 of the former employer's customers by telephone, utilizing a list they had compiled solely from memory. The former employer sued them for tortiously interfering with his contracts with his customers. A trial court ruled in favor of the employer, and the employees appealed. The Supreme Court of Virginia determined that the employees did not engage in improper methods by utilizing their memories to compile a list of the names of former customers and soliciting business from them. If the former employer wished to prevent the employees from soliciting his customers, he **should have required them to execute a covenant not to compete**. The court reversed and remanded the case. *Peace v. Conway*, 435 S.E.2d 133 (Va. 1993).

IV. COMPENSATION DISPUTES

There is no federal law that sets guidelines regarding wage disputes (like deducting an amount for damage to company property). Each state has its own laws and regulations regarding what is permissible. The following cases deal with wage disputes, including the payment of commissions and bonuses. For wage deductions generally (like for union dues, charitable contributions, stock purchases and loans made by the employer), employers usually need the written permission of employees.

Each state has its own laws concerning whether and how an employer can make a wage deduction for faulty workmanship, loss, theft or damage to employer property. As a general rule, employers should assume that they cannot make deductions from wages or commissions without the written permission of employees unless a court rules that the employees are liable for the loss or indebtedness.

State laws also allow for the garnishment of wages for certain debts (especially delinquent child support). Title III of the federal *Consumer Credit Protection Act* (CCPA) prohibits employers from discharging employees whose earnings have been subject to garnishment for any one debt. However, it does not prohibit discharging employees who have been subject to garnishment for more than one debt.

Title III of the CCPA also sets limits for how much money can be garnished (usually the lesser of 25% of disposable earnings or the amount by which disposable earnings are greater than $175.50 per week). Where garnishment is made for child support or alimony, Title III allows for more money to be withheld (usually 50 or 60% of disposable earnings).

If state laws allow garnishments that are more restrictive than federal law (in other words, if the employer cannot deduct as much under state law), the state law applies over the federal law. Also, if state law prohibits discharging an employee with two or more debts that are subject to garnishment, then state law applies there as well.

For cases involving minimum wage and overtime compensation under the Fair Labor Standards Act, please see Chapter Five, Section I.

A. Wage Disputes

Wage disputes usually arise as a result of unpaid wages or reductions in wages by the employer. As a general rule, when there is a wage dispute, the wise course of action is to pay the employee and then seek any amounts improperly received through the legal system (like small claims court).

Obviously, this is not completely satisfactory, but the alternative may be even less so. Where an employee makes a wage complaint to the state department of labor, a hearing will usually be required, costing time and money. Often the amount in dispute is not great enough to warrant the inconvenience such a hearing brings.

- Verizon signed a collective bargaining agreement that required it to notify the union before creating a new job title or classification (or restructuring an existing job) so that the union could bargain over the starting wage. The agreement also limited retroactive back pay awards to 150 days. **Verizon later assigned additional duties to its voice mail clerks, which the union claimed was a restructuring or reclassification** of the job to a more skilled position, and that they were entitled to a higher wage rate. The union filed a grievance, and an arbitrator ruled that Verizon should have negotiated this change. After negotiations failed, a second arbitrator awarded increased pay to the voice mail clerks retroactively, going back over five years. Verizon appealed and a D.C. federal court held that the arbitrator's award exceeded his authority under the bargaining agreement. The court remanded the issue of retroactivity to arbitration. *Verizon Washington, D.C. Inc. v. Communications Workers of America, AFL-CIO*, 569 F.Supp.2d 121 (D.D.C. 2008).

◆ An Indiana company fired two employees and paid them their accrued vacation/sick leave/personal time 14 days after it paid them their wages earned for their last pay period. They filed a class action lawsuit against the company, claiming it violated the state's Wage Claims Statute. The company claimed it could pay them after the date specified by the statute because of its employee manual. A court granted pretrial judgment to the company, but the Court of Appeals of Indiana reversed. Although the company could have completely denied payment of accrued vacation/sick leave/personal time according to the terms of its employee manual, having chosen to pay the employees, it was bound by the Wage Claims Statute. **The vacation/sick leave/personal time became "wages" under the statute and had to be paid within the time frame specified by law.** *Reel v. Clarian Health Partners, Inc.*, 873 N.E.2d 75 (Ind. Ct. App. 2007).

◆ A mechanic for a company in Wyoming was given a check for $2,500 and told that the company could no longer afford to employ him. He filed a claim with the state Department of Employment for the remainder of his unpaid wages. The company agreed that it owed him an additional $944 but disputed the remainder of his claim. A hearing officer ruled that the company owed him $8,700 in wages but that it could award a maximum of two months' wages by statute – in this case, $6,400 – because the mechanic did not file a civil suit. She also denied his request for interest, attorneys' fees and costs on the grounds that the department did not have the authority to make such an award. A district court and the Supreme Court of Wyoming upheld the hearing officer's decision. **The company was not entitled to offset the mechanic's wages for gas and parts for his pickup or for a lost toolbox.** Further, the department did not exceed its authority by requiring an employee's written authorization before certain sums could be deducted from wages. Finally, the department had the power to award interest, attorneys' fees and costs. The court remanded the case for a determination of the proper amount to be awarded. *Diamond B Services, Inc. v. Rohde*, 120 P.3d 1031 (Wyo. 2005).

◆ A California moving company employee put the wrong type of gas into a van, requiring the vehicle to be towed back to the employer's premises. The employee agreed to pay for half of the towing cost, but not out of his next paycheck. The employer deducted more than the entire cost of the tow from the employee's next paycheck. Though it later gave him a partial refund, it never gave him any more work assignments. When he questioned the payroll deduction and asked for more work, the employer fired him. He sued the employer and the company paymaster for wrongful discharge and infliction of emotional distress. The court dismissed the case, and the employee appealed to the California Court of Appeal, where he argued that **a state labor law**

protecting employees from unlawful payroll deductions created an important public policy against wrongful discharge. The court agreed. The prompt payment of wages is a fundamental public policy of the state. Because the employer's setoff against the employee's wages was improper, the employee's wrongful termination lawsuit based on that violation of public policy was viable. Also, the accompanying claim for emotional distress was not barred by the state workers' compensation act. However, the paymaster could not be held personally liable for wrongful termination. *Phillips v. Gemini Moving Specialists*, 74 Cal.Rptr.2d 29 (Cal. Ct. App. 1998).

◆ The director and sole shareholder of a South Carolina computer software business hired an employee to design and implement sales programs and train sales personnel. The shareholder applied for a Small Business Administration loan and repeatedly assured his employees that their back wages would be paid upon receipt of the loan proceeds. However, no wages were paid for almost a year. When the loan proceeds were finally paid, the shareholder offered the sales employee a commission sales job. The employee rejected the offer, and the shareholder refused to pay him any wages. The employee sued the shareholder and the corporation under the state wage act. The court held for the former employee and trebled the damage award, including an award of attorneys' fees. However, the court held that the shareholder was not personally liable for the judgment and dismissed him from the lawsuit. The Court of Appeals of South Carolina reversed, finding that there was sufficient evidence to pierce the corporate veil and **hold the shareholder individually liable for unpaid wages**. *Dumas v. Infosafe Corp.*, 463 S.E.2d 641 (S.C. Ct. App. 1995).

◆ A Louisiana farmer instructed an employee that he would withhold the replacement cost of damaged equipment from his wages if the employee continued to be careless in maintaining equipment. The farmer later deducted $61.25 from the employee's pay for damaging cultivator parts when the employee ran a tractor over an area known to contain tree stumps. The employee quit and sued for the wage withholding and a statutory penalty, plus attorneys' fees. The court ruled for the farmer, and the employee appealed. The Court of Appeal of Louisiana stated that in order to recover under the Louisiana Wage Statute, the employer must have acted arbitrarily, unreasonably or in bad faith. **When a legitimate dispute exists concerning the amount owed an employee upon termination, courts should avoid the award of penalties.** Here, the employee admitted that he knew there were tree stumps in the area and that he had been warned he would be liable for future damage caused by his carelessness. The wage withholding did not violate the statute, and the trial court decision was affirmed. *Cupp v. Banks*, 637 So.2d 678 (La. Ct. App. 1994).

◆ An Oregon general contractor working on five public works projects subcontracted with an excavating company that failed to pay its employees the prevailing wage in the area for the type of work being performed. Several employees of the subcontractor sued the general contractor, seeking the difference between their actual wages and the prevailing wage under an Oregon statute that was modeled after the federal Davis-Bacon Act, 40 U.S.C. § 276a *et seq.* Both acts require workers on government projects to be paid a minimum wage equivalent to the prevailing wage for similar work in the area. The court ruled for the general contractor, and the Supreme Court of Oregon ultimately upheld that decision. The statute only authorized the state commissioner of labor and industries to bring a civil action to compel a public agency to withhold from a contractor the equivalent of double the wages in dispute if the contractor refuses to pay the prevailing wage. **The subcontractor's employees were under contract only with the subcontractor and could not be third-party beneficiaries of a contract with the general contractor.** *Stockton v. Silco Construction Co.*, 319 Or. 365, 877 P.2d 71 (Or. 1994).

B. Commissions

In some positions (usually sales positions), employees receive commissions as a part of their compensation packages. Generally, commissions are paid against a draw – that is, the employee earns the higher commission wage after reaching a certain preset goal.

If the employee fails to reach the goal, he or she is paid only the draw amount. An employee who fails to reach the goal (or sales quota) for a certain number of pay periods becomes subject to termination.

1. Commission Arrangements

The commission arrangements outline the payment terms of the commission, such as what percentage amount of the sale comprises the commission. Withholding commission payments may subject the employer to substantial damage awards, including punitive damages.

- Outside sales reps for a company in California used their cars to perform their duties. They brought a lawsuit under Labor Code § 2802 seeking expenses incurred in using their own vehicles. The company asserted that it could meet its obligations under state law by paying the outside sales reps more than the inside sales reps. Eventually the case reached the Supreme Court of California, which held that the company could use a "lump-sum" method to reimburse the sales reps for work-required automobile expenses, provided that the amount paid was sufficient to provide full reimbursement for actual expenses necessarily incurred. Of course, the sales reps had to be permitted to challenge the lump-sum payments as being insufficient. The court also held that **the company could combine wages and business expense reimbursements in a single enhanced employee compensation payment of salary and commissions**, so long as the company established some means to identify the portion of the compensation that was intended as expense reimbursement, and provided that the amounts paid were sufficient to cover actual expenses incurred. *Gattuso v. Harte-Hanks Shoppers, Inc.*, 169 P.3d 889 (Cal. 2007).

- An account manager for a Kansas company sold training seminars by telephone. She was paid an hourly wage as well as commissions. The company changed its compensation policy from one of paying commissions upon a signed contract to one of paying commissions upon the buyer paying for the seminar. When the account manager quit, the company offset her hourly wages against what it claimed were prepaid, unearned commissions. She filed a claim for withheld wages with the Department of Labor, and the case reached the Court of Appeals of Kansas, which held that the offset was impermissible. **The employment agreement did not permit the offsetting of unearned commissions against accrued and earned hourly wages.** The company had to pay the account manager the $822.25 it withheld, plus interest. *Graceland College Center for Professional Development and Life-Long Learning, Inc. v. Kansas Dep't of Labor*, 131 P.3d 1281 (Kan. Ct. App. 2006).

◆ A South Carolina harbor pilot was paid commissions by a towing company for guiding ships into port. After several years, he made plans to form a competing business. While he continued working for the towing company, he made loan applications, filed registration and insurance forms and solicited most of the towing company's existing customers for the new venture. The towing company fired the pilot when it learned of the competing venture and refused to pay him $4,200 in accrued commissions. The pilot sued the towing company under the South Carolina Wage Payment Act, asserting breach of contract and other claims. The towing company counterclaimed on the basis of employee disloyalty. A jury awarded the pilot his claimed commissions. The court then trebled the damage award pursuant to the wage payment act and awarded him attorneys' fees.

The court of appeals reversed, stating that an employee's duty of loyalty continues throughout the term of employment. Although employees may make pre-termination plans to compete with an employer, an employee is disloyal if there is a direct solicitation of the employer's customers. The court determined that the common law duty of employee loyalty could properly be applied to deny a claim for unpaid commissions under the wage payment act. Here, the pilot had been disloyal by soliciting customers prior to employment termination. The South Carolina Supreme Court reversed, finding that **when an employee is disloyal, he forfeits compensation for only that period of time**. Here, the pilot should have been paid his claimed commissions for the period in which he was loyal to the company. *Futch v. McAllister Towing of Georgetown, Inc.*, 518 S.E.2d 591 (S.C. 1999).

◆ A Pennsylvania company hired independent sales reps under written contracts calling for compensation on the basis of a percentage of their gross sales. Sales reps were paid a monthly draw against expected commissions and were required to repay any excess draws within 90 days of contract termination. A sales rep who worked for almost two years had more than $34,000 in draws over and above commissions earned at the time of his termination. The employer filed a breach of contract action against him for repayment of the amount with interest. The court held for the employer but denied an award of interest, and the rep appealed. The Superior Court of Pennsylvania held that the state wage act was inapplicable to the dispute because it involved only the right to enforce payment of wages, and the rep conceded that he was paid all the commissions due him. Instead, the action involved the interpretation of the contract, which apparently failed to anticipate earnings remaining below the amount of advance draws. **Because the contract did not provide for the situation here, its repayment requirement was enforceable by its terms, and the rep had to repay the draw.** The court acknowledged that only Pennsylvania and Alabama apply this rule, and that 22 other states, including New York, California and Illinois, refuse to impose personal liability on salespersons to repay draws against commissions. *Banks Engineering Co., Inc. v. Polons*, 697 A.2d 1020 (Pa. Super. Ct. 1997).

- A Tennessee industrial supply sales rep worked under an oral contract for a commission of 35% of the gross profits from his sales. The company responded to declining profits by instituting a new compensation structure that paid commissions based on a sliding scale. The sales rep never agreed to the new commission scale and complained about it several times. He sued the employer for unpaid commissions of over $19,000. The court held for the rep, and the Court of Appeals of Tennessee affirmed. It characterized the **change in compensation as an attempted unilateral alteration of the parties' contract**. The employee had never indicated his assent to the contractual change, and his complaints were sufficient to indicate his lack of contractual assent. *Thompson v. Creswell Industrial Supply, Inc.*, 936 S.W.2d 955 (Tenn. Ct. App. 1996).

- A manufacturing company hired a sales rep under an oral agreement calling for commissions on all sales in the rep's territory based on a percentage of gross profits. The company failed to forward sales reports to the rep, and he discovered that company products had been sold in his territory through a freight handler. When he requested a commission for the sales, the company refused payment and he resigned. He sued his former employer in an Alabama trial court for breach of contract and fraud. The court conducted a jury trial resulting in a general damage award of $31,000, plus punitive damages of $160,000, the estimated profit made by the company from the disputed sales. The manufacturer appealed to the Supreme Court of Alabama, which affirmed, noting that the trial court's decision was based upon sufficient evidence that **the manufacturer had no intention of honoring the oral promise to pay** the sales rep commissions on all products shipped to his area. *Sealing Equipment Products Co., Inc. v. Velarde*, 644 So.2d 904 (Ala. 1994).

2. Damage Awards

State law defines the damages that are due where an employer improperly withholds payment of wages or commissions. Often, the employer has to pay, in addition to the withheld wages, interest, a <u>liquidated damages</u> penalty (usually an amount equal to the improperly withheld wages) and any attorneys' fees and costs the employee incurred.

- An Alabama employment agency salesperson was promoted to an account executive position. However, despite imposing a higher quota upon her sales production, the agency did not increase her salary or commission rate. When her commissions were cut from an average of $23,000 to approximately $4,000 in one quarter, she learned that the agency's management had arbitrarily changed her commission calculations and retroactively imposed the higher sales quota requirements on her. It also failed to credit her for certain new accounts. The salesperson sued the agency, claiming that it owed her $186,000 in underpaid commissions for three quarters of employment. A jury awarded her $300,000 in compensatory damages for fraud and $3 million in punitive damages. The court reduced the punitive damage award to $2 million. Before the Supreme Court of Alabama, the agency argued that the verdict had been inconsistent since it did not award any damages for breach of contract and the fraud claim was based on breaching the contract. The court found no error since the $300,000 awarded for compensatory damages did not have to be specified as breach of contract damages. **The agency had committed affirmative misconduct by concealing and falsifying the commission figures.** The Supreme Court requires state courts to review punitive damage awards for excessiveness by comparing them with the civil or criminal penalties that could be imposed for comparable misconduct. The court reduced the punitive damage award to $1.5 million and conditionally affirmed the trial court judgment. *Talent Tree Personnel Services, Inc. v. Fleenor*, 703 So.2d 917 (Ala. 1997).

◆ An independent sales rep sold an apparel line for a clothing company in Alabama, Georgia and Florida on a commission basis, receiving 5% of gross sales. Sales increased dramatically over eight consecutive years. After attempting to reduce the commission rate, the company decided to eliminate independent reps altogether. It offered the representative and his two associates a salary plus a commission of one-half percent of sales. The representative and his associates decided to quit rather than become salaried under these terms but continued to book orders until the effective date of their resignations. They **accused the company of tampering with their orders by crediting other salespersons**, improperly crediting returns against their accounts, canceling orders and other misconduct, which deprived them of almost $1 million in commissions. The reps sued the company in an Alabama court, which awarded them $15 million, including punitive damages for fraud and mental anguish. The Supreme Court of Alabama substantially affirmed, but imposed a $3.5 million reduction in the damages for mental anguish. *Duck Head Apparel Co., Inc. v. Hoots*, 659 So.2d 897 (Ala. 1995).

◆ A South Carolina radio advertising salesman was employed under a contract that called for the payment of sales commissions for separating employees only when the advertisements were actually broadcast. When his employment was terminated, the employer refused to pay commissions on seven contracts under which no advertisements had been broadcast. A South Carolina trial court directed a verdict in favor of the employer for three contracts, but allowed a jury to consider the remaining contract claims, which related to the employee's work for a division of the employer. This resulted in an award of damages for the employee plus attorneys' fees. Both parties appealed to the Supreme Court of South Carolina. On appeal, the employee argued that he was entitled to treble damages under the state wage act. The employer argued that it could not be liable for treble damages in a good-faith wage dispute. The court held that **treble damages are not payable where a good-faith wage dispute exists between employer and employee**. The trial court had properly withheld an award of treble damages and allowed the question of the four contracts to appear before the jury. It had also made an appropriate partial award of attorneys' fees. The trial court's judgment was affirmed. *Rice v. Multimedia, Inc.*, 456 S.E.2d 381 (S.C. 1995).

3. Salary Deduction Policies

Because there is no federal law in this area, employers need to know the laws and regulations of the states in which they have workers. Any questions that arise as to whether a deduction is allowable can be addressed to the state department of labor.

However, when in doubt, employers should pay wages first (certainly any undisputed portion of the wages or commissions) and seek reimbursement later.

- A company in New York gave its temporary employees the option of receiving a paycheck or cash. Those who chose the cash option were given a voucher that could only be redeemed at a cash dispensing machine owned by a subsidiary of the company. Each transaction cost a dollar plus the number of cents in the employee's wages – up to $1.99. A lawsuit resulted from the practice, and the Court of Appeals of New York – the state's highest court – ruled that **the company's voucher policy amounted to an unlawful deduction from the wages of the temporary workers**. The vouchers were not negotiable instruments that could be exchanged for cash. Also, the receipt of the voucher and subsequent receipt of cash could not be viewed as two separate transactions voluntarily made by the employees. *Angello v. Labor Ready, Inc.*, 7 N.Y.3d 579, 825 N.Y.S.2d 674 (N.Y. 2006).

- A California department store imposed a wage deduction on its sales personnel that represented a prorated share of commissions on returned items for which the salesperson could not be identified. The store justified the policy as a response to employee abuse for failing to follow procedures that would allow the identification of the affected salesperson. A sales employee sued the store, claiming that it had violated a California law prohibiting employers from recapturing wages already paid. The court granted pretrial judgment to the store, and the employee appealed. The California Court of Appeal observed that the state had a strong public policy against deductions from employee wages for cash shortages, breakages, and other business losses resulting from simple negligence by employees. Employers were not allowed to make their employees insurers against business losses. **The store's policy penalized conscientious employees who accurately reported their returns by charging a portion of the returns of dishonest employees against their wages.** The store had other options to prevent employee fraud that did not violate California law. The court reversed the trial court decision. *Hudgins v. Neiman Marcus Group, Inc.*, 41 Cal.Rptr.2d 46 (Cal. Ct. App. 1995).

◆ A Wisconsin convenience store manager was paid a fixed salary and also received a commission based on a percentage of store sales. Company policy was to hold store managers responsible for cash and merchandise shortages, returned checks, bad credit card charges and damaged or unreturned videos. For five years, the manager claimed that he lost over $26,000 due to the company policy. He sued in a Wisconsin trial court seeking twice the amount of the deductions under a state wage statute. The court determined that the store manager's commissions were not wages and dismissed the lawsuit. The court of appeals affirmed, and the manager appealed. The Supreme Court of Wisconsin reversed, determining that the statute's definition of wages encompassed many types of compensation. The statute did not operate as a minimum wage law or fairness guarantee as the court of appeals had ruled. Rather, it was intended to protect employees from arbitrary salary reductions attributable to performance. The court ruled that **commissions were included in the statutory definition of wages**. *Erdman v. Jovoco, Inc.*, 512 N.W.2d 487 (Wis. 1994).

C. Bonuses and Other Cash Incentives

Bonuses represent another form of compensation provided by many employers. Bonus rights generally must arise at the beginning of the employment relationship and be for an exact amount or based upon a formula or method of determining the exact amount of the bonus.

In other words, if any bonus due is payable at the discretion of the employer, and is not ascertainable through the use of a formula or from a written promise, it likely will not be enforceable through a court action.

◆ An Indiana surgeon was paid $250,000 a year, plus a bonus based on collections for services rendered. After the surgeon resigned, the institute he had worked for continued to receive collections for services he rendered prior to his resignation. However, it maintained he was not entitled to further compensation. The surgeon sued for his bonus, and the case reached the Supreme Court of Indiana, which held that **the post-termination bonus was to be calculated the same way as earlier bonuses**. Under the parties' contract, there was no indication that the surgeon was to be denied his bonus after his resignation. Thus, the surgeon was entitled to his bonus. However, it was not a "wage" governed by the state's Wage Payment Statute, so he was not entitled to double the bonus amount. *Highhouse v. Midwest Orthopedic Institute, P.C.*, 807 N.E.2d 737 (Ind. 2004).

◆ A financial analyst elected to receive an annual salary of $40,000 so that he would be eligible for participation in the company's bonus/profit-sharing pool, which required the company to meet certain financial goals. According to two memos, the shared distributions would be paid in quarterly installments at the sole discretion of the chief executive officer (CEO) and they were contingent on the recipient's continued employment. After the CEO allocated $160,000 to the analyst and paid him the first $40,000, the analyst resigned. He then sued to recover the remaining $120,000, claiming that the money was either "wages" to which he was entitled, or that his right to the bonus was vested. The New York Court of Appeals held that the bonus money could not be construed as "wages." The money was not sufficiently linked to the analyst's labor or services to the company. It was instead tied to the company's financial success. Further, his right to the bonus was not vested because **the plan clearly required him to continue working for the company to be eligible for future payments**. *Truelove v. Northeast Capital & Advisory, Inc.*, 715 N.Y.S.2d 366 (N.Y. 2000).

◆ A Pennsylvania chemist notified his employer that a competitor held a patent for a manufacturing process that was similar to a patent owned by the employer. The employer initiated a patent infringement action against the competitor. The competitor refused to permit any of the employer's current employees to review pretrial documents from the case, and the chemist agreed to retire from active employment to serve as a consultant in the patent litigation. The employer agreed to retain him on a per-diem basis for consulting work and agreed to pay him a bonus equaling 1% of the award should the employer prevail. The case was settled when the competitor agreed to undertake some shipping for the employer, but involved no cash payment. The employer refused to pay the former employee a bonus and he sued for breach of contract. He asserted that the employer was bound by a duty of good faith to reach a reasonable result in the patent litigation since he had voluntarily accepted early retirement to facilitate the case. The court observed that **the employer's duty required only the reasonable exercise of discretion to conduct the litigation and determine whether the former employee was entitled to a bonus**. The employer's independent self-interest was congruent with its duty of good faith, and there was no violation of the duty of good faith in settling the case. *Fremont v. E.I. DuPont DeNemours & Co.*, 988 F.Supp. 870 (E.D. Pa. 1997).

◆ A Maine employer instituted an employee suggestion program that awarded cash incentives for ideas that produced savings or increased profits. The maximum award for employee suggestions was $50,000, and the program also offered initial awards of $5,000 based on estimated savings. An employee with over 30 years of experience submitted a cost-saving idea that he expected would qualify for the maximum award. Although the employer paid him the maximum initial award of $5,000, further awards were not paid pending determination of first-year savings for the company. The employee retired, incorporating the expected maximum award into his retirement plans. After retiring, the company advised him that he would receive only $17,500 for his idea. He rejected the award and sued the employer in a Maine federal court for breach of contract and related claims. The court awarded pretrial judgment to the employer, and the former employee appealed. The First Circuit rejected the former employee's argument that the company had reserved excessive discretion over the program, making it void and legally unenforceable. **The terms of the program gave the employer appropriate discretion while giving employees incentives to participate.** However, the district court had improperly granted pretrial judgment to the employer concerning the breach of contract claim, since there was evidence that the employer had failed to live up to its obligations by withdrawing the offer. The court reversed and remanded this portion of the decision, but affirmed the dismissal of the claims based on negligent misrepresentation and reliance on the program for retirement funds. *Hodgkins v. New England Telephone Co.*, 82 F.3d 1226 (1st Cir. 1996).

◆ A discharged Georgia restaurant employee sued for unpaid annual bonuses. The former employer asserted that the claim was unenforceable. A jury awarded damages to the employee, and the court of appeals affirmed, holding that the promise to pay the bonuses was enforceable because it had been made at the beginning of the employment. The Supreme Court of Georgia reversed, observing that **in order to be enforceable, a claim of future compensation must not only be made at the beginning of the employment, it must be for an exact amount or based upon a formula or method of determining the exact amount of the bonus**. A promise to pay a certain percentage of a company's net earnings was sufficiently definite to be enforceable, but a promise to pay an amount within a certain range was not enforceable. Here, the bonuses were to be based in part on a formula but there was evidence that the company president retained discretion to set the amount. A bonus only partially tied to a definite formula was insufficient to be objectively ascertainable and was unenforceable. Because the parties had never agreed upon a sufficiently definite form of computing the bonus, the former employee was not entitled to the bonus. *Arby's, Inc. v. Cooper*, 454 S.E.2d 488 (Ga. 1995).

V. THE FAMILY AND MEDICAL LEAVE ACT

The Family and Medical Leave Act of 1993 (FMLA), 29 U.S.C. §§ 2601-2654, grants eligible employees the right to take up to 12 weeks of unpaid leave per year under specified circumstances related to family health care and childbirth, and (with the passage of amendments in 2008) for military caregiver leave or in exigent circumstances relating to the National Guard or Reserves. Employees become eligible by working:

1) for an employer with at least 50 employees,
2) for the employer for at least 12 months, and
3) at least 1,250 hours in the previous year.

Eligible employees are expressly authorized by the act to take leave upon the <u>birth</u> of a child by the employee or the employee's spouse, or by the placement of a child for <u>adoption</u> or <u>foster care</u> with the employee.

The act also applies when the employee is needed to care for a child, spouse or parent who has a <u>serious health condition</u>, and when the employee is unable to perform employment duties because of her own serious health condition.

◆ An Arkansas employee was diagnosed with cancer and requested medical leave. Her employer granted her request and allowed her to take seven months of leave. However, the company did not inform her of her eligibility under the FMLA, nor did it inform her of her right to have the leave designated as FMLA leave. When she exhausted the seven months of company-provided leave, she was fired. Her request for additional FMLA leave was denied. She sued, and a federal court ruled for the employer. The Eighth Circuit Court of Appeals affirmed, holding that the employer's failure to designate any part of the leave as FMLA leave did not prevent the FMLA leave from expiring. The court struck down the Department of Labor regulation that required the employer to provide more than 12 weeks of leave because of its failure to designate the leave as FMLA leave. The court refused to penalize the employer because its leave program was more generous than the FMLA. The U.S. Supreme Court also affirmed, noting that **employers who provide more than 12 weeks of family and medical leave cannot be penalized for failing to give proper FMLA notice.** *Ragsdale v. Wolverine World Wide, Inc.*, 535 U.S. 81, 122 S.Ct. 1155, 152 L.Ed.2d 167 (2002).

A. "Serious Health Condition"

Under the FMLA regulations, a serious health condition is one requiring an overnight stay in a hospital, hospice or residential medical care facility or a period of incapacity requiring more than three calendar days' absence and two visits to a healthcare provider.

Under the new regulations, the first healthcare provider visit must occur within seven days of the first day of incapacity and the second visit must occur within 30 days. For chronic health conditions, the employee must make at least two visits to a healthcare provider per year.

A serious health condition can also involve a period of incapacity due to pregnancy, a chronic serious health condition (like asthma, diabetes or epilepsy) or a permanent or long-term condition like Alzheimer's, a severe stroke or the terminal stages of a disease.

◆ A janitor for a property management company in Illinois notified his employer that he was having medical problems, including a weak bladder. He also told his supervisor he was having a biopsy to determine whether he had prostate cancer. After the biopsy, he returned to work with a temporary restriction on heavy lifting and a treatment plan, which his supervisor allegedly ignored. He said he was going home because he felt sick. The next day he was fired. After being diagnosed with prostate cancer, he sued under the FMLA and ADA. His FMLA suit was allowed to move forward. **Even though he didn't know of his diagnosis until after he was fired, he was entitled to FMLA protection.** However, he could not show that he was disabled under the ADA. *Burnett v. LFW Inc.*, 472 F.3d 471 (7th Cir. 2006).

◆ When a company refused to allow an employee time off to care for his 13-year-old son who had severe attention deficit disorder, the employee sued under the FMLA. A Michigan federal court ruled in favor of the company, and the Sixth Circuit Court of Appeals affirmed. Here, the son did not qualify as having a serious health condition because even though he saw his doctor every six months to monitor his medication, he was not incapacitated during the requested leave time. He was able to attend school and do the same activities most children do; he simply had to be watched all the time. *Perry v. Jaguar of Troy*, 353 F.3d 510 (6th Cir. 2003).

◆ A clerical worker at a Florida hospital was disciplined three times for unscheduled absences and was given a final written warning threatening suspension and possible termination. Later, she slipped and fell at work, fracturing an elbow and ankle. She returned to work on her doctor's recommendation after he put her arm in a sling. She left work early on several days and took two days off the following week without informing her supervisor. The following Monday she was fired. She sued the hospital under the FMLA, and a federal court ruled against her. The Eleventh Circuit affirmed. Here, the employee did not have a "serious health condition" under the FMLA because **her injury did not require her to miss three consecutive full calendar days of work**. Even though the several partial days and two non-consecutive days she took off added up to more than three days away from work during a 10-day period, she was not protected by the FMLA. The regulations clearly require some fraction more than three consecutive calendar days to constitute the period of incapacity. And she did not meet that requirement. The termination was justified. *Russell v. North Broward Hospital*, 346 F.3d 1335 (11th Cir. 2003).

◆ While unloading his truck, a driver experienced chest pains and, after another employee relieved him, drove himself to the hospital where he underwent an EKG. When no apparent heart damage was found, the driver was released under a "personal discharge plan" that warned he should not return to work until after a stress test was performed – 10 days later. He called several management employees to inform them he could not yet return to work. He forwarded the discharge plan to the company and passed the stress test. When he attempted to return to work, he was informed that he had been fired for violating the company's collective bargaining provisions concerning absences. He sued under the FMLA, and a trial court awarded him over $59,000 along with a reinstatement order. The Michigan Court of Appeals affirmed. Here, the driver's telephone notice regarding the reason he could not return to work was sufficient to trigger the protections of the FMLA. Also, he provided the discharge plan to the company within the 15-day period in the statute for requests for medical certification. Finally, **even though he did not actually have a serious health condition under the FMLA**, his absence qualified under the statute because a doctor concluded that an extended absence from work was needed following his emergency room visit. *Woodman v. Miesel Sysco Food Service Co.*, 657 N.W.2d 122 (Mich. Ct. App. 2003).

◆ A California truck driver's sister was murdered by her ex-husband. The truck driver moved to Reno temporarily to be with his father, who had fallen into a depression. He drove his father to counseling sessions and did household chores. While on leave, he agreed with the company's HR manager that he would resign from his job and would be rehired if he returned to work within six months. When he sought reinstatement, the company cited union-related restrictions and refused to reinstate him with seniority. It did, however, give him a position as a probationary truck driver. He sued under the FMLA, and a federal court granted pretrial judgment to the company. The Ninth Circuit reversed, finding an issue of fact as to whether the leave of absence qualified as FMLA leave. Here, if the father had a "serious health condition" and if the truck driver cared for him within the meaning of the FMLA, then he should have been reinstated to his position with seniority. *Scamihorn v. General Truck Drivers*, 282 F.3d 1078 (9th Cir. 2002).

◆ An employee of a Minnesota company became ill with the flu and missed two weeks of work. She went to her nurse practitioner and was given an inhaler, a decongestant, and a prescription for a cough suppressant with codeine. After she was fired for excessive absenteeism, she sued the company under the FMLA. A federal court dismissed her lawsuit, but the Eighth Circuit reversed, noting that she had submitted evidence that her illness was a "serious health condition," and that she was entitled to a trial. Even though she did not see her nurse practitioner twice before she was fired, **she did see the nurse for the second time on the day she was fired**. This was continuing treatment. *Rankin v. Seagate Technologies, Inc.*, 246 F.3d 1145 (8th Cir. 2001).

◆ A West Virginia employee with a history of absenteeism was warned about her poor attendance. Subsequently, she came down with the flu and missed a week of work. She saw her doctor twice during the week and requested FMLA leave when she returned to work. Her employer denied her request and fired her for excessive absenteeism. When she sued under the FMLA, a federal court ruled in her favor. The Fourth Circuit affirmed, holding that **an employee with the flu could be suffering from a "serious health condition"** where the employee cannot work for at least three consecutive days and receives continuing treatment from her doctor. The court noted that "treatment" includes examinations and evaluations of the seriousness of the illness. Here, even though the employee's second visit to the doctor was to evaluate her condition, this constituted continuing treatment for a serious health condition. *Miller v. AT&T Corp.*, 250 F.3d 820 (4th Cir. 2001).

◆ An Iowa employee left her job on a Wednesday complaining of cramps and diarrhea. She saw a doctor and returned to work the following Monday with a note indicating that she required the previous Thursday and Friday off. However, after only a few hours, she returned to the doctor with stomach pain and tests were scheduled for that Friday. When she returned to work the following Monday with another note excusing her absence, the company fired her for excessive absenteeism. Later, another doctor found that she had a minor condition that was stress related and that could be controlled with antacids. She sued under the FMLA, and a federal court found that her last absences should not have been counted against her because she had a "serious health condition." The Eighth Circuit Court of Appeals affirmed, noting that the burden was on the company to verify, at the time of the employee's absence, whether the absence was medically required. After receiving the doctor's notes, the company had to either count the employee's leave as FMLA leave or request FMLA certification to determine whether the employee truly had a serious health condition. By **failing to timely verify whether the employee's absence qualified as FMLA leave**, the company had to accept it as such despite the later diagnosis. *Thorson v. Gemini, Inc.*, 205 F.3d 370 (8th Cir. 2000).

B. Notice

The FMLA requires employees to give employers sufficient notice, usually 30 days, to prevent unduly disrupting employer operations. However, lesser notice may be sufficient when a 30-day notice is impossible.

Under the new regulations, employees have to follow the employer's usual and customary call-in procedures for reporting an absence unless unusual circumstances exist to excuse that lack.

The FMLA also requires employers to give notice to employees who request leave. Under the new regulations, the notice has to be given within five business days and must contain the following:

1) a statement that the leave will be counted against the employee's annual FMLA entitlement,
2) any requirements for the employee to furnish medical certification of a serious health condition,
3) a statement of the employee's right to substitute paid leave and whether the employer will require the substitution of paid leave,
4) any requirement for the employee to make any premium payments to maintain health benefits,
5) any requirement for the employee to present a fitness-for-duty certificate to be restored to employment,
6) if the employee is a "key employee," a statement explaining that status and the potential consequence that restoration may be denied following the leave,
7) a statement of the employee's right to restoration to the same or an equivalent job upon return from leave, and
8) a statement of the employee's potential liability for payment of health insurance premiums paid by the employer during the leave if the employee fails to return to work after the leave.

◆ An Illinois employee with a previously unblemished record got dizzy and felt her neck muscles tighten when a stray dog entered the facility where she worked. She began yelling to her supervisor that "f——— animals shouldn't be in the workplace." Two hours later she went home ill. She called in sick the next day, but the following day, she charged into the company president's office and began screaming and cursing at him for allowing a dog to enter the facility. She then missed three more days, and when she returned to work, she found the contents of her desk moved to another room to accommodate her fear of animals. She called the police, believing she was being harassed, then went home early. She went to a doctor but did not provide written or oral notice of her need for FMLA leave. After she was fired, she sued. A federal court granted pretrial judgment to the employer, but the Seventh Circuit reversed, finding issues of fact that required a trial. **Her unusual behavior may have provided the employer with constructive notice of her need for FMLA leave.** *Stevenson v. Hyre Electric*, 505 F.3d 720 (7th Cir. 2007).

◆ A service manager for a New Jersey company had a chronic heart condition, which his employer knew about. About two weeks after he returned from quintuple bypass surgery, he received a written warning about his job performance. He later told a supervisor that his doctor had found more blockages, that he was going to have to undergo medical monitoring, and that he might need more surgery. A week later he was fired for performance-related reasons. When he sued under the FMLA, a federal court granted pretrial judgment to the company. However, the Third Circuit reversed, finding issues of fact that required a trial. Here, **the employee's statement to his supervisor was sufficient to provide notice of his need for FMLA leave**. *Sarnowski v. Air Brooke Limousine, Inc.*, 510 F.3d 398 (3d Cir. 2007).

◆ A Maryland employee missed two-and-a-half days of work because of illness. She saw a doctor and returned to work with medical reports diagnosing her with a possible peptic ulcer. She worked four days. On the fifth day she told her supervisor she was sick and had to leave early for a doctor's appointment. She was absent for the next eight days, but failed to inform her superiors that she would be gone, instead telling three co-workers to inform her supervisor that she was sick. She was fired, then provided documentation of her absence, and was offered a lower-paying position. She turned it down, then sued under the FMLA. A federal court ruled against her, noting that **her minimal notice to the employer did not satisfy the requirements of the FMLA**. *Rodriguez v. Smithfield Packing Co.*, 545 F.Supp.2d 508 (D. Md. 2008).

◆ A Louisiana employee called her supervisor on a Monday to tell him she was sick. She also told him she was pregnant, but did not say that the sickness was related to pregnancy complications. When she called back on Tuesday, she was told to get a medical release. She told her supervisor she had a doctor's appointment on Wednesday, meaning more than a week later. However, her supervisor thought she meant the next day. She had no further contact with her employer for 10 days. When she was fired for violating the "no call/no show" policy, she sued under the FMLA. A federal court and the Fifth Circuit ruled against her. **She failed to give her supervisor enough information to put the employer on notice that she had a "serious health condition."** *Willis v. Coca-Cola Enterprises*, 445 F.3d 413 (5th Cir. 2006).

◆ An attendance-challenged Wisconsin employee in danger of being fired left work early because she was sick. She submitted a form from the company's health center stating that she should be off work for three days. Several months later, after more absences, she was fired. She was diagnosed with a head tumor and sued under the FMLA, claiming the three-day absence should not have been counted against her. A federal court and the Seventh Circuit ruled against her.

The note from the health center did not inform the company that she had a serious health condition, and she did not tell the company she was taking prescribed antibiotics. *Phillips v. Quebecor World RAI Inc.*, 450 F.3d 308 (7th Cir. 2006).

◆ After learning that she needed surgery, a pharmaceutical sales rep in Minnesota sought and obtained FMLA leave. However, the company sent her confusing notices as to when the leave started. One notice put the start date at August 2; another put it at August 20. Nevertheless, the company gave her more than 12 weeks leave, ultimately filling her position with someone else and firing her six months later. When she sued under the FMLA, she lost. The Eighth Circuit noted that **the ambiguities and contradictions in the company's notices did not create an FMLA claim**. *Grosenick v. SmithKline Beecham Corp.*, 454 F.3d 832 (8th Cir. 2006).

◆ A Florida employee asked for two weeks off to assist her pregnant daughter in Colorado because her daughter's husband had broken his collarbone. Even though she had already used her vacation time, the store manager granted her request. She asked the personnel office about FMLA leave, but did not assert that her daughter was suffering from any complications of pregnancy. The personnel office instructed her to obtain a doctor's note, but the doctor's note did not indicate there was any problem with the pregnancy either. Based on the note, the store manager denied her request for an additional two weeks' leave. She stayed with her daughter for four weeks and was fired. When she sued under the FMLA, she lost. The Eleventh Circuit noted that **she never gave the manager any indication that her daughter had a serious health condition**, so the store had no duty to inquire further. *Cruz v. Publix Super Markets, Inc.*, 428 F.3d 1379 (11th Cir. 2005).

◆ A union employee in New Jersey signed a last chance agreement after problems with absenteeism. Shortly thereafter, he got in a car accident. He was eligible for leave under the FMLA and requested such leave, but his employer did not provide him with the required notice of his entitlement to 12 weeks' leave. He decided to have surgery to correct the shoulder problem from the accident and was out for more than 12 weeks. The employer fired him after his 12 weeks of leave expired, and he sued under the FMLA. A federal court granted pretrial judgment to the employer, but the Third Circuit reversed in part. Here, **the employee was claiming that he was prejudiced by the lack of notice**: specifically, he said he would have reconsidered the surgery if he knew he only had 12 weeks of leave. This issue required a trial. *Conoshenti v. Public Service Electric & Gas Co.*, 364 F.3d 135 (3d Cir. 2004).

◆ An employee at an Ohio manufacturing plant got in a motorcycle accident and had to go to the emergency room, where a doctor gave him a note excusing him from work for three days. He called a plant security guard and notified the guard of the situation. However, by company policy, he was supposed to call the company's "leave department" if he was going to be gone for more than a day. Instead, he allegedly called a security guard every day – the procedure for absences of a day or less. He missed work two more times in the following months because of pain related to the accident, and was deemed to have violated the company's leave policy after his doctor failed to timely return a certification form. The company fired him, and he sued it under the FMLA. A federal court granted pretrial judgment to the company, but the Sixth Circuit reversed. It noted that **the company's leave policy was stricter than the FMLA's leave requirements**, which allow an employee to give timely "verbal or other" notice of leave. Here, if the employee gave notice as he claimed, it was sufficient to provide FMLA protection. The court remanded the case for trial. *Cavin v. Honda of America Manufacturing, Inc.*, 346 F.3d 713 (6th Cir. 2003).

◆ A North Carolina cable company provided its employees with a handbook outlining its policy on family and medical leave. Company policy required employees to use remaining vacation time concurrently with FMLA leave. When an employee was involved in a motorcycle accident, he took FMLA leave to recuperate. Six months later, he asked for time off to care for his wife after she underwent back surgery. A company nurse mistakenly wrote the employee that his FMLA leave would begin once his remaining vacation time hours had been exhausted. When informed that his leave was expiring, the employee failed to report to work for three consecutive shifts and was fired. He sued under the FMLA, asserting that the company had failed to provide proper notice under the act. A federal court ruled that the improper notice by the nurse did not provide the basis for a cause of action under the act. Here, the employee knew or should have known that he had to take his vacation leave concurrently with his FMLA leave. **He was not entitled to more than 12 weeks of leave.** *Kelso v. Corning Cable Systems Int'l Corp.*, 224 F.Supp.2d 1052 (W.D.N.C. 2002).

◆ A UPS employee asked for time off to be with his fiancée after the birth of their child. His supervisor waived the 10-day notice rule in the collective bargaining agreement, but expected him to be back at work in a couple of days. However, the employee thought his leave had an indefinite duration and did not contact his supervisor for a week. When he finally did so, the supervisor informed him that he had been fired for violating the bargaining agreement by failing to provide notice prior to his third day away from work. The employee sued under the FMLA, asserting that he could stay away from work for up to 12 weeks without informing his employer of when he would return. An Indiana federal court ruled in favor of UPS, and the Seventh Circuit affirmed. Under the FMLA, **an employer can require an employee to comply with its usual and customary notice procedures** for requesting leave. *Gilliam v. United Parcel Service,* 233 F.3d 969 (7th Cir. 2000).

C. Employer Paid Leaves and State Statutes

Sometimes employer paid leaves and state statutes provide different types of coverage for employees requiring leaves. Employer policies and state statutes may provide more protection than the minimum requirements of the FMLA. They may not provide less protection.

◆ After 10 months on the job, a Minnesota employee asked for leave to treat depression and chronic migraines. Since he didn't yet qualify for FMLA leave, the company granted him short-term disability leave. During his leave, the company informed him it was removing him from his position but that he would remain an employee and retain his benefits while on leave. Shortly after his 12-month anniversary, he was cleared to return to work, but the company had no job openings and discharged him. He sued under the FMLA, **asserting that he became eligible for FMLA leave during his disability leave**. A federal court disagreed. The determination of FMLA eligibility must be made as of the date leave commences. This was unlike a situation where an employee uses vacation time to get to the 12-month eligibility requirement. *Adly v. SuperValu, Inc.*, 2007 WL 2226040 (D. Minn. 8/3/07).

◆ An Alabama manager took a 15-week pregnancy leave, during which she received 13 weeks of pay under the employer's disability plan. Upon her return to work, she was demoted to assistant manager based on the expiration of the FMLA's maximum 12-week leave period. The employee resigned and sued, claiming that she had been constructively discharged in violation of the FMLA. The court considered FMLA language describing the relationship between the FMLA's maximum 12-week leave period and employer-provided paid leaves of absence. It noted a conflict between the statutory language and federal regulations published by the Department of Labor. **The FMLA does not require employers to provide 12 weeks of unpaid leave in addition to any paid leave provided by an employer plan.** Because the employee in this case had taken more than 12 weeks of leave, she had received all that she was entitled to receive under the FMLA. The court granted the employer pretrial judgment. *Cox v. AutoZone, Inc.*, 990 F.Supp. 1369 (M.D. Ala. 1998).

◆ A flight attendant, who normally worked less than 1,000 hours per year, missed substantial amounts of work due to illnesses she claimed were severe enough to qualify for coverage under the FMLA. The airline disputed the seriousness of the illnesses and fired her. She sued it in a Georgia federal court. The airline claimed that the injuries were not covered by the FMLA and that she did not work enough hours to qualify for coverage. The employee argued that the airline's policy provided substantial benefits to flight attendants working at least 540 hours per calendar year. Because **an FMLA regulation required employers to observe any benefit programs providing greater family or medical leave rights than the FMLA minimum**, she claimed coverage under the airline's internal policy. The court disagreed, stating that the regulation simply preserved contractual rights and did not alter FMLA jurisdictional requirements. Since she worked less than 1,250 hours per year, the act did not apply. *Rich v. Delta Air Lines, Inc.*, 921 F.Supp. 767 (N.D. Ga. 1996).

◆ New Jersey's Family Leave Act requires employers to grant employees leave for reasons including childbirth or the illness of a family member. "Employer" is defined by the act as a person, corporation or other business entity employing 50 or more employees. Unlike the federal FMLA, the state act does not specify that the minimum number of employees be located in a particular geographic location, and the act does not state whether they must work within the state. An employee filed a complaint with a state agency against her employer, claiming that it had violated the state act. The employer responded that while it employed 164 persons in six states, it had fewer than 12 New Jersey employees and that the act did not apply to it. The agency found probable cause of a violation of the act, and the New Jersey Superior Court, Appellate Division, affirmed. The absence of a geographic limitation in the statute indicated that **the legislature intended all employers doing business in the state having a total of 50 employees to come within the scope of the act**. Not all employers having less than 50 employees in the state were small; they could have hundreds or thousands of employees in other states. *Essex Crane Rental Corp. v. Director, Division on Civil Rights*, 294 N.J.Super. 101, 682 A.2d 750 (N.J. Super. Ct. App. Div. 1996).

D. Certification

Employers can require employees to provide medical certification issued by a health care provider to ensure that the employees have a serious health condition, but must allow 15 days for the certification to be provided.

Under the new regulations, employers can request recertification of an ongoing medical condition every six months in conjunction with an absence.

The new regulations also place strict limitations on who is allowed to contact the employee's healthcare provider, and prohibit the employee's direct supervisor from doing so.

◆ An Illinois employee with Graves' disease took three weeks of FMLA leave to have her thyroid removed. She returned to work, but the replacement hormones made her feel fatigued. She left work an hour early, taking work home in the evenings and on weekends. Her supervisor later told her she had to resume an eight-hour day and issued her a corrective action report (CAR) when she failed to do so. Her supervisor also told her she would have to provide FMLA certification. When she failed to turn it in on time, she was given a second CAR, then a third, at which time the company suspended, then fired her. She sued under the FMLA and lost. A federal court and the Seventh Circuit held that she failed to comply with the time restrictions imposed by the FMLA, so even though the company made some mistakes – it failed to let her know she might qualify for FMLA leave when it issued the first CAR, and it referred to the leave as "intermittent" rather than "reduced schedule" leave – **it properly fired her for failing to return the paperwork in a timely fashion**. *Ridings v. Riverside Medical Center*, 537 F.3d 755 (7th Cir. 2008).

◆ An Ohio employee with attendance problems missed two weeks of work for back pain, her 18-year-old daughter's post-partum depression, and her grandson's illness. This put her over the minimum number of points for unexcused absences under her employer's attendance policy. She sought FMLA leave to stave off her termination, but failed to submit proper certification from her doctor for her back pain. She offered a form that her doctor had signed. However, her doctor had not examined her so did not provide information about the date the medical condition began or its likely duration. After she was fired, she sued under the FMLA and lost. The Sixth Circuit noted that her daughter was not a minor child, and that **the company did not have to seek a second opinion before denying her leave. Nor was it barred from challenging her certification simply because it didn't obtain a second opinion.** *Novak v. MetroHealth Medical Center*, 503 F.3d 572 (6th Cir. 2007).

- A Tennessee welder requested FMLA leave for surgery. During the surgery, her doctor discovered that her condition was more serious than he had thought. He scheduled a follow-up appointment for her the day after she was to return to work. Six days before she was due back to work, she asked for an extension and was told to get a statement from her doctor. Believing she had 15 days to do so, she did not immediately obtain the statement. The company fired her the day she was scheduled to return to work even though her doctor faxed a statement to the company that day. She sued under the FMLA and obtained an award of $55,000. The Sixth Circuit upheld the award, noting that **federal regulations require employers to allow 15 days for certification submissions**. *Killian v. Yorozu Automotive Tennessee, Inc.*, 454 F.3d 549 (6th Cir. 2006).

- An employee of a company in Texas sought FMLA leave to recover from carpal tunnel surgery. The company conditionally approved the request, giving the employee 20 days to submit medical certification. She asked for an extra 15 days to submit the form, and the company agreed to extend the deadline. When the company failed to receive the form, it fired the employee. She sued under the FMLA, and a federal court ruled in her favor. The Fifth Circuit reversed, noting that the company had done everything required of it under 29 CFR § 825.305. **It did not have to give the employee a chance to "cure the deficiency" in her form because the form was never submitted.** Nor did it matter that the physician allegedly misplaced the form. The burden was on the employee to make certain that the form was submitted within the deadline. *Urban v. Dolgencorp of Texas*, 393 F.3d 572 (5th Cir. 2004).

- An emergency medical technician in Michigan suffered from migraine headaches and was allowed to take intermittent leave under the FMLA. However, her employer **spotted what it believed was an inconsistency in her medical certification** and asked her to correct it. She refused to do so, believing that if she did so, the employer would force her to work part time. After submitting to a fitness-for-duty exam, she told her supervisor to "quit f—— with [her]." She repeated the profanity the next day and was fired a few weeks later. When she sued for retaliation under the FMLA, a federal court and the Sixth Circuit ruled against her. She was legitimately fired for insubordination. *Hoffman v. Professional Med Team*, 394 F.3d 414 (6th Cir. 2005).

- An Illinois employee with "two strikes" under the company's disciplinary policy missed three days of work due to a bout of bronchitis. When he returned to work, his supervisor told him to apply for FMLA leave to avoid picking up his third strike. His doctor failed to precisely follow the instructions on the FMLA form the company gave him (which was a copy of the one provided by the Department of Labor). However, the doctor wrote the word "bronchitis" next to the "serious health condition" box. When the company fired the employee because the form was inadequately filled out, he sued. The Seventh Circuit held that he would be allowed to pursue his lawsuit against the employer. **Writing "bronchitis" next to the box was the equivalent of checking it.** *Kauffman v. Federal Express Corp.*, 426 F.3d 880 (7th Cir. 2005).

- A mechanic suffered a work-related injury that resulted in episodes of neck pain and numbness in his hands. He went on short-term disability leave, during which he received a letter from the employer, informing him that his leave qualified as FMLA leave, and that he had to produce a doctor's certificate to return to work. The day after his 12-week FMLA leave expired, he called the company to inquire about reinstatement, but was told that he was fired for not returning to the job within the 12-week period (the employer claimed that the 12-week period ran from before it sent the mechanic the FMLA notice letter). A week later, the mechanic received a letter confirming that he was fired. He sued the employer under the FMLA and the Arkansas Civil Rights Act, and a jury awarded him damages of $305,000. The Eighth Circuit affirmed the award, holding that **the jury had properly found that he had attempted to return to work**, that he had obtained a doctor's certificate releasing him to work, and that he was able to perform the essential functions of the job. *Duty v. Norton-Alcoa Proppants*, 293 F.3d 481 (8th Cir. 2002).

E. Post-Leave Issues

The FMLA requires covered employers to restore employees to their former positions or an equivalent position but does not confer a right, benefit or position to which the employee was not entitled in the absence of a leave.

- A staffing agency employee working in the IT division of an automotive industry company had to be hospitalized for asthma. While she was on FMLA leave, the company eliminated her position. It used another contractor from the staffing agency to perform her duties and later hired him directly. When she sued the agency and the company under the FMLA, a Michigan federal court granted pretrial judgment to the defendants. However, the Sixth Circuit found issues of fact requiring a trial. It noted that the defendants could be liable as joint employers for interfering with her reinstatement rights. Also, the employee presented **evidence that the restructuring was done to get around the requirements of the FMLA**. *Grace v. USCAR and Bartech Technological Services, LLC*, 521 F.3d 655 (6th Cir. 2008).

- A Pennsylvania company had a complicated system for determining overtime eligibility. It placed new hires and people who had been on leave for more than three weeks in the least favorable position on the overtime list. Eventually, those people who had the fewest overtime hours were given the opportunity to accept overtime. Every six months the slate was wiped clean and a new list was created. When an employee returned from FMLA leave, the slate had been wiped clean, putting him in a less favorable position for overtime. He sued, alleging a violation of the FMLA. A federal court ruled against him. **He was treated the same as any employee taking leave for more than three weeks** and was not entitled to be treated as if he had worked during the period of his leave. *Diiorio v. Manor*, 2007 WL 519252 (E.D. Pa. 2/12/07).

◆ An IT employee in Virginia took FMLA leave to have hip surgery. While he was gone, his position was eliminated and he was offered another project to work on with the same salary, title, bonus eligibility, and health and retirement benefits. However, he no longer oversaw the IT department budget and no longer had purchasing authority. Four months later, his job was eliminated because of a merger and by the end of the year, all IT functions had been transferred to Toronto. He sued under the FMLA and the ADA. A federal court and the Fourth Circuit ruled against him. **There was no FMLA violation in the assignment to the equivalent position**, and he could not prove he was disabled under the ADA. *Csicsmann v. Sallada*, 211 Fed.Appx. 163 (4th Cir. 2006).

◆ An assembly line employee of a recreational vehicle manufacturer in Indiana took FMLA leave for depression. While she was gone, the manufacturer consolidated two production lines and reassigned personnel to different tasks. As a result, when she returned she had to do a few more tasks than she performed before the leave. She developed tendonitis using a screw gun, and her doctor restricted her from using her right hand. Her supervisor excused her from using the screw gun but told her to continue using the "seal gun" with her left hand if necessary. She walked off the job. When the human resources director sent her a letter offering to accommodate her work restrictions, she instead sued under the FMLA. A federal court and the Seventh Circuit ruled against her. Here, **she was returned to an equivalent position following her leave**. The changes to her job were minimal and not physically demanding. *Mitchell v. Dutchmen Manufacturing*, 389 F.3d 746 (7th Cir. 2004).

◆ After receiving complaints about the HR department and one of its employees, a Louisiana company developed a plan to improve the department and reassigned the employee. Her supervisor later met with her to discuss areas where she needed improvement. She took FMLA leave for anxiety and stress. While on leave, she was granted a merit increase in salary, but the vice president of HR remained concerned about her performance. When she returned from leave, she was told that she would be fired if her performance did not improve. The plant manager micro-managed her work, and she was ridiculed at a meeting. She resigned, then sued under the FMLA. A federal court and the Fifth Circuit ruled against her. **She was not demoted when she returned from leave**, and the ridicule at the meeting was not enough to prove constructive discharge. *Haley v. Alliance Compressor, LLC*, 391 F.3d 644 (5th Cir. 2004).

◆ A production assistant at a Honda plant in Ohio took FMLA leave to have abdominal surgery. She received two extensions, then returned to work unexpectedly early, with a medical certification of her fitness for duty. Honda –

because of production line changes, her medical restrictions and her unanticipated return to work – did not have a position available for her. In the lawsuit that followed, Honda argued that it should be allowed to restore her job or an equivalent job within a "reasonable" time of her return. The Sixth Circuit disagreed. Under the FMLA, **an employer has to restore a returning employee to the same or an equivalent job within two days**. If Honda did not have reasonable notice that the employee was to return to work on the day she did, then it had to restore her job no later than two days after she showed up. *Hoge v. Honda of America Manufacturing*, 384 F.3d 238 (6th Cir. 2004).

F. Other FMLA Issues

The FMLA sometimes comes into conflict with the Americans with Disabilities Act and state workers' compensation law. Each statute has its own requirements. Thus, it is important to consult with an attorney before taking any questionable action.

◆ A company in Indiana used a point system to track and discipline employees for absenteeism. A recovering alcoholic employee who had worked there for 15 years was nine points (three absences) short of termination. He had a relapse on a Friday evening, and his wife called the hospital the next day to see if she could bring him in for treatment. He reached his doctor on Wednesday and, after obtaining insurance approval, was admitted to the hospital on Friday. However, he missed three scheduled days of work prior to his admittance. He sought FMLA protection. The company fired him and he sued. A federal court and the Seventh Circuit ruled against him, noting that **the three days he missed prior to his hospitalization (but after he and his wife contacted his doctor) did not count as "treatment" under the FMLA**. *Darst v. Interstate Brands Corp.*, 512 F.3d 903 (7th Cir. 2008).

◆ An Ohio flight attendant worked mostly as an on-call employee who could receive flight assignments up to two hours prior to departure. She had a history of unacceptable attendance but was granted intermittent leave for a pregnancy. After she returned to work, she continued to have attendance problems and was eventually fired for performance and dependability problems. She sued, alleging retaliation under the FMLA. The Sixth Circuit ruled against her, noting that she failed to work the requisite 1,250 hours to be eligible for FMLA leave. The airline detailed each flight she worked and added in the time required by the collective bargaining agreement for check-in, debriefing, training and ground time. Even with all that, **the employee worked only 1,128 hours during the year in question**. *Staunch v. Continental Airlines, Inc.*, 511 F.3d 625 (6th Cir. 2008).

◆ An employee of Boston University took intermittent leave under the FMLA to care for her sick mother. She asked for leave from August 4 through October 3 and, if necessary, again from October 28 through November 18. The university's director of personnel approved her request and notified her that if she failed to return on November 19, she would be deemed to have voluntarily resigned. While on leave, the employee sent a letter to her supervisor, informing her that she intended to take an extra day of leave because of an internal holiday granted by the university's board of trustees. Her supervisor sent a reply that holidays did not extend an employee's FMLA leave. When the employee did not return to work on November 19, the university deemed her to have quit. She sued, claiming a violation of the FMLA, and lost. The First Circuit Court of Appeals cited an FMLA regulation, which stated that **if "intermittent leave includes a full holiday-containing week, ... the amount of leave used includes the holiday."** *Mellen v. Trustees of Boston University*, 504 F.3d 21 (1st Cir. 2007).

◆ A Washington employee with bipolar disorder became extremely irritable at work and could not concentrate on her assignments. When her supervisors presented her with a performance plan, she threw it back over the desk, shouting profanities. The next day she began a medical leave, seeking treatment for her condition. **While on leave, she was fired for her previous outburst.** She sued under the FMLA and state law. The Ninth Circuit held that she was not fired in violation of the FMLA because the employer would have fired her regardless of whether she was on leave. However, she might have been fired in violation of the state law against discrimination. A new trial was required. *Gambini v. Total Renal Care, Inc.*, 486 F.3d 1087 (9th Cir. 2007).

◆ A car salesman for a Maine dealership worked there five years before leaving. After five years away, the salesman returned. He worked for seven months, then ruptured a disk in his back. He received medical treatment and took medical leave on 13 separate days over the next six weeks because the pain prevented him from working. When the dealership fired him, he sued under the FMLA, asserting that he was eligible because of his prior years of service. A federal court dismissed his lawsuit, but the First Circuit Court of Appeals reversed. It held that **FMLA regulations allow "break-in-service" employees to count previous periods of employment** toward the 12-month requirement as long as they meet the 1,250-hour requirement. *Rucker v. Lee Holding Co.*, 471 F.3d 6 (1st Cir. 2006).

◆ An airline pilot requested intermittent leave under the FMLA because her son had various health problems that required medical care. She later experienced health problems of her own that forced her to take medical leave. Although the airline initially granted her FMLA requests, it later denied her FMLA leave. She sued, **asserting that her reserve duty (or on-call time) should be counted toward the number of hours she had worked** in the previous year, thus bringing her up to the necessary 1,250 hours mandated by the act. A Utah federal court and the U.S. Court of Appeals, Tenth Circuit, ruled against her. Even though she had to refrain from drinking alcohol and be able to report to the airport and get cleared through security within an hour of being called while on reserve duty, the restrictions on her conduct weren't sufficient to be considered time worked. *Knapp v. America West Airlines*, 207 Fed.Appx. 896 (10th Cir. 2006).

◆ As part of a bank reorganization, a Kansas computer analyst was assigned to work on a system she was unfamiliar with, and was placed under a supervisor who had previously been a co-worker. She missed the first day of work for the new supervisor, was diagnosed with depression and anxiety, and was told to work half-days until her anxiety was under control. She then missed two deadlines and was fired six weeks later. When she sued under the FMLA, she lost. The Tenth Circuit held that **the termination was not causally connected to the FMLA leave**. Multiple managers observed the same problems with the analyst's performance, and her past three annual evaluations contained negative comments. *Metzler v. Federal Home Loan Bank of Topeka*, 464 F.3d 1164 (10th Cir. 2006).

◆ An employee of a company in North Carolina missed a lot of work due to health problems. Eventually, she had surgery on an abdominal mass. A few months later, she received a poor performance evaluation because of her absences. She was then laid off in a reduction in force. She signed a waiver of any claims against the company, received severance pay, then sued under the FMLA. A federal court granted pretrial judgment to the company, but the Fourth Circuit reversed. A Department of Labor (DOL) regulation (29 CFR § 825.220(d)) stated that **she could not be forced to waive her rights under the FMLA without court or DOL approval**. *Taylor v. Progress Energy, Inc.*, 493 F.3d 454 (4th Cir. 2007).

◆ A machine operator in Iowa took intermittent leave under the FMLA to deal with her depression, arriving late or leaving early when her depression worsened. Her supervisor questioned whether she was really sick and regularly complained to the HR manager about her use of FMLA leave. He also retaliated against her each time she took FMLA leave by doing little things to make her job more difficult. She was later fired for using her cell phone on company time. She sued, asserting that she had permission to use the cell phone and that no one else had ever been fired for a similar offense. A jury awarded her $107,571 in back pay. The trial court awarded an equivalent amount in liquidated damages, as well as $15,512 in front pay. The Eighth Circuit upheld the award, based on the evidence that **the supervisor intentionally retaliated against her**. *Hite v. Vermeer Manufacturing Co.*, 446 F.3d 858 (8th Cir. 2006).

◆ An ultrasound technician for a Missouri health care provider developed carpal tunnel syndrome and filed for workers' compensation benefits. Her employer's doctor imposed a "light gripping only" restriction on her. Since her job required her to grip an ultrasound machine for 95% of her workday, when the employer learned of the restrictions, it placed her on FMLA leave until she received medical clearance to return to work. It fired her after 12 weeks when she could not return to the job. She sued under the FMLA and state workers' compensation law, but a federal court and the Eighth Circuit ruled against her. **Neither the FMLA nor workers' compensation required an employer to keep a person employed when she cannot perform tasks required by her job.** *Bloom v. Metro Heart Group of St. Louis, Inc.*, 440 F.3d 1025 (8th Cir. 2006).

◆ A machine operator for a company in Maine obtained intermittent leave under the FMLA for migraine headaches. However, he never provided the company with the medical documentation to support his claim. The company became suspicious of his numerous absences after failing to reach him at home when he was supposed to be incapacitated by migraines. It hired an investigator, who followed him to the gym, a video store and three convenience stores. The company fired him and he sued under the FMLA. A federal court and the First Circuit ruled against him. **Hiring an investigator did not amount to retaliation under the FMLA.** The company was justifiably suspicious after being unable to reach the employee at home. *Colburn v. Parker Hannifin/Nichols Portland Division*, 429 F.3d 325 (1st Cir. 2005).

◆ A South Carolina employee began selling advertising for a company on June 1, 1999. She began to experience headaches, dizziness and exhaustion (which turned out to be caused by cancer). On May 19, 2000, she took a leave of absence at her doctor's suggestion. On May 30, her doctor certified the company's disability leave forms, and the employee left town believing her leave had been approved. It wasn't, and she was fired when she did not report to work on June 9. She sued under the FMLA. A jury ruled in her favor even though she was not eligible for FMLA leave at the time her leave began. It awarded her over $91,000. The Fourth Circuit Court of Appeals upheld the award, noting that the employee had been granted leave initially. It stated that she could not be both on leave and on an unexcused absence at the same time. *Babcock v. BellSouth Advertising*, 348 F.3d 73 (4th Cir. 2003).

◆ A teacher in Alabama during her first year of employment notified her principal that she was pregnant and that her due date was August 2. However, on May 15, the school board decided not to renew her contract for the following year because she did not establish a proper relationship with parents or students, and she sent students to the office over matters she should have been able to resolve herself. She gave birth July 27, less than a year after she started work, and a federal court determined that she was not eligible for FMLA leave because she had not yet worked for the school district for 12 months. The Eleventh Circuit affirmed, noting that even though she would have been eligible under the FMLA a few days after her leave would have started, **the request was made by an ineligible employee for a leave that would have started while she was still ineligible**. She was not protected by the FMLA. *Walker v. Elmore Board of Educ.*, 379 F.3d 1249 (11th Cir. 2004).

◆ The FMLA allows employers to use one of four methods for determining the 12-month leave period during which an employee is entitled to leave. They are: the calendar year; any fixed 12-month leave year; the 12-month period measured forward from the date an employee's first FMLA leave begins; or a "rolling" 12-month period measured backward from the date an employee uses any FMLA leave. An airline distributed a handbook that informed employees of their FMLA rights but did not identify which method it was using to measure the 12-month leave period. When an employee took a three-week leave and another day to care for her sick baby less than a year after she had taken maternity leave, the airline fired her for exceeding the 12 weeks allowed by the FMLA. She sued, and an Arizona court ruled in favor of the airline. The Ninth Circuit reversed, holding that **the airline should have specified the method it was going to use in determining the 12-month leave period**. Here, because it failed to do so, the court chose the method most favorable to the employee – the calendar year. Under that method, the employee had not used any leave time under the FMLA because a new year had occurred after her maternity leave expired. *Bachelder v. America West Airlines, Inc.*, 259 F.3d 1112 (9th Cir. 2001).

VI. ARBITRATION

Arbitration has become a popular method for resolving employment disputes, mainly because of the lower cost as compared to litigation. For cases involving arbitration with respect to labor relations, please see Chapter Five, Section II.F.

To be enforceable, an arbitration agreement has to be fair.

—It cannot place undue costs or obstacles on employees.
—It cannot require a forum that is convenient for the employer without considering the ability of employees to reach that forum.
—It cannot force employees to arbitrate but not make the same requirement of employers.
—It cannot change the law. In other words, it cannot provide less in the way of remedies than employees would be entitled to under federal and state law.

- As a condition of employment, a South Carolina man signed an arbitration agreement (agreeing to arbitrate employment-related disputes). He then began work as a grill operator for a restaurant. Sixteen days later, he suffered a seizure at work and was discharged shortly thereafter. He did not initiate arbitration proceedings, but instead filed a disability discrimination charge with the Equal Employment Opportunity Commission (EEOC), alleging that his firing violated the Americans with Disabilities Act (ADA). The EEOC filed an action against the restaurant seeking injunctive relief to eradicate past and present unlawful employment practices, and also seeking specific relief to make the employee whole. The employee was not a party to the case. A federal court refused to compel arbitration under the Federal Arbitration Act. The Fourth Circuit held that the arbitration agreement did not prevent the EEOC from bringing the action, but that it could not seek relief for the employee.

The U.S. Supreme Court then determined that the EEOC could seek relief on behalf of the employee despite the existence of the arbitration agreement. **The EEOC's statutory right to compel enforcement of Title VII and the ADA is not altered by an arbitration agreement** between employer and employee. *EEOC v. Waffle House, Inc.*, 534 U.S. 279, 122 S.Ct. 754, 151 L.Ed.2d 755 (2002).

◆ A gay employee of Circuit City claimed that he was subjected to harassment because of his sexual orientation. He quit and sued the company under California law. A federal court ordered him to arbitrate his claim because when he signed the application for the job, he agreed to arbitrate any disputes arising out of or relating to his employment. The Ninth Circuit reversed the order to arbitrate, finding that the Federal Arbitration Act excluded all employment-related agreements from its reach because of language exempting "seamen, railroad employees or any other class of workers engaged in foreign or interstate commerce." The case reached the U.S. Supreme Court, which held that employers could enforce arbitration agreements under the Federal Arbitration Act, even where employees wanted to sue for employment discrimination. **Only transportation employees engaged in interstate or foreign commerce are exempt from the application of the Federal Arbitration Act.** *Circuit City Stores, Inc. v. Adams*, 532 U.S. 105, 121 S.Ct. 1302, 149 L.Ed.2d 234 (2001).

On remand, the Ninth Circuit ruled that the arbitration agreement was not enforceable because it was both procedurally and substantively unconscionable. The agreement was a standard form contract that put the employee in a "take it or leave it" position by conditioning employment on signing the contract. Further, the agreement required employees to arbitrate while not requiring the employer to do so, and made them pay half the arbitrator's fees. *Circuit City Stores, Inc. v. Adams*, 279 F.3d 889 (9th Cir. 2002).

◆ A company in the Virgin Islands hired a Spanish-speaking construction worker and gave him an employment agreement to sign that included an arbitration clause. A bilingual applicant helped him with the paperwork but didn't explain everything. Later, the company fired the employee for dropping a bottle of urine on another contractor's employees from a great height. He sued for wrongful discharge, and a federal court held that the arbitration clause could not be enforced because he did not understand what he was signing. However, the Third Circuit reversed, **finding the clause enforceable despite the fact that the employee did not know what he was signing**. It was his duty to understand the agreement before signing it. Arbitration was required. *Morales v. Sun Constructors, Inc.*, 541 F.3d 218 (3d Cir. 2008).

◆ A Nebraska insurance company employee signed an agreement to arbitrate any employment-related claims against the company. She later filed charges with the EEOC, claiming sexual harassment by male subordinates. The EEOC brought a Title VII enforcement action and she sought to intervene in the case. The Eighth Circuit held that she could not do so. Although she had filed for Chapter 7 bankruptcy and could no longer afford her half of the arbitration fee, her employer had agreed to pay both halves and, even if it hadn't, **she could still be compelled to arbitrate her Title VII claims**. *EEOC v. Woodmen of the World Life Insurance Society*, 479 F.3d 561 (8th Cir. 2007).

◆ An Oklahoma pawnshop and check-cashing store introduced a mandatory dispute resolution program requiring employees to resolve their employment disputes through arbitration. The company made clear that **any employee who**

remained with the company after March 1, 2003 would be deemed to have accepted the arbitration program. A manager who explicitly rejected the arbitration language nonetheless continued to work for the company. After she was fired, she tried to sue for sex discrimination, but the Tenth Circuit Court of Appeals held that because she had continued to work for the company, she was required to arbitrate her claim. *Hardin v. First Cash Financial Services, Inc.*, 465 F.3d 470 (10th Cir. 2006).

◆ A beer company in Illinois created a new dispute resolution program that required all employees, as a condition of employment, to arbitrate any disputes arising out of that employment. It issued handbooks, arranged a presentation and placed posters throughout the workplace. Eighteen months later, an employee filed for workers' compensation benefits and was fired. She sued, and the trial court refused to compel arbitration. An appellate court agreed, but the Supreme Court of Illinois reversed, finding that the company could make arbitration a condition of continuing employment. Also, **workers' compensation law did not bar an employee from agreeing to submit a retaliatory discharge claim to arbitration**. *Melena v. Anheuser-Busch*, 847 N.E.2d 99 (Ill. 2006).

◆ A California department store employee who signed an arbitration agreement was fired a year later for "stealing time" by clocking in early. She filed an intent to arbitrate, claiming that the real reason for the firing was the fact that she had taken a second job to pay for school. The store believed her claim was without merit and refused to pay its share of the filing fee for arbitration. She sued it for wrongful discharge. The store then sought to dismiss the case on the grounds that she was required to arbitrate. A federal court and the Ninth Circuit refused to dismiss the case. **The store could not compel arbitration after breaching the agreement to arbitrate the wrongful termination claim.** *Brown v. Dillard's Inc.*, 430 F.3d 1004 (9th Cir. 2005).

◆ A new employee of a staffing firm in Washington, D.C., signed **an arbitration agreement that prohibited the awarding of punitive damages** in any proceeding required by the agreement. It also contained a severability clause, stating that if any part of the agreement were ruled to be invalid, that part would be severed from the rest of the agreement, which would continue to remain in effect. When the employee later sued for race discrimination, seeking punitive damages, the firm sought to compel arbitration. The U.S. Court of Appeals, D.C. Circuit, severed the invalid punitive damages waiver and ordered arbitration. *Booker v. Robert Half Int'l*, 413 F.3d 77 (D.C. Cir. 2005).

◆ A company in Massachusetts created a new dispute resolution policy and sent out a mass e-mail, referring employees to two links at the bottom of the message. The message informed employees they were covered by the new policy if they continued working after the policy's effective date, and warning that the company would seek to dismiss any employment-related lawsuit they might file. When an employee with sleep apnea was fired for too many absences, he sued under the ADA and the company sought to compel arbitration. A federal court and the First Circuit refused to do so. Here, **the mass e-mail did not mention the mandatory arbitration procedure in the body of the message**. Nor did it require employees to respond with an acknowledgement that they had read and understood the policy's terms. It also did not mention that the new policy would become automatically binding on any employee who showed up for work the next day. *Campbell v. General Dynamics Government Systems Corp.*, 407 F.3d 546 (1st Cir. 2005).

◆ A FedEx recruiter in Colorado allegedly promised three independent drivers that they would earn $1,500 a week by working 10-12 hours a day. They signed an operating agreement and were assigned delivery routes. However, they did not come close to the income promised and sued for breach of an implied contract and breach of the duty of good faith and fair dealing. The company claimed that the arbitration clause in the operating agreement required the lawsuit to be dismissed, but the Tenth Circuit disagreed. Here, **the arbitration obligation was narrowly limited to disputes over the termination of the operating agreement**, and the claims at issue did not relate to that. *Cummings v. FedEx Ground Package System, Inc.*, 404 F.3d 1258 (10th Cir. 2005).

◆ Employees of a restaurant chain in Tennessee brought a lawsuit to collect overtime they believed they were owed under the Fair Labor Standards Act. The restaurant asserted that the employees were bound by the arbitration agreements they had signed and thus could not sue. The case reached the Sixth Circuit, which ruled that **the arbitration agreements were not enforceable**. Here, the restaurant did not allow enough time for job applicants to review the arbitration agreements; they were not allowed to take the agreements home to review them; and the agreements failed to explicitly state that applicants were giving up their right to a jury trial by signing the agreements. This was not a knowing and voluntary waiver. Also, although applicants were required to arbitrate their claims against the company, the restaurant was not required to arbitrate its claims against employees. *Walker v. Ryan's Family Steak Houses, Inc.*, 400 F.3d 370 (6th Cir. 2005).

◆ An employee of a mortgage company in Massachusetts filed sex discrimination and harassment charges with the EEOC. The EEOC investigated the charges and determined that there was no evidence of discrimination. When the employee sued, the company sought to require arbitration based on an arbitration agreement the employee had signed before she began the job. The First Circuit Court of Appeals ruled that **the company could compel arbitration** even though it delayed its demand until after the EEOC completed its investigation. Requiring arbitration during an EEOC investigation would result in duplicative proceedings. *Marie v. Allied Home Mortgage Corp.*, 402 F.3d 1 (1st Cir. 2005).

◆ After the Supreme Court issued its ruling in *Circuit City Stores, Inc. v. Adams*, Circuit City modified its arbitration program to provide employees with an option to elect not to participate. An employee who received the "opt-out" form was notified that he could opt out of binding arbitration only if he signed and returned the form within 30 days. He was also encouraged to contact company representatives and/or an attorney before making his decision. He failed to return the form. When he later sued Circuit City under the California Fair Employment and Housing Act, the company moved for binding arbitration, and the Ninth Circuit held that he was required to submit to it. Because **he was given the chance to opt out of the arbitration program** and failed to do so, he had to submit to binding arbitration. *Circuit City Stores, Inc. v. Ahmed*, 283 F.3d 1198 (9th Cir. 2002).

◆ A company required an employee to sign an arbitration agreement, which contained a provision making each party responsible for its own attorneys' fees. Each party also had to pay half the cost of the arbitrator. When the employee sued the company for violating Title VII and 42 U.S.C. § 1981, an Illinois federal court ordered her to submit to arbitration. The U.S. Court of Appeals, Seventh Circuit, reversed, finding the arbitration agreement unenforceable because of the costs it inflicted on the employee. Under Title VII, prevailing plaintiffs are entitled to attorneys' fees. The agreement here, however, required each party to pay its own fees regardless of the outcome. As a result, **the arbitration agreement deprived the employee of a remedy available under Title VII**. *McCaskill v. SCI Management Corp.*, 298 F.3d 677 (7th Cir. 2002).

◆ A clerical employee with a New York university took medical leave under the FMLA and was terminated three months later when the leave allegedly expired and she still had not returned to work. She sued the university under the Americans with Disabilities Act and the FMLA, as well as state and city laws. The university sought to compel arbitration, relying on the collective bargaining agreement it had signed with her union. The Second Circuit held that **the employee could not be compelled to arbitrate** by virtue of the arbitration clause in the bargaining agreement. Here, the employee had not clearly and unmistakably waived her right to sue for violations of federal discrimination law. *Rogers v. New York Univ.*, 220 F.3d 73 (2d Cir. 2000).

◆ An employee signed an agreement to arbitrate all disputes, claims and questions regarding her rights and obligations with respect to the employer-employee relationship. Subsequently, she alleged that the owner and CEO of the company made sexually oriented statements to her, groped her and propositioned her. She sued him and the company for battery, negligence and invasion of privacy. The company sought to force her to arbitrate her claims, but the District Court of Appeal of Florida refused to order arbitration. **The arbitration agreement did not address sexual harassment** or other torts arising out of the employer-employee relationship. Nor was there anything in the agreement to suggest that the parties intended sexual harassment or other personal injury claims to be submitted to arbitration. The lawsuit against the company could continue. *Boone v. Etkin*, 771 So.2d 559 (Fla. Dist. Ct. App. 2000).

VII. OTHER EMPLOYMENT PRACTICES CASES

Any employment practice can lead to litigation. Thus, employers should try to implement practices and policies that will minimize the chances of being sued. Start with:

—written job descriptions,
—flexible disciplinary procedures,
—consistent application of company rules,
—a good handbook that contains anti-harassment policies, and
—an awareness of what the law allows and prohibits.

◆ A New Jersey county enacted **a living wage ordinance** affecting businesses that contracted with the county to provide home health care, food and janitorial services. Under the ordinance, the contractors had to provide their employees with health benefits and pay them 150% of the federal minimum wage. A lawsuit ensued, and the Superior Court, Appellate Division, held that the ordinance did not violate the contractors' constitutional right to equal protection by arbitrarily imposing requirements on some businesses but not others. The county had a legitimate interest in increasing the standard of living for low-wage workers while decreasing the tax burden of caring for the uninsured. *Visiting Homemaker Service of Hudson County v. Board of Chosen Freeholders*, 883 A.2d 1074 (N.J. Super. Ct. App. Div. 2005).

◆ An engineer worked at Intel for nine years until he was fired. He then joined with several other former and current Intel employees in forming an organization that was critical of Intel's employment policies. He became the organization's spokesperson and, in a 21-month period, sent out six mass e-mails on behalf of the organization to employee addresses on Intel's e-mail system. Besides criticizing Intel employment policies, the e-mails also suggested moving to other companies and joining the organization. Intel demanded that he stop sending the messages through its computer system. He refused, and it sued him for trespass. The case reached the Supreme Court of California, which ruled that **Intel could not succeed in its trespass lawsuit because the unwanted e-mails caused no property damage** to the company's computer system. Here, the harm Intel claimed to have suffered (lost productivity from employees reading and reacting to the e-mails) was not an injury to the company's interest in its computers. *Intel Corp. v. Hamidi*, 71 P.3d 296 (Cal. 2003).

◆ A Wal-Mart employee was fired after the company's loss prevention district supervisor determined that she had removed store property without authorization. The investigating supervisor obtained statements from several witnesses and also interviewed the employee, who wrote a two-page statement. After losing her job, the employee wrote to the store manager explaining her version of the events. She requested a copy of her personnel file and the documents relating to the investigation. Wal-Mart gave her copies of the documents in her personnel file, but did not give her any of the documents relating to the supervisor's investigation. The supervisor kept those documents in his home office. The employee sued under a Maine law requiring disclosure of "formal or informal employee evaluations and reports relating to the employee's character, credit, work habits, compensation and benefits."

A court determined that the investigation records were components of her personnel file pursuant to the statute and that Wal-Mart should have produced them. It ordered the documents to be disclosed and fined the company $500. The Supreme Judicial Court of Maine upheld the ruling in favor of the employee. It noted that **the statute did not limit disclosure to those documents actually placed in the employee's personnel file**, but rather included all employee records in the employer's possession. Even though Wal-Mart had sought to maintain witness confidentiality and protect itself from releasing possibly defamatory statements, it was required by law to disclose the documents. *Harding v. Wal-Mart Stores*, 765 A.2d 73 (Me. 2001).

◆ An engineer working in the Denver office of an international petroleum company requested and was given a five-month unpaid educational leave so that he could attend a semester of classes on a full-time basis. He signed a memorandum stating that there was no guarantee a position would be available when he returned, and that he would be considered for open positions, but that the company was under no obligation to hire him for them. However, his supervisor allegedly told him that he could return to his old job any time. During his leave, the company reduced part of its work force and informed the engineer that his position had been eliminated. He turned down a temporary job and an offer to relocate to Houston, and the company fired him. A federal court ruled for the company, and the U.S. Court of Appeals, Tenth Circuit, affirmed. The general rule in Colorado is that **there can be no implied promise where an express contract covers the same subject**. Here, because the written memo expressly outlined the terms of unpaid leave, there could be no implied promise from the engineer's supervisor that he could return to his old job any time. *Flint v. Amoco Corp.*, 173 F.3d 863 (10th Cir. 1999) (Unpublished).

◆ The 1986 Tax Reform Act placed an 80% cap (now 50%) on deductions for business meals and entertainment. A Las Vegas casino, however, believed its employees' meals were exempt from the cap and took a full deduction for its 1988 and 1989 expenses. The IRS disagreed and sent the company a bill for $400,000. In the lawsuit that followed, the Ninth Circuit Court of Appeals held that the casino could deduct 100% of its expenses. Because "**the furnished meals were, in effect, 'indispensable to the proper discharge' of the employees' duties,**" they met the tax code's requirement of being provided for the "convenience of the employer," and entitled the casino to the full deduction. *Boyd Gaming Corp. v. Commissioner of Internal Revenue*, 177 F.3d 1096 (9th Cir. 1999).

A. Discrimination and Nepotism

The following cases address discrimination issues other than those presented in Chapter One. For example, some states' civil rights laws protect against marital status or sexual orientation discrimination.

Appearance and dress code policies are generally permissible as long as they are not used in a discriminatory manner. For example, it may not be appropriate to ban cornrows because such a policy might be construed to have a discriminatory impact on African-Americans.

Nepotism (hiring family, friends and insiders) can be illegal where it leads to discrimination against protected minorities.

Anti-nepotism policies are generally legal. Only where they are used as a means of discriminating against protected minorities are they likely to be struck down.

- A native Alaskan, who was a member of the Kenaitze tribe, wore his hair long. He worked for a supermarket that had a dress code/grooming policy requiring men to wear their hair no longer than collar length. However, he was told that if he kept his hair tied back, he would not have to cut it. After he'd been on the job for more than two years, the store was sold, then closed. He was offered a transfer to another location, but only if he cut his hair. He refused to do so and was fired. When he sued, his constitutional claims failed because there was no state action. He also alleged a breach of the covenant of good faith and fair dealing, but lost that claim too. The company had a legitimate reason for its grooming policy, and **the employee never claimed, prior to his discharge, that he had religious reasons for wearing his hair long**. Further, his constitutionally protected liberty and privacy interest in wearing his hair long was outweighed by the company's legitimate interest in its grooming policy. *Miller v. Safeway, Inc.*, 170 P.3d 655 (Alaska 2007).

- A country club in Michigan refused to renew the contract of its golf professional after he moved out of his marital home and began having an adulterous affair with a married woman. He sued for marital status discrimination, claiming that the nonrenewal of his contract violated the state's Civil Rights Act. The case reached the Supreme Court of Michigan, which noted that **an employee who is fired solely because of conduct such as adultery is not protected by the Civil Rights Act**. However, because there was some evidence that the country club may have considered the golf pro's marital status in addition to the adultery when it made the decision not to renew the contract, the case was remanded for further consideration. *Veenstra v. Washtenaw Country Club*, 645 N.W.2d 643 (Mich. 2002).

- An employer belonging to the National Association of Securities Dealers (NASD) sold securities registered with the Securities and Exchange Commission. NASD requires all employees who participate in securities sales to be individually registered, and in order to obtain registration, agents must have no statutory disqualification. A felony conviction within 10 years of an application is a statutory disqualification unless an employer is willing to undertake certain obligations, such as paying substantial fees and making daily reviews of the applicant's securities work. An employer rejected an applicant based on his three-year-old conviction for helping deliver a controlled substance. He filed a complaint with the state Department of Industry, Labor and Human Relations. A hearing officer found no discrimination against the applicant because, based on his NASD disqualification, he was not qualified for the position. She held that an employer need not accommodate an applicant's conviction record. The applicant appealed. The Court of Appeals of Wisconsin agreed with the administrative finding that **an employment applicant must be qualified for a position in order to trigger statutory protections against unlawful discrimination**. The employer gave a legitimate, nondiscriminatory reason for refusing to hire felons based on its previous problems with NASD compliance prior to instituting its policy. Its refusal to voluntarily take steps which might have made him employable did not transform him into a qualified applicant, and nothing in Wisconsin law mandated such action. The court affirmed the ruling for the employer. *Knight v. Labor and Industry Review Comm'n*, 582 N.W.2d 448 (Wis. Ct. App. 1998).

◆ Washington's Law Against Discrimination prohibits employment discrimination based on marital status. A title company employee began to experience conflicts with her co-workers as a result of her husband's conduct. Her husband was an independent contractor who provided the company with janitorial services. A co-worker obtained a restraining order against him, and the company manager warned the employee, co-worker and husband that they would all be fired if they could not work together. The co-worker later complained of an obscene phone call by the husband, and the manager fired the employee and co-worker, and terminated the janitorial contract. The employee sued for discrimination based on marital status. The court granted pretrial judgment to the company, but the Court of Appeals of Washington reversed.

The company appealed to the Supreme Court of Washington, claiming that the action did not involve marital status discrimination because it did not involve the employee's marriage or the identity of her spouse. The employee argued that **marital status discrimination under state law included actions based on a spouse's misconduct**. The court agreed with the employee, stating that the law against discrimination was to be broadly construed to prohibit discrimination on the status of being married or single. This included the conduct of an employee's spouse. Because the question of discrimination should have been resolved by a jury, the trial court had improperly granted pretrial judgment to the company. *Magula v. Benton Franklin Title Co., Inc.*, 930 P.2d 307 (Wash. 1997).

◆ A hotel in Hawaii adopted a policy that provided that two direct relatives could not work in the same department together. If they married after being hired, one of the two would be asked to transfer or resign. A couple who had been cohabiting got married shortly after the husband was hired. A year later, the new owner of the hotel sought to enforce the rule. When neither the husband nor the wife transferred, the husband was fired. He sued the hotel in a state court, claiming violation of a Hawaii law against discrimination based on marital status. The court granted pretrial judgment to the hotel. The Supreme Court of Hawaii determined that it was the fact of marriage that caused the discharge. It then stated that the policy of **firing persons who marry others**

working in the same department violated Hawaii law unless a statutory exception could be shown. The court vacated and remanded the case so that the hotel could try to show that its policy fell within one of the statutory exceptions. *Ross v. Stouffer Hotel Co.*, 816 P.2d 302 (Haw. 1991).

◆ A Washington newspaper reporter openly supported gay and lesbian rights, feminist issues and abortion rights, and she was a political organizer and activist. Her employer advised her that these activities violated the company ethics code, which was designed to restrict conflicts of interest including high profile political activities that might cause the public to suspect that its news reporting was biased. The employer demoted her to a non-reporting position and refused to reinstate her former duties after she testified in support of a gay and lesbian civil rights bill before a state legislative committee. She sued the employer for violating the state Fair Campaign Practices Act, the state constitution, and for breach of contract and wrongful employment transfer. The court ruled for the employer on the campaign practices act and constitutional claims.

The Supreme Court of Washington agreed that the campaign practices act prohibited employment discrimination based on support for or opposition to a candidate, ballot proposition, political party or committee. However, the act unconstitutionally infringed on the employer's free speech rights. The conflict of interest code was representative of most policies maintained by U.S. daily newspapers and preserved managerial control and editorial integrity. **The publisher's right to control editorial content extended to the transfer or discharge of an employee for failing to comply** with editorial policies. The act was unconstitutional as applied to the employer. *Nelson v. McClatchy Newspapers, Inc.*, 936 P.2d 1123 (Wash. 1997).

◆ The District of Columbia Code prohibits employment discrimination on the basis of personal appearance, including grooming, hairstyles and beards. An exception exists where an employer has a reasonable business purpose for restricting the style of dress or grooming. A maintenance contractor doing business in the District had a written personal appearance policy requiring employees to maintain good hygiene, a neat hairstyle and a clean shaven face. One maintenance employee began wearing his hair in a ponytail and refused to cut it when his supervisor told him to get a haircut or wear a hat. He sued the employer for violation of the D.C. human rights act. The D.C. Court of Appeals ruled against him. The evidence indicated that the employer communicated a general rule that employees must conform to traditional grooming styles and that the supervisor's interpretation of the rule as forbidding ponytails was not unreasonable. There was a reasonable business purpose for the rule as there was evidence that customers were concerned about employee appearances. **Application of the grooming rule did not violate the human rights act.** *Turcios v. U.S. Services Industries*, 680 A.2d 1023 (D.C. 1996).

◆ A Florida roofing contractor maintained an appearance policy for employees who dealt directly with customers. An employee who quit rather than shave submitted a claim for unemployment compensation benefits, stating that the grooming policy was unfair. The District Court of Appeal of Florida held that there was **no evidence that the contractor had applied its grooming policy in a discriminatory manner**. The employee was not entitled to benefits. *Advanced Mobilehome Systems, Inc. v. Unemployment Appeals Comm'n*, 663 So.2d 1382 (Fla. Dist. Ct. App. 1995).

◆ The Supreme Court of Washington determined that **an employer's anti-nepotism policy was not a prohibited employment practice**. The employer maintained a policy forbidding a relative, cohabitant or person dating a co-worker from being hired or assigned to a position in the "chain-of-command" of a close relative, cohabitant or employee dating another company employee. The employer enforced the policy by firing two single co-workers who were dating each other. The co-workers filed an employment discrimination complaint against their former employer. The supreme court held that state law prohibits "marital status" discrimination, and not discrimination against people who are dating, living together, or in other social relationships. The legislature had clearly targeted the statute only to individuals who were married, and therefore the co-workers were not protected from the anti-nepotism policy. *Waggoner v. Ace Hardware Corp.*, 953 P.2d 88 (Wash. 1997).

B. Privacy Rights

Many states recognize a right of privacy. At times, employment policies will come into conflict with this right. For example, where a company official tells a prospective employer about a former company employee, there might be a defamation claim or an invasion of privacy claim brought.

Invasion of privacy lawsuits are difficult for employees to win, but the cost of defending them can be high. Thus, the dissemination of personal information about employees should be strictly forbidden.

◆ An Ohio claims adjuster joined a class action lawsuit against her employer under the Equal Pay Act. Her supervisor then allegedly began retaliating against her. Her attorneys asked her to provide any documentation that related in any way to the litigation. She gave confidential insurance files to the attorneys, even though the files had nothing to do with her case, because she thought the files might help "jog" her memory. When the company discovered the wrongdoing, it fired her. She sued for retaliation and lost. A federal court and the Sixth Circuit ruled that **the company properly fired her for violating its privacy policy**. *Niswander v. The Cincinnati Insurance Co.*, 529 F.3d 714 (6th Cir. 2008).

1. Invasion of Privacy

There are basically four types of invasion of privacy:

1) appropriation of an employee's name or picture for commercial advantage,

2) intrusion by an employer upon an employee's private affairs or seclusion,
3) publication by an employer of facts placing an employee in a false light, and
4) public disclosure of private facts about an employee.

The most common types of invasion of privacy claims employers face are false light claims (putting the employee in a false light) and lawsuits alleging public disclosure of private facts.

◆ While on a medical leave, an employee of an Ohio company had her ribs broken by her live-in boyfriend, who also worked for the company. The police were called and the boyfriend was convicted of domestic violence. While on probation, he was arrested again. The company learned of the domestic violence conviction and, pursuant to its anti-violence policy, questioned the employee on several occasions about whether the boyfriend was a threat. She was uncooperative. It decided to fire the boyfriend anyway and asked the employee to notify it if the boyfriend made any threats against it or its employees. She refused to do so and was fired. When she sued it for violating her privacy rights, she lost. **She failed to show that the questions intruded into her private life, or that her answers were substantially certain to become public knowledge outside the company.** *Rowe v. Guardian Automotive Products, Inc.*, 2005 WL 3299766 (N.D. Ohio 12/6/05).

◆ A maintenance supervisor at Wal-Mart's home office admitted to the company's loss prevention department that he had two light poles given to him by his supervisor. He agreed to let two loss prevention officers look at them. On the way to his house, the loss prevention officers summoned a deputy sheriff to meet them. When the deputy arrived, the loss prevention officers asked the employee to sign a consent form to allow a search of his house. The employee refused to do so three separate times. The loss prevention officers threatened to call the IRS and the media, and the deputy remained on the property. The employee finally called an attorney, stating that he thought he might lose his job if he did not consent to the search. He finally signed the consent form. The loss prevention officers confiscated several items, and the employee was fired. He sued for invasion of privacy, among other claims. A state court dismissed his lawsuit, but the Arkansas Court of Appeals reinstated the intrusion/invasion of privacy claim. Here, even though the employee had eventually signed the consent form, **there was a question as to whether that consent had been coerced and not voluntarily given**. *Addington v. Wal-Mart Stores,* 105 S.W.3d 369 (Ark. Ct. App. 2003).

◆ A Wal-Mart employee with a good performance record had attendance problems that increased after he injured his back at work. Wal-Mart sent the employee to a doctor for drug and alcohol testing per its policy requiring all injured employees to submit to such an exam. No drug or alcohol problem was found. Eventually, the employee's attendance problems resulted in his termination. He sued Wal-Mart for disability and workers' compensation discrimination, and for invasion of privacy. A jury found in his favor on the invasion of privacy claim, but determined that he was not entitled to compensatory damages because he did not suffer a loss. However, they decided that he was entitled to punitive damages. The trial court judge refused to award punitive damages, but the Supreme Court of Appeals of West Virginia held that he was entitled to a new trial on the issue of damages. Even though he **suffered no real harm as a result of the invasion of privacy**, he was entitled to at least a nominal compensatory damages award, which would then make him eligible for an award of punitive damages. *Rohrbaugh v. Wal-Mart Stores,* 572 S.E.2d 881 (W.Va. 2002).

- An employee was provided with two company computers: one at the office and one at home. He signed the company's electronic and telephone equipment policy, which stated that 1) computers were to be used for business purposes only unless personal use was expressly approved; 2) his computer use would be monitored; 3) the equipment would not be used for obscene, defamatory or inappropriate uses; and 4) improper use could lead to termination. He was fired when the company determined that he repeatedly accessed Internet porn sites from work. When he sued the company for wrongful termination, alleging that the porn sites had just "popped up" on his computer, the company sought the return of the computer at his home and demanded that he not delete any information. He claimed that he had an expectation of privacy that allowed him to delete personal files, but the California Court of Appeal disagreed. It noted that **he had signed the waiver, eliminating any reasonable expectation of privacy**. Also, a protective order could be issued to restrict the scope of the company's inspection and copying of information, and prohibit the unnecessary dissemination of personal information that had no rational bearing on the case. *TBG Insurance Services Corp. v. Superior Court*, 117 Cal.Rptr.2d 155 (Cal. Ct. App. 2002).

- An insurance company hired an entry-level claims representative and apparently never told him that he would have to view and assess damage to automobiles involved in fatal accidents or where there was serious bodily injury involving "blood and gore." He thought he would only be handling claims up to $2,500. After a while on the job, a co-worker asked him if he was gay. Taken by surprise, he answered "yes." Later, he began feeling stressed by the job and sought help through the company's Employee Assistance Program (EAP). Eventually, he sought long-term disability benefits and sued the company for emotional distress. When the EAP department turned over his records to the legal department, the claims rep claimed that that action, coupled with the question about his sexual orientation, **invaded his privacy**. An Ohio court ruled in favor of the company on the invasion of privacy claim, and the Ohio Court of Appeals affirmed. Here, the claims rep voluntarily answered the question of whether he was gay, and he signed a statement prior to participating in the EAP, which informed him that his records could be disclosed if litigation was brought against the company. *Morenz v. Progressive Casualty Insurance Co.*, 2002 WL 1041760 (Ohio Ct. App. 2002).

◆ An employee invited three co-workers, all of whom were supervisors, to his house. One co-worker became uncontrollable after having several drinks and had to be hospitalized after injuring himself. The employee's supervisor requested that the employee report the incident to higher-ranking supervisors, but he refused. The employer placed the employee on involuntary leave and eventually demoted him. He resigned, stating that he had been constructively discharged and that the employer had unlawfully invaded his privacy. The employee sued in a federal court, which found **no invasion of privacy under the state privacy act**. The act protects only information about an individual that is highly personal or intimate in nature. The employer here had stated legitimate business reasons for requesting more information about the drinking incident, which had raised serious concerns about the conduct of the supervisory employees and was only minimally intrusive. The court dismissed the action. *French v. United Parcel Service,* 2 F.Supp.2d 128 (D. Mass. 1998).

2. Wiretapping

Wiretapping is generally illegal under the federal Omnibus Crime Control and Safe Streets Act. However, the act creates an exception for conversations that are recorded by the user of communication services in the ordinary course of business.

The act also creates an exception for a person who "is a party to the communication or where one of the parties to the communication has given prior consent to such interception."

◆ The president of a company in Rhode Island surreptitiously monitored certain employees' phone calls and fired a vice president who used "salty language" to describe him to a colleague. The vice president then sued the company for violating the federal wiretap statute, 18 U.S.C. § 2510(5)(a), and a corresponding state law. A jury awarded him $50,000 for the violation of federal law and another $25,000 for invasion of privacy. The case reached the Supreme Court of Rhode Island, which held that the monitoring without consent was not within the company's ordinary course of business. Generally, monitoring must be done as part of the ordinary course of business, and the employer must notify the parties or obtain their consent. Thus, **the company violated the wiretap statute and invaded the vice president's privacy**. *Cady v. IMC Mortgage Co.*, 862 A.2d 202 (R.I. 2004).

◆ A Pennsylvania agent agreed to sell insurance policies as an independent contractor on an exclusive basis for an insurer. The contract was terminable at will. After the agent filed a complaint about the insurer with the state attorney general's office, the insurer performed a search of its main file server for any e-mails written by or to the agent that might indicate whether he had been revealing company secrets to competitors or violating the exclusivity agreement. It opened e-mails whose headers contained relevant information, and the attorney testified that the e-mails confirmed the agent's disloyalty. When it fired the agent, he sued under Title II of the Electronic Communications Privacy Act of 1986 (ECPA). A federal court ruled against him, and the Third Circuit affirmed. Title II of ECPA does not provide privacy protection for e-mails authorized "by the person or entity providing a wire or electronic communications service." Since the e-mails were stored on the insurer's own computer system, it could search those e-mails under the Title II exception. *Fraser v. Nationwide Mutual Insurance Co.*, 352 F.3d 107 (3d Cir. 2003).

- A consultant for an annuity association in New York City fielded calls from association clients and was told that his calls would be monitored as a way of evaluating the quality of service the consultants were providing. He was also allegedly told that his personal calls would not be monitored. During a party to celebrate a co-worker's promotion, a team leader exposed himself to the consultant and attempted to kiss him. He told the consultant that **another team leader had monitored one of the consultant's personal phone calls** and learned that he was gay, drank excessively and had problems in his personal life. The consultant complained about the incident and claimed that he was then subjected to retaliation in the form of discipline for tardiness, which had not been the cause of discipline before. He sued the association under federal, state and city law, and most of his claims were dismissed. However, a federal court refused to dismiss his claim against the association for violating the federal Wiretap Act (by intercepting and monitoring a personal call without his consent). A jury would have to decide that issue. *Devlin v. Teachers' Insurance & Annuity Ass'n of America*, 2003 WL 1738969 (S.D.N.Y. 2003).

- A New York alarm services company conducted 24-hour recording of incoming and outgoing telephone calls through a machine hooked up to its telephone system. Two employees sued under the federal wiretapping statute (Title III of the Omnibus Crime Control and Safe Streets Act) asserting the illegal interception of their private phone calls without their consent. They claimed that even if the recording was supported by a legitimate business purpose, the company failed to provide notice. The Second Circuit ruled in favor of the company. Although Title III generally prohibits the intentional interception of private phone conversations, it makes an **exception for conversations that are recorded by the user of communication services in the ordinary course of business**. Here, continual recording was standard practice within the central alarm industry because it ensured accurate reporting of emergencies and safeguarded sensitive information. Further, the company's underwriter recommended continual recording and some regulatory authorities even required it. Finally, the company did not violate the law by failing to notify employees that their private conversations were being recorded. *Arias v. Mutual Cent. Alarm Service, Inc.*, 202 F.3d 553 (2d Cir. 2000).

- A Kansas railway superintendent received a letter and audio tape in the mail containing evidence of an affair between two railway co-workers. The anonymous letter stated that it was from some other railway employees. The implicated male employee denied having an affair with the implicated female employee, and the supervisor then played the tape in his presence. The supervisor told the male employee that he could not be trusted any longer because he had lied. When the employee refused to resign, the supervisor fired him. The employee then sued the railway, supervisor and an attorney employed by the railway for invasion of privacy and violation of state and federal wiretap laws. A Kansas federal court found that the Omnibus Crime Control and Safe Streets Act of 1968 provides a civil cause of action for persons seeking redress for the interception of wire, oral or electronic communications, which are intentionally used in circumstances where the recipient has reason to know that the interception was obtained without consent. In this case, the employee had not given his consent to the railway or its employees to use the communication. Although listening to the tape was not "use" of the communication for the purposes of the act, there was a genuine issue of fact concerning **whether the railway and supervisor knew of the wiretap's illegality**. Therefore, the case would have to proceed to trial. The court also refused to dismiss the claim for punitive damages. *Fields v. Atchison, Topeka, and Santa Fe Railway Co.*, 5 F.Supp.2d 1160 (D. Kan. 1998).

- A Kansas company installed recorders to monitor employee-customer communications. However, it failed to advise employees prior to the installation and only notified them in writing several weeks after the equipment had been installed. Two employees sued the company for violations of state and federal telecommunications privacy acts. The company and three supervisors named in the suit filed motions for pretrial judgment. The court stated that the federal Omnibus Crime Control and Safe Streets Act of 1968, 18 U.S.C. § 2510, *et seq.*, prohibits the interception and disclosure of wire communications, with exceptions where consent is given or the interception is in the ordinary course of business. The court held that **a personal call could be intercepted in the ordinary course of business only to determine whether it was personal or business**. Because testimony indicated that the supervisors did not continue to listen to personal calls once identified, their monitoring was not unlawful. However, the recording of these calls, if proven, would violate the act. The court granted pretrial judgment to the employer on the claim that monitoring personal calls violated employee privacy. *Ali v. Douglas Cable Communications*, 929 F.Supp. 1362 (D. Kan. 1996).

C. Polygraphs

Lie detector tests are generally illegal under the federal Employee Polygraph Protection Act, which forbids an employer from directly or indirectly requiring, requesting, suggesting or causing any employee or prospective employee to take or submit to any lie detector test. Employers also cannot fire or otherwise discipline employees for refusing to take a lie detector test.

There are exceptions for public employers, security providers, power and water facilities, employers dealing with hazardous waste, and employers who are authorized to make, distribute or dispense controlled substances.

- A mail room supervisor for a defense contractor in Florida discovered 14 opened and undelivered Christmas cards in a wastebasket. She told her superior and notified him that a subordinate had been assigned to the front desk that day. He arranged for the subordinate to undergo a polygraph test, which indicated deception when he denied opening the mail. Later, **the company asked all the mail room employees to submit to a polygraph**. The mail room supervisor refused and was fired a week later for allegedly permitting package deliveries through the back door in violation of security procedures. She sued under the Employee Polygraph Protection Act (EPPA). The wrongful discharge claim settled, and the Eleventh Circuit held that the company also had liability under the EPPA for requesting the polygraph. Here, the company failed to show that it had a reasonable suspicion that the supervisor was involved with the wrongdoing. Instead, it sought the polygraph to absolve it of any potential liability for the opened and undelivered Christmas cards. *Polkey v. Transtecs Corp.*, 404 F.3d 1264 (11th Cir. 2005).

- The owner of a Florida bar suspected that employees were violating certain employment policies and hired a company to investigate their conduct. An agent for the company observed one employee taking multiple drink orders from different customers without recording them, ringing up no sales on the cash register when cash was taken from customers, and placing money in a tip jar when no sales were registered. Based on the report, the employer asked the employee to take a polygraph examination. She took the examination, then voluntarily resigned and sued the employer for violating the federal EPPA. The court observed that **there had been no improper disclosure of polygraph information by the employer**. Although the owner told other employees that the employee had failed a polygraph test, the comment had come after the filing of the lawsuit. The court rejected the employee's assertion that the employer had no reasonable suspicion giving rise to an investigation since there was evidence of business losses that could be attributable to employees. Although the EPPA forbids an employer from discharging or disciplining an employee for refusal to take a lie detector test, this issue was moot since the employee had voluntarily resigned. The court ruled in favor of the employer. *Long v. Mango's Tropical Cafe, Inc.*, 972 F.Supp. 655 (S.D. Fla. 1997).

- An Iowa grocery store employee was suspected of stealing money from a cash register. The store manager called the police. An officer stated that the police would need the store's agreement to examine the suspected employee by polygraph. The employee agreed to take a polygraph test to clear his name. His test results showed emotional distress or deception, and he did not pass the exam. Although no criminal charges were brought against the employee, the store manager and owner decided to take away his cash handling responsibilities and return him to stock work. The employee resigned and sued the store in federal court, alleging violations of the EPPA and state law.

  The court noted that **the EPPA prohibits an employer from using, accepting, or inquiring about the results of any lie detector test**, and makes it an unlawful practice to fire, discipline, or discriminate against an employee on the basis of a polygraph test result. Here, while the employer had not required the employee to take the test, it had clearly violated the EPPA by using the test results to discipline him. Conditions at the store became intolerable for the employee and he was constructively discharged when he was demoted. He was entitled to lost wages plus interest in excess of $22,000. He was also entitled to a $15,000 damage award for emotional distress and attorneys' fees. *Mennen v. Easter Stores*, 951 F.Supp. 838 (N.D. Iowa 1997).

D. Investigations

Employer investigations into employee wrongdoing should be conducted carefully. Employers should include in their handbooks a statement that employees have no right of privacy in their desks, work areas, lockers, etc. Thus, if the employer suspects wrongdoing, it may conduct a search without prior permission from the employee.

◆ The security manager for a medical center was accused of leaving an obscene message on the voice mail of a nurse. When several co-workers identified the speaker as the manager, the medical center began an investigation and submitted the obscene call for voice print analysis. The security manager refused to provide a voice exemplar for testing and was fired. He sued for wrongful discharge, claiming that such testing was prohibited by an Iowa law barring employers from conditioning employment on submission to a polygraph exam. A trial court ruled against the manager, and the Supreme Court of Iowa affirmed. First, **the manager was an at-will employee who could be fired for failing to cooperate in the investigation**. Second, the purpose of the voice print analysis was identification, not verification of truthfulness or deception. Finally, the medical center was not liable for defamation for stating the reason for his discharge and for having a security officer escort him from the building. *Theisen v. Covenant Medical Center, Inc.*, 636 N.W.2d 74 (Iowa 2001).

◆ An assistant security officer employed by a Virginia business learned that an employee had taken company property home without authorization. The security officer was invited to accompany a county sheriff's deputy and a federal agent who were executing a search warrant for illegal firearms at the employee's home. When the deputy, agent and security officer searched the home, the security officer saw several items belonging to the employer. The employee asked the security officer to leave, but he refused to do so when the deputy stated that he could remain. The employee sued the employer and security officer, asserting damages for the unauthorized search of his home. The court ruled for the employer and security officer, and the Supreme Court of Virginia affirmed. The law in question did not create a cause of action against a private entity for the improper execution of a search warrant. It afforded only substantive criminal law protections. Since the Fourth Amendment prohibition against unreasonable searches and seizures does not apply to private individuals, **the security officer's conduct was not precluded by state or federal law**. *Buonocore v. Chesapeake and Potomac Telephone Co. of Virginia*, 492 S.E.2d 439 (Va. 1997).

◆ A 16-year-old Maryland retail store employee was interrogated by store security employees for over four hours. When he sued for false imprisonment, a trial court awarded him $110,000 in compensatory damages and $9 million in punitive damages. The court of appeals noted that the U.S. Supreme Court has held that a punitive damage award cannot be grossly excessive in relation to deterrence and punishment interests. The amount of such an award must not be disproportionate to the harm done or the party's ability to pay the award. Another appropriate consideration is to compare the award with awards in other cases in the jurisdiction in somewhat comparable cases. The court had never upheld a punitive damage award of over $700,000, and the largest possible penalty for any state criminal law violation was $1 million. Most punitive damage awards were for less than $100,000. **Although the interrogation by the security guards was heinous, it was not life threatening**, and the employee had suffered no permanent injuries. The award could not stand. A remand was necessary to determine a proper punitive damages amount. *Bowden v. Caldor, Inc.*, 350 Md. 4, 710 A.2d 267 (Md. 1998).

E. Criminal Law Issues

If criminal wrongdoing is suspected, the proper authorities should be contacted. Employers should contact their attorneys before engaging in investigations into criminal wrongdoing.

◆ A Florida bookkeeper/office manager was criminally charged with one count of scheming to defraud and obtaining property in an amount of $50,000 or more. The criminal charge arose out of various irregular financial dealings. **While the criminal charge was pending, the company filed a civil action against the bookkeeper arising out of the same events** that formed the basis of the criminal charge. After the bookkeeper pleaded no contest to the criminal charges, the company sought pretrial judgment in the civil action. The court granted the motion but did not ascertain the amount of damages owed to the company. Nor did it set off the amount of restitution ordered, thus seemingly granting the company a double recovery. The bookkeeper appealed, and the District Court of Appeal of Florida agreed that the calculations of the damages owed had to be redone, partly because of that and partly because of the criminal appeal, in which the amount of restitution was remanded for recalculation. *Peterson v. Therma Builders, Inc.*, 958 So.2d 977 (Fla. Dist. Ct. App. 2007).

◆ After an insurance company laid off 450 workers, one of its senior executive vice presidents began receiving threatening telephone messages. The messages were recorded, and the company later identified the voice of a laid-off employee with 22 years of service who had been subsequently rehired. After firing the employee, it forwarded information to law enforcement authorities, who prosecuted him for violation of state criminal laws. A jury acquitted the employee, and he sued the company in a Massachusetts federal court, asserting violations of his constitutional rights. The court ruled for the company, and the First Circuit Court of Appeals affirmed. Here, the company had legal grounds to report the former employee to the police based on extensive efforts to identify the voice. Also, the officers exercised independent professional judgment in applying for a warrant, the magistrate issued the warrant independently, and the district attorney acted autonomously in prosecuting the case. Where **probable cause to arrest and prosecute** a suspect exists, there can be no unconstitutional deprivation of rights. *Roche v. John Hancock Mutual Life Insurance Co.*, 81 F.3d 249 (1st Cir. 1996).

◆ A Maryland department store loss prevention manager investigated an employee suspected of making fraudulent credit card charges to obtain store merchandise. He referred the matter to local police, who issued a warrant and arrested the employee. After the criminal charges were dropped because of the failure of witnesses to appear for trial, the employee sued the store and the loss prevention manager for false imprisonment and malicious prosecution. Following a trial, the court instructed the jury that punitive damages might be awarded in a malicious prosecution case on the basis of implied malice if there was a lack of probable cause to suspect the employee of wrongdoing. The jury returned a verdict for the employee which included $15,000 for compensatory damages and $45,000 in punitive damages. The Maryland Court of Special Appeals affirmed. The Court of Appeals of Maryland refused to overturn the judgment for malicious prosecution. However, the lower courts had improperly allowed punitive damage awards based on an inference of malice. Here, **there was no clear and convincing evidence of a wrongful motive**. *Montgomery Ward v. Wilson*, 339 Md. 701, 664 A.2d 916 (Md. 1995).

CHAPTER SEVEN

Workers' Compensation

I. EXCLUSIVE REMEDY

Workers' compensation is a system designed to protect both employer and employee. Generally, an employee gives up the right to sue his employer in exchange for the security of obtaining workers' compensation benefits for accidental injuries that arise out of and occur in the course of employment.

Where an accidental injury or illness arises out of and in the course of employment, workers' compensation is generally the exclusive remedy available to the employee. Thus, even where the employer is not at fault, it becomes liable for benefits under workers' compensation when an employee is injured.

The trade-off is that the employee cannot sue the employer in tort (e.g., for negligence) to recover for her injuries. She is limited to the statutory recovery provided by the workers' compensation system. Thus, even where the employer is at fault, the employee's recovery is limited to the statutory schedule of benefits for the type of injury suffered.

However, where the injury is not sufficiently work related, or where the injury is caused by an intentional tort, employer liability may result. For other cases involving employer liability, please see Chapter Two, Section I.

A. Exclusive Remedy Applied

Employees injured at work occasionally seek to avoid the application of workers' compensation in order to sue for negligence or another tort. By doing so, they hope to obtain a larger damage award than they could achieve with workers' compensation (including, potentially, punitive damages). In the following cases, courts applied the exclusive remedy doctrine to bar lawsuits against the employers.

◆ A CVS employee in Massachusetts attempted to apprehend a suspected shoplifter, who responded violently, stabbing him in the neck with a knife. The employee died at the scene shortly thereafter. At the time of his death, he was an 18-year-old high school student who lived at his mother's home. He was financially dependent on both parents and had no dependents himself. As a result, no workers' compensation benefits were paid. His parents sued CVS for wrongful death, and CVS sought to have the case dismissed, arguing that even though no workers' compensation benefits were paid, the employee would have been eligible had he survived or had dependents. Thus, his parents could not sue for wrongful death because of the exclusive remedy of workers' compensation. The Supreme Judicial Court of Massachusetts agreed with CVS that the employee's injury was technically compensable under the workers' compensation statute. So **even though no workers' compensation benefits were actually paid, the exclusive remedy prevented the parents' lawsuit**. *Saab v. Massachusetts CVS Pharmacy, LLC*, 896 N.E.2d 615 (Mass. 2008).

◆ For economic reasons, a Florida bank decided to eliminate the security guard position. It did so despite an earlier robbery in which a teller was pistol-whipped. Afterwards, two armed men entered the bank, robbed it, then shot the branch manager in the face. She sued the bank for negligence and for intentionally creating an unsafe environment. A federal court and the Eleventh Circuit ruled against her. The negligence claim failed because **injuries sustained during robberies in the workplace are deemed to "arise out of" employment**. Thus, workers' compensation provided immunity. And the exception for intentional torts failed because she could not show that the decision not to have a guard on duty amounted to conduct that was "substantially certain" to result in her injury or death. Accordingly, she was limited to workers' compensation benefits for her injuries. *Locke v. SunTrust Bank*, 484 F.3d 1343 (11th Cir. 2007).

◆ An Illinois worker suffered a heart attack and stroke, and was left lying on a loading dock for eight hours until help arrived. He filed for workers' compensation benefits and, when the company challenged the claim, sued the company for negligence before the workers' compensation commission ruled on the matter. The company then asserted that workers' compensation was his exclusive remedy. A federal court and the Seventh Circuit agreed with the company. However, the court of appeals noted that **the company, by insisting the worker had to rely on workers' compensation, was in essence conceding that some of the worker's injuries were compensable under that law**. *Dunlap v. Nestle USA, Inc.*, 431 F.3d 1015 (7th Cir. 2005).

◆ An employee at a company in Minnesota received a "birthday spanking" from five co-workers with a two-by-four that had been fashioned into a paddle. He suffered injuries to his buttocks, wrists and elbow, then sued the company and his co-workers for assault and battery, among other claims. The case reached the Supreme Court of Minnesota, which held that the state's workers' compensation act was the employee's exclusive remedy against the company. Even though the company knew about the tradition of "birthday spankings" employees visited on each other, it did not intend to harm the employee. **Its inaction with respect to stopping the spanking was not sufficient to satisfy the intentional injury exception to workers' compensation.** However, there was a question of fact regarding the co-workers' intent or gross negligence. The court remanded the case for a determination of that question. *Meintsma v. Loram Maintenance of Way, Inc.*, 684 N.W.2d 434 (Minn. 2004).

◆ A suspended police officer went to work for Sears as a security guard at its Hackensack, New Jersey, store. Two armed assailants killed him while he was trying to transport money from the warehouse to the main building after the store closed for the evening. Even though Sears had a regional directive requiring money to be transported in the morning and in the presence of two security guards, the Hackensack store had not implemented the directive. The guard's family obtained workers' compensation benefits. It then sued Sears for wrongful death, asserting that it had actual knowledge of the parking lot dangers and engaged in intentionally wrongful conduct by disregarding the corporate policy. A court ruled for Sears, and the Superior Court of New Jersey, Appellate Division, affirmed. The family's lawsuit was barred by the exclusive remedy provision of the state's workers' compensation law. They **failed to show that Sears committed an intentional wrong** – that it knew harm was "substantially certain" to result from its failure to follow corporate policy. Also, Sears did not violate OSHA or other governmental regulations. *Fisher v. Sears, Roebuck & Co.*, 833 A.2d 650 (N.J. Super. Ct. App. Div. 2003).

◆ A security guard for a car rental agency at the Cleveland airport backed out of the parking lot at the end of his noon-to-6 p.m. shift and hit a co-worker who was verifying a customer's paperwork. The co-worker received workers' compensation benefits for his injury and then sued the guard for negligence. The case reached the Ohio Supreme Court, which had to determine whether the injury occurred in the course of employment and whether it arose out of the employment. It noted that employees who are injured in their employers' parking lots on their way home from work have been injured "in the course of and arising out of" their employment. Therefore, an employee who **injures a co-worker in the parking lot while on his way home** has also injured the co-worker "in the course of and arising out of" employment. As a result, the workers' compensation statute was the co-worker's exclusive remedy, and the guard was immune to a lawsuit for negligence. *Donnelly v. Herron*, 88 Ohio St.3d 425, 727 N.E.2d 882 (Ohio 2000).

◆ A utility worker for a Virginia power company participated in a company-sponsored lunch time aerobics class and developed a severe headache. The company's health services coordinator took her to the "quiet room" for employees who become ill at work but did not call any medical or emergency personnel. Two hours later, the coordinator returned to check on the worker and found her in a coma-like state. The worker was then taken to the hospital, where she was diagnosed with a cerebral aneurysm and hemorrhaging. She sustained partial paralysis and brain damage, and she sued the company for negligence. After her lawsuit was dismissed, the Virginia Court of Appeals affirmed, finding that her injuries were covered by workers' compensation. The worker suffered an "injury by accident" because **the injury she sustained was the delay in treatment caused by the company's negligence**, not the aneurysm itself. Also, the injury arose out of and in the course of her employment. As a result, her exclusive remedy was workers' compensation. *Combs v. Virginia Electric and Power Co.*, 525 S.E.2d 278 (Va. Ct. App. 2000).

◆ The Court of Appeals of Georgia affirmed a ruling in favor of a convenience store sued by an employee who asserted a job-related emotional injury after being robbed at gunpoint. She filed a state court negligence action against the employer, claiming that it rejected her request for a transfer to the day shift without a cut in pay. The court dismissed the action under the exclusivity provision of the state workers' compensation act. On appeal, the court of appeals stated that even if an employer's **willful failure to afford employees a safe workplace** results in injury to an employee, the only recourse for the injury is under the workers' compensation act. *Boulware v. Quiktrip Corp.*, 486 S.E.2d 662 (Ga. Ct. App. 1997).

◆ A Vermont employee was placed at a factory by a temporary employment agency. Under the agreement between the temp agency and the manufacturer, the agency paid the temporary workers and provided their workers' compensation insurance. When the employee was injured at the factory, she obtained workers' compensation benefits from the temp agency and sued the manufacturer and one of its supervisors in state court. The court ruled for the manufacturer and supervisor under the borrowed servant doctrine. The Supreme Court of Vermont affirmed, finding that the manufacturer was the employee's statutory employer under the state workers' compensation act. **The act allowed an employee to have two contemporaneous employers**, and because the manufacturer qualified as an employer under the law, it was entitled to immunity. The employee could not collect workers' compensation benefits from the agency and bring a personal injury lawsuit against the manufacturer. *Candido v. Polymers, Inc.*, 687 A.2d 476 (Vt. 1996).

◆ A Kansas nuclear power plant employee suffered a heart attack at work and was treated by two physician's assistants employed at the plant. The employee died, and his estate filed a medical malpractice lawsuit against the employer, physician's assistants and their supervising physician, alleging that the employee lost a chance to survive the heart attack because of negligent treatment. The physician was dismissed from the lawsuit. The court held for the employer and assistants, ruling that the suit was barred by the exclusive remedy provision of the state workers' compensation act. The estate appealed to the Court of Appeals of Kansas, arguing that the action was not barred because the injury was not covered under the compensation act's heart amendment, which specifically precludes coverage for coronary disease unless the attack is caused by exertion that goes beyond the employee's usual work. The court noted that the amendment did not apply because the claim was based on the loss of chance of survival, and not the heart attack itself. **Medical malpractice claims against co-workers are barred** by the co-worker immunity and exclusive remedy provisions of workers' compensation law. *Scott v. Wolf Creek Nuclear Operating Corp.*, 928 P.2d 109 (Kan. Ct. App. 1996).

◆ A Utah worker was sent by a temporary agency to provide unskilled labor to a contractor at a construction site. Although the temporary agency had previously notified the contractor that it would not furnish workers for jobs performed at a height of over 12 feet above the ground, the contractor immediately assigned the temp worker to scaffolding 16 feet high. After the employee fell, suffering severe injuries, he sued the contractor, asserting that he was an employee of the temp agency and not the contractor. A state court ruled for the contractor. The employee appealed to the Supreme Court of Utah, arguing that the exclusivity provision of state workers' compensation law should not apply because no employment contract existed between him and the contractor. **He also claimed that the contractor did not have the right to control his duties**, and that this was demonstrated by its violation of the temp agency's prohibition on work performed by its employees over 12 feet above the ground. The court disagreed, ruling that the employee's injury was not exempt from workers' compensation law. The employee was a special employee of the contractor, and an employment contract existed. The court affirmed the judgment for the contractor. *Walker v. U.S. General, Inc.*, 916 P.2d 903 (Utah 1996).

◆ A Delaware department store employee worked in a shopping mall. The mall provided security, and the lease agreement between the store and mall required employees to park far away from entrances. The employee came to work almost an hour early on a Sunday morning and was assaulted and raped in the parking lot. She sued the mall and her employer. The employer filed a motion to dismiss the case based on the exclusivity provision of the state workers' compensation law. The court noted that in the majority of states, an employer's parking lot is included in the work premises. Although the mall owned the parking lot, **the employer exercised control over the area** and required its employees to report to work well before the store opened. In general, employment includes a reasonable time before or after scheduled work hours, especially where an employer approves of customary early arrivals as this employer had done. Thus, the employee was limited to recovery under the workers' compensation system. She could not bring a personal injury suit against the employer, as her injuries arose out of and in the course of her employment. *Rose v. Cadillac Fairview Shopping Center Properties Inc.*, 668 A.2d 782 (Del. Super. Ct. 1995).

B. Exceptions

Workers' compensation will not be the exclusive remedy in certain situations – most notably, where the employer is accused of intentional wrongdoing against the employee. If the employer commits an intentional tort (e.g., assault, battery, false imprisonment, intentional infliction of emotional distress), an employee injured as a result will be able to sue to recover for that injury.

Also, where an employer acts with deliberate indifference to its employees' welfare, and where harm is substantially certain to result, courts will assume that the employer intended to harm the employees, and they will be able to sue to recover for injuries sustained as a result.

For example, where an employer removes a safety device from a piece of machinery to speed up production, the employer will be deemed to have intended harm to employees using the machine. Any injury that results will allow for a tort lawsuit that could yield punitive damages.

Employers can also be sued for discrimination or where the injury does not arise out of and in the course of the employment relationship.

- An employee at a Florida store complained to his manager about an old wooden ladder that was wobbly and undersized. The manager in turn complained about it to her supervisor. Subsequently, the employee, while trying to retrieve merchandise from a high shelf, fell from the ladder. He sued for an intentional tort, claiming his injury was substantially certain to occur such that workers' compensation was not the sole remedy at his disposal. A jury awarded him $118,000 after making a reduction for comparative fault, and the store appealed. The district court of appeal reversed, finding no liability under the intentional tort exception to workers' compensation because the store did not conceal the dangerous nature of the ladder. On further appeal, the Florida Supreme Court held that **the store did not have to conceal the danger in order to be liable under the exception to workers' compensation**. The supreme court reversed the lower court decision and remanded the case. *Bakerman v. The Bombay Co., Inc.*, 961 So.2d 259 (Fla. 2007).

- A 12-year employee of a missile systems company was diagnosed with testicular cancer. He sued the company for fraudulently concealing the fact that he was exposed to carcinogenic chemicals in the workplace (an exception to the exclusive remedy provisions of workers' compensation law). A court dismissed his action, finding that he had to seek a remedy under the state's workers' compensation law. The California Court of Appeal reversed and remanded the case. It noted that an employee can avoid workers' compensation and recover in an action for damages where the employer knew he had suffered a work-related injury, the employer concealed that knowledge from the employee, and the injury was aggravated as a result of the concealment. Here, as a result of chronic overexposure to carcinogenic chemicals for many years, the employee suffered an injury. He also alleged that the company concealed the knowledge of his overexposure and that if he had known, he could have sought treatment earlier. As a result, **he was not bound by the exclusivity provisions of workers' compensation law**. He could sue for damages. *Palestini v. General Dynamics Corp.*, 120 Cal.Rptr.2d 741 (Cal. Ct. App. 2002).

- A lube technician for a trucking company contracted pneumonia and then bronchitis, partly as a result of acid mist and fumes from a chemical mixture used for cleaning the exteriors of trucks. He filed a workers' compensation claim for his lung condition, but benefits were denied because he failed to prove that his work exposure was the major contributing cause of his lung disorder. He then sued the company to recover for his bronchitis. The case eventually reached the Supreme Court of Oregon, which held that **he could proceed with his common law action despite the exclusive remedy provisions of workers' compensation law**. The court remanded the case for further proceedings. *Smothers v. Gresham Transfer, Inc.*, 332 Or. 83, 23 P.3d 333 (Or. 2001).

- A California employee claimed that her unborn child was exposed to toxic levels of carbon monoxide at her workplace. The allegation arose from the employer's use of a propane-powered machine in an inadequately ventilated location at which she was working. The employee and several others fainted from carbon monoxide fumes, and the employee alleged that her daughter was born with cerebral palsy and other disabilities as a result. She sued the employer for negligence on behalf of her child. The court held that the complaint was barred by the exclusivity provision of the state workers' compensation act. The court of appeal reversed, and the Supreme Court of California affirmed. Here, both the mother and child had been exposed to toxic levels of carbon monoxide. **The child had asserted a viable claim for injury to herself and was not claiming any damages for injury to her mother.** Because the child's claim for damages did not legally depend on injuries suffered by the mother, the workers' compensation act did not bar the claim. The court noted that many other state courts, including appellate courts in Colorado, Louisiana, Illinois, Indiana, Alabama, Pennsylvania and Georgia, have found prenatal injuries to be separate and distinct from injury to the mother. *Snyder v. Michael's Stores, Inc.*, 16 Cal.4th 991, 68 Cal.Rptr.2d 476, 945 P.2d 781 (Cal. 1997).

- An Arkansas employee sustained bilateral carpal tunnel syndrome from repetitive motion in her workplace. She filed a workers' compensation claim that was not challenged by her employer, and she resumed work while receiving treatment. Her physicians released her from treatment and rehabilitation with a permanent restriction from repetitive motion and a 5% permanent physical impairment in her arms. However, upon returning to work, the employer discharged her. She sued the employer for discrimination on the basis of disability in violation of the state civil rights act. The court dismissed the case on the grounds that the employee's sole remedy was workers' compensation, but the Supreme Court of Arkansas reversed. The compensation act did not afford any remedy for the employee here because she had alleged discharge on the basis of a disability. Because **the employee had alleged discrimination, and not refusal by the employer to allow her to return to work**, the complaint had been erroneously dismissed. The court remanded the case. *Davis v. Dillmeier Enterprises, Inc.*, 956 S.W.2d 155 (Ark. 1997).

◆ A West Virginia truck driver suffered a spinal injury and filed a claim for workers' compensation benefits. His employer contested the claim and asserted that no job-related injury had occurred. The claim was denied, but on appeal, benefits were awarded including a retroactive sum of over $95,000. The employee then sued the employer for fraud and for wrongfully opposing his workers' compensation complaint. The West Virginia Supreme Court of Appeals examined whether the exclusivity provision of the state workers' compensation law barred the separate action for fraud. It observed that **the compensation act pertained to employee injuries suffered as the result of workplace negligence** and that the fraud claim concerned alleged intentional acts by the employer. Because this was outside the scope of the compensation act, a separate action could survive if the injury giving rise to the claim was not suffered in the course of employment, if the employer fraudulently misrepresented facts, and if the misrepresentation was an attempt to deprive the employee of benefits covered by workers' compensation. *Persinger v. Peabody Coal Co.*, 474 S.E.2d 887 (W.Va. 1996).

◆ A Montana mining safety employee believed that his employer negligently disregarded his safety recommendations, leading to avoidable employee deaths and injuries. He reported depression and physical symptoms including chronic fatigue, insomnia, nausea and headaches, and he filed for workers' compensation benefits. The claim was denied, and the employee sued the employer for negligence. The court dismissed the lawsuit, determining that the state workers' compensation act barred the action – the act prohibited workers' compensation recovery for injuries that were purely mental or emotional. The Supreme Court of Montana determined that the employee had properly been denied a workers' compensation recovery because **his physical and mental injuries were expressly excluded by the statute**. As a result, personal injury remedies were available, and the district court had erroneously dismissed the case. *Kleinhesselink v. Chevron, USA*, 920 P.2d 108 (Mont. 1996).

◆ An employee worked for over 30 years for a Kentucky food distributor. He received positive employment evaluations until coming into conflict with a new marketing manager, who ordered him to obtain competitor price lists in violation of the company's ethics policy and employment manual. A manager then evaluated his job performance as poor, and he was presented with a resignation letter and severance package. The company also misleadingly offered him a position at a South Carolina bakery. After learning that no position was available as promised, the former employee suffered an emotional breakdown and attempted suicide. He sued the employer in a Kentucky court, which awarded him over $180,000 for wrongful discharge, $70,000 for intentional infliction of emotional distress and $500,000 in punitive damages. The court of appeals and the Supreme Court of Kentucky affirmed. The workers' compensation act did not bar the damage award, as the claim for **intentional infliction of emotional distress arose after the employment relationship had terminated**. There was evidence that the employer had induced the employee to resign with a nonexistent job offer and other intentional acts of fraud, deceit, slander and interference with his rights. *Kroger Co. v. Willgruber*, 920 S.W.2d 61 (Ky. 1996).

◆ A Washington aircraft manufacturer began using a toxic chemical compound in a production process. When workers complained of dizziness, nausea and other physical symptoms, a supervisor requested improved ventilation. The manufacturer denied the request and, despite warnings and continuing worker illnesses, defended the procedure as safe. Fourteen workers sued, claiming personal injuries, outrage, and negligent and intentional infliction of emotional distress. The Washington Supreme Court examined whether the complaint was barred by the exclusivity provisions of workers' compensation law. Here, **the employer was aware that employees would become sick from exposure to the toxic compound** and had taken no action to prevent continued exposure. Because this was a deliberate action, the employer had acted with the specific intent to harm. The claim for intentional infliction of emotional distress could continue. *Birklid v. Boeing Co.*, 904 P.2d 278 (Wash. 1995).

◆ A Colorado restaurant employee became pregnant shortly after accepting an assistant manager position. She developed complications, and her treating physician imposed a series of restrictions on her work hours and tasks. She claimed that her supervisors forced her to perform tasks and to work hours that violated the medical restrictions, resulting in the premature birth of her child and its death 10 days later. She sued the employer. The Supreme Court of Colorado held that the exclusivity provision of the workers' compensation act did not preclude a claim for the **death of an employee's child**. This type of claim was not derivative of any personal injury to the employee herself. *Pizza Hut of America, Inc. v. Keefe*, 900 P.2d 97 (Colo. 1995).

◆ The Supreme Court of Indiana reversed a pretrial ruling against an African-American auto salesman who claimed that his supervisors assaulted and slandered him and forced him to quit. The court found no evidence that the auto dealership intended to discriminate against him. However, because the employee had not claimed a physical injury, but only **embarrassment and humiliation**, the lawsuit was not barred by the exclusivity provisions of the workers' compensation act. The injuries alleged were not covered under the act, and the employee had potentially viable claims under the state Employer's Liability Act. *Perry v. Stitzer Buick GMC, Inc.*, 637 N.E.2d 1282 (Ind. 1994).

◆ A resident of the District of Columbia (D.C.) was hired there by a company, but he also worked for the company in the state of Virginia. He sustained a back injury while working in Virginia and received benefits under Virginia's workers' compensation law. Subsequently, he received a supplemental award under D.C.'s workers' compensation law. His employer and its carrier challenged this second award because Virginia law excluded any other recovery "at common law or otherwise." Thus, D.C. should have given the first award "full faith and credit." An administrative order upholding the second award was reversed by the U.S. Court of Appeals. The U.S. Supreme Court then held that **the Constitution's Full Faith and Credit Clause did not preclude successive workers' compensation awards** where the second state would have had the power to apply its workers' compensation law in the first place. Here, since the employee could have sought a compensation award from D.C. in the first place, the employer and its insurer would have had to measure their liability exposure by the more generous workers' compensation scheme anyway. Accordingly, Virginia's interest was not enough to prevent D.C. from making the supplemental award. The Court reversed the case. *Thomas v. Washington Gas Light Co.,* 448 U.S. 261, 100 S.Ct. 2647, 65 L.Ed.2d 757 (1980).

II. CONNECTION WITH EMPLOYMENT

Workers' compensation will not be paid merely because an injured person happens to be employed. The injury must be connected with the employment for benefits to become payable. The injury must either arise out of and in the course of the employment, or it must be an occupational disease.

A. Arising from Employment

For an injury to be compensable under workers' compensation, it must "arise out of and in the course of" employment. An injury that arises out of employment has a causal connection to the employment. In other words, there must generally be:

1) some proximity between the scene of the accident and the place of employment,
2) some degree of control exercised by the employer over the scene of the accident, and
3) some benefit the employer received from the injured employee's presence at the scene of the accident.

An injury that occurs in the course of employment generally occurs:

1) during working hours,
2) at the place of employment, and
3) while the employee is fulfilling his working duties.

Not every element listed above must be present in every case for employees to qualify for workers' compensation. However, the more elements present, the greater the likelihood that an injury will qualify for workers' compensation.

- A K-Mart employee in Oklahoma took an evening assignment guarding merchandise left outside overnight for a sale. Because the store was locked, he was told to go to the nearest convenience store if he had "issues with anything." Around 3:15 a.m., he went to use the bathroom at the nearest convenience store, but the place was closed. He then went to the nearest McDonald's, but only the drive-through was open there. He decided to get a hamburger and was shot while he was in his car. When he sought workers' compensation benefits, the Supreme Court of Oklahoma ruled that he was entitled to them. Here, his injuries occurred in the course of his employment and also arose out of his employment because **he had to leave the store to minister to his personal needs, and his shift put him at higher risk than the general population**. *K-Mart v. Herring*, 188 P.3d 140 (Okla. 2008).

- While making lunch in her kitchen, a telecommuter in Tennessee was assaulted by her neighbor without provocation or explanation. He knocked on her door and she let him in. He left after a few minutes but returned a moment later, saying he had forgotten his keys. When she turned away from him, he beat her until she lost consciousness. She sought workers' compensation benefits for her injuries, asserting that her work arrangement placed her in a position that facilitated the assault. However, the Tennessee Supreme Court ruled against her. **Although her injuries occurred in the course of her employment, they did not arise out of her employment** so as to be covered by workers' compensation. There was no evidence that she was singled out because of her work duties or business relationships. *Wait v. Travelers Indemnity Co. of Illinois*, 240 S.W.3d 220 (Tenn. 2007).

- A 50-year-old mechanic with a history of back problems reinjured his back when he jerked loose a card stuck in a knitting machine. He tried to return to work on light duty, but was told that there were no light-duty positions available. **He was fired a week later and committed suicide two weeks after that. His widow sought workers' compensation death benefits**, asserting that his injury caused him to become clinically depressed and that the termination exacerbated his depression to the point of suicide. The case reached the Massachusetts Court of Appeals, which upheld the award of death benefits. The court rejected the "independent, intervening factor" test – used in tort cases to break the chain of causation – noting that workers' compensation principles don't award or deny benefits based on fault. *In re Dube's Case*, 872 N.E.2d 1171 (Mass. App. Ct. 2007).

- Over a two-month period, a Chinese stir-fry cook at a restaurant in Arizona endured teasing at the hands of his supervisor and co-workers, who mimicked his accent and poor English. They thought it was just good fun, but he felt it was harassment and demeaning. After his supervisor mocked him for taking a bone home to make soup, he told his supervisor off. The supervisor pushed him away and he fell, injuring his shoulder and pelvis. He sought and was awarded workers' compensation benefits. The Arizona Court of Appeals held that under **the "friction and strain" rule**, his injuries arose out of his employment. The "friction and strain rule" provides that, even if the subject of the altercation in which the employee is injured is unrelated to the work, the injuries are compensable if work brought the participants together and created the relations and conditions which resulted in the altercation. *PF Chang's v. Industrial Comm'n of Arizona*, 166 P.3d 135 (Ariz. Ct. App. 2007).

◆ An Ohio cook apparently had a tense relationship outside of work with a co-worker. One day he accidentally or carelessly spilled hot water from a wok on the co-worker. After the cook turned away, the co-worker hit him in the back of the head with a large cooking utensil, knocking him unconscious. He suffered permanent paralysis to his left side and filed a claim for workers' compensation benefits. The industrial commission awarded benefits, a trial court reversed, and the Ohio Court of Appeals reinstated them. Here, **it did not matter that the injury was intentional** or that the two men allegedly had a poor relationship outside of work. What mattered was that the cook sustained his injury during the course of and arising out of his employment. *Luo v. Gao*, 2007 WL 675635 (Ohio Ct. App. 3/7/07).

◆ A 70-year-old cashier at a store in South Dakota completed her shift at 7:00 p.m. and punched out at 7:04. She bought a few items at 7:07 and, on her way out the door, tripped over a rug near the exit. She fell and sustained injuries to her head and leg, aggravating an ulcer in her ankle. Eventually she was forced to quit. She sought workers' compensation benefits, and an administrative hearing officer found that she was permanently disabled. The case reached the Supreme Court of South Dakota, which noted that **the cashier's activities were "reasonably incidental" to her work**. The store allowed employees to shop during breaks, and even though the cashier waited until the end of her shift, her deviation from her usual route before leaving was less than 10 minutes. She was entitled to benefits. *Fair v. Nash Finch Co.*, 728 N.W.2d 623 (S.D. 2007).

◆ On his way back to work after a bathroom break, a forklift operator for a company in Arkansas tried to cross a board that had been set on concrete and placed over a muddy ditch. While he was on the board, it slipped off the concrete and he fell, twisting his knee. He filed for workers' compensation benefits, which were denied on the grounds that he was not performing employment-related services at the time of his injury. The Arkansas Supreme Court disagreed with that finding. **A bathroom break is a necessary function and it directly or indirectly advances the interests of the employer.** Here, the worker was still on the clock and unable to leave the worksite. Also, he would have had to cut his break short if his supervisors needed him. *Wallace v. West Fraser South, Inc.*, 358 Ark. 68, 186 S.W.3d 695 (Ark. 2006).

◆ An Indiana DaimlerChrysler employee parked in a lot owned by a shopping mall across the street from the plant where he worked even though he wasn't supposed to. As he crossed the street on his way to work, he was struck by a car and killed. His widow applied for death benefits, which were denied. Here, the employee had not been acting in the course of his employment at the time of his death. Further, DaimlerChrysler provided plenty of parking for its plant that, even though it was farther away, did not require crossing a busy street. Benefits were denied the widow. *Mueller v. DaimlerChrysler Motors Corp.*, 842 N.E.2d 845 (Ind. Ct. App. 2006).

◆ A temporary employee in Tennessee was assigned to a hotel construction project in another town and returned at the end of the day to collect his paycheck. He waited for his paycheck outside the office along with other employees. A truck then pulled up and a woman passenger asked to use the bathroom. The manager denied the request pursuant to company policy, and an altercation ensued during which the driver shot and killed the employee. His children filed for workers' compensation benefits. The Tennessee Supreme Court ruled that the children were entitled to them because **the shooting outside the office arose out of the employment**. *Hurst v. Labor Ready*, 197 S.W.3d 756 (Tenn. 2006).

◆ An Arkansas employee was told to plan and coordinate a mandatory company retreat at an Ozarks resort. She rented a boat and waverunners, and obtained a map of the places where employees could jump off cliffs. When she attempted to follow some co-workers off a cliff, she fell and hit the rocks below. She filed for workers' compensation benefits, which a compensation judge denied. An appeals commission affirmed, but the Arkansas Court of Appeals reversed. Here, **the employee was acting within the course and scope of her employment when she fell off the cliff**. It did not matter that her employer did not expressly order her to jump off the cliff. She was entitled to benefits. *Engle v. Thompson Murray, Inc.*, 96 Ark.App. 200 (Ark. Ct. App. 2006).

◆ A New Jersey construction worker rode into New York City with his supervisor on September 11, 2001 to work at a job site there. After the terrorist attacks, the bridges and tunnels connecting New York and New Jersey closed, and the supervisor suggested they get an early dinner and return to the job to work until the bridges reopened. On the way back to the job site, they were in a car crash and the employee suffered injuries. He sought workers' compensation benefits, and the New Jersey Supreme Court held that he was entitled to them. Even though he was hurt off the job site, **he was directed or "compelled" to participate in the activity by his supervisor**. *Sager v. O.A. Peterson Construction Co.*, 862 A.2d 1119 (N.J. 2004).

◆ An employee of an Illinois industrial cleaning service was assigned to help carry 500 45-pound bags of asbestos down several flights of stairs to a dumpster. The temperature was 5 degrees Fahrenheit. He suffered chest pains, went to the hospital and had an angioplasty to open up a blocked artery. He filed for workers' compensation benefits, and an arbitrator awarded them. The court of appeals reversed the award, but the Supreme Court of Illinois reinstated it. There was sufficient evidence for the arbitrator to find a connection between the employee's work and his heart attack. Even though the employee's blocked artery was a preexisting condition, **his symptoms began while he was performing heavy labor under extreme conditions**, and the conditions contributed to the risk of heart attack in persons with blocked arteries. *Twice Over Clean, Inc. v. The Industrial Comm'n*, 827 N.E.2d 409 (Ill. 2005).

◆ A contract laborer who worked for a contractor in New Jersey did not have a driver's license and relied on his boss to drive him to job sites. After work at a customer's house one day, the contractor and the customer drove go-carts around a track on the property. The contractor then told the laborer to drive the go-cart. The laborer refused, saying he did not know how to drive, but the contractor persisted, insisting it was easy. When the laborer then crashed and broke his ankle, he sued for workers' compensation benefits. The case reached the Supreme Court of New Jersey, which ruled that **if an employee reasonably feels compelled to participate in a recreational activity, that activity becomes work related**, and workers' compensation benefits are available. The court remanded the case for a determination of whether the laborer had an objectively reasonable basis for believing he had to ride the go-cart. *Lozano v. Frank De Luca Construction*, 842 A.2d 156 (N.J. 2004).

◆ When a female worker brought a sexual harassment lawsuit against a Colorado company, a 25-year employee agreed to testify on her behalf. He claimed he was then ostracized and harassed in retaliation for his testimony. He brought a union grievance against a male co-worker for remarks made during a confrontation, but he refused to testify at the grievance hearing (allegedly because of pressure from the union president) and the grievance was dismissed. After being diagnosed with bipolar disorder, he sought workers' compensation benefits, which were awarded. The Colorado Court of Appeals affirmed, noting that even though the employee suffered from preexisting emotional problems, **his stress-related disability resulted primarily from his employment**. Also, it did not arise from non-compensable harassment, but from the work-related retaliation after his testimony in the harassment suit. *Public Service of Colorado v. Industrial Claim Appeals Office*, 68 P.3d 583 (Colo. Ct. App. 2003).

◆ An employee of a steel manufacturer accidentally killed a co-worker who stepped in front of a tow motor the employee was operating. After the accident, the employee sought treatment for severe depression and filed a workers' compensation claim. The claim was denied at the administrative level on the grounds that the employee had not sustained an injury as defined by the statute. The case reached the Ohio Supreme Court, which held that the state's workers' compensation law allowed an employee to recover for psychiatric injuries that arose from "an injury or occupational disease." **The law did not specify that the person suffering the psychiatric injury had to be the same person who suffered the compensable injury.** Since the law had to be construed liberally in favor of employees, the court ruled that the employee was entitled to benefits. *Bailey v. Republic Engineered Steels, Inc.*, 741 N.E.2d 121 (Ohio 2001).

◆ A customer service operator was pulled into her supervisor's office, where he locked the door and began yelling at her. He called her a name and threw things around the room. He also threatened her several times about telling anyone of his outburst. A few days later, she suffered a breakdown and was referred to a psychiatric facility. She received treatment for three years and obtained short- and long-term disability benefits for two of those years. When she applied for workers' compensation, an administrative judge found that she had suffered a work-related psychiatric injury and that she was entitled to benefits. The Pennsylvania Commonwealth Court agreed, noting that the behavior of the supervisor was an abnormal working condition for which benefits were available. The Supreme Court of Pennsylvania reversed, based on its decision in *Philadelphia Newspapers, Inc. v. WCAB*, 544 Pa. 203, 675 A.2d 1213 (Pa. 1996), where it held that **a single episode of criticism by a supervisor who used vulgar language** was not an abnormal working condition sufficient to award benefits for a psychic injury. *McKinney v. WCAB*, 770 A.2d 326 (Pa. 2001).

◆ A New York accountant bowled regularly on a Monday night team sponsored by one of his firm's clients. After he suffered a fatal heart attack at one of the games, his wife sought benefits under workers' compensation law, which prevents awards "where the injury was sustained in or caused by voluntary participation in an off-duty athletic activity not constituting part of the employee's work related duties," unless the employee is required to participate. The wife argued that the bowling game conferred a substantial benefit to the accounting firm because her husband and the client had a custom of discussing business before and after each game. A workers' compensation judge found that the wife was entitled to the award, but the board reversed. The court of appeals affirmed the board's ruling. **Benefit to the employer is one factor, but it did not mean that the games were work related**, as contemplated by the statute. To the contrary, the opposite conclusion was required because: 1) the accountant was not required to participate; 2) he was not paid to do so; and 3) the firm did not sponsor the games or even "overtly encourage" the accountant's participation. *Dorosz v. Green & Seifter*, 708 N.E.2d 162 (N.Y. 1999).

◆ An employee worked as a part-time driver in the office of an international manufacturer of radioactive hospital equipment. One day, after making his deliveries, he discovered that he had left his driver's license and wallet at home. Instead of turning off at the highway exit to the office, he went to the next one (leading to his home) and got into an automobile accident as he was exiting the ramp. He sought workers' compensation benefits for the accident. His supervisor testified at the hearing that he should have returned to the office and punched out before going home to get his license. Nonetheless, the workers' compensation commissioner found that the deviation from the driver's exact duties was minor and reasonable so as to warrant the award of benefits. The state board disagreed, finding instead that the injury occurred as a result of a separate side trip unrelated to employment. The Connecticut Court of Appeals reversed. The board improperly substituted its fact findings for those of the commissioner, who found that **the driver's decision to retrieve his license was in the best interests of both parties** and that the injury occurred at a time and place where it was reasonable for the driver to have been. *Kolomiets v. Syncor Int'l Corp.*, 723 A.2d 1161 (Conn. App. Ct. 1999).

◆ An Arkansas forklift driver kept watch over his area during his official 10-minute break to monitor the company's lumber dryers. When stepping away from the forklift one day to take a cigarette break, he slipped on a step covered with algae and injured his foot and ankle. He argued that he didn't get the two 10-minute breaks to which he was entitled because there was no one to relieve him. Nor did he have time to smoke in the designated areas, so he would stay in the job area to watch his station. He claimed that he was entitled to workers' compensation benefits. An administrative law judge and the workers' compensation commission disagreed. The case reached the Arkansas Supreme Court, which held that the commission had improperly found that the employee was not **performing employment services at the time of his injury**. The company derived benefits from the employee staying by his work station to smoke. The court remanded the case for a determination of benefits. *White v. Georgia-Pacific Corp.*, 6 S.W.3d 98 (Ark. 1999).

◆ An employee was struck by a car while she crossed an intersection near her office during a **coffee break**. She had been on her way back to her office after buying a gift for a departing supervisor for whom an office party was to be held. The employer paid its employees for morning and afternoon breaks, and many employees took their breaks outside the office. She filed a claim for workers' compensation benefits. The Supreme Court of Montana stated that because the employee had been injured during a paid break that was not a substantial deviation from her employment, and the employer placed restrictions on her break time, she was entitled to workers' compensation benefits. *Carrillo v. Liberty Northwest Insurance*, 922 P.2d 1189 (Mont. 1996).

◆ A Nevada employee on temporary assignment at a New Mexico laboratory suffered a fractured wrist when she **fell off a bicycle provided by the laboratory for its employees**. The lab was in a remote area and employees would use the bicycle during breaks to get exercise. The Supreme Court of Nevada reinstated an administrative decision awarding benefits. The employee was properly deemed to be in the course and scope of her employment when she was injured, considering the remote locale, the employer's ownership of the bicycle and the employer's expectation of employee use. The injury was not of the type contemplated by the legislature in amending the compensation act to preclude the award of workers' compensation benefits to employees injured in athletic or social events sponsored by employers. *Dixon v. State Industrial Insurance System*, 899 P.2d 571 (Nev. 1995).

◆ A Michigan machine operator suffered a substantial hearing loss and tinnitus from exposure to noise at work. The employer installed sound insulation several months before the employee filed an application for workers' compensation benefits. The hearing officer denied the claim, ruling that while the claimant was disabled by a hearing loss, he could not prove an employment-related disability under the state Workers' Compensation Act. The case reached the Supreme Court of Michigan, which observed that state workers' compensation law **limited awards to employees who experienced a limitation of their wage-earning capacity**. Here, the hearing loss was work related, but it did not limit the employee's wage-earning capacity. The workplace modifications had not been performed to accommodate his injury and thus did not bring his employment into a favored category of work that would entitle him to benefits. *Michales v. Morton Salt Co.*, 450 Mich. 479, 538 N.W.2d 11 (Mich. 1995).

- A Nebraska company held a picnic at which attendance was not mandatory, and an employee was severely injured while participating in a **football game**. The Supreme Court of Nebraska held that the injured employee was not entitled to receive workers' compensation benefits because the company had not received any substantial direct tangible benefit from holding the event. The court examined three factors for determining whether a recreational or social activity could be considered within the course of employment: 1) whether the accident occurred on the employer's premises as a regular incident of employment, 2) whether the employer expressly or impliedly required employee participation, and 3) whether the employer derived substantial direct benefit from the activity, irrespective of employee morale. Applying these factors, the court found that the employee was not entitled to benefits. *Shade v. Ayars & Ayars, Inc.*, 247 Neb. 94, 525 N.W.2d 32 (Neb. 1994).

B. Occupational Diseases

Just like injuries, occupational diseases have to be causally connected to employment in order to be compensable under workers' compensation. Generally, the disease must occur as a result of unusual, extraordinary or abnormal working conditions. In other words, there must be something about these working conditions that is different than normal working conditions.

Most jobs, for example, are somewhat stressful. A heart condition that occurs as a result of stress is usually not going to be compensable under workers' compensation. But the stress in certain jobs is so high that a heart condition is not an unlikely scenario (e.g., police officers and firefighters often have a statutory presumption that heart conditions are caused by occupational stress).

Occupational disease cases are harder to prove than occupational injury cases because there is seldom one defining incident that occurs to pinpoint causation.

- A tool cutter and grinder in Florida was exposed to beryllium dust over a period of 17 years until he was laid off. The Department of Labor offered to test his blood for potential work-related disorders, and he tested positive for beryllium sensitivity. He then received two medical directives. First, he could no longer work in an occupation with risk of beryllium exposure. Second, he should undergo regular medical testing or monitoring to determine whether the beryllium sensitivity had advanced to a state of chronic beryllium disease. When he sought workers' compensation benefits, his former employers asserted that he did not yet have chronic beryllium disease, so he should not be entitled to workers' compensation benefits. However, the Florida District Court of Appeal held that **his beryllium sensitivity caused an objective and verifiable change in his body that required medical treatment**. Thus, he suffered an injury for purposes of workers' compensation. *Huff v. Loral American Beryllium Co.*, 967 So.2d 244 (Fla. Dist. Ct. App. 2007).

◆ A Delaware retiree died from lung cancer caused by his occupational exposure to asbestos. He had worked for his employer for 40 years, never filing a workers' compensation claim and receiving a pension after he voluntarily retired. When his widow filed a claim for death benefits, the employer asserted that she had no independent right to recover them. The case reached the Supreme Court of Delaware, which ruled that a surviving spouse can recover death benefits independently and irrespective of whether the deceased employee received wages or disability benefits arising from the occupational injury or disease that caused his death. **Since death benefits were not limited to wage replacement benefits, the widow was entitled to recover them.** *Hirneisen v. Champlain Cable Corp.*, 892 A.2d 1056 (Del. 2006).

◆ An employee of a meat company in Kansas whose job required him to put his gloved hands into dirty water to handle intestines full of fecal matter developed weak, painful, swollen, discolored hands. He was diagnosed with bilateral dermatitis and was transferred to another position. When he sought workers' compensation benefits, an administrative law judge found that he had a 10% impairment to the body as a whole. However, he had not suffered any wage loss as a result because he was making more now than he had been when the disease first affected his hands. The Workers' Compensation Board determined that he was nevertheless entitled to 41.5 weeks of permanent partial disability compensation at the rate of $278.25 per week, resulting in an award of $11,547.38. The employer appealed. The Kansas Court of Appeals held that **even though the employee was earning more than before, he was not precluded from receiving benefits for his disease**. It affirmed the award. *Garcia v. Tyson Fresh Meats, Inc.*, 125 P.3d 580 (Kan. Ct. App. 2006).

◆ For approximately 40 years, an employee had a job retreading truck tires. The process required the use of various chemicals and produced a fine dust that covered him on a daily basis. He developed lung cancer and died. He never smoked, and the two houses he had lived in tested negative for significant radon exposure. After his widow was awarded workers' compensation death benefits, the company and its insurer appealed. The Missouri Court of Appeals affirmed the award. It held that the workers' compensation commission appropriately judged the credibility of the witnesses and found that the employee's experts were more credible. **Missouri law did not require the employee to prove which specific chemical caused the occupational disease in order to recover benefits.** *Kent v. Goodyear Tire and Rubber Co.*, 147 S.W.3d 865 (Mo. Ct. App. 2004).

- A Delaware tire shop repairman had to buff the insides of rubber tires to prepare them for patching. The process produced airborne particles of dirt and dust (including latex particles), which the repairman inhaled. After several months on the job, he was found to have an allergy to latex. He filed a claim for total disability workers' compensation benefits as well as his medical expenses. At his hearing, his expert witnesses testified that he was susceptible to allergies, noting that after he began working at the repair shop, he developed a number of allergies. The Delaware Industrial Accident Board denied him benefits, and the Superior Court of Delaware affirmed. It noted that although the repairman's allergy had been triggered by his exposure to latex particles at work, he was not entitled to benefits because there was an insufficient causal connection between the allergy and some distinctive feature of his job. Here, he had **a predisposition to allergies that was triggered by his employment**. This was not enough to require the payment of benefits. *Smith v. Service Tire Truck Center*, 2000 WL 145817 (Del. Super. Ct. 2000).

- A Pennsylvania district manager was promoted to manage a large territory that had been merged from two districts. Her workload increased from 55 to 70 hours weekly, and she began to suffer from severe depression. She successfully petitioned for workers' compensation benefits for suffering a psychic injury as a result of abnormal working conditions. The case reached the Supreme Court of Pennsylvania, which held that the manager had failed to establish that the merger of the districts and her promotion to a new job with greater responsibilities established abnormal working conditions. An **increase in workload and responsibilities caused by promotion or job change does not establish an abnormal working condition** under state workers' compensation law. Such a finding could be determined only by reference to the job into which she was promoted, not by comparison to her former responsibilities. *Hershey Chocolate Co. v. Comwlth. of Pennsylvania, WCAB*, 682 A.2d 1257 (Pa. 1996).

- A South Carolina employee suffered several job-related injuries to his arms, back and neck and received permanent disability benefits. Although a vocational rehabilitation specialist testified that the employee had symptoms of depression, fatigue and anxiety, the workers' compensation commission failed to address his claims of mental injury. When the employee later applied for benefits based on a change in the condition of his elbow and his mental condition, the commission did not consider the mental condition issue since it was not earlier included as an injury. A state court held that the mental injuries were not compensable because the employee had failed to establish unusual and extraordinary employment conditions. The South Carolina Court of Appeals held that the employee **did not have to prove that his mental condition resulted from an unusual or extraordinary employment condition**. If the mental injuries were causally related to the physical injury, they might be compensable even without proof of unusual or extraordinary job conditions. Because the symptoms were new manifestations of the same harm to the employee, proof of changed circumstances might justify a change in the award. The court remanded the case. *Estridge v. Joslyn Clark Controls, Inc.*, 482 S.E.2d 577 (S.C. Ct. App. 1997).

◆ A Nebraska bar and grill contracted with an exterminator to spray the premises each month for cockroaches. The exterminator sprayed the bar, and the following day an employee washed up the surfaces with towels and buckets of water, immersing her hands and arms in the water for over two hours. She experienced headaches, pain, seizures, blurred vision and memory loss. A physician diagnosed her as having organic brain damage due to toxic encephalopathy caused by poison. The employee submitted a claim for workers' compensation benefits. The workers' compensation court ruled that the employee was permanently totally disabled and entitled to benefits. The Court of Appeals of Nebraska affirmed, stating that unless the nature and effect of an industrial injury is readily apparent, expert testimony is required to establish a causal relationship between the incident and the disability. The compensation court was entitled to consider evidence that would assist it in understanding the claimant's condition. **A claimant is not required to prove that a medical diagnosis is universally recognized** in the medical community to prevail. *Sheridan v. Catering Management, Inc.*, 5 Neb. App. 305, 558 N.W.2d 319 (Neb. App. 1997).

◆ A 70-year-old South Dakota retiree worked part time at a grocery store. He unloaded a delivery truck for almost two hours one morning. That evening, he was taken to a hospital emergency room, where he was diagnosed as having a heart attack and massive gastrointestinal bleeding. He later died. His estate filed a claim for workers' compensation benefits that was denied by the state department of labor. The Supreme Court of South Dakota upheld that determination, observing that the employee had been a lifelong smoker who suffered from cardiovascular disease and chronic obstructive pulmonary disease for which he received medication. In workers' compensation cases resulting from heart attacks, claimants were required to establish a causal relationship between employment and the heart attack. Here, the department of labor was entitled to rely on testimony that **the employee was suffering angina while he was at work, rather than a heart attack**. *Helms v. Lynn's, Inc.*, 542 N.W.2d 764 (S.D. 1996).

◆ A Nebraska employee whose job was to change paint filters and maintain paint guns came into contact with a variety of solvents. He developed a rash and became dizzy when working around painting equipment and suffered seizures on three occasions. His employment was terminated, and he consulted two physicians who were unable to confirm that his seizures were caused by exposure to solvent toxicity. After a third physician attributed the seizures to repetitive solvent toxicity, the employee filed a claim for workers' compensation benefits. The employer contested the application and sought review by the state workers' compensation court, which awarded benefits. The court of appeals reversed the award. The employee appealed to the Supreme Court of Nebraska, which held that the compensation court was entitled to make a credibility determination among the physicians and agree with the third physician's opinion that **exposure to solvents caused the seizures**. The court reinstated the workers' compensation judgment. *Berggren v. Grand Island Accessories, Inc.*, 249 Neb. 789, 545 N.W.2d 727 (Neb. 1996).

◆ A Maryland computer operator claimed that some of his co-workers harassed him to the point that he became restless and sleepless, had headaches and developed posttraumatic stress syndrome. He claimed that the harassment prevented him from working, and he submitted a claim for workers' compensation benefits on the basis of an occupational disease. After the state workers' compensation commission denied the claim, the Maryland Court of Appeals held that purely mental diseases could be compensable as occupational diseases. However, a claimant must demonstrate a relationship between a particular disease and employment. The court found **no inherent relationship between the job duties of a computer operator and the alleged harassment by co-workers**. It was insufficient to show that a mental injury was related to general conditions on the job. The alleged injury was not compensable under the state workers' compensation act. *Davis v. Dyncorp*, 336 Md. 226, 647 A.2d 446 (Md. 1994).

◆ A Connecticut woman worked for a dentist as a hygienist for six years. Both the hygienist and the dentist received precautionary vaccinations against hepatitis. During this time, the hygienist's husband was diagnosed as being a carrier of the hepatitis type B virus (HBV). As a result, the hygienist was tested and also diagnosed as a carrier of HBV. She stopped working when she and the dentist agreed that her condition posed a threat to patients. She was awarded workers' compensation benefits, and the dentist appealed to the Supreme Court of Connecticut. On appeal, the dentist claimed that the hygienist failed to prove that HBV falls within the definition of an occupational disease. The court noted that the statutory language required the disease to be "peculiar to the occupation in which the employee was engaged and due to causes in excess of the ordinary hazards of employment as such." Although HBV is contagious and can be transmitted through means outside the workplace, **for dental hygienists HBV is a disease so distinctly associated with their profession that the necessary causal connection was present**. The court affirmed the award of benefits. *Hansen v. Gordon*, 602 A.2d 560 (Conn. 1992).

C. Preexisting Conditions

Although an injury may occur on the job or appear to be work related, it may be the result of a preexisting condition or an aggravation of a preexisting condition. However, a preexisting condition does not necessarily bar a claim for benefits. It may simply limit the amount of benefits an employer has to pay.

There may be a second injury fund or some sort of special fund set up by a state to compensate workers with preexisting conditions. Also, there are almost always questions in these cases, such as:

—how much of an employee's disability is attributable to the preexisting condition?
—how much can be attributed to the workplace incident?
—was the employer aware of the preexisting condition? and
—what was the employee's level of impairment before the second injury?

Generally, the employer is only responsible for the amount of disability attributable to the workplace incident.

These are complicated issues, the resolution of which demands specialized knowledge of a particular state's workers' compensation laws. The following cases examine some of the issues that arise in cases involving preexisting conditions.

◆ An electrician also worked as a minister for a church. He injured his knee while performing electrical work. The Montana State Fund, as the company's workers' compensation insurer, accepted workers' compensation liability for his injury. Eventually he had surgery, and for a while his knee performed well. The following year he took a buyout offer from the company and worked only for the church However, his knee deteriorated until he could no longer work as a minister either. He sought temporary total disability benefits, and the workers' compensation court determined that the state fund had to pay them. The Montana Supreme Court affirmed that decision, holding that **the temporary aggravation of his preexisting knee injury while working as a minister did not constitute the last injurious exposure**. Thus, the state fund (and not the church) was liable for the increased benefits. *Lanes v. Montana State Fund*, 192 P.3d 1145 (Mont. 2008).

◆ A Vietnam veteran working for a mining company in Pennsylvania filed a claim for workers' compensation benefits after experiencing harassing comments of a homosexual nature from the mine foreman. He claimed that he had been traumatized by numerous acts of homosexuality he observed in the military and that the foreman's comments about wanting to have sex with him aggravated his post-traumatic stress disorder. The company asserted that the psychological injury suffered was a preexisting condition for which it should not be held liable. The Supreme Court of Pennsylvania held that **the harassing behavior, which violated the union contract and which resulted in discipline for the foreman, constituted abnormal working conditions, thus entitling the employee to benefits**. The foreman's statements were more than mere joking, crude behavior. Also, it did not matter that the employee suffered from a preexisting condition. *RAG (Cyprus) Emerald Resources, L.P. v. WCAB*, 912 A.2d 1278 (Pa. 2007).

◆ An Arkansas Wal-Mart employee claimed that she fell off a ladder and hurt her back. No one saw the fall. Later in the day she had a friend drive her to the ER. After three days off work, she agreed to see the company doctor, but became argumentative and walked out. Eventually she saw the company doctor and another physician, neither of whom found bruising, swelling or muscle spasms consistent with the pain she claimed she was having. She also failed to tell them she had suffered a back injury 13 years earlier (and that she had filed a workers' compensation claim at that time) or that she had been hospitalized for back pain three years prior to the fall. When she sought workers' compensation benefits, the Arkansas Court of Appeals agreed with the workers' compensation commission that **she failed to prove the accident caused her**

back pain rather than a preexisting condition. She was not entitled to benefits. *English v. Wal-Mart Associates, Inc.*, 2006 WL 2848659 (Ark. Ct. App. 10/4/06).

◆ An employee at a shipyard in Maine suffered from an inherited neurological condition that caused involuntary shaking of his head and arms. The shaking became worse when he experienced stress. When his co-workers called him derogatory names and subjected him to practical jokes because of his symptoms, he worried that he could no longer safely perform his job. Eventually, his doctor advised him to stop working, and his symptoms improved. He filed for workers' compensation benefits, which the company fought. An administrative law judge found that the employee was subjected to dehumanizing remarks and pranks that aggravated his disorder, and that working conditions prevented him from returning to the shipyard. The First Circuit upheld the decision to award him total disability benefits. **The fact that his medical condition was preexisting did not prevent him from obtaining benefits.** *Bath Iron Works Corp. v. Preston*, 380 F.3d 597 (1st Cir. 2004).

◆ A Louisiana laborer developed fluid on his right knee and was diagnosed with traumatic arthritis. After receiving treatment and being placed on light duty for a week, the condition cleared and he resumed his regular duties. Over two years later, he completed a medical questionnaire for another employer. He indicated having a knee problem but erased his original "no" response to a question asking whether he had been bothered by the condition. The employer hired him. After three months, he slipped and fell on the job, injuring his right knee. He suffered a torn meniscus, for which he underwent two arthroscopic surgeries. He filed a workers' compensation claim, which the employer challenged on the basis of failure to disclose his preexisting condition on the medical questionnaire. The hearing officer dismissed the case.

The Supreme Court of Louisiana stated that a claimant's untruthful statement regarding a permanent partial disability may give rise to an affirmative employer defense under state law, when the statement prejudices the employer's ability to seek reimbursement from the state second injury fund. Because an employee may then have to forfeit all compensation benefits, the employer must show that failure to answer the question directly relates to the medical condition for which the claim was made. Notice must be provided to the employee that failure to make the disclosure could result in forfeiture, and the employer must demonstrate prejudice. **Here, the questionnaire was ambiguous, and the employee's response had not been untruthful.** Because the employer failed to demonstrate that the employee had a preexisting permanent partial disability, the court reversed the lower court judgments. *Wise v. J.E. Merit Constructors, Inc.*, 707 So.2d 1214 (La. 1998).

◆ An Arizona cabinet manufacturer hired a service worker who indicated in his application that he had been "wounded in combat NAM." He initially denied having mental or physical disabilities. In a subsequent employment interview, he revealed that he had posttraumatic stress disorder that required him to work outside a plant, away from people. Although he indicated that he had been wounded in a helicopter crash and had a bad back, he stated that he could lift over 50 pounds. He later suffered a back injury and filed a workers' compensation claim. The employer's insurer assigned him a permanent impairment and applied for reimbursement from the state special fund for the employee's preexisting posttraumatic stress disorder. An administrative judge awarded reimbursement, finding that the employee had properly advised the employer of the existence of his mental impairment under the written records requirement of state law, even though the written application had been supplemented with oral testimony. The court of appeals reversed.

The Supreme Court of Arizona stated that the purpose of the second injury fund was to provide incentives to employers to hire disabled workers by relieving them of the risk of increased liability from preexisting impairments and industrial injuries. The written records requirement should not be interpreted in a manner that defeated this legislative purpose. **Credible oral testimony offered in conjunction with written documents was sufficient to establish employer knowledge of a preexisting injury.** Here, the employer had been advised of the employee's general disability by the written record and supplementing oral evidence. It was entitled to reimbursement from the special fund, and the court reinstated the award. *Special Fund Division v. Industrial Comm'n of Arizona*, 953 P.2d 541 (Ariz. 1998).

- A painter was seriously injured after falling 30 feet when a support rope snapped. He filed a claim for workers' compensation benefits. An administrative law judge (ALJ) determined that he was permanently, totally disabled and entitled to full benefits. The employer argued that Section 8(f) of the Longshore and Harbor Workers' Compensation Act limited the claim to 104 weeks because the employee had a preexisting permanent partial disability (alcoholism), known to the employer, without which the employee would not be totally disabled. The employer argued that the employee's alcoholism robbed him of his motivation to rehabilitate himself. The District of Columbia Benefits Review Board held that despite being rendered a paraplegic who was incontinent, the injury was not severe enough to make full-time employment impossible. Appeal reached the U.S. Court of Appeals, D.C. Circuit.

The only question to be resolved was whether the employee's alcoholism was a direct contributing factor to his total disability. To answer this, the employer would have to show that a subsequent injury alone would not have caused total permanent disability. The employer could not satisfy this standard. There was evidence in the record that **work-related injuries caused total disability** and that the employee's physical limitations would prevent all but the most ambitious and motivated person from becoming reemployed. The court reinstated the ALJ's order. *Director, Office of Workers' Compensation Programs v. Jaffe New York Decorating*, 25 F.3d 1080 (D.C. Cir. 1994).

- An Arkansas employee suffered a work-related injury that resulted in some degree of permanent physical impairment but did not result in any reduction in his wage-earning capacity. Eight years later, the worker suffered another compensable injury. The impairment that resulted from this injury was allegedly greater than that which would have occurred but for the worker's previous compensable injury. The Workers' Compensation Commission determined that the second injury fund was not liable because the employee's previous injury was work related and did not result in a loss of earning capacity. The Arkansas Court of Appeals utilized a three-part test to determine whether the fund was liable. First, it agreed with the commission that the employee's earlier injury was a compensable injury. Second, the injury resulted in a permanent impairment. The court determined that **the prior impairment need not result in a loss of earning capacity** and may be caused by either a work-related or a non-work-related injury. A contrary holding would impermissibly distinguish between types of handicapped persons. The court did not address the third part of the test, which required that the compensable injury combine with the recent injury to produce the current disability status. The court affirmed the finding that the employee was permanently and totally disabled, reversed the finding as to the liability of the second injury fund and remanded the case. *White Consolidated v. Rooney*, 866 S.W.2d 838 (Ark. Ct. App. 1993).

◆ A New Hampshire employee with a history of back problems allegedly injured his back while shoveling gravel for his employer. He filed a claim for a permanent partial disability award with the department of labor. The hearing officer deemed medical evidence insufficient to support a finding that the injury was a result of the shoveling at work. The employee appealed, claiming that the hearing officer failed to apply the amended statute allowing permanent partial disability awards for spinal column or spinal cord injuries. Further, the employee claimed the hearing officer erred in determining that any permanent impairment that existed, existed before the alleged injury. On appeal, the Supreme Court of New Hampshire affirmed the hearing officer's finding and dismissed the employee's claims. The court agreed that **benefits should not be awarded because the employee did not prove his condition arose from his employment**. Moreover, the medical evidence showed no evidence of a definite new injury. *Petition of Hyde,* 605 A.2d 228 (N.H. 1992).

◆ A Nebraska nursing attendant suffered a back injury as a result of transferring a patient from a wheelchair to a bed. The employer gave her some time off and workers' compensation benefits for temporary disability. After returning to work, she allegedly began complaining of back pains. She eventually consulted a physician who concluded that she suffered from a naturally progressing back problem that could have been a congenital condition. The employee and employer presented conflicting evidence regarding whether the initial back injury exacerbated her naturally progressing condition. The state Workers' Compensation Court denied her claim for benefits. The Supreme Court of Nebraska affirmed. It recognized the compensation court's authority to weigh the conflicting evidence and testimony. Additionally, the expert testimony supported the finding that **the employee's condition resulted from the natural progression of her back condition**. *Liberty v. Colonial Acres Nursing Home,* 481 N.W.2d 189 (Neb. 1992).

◆ A truck driver's normal job was driving a 10-wheeler over medium distances on decent roads. One day, he received instructions to haul auger coal over rough roads on the edge of a mountain. He suffered a heart attack that day and underwent an angioplasty. He filed a claim with the Workers' Compensation Board, and an administrative law judge (ALJ) determined that **the heart attack was not work related**. The Supreme Court of Kentucky upheld the denial of benefits. Despite the stress and strain imposed as a result of a different job, he was not engaged in substantial arduous labor. He was merely required to shift gears, steer the truck, and avoid holes in the road. The court noted that the treating physician had testified that there was a possibility of a preexisting blocked artery. The court could only overrule an ALJ's decision for an abuse of discretion. Here, the ALJ considered all the evidence and came to a logical conclusion. *Roberts v. Estep*, 845 S.W.2d 544 (Ky. 1993).

◆ A 31-year-old Oregon man, who worked for a paper company, was required to bend, twist, and jump down from a waist-high table to a cement floor up to 60 times per shift. He began to have pain in his lower back and went to a chiropractor over 50 times in the next four years. A neurosurgeon determined that he had a congenital back problem as well as a herniated disk. The employer denied the compensability of his back problems and refused to pay for the surgery. A referee upheld the denials, concluding that the congenital problem was unrelated to the work activities. The Workers' Compensation Board agreed. The Court of Appeals of Oregon considered whether the man's work activity was the major contributing cause of any of his lower back problems. The board had relied primarily on the opinions of the man's two doctors in finding that the lower back problems were not caused in major part by his work activities, but by his congenital problems. However, the board had misinterpreted the doctors' opinions. The doctors had stated that they **could not determine to a reasonable degree of medical certainty that the work activities were the major contributing cause of his condition**. They did not say that the work activities were not the major cause. Therefore, the court reversed and remanded the case. *Skochenko v. Weyerhaeuser Co.,* 846 P.2d 1212 (Or. Ct. App. 1993).

D. The Coming and Going Rule

Generally, employers are not liable under workers' compensation for injuries sustained by employees while in transit to and from work.

However, under the coming and going rule, an employer can be liable for workers' compensation where an employee is injured on the way to or from work while on a special mission for the employer – for example, a car accident on the way to the bank to make a deposit before going home for the night.

Employers can also be liable where employees are required to be away from home for their jobs. Thus, an accident that occurs on the way to the work site from a hotel would likely be covered under workers' compensation.

◆ On his day off, a Nevada construction company employee was asked to deliver equipment from the construction yard to a job site. He did so using a company truck he was authorized to keep at his home. After dropping off the equipment, he headed for a location where he was doing a personal job. He got in an accident and was seriously injured two miles from the job site. When he sought workers' compensation benefits, the Nevada Supreme Court held that under the "special errand" exception to the coming and going rule, he would be **entitled to benefits if the accident occurred while he was on a part of the road he would only have been on because of the errand he was asked to perform**. The case was remanded for that determination. *Bob Allyn Masonry v. Murphy*, 183 P.3d 126 (Nev. 2008).

◆ A bank in Kansas leased 94% of a building and 737 of 757 spaces in the adjoining parking lot. While crossing the lot after leaving work, a bank employee slipped on a patch of sand that had been put down to prevent people from slipping on ice. She injured her hip, shoulder and elbow on the pavement, then filed a claim for workers' compensation. The case reached the Supreme Court of Kansas, which ruled that she was entitled to benefits. Here, **the bank had enough control over the parking lot for it to be considered part of the bank's premises**. Thus, since the employee was still on bank property, the "coming and going" rule did not apply to bar benefits. *Rinke v. Bank of America*, 148 P.3d 553 (Kan. 2006).

◆ An office equipment technician in Pennsylvania agreed to work for a company if he was given a company car. He signed a one-year contract that was not updated in following years. After becoming a supervisor and spending most of his time at the office rather than at clients' businesses, he was killed while driving to the office to repair a client's fax machines. His widow filed a claim for workers' compensation benefits. A workers' compensation judge denied benefits on the grounds that the technician was not killed in the course and scope of his employment. The case reached the Supreme Court of Pennsylvania, which disagreed. **Because the technician's employment contract included transportation to and from work, the "coming and going rule" did not apply to bar coverage.** *Wachs v. Workers' Compensation Appeals Board*, 884 A.2d 858 (Pa. 2005).

◆ An employee at a Pennsylvania car dealership wore the "wrong" casual clothes to work – his shirt did not carry the dealership's logo. He was given the option of buying a shirt with the logo on it or returning home for a proper shirt. He elected to go home. On his way back to the dealership, he was involved in a serious car accident that left him in a persistent vegetative state. His wife applied for workers' compensation benefits on his behalf, and the Workers' Compensation Appeals Board upheld the decision to award benefits. The dealership appealed, but the Pennsylvania Commonwealth Court upheld the award. Here, **the employee had been on a "special mission" for the dealership at the time of the accident**. Therefore, he had been acting in the course and scope of his employment so as to entitle him to benefits. He did not eat lunch or do anything else that would put him on his "own" time; instead, he immediately headed back to the dealership after changing his shirt. *Sloane Nissan v. WCAB*, 820 A.2d 925 (Pa. Commw. Ct. 2003).

◆ When a sales rep was placed on full commission, he negotiated for the right to work out of the office in his home. He only had to drive to the company office once a week. On one occasion, he drove to work and then stopped at his mailbox to pick up his personal and company mail on the way home. The mailbox was two blocks from his home but was not out of the way. As he was retrieving the mail, he slipped on the ice and fell, injuring himself. The employer's insurer refused to pay reasonable medical and workers' compensation benefits, arguing that the employee was injured while commuting. The Workers' Compensation Court ruled that the employee's injury was work related, since it occurred in the course and scope of his employment and was therefore compensable. It held the insurer liable for the employee's costs. The Montana Supreme Court affirmed. Here, the employee was traveling between two job sites: his company office and his home office. This was more than just going to and coming from work. **Since the injury occurred in the course of required travel, it was compensable.** *Bentz v. Liberty Northwest*, 57 P.3d 832 (Mont. 2002).

◆ A North Carolina yarn-service packer left work for the night. Exiting the plant, he found the gate at the back parking lot's chain-link fence locked. When he could not squeeze through the opening, he tried to climb the fence, fell and broke his leg. He filed a claim for workers' compensation benefits. The commission awarded him benefits, finding that even though he could have waited for someone to unlock the gate or walked around to the front door, his injury arose from his employment because he was not disobeying an order or thrill-seeking when he climbed the gate and was injured. The court of appeals affirmed. It noted that the coming and going rule did not act to bar the employee's claim because the employee was injured in the parking lot adjacent to the company's premises. The employee's negligence was not a bar to benefits because he was not intoxicated and did not willfully intend to injure himself or another. The Supreme Court of North Carolina reversed, noting that **the company provided a known safe and secure exit, which the employee elected not to use**. Also, climbing the fence was not an incidental activity of employment. *Arp v. Parkdale Mills, Inc.*, 576 S.E.2d 326 (N.C. 2003).

◆ A Kentucky employer furnished a truck to an employee to allow him to report directly to job sites without first reporting to an office. He was not compensated for travel time to and from home, but was paid for travel time between the office and job sites and was issued a credit card for fuel purchases. After performing work at an Indiana job site and the employer's office, he was killed in a traffic accident while going home. His survivors sought workers' compensation survivor's benefits, which the employer resisted. The Supreme Court of Kentucky awarded benefits. The employee's use of the vehicle had benefited the employer by allowing him to begin his work duties earlier in the day and work longer in the evening by avoiding a stop at the office. Since the employee had performed a service to the employer at the time of his death, **the work-related exception to the going and coming rule applied**. *Receveur Construction Co./Realm, Inc. v. Rogers*, 958 S.W.2d 18 (Ky. 1997).

◆ A Louisiana employer furnished van transportation to employees to a heliport for further transportation to job sites. A roustabout who chose instead to drive himself to the heliport was injured in a traffic accident and filed for workers' compensation benefits. The state workers' compensation office dismissed his claim, and the Court of Appeal of Louisiana affirmed. While an employee who is **required to check in at a certain place** and is injured en route to a work site is considered to be within the course of employment, this rule does not apply between home and the check-in place. The court rejected the roustabout's claim that the employer had expressly agreed to provide employee transportation, since a written employer policy only promised to provide transportation from its facility to a job site and not from an employee's home. *Bergeron v. Mar-Con, Inc.*, 705 So.2d 232 (La. Ct. App. 1997).

◆ An Oklahoma hospital laboratory supervisor was called at home during a lunch break to respond to an emergency. He was injured in an accident while returning to work, and he filed a claim for workers' compensation benefits. A judge determined that because he was responding to an emergency call, he was on a special mission for his employer, making the injury compensable as arising out of and in the course of employment. The Supreme Court of Oklahoma upheld that decision, noting that an injury may be compensable despite its occurrence off the employer's premises if the claimant is on a special mission for the employer. Here, **the employee had been called away from a lunch break**, and his injury arose out of and in the course of employment. *Stroud Municipal Hospital v. Mooney*, 933 P.2d 872 (Okla. 1996).

◆ A Maryland temporary services agency provided bus transportation for employees to and from work sites. The bus service was limited to agency employees, and usage was optional. An employee who was injured when one of the buses struck a curb filed a claim for workers' compensation benefits, which was denied as not arising out of employment. The Court of Special Appeals of Maryland noted the general rule that workers' compensation is not available to an employee injured while commuting. Exceptions apply where the employer provides free transportation or the conveyance is used for transportation. Here, the free transportation exception was inapplicable because the employer charged a fee and ridership was voluntary. However, **the employer conveyance exception applied because of the employer's substantial control over the bus service** and its exclusive use of the buses for transporting employees to job sites. Because the employer assumed the responsibility to transport employees, the transportation was incidental to employment. *Lee v. BSI Temporaries, Inc.*, 114 Md. App. 1, 688 A.2d 968 (Md. Ct. Spec. App. 1997).

◆ A Utah insurance company employee made deliveries for her employer when its normal courier service experienced delays. She **picked up documents on her way home from work on a route that created a five-mile detour** from her normal way home. The employer did not pay her for her extra time, mileage or other expenses. After dropping off documents on her way to pick up her children at day care, the employee was involved in an accident. When her insurer denied coverage, she applied for workers' compensation benefits. An administrative law judge held that her injuries arose out of and in the course of employment. The commission reversed, finding that the employee was not on a special errand for the employer because the deliveries were part of her routine and were outside the course of her employment. The Supreme Court of Utah agreed that the delivery was part of her normal job duties and not a special errand. The relative regularity, lack of onerous circumstances on the employee and lack of suddenness in the work assignment were all factors supporting the employer's view. The accident had not occurred as the result of a deviation from the employee's normal route home and was not substantial enough to make it any different from the normal risks presented to all commuters. *Drake v. Industrial Comm'n of Utah*, 939 P.2d 177 (Utah 1997).

- A maintenance supervisor at an Iowa plant responded to an emergency weekend call involving malfunctioning equipment. He made the repairs and left for home by an indirect route. He was severely injured in an accident and became quadriplegic. His wife received special training in caring for him, and their home was modified to accommodate his wheelchair use. The family also purchased a modified van and other adaptive equipment. He returned to work in a supervisory position at the same salary with the use of adaptive equipment. He filed for workers' compensation benefits since many of his expenses were not covered under his group health and accident insurance plan. The state industrial commissioner's office assigned an 80% industrial disability based on the severity of his injury and his compromised ability to compete for jobs. He was also awarded as reasonable medical expenses the cost of van conversion, home modification, appliances and home nursing services provided by his wife. An Iowa court and the Supreme Court of Iowa affirmed. **An employee responding to a weekend call apart from usual employment is acting for the benefit of the employer**, and the coming and going time of such a special errand is within the course of employment. Even though the employee had deviated from his normal return route, he had not abandoned his special errand. The injury was compensable. *Quaker Oats Co. v. Ciha*, 552 N.W.2d 143 (Iowa 1996).

- A laborer employed by a wrecking and demolition company worked with a group of co-workers at a Rhode Island demolition site for two weeks. The company furnished meal allowances, motel accommodations and a company vehicle. The group left a restaurant in the company car one night to return to their motel after eating and drinking. The laborer was injured in a fight with one of his co-workers after a complaint about his driving. He submitted a claim for workers' compensation benefits, which was denied by the New Hampshire compensation appeals board. He appealed to the Supreme Court of New Hampshire, which reversed, stating that in the case of traveling employees, travel risks impose special duties that are properly considered employment hazards. Because **the employer required the laborer to live away from home** and provided him with transportation, meals and lodging, personal activities such as dining and transit to and from work were to be broadly considered as arising out of and in the course of employment. Since the fight involved the employee's driving, it arose out of and in the course of employment. *Appeal of Griffin*, 671 A.2d 541 (N.H. 1996).

◆ An Idaho construction worker accepted employment with a construction company at a project in Washington that was 300 miles from his home. The contractor paid the worker $30 per day for "subsistence" without designating any portion as a transportation reimbursement. After completing work on the project, the worker was severely injured in a traffic accident as he returned to Idaho. His workers' compensation claim was denied by the state Industrial Commission, which determined that the accident did not arise out of and in the course of employment.

The Supreme Court of Idaho noted that a number of legal authorities and most states hold that when an employee travels away from an employer's premises, the employee is within the course and scope of employment continuously throughout the trip, except when making a distinct departure for personal business. Here, the Washington work site was considered the normal place of work. Because **the employee's work did not require him to travel away from the Washington work site**, he was not a traveling employee and was not entitled to workers' compensation benefits. *Andrews v. Les Bois Masonry, Inc.*, 896 P.2d 973 (Idaho 1995).

◆ A New York security guard was required to wear a uniform provided by his employer, and he was subject to discipline if he failed to keep it clean. Although he could choose various means to clean it, he used a dry-cleaning establishment at which the employer maintained an account for the purpose of encouraging guards to have their uniforms dry-cleaned. After dropping off some uniforms on his way home from work, he had a car accident and sustained serious injuries. The state's Workers' Compensation Board ruled that he sustained an accidental injury arising out of and in the course of his employment. The Supreme Court, Appellate Division, reversed, finding that the guard was not on a special errand for the employer because he was not required to have his uniform dry-cleaned. The New York Court of Appeals reinstated the holding of the Workers' Compensation Board. Here, the guard was engaged in a special errand at the time of his injury. **The employer encouraged its employees to have their uniforms dry-cleaned** by paying for those services, and it received a benefit in the form of its employees' appearance being neat and clean. *Neacosia v. New York Power Authority*, 649 N.E.2d 1188 (N.Y. 1995).

III. MODIFICATION AND TERMINATION OF BENEFITS

Benefits can be increased where the injured employee's situation worsens, and they can be decreased where the employee's situation improves. They can be terminated completely if the employee recovers or is able to return to work. They can also be terminated or offset for other reasons.

A. Modification of Benefits

There are four basic kinds of workers' compensation benefit awards: permanent total disability, temporary total disability, permanent partial disability, and temporary partial disability.

—Total disability occurs where the employee cannot regularly engage in an ordinary occupation, given the employee's physical impairment, level of education, training, experience and age.
—Partial disability is a lesser degree of impairment and is assigned a numerical value (a percentage of disability).
—Permanent disability means there is no reasonable expectation of improvement.
—Temporary disability means that the employee is in the process of healing and has not reached the stage of maximum medical improvement.

These awards can be modified up or down as the employee's changing condition merits. Thus, an employee whose condition deteriorates can seek increased payments, just as an employer can seek to pay less where an employee's condition improves.

◆ A Pennsylvania baggage handler injured his back and began collecting workers' compensation benefits. Eight years later, **he filed an amended claim seeking benefits for treatment of depression and anxiety**, which he said he developed as a result of being in constant pain from the injury. A workers' compensation judge held the company liable for 50% of the employee's psychiatric treatment because the injury was not the sole cause of the depression. An appeals board reversed, but the Commonwealth Court reversed the board and ordered 100% reimbursement for psychiatric treatment. Here, the employee had no preexisting psychiatric problems, and apportionment was not available because there was only one injury, from which the depression stemmed. *Huddy v. Workers' Compensation Appeal Board*, 905 A.2d 589 (Pa. Commw. Ct. 2006).

◆ An employee at a Nissan plant in Tennessee claimed that he suffered a loss of hearing as a result of noise from the assembly line. He filed for workers' compensation benefits. A trial court found that his ability to hear was not paramount to his job performance and awarded him a 9% vocational impairment of 150 weeks. The court of appeals raised the award to 45%, noting as it did so his loss of enjoyment of everyday activities. On further appeal, the Tennessee Supreme Court affirmed in part, noting that the 9% figure was too low. However, **Tennessee law does not allow for hedonic damages** (loss of enjoyment of life). The court remanded the case for a determination of whether the court of appeals took that into account when it issued the 45% award. *Lang v. Nissan North America, Inc.*, 170 S.W.3d 564 (Tenn. 2005).

◆ An ironworker slipped on a beam and fell, injuring his back. He filed for workers' compensation benefits. An MRI revealed degenerative disc disease and conflicting testimony was offered at his hearing. An administrative law judge awarded him 25% permanent partial disability. On review, the Labor and Industrial Relations Commission (LIRC) modified the award, finding total and permanent disability. The employer appealed. The Missouri Supreme Court affirmed, noting that a reviewing court was not required to view the evidence and all reasonable inferences drawn therefrom in the light most favorable to the LIRC award. As a result, it needed only to determine whether there was sufficient evidence to support the award. Here, **despite the conflicting evidence about the severity of the injury, there was sufficient evidence to support the award**. *Hampton v. Big Boy Steel Erection*, 121 S.W.3d 220 (Mo. 2003).

◆ The West Virginia legislature responded to the threatened integrity of the state workers' compensation fund by amending state law to limit permanent partial disability awards. Such awards were limited to claimants having suffered a whole body medical impairment of at least 50% without regard to the economic effect of the injury. A workers' compensation claimant with a 32% whole body disability rating brought a lawsuit asserting that the act violated his rights under the state constitution. The Supreme Court of Appeals of West Virginia observed that while **the amendment created a high threshold for receiving a permanent partial disability award**, the amendment did not modify the act's traditional reliance on the nature of an industrial injury as opposed to the claimant's economic circumstances. Because the government had a legitimate purpose in preserving the financial integrity of the state workers' compensation fund and the legislation appeared to meet this purpose, the court refused to declare the amendment unconstitutional on equal protection grounds. However, the legislature had violated the claimant's due process rights by waiving the 90-day waiting period that normally affects new state legislation. This had a retroactive effect on the claimant's case, and he was entitled to consideration of his claim. *State of West Virginia ex rel. Blankenship v. Richardson*, 474 S.E.2d 906 (W.Va. 1996).

◆ The New Mexico workers' compensation act used current American Medical Association (AMA) guides to evaluate medical impairment for determining the appropriate level of permanent or partial disability benefits for workers' compensation claims. Two employees who were injured in the scope of their employment filed claims for workers' compensation benefits and were rated through use of the AMA Guide. They contested the ratings and appealed. Before the Supreme Court of New Mexico, **they asserted that use of the AMA Guide was an unconstitutional delegation of legislative power**. They also asserted that they had been denied their equal protection rights to determine the existence or extent of an industrial disability. The court observed that many states have delegated highly technical issues such as industrial impairment to an independent authority in order to take advantage of its expertise. Here, there was no delegation of legislative power to an outside entity. Workers' compensation judges retained the authority to decide cases and use their discretion. The act did not violate the state constitution, and the court affirmed the rulings on the appropriate level of benefits. *Madrid v. St. Joseph Hospital*, 928 P.2d 250 (N.M. 1996).

◆ A housekeeper employed by the Catholic Archdiocese of Seattle complained of sexual harassment by her supervisor. She later injured her hand at work and required a three-month medical leave. She obtained workers' compensation benefits. Her supervisor repeated the harassment when she returned to work. When her hand required further surgery, she was absent from work for eight months under assurances that her position would be kept open. However, the archdiocese failed to preserve the job and refused to hire her for other vacancies. The housekeeper sued the archdiocese for discrimination, among other claims. A trial court awarded $150,000 in damages plus $47,000 in attorneys' fees. The court of appeals held that the trial court had erroneously refused to offset the damage award by the amount of lost wages under the workers' compensation system. The Supreme Court of Washington held that **the employee was not required to mitigate her damages under the collateral source rule**. The compensation had been made for two different injuries: discrimination and the hand injury. The trial court had not committed error by refusing to set off the damage award by the employee's workers' compensation benefits. The court reversed and remanded the case. *Wheeler v. Catholic Archdiocese of Seattle*, 880 P.2d 29 (Wash. 1994).

- A supermarket clerk slipped and fell on a wet floor, sustaining injuries that required medical treatment and vocational rehabilitation. She was paid temporary disability indemnity benefits and received a permanent disability indemnity of 61%. She sought a 50% increase in her award under Section 4553 of the California Labor Code, alleging serious and willful misconduct by the employer. At an administrative hearing, it was determined that there were no safety mats on the floor and that employees were advised to walk carefully because safety mats would be a nuisance. The workers' compensation judge found that the employee's injury occurred as a result of serious and willful misconduct and ordered a 50% increase in her total compensation benefits. The Workers' Compensation Appeals Board affirmed the finding of serious and willful misconduct. However, it held that the 50% increase in compensation applied only to compensation indemnity and not to non-indemnity benefits. The California Court of Appeal held that **the 50% increase recoverable under Section 4553 should include non-indemnity benefits such as medical treatment payments, medical legal fees, and vocational rehabilitation costs**. It noted that the state labor code defined compensation to include every benefit or payment conferred upon an injured employee, including vocational rehabilitation. The 50% increase did not constitute punitive damages and was not constitutionally excessive so long as the total benefits payable were not more than was necessary to fully compensate the clerk for her damages. The court annulled the board's decision and remanded the case for further proceedings. *Ferguson v. WCAB,* 39 Cal.Rptr.2d 806 (Cal. Ct. App. 1995).

- An Iowa employee's arm was amputated after she caught her hand in a meat grinder. She received partial disability benefits for the impairment to her right arm (a scheduled injury to a specific part of the body). However, the industrial commissioner denied her benefits for an alleged injury to her central nervous system as a result of pain at the "limb's former situs" (an unscheduled injury – based on injury to the body as a whole). The employee challenged the denial of benefits, alleging that Iowa statute Section 8534(u) entitled her to further compensation for the phantom limb pain. The court held that, pursuant to paragraph (m), the employee was entitled only to compensation for scheduled injuries. The Iowa Court of Appeals determined that psychological conditions resulting from work-related physical trauma are compensable as unscheduled injuries. Although no Iowa decision addressed compensation for phantom limb pain, New Mexico and Pennsylvania have held phantom limb pain to be a disabling impairment. Here, the court of appeals determined that **the phantom pain experienced by the employee at the limb's former situs was analogous to a psychological condition**. Consequently, it was a compensable unscheduled injury under paragraph (u). The case was reversed and remanded for a determination of the functional loss to the employee's body. *Dowell v. Wagler*, 509 N.W.2d 134 (Iowa Ct. App. 1993).

◆ A Rhode Island painter sustained severe injuries to his right leg when he fell between a roof and scaffolding. He filed for benefits with the Workers' Compensation Commission, which awarded him 125 weeks of disfigurement compensation. However, due to complications, the employee's right lower leg was amputated. He then filed with the Workers' Compensation Court seeking additional disfigurement compensation. The trial judge ordered the employer to pay **15 weeks of additional disfigurement compensation**. The Appellate Division affirmed. Before the Supreme Court of Rhode Island, the employee contended that the disfigurement award of 140 total weeks of compensation was highly inadequate. The court noted that the original disfigurement was 125 weeks for what the physician termed as a crushed leg. However, the assessed compensation for the disfigurement caused by the amputation was for 15 weeks (approximately eight times less than the value of the initial award). Accordingly, the court determined that the award was inadequate and remanded the case for further proceedings to determine the proper assessment. *Johnson v. State*, 634 A.2d 863 (R.I. 1993).

◆ A Pennsylvania welder became disabled as a result of exposure to zinc fumes. He received workers' compensation benefits based upon an average weekly wage that included a prorated $2,750 annual bonus. One year later, the welder filed a petition to review the compensation award, claiming that the entire bonus should be included in the quarter in which it was actually paid and that the same quarter should be used in calculating his average weekly wage. The Supreme Court of Pennsylvania determined that where the employee was paid a wage that was determined annually, **the average weekly wage was to be calculated by dividing the annual wage by 52**. Because the bonus had been paid as an annual performance bonus, the welder's wage was an annual wage that required prorating the bonus over 52 weeks. *Lane Enterprises, Inc. v. WCAB*, 644 A.2d 726 (Pa. 1994).

◆ The Michigan legislature enacted a statute allowing "benefit coordination" to enable employers to decrease benefits to those disabled employees who were eligible to receive wage-loss compensation from other employer-funded sources. Certain employers attempted to apply the law retroactively. The legislature then enacted a law disapproving this practice and requiring reimbursement. The employers sought judicial relief, and the controversy eventually reached the U.S. Supreme Court. The employers argued that the reimbursement provision violated the Contract Clause and the Due Process Clause of the U.S. Constitution. The Court disagreed. With respect to the Contract Clause, there was no contractual relationship here that had been impaired by the new statute. Although employment contracts existed prior to the new law's enactment, they did not address the specific workers' compensation terms at issue. Further, there was no due process violation because **the reimbursement provision was a rational means of meeting a legitimate objective** – preserving injured workers' rights to their full benefits. The Court thus held that the Michigan statute did not violate the Constitution. *General Motors Corp. v. Romein*, 503 U.S. 181, 112 S.Ct. 1105, 117 L.Ed.2d 328 (1992).

B. Termination of Benefits

Where an injured employee is able to return to work without restrictions, or is able to take another job that is less physically demanding, but which pays the same or better, and the employee either takes the job or refuses the offer, workers' compensation benefits can often be terminated.

◆ A Missouri truck driver, who was also a Jehovah's Witness, suffered a severe injury at work and was taken to the hospital, where he refused a blood transfusion because he considered that a sin. Seven days later he died, and the company began paying death benefits to his widow. Two years after the accident, the company stopped paying the death benefits on the grounds that he had unreasonably refused medical treatment. The widow sued and won. The Missouri Court of Appeals noted that the state workers' compensation act allowed an employee to receive treatment "by prayer or spiritual means." Because the statute was meant to liberally accommodate an employee's religious beliefs, **the employee could not be deemed to have acted unreasonably in refusing the transfusion**. *Wilcut v. Innovative Warehousing*, 247 S.W.3d 1 (Mo. Ct. App. 2008).

◆ A Louisiana forklift operator suffered a back injury when her forklift hit a hole. She became unable to work, eventually being diagnosed with fibromyalgia and osteoarthritis, allegedly caused by the accident. Her employer paid her $267 a week for 535 weeks for total temporary disability (TTD). After her doctor sent the employer a letter stating that she had "significant permanent restrictions as far as work activities," but that she could resume some form of work, the employer terminated her benefits. She appealed and the case reached the Supreme Court of Louisiana. The court held that she was entitled to supplemental earnings benefits, and the employer was not entitled to a credit for the TTD benefits it had already paid. However, **she was not entitled to permanent total disability benefits because she failed to prove by clear and convincing evidence that she was physically unable to engage in any employment at all**. *Frith v. Riverwood, Inc.*, 892 So.2d 7 (La. 2005).

◆ An Ohio man applied for a truck driver position and was required to list the most current five previous employers. He failed to include an employer he worked for during an eight-month period, and under whom he made a workers' compensation claim. However, he did list another employer under whom he made such a claim. While working in the new job, he suffered a neck injury and was certified with a temporary total disability. The employer discovered the unlisted employer and fired the driver for falsifying his application. It also sought to stop paying workers' compensation. The Ohio Court of Appeals refused to find that the driver had voluntarily abandoned his employment by failing to list the prior employer on his application. **The driver did not intend to deceive the employer when he failed to include the prior job; he merely forgot.** As a result, he was entitled to continuing benefits. *State ex rel. Strimbu, Inc. v. Industrial Comm'n of Ohio*, 2004 WL 1277770 (Ohio Ct. App. 2004).

◆ A construction worker's elbow came into contact with a live wire while he was working on a project in Kansas City, Missouri. He suffered an electric shock and spent several days off work recovering. However, when he tried to return to work, he experienced physical problems that kept him off the job. He was later diagnosed with a number of physical and emotional ailments, and he received workers' compensation benefits and vocational services for several years. His employer denied him further benefits after he missed a medical appointment at the Mayo Clinic. When he challenged the denial of future benefits, an administrative law judge ruled in his favor. The Missouri Court of Appeals also ruled on his behalf. Here, he missed the medical appointment because there was no one to accompany him to the hospital, and he could not get there without a traveling companion. **This was not a "refusal" to keep his medical appointment under state workers' compensation law.** *McCormack v. Carmen Schell Construction Co.*, 97 S.W.3d 497 (Mo. Ct. App. 2002).

◆ An employee injured his back on the job while working for a manufacturer. He took a few weeks off work, then returned to a light-duty assignment. After a few months, he quit, but refused to sign a "quit slip." In response, the manufacturer terminated his employment when he failed to show up for work for several days. Nearly two years later, he applied for workers' compensation benefits, and almost two years after that, he offered to return to work. The case reached the Supreme Court of Michigan, which held that the employee was **not entitled to benefits because he had refused the manufacturer's offer of reasonable employment**. Although he would have been able to obtain benefits for the period of time following his offer to return to work, a workers' compensation judge had found that his disability ended 10 months before that time. *Perez v. Keeler Brass Co.*, 608 N.W.2d 45 (Mich. 2000).

◆ A Maryland worker qualified for temporary total disability benefits due to a work-related injury. Two years later, he was incarcerated. His employer quit paying his temporary total disability benefits for several months during the sentence and withheld benefits for one month after his release from prison. The state workers' compensation commission denied the employee's demand for benefits during the period of incarceration but reinstated his benefits for the month following his release. The Court of Appeals of Maryland held that **incarceration did not affect the employee's entitlement to benefits**. The state workers' compensation act did not expressly allow the suspension or termination of temporary total disability benefits to otherwise qualified workers during periods of incarceration. The only statutory exception allowing termination of benefits was where a claimant unreasonably refused to submit to a medical examination. The employee was entitled to continue receiving benefits so long as the disability persisted and continued to impair his wage earning capacity. The court followed the majority of jurisdictions in reaching this conclusion, citing decisions of the Nevada and Wyoming Supreme Courts. *Bowen v. Smith*, 342 Md. 449, 677 A.2d 81 (Md. 1996).

◆ The Pennsylvania legislature amended the state workers' compensation act to authorize employers to stop paying total disability benefits to incarcerated claimants during their incarceration. A worker who received total disability benefits was jailed on the same day the amendment took effect. The employer quit paying benefits and filed a petition to suspend benefits. The employee sought reinstatement of benefits plus a statutory penalty. The workers' compensation appeals board held that the employer had violated the act but refused to award a penalty. The Commonwealth Court of Pennsylvania stated that **in general, suspension of benefits is appropriate when a claimant's earning power is no longer affected by a work-related injury**. The event that caused the suspension of the employee's benefits here was his incarceration, which occurred after the effective date of the amendment. The court affirmed the order denying the petition to suspend benefits. However, the employee was not entitled to a penalty because the amendment did not provide clear guidance or procedures for employers seeking to cut off benefits. *Banic v. WCAB*, 664 A.2d 1081 (Pa. Commw. Ct. 1995).

◆ A New Jersey employee sustained work-related injuries and was awarded workers' compensation benefits to last for nine years. **The employer miscalculated the amount of weekly payments**, causing the total amount due to be paid in seven and a half years. The employer therefore stopped payment. The employee moved to require the employer to continue the weekly payments until the nine years had expired. The Division of Workers' Compensation ordered the employer to continue the payments. The Superior Court of New Jersey, Appellate Division, held that the enforcement of the payment schedule would be contrary to principles of equity. In order to prevent the duplicity of payment for the same disability, the employee was not entitled to continued workers' compensation pay for the remaining year and a half. Also, the employer could attempt to recover the overpaid amount. *Montgomery v. Abex Corp., Division of Signal Stat*, 602 A.2d 290 (N.J. Super. Ct. App. Div. 1992).

IV. EMPLOYEE MISCONDUCT

Where an employee commits misconduct in the workplace by, for example, violating known safety rules, the employer can raise this as a defense in an action for benefits. Further, disregard of a doctor's advice may be enough to allow for the cessation of benefits.

◆ A Michigan employee of a company that promoted Martin Luther King's mission of racial equality and reconciliation refused to attend an annual staff development event in Dearborn because she had had bad experiences there as an African-American child. Her supervisor told her she would be docked a day's pay for refusing to attend. The CEO then docked her two days' pay and took away some of her responsibilities. The CEO also shook her finger at the employee and told her she didn't deserve a paycheck. As a result, the employee became deeply depressed and unable to work. She sought workers' compensation benefits. The Michigan Supreme Court held that she was not entitled to them. Here, **her illness arose out of her "intentional and willful" violation of a workplace rule** – that she attend the mandatory event. *Brackett v. Focus Hope, Inc.*, 753 N.W.2d 207 (Mich. 2008).

◆ A teenage employee of a restaurant in Ohio was told never to boil water in a pressure cooker to clean it. A supervisor saw him doing this and warned him against it, explaining that he could be severely injured if he did so. Later, an experienced co-worker saw him adding water again and told him to stop. Shortly thereafter, despite a warning from yet another co-worker not to open the lid, the employee did so and was severely burned by the boiling water that escaped under extreme pressure. Two others were also severely burned. He later obtained temporary total disability (TTD) benefits under workers' compensation, then was fired after an investigation. The company sought to discontinue paying benefits, but the Supreme Court of Ohio ruled that it had to keep paying them. **The employee's termination was causally related to his injury. Thus, his misconduct was not a voluntary job abandonment and did not preclude him from receiving TTD benefits.** *Gross v. Industrial Comm'n of Ohio*, 874 N.E.2d 1162 (Ohio 2007).

◆ While under the influence of methamphetamine, a construction worker in Arizona fell off his drywall stilts and injured himself. He applied for workers' compensation. An administrative law judge denied benefits. The case reached the Arizona Supreme Court, which consolidated it with another case involving an employee who had used alcohol the night before he had a workplace accident and tested positive for alcohol impairment. The court stated that the statute prohibiting recovery of benefits for alcohol or drug-impaired employees (unless they could prove that the impairment was not a contributing cause of the accident) was unconstitutional as applied here. **The statute eliminated claims for injuries partially caused by necessary risks or dangers** of employment, thereby conflicting with the state constitution. *Grammatico v. Industrial Comm'n of Arizona*, 117 P.3d 786 (Ariz. 2005).

◆ A New Jersey employee worked at a retail store where arm-wrestling matches were commonplace. He broke his arm during a match with his supervisor and submitted a claim for workers' compensation. The employer opposed the claim, asserting that the injury had involved a recreational activity and was not compensable. It appealed a final administrative ruling in the employee's favor to the Superior Court of New Jersey, Appellate Division, which observed that state law allows for compensation where an employee is injured as the result of horseplay so long as the horseplay is not instigated by the employee. However, **compensation is disallowed unless the horseplay is a regular incident of employment** and produces a benefit to the employer that goes beyond improvement in employee health and morale. Because the employee could not show that the arm-wrestling conferred any such benefit upon the employer, the court reversed the award of benefits. *Quinones v. P.C. Richard & Son*, 310 N.J.Super. 63, 707 A.2d 1372 (N.J. Super. Ct. App. Div. 1998).

◆ However, in a Nebraska case, a roofing laborer challenged a co-worker to an arm-wrestling match in response to his taunting for carrying less paint than other employees. Both men fell from the roof, and the taunted employee broke his ankle. He filed a claim for workers' compensation benefits, which was allowed. The Supreme Court of Nebraska ruled that an **insubstantial deviation that does not measurably detract from work** does not take an employee's case out of the workers' compensation regime. Here, the injury had arisen from work-related banter and was the result of an accidental slip during the course of momentary horseplay. The court affirmed the ruling for the employee. *Varela v. Fisher Roofing Co., Inc.*, 253 Neb. 667, 572 N.W.2d 780 (Neb. 1998).

◆ A Virginia construction company hired an employee who responded negatively to a job application question asking whether he had been charged or convicted of any crime. He was soon fired for absenteeism but was rehired the following year. On his second job application, he left the criminal record question blank. When the employee submitted a workers' compensation claim, the employer learned that he had been convicted of breaking and entering. A company human resources representative testified at a workers' compensation hearing that the employee would not have been rehired had the company known of his criminal record. The state Workers' Compensation Commission held that the employer had not relied upon the employee's misrepresentation in rehiring him. The Supreme Court of Virginia affirmed. In order to defeat the application, the employer had to prove that it relied upon the false representation in the application, that the **employer's reliance on the misrepresentation resulted in injury** and that there was a causal relationship between the injury and the misrepresentation. The employer had made no attempt to verify the employee's application and had not relied upon his misrepresentation. *Falls Church Construction Co. v. Laidler*, 493 S.E.2d 521 (Va. 1997).

◆ A Virginia employer hired an applicant and requested evidence of U.S. citizenship, including a social security card and other identification, as required by the Immigration and Naturalization Service. The employer hired the applicant because it thought the forged documents he provided were valid. When the employee broke his ankle, the workers' compensation commission denied his claim for benefits because he had misrepresented his eligibility to work legally in the U.S. at the time of hiring. The employee appealed to the Court of Appeals of Virginia, claiming that despite the misrepresentation, an employer-employee relationship existed and that the employer had failed to prove any causal connection between the misrepresentation and the injury. The court held that there was a causal connection between the claimant's inability to work legally and the injury received that defeated the claim for workers' compensation. The Supreme Court of Virginia disagreed with the reasoning of the court of appeals, but upheld the result. **As an illegal alien, the claimant was not an "employee"** for purposes of the workers' compensation act and thus was not entitled to benefits. *Granados v. Windson Development Corp.*, 509 S.E.2d 290 (Va. 1999).

◆ Georgia workers' compensation law disallows claims where a workplace injury or death is caused by intoxication by alcohol, marijuana, or a controlled substance. An employee who unjustifiably refuses to submit to drug testing must overcome **a rebuttable presumption that the accident or injury was caused by alcohol, marijuana or a controlled substance**. An employee of a self-insured employer was injured when he drove his forklift into a wall shortly after he had been observed smoking marijuana by a supervisory employee. He refused to take drug tests on three occasions during his week of hospitalization, asserting that he had been given narcotic pain medications in the ambulance. The employer contested his claim for workers' compensation benefits, and an administrative law judge agreed that he had unjustifiably refused the test and was subject to the rebuttable presumption that the injury was caused by marijuana. The Supreme Court of Georgia upheld that determination, finding that the employer did not have to give prior notice that refusing to submit to the test could result in the denial of benefits. *Georgia Self-Insurers Guaranty Trust Fund v. Thomas*, 501 S.E.2d 818 (Ga. 1998).

◆ A Nevada waitress suffered an on-the-job injury and received workers' compensation benefits. However, she accepted temporary work in violation of a collective bargaining agreement that gave her employer the right to fire her. She appealed the subsequent termination of benefits, and the employer agreed to reinstate them. However, when her doctor released her to light-duty status, the employer responded that no light-duty work was available. It then terminated the temporary total disability benefits it had been paying and denied a request for vocational rehabilitation benefits. A compensation appeals officer and a state court affirmed the denial of benefits. The Supreme Court of Nevada affirmed the decision that the employee had been justifiably terminated for accepting other employment. However, the employer had misleadingly represented that a light-duty job was available upon her release to work. The employer had thus improperly denied her application for rehabilitative services. The court followed the majority rule, citing cases from Ohio, Arizona and Minnesota in determining that **an employer who discharges an injured employee for misconduct is not liable for disability benefits** unless the employee's disability, and not the discharge, causes a wage loss or inability to secure subsequent work. The court reversed and remanded the decision denying the reinstatement of benefits. *Hudson v. Horseshoe Club Operating Co.*, 916 P.2d 786 (Nev. 1996).

◆ While operating a bulldozer, an employee scraped the dirt away from a nest of yellow jackets and received multiple stings. He had a severe reaction and was taken to a clinic by a co-worker. After receiving a shot, he was told by the doctor not to operate machinery or drive for the rest of the day. He was also given written instructions to that effect. The employee rejected a co-worker's offer to drive him home. He passed out behind the wheel of his car and had an accident in which he received injuries to his head, neck and back. An administrative law judge denied his request for workers' compensation benefits, stating that his disabilities flowed naturally from his failure to follow reasonable medical advice. The Supreme Court of Kentucky disagreed with his argument that driving himself home was not unreasonable and that the advice given to him by the doctor was not "medical advice." The doctor's advice was "medical advice." Workers' compensation benefits were denied. *Allen v. Glenn Baker Trucking, Inc.*, 875 S.W.2d 92 (Ky. 1994).

V. LONGSHORE AND HARBOR WORKERS' COMPENSATION ACT

The Longshore and Harbor Workers' Compensation Act (LHWCA) provides compensation for the death or disability of persons engaged in "maritime employment." For the LHWCA to apply,

—the injured person must have been injured in the course of employment,
—the injury must have occurred upon navigable waters (including adjoining areas like piers and wharfs),
—the employer must have employees engaged in maritime employment, and
—the employee must have been engaged in maritime employment.

The LHWCA was intended to supplement state workers' compensation laws and to provide a minimum federal remedy. Where state workers' compensation laws are more generous than the LHWCA, employees can avoid the LHWCA in favor of the state's system.

◆ The LHWCA allows awards to be modified upon a change in conditions or a mistake in a factual determination. A longshore worker injured his back and leg while working and received compensation under the LHWCA. He was retrained as a crane operator and was reemployed full time with additional work as a heavy truck operator. His earnings were about three times more than before his injury, and the employer moved to modify the disability award. An administrative law judge ordered disability payments discontinued even though the employee's physical condition had not improved. A benefits review board affirmed the modification order, but the U.S. Court of Appeals, Ninth Circuit, reversed, finding no authorization to modify the award absent changed physical conditions. The U.S. Supreme Court reversed and remanded, finding that modification of an LHWCA award is permissible where wage-earning capacity has been reduced, restored or improved.

The Ninth Circuit reversed the order to discontinue compensation payments, and the Supreme Court again accepted review. It observed that the uncertain nature of an employee injury and the need for swift resolution of compensation issues prohibited the complete foreclosure of an LHWCA remedy even where an employee's wage-earning capacity was not currently diminished. The employee was entitled to nominal compensation, which would hold open **the possibility of future modification should his earnings later fall below his pre-injury level**. An injured employee's disability is not necessarily reflected in actual wages earned after an injury, and an LHWCA fact-finder must make a determination that takes the future effect of a disability into account. The Court vacated the Ninth Circuit's judgment. *Metropolitan Stevedore Co. v. Rambo*, 521 U.S. 121, 117 S.Ct. 1953, 138 L.Ed.2d 327 (1997).

◆ A Mississippi shipbuilding company employee was exposed to asbestos at work. He was later diagnosed as suffering from asbestosis, chronic bronchitis and possible malignancy in his lungs. He filed a claim for disability benefits under the LHWCA, and his employer admitted liability. He then sued 23 manufacturers and suppliers of asbestos and entered into settlement agreements with eight of them. His wife joined in the settlements and released any cause of action she might have for wrongful death. None of these settlements were approved by the employer. After the employee died, the wife filed a claim for death benefits under the LHWCA, which was granted. The employer contested the claim on the ground that the wife had been a "person entitled to compensation" under the LHWCA who was required to obtain the employer's approval before entering into the settlements. Thus, because she had failed to do so, she forfeited her eligibility for death benefits. The U.S. Court of Appeals, Fifth Circuit, affirmed the grant of death benefits to the wife. The U.S. Supreme Court held that **before the injured worker's death, his wife had not been a "person entitled to compensation" for death benefits**. Thus, she did not have to obtain the employer's approval of the settlements and did not forfeit her right to collect death benefits under the LHWCA. *Ingalls Shipbuilding, Inc. v. Director, OWCP*, 519 U.S. 248, 117 S.Ct. 796, 136 L.Ed.2d 736 (1997).

◆ Five employees were injured while involved in shipbuilding or ship repair activities. Although the LHWCA applied to the injuries sustained, they applied for benefits under Pennsylvania's workers' compensation law. The employer asserted that the LHWCA was the exclusive remedy, but the state administrative agency ruled that the LHWCA did not preempt state workers' compensation laws. The case reached the U.S. Supreme Court, which noted that **the LHWCA supplemented, rather than supplanted, state workers' compensation law**. It was intended to provide complete coverage to maritime laborers so that they would not have to guess which jurisdiction they were supposed to be in before filing a claim. Here, by filing under state law, the workers may have gotten better benefits than under an exclusively federal system, but the LHWCA was enacted to raise awards to a federal minimum because state compensation laws were generally less generous. Thus, the workers were entitled to state benefits. The Court affirmed the state court decisions. *Sun Ship, Inc. v. Pennsylvania,* 447 U.S. 715, 100 S.Ct. 2432, 65 L.Ed.2d 458 (1980).

◆ The U.S. Supreme Court held that an employee who worked as a **welder on a fixed platform oil rig in Louisiana territorial waters was not entitled to LHWCA benefits** because his employment was not "maritime." Not everyone involved in every task that is part and parcel of offshore drilling can be considered a maritime employee. Congress' purpose under the LHWCA was to cover those workers on a covered situs who are involved in the essential elements of the loading, unloading or construction of vessels. The welding work here was far from the traditional work covered by the LHWCA. Further, even though the employee would have been eligible for LHWCA benefits if he had been injured on the continental shelf, such was not the case here. Accordingly, the employee was only entitled to recover state workers' compensation benefits. *Herb's Welding, Inc. v. Gray,* 470 U.S. 414, 105 S.Ct. 1421, 84 L.Ed.2d 406 (1985).

- A man worked for an iron works corporation for many years. After he retired, he learned that he suffered from a work-related hearing loss. An administrative law judge awarded him disability benefits under a combination of compensation systems set forth by the LHWCA. The Benefits Review Board affirmed, but the U.S. Court of Appeals reversed, finding that the worker should have been compensated under the LHWCA's scheduled injury plan. The U.S. Supreme Court held that **claims for hearing loss filed by either current workers or retirees were claims for scheduled injuries** that had to be compensated under the system of scheduled injury compensation, rather than under the system providing compensation for retirees who suffered from occupational diseases that did not become disabling until after retirement. As a scheduled injury type of loss, the worker is presumptively disabled simultaneously with the injury. It did not matter that the worker did not notice the hearing loss until after he retired. *Bath Iron Works Corp. v. Director OWCP*, 506 U.S. 153, 113 S.Ct. 692, 121 L.Ed.2d 619 (1993).

- The U.S. Department of Labor applied the "true doubt" rule to resolve claims under the Black Lung Benefits Act and the LHWCA. The rule shifted the burden of persuasion to a party opposing a claim for benefits so that in cases in which the evidence was evenly balanced, the claimant prevailed. In two separate cases arising under these federal acts, the U.S. Supreme Court determined that the department's analysis was incorrect. Under the true doubt rule, where evidence was evenly balanced, the claimant always won. However, because **the Administrative Procedure Act (APA) required a claimant to lose in the case of evenly balanced evidence**, the true doubt rule violated the APA. *Director, OWC Programs v. Greenwich Collieries*, 512 U.S. 267, 114 S.Ct. 2251, 129 L.Ed.2d 221 (1994).

- Three railroad employees worked at their employers' Virginia terminals, where coal was being loaded from railway cars to ships. Two of the employees were injured while they were cleaning spilled coal from loading equipment to prevent the machinery from fouling. The other employee was injured while repairing a mechanical device necessary for the loading of ships. All three employees brought suit in state court under the Federal Employers' Liability Act (FELA) (which provides a negligence cause of action for railroad employees), but the trial courts dismissed on the grounds that the LHWCA provided the exclusive remedy. The U.S. Supreme Court agreed, holding that the LHWCA provided the exclusive remedy. **Maritime employment includes not only those who physically handle cargo, but also land-based activity, which is an integral or essential part of loading or unloading a vessel.** Here, the employees were maintaining or repairing equipment which was essential to the loading process. Even though the work being performed might be considered traditional railroad work, it was being done at a relevant situs and it involved integral elements of the loading process. Thus, the LHWCA applied, and the employees could not bring suit under the FELA. *Chesapeake and Ohio Railway Co. v. Schwalb,* 493 U.S. 40, 110 S.Ct. 381, 107 L.Ed.2d 278 (1989).

VI. OTHER WORKERS' COMPENSATION CASES

Several other issues, representing a wide range of topics, can also arise in workers' compensation litigation. Some topics include discriminatory or unconstitutional statutes; classification of employees, employers, or dependents; and entitlement to benefits.

A. Discrimination

Employers should not inquire into whether applicants have filed workers' compensation claims. It is permissible to inquire as to whether an applicant can perform the essential functions of the position, and as to any accommodations that may be necessary for the applicant to do the job, but an inquiry into any past workers' compensation filing may violate state civil rights laws.

- The wife of a Missouri man died in a work-related accident in her employer's parking lot. Her husband filed a claim for death benefits under Missouri's workers' compensation law. However, the law provided that a widower could not receive death benefits unless he was either mentally or physically incapacitated from wage earning, or unless he could show actual dependency on his wife's earnings. His claim was denied because he did not fit into the statutory parameters. The case reached the U.S. Supreme Court, which held that the law indisputably mandated gender-based discrimination. Further, the discriminatory means employed were not substantially related to the achievement of the important governmental objective of providing for needy spouses. **Either all widows and widowers could be paid or only dependent surviving spouses could be paid.** The discriminatory law, then, simply did not stand up under the intermediate level of scrutiny applied by the Court in gender discrimination cases. The claim that it was administratively more convenient to have the law structured in this way was not sufficient to justify the different treatment for men. *Wengler v. Druggist Mutual Insurance Co.,* 446 U.S. 142, 100 S.Ct. 1540, 64 L.Ed.2d 107 (1980).

- A widow received workers' compensation death benefits under a 1989 amendment to the workers' compensation statute. She received benefits for 13 years until the Georgia Insurers Insolvency Pool began handling her claim. It then suspended her benefits, asserting that she had received more than the required 400 weeks of benefits required. The amendment stated that death benefits would terminate at age 65 or after 400 weeks of payments, "whichever occur[red] first." Prior to the amendment, the law required payment until age 65 or 400 weeks, whichever was the greater amount. And in 1990, the law was amended again to provide the greater of amount of benefits between age 65 and 400 weeks. The case reached the Georgia Supreme Court, which found that the 1989 amendment was unconstitutional because it was ostensibly enacted to correct grammatical errors and modernize language, but in fact it substantively changed the amount of time a surviving spouse was eligible to receive death benefits. *Sherman Concrete Pipe Co. v. Chinn*, 660 S.E.2d 368 (Ga. 2008).

- The Colorado legislature amended its workers' compensation law to disallow permanent total disability benefits to injured workers ages 65 and older. Two 64-year-old workers injured in the course of their employment turned 65 during administrative proceedings concerning their claims for permanent total disability benefits. In both cases, the state industrial claim appeals office affirmed denial of the claims based upon the amendment. The cases reached the Colorado Supreme Court, which held that the legislation **unconstitutionally denied workers' compensation benefits to individuals 65 and older who were permanently and totally disabled**, while allowing partially disabled workers over age 65 and other classes of younger disabled individuals to continue receiving benefits. This unequal treatment for social security recipients was not justified. Unlike workers' compensation benefits, social security retirement benefits were pension payments and were not intended to compensate workers for loss of income from work-related injury. *Industrial Claim Appeals Office v. Romero*, 912 P.2d 62 (Colo. 1996).

- A Minnesota carpenter injured his back and was rated as having a 9% permanent partial disability of the whole body. He later was offered a job by another employer, but was required to answer a series of questions about whether he had ever made a workers' compensation claim and whether he had ever had a back injury. He answered "no" to each of the questions. When he injured his back again, he was not awarded workers' compensation benefits from the new employer because of his failure to answer the questionnaire truthfully. However, the Minnesota Supreme Court ruled that **the questions regarding his physical condition inquired into more than the essential job related functions of the position**, and thus violated the Minnesota Human Rights Act. As a result, the employer could not rely on his false answers as a defense to his claim for workers' compensation benefits. The court reversed the denial of benefits. *Huisenga v. Opus Corp.*, 494 N.W.2d 469 (Minn. 1992).

B. Retaliation

Employers should not <u>retaliate</u> against employees for filing workers' compensation claims. In many states, the workers' compensation act prohibits this; in some states, such action is a violation of public policy. For cases involving termination as a result of a workers' compensation filing, please see Chapter Three, Section IV.C.

◆ A staffing service employee in Kentucky injured his chest on the job at a car manufacturing plant. He was taken to the emergency room, then placed on work restrictions for five days. He was released to work early, but was not dressed properly at that time. He claimed that his supervisor did not insist he return to work that day. She claimed that she told him to change his clothes and return to work. When he didn't return to work that day, he was fired for excessive absenteeism. He sued the staffing service, alleging retaliation for filing a workers' compensation claim. A state court granted pretrial judgment to the staffing service, but the Kentucky Court of Appeals reversed. It found **issues of fact as to whether the service fired him for filing the workers' compensation claim**. It also stated that he was not entitled to pursue punitive damages arising from his claim. *Bishop v. Manpower, Inc. of Cent. Kentucky*, 211 S.W.3d 71 (Ky. Ct. App. 2006).

◆ An Alabama employee injured his knee on the job and received medical expenses from his employer. He settled his workers' compensation claim against the employer. After returning to the job, he re-injured the knee a few years later and again settled a workers' compensation claim with the employer. However, he continued to have problems with the knee, then injured his back because his knee wouldn't bend properly. He was then fired for attendance problems. When he sued for retaliation under the state's workers' compensation law, **a jury awarded him $400,000 in compensatory damages and $200,000 in punitive damages**. The Supreme Court of Alabama upheld the jury's verdict, finding sufficient evidence that the reason for the discharge was pretextual and that the true reason was the employee's workers' compensation claims. *Flint Construction Co. v. Hall*, 904 So.2d 236 (Ala. 2004).

◆ A Kansas grocery store manager took time off work for surgery on his arm and filed a workers' compensation claim. He was demoted to another position with a reduction in pay upon returning to work. He sued the employer for demoting him in retaliation for filing the workers' compensation claim, and the court granted pretrial judgment to the employer. The court of appeals affirmed, and the employee appealed to the Supreme Court of Kansas. The court observed that state supreme courts in Illinois and California have recognized legal causes of action based upon retaliatory demotion, despite arguments that recognition of the cause of action would involve judicial micro-management of the workplace and lead to trivial lawsuits based on minor employment matters. The court held that **a cause of action for retaliatory demotion was necessary to supplement the existing cause of action for retaliatory discharge** in order to prevent an employer from demoting, rather than discharging, an employee in retaliation for filing a workers' compensation claim. The court reversed the lower court judgments and remanded the case. *Brigham v. Dillon Companies, Inc.*, 935 P.2d 1054 (Kan. 1997).

◆ An Alabama manufacturing employee missed approximately five months of work due to an injury for which he received workers' compensation benefits. On his first day back on the job he injured his back while repairing machinery and was absent for another five months. Upon his return to work, the employer fired him for allegedly falsifying his original job application regarding his prior compensation claims history. The employee sued for retaliatory discharge and won. The Court of Civil Appeals of Alabama affirmed, finding sufficient evidence that **the employer had retaliated against the employee for filing workers' compensation claims**. The employee had successfully rebutted the alleged falsification of the employment application with evidence that he had been instructed by a human resources employee to indicate "no" in response to an ambiguous question concerning whether he had previously filed a claim. Evidence indicated that the employee reasonably believed that he was honestly indicating only that he had never filed a lawsuit to obtain benefits. *Beaulieu of America, Inc. v. Kilgore*, 680 So.2d 288 (Ala. Civ. App. 1996).

- The Court of Appeals of Texas affirmed a trial court ruling for the employer of an injured driver who was fired while off work under doctor's orders following a job-related injury. Although the employer had created a new position to accommodate the driver's back injury, he never responded to the employer's request for a return-to-work date. The court found sufficient evidence that **the discharge action had been a legitimate response to changed business conditions** and that the employer did not fire the driver for discriminatory reasons in violation of the state workers' compensation act. *Hogue v. Blue Bell Creameries, L.P.*, 922 S.W.2d 566 (Tex. Ct. App. 1996).

C. Employment Relationship Issues

Independent contractors are generally not entitled to workers' compensation benefits, though they can sue the "employers" if their injuries resulted from employer negligence. Illegal immigrants may be entitled to workers' compensation despite their status.

- An illegal alien used fraudulent documents to obtain a janitorial position with a company in Georgia. After she was injured on the job, she filed a claim for workers' compensation benefits. She obtained an administrative ruling in her favor, and the company appealed to the Georgia Court of Appeals, which affirmed the award of benefits. Even though federal law prohibited the employment of illegal aliens, the Immigration Reform and Control Act did not preempt state workers' compensation law so as to make the employment contract void. Further, since **there was no causal connection between the janitor's fraud and the injury she suffered**, her fraud could not be used to deny her benefits. *Continental PET Technologies, Inc. v. Palacias*, 604 S.E.2d 627 (Ga. Ct. App. 2004).

- An illegal immigrant injured his back while working as a maintenance worker for a Pennsylvania company. A workers' compensation judge determined that **even though he did not have proper Immigration and Naturalization Service documentation to work in the United States, he was entitled to benefits** under Pennsylvania's workers' compensation act. The case reached the Commonwealth Court of Pennsylvania, which agreed that the worker was entitled to benefits. It joined courts in New Jersey, Florida,

Louisiana and Oklahoma in finding illegal immigrants eligible for workers' compensation. To disallow benefits would be to potentially subvert the public policy against illegal immigration because employers might seek out illegal aliens who would not have to be paid workers' compensation. The court also held that the company could not suspend benefits on the ground that the immigrant would be unavailable for suitable alternative employment.

The Pennsylvania Supreme Court upheld the ruling that the illegal alien was entitled to workers' compensation benefits. It then held that the commonwealth court should not have required the employer to present evidence for purposes of the suspension of benefits that jobs were referred to or available to the immigrant. When an employer seeks to suspend workers' compensation benefits that have been granted to an illegal alien, a showing of job availability by the employer is not required. However, since the workers' compensation judge did not address the company's contention that benefits had to be suspended, the court remanded the case for a determination on that issue. *Reinforced Earth Co. v. WCAB*, 810 A.2d 99 (Pa. 2002).

◆ An undocumented alien lost a finger in an assembly line accident and later experienced psychological injuries including posttraumatic stress disorder and severe depression. The employer accepted responsibility for medical and temporary disability benefits but contested his claim for continuing medical benefits and psychiatric treatment. A workers' compensation judge denied the claim. The Superior Court of New Jersey, Appellate Division, noted that **the workers' compensation system is fundamentally different than the unemployment compensation system (which disqualifies illegal aliens)**. The system was based on a contractual remedy that replaced the common law right of an employee to seek damages for personal injuries against employers. The compensation judge had improperly attempted to transport unemployment compensation principles to this claim. The court reversed and remanded the case. *Mendoza v. Monmouth Recycling Corp.*, 288 N.J. Super. 240, 672 A.2d 221 (N.J. Super. Ct. App. Div. 1996).

◆ A Colorado man worked for a ski resort as a part-time ski instructor in exchange for a ski pass that allowed him to ski free at any time at the resort. Subsequently, the resort notified its ski instructors that it needed persons with CPR qualifications and first aid training to work on ski patrol. The instructor was qualified for this position, and, because he already had a free pass, he negotiated an agreement with the ski patrol director to receive daily ski passes for his girlfriend in exchange for his work. He then fell while on ski patrol duty and injured his knees. His workers' compensation claim was contested on the ground that he was a volunteer and not entitled to benefits. An administrative law judge determined that he was an employee, and the court of appeals affirmed. The Supreme Court of Colorado agreed that the instructor was an employee of the resort under the basic definition of that term. Here, the instructor negotiated with his employer and agreed to work only in exchange for the benefit of daily passes for his girlfriend. The court rejected the resort's argument that the instructor was expressly excluded from the definition of employee by an amendment to the workers' compensation act which stated that a "person who volunteers his time or services as a ski patrol person ... for a passenger tramway operator ..." is not an employee. It did not matter that the instructor was not paid wages by the resort. **Because he specifically bargained for daily passes for his girlfriend, he was not a volunteer**, even if he would have been a volunteer had he only received ski passes for himself. The instructor was entitled to benefits. *Aspen Highlands Skiing Corp. v. Apostolou*, 866 P.2d 1384 (Colo. 1994).

- A South Carolina carpenter was hired by a subcontractor to work on a residential site. On his first day of work, he fell from a two-story high scaffold and was severely injured. He sought workers' compensation benefits from the contractor. The Workers' Compensation Commission awarded benefits, and the contractor appealed to the Supreme Court of South Carolina. The contractor contended that it was not the carpenter's statutory employer. However, the court noted that the contractor sent a letter to its insurer admitting the contractor-subcontractor relationship. Next, the contractor argued that the employee was required to establish that his immediate employer was financially irresponsible before bringing a claim against his statutory employer. However, the court noted that section 42-1-410 does not expressly require proof of the immediate employer's inability to pay. Rather, **the contractor was entitled to indemnity from the immediate employer (subcontractor)** and could either bring a separate action against him for indemnification or join him as a defendant in the action brought by the injured employee. Thus, the court upheld the decision of the Workers' Compensation Commission awarding benefits to the injured employee. *Long v. Atlantic Homes*, 428 S.E.2d 711 (S.C. 1993).

D. Other Issues

The following cases address various workers' compensation issues.

- Under Pennsylvania's Workers' Compensation Act, once an employer becomes liable for an employee's work-related injury, the employer or its insurer must pay for all reasonable and necessary medical treatment. The law was amended in 1993 to provide that where there is a disputed treatment, an insurer may withhold payment pending an independent "utilization review." A number of employees and employee representatives sued various insurers and self-insured entities under the Fourteenth Amendment and 42 U.S.C. § 1983, alleging that the withholding of payments without notice and an opportunity to be heard violated their due process rights. The case reached the U.S. Supreme Court, which stated that **the mere fact that a private business is subject to extensive state regulation does not by itself convert the business' actions into state action**. Here, the amendment to the workers' compensation statute allowing withholding and an independent review was not state authorization of insurers' actions. It was merely a decision not to intervene in disputes over whether particular treatments were reasonable and medically necessary. Further, even if there was state action, because the employees were not entitled to payment for medical treatment until the treatment at issue was found to be reasonable and necessary, there was no deprivation of their property rights under the Fourteenth Amendment. *American Manufacturers Mutual Insurance Co. v. Sullivan*, 526 U.S. 40, 119 S.Ct. 977, 143 L.Ed.2d 130 (1999).

- An undocumented worker in New York caught his right hand in a printing press and severed four fingers, two of which had to be amputated. The state workers' compensation board awarded him temporary disability benefits, and he interviewed with the board's office of rehabilitation regarding his return to work. He was referred to a vocational office for people with disabilities, but was ineligible for services because he was an illegal alien. After his temporary benefits ended, he sought additional disability benefits, but the New York Court of Appeals held that he was not entitled to them. One of the requirements for obtaining workers' compensation benefits beyond the initial award is that the worker participate in a board-approved work rehabilitation program. Since **the worker here was an illegal alien**, he could not do so. *Ramroop v. Flexo-Craft Printing, Inc.*, 896 N.E.2d 69 (N.Y. 2008).

- An illegal immigrant working for a company in Maryland injured his hand and required several surgeries. When he filed for workers' compensation, the company claimed that he did not qualify because of his resident status and the fact that he did not have a Social Security number. As such, he was not authorized to work in the U.S. under the Immigration Reform and Control Act. The case reached the Maryland Court of Appeals, which ruled that **the illegal immigrant was entitled to benefits**. The state's workers' compensation law only requires that an employee be "in the service of an employer" under "an express or implied contract of apprenticeship or hire." Because the employee met both of those conditions, it did not matter if he was unlawfully employed. *Design Kitchen and Baths v. Lagos*, 882 A.2d 817 (Md. 2005).

- An investment firm employee died in the terrorist attacks on 9/11. He had a fiancée and a 22-month-old daughter by a previous relationship. A dispute arose between the daughter and the fiancée over workers' compensation benefits. The case reached the New York Supreme Court, Appellate Division, which ruled that the daughter was entitled to $180 per week and the fiancée was entitled to $220. Workers' Compensation Law Section 4 provided that domestic partners of employees killed in the 9/11 terrorist attacks were eligible for the same benefits as surviving spouses. Even though the daughter would have received $400 per week if her father was killed at work on some other day, **the legislature permissibly created greater domestic partner rights for 9/11 victims' dependents**. *In re Novara*, 795 N.Y.S.2d 133 (N.Y. App. Div. 2005).

- A tool and die maker began experiencing pain in his forearms but did not report the problem to the shop foreman or complete an accident report until an incident of sharp pain occurred. After several months, the employee was diagnosed with carpal tunnel syndrome, and he filed for workers' compensation benefits. Between the time he had reported the pain and the diagnosis of carpal tunnel syndrome, the company had switched workers' compensation insurers. A question arose as to which of the two insurers was liable. The Pennsylvania

Commonwealth Court agreed with the Workers' Compensation Appeals Board that even though the injury was a cumulative one which developed over a period of time, **the date of injury for workers' compensation purposes was the date the injury was diagnosed**, making the second insurer liable. *Piad Corp. v. WCAB*, 761 A.2d 640 (Pa. Commw. Ct. 2000).

◆ A Texas staff leasing company chose not to provide workers' compensation insurance coverage to the employees it leased to other companies. When a corporation leased a number of workers from the leasing company, the state workers' compensation insurance fund sent it a premium, billing it for the workers as a co-employer. The Texas Supreme Court ruled that the corporation was not obligated to pay the premium. **The staff leasing company had the exclusive right to elect whether to obtain workers' compensation insurance coverage for its leased employees.** Because it had chosen not to do so, the corporation was not obligated to provide coverage either. *Texas Workers' Compensation Insurance Fund v. DEL Industrial, Inc.*, 35 S.W.3d 591 (Tex. 2000).

◆ A West Virginia truck driver submitted an accident report and claim for workers' compensation benefits after he was injured in a work-related incident. The employer's labor relations representative declared on the employer's portion of the form that there was no known job-related injury, and the employer denied the claim. The employee was subsequently awarded benefits by the state workers' compensation fund. He then sued the employer for fraud. The Supreme Court of Appeals of West Virginia held that an employee may maintain a private cause of action for fraud against an employer for the **employer's knowing and intentional filing of a false statement with the state workers' compensation fund**. The driver had described sufficient facts to support a claim for fraudulent misrepresentation by alleging that the employer had maliciously and knowingly filed a false report with the state. *Persinger v. Peabody Coal Co.*, 976 F.Supp. 1038 (S.D. W. Va. 1997).

◆ A clothing manufacturer operating plants throughout the U.S. contracted with an insurer to provide workers' compensation insurance at all its facilities. It gave notice to employees at an Oklahoma plant that it would close the following month, and 108 different employees submitted a total of 429 workers' compensation claims within the next few weeks. The insurer assigned reserve amounts for each claim and transferred claims data to the National Council on Compensation Insurance, resulting in a drastically increased experience rating modification and an increase in premiums from less than $800,000 to $6.8 million annually. The employer alleged that the insurer improperly agreed to settle claims totaling $4.8 million. It sued the insurer in a Kentucky court, alleging that excessive loss reserves, improper claim settlements and the increase in its insurance rating caused severe economic hardship. The employer later filed for bankruptcy. The Kentucky federal court granted the insurer pretrial judgment. The Sixth Circuit affirmed the findings that the insurer had not breached the insurance contract or failed to act in good faith by settling the claims. **Each of the actions by the insurer corresponded to its contractual**

rights or duties and did not satisfy the standard for intentional wrongful conduct necessary to prevail in a bad faith insurance action. *Big Yank Corp. v. Liberty Mutual Fire Insurance Co.*, 125 F.3d 308 (6th Cir. 1997).

◆ A Maine employee became quadriplegic in a work-related incident and was unable to work. She required a specially adapted wheelchair and personal care assistants because of her low blood pressure, dizziness and fainting. The employer agreed to purchase a specially adapted van to accommodate her needs. Five years later, the former employee petitioned the Workers' Compensation Board for the cost of a replacement van. The employer agreed to pay for the cost of adapting a new van but refused to pay for the van itself or for the housekeeping activities of two part-time assistants employed by her. The board found that the van was not a physical aid under state law and that the employer did not have to purchase it. It also held that the claim for housekeeping expenses should be denied. The Supreme Judicial Court of Maine observed that **state law required the replacement or renewal of physical aids when necessary due to wear and tear**. Because of her severe disability and the absence of any other available transportation except an ambulance, the van should be considered a reasonable and proper mechanical aid under state law. Accordingly, the employer had to pay for the entire cost of the adapted van. The employee was also entitled to the amounts claimed for housekeeping performed by her personal assistants. *Brawn v. Gloria's Country Inn*, 1997 ME 191, 698 A.2d 1067 (Me. 1997).

◆ In a case involving **sick building syndrome** and exposure to volatile organic compounds, the Supreme Court of Nebraska found that even though the employer had stipulated to partial liability, it had reserved the right to challenge the actual personal injury to the individual claimants, who bore the burden of proving their illnesses. *US West Communications, Inc. v. Taborski*, 253 Neb. 770, 572 N.W.2d 81 (Neb. 1998).

◆ A New Jersey man was shot and killed on the job by the mentally disabled boyfriend of a co-employee. His significant other filed for workers' compensation dependency benefits, contending that she was the **"de facto" wife of the decedent**. The Superior Court of New Jersey, Appellate Division, noted that "de facto" claims have only been sustained when "the surviving petitioner had entered into a ceremonial marriage unaware of any marital impediment on the part of the decedent employee." The parties here did not enter into a ceremonial marriage, and the woman was well aware of her single status. Thus, she was not entitled to dependency benefits. *Toms v. Dee Rose Furniture,* 621 A.2d 91 (N.J. Super. Ct. App. Div. 1993).

◆ A part-time newspaper carrier employed by a New Jersey newspaper also held another full-time job. While delivering newspapers, a truck collided with her car. She suffered severe injuries and suffered a 55% permanent partial disability. She applied for workers' compensation benefits. She had worked 17 and a half hours each week for the newspaper and had been paid at the hourly rate of $8.73. **The workers' compensation court calculated recovery on a**

reconstructed 40-hour workweek. The employer appealed to the Superior Court, Appellate Division. The appellate court reversed the decision and calculated benefits on an actual workweek based on part-time hours. The employee then appealed to the Supreme Court of New Jersey, which reversed the decision of the appellate court and upheld the workers' compensation award. *Katsoris v. South Jersey Publishing Co.,* 622 A.2d 219 (N.J. 1993).

- A woman worked for a company and suffered a compensable lower back injury. She was treated by several physicians, and she and the company ultimately agreed upon an authorized treating physician. The employee later requested the company to authorize treatment by another physician, and the company refused. Subsequently, surgery was performed on the employee by the unauthorized physician. The employee filed for workers' compensation, and the commission directed the company to pay for the surgery. The Court of Appeals of Virginia held that although the physician who performed the surgery was not the authorized physician, the company was required to pay for the surgery. The employee benefited appreciably from it, and the evidence showed that the extent of her injury was actually greater than that determined by her authorized treating physician. The court found that the employee had **acted in good faith by trying to seek the approval of her treating physician and the company before the surgery**, and that the surgery was both medically reasonable and necessary. The evidence supported the award of medical expenses to the unauthorized treating physician. *Shenandoah Products, Inc. v. Whitlock,* 421 S.E.2d 483 (Va. Ct. App. 1992).

CHAPTER EIGHT

Unemployment Compensation

Page

I. VOLUNTARY SEPARATION

Although the Federal Unemployment Tax Act establishes certain minimum federal standards that states must satisfy in order to participate in the program, the act leaves to state discretion the rules governing the administration of unemployment compensation programs.

Under state laws, there are three general requirements that must be satisfied for a claimant to be eligible for unemployment benefits:

1) A claimant must earn a specified amount of wages or work a specified number of weeks in covered employment during a one-year base period in order to be entitled to receive benefits,

2) A claimant must be able to work and be available for work in order to be eligible, and
3) A claimant must not be disqualified for the reasons set forth in the state's law.

The most common reasons for disqualification under state unemployment compensation laws are:

—voluntarily leaving the job without good cause attributable to the employer,
—participating in a strike,
—being discharged for misconduct, and
—refusing suitable work.

This first section deals with issues of voluntary separation.

A. Labor Stoppages

Many states have enacted unemployment compensation labor dispute disqualification statutes that prevent strikers from obtaining benefits.

Some statutes allow strikers to obtain benefits under certain circumstances, such as when the employer hires permanent replacement workers. However, other statutes require strikers to abandon the strike and put forth an unconditional offer to return to work.

1. Disqualification

If an employee is deemed to have caused his own unemployment by going out on strike, he generally will not be able to collect unemployment compensation.

◆ A Michigan statute made employees ineligible for unemployment compensation benefits if they provided "financing," by means other than the payment of regular union dues, for a strike that caused their unemployment. Employees of General Motors were required by their union to pay "emergency dues" to augment the union's strike insurance fund. Several local unions went on strike, curtailing operations at other plants. Strike fund benefits were paid to all the workers who were idle. They then sought unemployment compensation benefits but were denied such benefits by the Michigan Supreme Court. The U.S. Supreme Court agreed with the lower court that the employees' payment of emergency dues amounted to "financing" of the strikes that caused the unemployment. Even though federal labor law protects employee rights to authorize a strike, it does not prohibit a state from **disallowing unemployment benefits to employees who cause their own unemployment**. The decision to participate in the strike caused the unemployment in this case, making it voluntary rather than involuntary. The Court affirmed the Michigan Supreme Court's decision denying benefits. *Baker v. General Motors Corp.*, 478 U.S. 621, 106 S.Ct. 3129, 92 L.Ed.2d 504 (1986).

◆ Employees of a nursing home in Pennsylvania went out on strike after the union was unable to negotiate a new collective bargaining agreement. The nursing home then hired replacement workers and sent letters to each striking employee, promising the increased wages and better benefits from its last offer to the union if they would return to work. Six weeks later, the nursing home rescinded its imposition of the new contract terms and invited the striking workers back to work under the terms of the expired bargaining agreement. The strike continued for several months until the union made an unconditional offer to return to work. A number of strikers sought unemployment compensation for the entire period of the strike. The question of whether the nursing home had converted the strike into a lockout reached the Commonwealth Court of Pennsylvania. It held that the letters to the striking employees and the hiring of replacement workers did not convert the strike into a lockout. **The union failed to prove that it was willing to return to work in accordance with the terms of the expired bargaining agreement during the strike.** The employees were not entitled to unemployment benefits. *Presbyterian SeniorCare v. Unemployment Compensation Board of Review*, 900 A.2d 967 (Pa. Commw. Ct. 2006).

◆ Honolulu contracted with a private nonprofit corporation to provide bus services for the city. After notifying the corporation that its budget would be reduced by $10 million, Honolulu entered into negotiations for a new labor agreement. When they failed to reach one, the union called a strike. The corporation then locked its gates for security reasons until a new agreement was reached five weeks later. When individual drivers filed for unemployment benefits for the five weeks they were off work, the unemployment commission denied them. The union appealed, but the Hawaii Supreme Court agreed with the decision to deny benefits. Even though Honolulu had not required transit services to be provided during the strike, **the strike caused "substantial curtailment of business activity" disqualifying the drivers from unemployment benefits**. This was not a lockout because the lack of work was caused by the labor dispute. The lockout was strictly for safety reasons. *Hawaii Teamsters and Allied Workers, Local 966 v. Dep't of Labor and Industrial Relations*, 132 P.3d 368 (Haw. 2006).

◆ The collective bargaining agreement between a health care system in Pennsylvania and a nurses' association expired, and the union notified the employer that it intended to initiate a two-day work stoppage. The employer responded that it would hire replacement nurses, and it did so. The union offered to return to work under the terms of the expired bargaining agreement. They would then commence another two-day work stoppage eight days later. Shortly thereafter, the union and the employer signed a tentative agreement for the nurses to return to work. They returned to their jobs after being out of work for three weeks. Over 300 nurses sought unemployment compensation for two of the three weeks they were out of work, agreeing that they were disqualified during the first week because that work stoppage was a strike, but asserting that the second and third weeks were a lockout. The Commonwealth Court of Pennsylvania disagreed, finding that the whole three-week period was a strike, disqualifying the nurses from benefits. **The offer to return to work was not an offer to return to work for a reasonable period of time because of the threat to strike eight days later.** *Skrzysowski v. Unemployment Compensation Board of Review*, 862 A.2d 696 (Pa. Commw. Ct. 2004).

- The Supreme Court of Oregon affirmed the denial of unemployment compensation claims by a group of employees who were locked out of their workplaces during a labor dispute. Oregon law disqualifies employees from receiving unemployment compensation benefits because of a labor dispute with no exception for lockouts. The employers belonged to a multi-employer collective bargaining group, and not all of them had locked out their employees. Since this resulted in only a partial lockout, the employees argued that the work they had lost had not been as the result of a labor dispute. The court found no such distinction in state law even though not all of the employers had excluded employees from their workplaces. Since **the unemployment had resulted from a labor dispute**, the court affirmed the decision to deny benefits. *Abu-Adas v. Employment Dep't, Food Employers, Inc.*, 325 Or. 480, 940 P.2d 1219 (Or. 1997).

- Employees represented by the United Auto Workers called a strike after the union was unable to negotiate a new contract for Alabama aircraft product workers. Several weeks after the strike began, the employer hired permanent replacement employees. The union workers then filed claims for unemployment compensation that were denied because the unemployment was directly caused by a labor dispute. The Supreme Court of Alabama upheld the denial of benefits. It observed that unemployment compensation labor dispute disqualification statutes could be typed into two categories. The first, described as the "stoppage of work" statutes, included Michigan, Indiana, Ohio, Colorado, and California. In these states, the mere hiring of permanent replacement workers lifted the statutory labor dispute disqualification. The other statutes were described as "labor dispute in active progress" statutes, which were used in Wisconsin, Minnesota, Tennessee, Oregon and Arizona. In those states, replaced striking employees were required to show abandonment of the strike and an unconditional offer to return to work before the labor dispute disqualification could be lifted. Alabama followed the second type and its statute contained language that **a labor dispute could exist regardless of whether the disputants had an employer-employee relationship**. The use of replacement workers was not an event that ended the statutory disqualification for unemployment benefits. *Ex parte Williams,* 646 So.2d 22 (Ala. 1994).

2. Exceptions

Unemployment benefits can be awarded where:

—striking employees are permanently replaced (and thus no longer have jobs),
—employees are subjected to a lockout by the employer,
—the employer unilaterally imposes terms and conditions of employment

on striking workers, and
—employees refuse to cross a picket line for safety reasons.

◆ After the union for 44 workers at an Ohio company failed to reach an agreement on a new bargaining agreement, its members voted to strike. The company then hired permanent replacement workers and three weeks later notified the strikers by letter that their positions had been permanently filled. When the strikers applied for unemployment benefits, a hearing officer determined that **they were entitled to benefits from the point of the letter informing them that their jobs were lost**. The company appealed. The case reached the Supreme Court of Ohio, which agreed that the strikers were entitled to unemployment benefits from the date of the letter. At that point, the labor dispute became a lockout. The company's actions permanently severed the employment relationship and removed the disqualification to benefits. *M. Conley Co. v. Anderson*, 842 N.E.2d 1037 (Ohio 2006).

◆ Approximately 650 employees of a tire factory in Iowa walked off the job, claiming the company was committing unfair labor practices. The company asserted that the real reason for the strike was economic such that replacement workers could be hired. Weeks later, the company sent out a final offer and notified employees their positions would be filled by permanent replacement workers if they failed to return to work. Most of the strikers stayed away. When they filed for unemployment compensation benefits, the Employment Appeal Board and the Supreme Court of Iowa ruled that they were entitled to them. Here, **the company had severed its relationship with the strikers, ending their disqualification for benefits**. It hired replacement workers, transferred production to Texas and failed to notify the union that jobs remained for those strikers who wished to return to work. *Titan Tire Corp. v. Employment Appeal Board*, 641 N.W.2d 752 (Iowa 2002).

◆ In anticipation of a labor dispute, a company issued a pamphlet entitled "Rules of Conduct for Striking Employees." The rules set forth grounds for discharge based on certain conduct. Its employees struck as a result of the dispute, and the company determined that six workers who were participating in the strike also engaged in misconduct prohibited by the rules. The company terminated the workers, and they sought unemployment benefits under Illinois law. A state claims adjudicator granted their requests for benefits, and the company appealed to the Appellate Court of Illinois. Under the relevant statute, a worker becomes ineligible for unemployment benefits if his unemployment "is due to a stoppage of work, which exists because of a labor dispute … [where] he was last employed." However, **once an employee on strike is discharged for misconduct, he or she no longer has an expectation to return to work and is no longer disqualified** by virtue of participating in the strike. The court rejected the argument that its ruling would encourage striking employees to engage in misconduct or violence to circumvent the statute's eligibility requirement. It noted that employees discharged for misconduct are ineligible to receive benefits. *Caterpillar, Inc. v. Dep't of Employment Security*, 710 N.E.2d 890 (Ill. App. Ct. 1999).

◆ Union employees of an Iowa tire manufacturer struck for over 10 months. The employer began hiring permanent replacements after several months. It notified many of the striking employees by letter that they had been permanently replaced but would be entitled to preferential hiring rights if they made an unconditional offer to return to work and if a vacancy existed. A number of strikers obtained unemployment compensation benefits. The employer appealed to an administrative law judge, who found that the hiring of replacement workers and the employer's renewed production activity ended the stoppage of work, removing the strikers' disqualification from benefits. The Supreme Court of Iowa observed that the notification of permanent replacement removed the disqualification from unemployment benefits. Because **employees receiving letters of their permanent replacement no longer had an employment relationship with the employer and were not otherwise disqualified**, they were entitled to benefits. *Bridgestone/Firestone, Inc. v. Employment Appeal Board*, 570 N.W.2d 85 (Iowa 1997).

◆ The Supreme Court of Michigan consolidated appeals from the state Employment Security Board of Review involving claims by striking employees for unemployment compensation benefits where each of the employees accepted interim employment from at least one other employer after a labor dispute. Some of the employees, after first becoming ineligible for unemployment benefits during a labor dispute, requalified for benefits after obtaining interim employment for a combined period of two weeks through a union hiring hall. The hiring hall employment included jobs from more than one employer, and the struck employers argued that acceptance of work from multiple employers would encourage make-work employment and bad faith acceptance of interim employment. In another case, a number of employees appealed a decision reversing their awards on grounds that they had not acted in good faith in obtaining interim employment subsequent to a labor dispute. The supreme court found **no statutory requirement of good-faith acceptance of interim employment as a prerequisite to obtaining unemployment compensation benefits**. Also, the statute did not disallow requalification simply because employees accepted interim employment from more than one employer. The employees prevailed. *Empire Iron Mining Partnership v. Orhanen*, 565 N.W.2d 844 (Mich. 1997).

B. Discrimination and Harassment

Discrimination and harassment (e.g., sexual or racial) may constitute good cause for leaving employment, thereby entitling the employee to unemployment compensation benefits.

Some courts have also found that an employee who quits after failing to report workplace harassment to company officials is not disqualified from receiving benefits.

◆ A 28-year employee of a bank in Pennsylvania quit her job and applied for unemployment benefits, which the bank fought. She claimed that she was subjected to verbal abuse and harassment by a senior vice president and by the bank president, who also disciplined her unfairly after she spoke out about the harassment by the senior vice president. The unemployment compensation board of review reversed the hearing officer and found that the employee had a necessitous and compelling cause for voluntarily leaving her employment. The bank appealed. The Commonwealth Court of Pennsylvania affirmed the ruling in favor of the employee. Here, **the discipline, criticism and ridicule she was subjected to justified her action in quitting the job**. *First Federal Savings Bank v. Unemployment Compensation Board of Review*, 957 A.2d 811 (Pa. Commw. Ct. 2008).

- An employee of a manufacturer in Missouri went to the human resources (HR) department and told the HR administrator that his supervisor regularly "cussed him out, degraded him, humiliated and disrespected him," and that he wanted to be transferred to another department. The HR administrator told the employee she would first have to investigate the allegations, but the employee quit after the meeting. He later filed for unemployment compensation benefits. The question of his eligibility reached the Missouri Court of Appeals, which ruled against him. Here, if the employee's allegations were true, then he would have good cause to leave his work under state unemployment law. However, **he was first required to give the HR administrator a chance to investigate and resolve the situation**. Since he did not do so, he was not entitled to unemployment benefits. *Winco Manufacturing, Inc. v. Partee*, 141 S.W.3d 34 (Mo. Ct. App. 2004).

- A female employee at a New York company complained that someone deliberately left pubic hair on the toilet seat in the restroom near her work station. The company discussed the matter with her and the co-worker she believed was responsible for the action. Shortly thereafter, she shouted at the co-worker, and when she was warned about her behavior, she stopped coming to work and informed the employer that she had no choice but to leave the job. When she filed a claim for unemployment benefits, she was initially awarded $2,000. However, the labor department later found her ineligible and sought repayment of the money. The Supreme Court, Appellate Division, ruled that the employee's frustration with the situation did not constitute good cause to leave the job because **she did not show that her safety was ever compromised**. The employee had to repay the benefits she received. *In re Gully*, 778 N.Y.S.2d 212 (N.Y. App. Div. 2004).

- A human resources manager filed an employment discrimination complaint against her employer. The parties settled their dispute under an agreement that required the employee to resign. She negotiated language in the agreement that characterized her separation as voluntary retirement, in order to become eligible for certain retirement benefits. She then applied for unemployment compensation benefits and testified before an administrative appeals board that she had retired only because the settlement agreement required her to do so. The board awarded benefits, and the Court of Appeals of Arizona affirmed. Even though the employee had voluntarily entered into the settlement agreement, her primary reason for doing so was to settle her discrimination complaint and not to retire. Because she intended to continue working, the employer was the moving party in the termination. **Employment separation that results from an employer's intent and action is properly characterized as a discharge.** Since the employee had no independent desire to quit her job, but had been compelled to do so by the settlement agreement, she was entitled to benefits. *California Portland Cement Co. v. Arizona Dep't of Economic Security*, 960 P.2d 65 (Ariz. Ct. App. 1998).

◆ A North Carolina employee endured sexual harassment by her immediate supervisor for several years. Although she was offended and intimidated, she never told him to stop and failed to report the harassment to upper management as specified in her employer's anti-harassment policy. She felt that any report to management would not be believed. She eventually quit and applied for unemployment compensation benefits. An appeals referee determined that she had not left her work for good cause attributable to the employer because of her failure to abide by its anti-harassment policy. Because the employer was deprived of an opportunity to remedy the situation, she was not entitled to benefits. The state employment security commission affirmed the referee's decision. The case reached the Court of Appeals of North Carolina, which held that **sexual harassment constitutes good cause for quitting under the state unemployment compensation law**. The failure to report sexual harassment according to the employer's policy did not disqualify the employee from receiving benefits. *Marlow v. North Carolina Employment Security Comm'n*, 493 S.E.2d 302 (N.C. Ct. App. 1997).

◆ A Missouri restaurant employee claimed that his employer subjected him to repeated name-calling and shouting during his year of part-time employment. After failing to report to work one day, he filed for unemployment compensation benefits and called the employer several days later to report that he would not return. The state Labor and Industrial Relations Commission denied his claim for unemployment, and an appeals tribunal affirmed the decision. The employee appealed to the Missouri Court of Appeals, which agreed with him that **abusive behavior by an employer that would be unacceptable to a reasonable person is sufficient good cause to quit** under state law. It rejected the employer's and commission's argument that no reasonable person would have quit under the circumstances and that the employee had demonstrated bad faith in failing to resolve the problem before quitting. The duration of the harassment was not a defense for the employer's behavior. The court of appeals reversed the commission's decision. *Streitz v. Juneau*, 940 S.W.2d 548 (Mo. Ct. App. 1997).

C. Layoffs and Transfers

Voluntary separations based on layoffs generally will not disqualify an employee from benefits. However, some courts have found that where the employer does not actually lay off any employees, and uncertainty about future employment does not establish good cause for quitting, benefits may be denied.

In other words, where an employee has notice that layoffs are likely to occur and decides to resign instead of being laid off, she may not be entitled to benefits if the layoffs do not in fact occur. However, if layoffs are announced and the employee volunteers to be laid off early, she may still be entitled to benefits.

Where an employee refuses a transfer to another work site or position, he may not be entitled to benefits where the transfer request was reasonable. However, where the requested transfer is to a distant location (e.g., another city) or to a position that is unreasonable (e.g., more dangerous but with less pay and seniority), the employee may be entitled to benefits.

◆ A supervisor for a company that cleaned and maintained shopping carts drove his mobile maintenance unit to the customers' places of business to repair their shopping carts and also sell them carts and spare parts. His contract called for him to work a 260-day work year and awarded him compensatory time on a one-to-one basis for each day he worked over the 260 days. He was laid off for three months, and during that time he received compensatory pay for working Saturdays and Sundays during the prior year. He also obtained unemployment compensation benefits. The Nebraska Department of Labor determined that he had been overpaid unemployment benefits by $2,000 and sought to recover that amount. However, the Supreme Court of Nebraska ruled that **the deferred compensatory wages he received were actually earned during his time of employment, not while he was laid off**. As a result, the supervisor was not "employed" during his layoff and was thus entitled to the benefits. *Wadkins v. Lecuona*, 740 N.W.2d 34 (Neb. 2007).

◆ A number of employees of Verizon accepted voluntary termination offers and then filed for unemployment benefits, claiming that they quit only because layoffs were imminent. Some had received written or verbal notice informing them of downsizing in their departments. The case reached the Commonwealth Court of Pennsylvania, which examined whether the circumstances surrounding the voluntary quitting indicated a likelihood that fears about serious impending threats to the job were well-founded. In other words, were their fears about imminent layoffs justified. It determined that, with one possible exception, the claimants were not entitled to recover benefits because **their belief that layoffs were imminent was mere speculation**. Thus, they could not show that they had a necessitous and compelling cause for voluntarily ending their employment. *Johnson v. Unemployment Compensation Board of Review*, 869 A.2d 1095 (Pa. Commw. Ct. 2005).

◆ An Indiana bank restructured its loan department, eliminating some positions and moving others to another city. After an employee's position was eliminated, she signed a release, which stated that she had offered to resign and which provided for a severance payment in exchange. The agreement also stated that acceptance of the severance pay constituted an accord and satisfaction of all claims against the bank. The employee applied for and received unemployment compensation benefits, testifying in administrative proceedings that she had left the employment because her job had been eliminated and that she did not voluntarily resign. The bank appealed to the Court of Appeals of Indiana, which held that the employee had been laid off due to lack of work. The release she signed to obtain severance pay was ambiguous because it implied that she might receive additional pay and was therefore not the final resolution of all employment matters involving the parties. Because **the employee had not resigned but had voluntarily left for good cause**, the award of benefits was affirmed. *Salin Bank and Trust Co. v. Review Board of Indiana Dep't of Workforce Development*, 698 N.E.2d 1 (Ind. Ct. App. 1998).

◆ A Massachusetts electronic technician complained repeatedly to her supervisors about her job conditions, believing that male co-workers received better pay and advancement opportunities. The employer transferred her to the company's automotive products division, allegedly to accommodate her need for advancement. However, the new assignment was at the same level as her previous position, and the employee refused to report because of concerns about chemical exposure and possible allergic reactions. The employer fired her. The state commissioner of employment and training found that the employee had left her job voluntarily and was disqualified from receiving unemployment benefits. The Appeals Court of Massachusetts stated that a departure from work must be both voluntary and without good cause attributable to the employer to be deemed a voluntary separation. An employee forced to quit because of compelling personal circumstances is deemed to have left work involuntarily. Here, both employer and employee stated that **the employee was discharged for failing to report to her new job assignment**. The record lacked substantial evidence that the employee had voluntarily quit. The commission had erroneously disqualified her from benefits on that basis. The court remanded the case for another hearing. *Potris v. Commissioner of Dep't of Employment and Training*, 679 N.E.2d 605 (Mass. App. Ct. 1997).

◆ A Washington regional sales manager accepted an early retirement settlement from his employer after it announced that his department would be eliminated within one year. The company announced a 10% staff reduction but did not actually lay off any employees. The company eventually attained its work force reduction goal without any layoffs. The sales manager's application for unemployment compensation benefits was granted. A trial court reversed, and the manager appealed. The Court of Appeals of Washington stated that unemployed workers are not entitled to receive unemployment benefits if they voluntarily leave work without good cause. **An employee is not disqualified from receiving benefits where the employer announces a layoff, even where the employee volunteers to be laid off.** However, because the employer did not actually lay off any employees, and uncertainty about future employment did not establish good cause for quitting, the trial court order denying benefits was affirmed. *Goewert v. Employment Security Dep't of State of Washington*, 919 P.2d 106 (Wash. Ct. App. 1996).

◆ An Alabama steel producer advised employees of substantial losses and proposed a layoff to avoid a plant closing. A group of employees accepted a work force reduction inducement agreement that called for either periodic or lump sum payments. They applied for unemployment compensation benefits, but their claims were denied. The Alabama Court of Civil Appeals determined that whether voluntary employment termination disqualifies an employee from receiving unemployment compensation benefits depends on whether the separation is reasonable as measured by what the average worker would have done in similar situations. The appellate court considered testimony by longtime plant employees faced with increased workloads and wage reductions of up to $645 per month. One employee testified that he would lose an assistant, which could jeopardize his safety. These factors were reasonable and sufficient to motivate the average employee to accept the work force reduction agreement. Accordingly, **the employees had carried their burden of proving that the employment separation was for good cause connected with their work**, and the court held that they were entitled to unemployment compensation benefits. *Director, State Dep't of Industrial Relations v. Jones*, 669 So.2d 170 (Ala. Civ. App. 1995).

D. Medical and Personal Reasons

Certain medical and personal reasons may be deemed necessitous and compelling to allow the employee to recover unemployment benefits. If an employer offers the employee an alternative position to help alleviate the problems associated with the reason, however, the employee's refusal of the accommodation may result in a denial of benefits.

1. Medical Reasons

As a general rule, employees who quit their jobs for medical reasons will *not* be entitled to unemployment compensation benefits. However, if the medical condition is attributable to the employment or is somehow caused by the employment, benefits might be payable.

◆ A Missouri woman worked for a company for about three years and then requested a leave of absence due to pregnancy. The company granted her a "leave without guarantee of reinstatement," which meant that she would only be rehired if a position was available when she was ready to return to work. When she later notified the company of her willingness to return to work, no positions were available. She filed a claim for unemployment compensation benefits, which was denied. A trial court held that the statute – which disqualifies a claimant who has left work voluntarily without good cause attributable to the work or the employer – was inconsistent with the Federal Unemployment Tax Act (FUTA). The court of appeals affirmed, but the Missouri Supreme Court reversed. The U.S. Supreme Court held that the Missouri statute was consistent with the FUTA. Congress only intended to prohibit states from singling out pregnancy for unfavorable treatment when it decreed that no state could deny any compensation "solely on the basis of pregnancy or termination of pregnancy." Here, the Missouri statute was neutral toward pregnancy. Since **the employee had left work for a reason that had no causal connection to either**

her work or her employer, she was not entitled to unemployment compensation benefits. She had not been denied benefits "solely" because of her pregnancy. The Court affirmed the decision against the employee. *Wimberly v. Labor and Industrial Relations Comm'n,* 479 U.S. 511, 107 S.Ct. 821, 93 L.Ed.2d 909 (1987).

◆ A front desk agent at a hotel in Florida contracted bronchitis and pneumonia as a result of mold and mildew in her work environment. When she notified her employer of her medical condition, he did nothing about the problem until after the Occupational Safety and Health Administration inspected the job site. Even then, he did not clean the air conditioner or ventilation systems, so the air continued to have contaminants. The employee became dissatisfied with the working conditions and quit her job, later filing for unemployment compensation benefits, which the Florida Court of Appeal granted. The employee made reasonable efforts to preserve her employment, and quit only because the working conditions were so harsh as to require her separation. **Although the employer took some steps to remedy the problem, he failed to show that the problem was in fact remedied.** *Kloepper v. Unemployment Appeals Comm'n*, 871 So.2d 997 (Fla. Dist. Ct. App. 2004).

◆ A Pennsylvania office manager suffered a non-work injury, for which she was hospitalized and granted a medical leave of absence. One month later, her employer advised her that it would have to hire another employee to perform certain duties that she was now physically unable to perform. It offered her other employment at a substantial wage decrease to conform with her medical release for limited work duties. The employee stated that she could not afford a pay cut, quit, and applied for unemployment benefits. The state unemployment compensation board of review granted benefits, finding that the employer had effectively demoted the employee because of her physical restrictions, and had given her good cause to quit her job. The Commonwealth Court of Pennsylvania observed that the employee had not been demoted and was unable to perform her former job duties. A **voluntary leaving of work because of disability shall not be deemed good cause to quit where other suitable work is available from the employer**. The employer had made suitable work available to the employee, which she declined, making her ineligible for benefits. The court reversed the board's order. *Phoenix Women's Health Center v. UCBR*, 695 A.2d 466 (Pa. Commw. Ct. 1997).

◆ A 10-year employee of a Montana manufacturer was injured in an on-the-job accident. He underwent back surgery and returned to light-duty work for nine months before leaving for a second back surgery. Upon his release, he contacted the employer to resume work, but was informed that no light-duty work was available. He filed a claim for unemployment compensation benefits, which was denied on grounds that he had left employment for medical reasons and could not return to work without restrictions. The state board of labor appeals affirmed this decision, and a state court affirmed the denial of benefits. The employee appealed to the Supreme Court of Montana, which found that an employee is not disqualified from receiving unemployment compensation benefits if four statutory conditions are met. This includes an **offer to return to employment after an injury where "regular or comparable suitable work" is not available**. The court stated that an employee's regular work is that which is done normally, typically or naturally. If an employer changes an employee's job duties, that work becomes what the employee does normally, typically and naturally. Under this analysis, the modified light-duty position became the employee's regular work. Because the modified position was no longer available, the employee was entitled to receive unemployment compensation benefits. *Brothers v. Cargill, Inc.*, 915 P.2d 226 (Mont. 1996).

2. Personal Reasons

Where an employee quits for personal reasons, unemployment compensation benefits generally are *not* payable. However, where the employer has caused, at least in part, the separation, the employee might be entitled to benefits.

◆ A New York employee visited his mother in Puerto Rico and learned that she had been diagnosed with lung cancer. He decided to relocate to care for her, and quit his job without notice. When he applied for unemployment compensation benefits, the Unemployment Insurance Appeal Board ruled that he was disqualified from receiving benefits because he voluntarily left his employment without good cause. The New York Supreme Court, Appellate Division, upheld that determination, finding **no evidence that the employee's relocation was medically necessary for the care of his mother**. Further, by neglecting to inform the employer of his departure or inquire about a leave of absence, he failed to take reasonable steps to protect his employment. *In re Soler*, 805 N.Y.S.2d 448 (N.Y. App. Div. 2005).

◆ A Florida employee claimed that her husband physically and mentally abused her and repeatedly threatened her life. She obtained a divorce and moved to California, believing that her life was in danger. She filed a claim for unemployment compensation benefits, asserting that she had not voluntarily left her employment. The state unemployment appeals commission held that the employee had not quit her job for good cause attributable to the employer and denied her claim. The District Court of Appeal of Florida observed that the legislature had amended the statute to allow benefits for a good cause separation only where the separation is attributable to the employer. There was **no evidence that the employee's separation from work had been caused by the employer**, and the court refused to extend an exception for domestic abuse cases. The employee was not entitled to benefits. *Hall v. Florida Unemployment Appeals Comm'n*, 697 So.2d 541 (Fla. Dist. Ct. App. 1997).

◆ A New Jersey appeals court affirmed a state administrative decision denying unemployment benefits to a legal secretary who quit her job due to domestic violence caused by her husband. She obtained a restraining order following a violent attack by her husband, who continued to harass her at work. Although she enjoyed her job and was good at it, she felt compelled to quit and move away to prevent a life-threatening situation that affected her job performance. The court observed that the state unemployment compensation law disqualifies claimants who voluntarily leave work without good cause attributable to work. Since the state agency had found that **the decision to leave work because of an abusive spouse was a personal reason that was not attributable to work**, the court affirmed the denial of benefits. *Pagan v. Board of Review*, 296 N.J.Super. 539, 687 A.2d 328 (N.J. Super. Ct. App. Div. 1997).

◆ A Pennsylvania sales rep refused to attend a mandatory seminar held in New York, stating that she suffered from severe anxiety when commuting long distances in automobiles. The employer's president then left a telephone message that she need not report to work the following work day, but should bring in her things at a later time. The sales rep interpreted the message as notice of her termination. Although the president gave the rep a final paycheck, he later denied intending to discharge her and asserted that she had voluntarily quit. An unemployment compensation referee held that the president's message did not convey the necessary intent or immediacy for discharge. The referee denied benefits. The state unemployment compensation board of review affirmed, and the rep appealed. The Commonwealth Court of Pennsylvania held that **the sales rep did not intend to leave her job** and that the president's message was consistent with termination. Because the board had erroneously based its decision on whether the employer intended to discharge the rep, instead of whether the rep intended to quit, the court reversed the board's order. *Gold v. UCBR*, 700 A.2d 1065 (Pa. Commw. Ct. 1997).

◆ A Pennsylvania mechanic worked at a facility five miles from his home until his employer announced that it was transferring the terminal to a Connecticut location 337 miles away. The employee accepted a job transfer and worked at the Connecticut location for seven weeks before quitting because of the stress of being away from home. The Commonwealth Court of Pennsylvania found that **an insurmountable commuting problem could constitute a necessitous and compelling reason for employment termination** that would not prohibit unemployment compensation benefits. The employee had not been given a reasonable opportunity to find a job closer to home before accepting the transfer, and the unemployment compensation law did not require employees to sever their ties with family and community without an opportunity to seek work closer to home. *Speck v. UCBR*, 680 A.2d 27 (Pa. Commw. Ct. 1996).

E. Other Circumstances

Many employees quit their jobs for reasons they believe are necessitous and compelling. However, unless the working conditions are so difficult that a reasonable person would be forced to quit, the employee will probably not be entitled to unemployment compensation benefits.

◆ A Missouri receptionist asked her boss for a raise and was turned down. Shortly thereafter, she submitted a letter of resignation, giving 30 days' notice. However, with a little more than two weeks left in her tenure, the boss told her to leave. She filed a claim for unemployment compensation for the period between her termination and her resignation date. The Missouri Department of Employment Security held that she was not entitled to benefits for the time between the firing and the effective resignation date. However, the Missouri Court of Appeals reversed. **She did not agree to advance her resignation date. Thus, she did not voluntarily quit at that particular time.** The court remanded the case for a determination of whether she was otherwise eligible for benefits. *Fitzpatrick v. Don Brown Automotive Group*, 237 S.W.3d 595 (Mo. Ct. App. 2007).

- An employee with impaired vision took the bus to work every day. The company considered him a model employee. Years later, the company changed his shift so that he had to arrive at 3:30 p.m. and work until after midnight, when buses no longer ran. For nine months he tried to make the arrangement work, carpooling with a supervisor for a while and then carpooling with a co-worker who had slightly different hours. At times he was forced to leave at midnight to get a ride home. Fearing he would be fired for leaving early, he finally quit, then filed for unemployment compensation benefits. The case reached the New Jersey Supreme Court, which held that **he was entitled to benefits because he had "good cause" to quit**. The shift change altered the employee's working conditions, and he did all that was reasonable and necessary to stay employed. *Utley v. Board of Review, Dep't of Labor*, 946 A.2d 1039 (N.J. 2008).

- An equine veterinarian in New Jersey was informed that she was going to be discharged and that she would be given 60 days' notice under her contract when a new veterinarian was hired to replace her. Two months later, she submitted a letter of resignation, giving 60 days' notice. When she applied for unemployment compensation benefits, the Board of Review, Department of Labor, disqualified her on the grounds that she had voluntarily quit without good cause attributable to her employment. However, the Superior Court of New Jersey, Appellate Division, reversed. It noted that **she was compelled to resign because of a real, imminent, and substantial risk of losing her job**. She was told that a replacement was being sought and that she was going to be let go when the new veterinarian was hired. Further, the requirement in unemployment compensation law that the employee be threatened with discharge within 60 days did not apply here because both parties were required to provide 60 days' notice. *Shuster v. Board of Review, Dep't of Labor*, 396 N.J.Super. 240, 933 A.2d 641 (N.J. Super. Ct. App. Div. 2007).

- A truck driver for a transportation company in Florida got a ticket in Georgia and tried to arrange with the dispatcher to be given a route that would take him to Georgia during the time he was scheduled to be in court. The dispatcher did not do so, and the driver missed his court date. He managed to reschedule, but the dispatcher again refused to give him a route that would allow him to appear in court. After returning from that job, the driver waited at the facility for four days, hoping to speak with the owner to resolve the problem. When the owner refused to speak with him, he quit. He filed for unemployment compensation, and the Florida District Court of Appeal granted him benefits.

There was clearly **good cause for the driver's resignation**. *Thomas v. Peoplease Corp.*, 877 So.2d 45 (Fla. Dist. Ct. App. 2004).

◆ An employee at a grocery store was accused of taking a missing bank deposit. She was told by the employer and a Division of Criminal Investigation agent that if she admitted to taking the money, she could keep her job, so she should either admit to taking the money or leave. She refused to admit to taking the money and left, believing she was fired. When she filed for unemployment compensation benefits, the Supreme Court of South Dakota determined that she had voluntarily left her job with good cause. Even though no one ever told her she was fired, she reasonably believed she had been. **Requiring an involuntary admission of guilt to theft changed the employment contract and gave her good cause to leave** her job. *Habben v. G.F. Buche Co., Inc.*, 677 N.W.2d 227 (S.D. 2004).

◆ An employee of a company in New York moved to Florida for personal reasons and was allowed to telecommute. The company paid for a computer, telephone line and other necessary items so she could perform her duties. Two years later, the company decided to end the telecommuting arrangement and offered the employee work in the New York office. She turned it down, and the company let her go. She applied for unemployment compensation benefits in Florida, but was turned down because she had voluntarily quit her job. The employee then filed an interstate claim for benefits under New York law. The case reached the Court of Appeals of New York, which ruled that **she was not entitled to benefits under New York law because she was regularly physically present in Florida** while she was working for the company. Thus, her work was "localized" in Florida. Benefits were denied. *Allen v. Commissioner of Labor*, 763 N.Y.S.2d 237, 794 N.E.2d 18 (N.Y. 2003).

◆ A temporary placement service hired employees to perform short-term and long-term assignments with client companies. It placed an employee as a staff accountant with the federal Small Business Administration (SBA). After the employee's SBA supervisor told her she was going to be reassigned to a work cubicle that the employee believed was totally inadequate, the employee orally resigned. About three hours later, she changed her mind and attempted to withdraw the resignation, but the supervisor refused to let her. When the service had no further assignments for her, she applied for unemployment benefits. A hearing officer denied them on the grounds that she had quit because of dissatisfaction with standard working conditions. Thus, she was not unemployed through no fault of her own. The Colorado Court of Appeals affirmed the decision against her, noting that **her voluntary resignation set in motion the chain of events that led to her unemployment**. *Cunliffe v. Industrial Claims Appeals Office*, 51 P.3d 1088 (Colo. Ct. App. 2002).

◆ A district manager, who quit her job with an Indiana property management company because she disagreed with its rule prohibiting employees from dating tenants, did not terminate her employment for "good cause." Her reasons were personal and subjective rather than job-related and objective, and thus insufficient to establish that she was entitled to unemployment benefits. The company had a written policy that its employees were to refrain from relationships with tenants. The company considered a manager's failure to report a violation of this rule a violation of company policy. Either violation could result in termination. After the company discovered that an employee at one complex was dating a tenant, it terminated both the employee and the property manager, who knew about the relationship but didn't report it. The company then notified the district manager, who also admitted to knowing about the relationship but not reporting it because she disagreed with the rule. The company told her that **if she could not enforce the "no dating" rule, she should not continue her employment**. She quit and applied for unemployment benefits. The Indiana Court of Appeals ruled that the manager's reasons were clearly personal and subjective. *M&J Management v. Review Board of Dep't of Workforce Development*, 711 N.E.2d 58 (Ind. Ct. App. 1999).

- A secretary agreed to work for an Oklahoma law firm for three months while its regular secretary was on maternity leave. When the regular secretary's three-month leave ended, the temporary secretary filed a claim for unemployment compensation benefits. The state employment security commission determined that she had not been discharged due to misconduct and approved the claim. An administrative hearing officer found that the temporary secretary had not voluntarily quit her job, but a state court reversed, finding that she had voluntarily left the job. The Supreme Court of Oklahoma held that the district court had properly set aside the administrative award of benefits. The parties had contemplated only temporary employment during the regular secretary's maternity leave. **Because the temporary secretary had agreed to work during the pregnancy leave of the regular employee, she had voluntarily left her employment** upon the regular secretary's return and was not entitled to benefits. *Wright & Edwards v. Oklahoma Employment Security Comm'n*, 934 P.2d 1088 (Okla. 1997).

- A Hawaii transportation company fired a bus driver after learning that his license had been suspended for driving his car without no-fault insurance coverage, as required by state law. His claim for unemployment benefits was denied, and the employee appealed. The Intermediate Court of Appeals of Hawaii observed that the denial of benefits was based upon the doctrine of "constructive voluntary leaving." The doctrine is employed in Michigan and California and has been applied where an employee's conduct makes it impossible for an employer to utilize the employee's services due to the voluntary commission of an act which foreseeably jeopardizes the employment. The court found the doctrine inconsistent with Hawaii unemployment compensation law, which requires that an employee actually intend to leave work voluntarily and to be the moving party in the termination of the employment relationship in order to be considered to have quit voluntarily. Joining jurisdictions like Maryland, Maine, Connecticut and Vermont, **the court rejected the constructive voluntary leaving doctrine** and remanded the case for a determination of whether the employee had committed misconduct connected with work. *Keanini v. Akiba*, 935 P.2d 122 (Haw. Ct. App. 1997).

II. RELIGIOUS BELIEF SEPARATION

The U.S. Supreme Court has recognized the right of employees to receive unemployment compensation benefits where continued employment interferes with a sincerely held religious belief. Denial of benefits in these cases has been held to violate the Free Exercise Clause of the First Amendment to the U.S. Constitution.

The most common scenario involves employees who are not willing to work on their religion's holy day (usually a Saturday or Sunday). Where possible, employers should be flexible and accommodating, not only to avoid paying unemployment compensation, but also to avoid claims of religious discrimination. For cases involving religious discrimination, please see Chapter One, Section V.

Where flexibility is not possible, note that employers can ask applicants if they are capable of performing the duties of the job, and if they need any accommodations to perform those duties.

If the applicant claims that he can perform the job's duties and later asserts that a religious belief prevents him from working on his holy day, you may then have to pay unemployment benefits if he quits rather than break a sincerely held religious belief.

◆ An Illinois man was offered a temporary retail position by a placement agency. He refused the position because the job would have required him to work on Sunday, a day he considered to be "the Lord's day." He applied for unemployment compensation benefits, claiming that there was good cause for his refusal to work on Sunday. The Illinois Department of Economic Security denied his application, and a board of review upheld that decision. It found that the applicant's refusal to work was based solely on an entirely personal belief that was not a tenet or dogma of a church, sect or denomination. The Illinois courts also upheld the denial of benefits, and appeal was taken to the U.S. Supreme Court. The applicant charged that the denial of benefits violated his free exercise of religion rights, as guaranteed by the First Amendment. The Court agreed. So long as the applicant had **a sincere belief that required him to refrain from the work offered**, it did not matter that the belief was not in response to the commands of a particular religious organization. Further, the state had not shown any justification for burdening the applicant's beliefs by denying unemployment benefits. Granting benefits was not likely to cause a mass movement away from Sunday employment by others. The Court reversed the lower courts and granted benefits to the applicant. *Frazee v. Illinois Dep't of Economic Security,* 489 U.S. 829, 109 S.Ct. 1514, 103 L.Ed.2d 914 (1989).

◆ A Florida jeweler hired a woman to work at a retail jewelry store. Subsequently, the woman became baptized in the Seventh-Day Adventist Church. She informed her supervisor that she could no longer work from sundown on Friday to sundown on Saturday due to her religious beliefs. After initially accommodating her, the jeweler discharged her. When she filed for unemployment compensation benefits, the jeweler contested payment, asserting that "misconduct" connected with her work was the reason for the discharge. Benefits were denied. The case reached the U.S. Supreme Court, which held that the denial of benefits violated the Free Exercise Clause of the First Amendment. Under a strict scrutiny analysis, the rejection of benefits failed. First, even though Florida law only disqualified applicants for a limited time, rather than making them completely ineligible, the denial could not be justified. Second, **it did not matter that the employer did not change the conditions of employment so as to conflict with the employee's religious beliefs**, or that the employee converted to the religion during the course of the employment. Benefits had to be paid. Finally, the Court noted that paying benefits here would not be a fostering of religion in violation of the Establishment Clause. *Hobbie v. Unemployment Appeals Comm'n of Florida,* 480 U.S. 136, 107 S.Ct. 1046, 94 L.Ed.2d 190 (1987).

◆ An employee of a foundry fabricated sheet steel for a variety of industrial uses. When the foundry closed, the company transferred him to a department that fabricated turrets for military tanks. The employee, a Jehovah's Witness, believed that working on weapons would violate the principles of his religion. Because there were no "nonweapons" jobs in the company and because the company refused to lay him off, he quit. He then applied for unemployment compensation, which was denied. The Indiana Court of Appeals awarded benefits, but the state supreme court reversed. On further appeal, the U.S. Supreme Court held that the denial of benefits violated the applicant's First Amendment right to the free exercise of his religion. **It did not matter that another Jehovah's Witness was willing to work on tank turrets.** The religious belief in question need not be shared by all the members of a religious sect. Here, the important thing to consider was that the employee had quit for religious reasons. The Court stated that a person may not be compelled to choose between the exercise of a First Amendment right and participation in an otherwise available public program. It granted benefits to the applicant. *Thomas v. Review Board of Indiana Employment Security Division,* 450 U.S. 707, 101 S.Ct. 1425, 67 L.Ed.2d 624 (1981).

◆ A drug rehabilitation organization fired two employees because they ingested peyote, a hallucinogenic drug, for sacramental purposes at a Native American church ceremony. When the two men applied for unemployment benefits, their applications were denied on the ground that they had committed work-related misconduct. The Oregon Supreme Court held that the prohibition against religious use of peyote was invalid under the Free Exercise Clause. Thus, the state could not deny unemployment benefits to the applicants. The case reached the U.S. Supreme Court, which stated that Oregon could prohibit sacramental peyote use without violating the Free Exercise Clause and, accordingly, could deny unemployment benefits to persons discharged for such use. **A law of general applicability, which is religiously neutral, can prohibit the possession of controlled substances (including peyote) without making exceptions for religious use.** The law only incidentally affected religion. The

Court reversed the state supreme court and held that unemployment benefits could be denied. *Employment Division, Dep't of Human Resources v. Smith,* 494 U.S. 872, 110 S.Ct. 1595, 108 L.Ed.2d 876 (1990).

◆ A part-time instructor at a college in Wisconsin sought unemployment compensation benefits when her job ended after the fall semester. The college then offered her work for the spring semester. **She rejected the job offer because she had to make a religious pilgrimage.** The Labor and Industrial Review Commission denied her benefits, finding that she did not have good cause to reject the job offer. However, it did not make factual findings as to whether she had to make the pilgrimage at the time she claimed she did. Nor did it address whether the "good cause" standard of Wisconsin law violated her religious free exercise rights. The case reached the Wisconsin Court of Appeals, which reversed the denial of benefits and remanded the case for further consideration. *Rashad v. LIRC*, 699 N.W.2d 254 (Wis. Ct. App. 2005).

III. MISCONDUCT

Employee misconduct often provides a valid reason for denying benefits, in whole or in part. Generally, misconduct entails a willful and wanton or intentional disregard of an employer's interests, a deliberate violation of rules or policies, or a disregard of behavioral standards that an employer has the right to expect. Incompetence or inability may not necessarily constitute misconduct.

A. Employer's Interests

Where an employee commits misconduct that is against the employer's business interests, he may be disqualified from benefits in whole or in part. Generally, employees commit such misconduct by ignoring or refusing orders, or by acts or omissions that harm the employer.

◆ A car detailer at a Minnesota dealership was asked to pick up litter from the premises. He told his supervisor that he was busy and that the manager could go "f— himself." He was then fired. He sought unemployment compensation benefits, which an administrative law judge denied. The Minnesota Court of Appeals reversed. It noted that misconduct occurs when an employee refuses to comply with a reasonable request by the employer. And the request here was reasonable. However, while misconduct such as what happened here could be a bar to receiving benefits, the state's unemployment compensation statute also provides that **a single incident of misconduct isn't a bar to benefits when the incident doesn't have a "significant adverse impact on the employer."** Here, there was no evidence that the employee's refusal to pick up trash had a significant impact on his job of detailing cars. *Williams v. Brooklyn Center Motors*, 2007 WL 1747125 (Minn. Ct. App. 6/19/07).

◆ After less than two months on the job, a paralegal at an Indianapolis law firm asked for the afternoon off to pick up her son, her car, and sign an apartment lease. What she didn't mention was that she was also going to attend

Carburetion Day, the last day of practice before the Indianapolis 500. While she was there, someone used a cell phone to take a photo of her and e-mailed it to her at work. Her boss discovered the photo in her e-mail and fired her. When she applied for unemployment benefits, she was initially awarded them. The law firm appealed and won. The Indiana Court of Appeals held that **she breached her duty of loyalty and that she was thus fired for just cause**. She was not entitled to benefits. *McHugh v. Review Board of the Indiana Dep't of Workforce Development*, 842 N.E.2d 436 (Ind. Ct. App. 2006).

◆ An employee at a store in New Hampshire with no warnings or disciplinary issues against her sold cigarettes to an underage customer in violation of store policy. In violation of store policy, she failed to verify the customer's age and used the override feature on the cash register to complete the sale without verifying the age. The customer was part of a sting operation, and the police issued her a summons for selling tobacco products to a minor. She was fired the next day and later applied for unemployment benefits. The case reached the Supreme Court of New Hampshire, which found that she was not entitled to benefits because she was fired for misconduct connected with her work. **She deliberately violated a company rule** reasonably designed to protect the legitimate business interests of the employer. *In re Riendeau*, 877 A.2d 207 (N.H. 2005).

◆ A manager at an Oregon retail automotive parts chain store conducted a training class for new employees and allegedly made racially and ethnically offensive statements during the class. After a new employee complained, his supervisor requested a written statement of what occurred, advising the manager that he should do this both as a subordinate and as the person being investigated. The manager was fired after he refused to submit a written statement. He sought unemployment benefits. An administrative law judge granted him benefits, but the Oregon Employment Appeals Board reversed. The Oregon Court of Appeals upheld the board's decision, finding substantial evidence that the manager engaged in misconduct when he **intentionally refused to provide his supervisor with a written statement of what he said during the class**. The court rejected the manager's argument that he was asked to voluntarily provide the statement, rather than directed to do so. The directive here came from the manager's supervisor, and he could expect the manager to comply. *Bingham v. Employment Dep't*, 987 P.2d 578 (Or. Ct. App. 1999).

◆ Beginning shortly after she was hired, a customer service representative constantly criticized her co-workers, yelling at them and sending them "nasty grams." After she initiated a hostile confrontation with a co-worker, she received a written warning that the company would no longer tolerate her conduct and that the next incident would result in her termination. In response, she wrote a letter to the company accusing management of having big egos and self-serving agendas. She was fired and sought unemployment compensation. An administrative law judge (ALJ) denied her benefits because **her conduct was done in willful disregard of the employer's interest and caused harm to the employer's business**. Both the state board and the Washington Court of

Appeals affirmed the ALJ's findings. The representative argued that the court should consider principles enunciated under the National Labor Relations Act, which makes allowances for an employee's otherwise insubordinate behavior when it occurs during a disciplinary grievance procedure. The appeals court disagreed. This was not a collective bargaining situation. *Haney v. Employment Security Division*, 978 P.2d 543 (Wash. Ct. App. 1999).

- A Maryland nursing home discharged two nurses for failing to respond to a page requesting assistance for a patient who was experiencing chest pains. The facility then challenged their applications for unemployment benefits and produced witnesses who testified that they had left the building on a personal errand rather than assist the patient. A hearing officer found that the nurses had failed to assist the patient. The decision was affirmed by an appeals board, resulting in the denial of benefits for a nine-week period. The case reached the Court of Appeals of Maryland, which noted that there was substantial evidence of misconduct by the nurses. **Misconduct in an unemployment compensation claim need not be intentional to support temporary disqualification.** The statute that governed this case provided for disqualification for up to 10 weeks based on the seriousness of the misconduct. A separate statute governed cases of gross or aggravated misconduct. The court affirmed the temporary disqualification from unemployment benefits. *Dep't of Labor, Licensing and Regulation v. Hider*, 349 Md. 71, 706 A.2d 1073 (Md. 1998).

- A Montana gas plant field operator told his supervisor that he would remain working for the employer if he received a $100 monthly raise. He also stated that he needed a reply that day and that he had been offered a job by a competitor that was also prepared to hire the employer's only other field operator. The supervisor then offered the co-worker a raise, which was accepted, and hired a replacement field operator previously discharged by the competitor. Afterward, the supervisor fired the operator who had sought the raise, stating that his replacement was cheaper. The operator filed a claim for unemployment benefits, which was denied. The Supreme Court of Montana held that while **the employee's attempt to exert leverage on the employer had been somewhat deceptive** (since the competitor's offer was $700 less than his present salary), he had not committed misconduct within the meaning of state law. There was no showing of willful or wanton disregard of the right, title and interest of a fellow employee or the employer. The court reversed the denial of benefits. *Moody v. Northland Royalty Co.*, 930 P.2d 1100 (Mont. 1997).

- An Idaho aviation line service employee **pulled an aircraft across a runway without permission from the air traffic control tower**. When the employee repeated this violation the next day, he was fired, and he filed for unemployment compensation benefits. After a finding that the incidents were serious violations of FAA rules and regulations, constituting reckless disregard for airport safety, his claim was denied on the basis of misconduct. The Supreme Court of Idaho determined that the finding of intentional disregard of the employer's interests was supported by substantial evidence. This was true despite the absence of evidence that the employer ever communicated an expectation to employees that they should not cross the runway without clearance from the control tower. This was a circumstance in which the expectation flowed naturally from the employment and did not need to be communicated by the employer. Because the action showed substantial disregard for the employer's interests, the employee was not entitled to benefits. *Bullard v. Sun Valley Aviation, Inc.*, 914 P.2d 564 (Idaho 1996).

- A Nevada taxi driver worked for an employer under a collective bargaining agreement that provided for immediate termination where the driver had two chargeable accidents in any three-year period. A chargeable accident was defined as one in which the insurer determined the driver to be at fault, requiring the company to pay damages. After the driver became involved in his second chargeable accident within a one-year period, the company fired him. He filed a claim for unemployment benefits with the state Employment Security Division. The division denied his application based upon work-related misconduct. The Supreme Court of Nevada noted the distinction between appropriate grounds for termination and grounds for the denial of unemployment compensation benefits. According to the court, **ordinary negligence in isolated circumstances and good-faith errors in judgment are not considered misconduct**. Here, the necessary element of wrongful conduct was not present, and the bargaining agreement's definition of grounds for termination could not be transported to an unemployment claim. The accidents did not constitute misconduct sufficient to deny unemployment benefits. *Kolnik v. Nevada Employment Security Dep't*, 908 P.2d 726 (Nev. 1996).

- A Pennsylvania employer laid off an office manager for budgetary reasons. She filed for unemployment and received benefits for several weeks. However, an audit determined that the employee had embezzled over $40,000. The department then determined that the employer would have denied the claim had it known of the embezzlement and that she would have been disqualified from receiving benefits. The employee appealed. A hearing referee refused to consider the after-acquired evidence. The Commonwealth Court of Pennsylvania determined that state unemployment compensation law **categorized theft or embezzlement from an employer as willful misconduct that precluded the receipt of unemployment benefits**. An employee should not benefit from criminal conduct that is concealed from the employer prior to separation. The court recognized a narrow exception that allowed employers to present after-acquired evidence of criminal conduct if presented within a reasonable time after the employee's separation. *Preservation Pennsylvania v. UCBR*, 673 A.2d 1044 (Pa. Commw. Ct. 1996).

B. Rules or Policies

Violation of employer policies can result in denial of unemployment benefits. Common employer policies include drug-free workplace policies (for cases dealing with drug testing, please see Chapter Six, Section II) and attendance policies.

1. Drug Policies

Employees who violate drug policies can be fired even if they are recovering addicts who are in treatment. This does not violate the Americans with Disabilities Act because the employee is not being fired for what she is but for actions that violate a standard set forth by the employer.

When an employee fired for violating a drug policy seeks unemployment compensation, benefits generally will be denied either in whole or in part.

◆ An employee of a window manufacturer was issued a reprimand for failing to call in on a day he was absent. Company policy required employees issued reprimands to submit to a drug test or be fired. He refused to take the test and left work without telling anyone of his decision. When he filed for unemployment compensation, the case reached the Missouri Court of Appeals. The court held that the employee left his job without good cause attributable to his employer, making him ineligible for unemployment compensation. **By refusing to take the drug test, he abandoned his job.** *Winco Manufacturing, Inc. v. Capone*, 133 S.W.3d 555 (Mo. Ct. App. 2004).

◆ A certified nurse's aide at a nursing home was treated for a workplace injury. Attached to the bill for services was her medical history, which indicated that she regularly used illegally obtained prescription medicine and marijuana. She admitted to her employer that she **used marijuana daily after work** but asserted that she did not report to work under its influence. She denied using illegal prescription drugs. The employer fired her, and she applied for unemployment compensation benefits, which were denied. On appeal, the Pennsylvania Supreme Court held that she was entitled to benefits. Here, the aide had not committed work-related misconduct. As for her off-duty misconduct, the employer failed to show both that her marijuana smoking was "inconsistent with acceptable standards of behavior" and that it directly affected her ability to perform her assigned duties. As a result, she was entitled to collect unemployment compensation. *Burger v. Pennsylvania Unemployment Compensation Board of Review*, 801 A.2d 487 (Pa. 2002).

◆ A trucking company installed a surveillance camera to try to determine whether marijuana was being sold on the premises. It recorded several people smoking a pipe. One of the individuals in the film identified a co-worker as the seller after he was promised that he would not be disciplined so long as he cooperated with the police. Another employee also implicated the co-worker as the seller in exchange for a promise of no adverse action. The co-worker denied selling drugs. When the company fired him anyway, he filed for unemployment compensation benefits. His claim was denied, and he appealed to the Commonwealth Court of Pennsylvania, which affirmed the denial. **The court noted that he had engaged in willful or deliberate misconduct**, and it found the testimony of the company's witnesses to be more credible than his assertions. The company also did not treat him unfairly by firing him while retaining the two employees who had been caught smoking marijuana on the job, because by doing so, the company was able to rid itself of an undesirable and potentially dangerous element. *Daniels v. Unemployment Compensation Board of Review*, 755 A.2d 729 (Pa. Commw. Ct. 2000).

◆ An Oklahoma employer with a drug-free workplace policy fired an employee after learning that **she failed to report a guilty plea to a drug-related offense**. The employee had previously admitted having a substance abuse problem, for which the employer required her to seek treatment under an employer-sponsored program. She had instructed her attorney to contact the employer about the drug-related offense, but he failed to do so. Her claim for unemployment benefits was denied, based on evidence that the employer had adequately communicated its drug-free policy in employee handbooks. A trial court found no evidence that the employer had advised the employee of the drug-free policy. The Court of Civil Appeals of Oklahoma held that the employee had admitted knowledge of the workplace policy by revealing her abuse problem to a supervisor and directing her attorney to inform her supervisor of the guilty plea. Because there was substantial evidence of her misconduct, the trial court decision was reversed. *Davis v. Oklahoma Employment Security Comm'n*, 949 P.2d 683 (Okla. Ct. App. 1997).

◆ A Nevada hotel implemented a drug-free workplace policy and gave its employees 90 days advance notice of a drug test. An employee who often handled large amounts of cash and had access to the hotel computer system failed a radioimmunoassay hair analysis (RIA) for drug use, and a second test revealed cocaine use. The hotel fired her, and she filed for unemployment benefits. Her claim was denied. A trial court found that failure to pass a drug test without proof of drug-related activity was insufficient to show work-related misconduct sufficient to disqualify unemployment. The court also held that RIA was scientifically unreliable. The Supreme Court of Nevada observed that courts in New York and Florida have accepted RIA drug testing and that medical evidence indicated that this form of analysis was more accurate than urinalysis. The court also determined that **misconduct for unemployment purposes requires that the employer show a deliberate violation or disregard of employee standards of behavior** that the employer has the right to expect. The employer here had a sound reason for demanding compliance with the drug-free policy. It had also given the employee adequate notice to comply with the new policy, and her claim for benefits was properly denied. *Nevada Employment Security Dep't v. Holmes*, 914 P.2d 611 (Nev. 1996).

◆ An Indiana employer maintained a drug-free workplace policy making employees who were under the influence of alcohol or other drugs at work subject to discipline, which could include termination. The employer fired 16 employees for selling and distributing illegal drugs in violation of the policy, including one who had worked for the employer for 18 years. He obtained unemployment compensation benefits because a review board found that the employer had not uniformly enforced the drug-free workplace policy. The Court of Appeals of Indiana determined that the state unemployment compensation law, while requiring an employer to reasonably and uniformly enforce its rules, did not prohibit employers from creating **different categories of offenders within an employment policy**. While the employer had not previously fired employees for drug use, each of the 16 offenders in this case had been fired for the more serious offense of drug distribution, and this was sufficient uniformity for purposes of the statute. *General Motors Corp. v. Review Board of Indiana Dep't of Workforce Development*, 671 N.E.2d 493 (Ind. Ct. App. 1996).

◆ A Louisiana employer imposed a pre-employment drug screening test on all job applicants and required them to make a statement that they were capable of passing the test. The employer also maintained a drug-free workplace policy. A new employee worked for only one week before the employer learned that he had failed his drug-screen test. The company fired the employee, and he applied for unemployment compensation. He was awarded benefits. The employer appealed to the Court of Appeal of Louisiana, which stated that the employer's policy made drug-free status a condition of employment. The employee had asserted that he could pass a drug test at the time of his application and understood that he could be fired for failing to pass the test. Thus, **he had made false assertions that constituted misconduct** connected with his employment. Because he had been fired for deliberately falsifying employment information, he was not entitled to unemployment compensation benefits. The court reversed and remanded the case. *Bean Dredging Corp. v. Administrator, Division of Employment Security,* 679 So.2d 1019 (La. Ct. App. 1996).

◆ An Idaho lumber company employee tested positive for marijuana use and admitted smoking marijuana on a day off. The company fired the employee for failing to pass a drug test, and his claim for unemployment benefits was denied by the state Department of Employment. However, an appeals examiner ruled that the company had failed to establish employment-related misconduct, and the state industrial commission affirmed this decision. On appeal, the Supreme Court of Idaho agreed with the industrial commission that there was no evidence that the employee had failed to comply with the company's substance abuse policy. **The employer could not require the employee to comply with untold expectations** to refrain from illegal drug use on an off day. *Merriott v. Shearer Lumber Products*, 903 P.2d 1317 (Idaho 1995).

2. Attendance Policies

Excessive absenteeism and tardiness can be construed as deliberate misconduct such that the employee will be denied benefits. Generally, there must be a pattern and practice of lateness or absenteeism for unemployment to be denied on grounds of misconduct. Attendance problems in and of themselves may not disqualify an employee from benefits, even though they justify the firing.

◆ A New York machine operator was fired when she failed to return to work at the end of an authorized bereavement leave and also failed to notify the employer that her return would be delayed. She filed for unemployment compensation benefits, which were denied. The New York Supreme Court, Appellate Division, upheld the denial of benefits, noting that **an employee's**

failure to return to work or contact the employer following an authorized leave of absence can constitute disqualifying misconduct. Here, although the employee claimed she could not contact the employer because she was staying in a rural area that did not have phones, she had made several trips to a nearby city during her leave, where she had access to telephones. *In re Jimenez*, 811 N.Y.S.2d 481 (N.Y. App. Div. 2006).

◆ A Florida employer had a policy of progressive discipline that prohibited excessive absenteeism and tardiness. It applied a point system to each worker's attendance record. When a new employee was absent four times, late four times and left early on one occasion in his first four months, he was fired. He filed for unemployment benefits, claiming that his last tardiness (on the day he was fired) occurred because the person who was supposed to pick him up did not show up that day, forcing him to walk to work. Further, he had left work early a few days before that with the approval of his supervisor because he felt ill. As a result, he asserted that he had not committed misconduct under the statutory unemployment scheme. The case reached the Florida Supreme Court, which held that he had been properly denied benefits. **Even though his final two attendance problems might have been justified, they fit into the pattern of absenteeism and tardiness** that he had started. *Mason v. Load King Manufacturing Co.*, 758 So.2d 649 (Fla. 2000).

◆ A Florida employer discharged an employee for missing three consecutive work days due to transportation problems. The state unemployment appeals commission affirmed an administrative decision disqualifying him from unemployment compensation benefits, finding that he had been discharged for misconduct connected with work. The District Court of Appeal of Florida held that the absences did not demonstrate willful or wanton disregard of the employer's interests through deliberate violation of standards of behavior that the employer had a right to expect, or demonstrate wrongful intent or substantial disregard of the employer's interests. **Although the absences might have justified discharge, they did not constitute misconduct** serious enough to deny unemployment benefits. The court reversed and remanded the decision, allowing the employee to claim benefits. *Roberts v. Diehl*, 707 So.2d 869 (Fla. Dist. Ct. App. 1998).

◆ A Missouri housekeeping employee was late or absent from work 12 times in one year, creating grounds for termination for excessive absenteeism under her employer's written policy. The employer fired her and opposed her claim for unemployment compensation benefits. The state labor and industrial relations commission determined that the employee had been discharged for misconduct and that she was not entitled to receive unemployment compensation benefits. The housekeeper appealed to the Missouri Court of Appeals, which held that absenteeism by itself does not constitute misconduct. **Excessive absence justified by illness or family emergency does not constitute willful misconduct** where properly reported to an employer. In this case, at least half of the 12 occurrences involved illness and all had been timely reported to the employer. Because absence due to illness does not constitute misconduct connected with work, the court reversed the commission's decision. *Kelley v. Manor Grove, Inc.*, 936 S.W.2d 874 (Mo. Ct. App. 1997).

◆ A Rhode Island employer forced an employee to resign after an investigation disclosed the falsification of his time cards. The hearing referee determined that the employee had voluntarily left his job without good cause and was disqualified from receiving unemployment compensation benefits. The state board of review upheld that determination. A state court held that there was no evidence to support the board's decision based on the employee's exemplary work history and the employer's failure to warn him that he might be fired for falsifying time records. On appeal, the Supreme Court of Rhode Island agreed with the district court in reversing the review board's decision. **In two of the instances of time card falsification the difference in time reported was only a few minutes**, and the employer had failed to warn the employee that these discrepancies might result in firing. *Cardoza v. Dep't of Employment and Training Board of Review*, 669 A.2d 1165 (R.I. 1996).

◆ An Illinois computer attendant worked at a facility where employees were required to work eight-hour shifts including a 30-minute unpaid lunch break and two 15-minute paid breaks. Employees frequently asked for permission to combine lunch and break times at the end of the shift so they could leave early. These requests were usually denied, and the company circulated a memo stating that failure to fill out time sheets correctly would result in discipline. A company manager observed the attendant leaving at least one hour early on several occasions for which she submitted time sheets indicating that she had worked a full shift. The company fired her for falsifying time records, and she applied for unemployment benefits. A court held that the company had failed to follow its own progressive disciplinary policy. The Appellate Court of Illinois found **no requirement for compliance with progressive disciplinary policies in Illinois unemployment compensation law**. The statute provided for the denial of unemployment benefits to employees fired for misconduct, defined as the deliberate and willful violation of a reasonable rule or policy of the employer, where the violation harms the employer and the employee is explicitly warned to stop. The court denied benefits to the attendant. *DeBois v. Dep't of Employment Security*, 653 N.E.2d 1336 (Ill. App. Ct. 1995).

◆ A Maryland employee repeatedly worked an erratic work schedule despite at least one warning that she was required to work from 9:00 a.m. to 5:00 p.m. each day. She was fired after several instances in which she arrived late, left early, or took more than one hour for lunch. A hearing examiner determined that she worked only 30 of her 40 scheduled hours per week and was disqualified from receiving unemployment benefits for 10 weeks due to misconduct. A board of appeals determined that the employee had been discharged for gross misconduct and was entirely disqualified from benefits. The Court of Special Appeals of Maryland found that **the employee's chronic pattern of arriving to work late and leaving early could constitute gross misconduct** under the statutory definition. Because the employer could insist on the employee's adherence to a specified schedule, the evidence supported the board's determination. There was no requirement for an employer to issue more than one warning in order to deem abuse of a work schedule gross or willful misconduct. *Dep't of Economic and Employment Development v. Propper*, 108 Md. App. 595, 673 A.2d 713 (Md. Ct. Spec. App. 1996).

3. Other Policies

Where employers set reasonable workplace policies that are justified by a legitimate business reason, and where those policies are adequately communicated to the employees, the violation of those policies will not only justify discharge, but may also amount to misconduct that warrants the denial of unemployment compensation.

- While helping a new sales clerk look for a missing credit card receipt, a clerk for an adult novelty store opened the cash register using the emergency switch. However, the store had a policy requiring employees to open the cash register only by pressing the cash-total key or the no-sale key. Even though the clerk did not take any money from the register, he was fired after the manager reviewed security video while investigating the missing credit card receipt. He filed a claim for unemployment compensation, which the store fought. The Minnesota Court of Appeals ruled that he was entitled to benefits. **A single incident of misconduct that does not have a significant adverse impact on the employer does not disqualify a fired employee from receiving unemployment benefits.** *Pierce v. DiMa Corp.*, 721 N.W.2d 627 (Minn. Ct. App. 2006).

- After a kitchen worker at a Hawaii resort complained about a work scheduling policy, the food and beverage director changed the policy, resulting in numerous changes to employees' schedules. A hostess who had been with the resort for 22 years came up behind the worker and **jokingly choked her**, saying, "This is all because of you." The worker seemed to laugh it off, but reported it to the director after her shift. The resort then fired the hostess for violating its zero tolerance workplace violence policy. When she filed for unemployment compensation, she was denied benefits. The Supreme Court of Hawaii held that by pretending to choke her co-worker, the hostess showed a conscious disregard of the resort's zero tolerance policy, which expressly prohibited talk of violence, including joking about violence. *Medeiros v. Hawaii Dep't of Labor and Industrial Relations*, 118 P.3d 1201 (Haw. 2005).

- An employee at a Wendy's restaurant in Tennessee asked for permission to wear her shirt untucked in violation of the company's dress code. She received permission to do so. However, when a new manager arrived 11 months later, he told her to tuck in her shirt on several occasions. She refused to do so, became upset and used "foul language." She left work and was fired when she failed to return. When she filed for unemployment benefits, her request was denied. The Court of Appeals of Tennessee held that **she engaged in misconduct on the job by refusing to comply with the dress code**. *Hallowell v. Vestco, Inc.*, 2005 WL 1046795 (Tenn. Ct. App. 5/4/05).

- A Utah company issued an employee handbook, which provided that e-mail was to be used for business purposes only. It later sent all employees an e-mail reminding them that the policy was still in effect. After a former employee notified the company that she had received sexually offensive e-mails from current employees, the company fired two workers. One had sent 11 "clearly offensive" messages and the other had sent 25. When the two fired workers applied for unemployment benefits, the Utah Court of Appeals held that they were fired for just cause and that they were not eligible for benefits. The company did not have to warn them that their e-mails differed significantly from those of their co-workers. Here, the workers had **violated a universal standard of behavior by sending e-mails containing sexually explicit and offensive jokes, pictures and videos** (including videos depicting sexual acts). *Autoliv ASP, Inc. v. Dep't of Workforce Services*, 29 P.3d 7 (Utah App. 2001).

- A heavy equipment manufacturer suspended 19 union-affiliated employees for violation of a workplace rule forbidding T-shirts, buttons or other apparel containing messages that attacked or insulted co-workers. The employees had worn shirts referring to an unfair labor practices complaint against the employer based on the suspension of an employee who wore a shirt calling for the replacement of the company's chairman. The suspended employees applied for unemployment compensation benefits for the period of their suspension. In a separate action, the National Labor Relations Board (NLRB) made a finding of unfair labor practices by the employer. The employees obtained unemployment benefits, and the employer appealed.

  The Supreme Court of Pennsylvania observed that unemployment benefits are not payable where an employee is discharged or suspended for willful misconduct connected with work. **Violation of an employer rule may constitute willful misconduct where the rule or policy is reasonable** under the circumstances. The employer's enforcement of the rule must also be reasonable. In this case, the NLRB had found that wearing the T-shirts was protected union activity. The employer's application of the rule did not support its goal of avoiding workplace confrontations, and the actions of the claimants did not constitute willful misconduct. The court affirmed the award of benefits. *Caterpillar, Inc. v. UCBR*, 703 A.2d 452 (Pa. 1997).

- An Illinois employee **refused to remove a pro-union sign from his personal vehicle that displayed the term "scab" in violation of an employer rule**. He was discharged for misconduct and applied for unemployment compensation benefits. The Appellate Court of Illinois agreed with the board's finding that the employer's rule was unreasonable. An employee may be disqualified on the basis of misconduct for violating only a reasonable employer rule, and the board was entitled to deference. The court also agreed with the employee that placing the sign in the window of his personal vehicle was not connected with work because it did not relate to the performance of his job duties as a lathe operator and did not govern his performance of work. The court reinstated the award of benefits. *Caterpillar, Inc. v. Fehrenbacher*, 676 N.E.2d 710 (Ill. App. Ct. 1997).

◆ A Virginia sales rep worked for a security system installer under a commission agreement, which compensated him at a higher rate for equipment leases than for sales. He conducted extensive negotiations with a customer for a purchase agreement of equipment, which the employer later argued resulted in an overpayment to the representative of over $16,000. Even though the transaction had been closely monitored by his supervisors and a branch manager, the employer fired the sales rep for failing to follow company policy in structuring the transaction and failing to use a corporate-approved contract. The sales rep filed a claim for unemployment compensation, which was awarded. The employer appealed to the Court of Appeals of Virginia, asserting that the sales rep was guilty of misconduct connected with work and was therefore disqualified from receiving benefits. The court agreed with the sales rep that **his conduct had been authorized and directed by supervisors and** that his deviation from company rules had been approved by them. Because the supervisors had indicated their approval of the transaction, the court rejected the employer's claim that the sales rep had engaged in misconduct that disqualified him from benefits. *Wells Fargo Alarm Services, Inc. v. Virginia Employment Comm'n*, 24 Va. App. 377, 482 S.E.2d 841 (Va. Ct. App. 1997).

◆ A medical records manager rose to a department head position after 16 years at a New Mexico care center. A new administrator held her responsible for **failing to maintain appropriate resident charts**. These deficiencies led the state department of health and human services to place the center on probation. Although the center's employment policy required two written notices prior to discharge for unsatisfactory performance, the administrator fired the manager. She filed a claim for unemployment benefits. The Supreme Court of New Mexico found no evidence of willful misconduct, insubordination or gross negligence so as to disallow the claim for unemployment benefits. The evidence indicated that the manager was working overtime to try to bring her performance in line with expectations. Her failure to maintain appropriate records involved her inability to obtain documents and required signatures by doctors over whom she had no control. Denying unemployment compensation benefits for misconduct requires a showing of deliberate misconduct that was absent here. It was unfair for the employer to discharge the employee without following its progressive disciplinary policy. *Chicharello v. Employment Security Division*, 930 P.2d 170 (N.M. 1996).

◆ A South Dakota manufacturer sold computer products through telephone reps. The employer assigned daily quotas for sales reps and kept statistics on their performance. It conducted an audit of its phone lines and learned that many employees manipulated their telephone statistics by calling the company's 800 number and placing themselves on hold. The employer circulated a form outlining correct phone procedures, including the requirement to refrain from calling its 800 number. The same month, it fired 10 employees for violating the policy, including two top sales reps who claimed that they were unaware that calling themselves on the 800 number enhanced their statistics and stated that they only wished to listen to music on the hold line while they performed other duties. They filed claims for unemployment compensation. The Supreme Court of South Dakota observed that inefficiency, unsatisfactory conduct, failure to perform job duties as the result of inability or incapacity, good-faith errors in judgment and conduct mandated by religious beliefs do not constitute misconduct under state unemployment compensation law. **Unknowingly violating an employment policy constituted a good-faith error in judgment and was not misconduct.** Because there was evidence that the employees had not seen the form that admonished them not to call the 800 number were simply listening to music, the employees were entitled to benefits. *Abild v. Gateway 2000, Inc.*, 547 N.W.2d 556 (S.D. 1996).

C. Behavioral Expectations

An employer can require employees to conform to reasonable standards of behavior. For example, an employer has the right to expect its employees will not engage in conduct that seriously endangers people's safety. Firing an employee who violates these expectations may result in the denial of unemployment benefits.

- After a rude customer called a Macy's employee a "bitch," the employee told the customer to get her "fat ass out of here." She was then fired. When she applied for unemployment compensation benefits, they were denied. She appealed. At the hearing, Macy's was represented by a non-attorney employee of a company that specialized in unemployment matters. The hearing officer found for Macy's, but a court reversed on the grounds that Macy's wasn't represented by a lawyer. The Supreme Court of Pennsylvania eventually heard the case and decided that **Macy's did not have to hire a lawyer to represent it at unemployment compensation hearings** because such hearings were not trials and did not involve complex legal analysis. Macy's did not have to pay benefits to the fired employee. *Harkness v. Unemployment Compensation Board of Review*, 920 A.2d 162 (Pa. 2007).

- A spray painter worked for an Ohio company for 11 years, the last two of which were marred by harassing behavior from a co-worker who was sabotaging his work and attempting to make trouble for him. He complained repeatedly to management, but little was done. Finally, the painter saw the co-worker remove a lock from a box containing paint spray equipment, for which the painter was responsible. He told his supervisor he was going to "kill the f---ing son of a bitch, stab him in the heart with a screwdriver." He was fired, and applied for unemployment benefits. The Ohio Court of Appeals held that he was entitled to benefits. Here, the painter's inappropriate statement to his supervisor was predictable under the circumstances, and he never directly threatened the co-worker. The company was partly to blame for the incident because it failed to adequately address the earlier harassment. **Because the termination was not for just cause, benefits were awarded.** *Thompson v. Aeroquip Inoac Co.*, 2003 WL 1861005 (Ohio Ct. App. 2003).

- A room service manager for a Missouri casino experienced substantial bleeding associated with her pregnancy, and on December 30, her physician advised her to stay off work for the next week. That night (her night off), she was observed at a rival casino with her husband. The casino determined that she had not conducted herself with the loyalty and integrity appropriate to a managerial employee and fired her. The casino believed that in light of her attendance at the rival casino, she could have worked New Years' Eve. The state employment security commission concluded that she had engaged in misconduct associated with her work and disqualified her from unemployment benefits for seven weeks. The Missouri Court of Appeals reversed. First, **even if the firing was justified because of poor judgment and irresponsible actions, those actions are generally not grounds for denying unemployment**. Second, the standard for denying benefits for off-duty conduct is whether the conduct is clearly egregious or illegal. Here, although irresponsible, the manager's conduct was neither. *Miller v. Kansas City Station Corp*, 996 S.W.2d 120 (Mo. Ct. App. 1999).

◆ After being informed that he could not alter his schedule to make a scheduled court appearance that his immediate supervisor had previously authorized, an Ohio employee stated, "that's bullshit, ... that's f---ing bullshit," and left the office. After imposing a five-day suspension on the employee, the employer discharged him and opposed his subsequent application for unemployment compensation benefits. A state circuit court reversed a final administrative decision in the employer's favor, finding that the expletives were not directed at any person and were of no relative severity or part of a pattern. On appeal, the Court of Appeals of Ohio held that **profanity that was not directed toward anyone did not constitute misconduct** sufficient to disqualify a discharged employee from unemployment. Ohio courts have identified four factors when analyzing discharges based upon profanity, including the severity of the language used, whether the language is part of a pattern of behavior, and whether the outburst was provoked. In this case, each of the factors favored the employee, who had a good employment record and threatened no one. *Lombardo v. Ohio Bureau of Employment Services*, 119 Ohio App.3d 217, 695 N.E.2d 11 (Ohio Ct. App. 1997).

◆ Following a Kentucky employee's outburst, her employer fired her for insubordination and refused to reinstate her despite her assertions that the outburst was an incident of her major depression and dissociative disorder. The state unemployment insurance division initially disqualified her from receiving benefits, and a hearing referee determined that she had been discharged due to misconduct. The agency's final review commission reversed the order, finding no misconduct related to work since, due to her dissociative disorder, the employee could not be held to have willfully disregarded the employer's legitimate business interests. A state court reversed the administrative order, finding insufficient evidence of her mental condition to justify her actions. The court of appeals affirmed, finding that **the lack of medical testimony in support of the employee's position was fatal to her claim**. Since she was unable to establish a connection between her misconduct and her mental condition, the court affirmed the circuit court order denying her appeal. *Burch v. Taylor Drug Store, Inc.*, 965 S.W.2d 830 (Ky. Ct. App. 1998).

◆ A customer service representative at a Delaware bank made a sexually explicit proposition to another representative. The remark was overheard by another employee who monitored telephone calls for quality control purposes. The bank fired the rep for violation of its written sexual harassment policy, which had been published and distributed to all employees. The rep filed a claim for unemployment compensation benefits, which resulted in a determination that he had been dismissed for just cause. His administrative appeals were unsuccessful, and he appealed to the Delaware Superior Court. The court ruled that **an employee's sexually explicit proposition to a co-worker constituted misconduct** that justified the denial of unemployment benefits. It observed that a New York appellate division court had found similar conduct sufficient to justify the denial of an unemployment compensation claim even in the absence of a written sexual harassment policy. *Tuttle v. Mellon Bank of Delaware,* 659 A.2d 786 (Del. Super. Ct. 1995).

◆ A North Dakota food service worker got into a fight with a co-worker, grabbing a knife in the process. Both employees were restrained by others working in the kitchen and, later that day, the employee who had grabbed the knife was discharged for violating a company policy against fighting. She claimed that she had acted in self-defense and obtained unemployment compensation benefits from the state job service. A trial court reversed the eligibility decision, finding that the employee had allowed the fight to escalate and had engaged in mutual combat (misconduct). The Supreme Court of North Dakota stated that misconduct in the context of unemployment compensation is conduct that evinces a willful or wanton disregard of an employer's interests as found in deliberate violation or disregard of employee standards of behavior of which the employer has a right to expect. The court affirmed the denial of benefits, observing that it had previously upheld a denial of benefits where the discharge was for a single incident of violence that violated an employer rule. **Although the employee had a right to defend herself against physical assault, the evidence here indicated that she had engaged in mutual combat.** *ProServe Corp. v. Rainey*, 536 N.W.2d 373 (N.D. 1995).

D. Incompetence or Inability

Generally, an employee's failure to perform as the result of inability or incapacity does not constitute misconduct sufficient to deny benefits. However, an employee's lack of effort or unwillingness to perform may result in the denial of unemployment.

◆ A dock worker and truck driver for a transportation company in North Carolina received several written warnings about his job performance. Eventually he was fired and filed for unemployment benefits. The Employment Security Commission determined that he was discharged for substantial fault not rising to the level of misconduct, and disqualified him from benefits for nine weeks. The case reached the Court of Appeals of North Carolina, which upheld that determination. The employee was careless in performing his job duties despite numerous written warnings. **His performance problems amounted to**

more than just inadvertent mistakes, minor rules infractions or insufficient skill. The nine-week disqualification would stand. *Reeves v. Yellow Transportation, Inc.*, 613 S.E.2d 350 (N.C. Ct. App. 2005).

◆ The manager at a Mall of America store failed to perform up to the standards expected of her and was told that she would be fired if she did not improve. When she continued to have problems running the store, she was fired. She filed for unemployment compensation benefits and received them. The Minnesota Court of Appeals noted that under state law, **inefficiency, simple unsatisfactory conduct or poor performance due to inability or incapacity are not misconduct so as to deprive the claimant of unemployment benefits**. *Bray v. Dogs & Cats Limited*, (1997), 679 N.W.2d 182 (Minn. Ct. App. 2004).

◆ A typist employed by an Ohio law firm persistently made typing errors requiring three or four drafts to correct. The firm gave her two reprimands advising her that her job was in jeopardy if she failed to improve, then fired her. The state bureau of employment services allowed her claim for unemployment benefits, and an administrative referee affirmed, finding no just cause for the termination, since there was no evidence of willful or wanton misconduct. An appeals board found that the employee's inability, not her unwillingness, to improve her performance had resulted in the employment termination and that this did not constitute just cause for unemployment compensation purposes. The court of appeals reversed, and the employee appealed. The Ohio Supreme Court stated that **unsuitability for a job position may constitute fault sufficient to support a just cause termination under the unemployment compensation act**. Employers may justifiably fire deficient employees who cannot perform required work. Because evidence indicated that the employee had made serious errors and could not do required work, the employment termination was supported by just cause, and the denial of benefits was affirmed. *Tzangas, Plakas & Mannos v. Administrator, Ohio Bureau of Employment Services*, 73 Ohio St.3d 694, 653 N.E.2d 1207 (Ohio 1995).

◆ A South Dakota truck driver was convicted of driving under the influence of alcohol. As a result, his driver's license was suspended for one year. He was granted a work permit; however, federal regulations require commercial truck drivers to possess a commercial driver's license (CDL). Because the employee could not obtain a CDL, the company offered him alternative continued employment operating a grinder. He experienced difficulties with the machine and was discharged. His claim for unemployment insurance benefits was denied, and a state court upheld that denial.

The Supreme Court of South Dakota held that if the employee had been discharged for his off-duty traffic violation and consequent inability to obtain a CDL, the discharge would have been for work-connected misconduct that would disqualify him from receiving unemployment insurance benefits. The employee's voluntary conduct in driving drunk was a knowing and substantial disregard of an obligation he owed his employer. However, he had been discharged because of his inability to operate a grinder. South Dakota law states that the **failure to perform as the result of inability or incapacity is not**

misconduct. Accordingly, the employee was entitled to unemployment benefits. *Rasmussen v. South Dakota Dep't of Labor*, 510 N.W.2d 655 (S.D. 1993).

- A man worked as a body shop painter in an Ohio automobile shop. He had a third-grade level of education and was functionally illiterate. As the state of technology of automobile paints advanced, his job required an ability to read in order to correctly blend and match the colors. On several occasions he mixed the wrong colors together, which resulted in costly corrections. The employer offered on numerous occasions to send him to school to learn to read, but he ignored the offers. Thereafter, he was issued repeated warnings for poor work performance, followed by a suspension and discharge. He filed a claim for unemployment compensation, which was denied. A board of review and the Court of Appeals of Ohio affirmed that decision. Discharge for just cause requires a finding that the employee was at fault in some way. The employee argued that the technological advances were beyond his control, and that he was therefore not at fault and should not be deprived of benefits. However, the court found that while inability to perform may not be just cause for discharge, **a lack of effort or unwillingness to perform is just cause for denial of benefits**. Here, the employee refused the help and assistance of his employer and co-workers. He did not demonstrate a good-faith effort to improve his performance. *Lee v. Nick Mayer Lincoln*, 598 N.E.2d 1238 (Ohio Ct. App. 1991).

IV. INDEPENDENT CONTRACTORS

In order to be eligible for unemployment compensation benefits, the separated worker must have been employed on terms that meet statutory definitions of employee. An independent contractor is not an employee and therefore receives no entitlement to unemployment compensation upon separation.

There can also be no employer liability for state unemployment compensation taxes where only independent contractors (and not employees) perform work for the "employer."

- A courier service in California paid drivers to pick up and deliver packages in a timely manner. It filed a complaint for a refund against the Director of the Employment Development Department to recover employment taxes it paid for the drivers. It argued that the drivers operated as independent contractors rather than employees, and that it should not have been assessed under the state's unemployment insurance code. A trial court ruled against the service, and it appealed. The California Court of Appeal held that **the drivers were employees. They worked a regular schedule, and many of those schedules involved regular daily routes.** They infrequently turned down jobs and were paid on a regular schedule. The evidence clearly permitted finding that the drivers were employees such that employment taxes had to be paid. *Air Couriers Int'l v. Employment Development Dep't*, 59 Cal.Rptr.3d 37 (Cal. Ct. App. 2007).

◆ The South Dakota Unemployment Insurance Division determined that **a flower dealer's rose peddlers were employees**. Thus, the dealer was responsible for paying unemployment insurance compensation taxes. The dealer contested the determination, asserting that the peddlers were independent contractors. The case reached the Supreme Court of South Dakota, which ruled against the dealer. The court noted that, first and foremost, the agreement signed by the peddlers contained a non-compete clause that prohibited them from selling flowers for any of the dealer's competitors for two years within a 70-mile radius of Sioux Falls, if they stopped selling for the dealer. Also, they were not liable for unsold flowers; the dealer supplied the necessary items for them to sell the roses; the peddlers did not have their own offices; and they did not have sales tax licenses. Even if the non-compete clause was void as overreaching, it demonstrated an intent to keep the peddlers from engaging in independent work of the same nature if their relationship with the dealer ended. The dealer had to pay unemployment taxes. *Moonlight Rose Co. v. SDUID*, 668 N.W.2d 304 (S.D. 2003).

◆ A Georgia salesperson worked for a book retailer as an independent contractor. He was compensated on the basis of the difference between the cost of books that he took on consignment and the price he obtained for them. The retailer made no payroll deductions and offered no health insurance or retirement plans. It did not require its sales staff to work any particular hours, did not furnish customer lists and did not provide office space or equipment. However, salespersons came to the retailer's premises each week to pick up inventory and turn in their sales receipts. The Georgia Department of Labor determined that **the retailer was liable for contributions to the state unemployment compensation fund on behalf of the salespersons**. The retailer appealed. The Court of Appeals of Georgia rejected the retailer's argument that it was not an employer under the compensation statute's exception for independent contract carriers who were compensated on the basis of the number of deliveries accomplished. Salespersons were compensated for the difference between the retail price and the consignment amount, not the number of their deliveries. The court also determined that in-office inventory pickups by salespersons resulted in the provision of services at the retailer's business. This was fatal to the retailer's claim that it was exempt from unemployment compensation contributions. *American Book Display v. Poythress*, 479 S.E.2d 198 (Ga. Ct. App. 1996).

◆ The New York Supreme Court, Appellate Division, affirmed awards of unemployment compensation benefits in cases filed by drivers who owned their own vehicles and worked under contract for trucking and delivery companies. In the first case, an independent driver contracted with a transportation company to share revenues for loading and transporting freight. When he terminated his relationship with the company, the state labor department determined that he was not entitled to receive unemployment benefits. This decision was overturned in administrative appeals before reaching the appellate division, which observed that although the driver owned the vehicle, the company's name was painted on its doors and he responded to the company's instructions. The agreement required that he not work for another company without permission. There was substantial evidence that **the company exercised sufficient overall control over the driver to establish his status as an employee and his corresponding entitlement to benefits**. *Claim of Short*, 649 N.Y.S.2d 955 (N.Y. App. Div. 1996).

◆ In the second case, drivers who owned their own vehicles contracted with a delivery service to accept only deliveries authorized by the service. The service also required each vehicle to carry its emblem. Drivers were subject to a review process and responded only to service dispatch requests. Applying the rule of control to determine the existence of an employment relationship, the appellate court found that **the service maintained sufficient control over the drivers to establish their status as employees**. The service was liable for additional unemployment insurance contributions. *Claim of McKenna*, 649 N.Y.S.2d 953 (N.Y. App. Div. 1996).

V. SETOFF

State laws provide that unemployment compensation benefits can be offset by or can offset other awards. Disability benefits, vacation benefits, pension benefits and workers' compensation benefits may all allow a setoff in certain circumstances.

◆ Ohio auto workers were laid off after a strike in Michigan caused a shortage of parts. When the strike ended, the automaker agreed to pay the Ohio employees a special one-time payment for the week of the Fourth of July, for which the employees would have been paid had they been able to work. The agreement stated that the payment might make the employees ineligible for unemployment compensation already received, and further stated that the employees would have to repay any overpayment. The employees asserted that the special payment should not prevent them from receiving unemployment compensation for the week in question, but the Ohio Bureau of Employment Services ruled that the employees should not receive unemployment benefits for that week. The case reached the Ohio Court of Appeals, which held that **the special payment was "remuneration" such that the employees were not entitled to unemployment benefits for that week**. *Rodriguez v. Ohio Dep't of Job & Family Services*, 847 N.E.2d 458 (Ohio Ct. App. 2006).

◆ A Colorado worker with diabetes and other physical disabilities was laid off from the part-time job he held to supplement his Social Security Disability Insurance (SSDI) benefits. He applied for unemployment benefits, which he was initially awarded. However, when the Division of Employment learned that he was receiving SSDI benefits, it ruled that **because of the offset required by state law, he was not entitled to unemployment benefits**. State law provided for an offset of 50% of the prorated weekly social security benefit. In this case, the worker's weekly SSDI benefit was $311, more than twice his unemployment benefit of $108. Since half of $311 was still more than $108, he was ineligible for unemployment benefits. Further, there was no

Americans with Disabilities Act violation because the offset did not discriminate against him on the basis of disability. He would also have been ineligible for unemployment if he were receiving retirement benefits. *Cericalo v. Industrial Claim Appeals Office of State of Colorado*, 114 P.3d 100 (Colo. Ct. App. 2005).

◆ A seaman worked under a collective bargaining agreement that compelled him to take vacation after 120 consecutive days aboard an employer's ship. Under the agreement, instead of paying the seaman for compelled vacation, the employer paid into a union trust fund, from which the seaman could apply for the benefits from the union. If he failed to do so within 15 months, he would lose the benefits. After 111 days aboard, the seaman began a period of unemployment and, rather than apply for the 56 days of union benefits he had coming, he sought unemployment benefits. The employer asserted that his unemployment benefits should be reduced by the amount of vacation pay it had paid into the union trust fund. The Oregon Court of Appeals disagreed. **The payment into the union trust fund did not entitle the employer to an offset.** *Alaska Tanker Co. v. Employment Dep't*, 61 P.3d 276 (Or. Ct. App. 2003).

◆ A Utah carpenter was laid off by two different employers in one year and received unemployment compensation benefits for parts of two years based on his employment with both employers. He then applied for social security benefits and received a retroactive award that encompassed some months during which he received unemployment compensation. He later filed a third claim for unemployment, which was denied. He appealed, and an administrative law judge ruled that he was ineligible for unemployment benefits and that the retroactive social security retirement income he received reduced his weekly benefit to zero. However, because the employee had notified the department of his social security application, the amount would only have to be repaid from any future unemployment compensation award. An appeal board affirmed the administrative decision, and the employee appealed to the Court of Appeals of Utah.

On appeal, the employee argued that it was improper to set off an unemployment compensation award with social security benefits because social security benefits are not retirement pay and the two programs have separate purposes. The board argued that the setoff was required by state law, which included social security in the definition of retirement benefits. The court agreed with the board, finding that Congress enacted the Unemployment Compensation Amendments of 1976 to **allow the states to reduce unemployment compensation awards by the amount of any public or private pensions received**, including social security retirement benefits. Since Utah's unemployment compensation code permitted a 100% reduction in benefits for retirement pay received, the court affirmed the decision. *Harrington v. Industrial Comm'n*, 942 P.2d 961 (Utah App. 1997).

◆ An Ohio mining company announced a mine closing due to economic problems and paid its employees for their unused vacation time in lump sums at the time of the closing. Employees who filed claims for unemployment benefits received a favorable determination of eligibility, but the state compensation review board modified the award of benefits to reflect the deduction of vacation pay received for those employees with scheduled vacations during the layoff period. The employer appealed to a state court, which affirmed the board of review's decision. The employer appealed to the Court of Appeals of Ohio, which held that the employer **could reduce unemployment compensation benefits by vacation pay only for those employees who had selected their vacations during the period of the layoff**, since those benefits were voluntarily elected by the employees. Those employees who had received vacation pay lump sums at the employer's designation could not be deemed as having received remuneration during the layoff as contemplated by the state unemployment compensation law. Reducing unemployment benefits for these employees was not lawful or reasonable, and their claims for unemployment benefits not reduced by the lump sums were affirmed. *Akzo Salt, Inc. v. Ohio Bureau of Employment Services*, 669 N.E.2d 250 (Ohio Ct. App. 1995).

CHAPTER NINE

Employer Insurance Coverage

I. AREAS OF COVERAGE

Insurance policies are generally of two types – first party insurance and third party insurance. First party insurance policies cover losses incurred by the insured (e.g., a policy that compensates a business for losses suffered in a warehouse fire). Property and casualty policies, health and life insurance, and fidelity bonds are examples of first party insurance.

Third party insurance policies cover the insured for losses suffered by third parties. Liability insurance is third party insurance because it provides that the insurer will defend the insured for claims against it and indemnify the insured for any amount it becomes liable to pay.

Many insurance policies are hybrid first and third party policies. For example, a business automobile policy covers the company and employees for injuries or losses incurred in a motor vehicle accident, but also provides liability coverage in case an employee is involved in an accident and injures a third party.

Businesses seek to find coverage under their liability policies for a variety of issues, particularly related to employment practices and personal injury claims. Coverage, however, may be limited based on the definitions of "injury" and/or "occurrence." Also, specific exclusions such as "assault and battery" exclusions often preclude coverage for certain types of conduct.

◆ A company in Oklahoma purchased about 1,400 corporate-owned life insurance policies on all its full-time employees. When an employee died, the company collected $340,000. Four years later it filed for bankruptcy protection and the widow learned about the policy. She sued to collect the proceeds. A federal court granted pretrial judgment to the company, but the Tenth Circuit reversed. Here, **the company did not have an "insurable interest" in the employee's life**. He was not a key corporate officer the company substantially depended on, but rather a rank-and-file employee. *Tillman v. Camelot Music, Inc.*, 408 F.3d 1300 (10th Cir. 2005).

A. Liability Policies

Commercial or comprehensive general liability (CGL) policies cover a broad range of losses. In this chapter, we will concern ourselves with issues that arise out of the employment relationship, and the attempt by employers to protect themselves against loss to third parties through insurance. This means we will focus on third party (liability) insurance rather than on first party insurance.

One of the greatest benefits liability policies provide is the <u>duty to defend</u>, which is generally broader than the duty to indemnify (pay for loss). Because the costs of litigation are so high, insurers often seek to avoid paying defense costs by asserting an exclusion or a lack of coverage.

◆ A Maryland company purchased a business liability policy with $1 million of coverage. The policy limited coverage for fellow employees to the statutory minimum required by state law. After an employee fell asleep at the wheel returning from a job, his co-worker passenger suffered severe injuries and sued the company and insurer. The case reached the Court of Appeals of Maryland, which held that the limitation did not violate public policy. **As long as the policy provided at least the minimum recovery to the innocent passenger, it was valid.** The limitation was upheld. *Wilson v. Nationwide Mutual Insurance Co.*, 910 A.2d 1122 (Md. 2006).

◆ A cell phone manufacturer was sued in two class actions by consumers who were seeking compensation for damages allegedly caused by using the phones. The lawsuits claimed that the cell phones emit harmful radio frequency radiation that potentially causes injury to human cells when the cell phones are used without a headset. The manufacturer tendered the defense of the complaints to its CGL and excess umbrella liability insurer, because it believed the class actions alleged "bodily injury" and sought "damages because of bodily injury" under the insurer's policies. The insurer defended one class action under a reservation of rights but refused to defend the other because the plaintiffs in that action expressly disclaimed damages for personal injury resulting from the use of the cell phones. The question of whether the insurer had to defend the manufacturer reached the Texas Court of Appeals, which held that **the cellular damage alleged by the consumers amounted to bodily injury under the policies**. The court also held that the cost of headsets sought by the plaintiffs constituted "damages because of bodily injury" within the meaning of the policies. Thus, the insurer had to defend the first lawsuit. However, the insurer did not have to defend the second lawsuit, where the plaintiffs had only alleged misrepresentation and unjust enrichment. *Samsung Electronics America, Inc. v. Federal Insurance Co.*, 202 S.W.3d 372 (Tex. Ct. App. 2006).

1. Negligent Supervision

Negligent supervision occurs when an employer knows or reasonably should know that an employee is likely to cause harm but fails to properly supervise the employee to prevent the harm. Similar causes of action are negligent hiring and negligent retention. All three involve holding the employer vicariously liable for the actions of its employee.

Insurance is generally available where the employer negligently fails to supervise its employees (even if the employees commit intentional wrongdoing against a third party). Although intentional wrongdoing is ordinarily not insurable, coverage may be available for the negligence of the employer in allowing the employee to commit the intentional wrongdoing.

- A beauty salon/health spa obtained a business liability policy that covered claims for bodily injury caused by an occurrence. A customer later sued the salon, asserting that a masseur made improper sexual contact while performing a full body massage. She asserted that the salon was liable for negligently hiring and retaining the masseur, as well as for failing to properly supervise his activities. The insurer denied coverage on the grounds that the injury was intended or expected from the standpoint of the insured, and on the grounds that the injury resulted from a body massage other than a facial massage – both exclusions under the policy. The case reached the New York Court of Appeals, which held that **the masseur's alleged intention to commit an assault could not be attributed to his employer**. Further, even though the policy excluded injury arising out of a body massage, the injury here was from an alleged sexual assault and not from the actual massage. The insurer had to defend and indemnify the salon. *RJC Realty Holding Corp. v. Republic Franklin Insurance Co.*, 2 N.Y.3d 158 (N.Y. 2004).

- At an anti-abortion demonstration at a Wisconsin clinic, a father accused a woman of cursing and kicking his daughter in the face. The allegations against the woman were covered extensively in broadcasts by a radio station owned by Wisconsin Voice of Christian Youth (WVCY). Two employees of WVCY also caused the woman's assets to be encumbered and served a false subpoena at her residence. Based on these incidents, she sued WVCY for negligent supervision. One of WVCY's comprehensive general liability insurers sued for a determination that it did not have to defend or indemnify WVCY. The

Wisconsin Supreme Court held that **the CGL policy provided coverage for negligent supervision**. Since the claim focused on WVCY's negligence in supervising its employees whether or not the employees committed the underlying wrong intentionally, the intentional acts exclusion did not bar coverage. The insurer had a duty to defend. *Doyle v. Engelke*, 580 N.W.2d 245 (Wis. 1998).

- A Florida bird supply business maintained a CGL policy that covered "occurrences." Two separate lawsuits were filed against the business by parents of two minor children, alleging that the minors were sexually molested by two of the business' employees on the premises during nonbusiness hours. The complaints alleged that the business had actual or constructive knowledge of its employees' propensities and use of the business premises, and that the business was negligent in hiring, retaining, training and supervising its employees. The insurer initially agreed to defend the business, and then sued for a ruling that it had no duty to defend. The District Court of Appeal of Florida held that the insurer owed a duty to defend based on the allegations of constructive knowledge. If the evidence established that the business had no actual knowledge of the abuse but with the exercise of due care could have learned of it and taken remedial steps to prevent the victimization of the plaintiffs, then **its negligence would qualify as an "occurrence" under the policy**. Also, the complaints were not barred by the intentional acts exclusion as the insured itself was never involved in any sexual abuse. *Sunshine Birds and Supplies, Inc. v. U.S. Fidelity and Guaranty Co.*, 696 So.2d 907 (Fla. Dist. Ct. App. 1997).

- An Indiana painting company, insured under a liability policy, entered into a contract to paint an individual's home. The home was allegedly burglarized and set on fire by one of the painting company's employees. After the homeowner sued the employee and the company for negligent hiring and retention, the insurer sued for a declaration that the fire loss to the homeowner was not covered by the policy. The Court of Appeals of Indiana determined that the policy language limited coverage to personal injury or property damage caused by an "occurrence." The term **"occurrence" meant "an accident,"** defined as an unexpected happening without intention or design. Here, the property damage was alleged to have arisen from the company's hiring and retention of the employee. Even if proven to be careless and negligent, these acts were intentional as opposed to accidental. As a result, the homeowner's action against the company was not the result of an "occurrence" as defined by the policy. The policy did not cover the damage. *Erie Insurance Co. v. American Painting Co.*, 678 N.E.2d 844 (Ind. Ct. App. 1997).

2. Sexual Harassment

Generally, sexual harassment will not be covered by insurance because it is intentional in nature. CGL policies cover accidents and occurrences, usually caused by negligence. Because sexual harassment is intentional, any harm that arises from the harassment will have to be compensated by the company and not its insurers.

◆ A former waitress at an Ohio restaurant sued the restaurant and its owners for sexual harassment, alleging that she was subjected to unwelcome and vulgar remarks as well as unwanted touching of her breasts, buttocks and genitalia. She also asserted that she was sexually assaulted by a male co-worker right before she quit. The restaurant sought a defense from its liability insurer, which refused to defend one of the owners and the parent company. The case reached the Court of Appeals of Ohio, which ruled that the claims against the parent company were not precluded by public policy because the parent company was not the party that committed the intentional tort against the waitress. Next, the court held that the Stop-Gap endorsement was intended to cover damages for bodily injury, including mental anguish, to employees, that is alleged or is determined to be substantially certain to occur as the result of an employer's intentional tort. Notably, the Stop-Gap was careful to distinguish between this type of situation and one in which an injury is "directly intended." Thus, **the insurer had to defend both the owner and the parent company, which could be vicariously liable** for the harm the waitress suffered as a result of the intentional conduct of the co-worker. *GNFH v. West American Insurance Co.*, 873 N.E.2d 345 (Ohio Ct. App. 2007).

◆ A Georgia supervisor allegedly made submission to his sexual advances a condition of employment. When three employees reported the harassment, the company allegedly discriminated against them for doing so. They sued the company and won. The company then sued its umbrella liability insurer to recover that amount under the policy, despite an exclusion for bodily or personal injury inflicted by one employee on another "arising out of and in the course of" their employment. The Georgia Supreme Court looked to workers' compensation law, where the terms had been previously construed. It noted that "in the course of" related to the time, place and circumstances under which the injury took place. "Arising out of" referred to a causal connection between the conditions under which the work was required to be performed and the resulting injury. **Sexual harassment claims do not arise out of employment, even though they occur in the course of employment**, because such injuries are not a risk of employment that a reasonable person would foresee arising. Injuries from harassment are due to the willful act of a third person for personal reasons and are not work related. The exclusion did not bar coverage. *SCI Liquidating Corp. v. Hartford Fire Insurance Co.*, 526 S.E.2d 555 (Ga. 2000).

◆ An importer and wholesaler of alcoholic beverages hired models called "Jagerettes" to appear at promotional events to encourage liquor sales. The Equal Employment Opportunity Commission (EEOC) filed charges against the importer, alleging that the company president, as well as a number of management employees, engaged in sexually harassing behavior against more than 100 female employees, including the "Jagerettes" who attended these functions. Among other things, the EEOC claimed that the president and company managers tried to hug, kiss and fondle the women during these events. The importer's CGL policy covered claims for bodily injury or property damage caused by "occurrences," but excluded coverage that was expected or intended by the insured. The importer sued after its insurer refused to defend the action. A federal court ruled for the insurer, noting that **sexual harassment, like sexual abuse and child abuse, is intentional in nature** and does not qualify as an occurrence under a CGL policy. The intent to harm can be inferred from the harassing acts because harm is inherent in the nature of the acts alleged. *Sidney Frank Importing Co. v. Farmington Casualty Co.*, 199 F.3d 1323 (2d Cir. 1999).

◆ A former secretary brought a sexual harassment suit against her employer and the company's sole owner and director. She alleged that the owner touched her inappropriately, attempted to kiss her and solicited sexual intercourse and oral sex. The company's insurer defended the suit under a reservation of rights and sought a declaratory judgment on its legal duty to defend. It maintained that a harassment exclusion in the employer's liability policy precluded coverage. The trial court decided that the policy exclusion for damages "arising out of harassment and discrimination against any employee" was ambiguous, and that it did not exclude vicarious liability for the actions of employees. The Court of Appeals of Kentucky reversed. It saw **no ambiguity in the exclusion for damages "arising out of" sexual harassment**. The exclusion covered vicarious liability as well as direct liability. Moreover, the court determined that there was no vicarious liability claim since the actions of the corporation could not be separated from those of its owner and director in this instance. The insurer had no duty to defend. *Midwestern Insurance Alliance, Inc. v. Coffman*, 7 S.W.3d 393 (Ky. Ct. App. 1999).

◆ After the president of an insured private preschool sued a former female employee for slander, she brought a counterclaim against him and the school for sexual harassment. The insurer refused to defend the counterclaim, saying sexual harassment claims were excluded from coverage. The Court of Appeals of Texas noted that the policy excluded coverage for "intentional conduct." The former employee alleged that the president forcefully tried to kiss her, fondled her buttocks, touched and rubbed her thighs, and rubbed her shoulders in a sexual manner. She also alleged that he used sexually abusive, sexually suggestive and vulgar language when speaking with her. Taking the former employee's allegations as true, the president's acts were voluntary and intentional, and the injury to the former employee was the natural result of these acts. Therefore, the alleged conduct was excluded from coverage. However, **an issue of fact existed as to whether the insurer misrepresented the scope of coverage provided by the policy**. A trial needed to be held on that issue. *Cottage School System Inc. v. Cigna Lloyds Insurance Co.*, 1999 WL 1081032 (Tex. Ct. App. 1999).

◆ A former employee of a Virginia company filed a charge with the Equal Employment Opportunity Commission, alleging that she had been constructively discharged as a result of sexual harassment and discrimination. The company sought coverage under its commercial excess umbrella policy, which provided coverage for personal injury, bodily injury, and advertising injury. The policy also contained an employment exclusion precluding coverage for any liability "arising out of injury of an employee in the course of employment." When the insurer denied coverage, the company sued. A federal court ruled for the insurer, finding that the term "injury" was not ambiguous and that the employment exclusion barred coverage. The U.S. Court of Appeals, Fourth Circuit, affirmed. Although "injury" was not defined in the policy, the court held that the term encompassed the subsets of personal injury, bodily injury, and advertising injury, all of which were carefully defined by the policy. Based on the absence of such qualifiers in the exclusion, **the court interpreted "injury" according to its plain meaning**, which generally incorporates a wrong or damage done to a person or his property, reputation or rights. *Gates, Hudson & Associates, Inc. v. Federal Insurance Co.*, 141 F.3d 500 (4th Cir. 1997).

◆ An Arizona corporation was insured under a commercial general liability policy. A female sales rep alleged that the corporation's president had sexually harassed and assaulted her on numerous occasions at the office and on business trips. The president admitted to having sexual relations with the rep, but claimed that she had consented. The corporation reported the claim to its insurer, which stated that the intentional act exclusion in the policy precluded coverage. It then sued for a declaration that it had no duty to defend or indemnify the corporation in the underlying sexual harassment suit. The trial court ruled in favor of the insurer, and the insured appealed. The Court of Appeals of Arizona affirmed, noting that if the acts had happened as the rep said, then they were intentional and occurred without her consent. However, if the acts had happened as the president proclaimed, there were no claims because the rep had consented. Thus, **the intentional act exclusion precluded coverage for the president's alleged sexual misconduct**. *Northern Insurance Co. of New York v. Morgan,* 918 P.2d 1051 (Ariz. Ct. App. 1995).

3. Discrimination

Discrimination, like harassment, is generally not covered by insurance, so any discrimination that occurs will result in company liability that cannot be recouped. For more cases on discrimination and harassment not involving insurance coverage issues, please see Chapter One.

◆ After guaranteeing a reservation with a credit card, a hotel in New York refused to rent two suites to a predominantly African-American church for a youth retreat on the grounds that they would make too much noise. The church sued the hotel for race discrimination, among other claims, and the hotel sought coverage under its CGL insurance policy. After the insurer denied coverage, a lawsuit resulted. A Kansas federal court ruled that **there could be no insurance coverage for a denial of accommodations on the basis of racial discrimination**, and that all the underlying acts were intentional. The Kansas Court of Appeals affirmed. Here, the harm flowed directly and immediately from an allegedly intentional act, not from negligence or recklessness. *Rockgate Management Co. v. CGU Insurance, Inc.*, 88 P.3d 798 (Kan. Ct. App. 2004).

◆ **The insured owner of a bar and restaurant was sued for race discrimination after allegedly denying entry to black patrons on three occasions** while allowing whites of similar age and attire to enter. The insurer refused to defend or indemnify under the policy. The bar owner settled two of the cases on terms favorable to the patrons, then sought coverage under a policy clause that protected against "bodily injury," including "wrongful eviction … of a person from a room, dwelling or premises." The Oregon Court of Appeals ruled that "wrongful eviction" is limited to improperly removing a person from property where he or she has a possessory interest. A customer or prospective customer of a commercial establishment does not ordinarily have a possessory interest in the establishment he or she is trying to enter. Thus, this policy provision did not apply. The court also found no duty to defend or indemnify under the policy's liquor liability coverage. That provision applied to liability "imposed on the insured by reason of the selling, serving or furnishing of any alcoholic beverage." *STK Enterprises Inc. v. Crusader Insurance Co.*, 14 P.3d 638 (Or. Ct. App. 2000).

◆ An Oregon man owned an apartment building that was insured under a "Special Business Owners" insurance policy. A husband and wife managed the building. A prospective tenant with a seven-week-old child inquired about a vacant second-floor apartment. The wife informed her that the building did not allow small children on the second floor because of safety concerns, such as falling off the balcony or down the stairs. Since no first-floor apartments were available, the woman could not live there. She sued the owner for intentional housing discrimination. After the insurer refused to defend or indemnify the owner, he sued it for breach of contract. A trial court ruled for the insurer. The Supreme Court of Oregon affirmed. The policy did not cover a claim of housing discrimination made by a prospective tenant. Although the policy insured against "wrongful entry or eviction or *other* invasion of the right of private occupancy," it limited claims to those involving an existing possessory interest. **Since the prospective tenant held no existing possessory interest in the property, her discrimination claim was not covered.** *Groshong v. Mutual of Enumclaw Insurance Co.*, 985 P.2d 1284 (Or. 1999).

◆ An employee of an Oregon insured requested permission to miss a meeting in order to attend a religious ceremony with his wife and children. Initially, the insured granted its permission, but later revoked it. When the employee insisted on attending the ceremony, the insured fired him. The employee filed an employment discrimination suit against the insured, and the insured tendered a request to defend to its insurer. The insurer accepted with a reservation of rights; however, it then refused to defend further. The insured retained its own defense counsel and ultimately lost the discrimination case on appeal. It then sued the insurer for breach of contract, seeking to recover from the insurer its cost of defending in the underlying action. The case reached the Oregon Court of Appeals, which noted that the insurer had agreed to pay for personal injury, including discrimination, if the coverage was not prohibited by law or public policy. Both parties agreed that liability for intentional discrimination was uninsurable and excluded from the policy, but liability for unintentional discrimination was insurable and within coverage. In affirming the trial court, the court of appeals concluded that **there was sufficient proof of unintentional conduct made in the original complaint by the employee to find that coverage was warranted**. Therefore, the insurer was required to defend the insured and was liable for the defense costs incurred. *Ron Tonkin Chevrolet v. Continental Insurance Co.*, 870 P.2d 252 (Or. Ct. App. 1994).

4. Employment Termination

Most CGL policies exclude coverage for claims arising out of employment terminations, though they may cover events in close proximity (like defamation, invasion of privacy, false imprisonment and malicious prosecution).

◆ Two former employees of an insured company sued for defamation after they were fired. The company sought defense and indemnity from its liability insurer, which asserted that it had no duty to defend because of the exclusion for terminations or employment-related practices. A California federal court ruled for the insurer and the Ninth Circuit affirmed. Here, **the alleged defamation occurred when the company was looking for a justification to fire the employees**. Further, even though the alleged defamation continued for up to three months, the statements at issue related to the termination. Thus, the insurer had no duty to defend. *Pace Integrated Systems, Insurance v. RLI Insurance Co.*, 196 Fed.Appx. 514 (9th Cir. 2006).

◆ A building engineer at a 19-story office building in Dallas worked for a number of management companies until he was fired. He later sued the owners and managers of the building, alleging that he was wrongfully terminated and that, after his firing, the owners and managers circulated color "wanted posters" of him to the general public, including tenants and customers in the building. The posters asked anyone spotting the engineer in the building to call security and, in addition to a picture of him, contained his name, address, driver's license number, Social Security number and car tag number. The owners and managers also hired eight uniformed Dallas police officers to patrol the lobby and parking garage. When the owners and managers sought insurance coverage in the lawsuit, their CGL insurer claimed that it did not have to defend or indemnify them because the circumstances relating to the termination were internal employment practices and not a "business activity." The Fifth Circuit disagreed, holding that the owners and managers had acted consistently with their business of owning and managing the property in light of a potential duty of care to tenants and customers, and a perceived risk. Thus, **the insurer had to defend the lawsuit by the fired engineer**. *St. Paul Guardian Insurance Co. v. Centrum GS Limited*, 283 F.3d 709 (5th Cir. 2002).

◆ An Illinois employee sued his former employer, alleging that he was fired for filing a workers' compensation claim. The employer's CGL insurer denied coverage. After the employer won the underlying suit, it sued its insurer to recover attorneys' fees and costs. The Appellate Court of Illinois found that **the retaliatory discharge claim fell outside the policy's coverage**. Although the policy provided coverage for "personal injury," the list of expressly covered personal injuries (i.e., false arrest, malicious prosecution, slander/libel, and privacy violations) did not include retaliatory discharge. Moreover, retaliatory discharge would not normally be construed, either expressly or by implication, as one of the enumerated injuries covered. Because a reasonable purchaser of insurance would not conclude that such a risk was covered, the employer here could not have reasonably reached such a conclusion, and the insurer did not have a duty to defend or indemnify it. *Emtech Machining & Grinding, Inc. v. Transcontinental Insurance Co.*, 695 N.E.2d 545 (Ill. App. Ct. 1998).

◆ A New York veterinarian clinic owner fired one of his veterinarians. At a staff meeting, and later to at least one client, the clinic owner criticized the veterinarian's performance. He also wrote a form letter to clients indicating that a number of differences of opinion had made it impossible for the veterinarian to continue as an employee and that a well-trained, experienced veterinarian had replaced her at the clinic. The veterinarian sued the clinic owner for defamation. A jury returned a verdict in her favor and awarded compensatory and punitive damages, which the appellate division substantially modified. Although the clinic owner's insurer provided a defense under a liability policy, it ultimately found no coverage. The clinic owner then sued the insurer.

The court found that the insurer was not required to indemnify the clinic for the compensatory damages based on the employment-related exclusion. **The policy expressly excluded coverage for "personal injury" arising out of such activities as termination, defamation, and evaluation.** Regardless of the clinic owner's motive for mildly criticizing the veterinarian to the staff and clients, the statements constituted an assessment of the veterinarian's performance as an employee and an explanation of why she was discharged. As a result, the statements fell squarely within the exclusion. Even though the statements were made after the veterinarian was discharged, they were nevertheless clearly "employment-related." However, the form letters sent to the clients, asking them to continue using the clinic, fell within the coverage of "advertising injury," thereby entitling the clinic to indemnification for the post-verdict expenses. *Berman v. General Accident Insurance Co. of America*, 671 N.Y.S.2d 619 (N.Y. Sup. Ct. 1998).

◆ After a Montana employer fired an employee for alleged misconduct, the employee sued for wrongful discharge. The employer sought coverage under the professional liability provision of its liability policy, which granted coverage for injuries "arising out of any negligent act, error or omission in rendering or failure to render professional services." The policy also included a "combined provisions endorsement" that **excluded claims arising out of employment terminations**. The insurer refused coverage based on the employment termination exclusion. The Supreme Court of Montana held that the exclusion precluded coverage. The "combined provisions endorsement," which stated that the policy did not cover claims arising from employment terminations, extended to the entire policy including the professional liability provision. The policy was not ambiguous because both the combined provisions endorsement and the professional liability provision were clearly identified as attachments under the same policy number. The two provisions also indicated that they related to one another. Thus, the insurer did not have to defend or indemnify the employer. *Counterpoint, Inc. v. Essex Insurance Co.*, 967 P.2d 393 (Mont. 1998).

5. Drinking and Driving Accidents

Where an employee gets in an accident after drinking and driving, business automobile insurers generally look to the scope of permission the employee had in determining whether coverage is available. If the employee was not allowed to use the vehicle after drinking, the insurer will be able to argue that there is no coverage because the policy only covers drivers who have permission to use the vehicle.

- A Texas auto shop employee commuted two hours each way to work, driving a company truck and dropping off tires once or twice a week, either at the shop near where he lived or the one where he worked. One night after work, he drove the company truck to his father's house for dinner, had a few beers and fell asleep for four hours. When he awoke after midnight, he went out for cigarettes for his father. He fell asleep at the wheel and was involved in an accident. When the other driver sued, the company's insurer refused to defend the case. He then sued the company and its insurer, and the Fifth Circuit held that the defendants were not entitled to pretrial judgment. There was a fact question over **whether the employee had implied permission to use the truck for minor errands after work**. *Adams v. Travelers Indemnity Co. of Connecticut*, 465 F.3d 156 (5th Cir. 2006).

- An employee of a Virginia company was assigned to a work site in Denver. While there, he went to a bar with some co-workers on a Saturday night. On the way home with a co-worker to company-provided housing, but while driving his own car, he was involved in a fatal accident. The victim's family sued the company's insurer to recover under its employee auto insurance policy. A Virginia court and the Fourth Circuit ruled in favor of the insurer. Here, the policy stated that in order for an employee to recover under the policy while driving his own car, he must be performing the employer's "business or personal affairs" at the time of the accident. Since **the employee was not acting within the scope of his employment while driving home from the bar**, the policy did not cover the accident. *Pham v. Hartford Fire Insurance Co.*, 419 F.3d 286 (4th Cir. 2005).

- An Indiana truck driver consumed alcoholic beverages and then unhooked a cab from one of his employer's semi-trailer trucks. While driving the cab, he collided with another vehicle and injured a couple. The couple sued the truck driver and his employer. The employer's liability insurer filed a declaratory judgment action to establish that it had no obligation to defend or indemnify. The Supreme Court of Indiana determined that the truck driver was not an insured under the employer's liability policy. The policy provided coverage to the employer as well as anyone else using a covered truck with the employer's permission. The employer's no-alcohol rule expressly restricted the grant of permission. Here, **the truck driver's permission to use the employer's truck was restricted when he consumed alcohol**. Therefore, the driver was not an insured under the policy. However, with respect to the lawsuit against the employer, there were genuine issues of material fact concerning whether the truck driver was acting within the scope of his employment despite the employer's no-drinking rule. Those required a trial. *Warner Trucking, Inc. v. Carolina Casualty Insurance Co.*, 686 N.E.2d 102 (Ind. 1997).

- A Georgia employee drove a company truck after consuming alcohol, in violation of company policy, and collided with four vehicles. In the lawsuit that followed, the trial court granted pretrial judgment to the employer and insurer. The Court of Appeals of Georgia determined that the employer's automobile policy provided coverage for anyone using a covered auto with the employer's permission. Because the employer had **a rule that prohibited the possession and consumption of alcoholic beverages in company vehicles**, the employee had exceeded the scope of his permission by driving the vehicle while under the influence of alcohol. Therefore, he was not a permissive driver entitled to coverage under the policy. The court of appeals then noted that the employer could be responsible for damages resulting from the collision if a jury found the employer vicariously liable for the employee's actions. Here, there was an issue of fact as to whether the employee was engaged in an errand required by his employer. The judgment of the lower court was affirmed in part and reversed in part. *Barfield v. Royal Insurance Co. of America,* 492 S.E.2d 688 (Ga. Ct. App. 1997).

- A New York husband and wife who owned and operated a service station were insured under a business policy. A woman brought her car to the station to have its front axle worked on. She left the vehicle at the station with the understanding that the husband would test-drive the vehicle. Four or five days later, after closing for the night, the husband drove the vehicle to a local pub. There he met a friend and drank eight highballs. He then left the bar to take his friend home and was involved in an accident that caused injuries to both the friend and the driver of the other vehicle. The injured parties sued the insureds and their business. Eventually, a lawsuit was brought regarding coverage under the business liability policy. The New York Supreme Court, Appellate Division, held that **if the customer's vehicle was being test driven when it was involved in the accident, it would have been covered** under the policy. However, the vehicle was clearly being operated for the insured's personal use and was in no way being used in connection with his business. Therefore, the accident was not covered by the policy. *Dumblewski v. ITT Hartford Insurance Group*, 623 N.Y.S.2d 374 (N.Y. App. Div. 1995).

B. Exclusions

Most policies exclude coverage for certain acts. Some exclusions address specific types of conduct such as assault and battery, while other exclusions cover a broader range of conduct (like intentionally harmful conduct). Employment-related exclusions often exclude coverage for conduct based on the employer/employee relationship.

1. Assault and Battery Exclusion

The assault and battery exclusion bars coverage for actions that amount to assault or battery. Further, all harm arising out of the assault or battery will not be covered unless the employer is being sued for negligent supervision. Even then, a court may find that no coverage is available.

- A customer at a restaurant in Connecticut was confronted by three drunk patrons, who punched and struck him until all four men were thrown out of the restaurant. In the parking lot, the three men continued to assault the customer. He suffered injuries and sued the restaurant for negligence. A court ruled in his favor. After he was unable to collect from the restaurant, he sought to recover the restaurant's liability policy proceeds as a judgment creditor. The case reached the Connecticut Court of Appeals, which ruled in favor of the insurer. Here, **even though he alleged that the restaurant was negligent, his injuries arose from the assault and battery**, which were excluded by the liability policy. *Clinch v. Generali-U.S. Branch*, 110 Conn.App. 29, 954 A.2d 223 (Conn. App. Ct. 2008).

- A patron of a Pennsylvania nightclub was forcibly evicted, wrestled down the stairs (at times in a choke hold) and thrown face down on the ground. The bouncers then laid on top of him, restricting his ability to breathe and ultimately suffocating him. His estate sued the nightclub to recover for his death, and the nightclub's insurer asserted that it had no duty to defend or indemnify because of the assault and battery exclusion of the CGL policy. The Superior Court of Pennsylvania ruled against the insurer. Here, **the alleged negligence that caused the patron's death was an accident** and therefore an occurrence under the policy. Thus, the assault and battery exclusion did not apply to bar coverage. *QBE Insurance Corp. v. M & S Landis Corp.*, 915 A.2d 1222 (Pa. Super. 2007).

- A detective agency provided a man with the Social Security number and place of employment of a certain woman. The man then drove to her workplace, where he fatally shot her and then himself. Her estate sued the detective agency for negligence in providing the man the information needed to find and kill her. It also sued for invasion of privacy and violation of the state Consumer Protection Act. The trial court found that the agency's CGL policy excluded damages arising from assault and battery. Since the claimed damages arose from the alleged assault and battery against the deceased, there was no coverage. The Supreme Court of New Hampshire affirmed only in part, noting that where damages arise entirely out of an act that would not be covered, the negligence claim is not covered. Here, the plaintiff in the underlying lawsuit **could not prevail on the negligence claim without proving damages from the murder**. Therefore, the claim was excluded. However, the invasion of privacy and consumer protection counts of the underlying claim could succeed without the plaintiff proving assault and battery. The court remanded those counts. *Preferred National Insurance Co. v. Docusearch, Inc.*, 829 A.2d 1068 (N.H. 2003).

◆ The officers and directors of a corporation that operated a restaurant in California obtained a commercial insurance policy that excluded bodily injury arising from assault or battery. When an employee of the restaurant punched a customer (allegedly in self-defense), the customer sued the officers and directors for negligent hiring and supervision as well as vicarious liability with respect to the intentional tort of their employee. Their insurer denied that it had a duty to defend or indemnify them. After the underlying suit settled, the officers and directors sued the insurer for breach of contract and bad faith. The court ruled for the insurer, and the California Court of Appeal affirmed. Although the duty to defend is broad and may exist even where no damages are ultimately awarded against an insured, the insurer owed no duty to defend in this case. Here, **the policy clearly stated that there would be no coverage for bodily injury or property damage "arising out of assault or battery**, or out of any act or omission in connection with the prevention or suppression of an assault or battery." Regardless of whether the employee had acted in self-defense, the exclusion was triggered and the insurer owed no duty to defend. *Zelda, Inc. v. Northland Insurance Co.*, 66 Cal.Rptr.2d 356 (Cal. Ct. App. 1997).

◆ An insured corporation employed a retired New York City police officer as a security guard in its nightclub. In the early morning hours an off-duty police officer apprehended a suspect outside the nightclub and, with gun drawn, brought the suspect into the club to use the phone. The security guard ordered the police officer to drop his gun. When the officer did not comply, the guard shot him twice. The officer claimed that he had identified himself as a police officer prior to the shooting, but the guard stated that he did so only after he was shot. The officer sued the insured corporation for negligence. The insured's liability carrier sought a declaratory judgment that it was not obligated to defend or indemnify the insured because of the assault and battery exclusion in the policy. The Court of Appeals of New York stated that **the guard's lack of intent to cause harm was irrelevant in determining the intentional nature of his act**. Quite simply, the injury being sued for was an assault and battery. All of the other claims surrounding that injury, including negligent hiring and supervising, were based on that assault and battery. Thus, the insurer was not required to defend or indemnify the insured. *U.S. Underwriters Insurance Co. v. Val-Blue Corp.*, 85 N.Y.2d 821, 623 N.Y.S.2d 834, 647 N.E.2d 1342 (N.Y. 1995).

2. Employment-Related Exclusions

Many CGL policies exclude coverage for claims arising out of the employment relationship. Where a policy has such an exclusion, the insurer probably will not have to defend or indemnify the employer for injury resulting from that relationship.

◆ An Ohio employee suffered a severe bodily injury and sued his employer for a substantial certainty intentional tort. The company settled the claim for an amount greater than its first-level policy of liability insurance that provided coverage for employer's liability. The insurer paid its liability policy limits. However, it then asserted that its umbrella policy did not provide coverage for substantial certainty intentional torts. The company claimed that **a second exclusion in the umbrella policy conflicted with the first exclusion and provided "follow-form" coverage** – that is, it provided the same coverage as was available under the liability policy. A federal court held that this ambiguity between the two exclusions had to be resolved in the insured company's favor. Thus, coverage was available under the umbrella policy. *General Mills Inc. v. Liberty Insurance Underwriters Inc.*, 498 F.Supp.2d 1088 (S.D. Ohio 2007).

◆ An insured corporation in California provided janitorial services to commercial entities. It contracted with another company to actually provide the individuals needed to perform the work. When it was sued by some of the subcontractor's janitors for false imprisonment (for locking them inside the stores at night), it sought coverage from its liability insurer. The insurer claimed it had no duty to defend or indemnify because of the employment-related practices exclusion. A trial court agreed, but the California Court of Appeal reversed, holding that **the employment-related practices exclusion did not apply to a lawsuit brought by employees of a different entity** (the subcontractor). *North American Building Maintenance, Inc. v. Fireman's Fund Insurance Co.*, 40 Cal.Rptr.3d 468 (Cal. Ct. App. 2006).

◆ A company in Texas was sued by a former employee, who alleged that he was fired for filing a workers' compensation claim and that he was defamed to other prospective employers. The company sought a defense under its CGL policy and the Employee Benefit Liability (EBL) endorsement to the policy. A trial court ruled in favor of the insurer, but the Texas Court of Appeals reversed in part. It held that although the CGL policy excluded coverage for defamation and "employment related" acts or omissions, the EBL endorsement required the insurer to defend the company. The EBL endorsement did not limit coverage to negligent acts as the insurer asserted, but rather limited the extent of coverage for negligent acts thereunder. *Altivia Corp. v. Greenwich Insurance Co.*, 161 S.W.3d 52 (Tex. Ct. App. 2004).

◆ An employee of an insured was injured when she fell off a loading dock while working. She filed intentional tort claims against the insured, alleging that the failure to place a guardrail on the loading dock made her injuries substantially certain to occur. A jury awarded her more than $2.7 million. The CGL insurers refused to pay. The case reached the Supreme Court of Ohio, which noted that one CGL policy expressly excluded coverage for bodily injury to an employee of the insured "arising out of and in the course of employment." Even though the employee's lawsuit was for an intentional tort, **her injury was still causally related to her employment** and came under the language of the exclusion. As to the other policy, the court found there was a genuine issue of material fact as to whether the employee's injuries were caused by "continuous and repeated exposure to substantially the same general harmful conditions." Therefore, the case was remanded for further action. *Penn Traffic Co. v. AIU Insurance Co.*, 99 Ohio St. 3d 227, 790 N.E.2d 1199 (Ohio 2003).

◆ After the president of a farming cooperative in Utah was fired for strange behavior, he sued for defamation, claiming that the cooperative was vicariously liable for its employees' defamatory statements. The cooperative's insurer asserted that it did not have to defend the lawsuit because of an exclusion in the policy for injury arising out of the cooperative's employment practices. A federal court ruled that the exclusion was ambiguous and that the insurer had to provide a defense. The Tenth Circuit reversed, finding that **the term "employment practices," though not defined in the policy, was not ambiguous**. Because the allegedly defamatory statements were made while evaluating the former president's employment status and were closely tied to his allegedly wrongful dismissal, they arose out of the cooperative's employment practices and the insurer did not have to defend the lawsuit. *Moroni Feed Co. v. Mutual Service Casualty Insurance Co.*, 287 F.3d 1290 (10th Cir. 2002).

◆ When a former employee sued an insured pizzeria after its manager allegedly harassed and assaulted her, the pizzeria's insurer refused to defend or indemnify it. The pizzeria sued, and the case reached the Supreme Court of Oregon. The court noted that there was no insurance coverage for most of these charges because the CGL policy excluded personal injury "to an employee of the insured arising out of and in the course of employment by the insured." The insurer had no duty to defend the pizzeria because **the "employee exclusion" barred coverage for on-the-job misconduct**, and the owner had no vicarious liability for a sexual assault that occurred off duty. The employee alleged that she was assaulted at the manager's apartment. That was a single episode in a series of acts. It could not be inferred that the assault was caused by the harassment such that the pizzeria would be vicariously liable. *Minnis v. Oregon Mutual Insurance Co.*, 334 Or. 191, 48 P.3d 137 (Or. 2002).

◆ A delivery truck carrying two employees slid into a ditch and flipped over several times, severely injuring the passenger. The employer's business automobile insurer refused to cover the passenger, citing the co-employee exclusion. Under this exclusion, the passenger had to seek coverage under the employer's workers' compensation insurance policy. The insurer paid out $85,000 under the workers' compensation policy, but it refused to provide additional coverage under the business automobile policy. A Vermont federal court ruled for the insurer in the lawsuit that followed. The U.S. Court of Appeals, Second Circuit, found that the co-employee exclusion did not violate the Vermont Financial Responsibility Act, which requires a $20,000 minimum coverage under automobile insurance policies. Even though **the employer's business automobile policy did not provide the minimum coverage to the passenger**, the workers' compensation policy did. Therefore, this part of the lower court decision was affirmed. However, the trial court had improperly allowed the insurer to deduct the full $20,000 the passenger had collected from the driver from the $85,000 paid for workers' compensation. The trial court should have deducted the expenses the passenger incurred in recovering that $20,000. It reversed that part of the decision and remanded the case. *Davis v. Liberty Mutual Insurance Co.*, 267 F.3d 124 (2d Cir. 2001).

◆ A Massachusetts parish pastor fired the parish's music director. The director claimed that the pastor made comments to church members indicating that it was not safe for her to be around children. She sued the pastor, the parish, and the Protestant Diocese of Massachusetts for defamation. The parish's general liability insurer denied coverage because of an exclusion for "personal injury sustained by any person as a result of an offense directly or indirectly related to the employment of such person by the Named Insured." The parish sought a determination of its rights under the policy in a federal district court. The court found in favor of the insurer, and the parish appealed. The First Circuit affirmed, finding that the exclusion precluded coverage because **defamatory statements explaining an employment termination or directed to performance are "related to" employment**. Here, the pastor's statements were comments regarding the director's abilities and job performance, which explained why she was fired. Because the statements were related to the director's employment, the exclusion applied to preclude coverage. *Parish of Christ Church v. Church Insurance Co.,* 166 F.3d 419 (1st Cir. 1999).

◆ A California employee alleged that he was confronted by two co-workers and driven (without his consent) to a motel room where he was interrogated about inventory shortages and any mistakes he may have committed during his employment. During the interrogation, he admitted consuming items marked for disposal. Although the employee alleged that the co-workers told him that the corporation would not take any retaliatory action, he was fired. The employee sued the corporation for false imprisonment. The corporation's CGL insurer denied coverage based on the employment-related exclusion. The insurer then filed a declaratory relief action in a federal court. The employment-related exclusion barred coverage for "bodily injury" and "personal injury" arising out of several specifically enumerated actions including termination of employment as well as "other employment-related practices, policies, acts or omissions." Because **the policy defined "personal injury" to include "false arrest, detention or imprisonment,"** and because the exclusion did not specifically exclude false arrest or imprisonment, the court found that the claim was not excluded. *Zurich Insurance Co. v. Smart & Final Inc.*, 996 F.Supp. 979 (C.D. Cal. 1998).

3. Intentional Acts Exclusion

Intentionally harmful acts are not insurable. Thus, where employees commit an intentional tort against a third party, there generally will be no liability insurance coverage. However, coverage may be available where the employer is sued for negligent hiring, training or supervision.

◆ An insured Ohio company was sued by the widow of an employee for wrongful death after a gearbox he was welding fell on him. She claimed that the company committed an intentional tort against her husband. The company sought a defense from its insurer under a commercial general liability policy and an umbrella policy. The insurer contended it had no duty to defend or indemnify, and the Court of Appeals of Ohio agreed. **The CGL policy excluded coverage for bodily injuries expected or intended from the**

standpoint of the insured, and the umbrella policy excluded coverage for injuries arising out of or in the course of employment and only provided coverage for events covered by the underlying insurance. *Cincinnati Insurance Co. v. Schwerha*, No. 04 MA 257, 2006 WL 1868321 (Ohio Ct. App. 6/28/06).

◆ A company that received junk faxes from a business in Illinois brought a class action lawsuit against the business, which sought a defense from its insurer. The policy covered "advertising injury" among other harms, and it defined advertising injury to include "oral or written publication of material that violates a person's right of privacy." The insurer sued for a ruling that it did not have to defend the business, and the Seventh Circuit agreed that it did not have to defend the lawsuit. **The sending of junk faxes was outside the policy's coverage.** Further, even if the business did not know that its junk faxes violated the Telephone Consumer Protection Act, it had to know that its faxes would use up the recipients' paper and ink. Thus, the intentional tort exclusion in the policy prevented coverage. *American States Insurance Co. v. Capital Associates of Jackson County, Inc.*, 392 F.3d 939 (7th Cir. 2004).

◆ A construction company employee attacked an employee of another company working at the same site after being confronted about some missing and damaged electrical wiring. The assaulted employee sued the owner of the construction company for negligently hiring, training and supervising the employee who attacked him. He also asserted that the owner was vicariously liable. The owner's insurer refused to defend the lawsuit on the grounds that the assault had been intentional; thus, there was no accident or "occurrence" under the policy. The case reached the Supreme Court of Texas, which held that the proper examination is not whether the insured owner's employee intended to attack the victim, but whether the owner intended the attack. Here, **since the owner did not intend to harm the victim, the insurer had a duty to defend the owner**. The court remanded the case for a determination of attorneys' fees owed. *King v. Dallas Fire Insurance Co.*, 85 S.W.3d 185 (Tex. 2002).

◆ Two social workers operated a center for adults who had been sexually abused as children. They carried professional liability policies that limited coverage to $25,000 for any claims involving alleged or actual sexual misconduct. When a patient sued them, asserting that one of the social workers had subjected her to sexual misconduct, they sought to avoid the $25,000 limitation. A New York appellate court held that **the limitation applied as to the social worker who committed the misconduct**, but that it did not apply as to the other social worker. *American Home Assurance Co. v. McDonald*, 712 N.Y.S.2d 507 (N.Y. App. Div. 2000).

◆ A Texas minister allegedly sexually assaulted a learning disabled adult. The victim sued the minister, the Evangelical Lutheran Church in America (ELCA), and the Texas-Louisiana Gulf Coast Synod for negligence in training, supervising, placing, and monitoring the minister. The minister was never an agent or employee of the ELCA or Synod, but had graduated from the Lutheran Theological Seminary and was listed on the ELCA clergy roster as a retired

Lutheran pastor. The ELCA and Synod sought coverage under their CGL and commercial umbrella liability policies. Both policies provided coverage for an "occurrence," defined as "an accident, including continuous or repeated exposure to substantially the same general conditions." The policies also contained an intentional acts exclusion. In the lawsuit that followed, a federal court held for the ELCA and Synod. The Fifth Circuit Court of Appeals affirmed, finding that the policies provided coverage for the claims of negligence. Relying on a prior Illinois case, the court noted that **allegations of negligent hiring fall within the definition of "occurrence." Thus, the insurer had a duty to defend the ELCA and Synod.** Negligent training also did not constitute an intentional tort in this case because the minister's acts were not the insureds' intentional acts. As a result, the intentional acts exclusions did not preclude coverage. *Evangelical Lutheran Church in America v. Atlantic Mutual Insurance Co.,* 169 F.3d 947 (5th Cir. 1999).

◆ A branch manager of an insured Michigan automotive service company learned of the company's plan to discharge him and met with his immediate supervisor, who fired him. Shortly afterward, the manager shot and killed the supervisor in the middle of a public street. The supervisor's estate filed a wrongful death action against the company, alleging that it had ordered the supervisor to fire the manager even though it had knowledge that the manager was mentally unstable and that an injury was substantially certain to occur. The company's insurer agreed to defend the claim but reserved the right to withdraw from the defense, citing an intentional tort exclusion in the policy. The underlying wrongful death suit was decided in favor of the estate, and appeal was taken. During the pendency of the appeal, the company sued the insurer, seeking a determination that it had a duty to defend it during the appeal of the underlying action. The district court entered pretrial judgment in favor of the insurer and the company appealed to the U.S. Court of Appeals, Sixth Circuit.

On appeal, the insurer argued that it never had a duty to defend the wrongful death complaint against the company because the complaint alleged intentional acts. Thus, the insurer had no duty to continue its defense on appeal once the trial court found the company guilty of an intentional act. The court of appeals disagreed, noting that **the insurer still had a duty to defend the company even though the wrongful death complaints spoke in terms of an intentional act**. The intentional tort exclusion, which excluded from coverage bodily injury intentionally caused or aggravated by the company, did not include situations where an employer allegedly had actual knowledge that an injury was certain to occur and willfully disregarded that information. The district court's decision was reversed. *Ziebart Int'l Corp. v. CNA Insurance Companies*, 78 F.3d 245 (6th Cir. 1996).

◆ An insured Ohio company, covered under a CGL policy, performed sandblasting operations on a bridge and used a barge in the river directly below the bridge to place its scaffolding in order to perform the sandblasting. An employee fell from the scaffolding and died. His estate brought a wrongful death action against the insured, claiming that the insured had intentionally and/or with substantial certainty failed to provide safety equipment, including safety belts, lifelines and safety nets. The insurer sued for a declaration that it did not have to defend or indemnify the insured. The trial court ruled in favor of the insured, and the insurer appealed to the Court of Appeals of Ohio.

On appeal, the insurer argued that an intentional act exclusion precluded coverage. The exclusion denied coverage for any injuries sustained because of an act committed intentionally by, or at the direction of, the insured. Because the estate alleged an intentional act by the insured in the underlying action, the insurer reasoned that it did not have to provide coverage. The court of appeals disagreed, noting that an intentional act is one where the actor desires to cause the consequences of the act, or believes that the consequences are substantially certain to occur. **Although the insured may have directed the employee to work in an unsafe environment, without proper safety training or equipment, the resulting injuries were nonetheless accidental.** Because the insurer failed to demonstrate that the injuries were expected or intended, it had to defend and indemnify its insured. *Beacon Insurance Co. of America v. Kleoudis*, 652 N.E.2d 1 (Ohio Ct. App. 1995).

4. Other Exclusions

In addition to the standard exclusions in insurance policies (e.g., intentional acts, assault and battery, employment-related practices), there are often a number of exclusions tailored to a particular business. The following cases explore some of these exclusions.

- A refinery in Minnesota hired a service provider to overhaul a compressor at its facility. The provider worked around the clock on the compressor for over two weeks. In connection with the work, a large container of cloth rags were used to wipe the compressor during the overhaul. After the work was complete, the refinery put the compressor back into service. Initially, the compressor worked fine. But a week later, the refinery had to shut it down when problems occurred. It inspected the compressor and found a cloth rag and cloth fragments lodged inside. It was able to repair the compressor itself, but the compressor was out of service for five days, causing the refinery to incur business losses of more than $6.5 million. One of the service provider's liability insurers refused to pay its share, and a lawsuit resulted. The Court of Appeals of Minnesota eventually ruled that **leaving the cloth rag inside the compressor was "work" that the insured performed incorrectly and thus was excluded from coverage**. *Tonicstar Ltd. v. Lovegreen Turbine Services, Inc.*, 535 F.3d 790 (8th Cir. 2008).

- A North Carolina couple sued a company for negligent hiring, retention and supervision after a company employee crossed the median and hit the wife's vehicle. The employee was cited for driving under the influence and reckless driving. He had multiple moving violations on his record, including one while driving a company vehicle. The company's CGL insurer sought a ruling that it did not have to defend or indemnify the company because of the motor vehicle exclusion. The case reached the Supreme Court of North Carolina, which ruled that **the exclusion barred coverage for the incident**. Although the couple alleged that the company was negligent in hiring, retaining and supervising the employee, those actions were harmful to the wife only because the employee was required to drive the company van in the course of his employment; and the collision was the sole cause of the wife's injury. *Builders Mutual Insurance Co. v. North Main Construction, Ltd.*, 361 N.C. 85, 637 S.E.2d 528 (N.C. 2006).

◆ A cemetery corporation owned several liability policies, which excluded coverage for bodily injury caused by willful violation of a penal statute committed by or with the knowledge of an insured. The cemetery admitted it had a practice of over-burying that dated back to the early 1900s. This included reusing grave sites, removing remains and memorials from graves, digging in occupied graves and selling already occupied sites. A court found these actions were taken intentionally and with the knowledge of past officers and directors of the cemetery. The current officers and directors denied any knowledge of such practices. Criminal charges against them were dismissed when they agreed to participate in a diversion program. When civil lawsuits were filed against the cemetery, its officers sought insurance coverage. A trial court found in favor of the insurer, since the cemetery had admittedly violated criminal statutes prohibiting desecration of venerated objects and violation of graves. The appeals court reversed, but the Kentucky Supreme Court enforced the exclusion, noting that willful violations of criminal statutes had been committed. **The exclusion did not require a criminal conviction, and the court refused to read such a requirement into the policy.** *Employers Insurance of Wausau v. Martinez*, 54 S.W.3d 142 (Ky. 2001).

◆ A woman was killed and her two children were injured in a collision between her truck and a tractor-trailer driven by a logging company employee. The accident occurred when a skidder that protruded two feet over each side of the trailer met the woman's truck coming from the opposite direction. The overhanging portion of the skidder struck the truck, causing the injuries and death. When the decedent's husband sued the logging company, its insurer filed a declaratory judgment asserting lack of coverage. The Georgia Court of Appeals ruled that the CGL policy purchased by the logging company excluded bodily injury arising out of the "use" of an "auto," including a trailer. Here, **the skidder would not have made contact with the truck but for the fact that it was being transported by the tractor-trailer**. The collision therefore flowed from the logging company's "use" of the tractor-trailer, as contemplated by the "auto exclusion." *Jacobs v. American Interstate Insurance Co.*, 549 S.E.2d 767 (Ga. Ct. App. 2001).

◆ The driver and passengers of an automobile sued an insured corporation, alleging that it negligently parked a tractor/trailer on the roadway and that they then hit it. When the corporation filed an insurance claim, its CGL insurer sought to absolve itself of the duty to defend or indemnify. The Florida District Court of Appeal noted that the policy in question excluded bodily injury and property damage "arising out of the ownership, maintenance, use or entrustment to others of any … auto" owned by the insured. The exclusion defined "use" to "include operation and loading and unloading." The court found that the term "arising out of" was broader in meaning than the term "caused by," and meant "originating from, having its origin in, growing out of, flowing from, incident to, or having a connection with" the use of the vehicle. **The exclusion was broad enough to include "negligent parking" and thus covered the case.** The insurer did not have to defend or indemnify the corporation. *Alligator Enterprises Inc. v. General Agent's Insurance Co.*, 773 So.2d 94 (Fla. Dist. Ct. App. 2000).

◆ While using a stone-cutting saw, an employee caught his foot between the rotating pinion and the rack of the saw. He sustained injuries and sued the saw's manufacturer, alleging that the saw was defective because it had no guard to prevent such injuries. The manufacturer sought coverage under its general liability insurance policy. A trial court found the insurer had no obligation to defend the lawsuit or provide bodily injury coverage because of the "products completed operations hazard" exclusion in the policy. The Georgia Court of Appeals affirmed, finding that **the "products completed operations hazard" exclusion applied to "bodily injury" caused by the manufacturer's product after it left the manufacturer's premises**. This described the employee's injury, which occurred while he was working for a company that had bought the stone-cutting saw from the manufacturer. The failure to install the safety mechanism did not make the work incomplete. Thus, even if the saw needed correction, repair or replacement to comply with Occupational Safety and Health Act regulations, it was still "complete" within the meaning of the policy. *Wilson Industrial Electric Inc. v. Cincinnati Insurance Co.*, 539 S.E.2d 612 (Ga. Ct. App. 2000).

◆ An employee of a corporation insured under a CGL policy, acting within the scope of his duties, attached a cement mixer to his own truck and took the mixer to be repaired. On the way, his truck collided with a car, killing its driver. When the deceased's estate sued the corporation, the insurer sought a declaration absolving it from the duty to defend. The trial court ruled against the insurer. The Florida District Court of Appeal affirmed. The corporation was legally obligated to pay damages because its employee caused the harm while acting within the scope of his duties. **Even though the policy excluded the employee as an insured, the corporation was liable for the employee's negligence under a master/servant theory.** The court also found that the policy's exclusion for bodily injury arising out of any auto "owned or operated by or rented or loaned to any insured" was ambiguous. The employee involved in the accident was driving his own vehicle. It was not owned, operated or rented by an insured (since the employee was excluded from coverage). The court also accepted the corporation's assertion that the employee had not "loaned" the vehicle to it. *Union American Insurance Co. v. Maynard*, 752 So.2d 1266 (Fla. Dist. Ct. App. 2000).

◆ A supervisor at a fast-food restaurant allegedly ordered two minor female employees into his office and told them he was investigating a theft. He handed them a telephone, and a person who identified himself as a sheriff's deputy instructed them to submit to a strip search. One employee removed most of her clothing and allowed the supervisor to touch her to conduct the search. The other permitted him to pat her down. The employees later sued their employer for infliction of emotional distress. The employer unsuccessfully sought a declaratory judgment to force its insurer to defend it. The Court of Appeals of Ohio noted that the restaurant's commercial liability policy covered it for "false imprisonment" if the offense arose out of the employer's business. The court found that **if the strip search was for the business purpose of finding a thief, it would be privileged and would not constitute false imprisonment**. If the strip search was motivated by a desire to see the two minor females naked, there would be no business purpose. In either case the incident would not be covered under the policy. The claim was also excluded because it involved intentional conduct. *Consolidated Investment Corp. v. Kemper Insurance Co.*, 1999 WL 1314677 (Ohio Ct. App. 1999).

◆ A Washington fruit-packing company delivered more than 2,000 tons of apples to a storage company, which agreed to maintain a temperature of approximately 32 degrees. Several months later, when the storage rooms were opened to pack and ship the apples, the packing company discovered that they were frozen. Its insurer paid the policy limits. The packing company then sued the storage company for breach of contract and negligent monitoring and storage. The storage company's CGL insurer denied coverage based on the care, custody or control exclusion. The packing company sued the insurer. A trial court decided that coverage did not exist because the apples were in the care, custody, or control of the storage company.

On appeal, the packing company argued that the apples were in the exclusive care, custody or control of one employee of the storage company. It asserted that the employee was the only person with the knowledge necessary to maintain the controlled atmospheres in the storage rooms. Further, the employee was not a named insured under the policy, and therefore the exclusion should not apply. The Court of Appeals of Washington disagreed, noting that even if by virtue of his job the employee did exercise some care, custody or control over the apples in cold storage, **they were placed in the primary care, custody or control of the storage company**. To the extent the employer and employee were both in charge of the apples, they shared joint responsibility. However, the employee's caretaking activities did not remove the fruit from the storage company's control. Thus, the exclusion applied and there was no coverage. *Cashmere Pioneer Growers, Inc. v. Unigard Security Insurance Co.*, 891 P.2d 732 (Wash. Ct. App. 1995).

II. THEFTS BY EMPLOYEES

Businesses generally seek coverage for employee thefts under general liability policies or fidelity bonds. However, liability policies generally contain employee dishonesty exclusions that preclude coverage for employee thefts. Fidelity bonds, on the other hand, insure against fraudulent and dishonest acts of employees of an insured.

◆ A Texas Christian College purchased a "school leaders errors and omissions" policy that insured it against wrongful acts committed by directors and officers of the school. Subsequently, a member of the board of trustees convinced the board to invest $2 million of its endowment funds in a company that he partly owned and that had a negative net worth. When the investment failed, the college obtained the board member's resignation and then sued him and his company for misrepresentation. The college obtained a judgment against the board member for $1.8 million and against the company for $2 million. Unable to collect on the judgments, it sought to collect under its errors and omissions policy. The insurer denied coverage under the "fraud or dishonesty" exclusion and the "personal profit or advantage" exclusion. A Texas federal court held that the two exclusions applied to bar coverage, and the U.S. Court of Appeals, Fifth Circuit, affirmed. The **exclusion for "any claim arising out of the gaining in fact of any personal profit or advantage to which the Insured is not legally entitled"** barred coverage. Here, the board member clearly gained a personal advantage by his company's receipt of the $2 million in endowment funds. Despite the fact that the board member did not ultimately make a profit, he did gain a personal advantage. As a result, the insurer had no obligation under the policy. *Jarvis Christian College v. National Union Fire Insurance Co.*, 197 F.3d 742 (5th Cir. 1999).

A. Liability Policies

CGL policies generally have employee dishonesty exclusions that bar coverage for injury to third parties caused by dishonest and fraudulent employee actions.

◆ A Virginia real estate developer engaged a title company to provide it with escrow services. Over the course of several years, the developer entrusted over $1.1 million in escrow funds to the title company pursuant to this arrangement. During the same period, the title company's bookkeeper embezzled approximately $1.4 million in over 130 transactions, and the title company thereafter went into bankruptcy, unable to return the entrusted funds to the developer. The title company submitted claims for its losses to two insurance companies – one that provided a fidelity bond and another that had issued an errors and omissions policy. The fidelity bond yielded payment of $100,000 for the loss resulting from the bookkeeper's dishonesty. The other insurer, however, denied coverage, contending that the loss was excluded from errors and omissions coverage as "arising out of" a dishonest or criminal act. A federal court ruled for the insurer, and the Fourth Circuit affirmed. **The developer's claim was barred by the exclusion for damages arising "directly or indirectly" out of criminal acts.** *Gulf Underwriters Insurance Co. v. KSI Services, Inc.*, 233 Fed.Appx. 239 (4th Cir. 2007).

◆ An employee of an insured company fraudulently cashed checks from the company as well as from a separate business entity, for which the company provided administrative services for the processing and payment of its bills. The company's employee dishonesty protection insurer paid for the loss the company incurred but refused to pay the loss suffered by the other business entity. The company sued and the Appeals Court of Massachusetts ruled in favor of the insurer. Since **the policy excluded indirect losses to third parties**, the insurer did not have a duty to pay that claim. It did not matter that it was the insured's employee's dishonesty that caused the loss. *Atlas Metals Products Co., Inc. v. Lumbermans Mutual Casualty Co.*, 829 N.E.2d 257 (Mass. App. Ct. 2005).

◆ A condominium association filed a breach of contract action against its insurer under an employee dishonesty endorsement. The trial court credited the insurer's argument that the person who embezzled $43,493.47 from the association was not an "employee" under the policy, and it dismissed the suit. The Missouri Court of Appeals reversed. The policy's definition of "employee" included "any person employed by an employment contractor while the person was performing services for the insured under the insured's direction and control." The insurer argued that the term "employment contractor" was unambiguous and referred only to a temporary employment agency. The insured contended that the term could include an employee of a management company hired to manage the property of the condominium association. The appeals court concluded that the term did not have any readily discernible, ordinary meaning. The insured's definition was reasonable since the substance of the transaction was identical: a temporary employment agency hires and pays employees to work in other companies, and the management company in this case did the same. **The term "employee" was ambiguous and had to be construed against the insurer.** *Mansion Hills Condominium Ass'n v. American Family Mutual Insurance Co.*, 62 S.W.3d 633 (Mo. Ct. App. 2001).

◆ An insured servicer of HVAC equipment discovered a discrepancy between its freon inventory and its general ledger. After determining that 439 canisters of freon worth $83,584 were missing, it filed a claim for "employee dishonesty" coverage under its commercial crimes policy. When the insurer denied coverage, the insured sued for breach of contract. A trial court ruled for the insurer, finding insufficient evidence that the freon was stolen or that the thief was an employee. The Appellate Court of Illinois affirmed – on different grounds. It said that the insured was obliged to show evidence of three things: (1) that a loss occurred, (2) that it was caused by employee dishonesty and (3) that each "occurrence" of theft was in excess of the $10,000 deductible. The only evidence of the loss was a discrepancy between the general ledger on the computer and the actual inventory of freon. This loss arguably came within the policy exclusion for inventory shortages. Further, **the insured was unable to establish how many occurrences of alleged theft there were**, whether there were in fact any thefts at all, and if there were, how many were in excess of the $10,000-per-occurrence deductible. Accordingly, the insured was not entitled to coverage. *Reedy Industries, Inc. v. Hartford Insurance Co. of Illinois*, 715 N.E.2d 728 (Ill. App. Ct. 1999).

◆ A New Jersey manufacturer's commercial property loss insurance policy contained a **dishonesty exclusion for losses from fraudulent, dishonest or criminal acts** committed by the manufacturer, its employees, or authorized representatives. Despite the dishonesty exclusion, the manufacturer sought coverage for several thefts committed by an employee whose co-conspirators were former employees. When the insurer refused to provide coverage, the manufacturer sued it in a state trial court ruled for the insurer. The Superior Court of New Jersey, Appellate Division, affirmed, finding that even though the employee's actions were outside the scope of his employment, he committed the fraudulent, dishonest or criminal acts as the manufacturer's employee. Whether or not the employee's co-conspirators were actual employees at the time of the theft was not legally significant because an employee initiated the thefts and his dishonesty defeated coverage. The manufacturer could have purchased a fidelity bond to protect itself against dishonest or fraudulent acts of its employees. *Cobra Products, Inc. v. Federal Insurance Co.*, 722 A.2d 545 (N.J. Super. Ct. App. Div. 1998).

- A Florida business was covered under four consecutive one-year comprehensive insurance policies that covered losses incurred in any one occurrence. The policies covered employee dishonesty. Each had a limit of $25,000 per covered occurrence. An employee of the insured embezzled money over a four-year period. Since the embezzlement occurred over four consecutive years, the insured sought coverage under the four separate policies. The insurer denied coverage on all but the most current policy. It contended that although the employee's embezzlement occurred over a four-year period, it constituted a single occurrence. The insured sued, seeking coverage under all the policies. The trial court entered pretrial judgment in favor of the insured. On appeal, the insurer argued that because the embezzlement loss was only one occurrence, recovery could be made under only one of the policies. The court of appeal agreed, noting that **the insurer's liability for the embezzlement over the four-year period was limited to one one-year insurance policy**. Even though discovery of loss provisions limited coverage to two of the policies, each policy contained a non-accumulation clause that prohibited insurance from accumulating from year to year. Each stated that the insurer was only liable for the larger of the amount recoverable under either policy, but that the policies would not be cumulative. The trial court's decision was reversed. *Reliance Insurance Co. v. Treasure Coast Travel Agency, Inc.*, 660 So.2d 1136 (Fla. Dist. Ct. App. 1995).

B. Fidelity Bonds

Fidelity bonds generally cover employee dishonesty, fraud and embezzlement.

- An accounting employee of an Arizona company embezzled more than $500,000 during a five-year period by forging company checks. The company had purchased employee fidelity policies covering two of those years. The policies at issue limited coverage to $50,000 per occurrence of loss and defined occurrence as "all loss caused by, or involving, one or more 'employees,' whether the result of a single act or series of acts." When the company sought coverage for the embezzlement, the insurer maintained that the series of thefts amounted to a single occurrence and that it owed the company only $50,000. A lawsuit ensued, and the case reached the Supreme Court of Arizona, which agreed with the insurer that **the series of thefts amounted to a single occurrence under the policies**. In fact, because of the $250 deductible, treating the losses as separate occurrences would generally hurt employers where employees stole small amounts over a period of time, because none of those small thefts would be covered. *Employers Mutual Casualty Co. v. DGG & CAR, Inc.*, 218 Ariz. 262, 183 P.3d 513 (Ariz. 2008).

◆ An employee allegedly stole checks belonging to an insured and used them to pay money from the insured's bank account to herself and others. Her actions extended over two policy terms, and the loss to the insured exceeded $50,000 per policy period. Nevertheless, the insurer refused to pay more than $50,000, asserting that the conduct during the two policy periods constituted a "single occurrence" and was therefore subject to a single $50,000 policy limit. A trial court ruled for the insurer, but the Court of Appeals of Oregon reversed. The policy stated the insurer would "pay only for loss or damage you sustain through acts committed or events occurring during the policy period." In addition, it stated that "no limit of insurance cumulates from year to year or period to period." The implication of this language is that a policy is intended to create a new insurance contract, discrete from the contract for the previous policy period. Therefore, **the insurer had to pay the limits for the second policy period**. *Robben & Sons v. Mid-Century Insurance Co.*, 74 P.3d 1141 (Or. Ct. App. 2003).

◆ An insured company conducted clinical tests on new drugs for pharmaceutical companies. Protocols for four clinical trials required the insured's nurses to observe patients for eight hours and record observations every 30 minutes. In many cases nurses sent patients home early (sometimes seven hours early), yet recorded and submitted observations allegedly covering the full eight hours – standard practice was to fill out observation forms ahead of time and change them only if the actual observation did not fit the expected observation. By the time this was discovered (based on a tip from an ex-employee), the four studies were unfit for Food and Drug Administration review. The insured replicated the studies at a combined cost of $1.2 million and **sought coverage under its Blanket Employee Dishonesty Policy**. The insurer refused coverage, and the insured sued. The Third Circuit Court of Appeals found that the nurses' practice of submitting records containing observations they did not make was dishonest. The costs of the labor, equipment, and expertise the insured sought to recover were "direct" losses because they were directly tied to the studies rendered worthless by the nurses' actions. These were losses to property within the meaning of the policy. Finally, the nurses' actions in all four studies constituted a single series of related acts. Therefore, they were subject to the policy limit of $280,000 per event or series of related events. *Scirex Corp. v. Federal Insurance Co.*, 313 F.3d 841 (3d Cir. 2002).

◆ The executive director and assistant director of a County Parking and Transit Authority were convicted of embezzling funds through a number of methods, including paying themselves salaries in excess of what they earned. When the abuses were discovered by an outside audit, the authority sought coverage under its fidelity insurance policy, which covered losses resulting from employee dishonesty. The insurer paid some of the claims, but it refused to cover funds the employees received under the guise of salaries, citing **a policy exclusion for salaries earned in the normal course of employment**. The authority successfully sued the insurer to recover these additional funds, and the Alabama Supreme Court affirmed. The court found that the embezzled funds received in the form of payroll checks were not "salaries." To exclude such funds from coverage, the insurer would have to rewrite the policy to exclude all sums "designated as salaries." Moreover, none of the embezzled funds were "earned." They were stolen. Therefore, the embezzled funds received under the guise of salaries were not "salaries" within the meaning of the exclusion. *Cincinnati Insurance Co. v. Tuscaloosa County Parking and Transit Authority*, 827 So.2d 765 (Ala. 2002).

◆ The owner of a Texas convenience store (with a Western Union and a check cashing business) took out an "employee dishonesty coverage" insurance policy with a $500 deductible and a $25,000 limit. The policy was renewed five times. When the owner discovered that two employees, acting separately, had each stolen in excess of $31,000 during the fourth and fifth renewal periods, the insurer paid the policy limit less the deductible ($24,500) on the fifth renewal policy, but refused to pay anything on the fourth, reasoning that there had been only one "occurrence" of employee dishonesty within the meaning of the policy. The insured sued for breach of contract and won. The U.S. Court of Appeals, Fifth Circuit, affirmed. The policy defined "occurrence" as "all loss caused by, or involving, one or more employees, whether the result of a single act or a series of acts." The court found that **theft by multiple employees would constitute a single "occurrence" only if the employees conspired together to steal**. The proper focus is on the events that cause the loss and give rise to the insured's liability, rather than on the number of injurious effects. The insurer had to pay the insured $24,500 under the fourth renewal policy. *Ran-Nan Inc. v. General Accident Insurance Co.*, 252 F.3d 738 (5th Cir. 2001).

◆ When an insured furniture company discovered that three of its employees had embezzled $205,000 over a period of six years, it sought indemnification under its business insurance policy. The insurer interpreted the embezzlement as a single series of related acts and paid only $50,000 – the policy limits for one occurrence. The insured sought coverage for three instances of employee dishonesty ($150,000) and sued to recover the extra $100,000. The Washington Court of Appeals noted that the payroll manager, with the assistance of two other employees, issued advances to the three of them but failed to forward notices of these draws to the outside payroll company. The court defined "series of related acts" as "a succession of logically or causally connected acts, linked by time, place, opportunity, pattern, and method." Here, the loss would not have occurred but for the acts of the payroll manager. The other two employees had no independent access to the funds. The embezzlements started and ended at the same time for all three employees, using the same method. Thus, **the**

embezzlement constituted one occurrence under the policy. The insured's coverage was limited to $50,000. *Valley Furniture & Interiors, Inc. v. Transportation Insurance Co.*, 26 P.3d 952 (Wash. Ct. App. 2001).

◆ Over a three-year period, an employee and his accomplices managed to defraud his employer out of $1.5 million. The employer turned to its fidelity insurer, which had issued three identical policies, one for each of the three years in question and each with a coverage limit of $250,000. The employer sought to collect the $250,000 limit for each of the three policy periods. Its insurer contended that the loss was attributable to only one "occurrence" and paid out a total of $250,000. The employer sued for breach of contract. The case reached the Ninth Circuit Court of Appeals, which noted that if the parties intended to make one continuous contract, then there would be only one occurrence. However, **if the parties intended separate contracts for each year, there would be three separate occurrences** and the insurer would be liable for three policy limits. Here, ambiguous language required a construction in favor of finding separate one-year contracts. The insurer was liable for its limit of liability for each policy period. However, because the loss was discovered more than a year after the first policy expired, and because the policy only promised to pay for loss discovered no later than one year from the end of the policy period, the employer was precluded from coverage under the first policy. *Karen Kane Inc. v. Reliance Insurance Co.*, 202 F.3d 1180 (9th Cir. 2000).

◆ Seven months after changing insurers, a law firm discovered that a clerk had embezzled $47,830. The firm notified its current insurer, which paid on all claims, including those that arose during coverage by the prior insurer. It then obtained an assignment from the firm of all of its claims and rights against the clerk. Later, the insured discovered more losses with the help of an accounting firm. Thirteen months after discovering the first loss, it finally notified its previous insurer of the losses. The insurer denied coverage because it had not received timely notice. In the lawsuit that followed, the U.S. Court of Appeals, Eighth Circuit, noted that **in Minnesota, late notice defeats coverage only if it prejudices the insurer**. Here, the prior insurer had been prejudiced by the 13-month delay. It would not be able to sue either the bank or the clerk because of the passage of time and the assignment of rights. *Winthrop & Weinstine v. Travelers Casualty and Surety Co.*, 187 F.3d 871 (8th Cir. 1999).

◆ A New York mergers and acquisitions specialist engaged in several insider-training schemes that resulted in losses to his employer. After the specialist pled guilty to violations of the securities laws, his employer was sued by public shareholders of the companies that were the subject of the insider-trading schemes. The employer settled the lawsuits for several million dollars and then sought coverage under its fidelity bonds. The insurers filed a declaratory judgment action in a state trial court, which granted partial pretrial judgment to the insurers. The New York Supreme Court, Appellate Division, affirmed, finding that the bonds did not cover third-party claims against the employer. First, the specialist lacked the manifest intent to cause his employer the losses. Instead, his actions caused his employer's customers' injuries.

Second, the bonds limited coverage to direct compensatory damages and specifically excluded other types of damages such as the consequential damages paid by the employer in the settlements. In short, **the bonds did not cover indirect and consequential injuries** to the employer resulting from legal settlements with third parties who were the actual targets of the employee's acts. *Aetna Casualty & Surety Co. v. Kidder, Peabody & Co., Inc.*, 676 N.Y.S.2d 559 (N.Y. App. Div. 1998).

III. DIRECTORS' AND OFFICERS' POLICIES

Directors' and Officers' policies, or Executive Protection policies, provide coverage for elected or appointed company directors and officers. Often, the policies contain an "insured against insured" exclusion, which indicates that the insurer will not be liable for loss on account of any claim made against any insured person brought or maintained by or on behalf of any other insured.

◆ An employee of a company in Missouri forged the signature of a vice president on a contract to sell merchandise through catalogs. As a result, two other businesses suffered losses. They sued the company and the employee, and the company settled the claims by agreeing to pay one business $400,000 and the other business $1,775,000. The company then sought coverage under its directors and officers liability policy. The insurer acknowledged coverage under the smaller claim, but admitted to only a fraction of the amount sought on the larger claim. In the lawsuit that followed, a federal court held that **the company was entitled to coverage under the Crime Coverage section of the policy**. However, it could not obtain a double recovery with respect to the $400,000 already paid to the first business and the $250,000 deductible, as well as to the attorneys' fees claimed. Thus, it was entitled to only $1,268,464 on the second claim. *Graybar Elec. Co., Inc. v. Federal Insurance. Co.*, 567 F.Supp.2d 1116 (E.D. Mo. 2008).

◆ The officers and directors of a closely held corporation bought back a number of shares from two groups of shareholders without informing the shareholders about an upcoming merger. They later sold the shares for a huge profit. When the shareholders sued them, they entered into a settlement agreement in the amount of $1,095,000. The officers and directors then sought indemnification under their directors and officers liability policy. Their insurer refused to pay. A trial court ruled for the insurer but denied its request for attorneys' fees. Both parties appealed. The Court of Appeals of Ohio affirmed, agreeing with the trial court that **the officers and directors had been acting in their personal capacities when they purchased the stock**, not in their capacities as directors and officers of the company. The court also found no abuse of discretion in the trial court's decision to deny the insurer's request for attorneys' fees. *Cincinnati Insurance Co. v. Irwin Co.*, 2000 WL 1867297 (Ohio Ct. App. 2000).

◆ An agricultural credit bank purchased a directors and officers liability policy, which covered breaches of fiduciary duty and had a $5 million policy limit. The head of the bank's trust department – which invested the savings of its customers – became enamored of derivatives and invested nearly 50% of the bank's trust funds in them. After the trust accounts showed huge paper losses, customers began demanding their money back. The bank notified the Office of the Controller of the Currency (OCC) and the insurer of the problem. OCC determined that the bank had breached its fiduciary duty to its trust customers by investing in high-risk securities, and that the trust manager's lack of expertise led him to rely too heavily on broker recommendations. OCC found no evidence of intentional wrongdoing. It told the bank to liquidate the securities and pay off the trust customers, which it did, incurring a loss in excess of $5 million. The insurer denied coverage. An Illinois federal court then ordered the insurer to pay $4.9 million plus costs and attorneys' fees. The Seventh Circuit Court of Appeals agreed that the trust manager had acted with "a pure heart but an empty head." Therefore, the exclusions for actions taken in "bad faith" or for "dishonest, fraudulent, criminal or malicious acts" were not applicable. Bad faith required some level of intentional wrongdoing. *Citizens First National Bank of Princeton v. Cincinnati Insurance Co.*, 200 F.3d 1102 (7th Cir. 2000).

◆ Former directors of a Maryland bank were investigated by the bank's receiver due to a $6.4 million loan made to a corporation to fund the construction of an office building in Virginia. The loan potentially violated the loans-to-one-borrower limitation by over $2 million. When the investigation revealed evidence of negligence, the bank's directors and officers (D&O) insurer negotiated a release of the directors upon payment of $150,000. The insurer paid the settlement but refused to pay the directors' attorneys' fees, which amounted to $96,294.75 plus expenses of $4,872.48. The former directors filed suit in a Maryland federal court, seeking reimbursement for attorneys' fees and expenses. The court found that the potential claim by the receiver did not constitute a claim within the meaning of the policy. **A "claim" required more than notice by the receiver that it intended to hold the directors liable.** Here, the receiver never filed a claim in court. Further, the fees and expenses did not constitute a "loss" under the policy because they were not incurred in the defense of a civil legal action. Finally, the insured-versus-insured exclusion barred coverage. The court granted pretrial judgment in favor of the insurer. *Hyde v. Fidelity & Deposit Co. of Maryland*, 23 F.Supp.2d 630 (D. Md. 1998).

◆ A parent company maintained an executive protection insurance policy that included coverage for its subsidiaries and their elected or appointed directors and officers. One of the subsidiaries acquired an 80% ownership interest in a local communications network company (Telecom). The original owners of Telecom eventually sold their minority shares to the subsidiary, which then sold a portion of its stock through an initial public offering. The sale prompted several minority shareholders to sue the subsidiary's CEO, the subsidiary and the parent company, alleging that the subsidiary had concealed material information prior to the sale of their shares. The former president and CEO of Telecom, who had also previously served as a director and vice chairman, joined the suit. The suit settled; however, the subsidiary's insurer denied coverage. The subsidiary sued it in an Illinois federal court. The court found that **the insurer had properly denied coverage pursuant to the "insured against insured" exclusion**. Because the former Telecom officer had been a duly elected officer and director of the insured organization, he was an "insured" under the policy and coverage was barred. Further, if any insured joins or even aids plaintiffs in an action against an insured, coverage for the entire proceeding is barred. The Seventh Circuit affirmed in part, but it disagreed that coverage for an entire proceeding is barred if an insured joins the action. Because the contract here required allocation between covered and uncovered losses, those amounts awarded to the former officer were not covered by the policy. *Level 3 Communications, Inc. v. Federal Insurance Co.*, 168 F.3d 956 (7th Cir. 1999).

APPENDIX A

UNITED STATES CONSTITUTION

[Relevant provisions with respect to employment law]

ARTICLE I

Section 1. All legislative Powers herein granted shall be vested in a Congress of the United States, which shall consist of a Senate and House of Representatives.

* * *

Section 8. The Congress shall have Power To lay and collect Taxes, Duties, Imposts and Excises, to pay the Debts and provide for the common Defence and general Welfare of the United States; but all Duties, Imposts and Excises shall be uniform throughout the United States;

To borrow money on the credit of the United States;

To regulate Commerce with foreign Nations, and among the several States, and with the Indian Tribes;

To establish an uniform Rule of Naturalization, and uniform Laws on the subject of Bankruptcies throughout the United States;

* * *

To promote the Progress of Science and useful Arts, by securing for limited Times to Authors and Inventors the exclusive Right to their respective Writings and Discoveries;

* * *

To make all Laws which shall be necessary and proper for carrying into Execution for the foregoing Powers, and all other Powers vested by this Constitution in the Government of the United States, or in any Department or Officer thereof.

* * *

Section 9. * * * No Bill of Attainder or ex post facto Law shall be passed.

* * *

Section 10. No State shall * * * pass any Bill of Attainder, ex post facto Law, or Law impairing the Obligation of Contracts, or grant any Title of Nobility.

ARTICLE II

Section 1. The executive Power shall be vested in a President of the United States of America.

* * *

ARTICLE III

Section 1. The judicial Power of the United States, shall be vested in one supreme Court, and in such inferior Courts as the Congress may from time to time ordain and establish. The Judges, both of the supreme and inferior courts, shall hold their Offices during good Behaviour, and shall, at stated Times, receive for their Services a Compensation, which shall not be diminished during their Continuance in Office.

Section 2. The judicial Power shall extend to all Cases, in Law and Equity, arising under this Constitution, the Laws of the United States, and Treaties made, or which shall be made, under their Authority; - to all Cases affecting Ambassadors, other public Ministers and Consuls; - to all Cases of admiralty and maritime Jurisdiction, - to Controversies to which the United States shall be a party; - to Controversies between two or more States; - between a State and Citizens of another State; - between Citizens of different States; - between Citizens of the same State claiming Lands under the Grants of different States, and between a State, or the Citizens thereof, and foreign States, Citizens or Subjects.

* * *

ARTICLE IV

Section 1. Full Faith and Credit shall be given in each State to the public Acts, Records and judicial Proceedings of every other State. * * *

Section 2. The Citizens of each State shall be entitled to all Privileges and Immunities of Citizens in the several States.

* * *

Section 4. The United States shall guarantee to every State in this Union a Republican Form of Government, and shall protect each of them against Invasion; and on Application of the Legislature, or of the Executive (when the Legislature cannot be convened) against domestic Violence.

ARTICLE V

The Congress, whenever two thirds of both Houses shall deem it necessary, shall propose Amendments to this Constitution, or, on the Application of the

Legislatures of two thirds of the several States, shall call a Convention for proposing Amendments, which, in either Case, shall be valid to all Intents and Purposes, as part of this Constitution, when ratified by the Legislatures of three fourths of the several States, or by Conventions in three fourths thereof, as the one or the other Mode of Ratification may be proposed by the Congress; Provided that no Amendment which may be made prior to the Year One thousand eight hundred and eight shall in any Manner affect the first and fourth Clauses in the Ninth Section of the first Article; and that no State, without its Consent, shall be deprived of its equal Suffrage in the Senate.

ARTICLE VI

* * *

This Constitution, and the Laws of the United States which shall be made in Pursuance thereof; and all Treaties made, or which shall be made, under the Authority of the United States, shall be the supreme Law of the Land; and the Judges in every State shall be bound thereby, any Thing in the Constitution or Laws of any State to the Contrary notwithstanding.

The Senators and Representatives before mentioned, and the Members of the several State Legislatures, and all executive and judicial Officers, both of the United States and of the several States, shall be bound by Oath or Affirmation, to support this Constitution; but no religious Test shall ever be required as a Qualification to any Office or public Trust under the United States.

* * *

AMENDMENT I

Congress shall make no law respecting an establishment of religion, or prohibiting the free exercise thereof; or abridging the freedom of speech, or of the press; or the right of the people peaceably to assemble, and to petition the Government for a redress of grievances.

* * *

AMENDMENT IV

The right of the people to be secure in their persons, houses, papers, and effects, against unreasonable searches and seizures, shall not be violated, and no Warrants shall issue, but upon probable cause, supported by Oath or affirmation, and particularly describing the place to be searched, and the persons or things to be seized.

AMENDMENT V

No person shall be held to answer for a capital, or otherwise infamous crime, unless on a presentment or indictment of a Grand Jury, except in cases arising in the land or naval forces, or in the Militia, when in actual service in time of War or public danger; nor shall any person be subject for the same offence to be twice put in jeopardy of life or limb; nor shall be compelled in any criminal case to be a witness against himself, nor be deprived of life, liberty, or property, without due process of law; nor shall private property be taken for public use, without just compensation.

AMENDMENT VI

In all criminal prosecutions, the accused shall enjoy the right to a speedy and public trial, by an impartial jury of the State and district wherein the crime shall have been committed, which district shall have been previously ascertained by law, and to be informed of the nature and cause of the accusation; to be confronted with the witnesses against him; to have compulsory process for obtaining witnesses in his favor, and to have the Assistance of Counsel for his defense.

AMENDMENT VII

In Suits at common law, where the value in controversy shall exceed twenty dollars, the right of trial by jury shall be preserved, and no fact tried by jury, shall be otherwise re-examined in any Court of the United States, than according to the rules of the common law.

AMENDMENT VIII

Excessive bail shall not be required, nor excessive fines imposed , nor cruel and unusual punishments inflicted.

AMENDMENT IX

The enumeration in the Constitution, of certain rights, shall not be construed to deny or disparage others retained by the people.

AMENDMENT X

The powers not delegated to the United States by the Constitution, nor prohibited by it to the States, are reserved to the States respectively, or to the people.

AMENDMENT XI

The Judicial power of the United States shall not be construed to extend to any suit in law or equity, commenced or prosecuted against one of the United States by Citizens of another State, or by Citizens or Subjects of any Foreign State.

* * *

AMENDMENT XIII

Section 1. Neither slavery nor involuntary servitude, except as a punishment for crime whereof the party shall have been duly convicted, shall exist within the United States, or any place subject to their jurisdiction.

Section 2. Congress shall have power to enforce this article by appropriate legislation.

AMENDMENT XIV

Section 1. All persons born or naturalized in the United States, and subject to the jurisdiction thereof, are citizens of the United States and of the State wherein they reside. No State shall make or enforce any law which shall abridge the privileges or immunities of citizens of the United States; nor shall any State deprive any person of life, liberty, or property, without due process of law; nor deny to any person within its jurisdiction the equal protection of the laws.

* * *

Section 5. The Congress shall have power to enforce, by appropriate legislation, the provisions of this article.

APPENDIX B

TABLE OF RECENT AND IMPORTANT UNITED STATES SUPREME COURT EMPLOYMENT CASES

Affirmative Action

Adarand Constructors, Inc. v. Pena, 515 U.S. 200, 115 S.Ct. 2097, 132 L.Ed.2d 158 (1995).

Martin v. Wilks, 490 U.S. 755, 109 S.Ct. 2180, 104 L.Ed.2d 835 (1989).

City of Richmond v. J.A. Croson Co., 488 U.S. 469, 109 S.Ct. 706, 102 L.Ed.2d 854 (1989).

Johnson v. Transportation Agency, Santa Clara County, 480 U.S. 616, 107 S.Ct. 1442, 94 L.Ed.2d 615 (1987).

U.S. v. Paradise, 480 U.S. 149, 107 S.Ct. 1053, 94 L.Ed.2d 203 (1987).

Wygant v. Jackson Board of Education, 476 U.S. 267, 106 S.Ct. 1842, 90 L.Ed.2d 260 (1986).

Firefighters Local Union No. 1784 v. Stotts, 467 U.S. 561, 104 S.Ct. 2576, 81 L.Ed.2d 483 (1984).

County of Los Angeles v. Davis, 440 U.S. 625, 99 S.Ct. 1379, 59 L.Ed.2d 642 (1979).

Discrimination

CBOCS West, Inc. v. Humphries, 128 S.Ct. 1951 (U.S. 2008).

Meacham v. Knolls Atomic Power Laboratory, 128 S.Ct. 2395, 171 L.Ed.2d 283 (U.S. 2008).

Sprint/United Management Co. v. Mendelsohn, 128 S.Ct. 1140 (U.S. 2008).

Ledbetter v. Goodyear Tire & Rubber Co. Inc., 127 S.Ct. 2162, 167 L.Ed.2d 982 (U.S. 2007).

Arbaugh v. Y&H Corp., 546 U.S. 500, 126 S.Ct. 1235, 163 L.Ed.2d. 1097 (2006).

Ash v. Tyson Foods, Inc., 546 U.S. 454, 126 S.Ct. 1195, 163 L.Ed.2d 1053 (2006).

Burlington Northern and Santa Fe Railway Co. v. White, 548 U.S. 53, 126 S.Ct. 2405, 165 L.Ed.2d 345 (2006).

Smith v. City of Jackson, 544 U.S. 228, 125 S.Ct. 1536, 161 L.Ed.2d 410 (2005).

General Dynamics Land Systems, Inc. v. Cline, 540 U.S. 581, 124 S.Ct. 1236, 157 L.Ed.2d 1094 (2004).

Raytheon Co. v. Hernandez, 540 U.S. 44, 124 S.Ct. 513, 157 L.Ed.2d 357 (2003).

Clackamas Gastroenterology Associates, P.C. v. Wells, 538 U.S. 440, 123 S.Ct. 1673, 155 L.Ed.2d 615 (2003).

Desert Palace Inc. d/b/a Caesers Palace Hotel & Casino v. Costa, 539 U.S. 90, 123 S.Ct. 2148, 156 L.Ed.2d 84 (2003).

Swierkiewicz v. Sorema N.A., 534 U.S. 506, 122 S.Ct. 992, 152 L.Ed.2d 1 (2002).

Chevron U.S.A. v. Echazabal, 536 U.S. 73, 122 S.Ct. 2045, 153 L.Ed.2d 82 (2002).

U.S. Airways, Inc. v. Barnett, 535 U.S. 391, 122 S.Ct. 1516, 152 L.Ed.2d 589 (2002).

Toyota Motor Manufacturing v. Williams, 534 U.S. 184, 122 S.Ct. 681, 151 L.Ed.2d 615 (2002).

Pollard v. E.I. du Pont de Nemours & Co., 532 U.S. 843, 121 S.Ct. 1946, 150 L.Ed.2d 62 (2001).

Reeves v. Sanderson Plumbing Products, 530 U.S. 133, 120 S. Ct. 2097, 147 L.Ed.2d 105 (2000).

Albertsons, Inc. v. Kirkingburg, 527 U.S. 555, 119 S.Ct. 2162, 144 L.Ed.2d 518 (1999).

Murphy v. United Parcel Service, Inc., 527 U.S. 516, 119 S.Ct. 2133, 144 L.Ed.2d 484 (1999).

Sutton v. United Air Lines, Inc., 527 U.S. 471, 119 S.Ct. 2139, 144 L.Ed.2d 450 (1999).

Cleveland v. Policy Management Systems Corp., 526 U.S. 795, 119 S.Ct. 1597, 143 L.Ed.2d 966 (1999).

Kolstad v. American Dental Ass'n, 527 U.S. 526, 119 S.Ct. 2118, 144 L.Ed.2d 494 (1999).

Faragher v. City of Boca Raton, 524 U.S. 775, 118 S.Ct. 2275, 141 L.Ed.2d 662 (1998).

Burlington Industries, Inc. v. Ellerth, 524 U.S. 742, 118 S.Ct. 2257, 141 L.Ed.2d 633 (1998).

Bragdon v. Abbott, 524 U.S. 624, 118 S.Ct. 2196, 141 L.Ed.2d 540 (1998).

Oncale v. Sundowner Offshore Services, Inc., 523 U.S. 75, 118 S.Ct. 998, 140 L.Ed.2d 201 (1998).

Oubre v. Entergy Operations, Inc., 522 U.S. 422, 118 S.Ct. 838, 139 L.Ed.2d 849 (1998).

Walters v. Metropolitan Educ. Enterprises, Inc., 519 U.S. 202, 117 S.Ct. 660, 136 L.Ed.2d 644 (1997).

Robinson v. Shell Oil Co., 519 U.S. 337, 117 S.Ct. 843, 136 L.Ed.2d 808 (1997).

O'Connor v. Consolidated Coin Caterers Corp., 517 U.S. 308, 116 S.Ct. 1307, 134 L.Ed.2d 433 (1996).

Commissioner of Internal Revenue v. Schleier, 515 U.S. 323, 115 S.Ct. 2159, 132 L.Ed.2d 294 (1995).

McKennon v. Nashville Banner Publishing Co., 513 U.S. 352, 115 S.Ct. 879, 130 L.Ed.2d 852 (1995).

Harris v. Forklift Systems, Inc., 510 U.S. 17, 114 S.Ct. 367, 126 L.Ed.2d 295 (1993).

Hazen Paper Co. v. Biggins, 507 U.S. 604, 113 S.Ct. 1701, 123 L.Ed.2d 338 (1993).

St. Mary's Honor Center v. Hicks, 509 U.S. 502, 113 S.Ct. 2742, 125 L.Ed.2d 407 (1993).

Astoria Federal Saving and Loan Ass'n v. Solimino, 501 U.S. 104, 111 S.Ct. 2166, 115 L.Ed.2d 96 (1991).

Gilmer v. Interstate/Johnson Lane Corp., 500 U.S. 20, 111 S.Ct. 1647, 114 L.Ed.2d 26 (1991).

Stevens v. Dep't of the Treasury, 500 U.S. 1, 111 S.Ct. 1562, 114 L.Ed.2d 1 (1991).

EEOC v. Arabian American Oil Co., 499 U.S. 244, 111 S.Ct. 1227, 113 L.Ed.2d 274 (1991).

Int'l Union, UAW v. Johnson Controls, 499 U.S. 187, 111 S.Ct. 1196, 113 L.Ed.2d 158 (1991).

Public Employees Retirement System of Ohio v. Betts, 492 U.S. 158, 109 S.Ct. 2854, 106 L.Ed.2d 134 (1989).

Jett v. Dallas Independent School Dist., 491 U.S. 701, 109 S.Ct. 2702, 105 L.Ed.2d 598 (1989).

Patterson v. McLean Credit Union, 491 U.S. 164, 109 S.Ct. 2363, 105 L.Ed.2d 132 (1989).

Lorance v. AT&T Technologies, Inc., 490 U.S. 900, 109 S.Ct. 2261, 104 L.Ed.2d 961 (1989).

Wards Cove Packing Co., Inc. v. Atonio, 490 U.S. 642, 109 S.Ct. 2115, 104 L.Ed.2d 733 (1989).

Price Waterhouse v. Hopkins, 490 U.S. 228, 109 S.Ct.1775, 104 L.Ed.2d 268 (1989).

Watson v. Fort Worth Bank and Trust, 487 U.S. 977, 108 S.Ct. 2777, 101 L.Ed.2d 827 (1988).

Goodman v. Lukens Steel Co., 482 U.S. 656, 107 S.Ct. 2617, 96 L.Ed.2d 572 (1987).

School Board of Nassau County, Fla. v. Arline, 480 U.S. 273, 107 S.Ct.1123, 94 L.Ed.2d 307 (1987).

Ansonia Board of Educ. v. Philbrook, 479 U.S. 60, 107 S.Ct. 367, 93 L.Ed.2d 305 (1986).

Local No. 93, Int'l Ass'n of Firefighters v. City of Cleveland, 478 U.S. 501, 106 S.Ct. 3063, 92 L.Ed.2d 405 (1986).

Local 28 of Sheet Metal Workers v. EEOC, 478 U.S. 421, 106 S.Ct. 3019, 92 L.Ed.2d 344 (1986).

Meritor Savings Bank, FSB v. Vinson, 477 U.S. 57, 106 S.Ct. 2399, 91 L.Ed.2d 49 (1986).

Western Air Lines, Inc. v. Criswell, 472 U.S. 400, 105 S.Ct. 2743, 86 L.Ed.2d 321 (1985).

Connecticut v. Teal, 457 U.S. 440, 102 S.Ct. 2525, 73 L.Ed.2d 130 (1982).

County of Washington v. Gunther, 452 U.S. 161, 101 S.Ct. 2242, 68 L.Ed.2d 751 (1981).

Texas Dep't of Community Affairs v. Burdine, 450 U.S. 248, 101 S.Ct. 1089, 67 L.Ed.2d 207 (1981).

Int'l Brotherhood of Teamsters v. U.S., 433 U.S. 324, 97 S.Ct. 1843, 52 L.Ed.2d 396 (1977).

Dothard v. Rawlinson, 433 U.S. 321, 97 S.Ct. 2720, 53 L.Ed.2d 786 (1977).

Trans World Airlines, Inc. v. Hardison, 432 U.S. 63, 97 S.Ct. 2264, 53 L.Ed.2d 113 (1977).

Massachusetts Board of Retirement v. Murgia, 427 U.S. 307, 96 S.Ct. 2562, 49 L.Ed.2d 520 (1976).

Albemarle Paper Co. v. Moody, 422 U.S. 405, 95 S.Ct. 2362, 45 L.Ed.2d 280 (1975).

Espinoza v. Farah Manufacturing Co., 414 U.S. 86, 96 S.Ct. 334, 38 L.Ed.2d 287 (1973).

McDonnell Douglas Corp. v. Green, 411 U.S. 792, 93 S.Ct. 1817, 36 L.Ed.2d 668 (1973).

Griggs v. Duke Power Co., 401 U.S. 424, 91 S.Ct. 849, 28 L.Ed.2d 158 (1971).

Employee Benefits

LaRue v. DeWolff, Boberg & Associates, 128 S.Ct. 1020, 169 L.Ed.2d 847 (U.S. 2008).

Metropolitan Life Insurance Co. v. Glenn, Inc., 128 S.Ct. 2343, 171 L.Ed.2d 299 (U.S. 2008).

Beck v. PACE Int'l Union, 127 S.Ct. 2310, 168 L.Ed.2d 1 (U.S. 2007).

Sereboff v. Mid Atlantic Medical Services, Inc., 547 U.S. 356, 126 S.Ct. 1869, 164 L.Ed.2d 612 (2006).

Aetna Health Care v. Davila, 542 U.S. 200, 124 S.Ct. 2488, 159 L.Ed.2d 312 (2004).

Cent. Laborers' Pension Fund v. Heinz, 541 U.S. 739, 124 S.Ct. 2230, 159 L.Ed.2d 46 (2004).

Black & Decker Disability Plan v. Nord, 123 S.Ct. 1965, 155 L.Ed.2d 1034 (2003).

Great-West Life & Annuity Insurance Co. v. Knudson, 534 U.S. 204, 122 S.Ct. 708, 151 L.Ed.2d 635 (2002).

Egelhoff v. Egelhoff, 532 U.S. 141, 121 S.Ct. 1322, 149 L.Ed.2d 264 (2001).

Eastern Enterprises v. Apfel, 524 U.S. 498, 118 S.Ct. 2131, 141 L.Ed.2d 451 (1998).

Geissal v. Moore Medical Corp., 524 U.S. 74, 118 S.Ct. 1869, 141 L.Ed.2d 64 (1998).

Bay Area Laundry and Dry Cleaning Pension Trust Fund v. Ferbar Corp. of California, Inc., 522 U.S. 192, 118 S.Ct. 542, 139 L.Ed.2d 553 (1997).

California Division of Labor Standards Enforcement v. Dillingham Construction N.A., Inc., 519 U.S. 316, 117 S.Ct. 832, 136 L.Ed.2d 791 (1997).

Boggs v. Boggs, 520 U.S. 833, 117 S.Ct. 1754, 138 L.Ed.2d 45 (1997).

DeBuono v. NYSA-ILA Medical and Clinical Services Fund, 520 U.S. 806, 117 S.Ct. 1747, 138 L.Ed.2d 21 (1997).

Inter-Modal Rail Employees Ass'n v. Atchison, Topeka and Santa Fe Railway Co., 520 U.S. 510, 117 S.Ct. 1513, 137 L.Ed.2d 763 (1997).

Lockheed Corp. v. Spink, 517 U.S. 882, 116 S.Ct. 1783, 135 L.Ed.2d 153 (1996).

Varity Corp. v. Howe, 516 U.S. 489, 116 S.Ct. 1065, 134 L.Ed.2d 130 (1996).

Peacock v. Thomas, 516 U.S. 349, 116 S.Ct. 862, 133 L.Ed.2d 817 (1996).

Milwaukee Brewery Workers' Pension Plan v. Jos. Schlitz Brewing Co., 513 U.S. 414, 115 S.Ct. 981, 130 L.Ed.2d 932 (1995).

Curtiss-Wright Corp. v. Schoonejongen, 514 U.S. 73, 115 S.Ct. 1223, 131 L.Ed.2d 94 (1995).

John Hancock Mutual Life Insurance Co. v. Harris Trust and Savings Bank, 510 U.S. 86, 114 S.Ct. 517, 126 L.Ed.2d 524 (1993).

Mertens v. Hewitt Associates, 508 U.S. 248, 113 S.Ct. 2063, 124 L.Ed.2d 161 (1993).

Commissioner of Internal Revenue v. Keystone Consolidated Industries, Inc., 508 U.S. 152, 113 S.Ct. 2006, 124 L.Ed.2d 71 (1993).

Bath Iron Works v. Director, OWCP, 506 U.S. 153, 113 S.Ct. 692, 121 L.Ed.2d 619 (1993).

District of Columbia v. Greater Washington Board of Trade, 506 U.S. 125, 113 S.Ct. 580, 121 L.Ed.2d 513 (1992).

Nationwide Mutual Insurance Co. v. Darden, 503 U.S. 318, 112 S.Ct. 1344, 117 L.Ed.2d 581 (1992).

Ingersoll-Rand Co. v. McClendon, 498 U.S. 133, 111 S.Ct. 478, 112 L.Ed.2d 474 (1990).

FMC Corp. v. Holliday, 498 U.S. 52, 111 S.Ct. 403, 112 L.Ed.2d 356 (1990).

Mead Corp. v. Tilley, 490 U.S. 714, 109 S.Ct. 2156, 104 L.Ed.2d 796 (1989).

Massachusetts v. Morash, 490 U.S. 107, 109 S.Ct. 1668, 104 L.Ed.2d 98 (1989).

Firestone Tire and Rubber Co. v. Bruch, 489 U.S. 101, 109 S.Ct. 948, 103 L.Ed.2d 80 (1989).

Fort Halifax Packing Co. v. Coyne, 482 U.S. 1, 107 S.Ct. 2211, 96 L.Ed.2d 1 (1987).

Connolly v. Pension Benefit Guaranty Corp., 475 U.S. 211, 106 S.Ct. 1018, 89 L.Ed.2d 166 (1986).

Cent. States, Southeast and Southwest Areas Pension Fund v. Cent. Transport, Inc., 472 U.S. 559, 105 S.Ct. 2833, 86 L.Ed.2d 447 (1985).

Metropolitan Life Insurance Co. v. Massachusetts, 471 U.S. 724, 105 S.Ct. 2380, 85 L.Ed.2d 728 (1985).

City of Los Angeles Dep't of Water v. Manhart, 435 U.S. 702, 98 S.Ct. 1370, 55 L.Ed.2d 657 (1978).

Employer Liability

National Railroad Passenger Corp. v. Morgan, 536 U.S. 101, 122 S.Ct. 2061, 153 L.Ed.2d 106 (2002).

Haddle v. Garrison, 525 U.S. 121, 119 S.Ct. 489, 142 L.Ed.2d 502 (1998).

Metro-North Commuter Railroad Co. v. Buckley, 521 U.S. 424, 117 S.Ct. 2113, 138 L.Ed.2d 560 (1997).

Atchison, Topeka and Santa Fe Railway Co. v. Buell, 480 U.S. 557, 107 S.Ct. 1410, 94 L.Ed.2d 563 (1987).

Employment Practices

Ragsdale v. Wolverine World Wide Inc., 535 U.S. 81, 122 S.Ct. 1155, 152 L.Ed.2d 167 (2002).

EEOC v. Waffle House, Inc., 534 U.S. 279, 122 S.Ct. 754, 151 L.Ed.2d 755 (2002).

Circuit City Stores Inc. v. Adams, 532 U.S. 105, 121 S.Ct. 1302, 149 L.Ed.2d 234 (2001).

Eastern Associated Coal Corp. v. United Mine Workers of America, Dist. 17, 531 U.S. 57, 121 S. Ct. 462, 148 L. Ed. 2d 354 (2000).

Brogan v. U.S., 522 U.S. 398, 118 S.Ct. 805, 139 L.Ed.2d 830 (1998).

California Federal Savings and Loan Ass'n v. Guerra, 479 U.S. 272, 107 S.Ct. 683, 93 L.Ed.2d 613 (1987).

Attorney General of New York v. Soto-Lopez, 476 U.S. 898, 106 S.Ct. 2317, 90 L.Ed.2d 899 (1986).

Free Speech

Dun & Bradstreet, Inc. v. Greenmoss Builders, Inc., 472 U.S. 749, 105 S.Ct. 2939, 86 L.Ed.2d 593 (1985).

Brockett v. Spokane Arcades, Inc., 472 U.S. 491, 105 S.Ct. 2794, 86 L.Ed.2d 394 (1985).

Connick v. Myers, 461 U.S. 138, 103 S.Ct. 1684, 75 L.Ed.2d 708 (1983).

Labor Relations

Chamber of Commerce of U.S. v. Brown, 128 S.Ct. 2408 (U.S. 2008).

IBP, Inc. v. Alvarez, 546 U.S. 21, 126 S.Ct. 514, 163 L.Ed.2d 288 (2005).

Hoffman Plastic Compounds, Inc. v. NLRB, 535 U.S. 137, 122 S. Ct. 1275, 152 L.Ed.2d 271 (2002).

Marquez v. Screen Actors Guild, 525 U.S. 33, 119 S.Ct. 292, 142 L.Ed.2d 242 (1998).

Wright v. Universal Maritime Service Corp., 525 U.S. 70, 119 S.Ct. 391, 142 L.Ed.2d 361 (1998).

Air Line Pilots Ass'n v. Miller, 523 U.S. 866, 118 S.Ct. 1761, 140 L.Ed.2d 1070 (1998).

Allentown Mack Sales and Service, Inc. v. NLRB, 522 U.S. 359, 118 S.Ct. 818, 139 L.Ed.2d 797 (1998).

Textron Lycoming Reciprocating Engine Division, AVCO Corp. v. United Automobile, Aerospace and Agricultural Implement Workers of America, Int'l Union, Local 787, 523 U.S. 653, 118 S.Ct. 1626, 140 L.Ed.2d 863 (1998).

Auciello Iron Works, Inc. v. NLRB, 517 U.S. 781, 116 S.Ct. 1754, 135 L.Ed.2d 64 (1996).

United Food and Commercial Workers Union Local 751 v. Brown Group, Inc., 517 U.S. 544, 116 S.Ct. 1529, 134 L.Ed.2d 758 (1996).

Holly Farms Corp. v. NLRB, 517 U.S. 392, 116 S.Ct. 1396, 134 L.Ed.2d 593 (1996).

Brotherhood of Locomotive Engineers v. Atchison, Topeka & Santa Fe Railroad Co., 516 U.S. 152, 116 S.Ct. 595, 133 L.Ed.2d 535 (1996).

NLRB v. Town & Country Electric, Inc., 516 U.S. 85, 116 S.Ct. 450, 133 L.Ed.2d 371 (1995).

North Star Steel Co. v. Thomas, 515 U.S. 29, 115 S.Ct. 1927, 132 L.Ed.2d 27 (1995).

NLRB v. Health Care & Retirement Corp., 511 U.S. 571, 114 S.Ct. 1778, 128 L.Ed.2d 586 (1994).

ABF Freight System, Inc. v. NLRB, 510 U.S. 317, 114 S.Ct. 835, 127 L.Ed.2d 152 (1994).

Livadas v. Bradshaw, 512 U.S. 107, 114 S.Ct. 2068, 129 L.Ed.2d 93 (1994).

Hawaiian Airlines, Inc. v. Norris, 512 U.S. 246, 114 S.Ct. 2239, 129 L.Ed.2d 203 (1994).

Thunder Basin Coal Co. v. Reich, 510 U.S. 200, 114 S.Ct. 771, 127 L.Ed.2d 29 (1994).

Lechmere, Inc. v. NLRB, 502 U.S. 527, 112 S.Ct. 841, 117 L.Ed.2d 79 (1992).

Litton Financial Printing v. NLRB, 501 U.S. 190, 111 S.Ct. 2215, 115 L.Ed.2d 177 (1991).

Air Line Pilots Ass'n Int'l v. O'Neill, 499 U.S. 65, 111 S.Ct. 1127, 113 L.Ed.2d 51 (1991).

Martin v. OSHRC, 499 U.S. 144, 111 S.Ct. 1171, 113 L.Ed.2d 117 (1991).

Groves v. Ring Screw Works, 498 U.S. 168, 111 S.Ct. 498, 112 L.Ed.2d 508 (1990).

English v. General Electric Co., 496 U.S. 72, 110 S.Ct. 2270, 110 L.Ed.2d 65 (1990).

NLRB v. Curtin Matheson Scientific, Inc., 494 U.S. 775, 110 S.Ct. 1542, 108 L.Ed.2d 801 (1990).

Trans World Airlines v. Independent Federation of Flight Attendants, 489 U.S. 426, 109 S.Ct. 1225, 103 L.Ed.2d 456 (1989).

Communications Workers of America v. Beck, 487 U.S. 735, 108 S.Ct. 2641, 101 L.Ed.2d 634 (1988).

Fall River Dyeing & Finishing Corp. v. NLRB, 482 U.S. 27, 107 S.Ct. 2225, 96 L.Ed.2d 22 (1987).

Icicle Seafoods, Inc. v. Worthington, 475 U.S. 709, 106 S.Ct. 1527, 89 L.Ed.2d 739 (1986).

NLRB v. International Longshoremen's Ass'n, AFL-CIO, 473 U.S. 61, 105 S.Ct. 3045, 87 L.Ed.2d 47 (1985).

NLRB v. Action Automotive, Inc., 471 U.S. 1049, 105 S.Ct. 984, 83 L.Ed.2d 986 (1985).

Tony and Susan Alamo Foundation v. Secretary of Labor, 471 U.S. 290, 105 S.Ct. 1953, 85 L.Ed.2d 278 (1985).

Allis-Chalmers Corp. v. Lueck, 471 U.S. 202, 105 S.Ct. 1904, 85 L.Ed.2d 206 (1985).

Barrentine v. Arkansas-Best Freight System, 450 U.S. 728, 101 S.Ct. 1437, 67 L.Ed.2d 641 (1981).

Termination

Pennsylvania State Police v. Suders, 524 U.S. 129, 124 S.Ct. 2342, 159 L.Ed.2d 204 (2004).

Beck v. Prupis, 529 U.S. 494, 120 S. Ct. 1608, 146 L. Ed. 2d 561 (2000).

Baker v. General Motors Corp., 522 U.S. 222, 118 S.Ct. 657, 139 L.Ed.2d 580 (1998).

Lingle v. Norge Division of Magic Chef, Inc., 486 U.S. 399, 108 S.Ct. 1877, 100 L.Ed.2d 410 (1988).

United Paperworkers Int'l Union v. Misco, Inc., 484 U.S. 29, 108 S.Ct. 364, 98 L.Ed.2d 286 (1987).

Caterpillar Inc. v. Williams, 482 U.S. 386, 107 S.Ct. 2425, 96 L.Ed.2d 318 (1987).

Unemployment Compensation

Frazee v. Illinois Dep't of Employment Security, 489 U.S. 829, 109 S.Ct. 1514, 103 L.Ed.2d 914 (1989).

Hobbie v. Unemployment Appeals Comm'n of Florida, 480 U.S. 136, 107 S.Ct. 1046, 94 L.Ed.2d 190 (1987).

Baker v. General Motors Corp., 478 U.S. 621, 106 S.Ct. 3129, 92 L.Ed.2d 504 (1986).

Thomas v. Review Board of Indiana Employment Security Division, 450 U.S. 707, 101 S.Ct. 1425, 67 L.Ed.2d 624 (1981).

Workers' Compensation

American Manufacturers Mutual Insurance Co. v. Sullivan, 526 U.S. 40, 119 S.Ct. 977, 143 L.Ed.2d 130 (1999).

Metropolitan Stevedore Co. v. Rambo (Rambo II), 521 U.S. 121, 117 S.Ct. 1953, 138 L.Ed.2d 327 (1997).

Ingalls Shipbuilding, Inc. v. Director, OWCP, 519 U.S. 248, 117 S.Ct. 796, 136 L.Ed.2d 736 (1997).

Director, Office of Workers' Compensation Programs, Dep't of Labor v. Newport News Shipbuilding and Dry Dock Co., 514 U.S. 122, 115 S.Ct. 1278, 131 L.Ed.2d 160 (1995).

Chandris, Inc. v. Latsis, 515 U.S. 347, 115 S.Ct. 2172, 132 L.Ed.2d 314 (1995).

Metropolitan Stevedore Co. v. Rambo, 515 U.S. 291, 115 S.Ct. 2144, 132 L.Ed.2d 226 (1995).

Director, Office of Workers' Compensation Programs v. Greenwich Collieries, 512 U.S. 267, 114 S.Ct. 2251, 129 L.Ed.2d 221 (1994).

Thomas v. Washington Gas Light Co., 448 U.S. 261, 100 S.Ct. 2647, 65 L.Ed.2d 757 (1980).

Wengler v. Druggist Mutual Insurance Co., 446 U.S. 142, 100 S.Ct. 1540, 64 L.Ed.2d 107 (1980).

The Judicial System

To allow you to determine the relative importance of a judicial decision, the cases included in ***Deskbook Encyclopedia of Employment Law*** identify the particular court from which a decision has been issued. For example, a case decided by a state supreme court generally will be of greater significance than a state circuit court case. Hence a basic knowledge of the structure of our judicial system is important to an understanding of employment law.

Almost all the reports in this volume are taken from appellate court decisions. Although most employment law decisions occur at trial court and administrative levels, appellate court decisions have the effect of binding lower courts and administrators so that appellate court decisions have the effect of law within their court systems.

State and federal court systems generally function independently of each other. Each court system applies its own law according to statutes and the determinations of its highest court. However, judges at all levels often consider opinions from other court systems to settle issues that are new or arise under unique fact situations. Similarly, lawyers look at the opinions of many courts to locate authority that supports their clients' cases.

Once a lawsuit is filed in a particular court system, that system retains the matter until its conclusion. Unsuccessful parties at the administrative or trial court level generally have the right to appeal unfavorable determinations of law to appellate courts within the system. When federal law issues or constitutional grounds are present, lawsuits may be appropriately filed in the federal court system. In those cases, the lawsuit is filed initially in the federal district court for that area.

On rare occasions, the U.S. Supreme Court considers appeals from the highest courts of the states if a distinct federal question exists and at least four justices agree on the question's importance. The federal courts occasionally send cases to state courts for application of state law. These situations are infrequent and, in general, the state and federal court systems should be considered separate from each other.

The most common system, used by nearly all states and also the federal judiciary, is as follows: a legal action is commenced in district court (sometimes called trial court, county court, common pleas court or superior court) where a decision is initially reached. The case may then be appealed to the court of appeals (or appellate court), and in turn this decision may be appealed to the supreme court.

Several states, however, do not have a court of appeals; lower court decisions are appealed directly to the state's supreme court. Additionally, some states have labeled their courts in a nonstandard fashion.

In Maryland, the highest state court is called the Court of Appeals. In the state of New York, the trial court is called the Supreme Court. Decisions of this court may be appealed to the Supreme Court, Appellate Division. The highest court in New York is the Court of Appeals. Pennsylvania has perhaps the most complex court system. The lowest state court is the Court of Common Pleas. Depending on the circumstances of the case, appeals may be taken to either the Commonwealth Court or the Superior Court. In certain instances the Commonwealth Court functions as a trial court as well as an appellate court. The Superior Court, however, is strictly an intermediate appellate court. The highest court in Pennsylvania is the Supreme Court.

While supreme court decisions are generally regarded as the last word in legal matters, it is important to remember that trial and appeals court decisions also create important legal precedents. For the hierarchy of typical state and federal court systems, please see the diagram below.

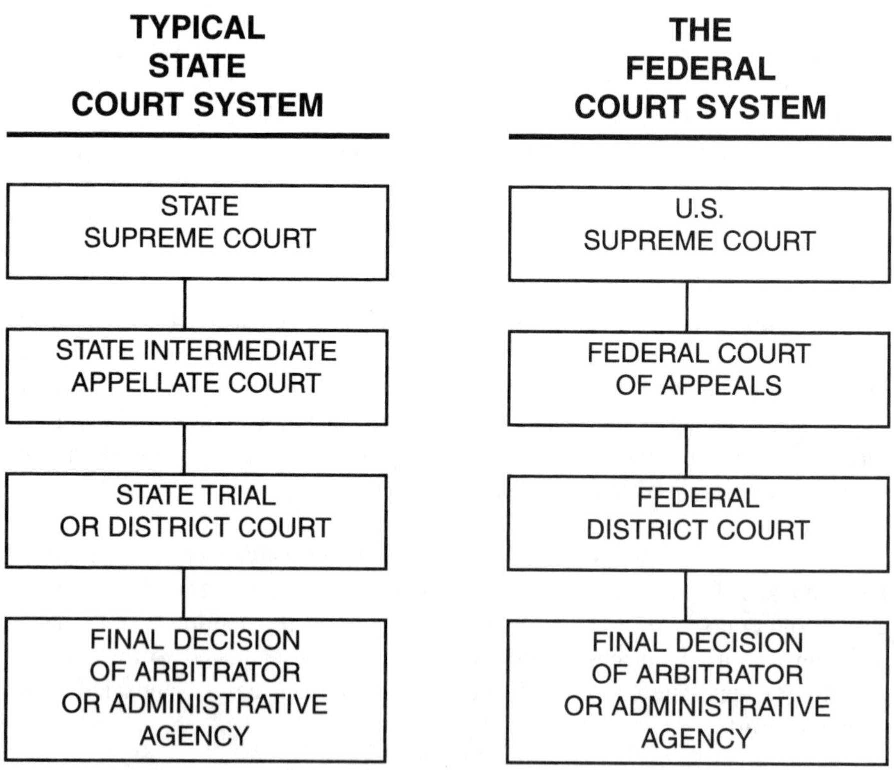

Federal courts of appeals hear appeals from the district courts that are located in their circuits. Below is a list of states matched to the federal circuits in which they are located.

First Circuit	—	Maine, Massachusetts, New Hampshire, Puerto Rico Rhode Island
Second Circuit	—	Connecticut, New York, Vermont
Third Circuit	—	Delaware, New Jersey, Pennsylvania, Virgin Islands
Fourth Circuit	—	Maryland, North Carolina, South Carolina, Virginia, West Virginia
Fifth Circuit	—	Louisiana, Mississippi, Texas
Sixth Circuit	—	Kentucky, Michigan, Ohio, Tennessee
Seventh Circuit	—	Illinois, Indiana, Wisconsin
Eighth Circuit	—	Arkansas, Iowa, Minnesota, Missouri, Nebraska, North Dakota, South Dakota
Ninth Circuit	—	Alaska, Arizona, California, Guam, Hawaii, Idaho, Montana, Nevada, Northern Mariana Islands, Oregon, Washington
Tenth Circuit	—	Colorado, Kansas, New Mexico, Oklahoma, Utah, Wyoming
Eleventh Circuit	—	Alabama, Florida, Georgia
District of Columbia	—	Hears cases from the U.S. District Court for Circuit the District of Columbia.
Federal Circuit	—	Sitting in Washington, D.C., the U.S. Court of Appeals, Federal Circuit, hears patent and trade appeals and certain appeals on claims brought against the federal government and its agencies.

How to Read a Case Citation

Generally, court decisions can be located in case reporters at law school or governmental law libraries. Some cases can also be located on the Internet through legal Web sites or official court Web sites.

Each case summary contains the citation, or legal reference, to the full text of the case. The diagram below illustrates how to read a case citation.

case name (parties) ↘ | case reporter name and series ↓ | court location ↙

Thompson v. The Coca Cola Co., 522 F.3d 168 (1st Cir. 2008).

volume number ↗ | first page ↑ | year of decision ↖

Some cases may have two or three reporter names, such as U.S. Supreme Court cases and cases reported in regional case reporters as well as state case reporters. For example, a U.S. Supreme Court case usually contains three case reporter citations.

first reporter | second reporter

Arbaugh v. Y&H Corp., 546 U.S. 500, 126 S.Ct. 1235,
163 L.Ed.2d 1097 (2006).

third reporter | year of decision ↖

The citations are still read in the same manner as if only one citation has been listed.

Occasionally, a case may contain a citation that does not reference a case reporter. For example, a citation may contain a reference such as:

case name ↓ | court file number ↓ | Westlaw®[1] ↓ | first page ↓

Engle v. Thompson Murray, Inc., No. CA 06-81, 2006 WL 2691684
(Ark. Ct. App. 9/20/06).

court location ↑ | date of decision ↑ | year of decision ↑

The court file number indicates the specific number assigned to a case by the particular court system deciding the case. In our example, the Arkansas Court of

[1] Westlaw® is a computerized database of court cases available for a fee.

Appeals has assigned the case of *Engle v. Thompson Murray, Inc.,* the case number of "No. CA 06-81" which will serve as the reference number for the case and any matter relating to the case. Locating a case on the Internet generally requires either the case name and date of the decision, and/or the court file number.

Below, we have listed the full names of the regional reporters. As mentioned previously, many states have individual state reporters. The names of those reporters may be obtained from a reference law librarian.

P. **Pacific Reporter**
Alaska, Arizona, California, Colorado, Hawaii, Idaho, Kansas, Montana, Nevada, New Mexico, Oklahoma, Oregon, Utah, Washington, Wyoming

A. **Atlantic Reporter**
Connecticut, Delaware, District of Columbia, Maine, Maryland, New Hampshire, New Jersey, Pennsylvania, Rhode Island, Vermont

N.E. **Northeastern Reporter**
Illinois, Indiana, Massachusetts, New York, Ohio

N.W. **Northwestern Reporter**
Iowa, Michigan, Minnesota, Nebraska, North Dakota, South Dakota, Wisconsin

S. **Southern Reporter**
Alabama, Florida, Louisiana, Mississippi

S.E. **Southeastern Reporter**
Georgia, North Carolina, South Carolina, Virginia, West Virginia

S.W. **Southwestern Reporter**
Arkansas, Kentucky, Missouri, Tennessee, Texas

F. **Federal Reporter**
The thirteen federal judicial circuits courts of appeals decisions. See *The Judicial System, p. 581,* for specific state circuits.

F.Supp. **Federal Supplement**
The thirteen federal judicial circuits district court decisions. See *The Judicial System, p. 581,* for specific state circuits.

Fed. Appx. **Federal Appendix**
Contains unpublished decisions of the U.S. Circuit Courts of Appeal.

U.S. **United States Reports**
S.Ct. **Supreme Court Reporter** > U.S. Supreme Court Decisions
L.Ed. **Lawyers' Edition**

GLOSSARY

Administrative Law Judge - (ALJ) an officer who presides at administrative hearings. ALJs are empowered by employment and agency statutes to serve as initial fact finders in many employment cases, including workers' compensation and unemployment benefits claims and many labor disputes. Although courts must give ALJ findings of fact considerable weight, they are not bound by an ALJ's conclusions of law.

Age Discrimination in Employment Act (ADEA) - The ADEA, 29 U.S.C. § 621 *et seq.*, is part of the Fair Labor Standards Act. It prohibits discrimination against persons who are at least 40 years old, and it applies to employers that have 20 or more employees and affect interstate commerce.

Americans with Disabilities Act (ADA) - The provisions of the ADA, 42 U.S.C. § 12101 *et seq.*, specifically addressing employment discrimination went into effect on July 26, 1992. Among other things, the ADA prohibits discrimination against a qualified individual with a disability because of that person's disability with respect to job application procedures, the hiring, advancement or discharge of employees, employee compensation, job training, and other terms, conditions and privileges of employment.

Bona fide - Latin term meaning "good faith." Generally used to note a party's lack of bad intent or fraudulent purpose.

CBA - Collective bargaining agreement.

Class Action Suit - Federal Rule of Civil Procedure 23 allows members of a class to sue as representatives on behalf of the whole class provided that the class is so large that joinder of all parties is impractical, there are questions of law or fact common to the class, the claims or defenses of the representatives are typical of the claims or defenses of the class, and the representative parties will adequately protect the interests of the class. In addition, there must be some danger of inconsistent verdicts or adjudications if the class action were prosecuted as separate actions. Most states also allow class actions under the same or similar circumstances.

Collateral Estoppel - Also known as issue preclusion. The idea that once an issue has been litigated, it may not be re-tried. Similar to the doctrine of *res judicata* (see below).

Due Process Clause - The clauses of the Fifth and Fourteenth Amendments to the Constitution that guarantee the citizens of the United States *due process of law* (see below). The Fifth Amendment's Due Process Clause applies to the federal government, and the Fourteenth Amendment's Due Process Clause applies to the states.

Due Process of Law - The idea of "fair play" in the government's application of law to its citizens, guaranteed by the Fifth and Fourteenth Amendments. Substantive due process is just plain *fairness*, and procedural due process is accorded when the government utilizes adequate procedural safeguards for the protection of an individual's liberty or property interests.

Employee Retirement Income Security Act (ERISA) - Federal legislation that sets uniform standards for employee pension benefit plans and employee welfare benefit plans. It is codified at 29 U.S.C. § 1001 *et seq.*

Enjoin - (see Injunction).

Equal Pay Act - Federal legislation that is part of the Fair Labor Standards Act. It applies to discrimination in wages that is based on gender. For race discrimination, employees paid unequally must utilize Title VII or 42 U.S.C. § 1981. Unlike many labor statutes, there is no minimum number of employees necessary to invoke the act's protection.

Equal Protection Clause - The clause of the Fourteenth Amendment that prohibits a state from denying any person within its jurisdiction equal protection of its laws. Also, the Due Process Clause of the Fifth Amendment that pertains to the federal government. This has been interpreted by the Supreme Court to grant equal protection even though there is no explicit grant in the Constitution.

Establishment Clause - The clause of the First Amendment that prohibits Congress from making "any law respecting an establishment of religion." This clause has been interpreted as creating a "wall of separation" between church and state. The test now used to determine whether government action violates the Establishment Clause, referred to as the *Lemon* test, from *Lemon v. Kurtzman,* 403 U.S. 602, 91 S.Ct. 2105, 29 L.Ed.2d 745 (1971), asks whether the action has a secular purpose, whether its primary effect promotes or inhibits religion, and whether it requires excessive entanglement between church and state.

Ex Post Facto Law - A law that punishes as criminal any action that was not a crime at the time it was performed. Prohibited by Article I, Section 9, of the Constitution.

Exclusionary Rule - Constitutional limitation on the introduction of evidence that states that evidence derived from a constitutional violation must be excluded from trial.

Fair Labor Standards Act (FLSA) - Federal legislation that mandates the payment of minimum wages and overtime compensation to covered employees. The overtime provisions require employers to pay at least time-and-one-half to employees who work more than 40 hours per week.

Federal Employers' Liability Act (FELA) - Legislation enacted to provide a federal remedy for railroad workers who are injured as a result of employer or co-employee negligence. It expressly prohibits covered carriers from adopting any regulation, or entering into any contract, which limits their FELA liability.

Federal Tort Claims Act - Federal legislation that determines the circumstances under which the United States waives its *sovereign immunity* (see below) and agrees to be sued in court for money damages. The government retains its immunity in cases of intentional torts committed by its employees or agents, and where the tort is the result of a "discretionary function" of a federal employee or agency. Many states have similar acts.

42 U.S.C. §§ 1981, 1983 - Section 1983 of the federal Civil Rights Act prohibits any person acting under color of state law from depriving any other person of rights protected by the Constitution or by federal laws. A vast majority of lawsuits claiming constitutional violations are brought under Section 1983. Section 1981 provides that all persons enjoy the same right to make and enforce contracts as "white citizens." Section 1981 applies to employment contracts. Further, unlike Section 1983, Section 1981 applies even to private actors. It is not limited to those acting under color of state law. These sections do not apply to the federal government, though the government may be sued directly under the Constitution for any violations.

Free Exercise Clause - The clause of the First Amendment that prohibits Congress from interfering with citizens' rights to the free exercise of their religion. Through the Fourteenth Amendment, it has also been made applicable to the states and their sub-entities.

Incorporation Doctrine - By its own terms, the Bill of Rights applies only to the federal government. The Incorporation Doctrine states that the Fourteenth Amendment makes the Bill of Rights applicable to the states.

Injunction - An equitable remedy (see Remedies) wherein a court orders a party to do or refrain from doing some particular action.

Issue Preclusion - (see Collateral Estoppel).

Jurisdiction - The power of a court to determine cases and controversies. The Supreme Court's jurisdiction extends to cases arising under the Constitution and under federal law. Federal courts have the power to hear cases where there is diversity of citizenship or where a federal question is involved.

Labor Management Relations Act (LMRA) - Federal labor law that preempts state law with respect to controversies involving collective bargaining agreements. The most important provision of the LMRA is Section 301, which is codified at 29 U.S.C. § 185.

National Labor Relations Act (NLRA) - Federal legislation that guarantees to employees the right to form and participate in labor organizations. It prohibits employers from interfering with employees in the exercise of their rights under the NLRA.

Negligence per se - Negligence on its face. Usually, the violation of an ordinance or statute will be treated as negligence per se because no careful person would have been guilty of it.

Occupational Safety and Health Act (OSH Act) - Federal legislation that requires employers to provide a safe workplace. Employers have both general and specific duties under OSH Act. The general duty is to provide a workplace that is free from recognized hazards that are likely to result in serious physical harm. The specific duty is to conform to the health and safety standards promulgated by the Secretary of Labor.

Overbroad - A government action is overbroad if, in an attempt to alleviate a specific evil, it impermissibly prohibits or chills a protected action. For example, attempting to deal with street litter by prohibiting the distribution of leaflets or handbills would be overboard.

Preemption Doctrine - Doctrine that states that when federal and state law attempt to regulate the same subject matter, federal law prevents the state law from operating. Based on the Supremacy Clause of Article VI, Clause 2, of the Constitution.

Prior Restraint - Restraining a publication before it is distributed. In general, constitutional law doctrine prohibits government from exercising prior restraint.

Pro Se - A party appearing in court, without the benefit of an attorney, is said to be appearing pro se.

Religious Freedom Restoration Act - Federal law that creates a statutory prohibition against governmental action that substantially burdens the exercise of religion, even if the burden results from a rule of general applicability, unless the government can show that the action is the least restrictive means of furthering a compelling governmental interest.

Remand - The act of an appellate court in returning a case to the court from which it came for further action.

Remedies - There are two general categories of remedies, or relief: legal remedies, which consist of money damages, and equitable remedies, which consist of a court mandate that a specific action be prohibited or required. For example, a claim for compensatory and punitive damages seeks a legal remedy; a claim for an injunction seeks an equitable remedy. Equitable remedies are generally unavailable unless legal remedies are inadequate to address the harm.

Res Judicata - The judicial notion that a claim or action may not be tried twice or re-litigated, or that all causes of action arising out of the same set of operative facts should be tried at one time. Also known as claim preclusion.

Section 504 of the Rehabilitation Act of 1973 - Section 504 applies to public or private institutions receiving federal financial assistance. It requires that, in the employment context, an otherwise qualified individual cannot be denied employment based on his or her handicap. An otherwise qualified individual is one who can perform the "essential functions" of the job with "reasonable accomodation."

Section 1981 & Section 1983 - (see 42 U.S.C. §§ 1981, 1983).

Sovereign Immunity - The idea that the government cannot be sued without its consent. It stems from the English notion that the "King can do no wrong." This immunity from suit has been abrogated in most states and by the federal government through legislative acts known as "tort claims acts."

Standing - The judicial doctrine that states that in order to maintain a lawsuit a party must have some real interest at stake in the outcome of the trial.

Statute of Limitations - A statute of limitation provides the time period in which a specific cause of action may be brought.

Summary Judgment - Also referred to as pretrial judgment. Similar to a dismissal. Where there is no genuine issue as to any material fact and all that remains is a question of law, a judge can rule in favor of one party or the other. In general, summary judgment is used to dispose of claims that do not support a legally recognized claim.

Supremacy Clause - Clause in Article VI of the Constitution that states that federal legislation is the supreme law of the land. This clause is used to support the *Preemption Doctrine* (see above).

Title VII, Civil Rights Act of 1964 (Title VII) - Title VII prohibits discrimination in employment based upon race, color, sex, national origin, or religion. It applies to any employer having 15 or more employees. Under Title VII, where an employer intentionally discriminates, employees may obtain money damages unless the claim is for race discrimination. For those claims, monetary relief is available under 42 U.S.C. § 1981.

U.S. Equal Employment Opportunity Commission (EEOC) - The EEOC is the government entity that is empowered to enforce Title VII (see above) through investigation and/or lawsuits. Private individuals alleging discrimination must pursue administrative remedies within the EEOC before they are allowed to file suit under Title VII.

Vacate - The act of annulling the judgment of a court either by an appellate court or by the court itself. The Supreme Court generally will vacate a lower court's judgment without deciding the case itself and remand the case to the lower court for further consideration in light of some recent controlling decision.

Void-for-Vagueness Doctrine - A judicial doctrine based on the Fourteenth Amendment's Due Process Clause. In order for a law that regulates speech, or any criminal statute, to pass muster under the doctrine, the law must make clear what actions are prohibited or made criminal. Under the principles of the Due Process Clause, people of average intelligence should not have to guess at the meaning of a law.

Writ of Certiorari - The device used by the Supreme Court to transfer cases from the appellate court's docket to its own. Since the Supreme Court's appellate jurisdiction is largely discretionary, it need only issue such a writ when it desires to rule in the case.

INDEX